HISTORY

OF

PROTESTANT THEOLOGY

VOLUME I.

HISTORY

OF

PROTESTANT THEOLOGY

PARTICULARLY IN GERMANY

Viewed according to its Fundamental Movement

AND IN CONNECTION WITH THE RELIGIOUS, MORAL, AND
INTELLECTUAL LIFE

By Dr. J. A. DORNER

OBERCONSISTORIALRATH AND PROFESSOR OF THEOLOGY AT BERLIN

TRANSLATED BY THE
REV. GEORGE ROBSON, M.A., INVERNESS
AND
SOPHIA TAYLOR

VOLUME I.

WITH A PREFACE TO THE TRANSLATION BY
THE AUTHOR

Wipf & Stock
PUBLISHERS
Eugene, Oregon

Wipf and Stock Publishers
199 W 8th Ave, Suite 3
Eugene, OR 97401

History of Protestant Theology, Volume 1
By Dorner, Isaak A.
Softcover ISBN-13: 979-8-3852-0413-7
Hardcover ISBN-13: 979-8-3852-0414-4
eBook ISBN-13: 979-8-3852-0415-1
Publication date 9/26/2023
Previously published by T&T Clark, 1887

This edition is a scanned facsimile of the original edition published in 1887.

AUTHOR'S PREFACE

TO THE ENGLISH TRANSLATION

EINE Rechtfertigung dafür, dass ich es wage, mit diesem Vorwort mich an die theologische Welt englischer Zunge zu wenden, könnte ich zwar darin suchen, dass die erste Anregung zu diesem Schritt mir von Freunden aus dem Volke gekommen ist, an welches mich zu wenden ich hier beabsichtige, von denselben Männern nemlich, welche dafür Sorge getragen haben, dass vorliegendes Werk durch Uebersetzung auch in die englische Litteratur eingeführt werde.

Aber die Schuld sowohl an dieser Einführung und Uebersetzung (die ich gestattet habe, ohne im Stande zu sein, dabei eine Controlle zu übernehmen) als auch an dem Wagestück dieses Vorworts werde ich, wie ich sehe, immerhin wenigstens mitzutragen habe. Und so berufe ich mich lieber, gleichsam als wäre die erste Anregung mir nicht von aussen gekommen, darauf, dass ich seit meinen Jugendjahren mit besonderer ‚Liebe mich mit englischer Litteratur beschäftigt, durch einen längeren Aufenthalt in Grossbrittanien mich mit Land und Volk und dessen Geist bekannt gemacht und befreundet habe und daher mich nicht ganz als einen Fremden ihnen gegenüber fühle.

Das vorliegende Werk giebt mir aber, hoffe ich, durch seinen Grundgedanken ein besonderes Recht, es auch der Aufmerksamkeit der Evangelischen englischer Zunge zu empfehlen. Denn geleitet von dem Geiste evangelischer Katholicität sucht dasselbe den geschichtlichen Nachweis zu liefern, dass trotz der verschiedenen Nationalitäten sowie der mannigfaltigen Gestaltungen des evangelish-protestantischen Christenthums bei den Völkern, die sich den Segen der Reformation des sechzehnten Jahrhunderts angeeignet haben, trotz der Trennung in Sprache, Gebräuchen und Gewohnheiten sowie ihrer Schicksale die. evangelisch-protestantische Christenheit eine Einheit bilde. Der englische Theil des Protestantismus, zusammengenommen mit der evangelischen Christenheit seiner Tochter-republik jenseits des Atlantischen Oceans, bildet die eine grosse Gruppe des Protes-

tantismus, neben welcher nur die deutsche Hälfte in gleicher
Bedeutung und ähnlichem Umfang dasteht. Hat der deutsche
Protestantismus durch philosophischen Geist und freie Entwickelung der Wissenschaft den universalen Blick und das weite Herz
gewonnen, das frei von sektenhafter Enge den evangelischen
Geist, wo er sich findet, wieder erkennt, so hat der angloameri-
kanische Theil des Protestantismus dieselbe weite Umschau
durch die Weltstellung erlangt, die ihm seine politische, koloniale
und merkantile Geschichte in Verbindung mit seinem praktischen Geschick und Trieb eingetragen hat. Dass Ein Lebens-
blut in den beiden grossen Theilen des evangelischen Protestantismus fliesst, zeigt sich auf das schlagendste durch das Factum,
welches die Geschichte der protestantischen Theologie bezeugt:
dass beide, und zwar nicht durch blosse Einwirkung auf einander,
sondern selbstständig dieselbe Reihenfolge von inneren Lebens-
epochen bis jetzt durchlaufen haben; allerdings in national
verschiedener Gestalt, indem der Typus des deutschen Genius
bisher mehr zur Theorie und Speculation hingewendet war, der
Geist unserer germanischen Brüder jenseits des Kanals und
Oceans mehr zu praktischen Problemen und Evolutionen. Aber
dieser Unterschied hat sie nur eine zeitlang trennen oder ihre
Arbeit gegenseitig ignoriren lassen können. Die religiösen
Wurzeln und Impulse sind von der Reformation her, in welcher
göttliche Autorität und evangelische Freiheit principiell geeinigt
sind, in beiden wesentlich gemeinsam geblieben. Dazu kommt,
die deutsche Theologie hat nach manchen theoretischen und
speculativen Ausschreitungen in ihren hoffnungreichsten neuesten
Entwickelungen immer mehr erkannt, wie das *ethische Princip*
der Gotteslehre, Anthropologie, Christologie und Ecclesiastik
einzuverleiben ist, um sowohl festen Grund als sichern Fortschritt
zu gewinnen. Je mehr aber die deutsche Wissenschaft auch das
ethische Gebiet cultivirt und seine Lebensgesetze zu erkennen
bestrebt ist, desto mehr erschliesst sich ihr auch der Sinn
für die eigenthümliche Geistesarbeit in Grossbrittanien und
Nordamerika, desto mehr ist sie geneigt auch von dem diesen
Nationen gewordenen Charisma Gewinn zu ziehen. Ein ana-
loger Vorgang aber bereitet sich, wenn ich mich nicht täusche,
umgekehrt auch in diesen Ländern vor, welche einst speculative
Theologen ersten Ranges, einen Anselm von Kanterbury, einen
Duns Scotus, ja schon früher einen Skotus Erigena gestellt haben,

seit dem fünfzehnten Jahrhundert aber in andere Bahnen übergegangen sind. Denn das scheint die neuere kirchliche Geschichte dieser Länder zu zeigen, dass ohne den Dienst strenger, productiver, schlagfertiger, theologischer Wissenschaft die Kirche den neueren gewaltigen Bewegungen der Naturwissenschaften und der historischen Kritik, wie dem Geiste des practischen und theoretischen Materialismus wehrlos gegenüber steht. Das Alles lässt ein Wachsthum der geistigen, auch literarischen Gemeinschaft zwischen den beiden Hauptgruppen der evangelischen Christenheit wünschen und weissagen, wie der immer deutlicher hervortretende Zusammenschliess der feindlichen Mächte, mit denen sie zu thun hat, es verlangt. Warum hat eine von der evangelischen Wahrheit abgewendete Civilisation bei uns in Deutschland so grosse Dimensionem angenommen? weil der Erkenntnisstrieb zwar lebendig aber zu wenig mit ethischem Geiste gesättigt war, wozu nicht wenig die Verkümmerung unserer nationalen, politischen und bürgerlichen Verhältnisse, ihre unbehagliche Unklarheit und Unfertigkeit beigetragen hat, Hemmungen, Verwirrungen, Zersplitterungen, von denen erst die grossen Ereignisse der neuesten Zeit, wie wir zu Gott hoffen, uns befreit haben. Andererseits was ist der innigste Grund davon, dass in England und zum Theil in Nordamerika theils eine ungläubige, theils eine romanisirende Richtung sich verbreitet hat, welche letztere auch bereits nach Deutschland herüber ihre Wurzeln treibt, als weil der herrschende Empirismus für das in sich Wahre und Ewige keinen Sinn hat, oder an seiner Zugänglichkeit skeptisch verzweifelt und daher um nur einigen Halt für das Leben zu haben, gewisse selbsterwählte Autoritäten zur Herrschaft über sich einsetzt?

Ueber die Gefahr einer Wiederkehr des Deismus ist Grossbritanien nicht hinaus, wird auch in der ritualistischen Richtung dagegen keine Schutzwehr finden, sowenig als in einem blossen Hüten der Schätze vergangener Jahrhunderte oder in einem buchstäbischen an die Confessionen des sechzehnten und siebzehnten Jahrhunderts unfruchtbar und thatlos sich heftenden Wesen. Beide Nationen, die deutsche und die englische bedürfen es, dass das Volk von den niedrigsten bis zu den höchsten Schichten in dem evangelischen Christenthum wieder seine Heimath finde, dass diejenigen Seiten aus dem reformatorischen Glauben hervorgebildet werden, die im Stande sind, der jetzigen

Stufe seines Lebens und seiner Cultur die Leuchte zu geben, und die dem öffentlichen Geist der Nation wie dem Leben der Einzelnen die rechte Spannkraft und Harmonie zu verleihen geeignet sind.

Nie vielleicht ist die Nothwendigkeit so einleuchtend gewesen, gegen die gemeinsamen Feinde des Protestantismus gemeinsam die Fahne des Evangeliums hochzuhalten. Aber auch keine Zeit ist einer lebendigeren Gemeinschaft der verschiedenen evangelischen Völker günstiger gewesen. Ich denke dabei nicht bloss an die fast wunderbar gesteigerten Verkehrsmittel für Personen und Erzeugnisse der Presse, nicht bloss an die evangelische Allianz, durch welche namhafte Männer aus England, Schottland, Holland, Frankreich, der Schweitz und Nordamerika, aus Deutschland, Dänemark und Schweden in persönliche Gemeinschaft wie zu einer Gemeinsamkeit von Arbeit und Gebet in Beziehung auf viele wichtige Probleme der jetzigen Christenheit gebracht worden sind. Sondern ich denke dabei besonders daran, dass in dem germanischen und englischen Theil der evangelischen Kirche auch in Europa der Zug der Zeit unleugbar immer mehr dahin geht, dass die Kirche von den zu engen Banden, die sie an den Staat anschlossen, mehr und mehr befreit wird. Die christliche Kirche kann sich, wenn sie auf ihr Wesen sich besinnt, nicht in territoriale und staatliche Schranken einengen lassen: sie vertritt das universale Princip und kann die Grenzpfähle der Staaten nicht als die Grenze ihres Liebessinnes und Gemeinschaftslebens anerkennen. Der Staat dagegen hat nothwendig eine particulare Existenz und weiss sich in dieser als eine vollständige mit absoluter Souverainetät ausgestattete Grösse. Einen Universalstaat aber kann es nicht geben, weil jede Nationalität ihre staatliche absolute Souverainetät ihm müsste zum Opfer bringen. Die Kirche dagegen schreitet zwar durch die Geschichte gleichfalls nothwendig in nationalen Formen und Gestaltungen; sie ist sich aber dabei, auch wo dies nicht praktisch hervortritt, ihrer über Staaten und Nationen übergreifenden Einheit bewusst, wie schon das apostolische Bekenntniss sagt: ich glaube an eine heilige allgemeine christliche Kirche. Die Nationalitäten sind für sie keineswegs Schranken, sondern Individualitäten, ausgestattet mit verschiedenen Charismen, die dem Einen alle umschliessenden Zwecke, der Mehrung des Reiches Gottes, zu dienen haben.

Author's Preface.

Je mehr nun die staatliche und kirchliche Entwickelung des protestantischen Europa zu wachsender Selbständigkeit der Kirche führen wird, je mehr diese nach Verlust ihres anfänglichen staatlichen Stützpunktes ihre Kraft in sich selbst, das heisst in dem evangelischen Volk wird zu suchen haben, desto mehr wird es ihr, entbunden von den partikularen staatlichen Gesichtspunkten inneres Bedürfniss wie äussere Nothwendigkeit werden, das Princip wahrer d. h. evangelischer Katholicität sich frei und kräftig entfalten zu lassen kraft desselben Triebes, wenn auch nicht in denselben Formen, wie in der ältesten Christenheit. Diese Einheit der evangelischen Christenheit ist vereinbar mit den verschiedensten Verfassungen und Lebensformen der verschiedenen Nationen und fordert keineswegs, wie die römische Kirche will, eine Einheit oder auch nur Gleichheit des Kirchenregimentes bei Allen. Im Gegentheil selbst in einer und derselben Nation mögen unbeschadet des Alle vereinigenden conföderativen Principes die mannigfaltigsten Kirchenformen herrschen. Wenn sie nur mit den Grundlagen der Reformation vereinbar sind, werden sie auf gegenseitige Anerkennung und Förderung Anspruch machen können. Einheit in lebensvoller Mannigfaltigkeit ist es, wofür die Reformation den Weg eröffnet hat, ja was die natürliche gesunde Lebensform des Christenthums in der Menschheit ist.

Die Wege, welche jene beiden Hälften des Protestantismus zu dem Ende einzuschlagen haben, sind verschiedene, ja zum Theil entgegengesetzte. In der angloamerikanischen Hälfte haben die ein ganzes Volk umschliessenden Nationalkirchen (Schottland bis zur Disruption ausgenommen) nicht lange gedauert, sondern sich in eine Menge von evangelischen Denominationen getheilt, die im Dogma wenig verschieden um der Verfassung willen sich gespalten und von einander gesondert haben, und die Production immer neuer Sonderkirchen ist noch in stetem Fortgang. Träte nicht eine Gegenbewegung ein, so würde die endlose Zersplitterung immer mehr die evangelische Einheit in Vergessenheit bringen, jede gemeinsame Action des Protestantismus in der Heidenmission oder gegen die compact auftretende römische Kirche oder gegen den Unglauben paralysiren; die Hervorkehrung der Freiheit ohne die Einheit würde den Protestantismus zur Ohnmacht zurückführen. Ja auch die Freiheit, namentlich der wissenschaftlichen Bewegung würde durch solches Verleugnen der Einheit in Sektengeist Schaden nehmen müssen, weil, wenn jede auch geringere Abweichung von dem Hergebrachten sich zu einer eigenen Kirchenpartei abschliesst, jedem Einzelnen, scheinbar im Interesse der Wahrheit, angesonnen werden wird, die Lehrsätze anderer Denominationen als Grenzen anzusehen, die von ihm nicht überschritten werden dürfen, so dass die Freiheit seiner theoretischen und practischen Bewegung immer mehr eingeengt werden muss. Mag er immerhin sich bewusst sein, mit Lust und Ueberzeugung in seiner Cofession zu stehen, *so* wird er dann nicht ihr zugehören dürfen, dass er das Wahre, was er an Anderen erkennt und was dieselben von der eigenen Confession mit unterscheidet, der Letzteren zuführen dürfte. So führt die Freiheit ohne die Einheit, ohne die innere Katholicität in die Unfreiheit, in die Enge des Sektengeistes. Darum kann es nur mit Freuden begrüsst werden, dass in der neuesten Zeit in kräftigen und gesunden Theilen des englischen, schottischen, amerikanischen Protestantismus eine Gegenbewegung gegen diese centrifugale Richtung immer mehr Platz greift und in vielen der besten Männer aus allen Denominationen der Geist evangelischer Katholicität seine Vertreter findet. Aber damit das Wort: "in necessariis unitas, in dubiis libertas, in omnibus caritas" zu praktischer Durchführung gelange, dazu ist Wissenschaft, dogmatische Bildung, gründliche Kenntniss und Verständniss der evangelischen Grundwahrheiten erforderlich. Denn nur so ist Pflicht und Maass der kirchlichen Gemeinschaft sicher erkennbar. Hier eröffnet sich also ein Gebiet der gemeinsamen Arbeit wie des wünschenswerthen Austausches der theologischen Litteraturen.

Ein ganz anderer Weg scheint der germanischen Familie des Protestantismus von *ihrem* Ausgangspunkte aus vorgezeichnet. Hier sind die grossen evangelischen Nationalkirchen noch in wesentlich ungebrochener Einheit, nur dass die oben erwähnte enge Verbindung mit dem Staate in Deutschland Hemmungen gebracht und Schranken der einzelnen Landeskirchen gegen einander aufgezogen hat. Wenn nun jene Verbindung mit dem Staate sich lockert, oder soweit sich löst, als die kirchliche Selbstständigkeit es verlangt, so steht ohne Zweifel auch hier das Auftreten sehr verschiedener Denominationen oder Sekten in Aussicht. So wenig Dieses mit äusseren oder gar staatlichen Mitteln wird verhindert werden dürfen, so bleibt doch die Einheit der evangelischen Kirche, die auch in der landeskirchlichen

Zersplitterung nie vergessen wurde, sondern die an den Universitäten und der Litteratur eine nie versiegende Quelle der Erfrischung, ja ein sie abspiegelndes Abbild fand, ein grosses Gut, das wir Deutschen um so weniger gering schätzen werden, je mehr uns die Entwickelung der Dinge in Grossbrittanien und Nordamerika den Werth dieses Gutes schätzen lehrt. Hier also wird es darauf ankommen, im Interesse des Gutes der Einheit und innerhalb derselben der Freiheit die Stelle zu finden, welche mit den Grundlagen der Reformation vereinbar ist: und dazu ist ein bedeutsamer Anfang bereits gemacht. Nicht in kirchengesetzlicher, geordneter Weise, aber in freiem gesundem Takte besonders in Württemberg, dagegen institutionell und gesetzlich geordnet in der preussischen Landeskirche, die in ihrer Einheit nicht uniforme Gleichheit oder Aufgeben der confessionellen Differenzen verlangt, sondern den Reformirten wie den Lutheranern ihr Bekenntniss ungeschmälert lässt, auch die Ausgestaltung der Verschiedenheit der evangelischen Typen in Cultus zulässt, aber auch wieder der Einheit ihre Bedeutung und Kraft gesetzlich und institutionell sichert.

Das Ausgeführte möge genügen um zu begründen, warum jetzt gerade ein deutscher theologischer Autor es wünschen darf, dass ein Werk seines vieljährigen Studiums und Nachdenkens auch in der evangelischen Welt englischer Zunge freundliche Aufnahme finde. Ich kann aber nicht ohne ein Bekenntniss schliessen. Ich bin mir der Unvollkommenheit und Unvollständigkeit der Darstellung der englischen Theologie nur zu sehr bewusst. An ihr trägt nicht der Mangel an gutem Willen aber die Unzugänglichkeit vieler englischen theologischen Werke und der fast gänzliche Mangel an zusammenhängenden deutschen Vorarbeiten die Schuld. Möchte daher bald ein englischer Gelehrter sei es in Grossbrittanien oder Nordamerika diese Lücke ausfüllen; ich glaube sagen zu dürfen, dass sich sein Werk einer nicht weniger günstigen Aufnahme in Deutschland zu erfreuen haben würde, als diejenige ist, die ich mir für dieses Buch wünsche, indem ich es in die englische Welt hinausgehen lasse.

Dr. Dorner.

Berlin, d. 30 März, 1871.

TRANSLATION

OF THE

AUTHOR'S PREFACE.

FOR my venturing to address myself in this preface to the English-speaking theological world I might seek a justification in the circumstance, that the first incitement to this step came to me from friends out of the people to which I design in this preface to address myself, namely from those who have made it their care to introduce the present work, by means of a translation, also into English literature.

But I will always, as I perceive, have at least to share in bearing the responsibility of so introducing it, and of this translation (which I have sanctioned without being in a position to undertake any control in connection with it), as well as of the venturous act of this preface. And therefore I will rather, just as if the first incitement had not come to me from without, appeal to the circumstance, that since my youthful years I have with a special love occupied myself with English literature, and have by a stay of some length in Great Britain acquired acquaintance with and a friendship for the land and people and their genius, and therefore do not feel toward them altogether as a stranger.

The present work, however, gives me, I hope, through its fundamental ideas, a special right to commend it to the attention of English-speaking Evangelicals. For it seeks, under the guidance of the spirit of evangelical catholicity, to furnish the historical evidence that, in spite of the variety of nationalities, as well as the manifold conformations of evangelical Protestant Christianity amongst those peoples which have appropriated the blessing of the Reformation of the sixteenth century,—in spite of the division in language, usages, and habits, as well as in its destinies, evangelical Protestant Christendom forms an unity. The English section of Protestantism, together with the evan-

gelical Christendom of its daughter Republic on the other side
of the Atlantic Ocean, forms the one great group of Protestantism, alongside of which only the German moiety stands
possessed of equal importance and similar circumference. If
German Protestantism has, by means of a philosophic spirit and
a free development of science, acquired an universal glance and
that broad heart, which—free from sectarian narrowness—recognizes the evangelical spirit wherever it is to be found, the
Anglo-American section of Protestantism has arrived at the
same wide comprehensiveness of view by means of that position
in the world, which its political, colonial, and mercantile history,
united to its practical skill and instinct, has procured for it.
That one life-blood flows in the two great sections of evangelical
Protestantism is most convincingly evidenced by the fact, which
the history of Protestant theology attests, that both have until
now—and that not through merely re-acting upon one another,
but independently—passed through the same succession of crises
in their inward life. No doubt this has occurred under a national
difference of form, inasmuch as the type of the German genius
has been hitherto inclined rather to theory and speculation, and
the mind of our Germanic brothers on the other side of the
Channel and the Ocean rather to practical problems and evolutions.
But only for a time has this difference been able to separate
them or allow a mutual ignoring of the work of the other. The
religious roots and impulses have, since the time of the Reformation, in which divine authority and evangelical liberty are united
in principle, remained essentially akin in both. Besides, German
theology, after many theoretical and speculative excesses, has in
its most recent and very hopeful developments increasingly perceived how the *ethical principle* must be incorporated into the
doctrine of God, anthropology, Christology, and Ecclesiastics, in
order to secure a firm basis as well as sure progress. The more,
however, that German science cultivates the ethical province
also, and is striving to know the laws of the life of the latter, the
more is its feeling for the peculiar work of the human mind in
Great Britain and North America opened up, and the more is it
inclined to profit by the charisma bestowed upon these nations.
Conversely, however, an analogous procedure is, if I am not
mistaken, in preparation also in those lands, which once produced speculative theologians of the first rank, an Anselm, a

Duns Scotus, nay, even earlier, a Scotus Erigena, but which have, since the fifteenth century, passed over into other paths. For the more recent Church history of these countries seems to show that, without the aid of a severe and productive theological science, prepared for combat, the Church stands defenceless against the more recent and powerful movements of the physical sciences and of historical criticism, as well as against the spirit of practical and theoretical materialism. All this permits us to wish for and to prophesy an increase of intellectual and even literary communion between the two main groups of evangelical Christendom, even as the alliance, becoming more and more conspicuously manifest, between the hostile powers with which it has to contend, renders the same desirable. Why has a civilization that is alienated from evangelical truth assumed such large dimensions amongst us in Germany? Because the impulse towards knowledge has been, although in a vital manner, yet too little impregnated by an ethical spirit. To this the embarrassed condition of our national, political, and civic relations, their uncomfortable obscurity and unfinished character, have not a little contributed,—restrictions, complications, and minute divisions, from which only the great events of the most recent times have, as we devoutly hope, set us free. On the other hand, what is the innermost ground of the diffusion in England, and to a certain extent in North America, of a tendency, partly infidel, and partly Romanizing, which in its latter aspect is already striking its roots over into Germany, if not that the prevalent Empiricism has no feeling for what is in itself true and eternal, or sceptically despairs of its accessibility, and hence, merely in order that life may not be without something to hold by, appoints certain self-chosen authorities to sovereignty over itself? Great Britain is not beyond the danger of a return of Deism, neither will it find a bulwark against it in the ritualistic tendency, as little as in a mere guarding of the treasures of past centuries, or in a literal cleaving, in a barren and inactive way, to the confessions of the sixteenth and seventeenth centuries. Both nations, the German and the English, stand in need of this, that the people, from the lowest strata to the highest, should again find its home in evangelical Christianity, and that those aspects of the Reformation faith should be worked out and presented, which are in a position to furnish the lamp for the present stage of the life and culture of the people, and are fitted to lend to the public mind of the nation as well as to the life of individuals the proper power of expansion and the proper harmony.

Never, perhaps, has there been so evident a necessity for holding aloft in common the banner of the Gospel against the common enemies of Protestantism. But never also has there been a time more favourable for a more lively communion amongst the different evangelical nations. I refer not merely to the almost marvellously increased means of intercourse for persons and for productions of the press, nor merely to the Evangelical Alliance, by means of which well-known men from England, Scotland, Holland, France, Switzerland, and North America, and from Germany, Denmark, and Sweden have been brought into personal communion, as well as to a community of work and prayer in reference to many important problems at present affecting Christendom; but I refer in particular to the circumstance that in the German and English portions of the Evangelical Church, even in Europe, the tendency of the times is undeniably moving increasingly in the direction of setting the Church more and more free from the too close bonds which attached her to the State. The Christian Church cannot, if it considers its nature, suffer itself to be confined within territorial and State limits; it represents the universal principle, and cannot recognize the landmarks of states as the boundary of its feeling of love and communion of life. The State, on the other hand, has necessarily a particular existence, and feels itself in this particularity of existence to be a complete entity, furnished with absolute sovereignty. An Universal State, however, there cannot be, because every nationality would require to sacrifice to it its own absolute state sovereignty. The Church, on the other hand, whilst it necessarily marches through history in like manner in national forms and shapes, is nevertheless conscious, even where this does not come out practically, of an unity stretching beyond states and nations, even as the Apostolic Creed confesses, "I believe in the holy Catholic Church." Nationalities are in no way limits for the Church, but are individualities, furnished with different charismata, which have to subserve the one all-embracing end, the advancement of the kingdom of God.

Now, the more the State and Church development of Protestant Europe will lead to the increasing independence of the Church, and the more the latter, after the loss of its original point of support in the State, will have to seek its power in itself, that is to say, in the evangelical people, the more will it become for the Church, having been detached from particular and State points of view, an inward need and an external necessity to allow the principle of true—that is to say, evangelical—catholicity to develop itself freely and powerfully, in virtue of the same impulse, though it may not be in the same forms, as in primitive Christendom. This unity of evangelical Christendom may be combined with the most different constitutions and forms of life on the part of the different nations, and in no way requires, as the Romish Church has it, an unity or even a similarity of church government in the case of all. On the contrary, even in one and the same nation there may prevail, without prejudice to the confederative principle, which unites all, the most manifold church forms. If they are only capable of union with the bases of the Reformation, they will be able to claim mutual recognition and furtherance. Unity amid a diversity full of life is that for which the Reformation opened the way, nay, is the natural and healthy form of life for Christianity amongst mankind.

The paths which these two sections of Protestantism have to take toward this end are different, and even in part opposed. In the Anglo-American section the National Churches, embracing a whole people, have not (with the exception of Scotland down to the Disruption) lasted long, but have been parted into a number of evangelical denominations, which, differing slightly in dogma, have divided and separated from one another on account of constitution, and the production of new separate churches is still always going on. If a counter-movement did not commence, the endless division and subdivision would more and more induce forgetfulness of the evangelical unity, and paralyze all common action on the part of Protestantism in missions to the heathen or against the Romish Church, presenting as it does such a compact appearance, or against unbelief; the giving prominence to liberty without unity would conduct Protestantism back into a state of impotence. Nay, even liberty, especially that of scientific movement, would itself suffer harm from this denial of unity in a sectarian spirit; for if every divergence, even of lesser importance, from what has been handed down crystallizes into a church party of its own, every individual would be prompted, apparently in the interests of truth, to regard the tenets of other denominations as boundaries which must not be overstepped by him, so that the freedom of his theoretical and practical movement would become more and more restricted. No matter although he may be conscious of holding to his own confession with desire and conviction, still he cannot in that case be attached to it in such a way as to be at liberty to import to it what he perceives to be true in others and what in common distinguishes them from his own. Thus liberty, without unity, without inward catholicity, leads to bondage, to the narrowness of a sectarian spirit. On that account the circumstance can only be welcomed with joy, that in most recent times, in powerful and healthy portions of English, Scotch, and American Protestantism, a counter-movement against this centrifugal tendency is more and more gaining ground, and the spirit of evangelical catholicity is finding its representatives in many of the best men out of all denominations. But in order that the saying, "In necessariis unitas, in dubiis libertas, in omnibus caritas," may come to be practically carried out, science, dogmatic culture, and a thorough acquaintance with and understanding of the fundamental evangelical truths are requisite. For only in this way are the duty and the measure of Church communion to be surely perceived. At this point accordingly there is presented a field for common labour, as well as for the desirable interchange of our theological literatures.

Quite a different path seems prescribed to the German family of Protestantism by *its* starting-point. Here the great evangelical National Churches still enjoy essentially unbroken unity, save that the above-mentioned close connexion with the State in Germany has brought with it restrictions and set up boundaries for the individual National Churches against one another. When once that connection with the State is loosened, or is so far dissolved as the independence of the Church renders desirable, there is here too, without doubt, to be anticipated the rising up of very different denominations or sects. Whilst this is not to be hindered by outward or even State means, still the unity of the Evangelical Church—which was never forgotten amid the division into national churches, but found in the universities and in literature a never-failing source of refreshment, nay, an image which reflected it—remains a great blessing, which we Germans will so much the less slight, the more the development of things in Great Britain and North America teaches us to prize the worth of this blessing. Here accordingly the vital point will be to find, in the interests of the blessing of unity and within the circle of it, that place for liberty which is in harmony with the bases of the Reformation; and an important beginning has already been made in this direction. It has been done in particular in Würtemberg, not in the way of being prescribed by church laws and formal arrangement, but in the exercise of a free and healthy tact; and, on the other hand, as matter of regular institution and legal arrangement in the Prussian National Church, which does not desire in its unity an uniform similarity or the giving up of confessional differences, but leaves their confession unimpared both to the Reformed and to the Lutheran, even allowing the development of the difference of the evangelical types in the cultus, but at the same time securing to the unity by law and institution its significance and power.

What has been said may suffice to furnish the reason why precisely at this present moment a German theological author may wish that a work, which is the product of many years of study and reflection on his part, should also find a friendly reception in the English-speaking evangelical world. I cannot close, however, without a confession. I am only too conscious of the imperfection and incompleteness of the exhibition given of English theology. The blame thereof is not due to the want of goodwill, but to the inaccessibility of many English theological works, and to the almost total want of connected German preparatory works. Would therefore that soon some Englishman of learning, whether in Great Britain or in North.America, would fill up this gap! I think I may say that his work would be sure to enjoy in Germany a no less favourable reception than that which I wish for myself on behalf of this book, when I now let it go forth into the English world.

Dr. DORNER.

BERLIN, 30*th March* 1871.

TRANSLATOR'S PREFACE.

THE Historical Commission of the Royal Academy of Sciences at Munich has, under the auspices of Maximilian II., King of Bavaria, undertaken the issue of a complete history of the sciences in Germany. Of the twenty-five histories embraced in the prospectus, one of the earliest to appear was the *History of Protestant Theology*, which was entrusted by the Commission to Dr. Dorner, and has been executed by him in a manner worthy of the occasion and the subject. The work met with a very favourable reception in Germany, having already passed through more than one edition, and is generally regarded there as one of the most important and valuable of the theological productions of the last five years. A companion or rival work, the *History of Catholic Theology*, was entrusted by the Commission to Dr. Werner, but even Roman Catholic reviewers have joined with Protestants in assigning the palm to the former, as in every respect a triumph of Protestant science over that of the Romish Church. Whilst Dr. Werner simply narrates with clear insight and comprehensiveness the various conflicts and particular incidents occurring in the field of Roman Catholic theology subsequently to the Council of Trent, Dr. Dorner endeavours first of all to exhibit the historic origin and the proper nature of Protestantism in order to a right understanding of the course of its subsequent life, and although minutely following the various developments and manifestations of that life, he never loses sight of their connection with or bearing upon the essential principles and matter of Protestantism. He not only narrates the history of Protestant theology, but aims at conveying to the reader a proper understanding of that history. It is therefore not surprising that this production of his pen should have been spoken of as "a classic, both in respect of matter and of form," and should have taken a foremost place as a standard work on the subject to which it refers. Neither is it surprising that it should have called forth antagonistic works from those who take different views of the nature of Protestantism, such as Schwarz (*Geschichte der neuesten Theologie*, Leipzig, 1869).

The estimate formed of this work in Germany, and the reception there accorded to it, would be a sufficient justification for its translation into English, even apart from those considerations founded on the nature of its contents, to which Dr. Dorner has in the preceding preface made forcible and seasonable reference. In any circumstances an English translation of a German theological work presents itself to the English reader under peculiar disadvantages. Besides the loss unavoidably occasioned by the transformation of the original into words, which, however closely they may answer to, are still always different from, those of the author himself, there is the complexity introduced by the endeavour to make the English sentences correspond in some measure to those of a language much more involved in its grammatical structure than our own. And not only so, but the habits of thought and the methods of presenting it natural to the German mind are very different from those to which we are accustomed in English authors, and generally require a conscious effort on our part to adopt this more or less unwonted form of mental contemplation. In the present case, however, the style peculiar to Dr. Dorner imposes more than ordinary difficulties upon the translator. Whilst evidently possessing a power of clear, nervous and eloquent writing, he is too much in the habit of allowing his thoughts to come out in sentences cumbrously and often obscurely built up and prolonged, as if the aim had been rather to free the mind of the writer of a load of thoughts connected with the matter in hand than to present those thoughts in the form most fitted to instruct and engage the reader. Many of his sentences also are characterized by a certain ruggedness and by almost obtrusive inelegance, more indicative of simple indifference to style than of want of care. It is almost necessary for me to make those remarks, for I have neither sought to impart to the translation any gracefulness or fluency not possessed by the original, nor have I willingly done any injustice to the latter. Had the work been of a popular character, I would have deemed it my duty to be less regardful of the manner of the original, and to aim at conveying the matter of it in a style more easy and perspicuous than that of a literal translation could be. I could not but feel however that it would be more acceptable to the class of readers for which the book is mainly designed and will be of chief value, that I should simply attempt as faithful a rendering of the original as could well be given, so that they might have the thoughts of the author in a shape corresponding to the form in which he himself presented them. And this accordingly is what I have endeavoured to give.

I have only to add that I have ventured to append a few notes in the hope that they may prove helpful at least to some. A few of these notes which were too late for insertion in their proper place I was obliged to relegate to an appendix, and I have not resisted in every instance the temptation thus presented to make the note a little longer than it would otherwise have been.

It ought to be distinctly stated that whilst I had the sole care of the first volume, the translation of the second is entirely the work of Miss Taylor, who has already earned a name as the translator of various works issued by Messrs. Clark.

GEORGE ROBSON.

INVERNESS, 23d *June*, 1871.

CONTENTS OF VOLUME I.

	PAGE
Introduction, ...	1

BOOK I.

The Primitive Period of Protestantism, ...	15

FIRST DIVISION.

The Preparation of the Evangelical Principle in a Negative and in a Positive Aspect, ...	17

SECTION I.

The Negative Side of the Preparation, . . , .	17

CHAPTER I.

The Pre-Reformation Church in general, ...	17

CHAPTER II.

The Development of Church Doctrine in respect of its Form and Subject-matter, ...	35

CHAPTER III.

The Life of the Church of the Middle Ages in its Concrete Opposites,	48

SECTION II.

The Positive Preparation for the Reformation, . . .	50

CHAPTER I.

The Mysticism of the Middle Ages, ...	51

CHAPTER II.

The Biblical Factor in the preparation of the Reformation, . . 63

CHAPTER III.

The Christian Education of the People and Christian Science, . 69

SECOND DIVISION.

The Reformation in its Initial Unity and Principial Basis, 1517-1525, 81

SECTION I.

The Lutheran Reformation, ... 81

CHAPTER I.

The Personal Development of Luther till 1517, . . . 81

CHAPTER II.

Development of the Purgative and Critical Side of the Reformation Principle in Luther, 1517-1522, ... 86
The University of Wittenberg; in particular, Melanchthon and the Alliance of the Reformation with Science, . . . 113

CHAPTER III.

The Development and Limitation of the Evangelical Principle in its Church-forming Aspects, from 1522 to 1536, in conflict with Antagonistic Parties, ... 122
  I. The Fanatics of a Practical Sort; in particular, the False Ethical Mysticism, ... 125
  II. Dogmatic Confutation of the Fanatics of the Species of False Ethical Mysticism, ... 142
  III. The Ethical side of the Controversy with the Fanatics. The office of the Ministry and Church Order, . . . 172
  IV. The false Theoretical Mysticism, ... 182
    1. The Christian side of the Theoretical Mysticism, . 182
    2. The Naturalistic side of Theoretical Mysticism, . 189
  V. The Reformation in Opposition to the False Theoretical Mysticism, 195
  VI. The Controversy with Erasmus, 1525, . . . 202

CHAPTER IV.

Exhibition of the Evangelical Principle in the Formation of the Church, 220
   A. The Natural side of the Evangelical Principle by Itself, or in its Relative Independence, ... 227
   B. The Essential Independence of the Holy Scriptures in respect of Faith and the Church, ... 245
   C. The Internal Connection of the Scriptures and Faith, without detracting from their Relative Independence, . . 249
   The Province of Christian Morals under the point of view of the Reformation Principle, ... 264

SECTION II.

The Swiss Reformation, as far as the Formation of its First Symbols, and its Relation to the German Reformation, ... 282

CHAPTER I.

The Fundamental Reformation Ideas of Zwingli, . . . 282

CHAPTER II.

Zwingli's Conflict with the Fanatics, in particular with the Anabaptists, 300

CHAPTER III.

Relation of the Swiss and German Reformations; their Harmony at the Outset, their Controversy, and Preliminary Peace, . . 303
   1. The Original Harmony, ... 303
   2. The Controversy regarding the Supper, . . . 306
   3. The Preliminary Peace, or the Marburg Conference. A.D. 1529, and the Wittenberg Concord, A.D. 1536, . . . 328

THIRD DIVISION.

The Development of the Two Evangelical Systems of Doctrine until their symbolic settlement, or the period from the first formation of the Evangelical Confession, about 1530, until the second, 1580 and 1619, 338

SECTION I.

The Lutheran Church, ... 338
   First Doctrinal Article.—The Antinomian and Majorist Controversies, 1527-1559, ... 344
   Second Doctrinal Article.—The Controversies regarding the Object of Faith. A. Osiander and F. Stancarus, . . . 353
   Third Doctrinal Article.—The Synergistic and Flacian Controversies regarding Anthropology and Soteriology, . . . 370

SECTION II.

The Reformed Church of the Second Symbolic Formation, . . 384

SECTION III.

The Reformed Church from the Death of Calvin to the Synod of Dort, 415

INTRODUCTION.

A HISTORY of Protestant Theology in Germany presupposes that the latter is, somehow or other, a thing which forms a unity in itself, and is not merely determined by the similarity of the geographical theatre; else we could not speak of a history of its life. Nor would even this justify our undertaking, if, as many suppose, it were only a phenomenon dependent upon another,—only, it might be, the negative side of Roman Catholicism, and therefore for its own existence always postulated that with which it combats. It is not merely the protest which runs alongside of, and is directed against, the Romish Church, ordained by a higher Hand as a warning check to it, for its purification or even for its chastisement: it has a proper principle of life in itself; it is a peculiar Christian formation, differing from the Roman and Greek Catholic Churches as well as from the sects. We have not here to inquire whether it and Roman Catholicism differ from one another in kind, or as stages in the apprehension of Christianity. In the former case, their difference would be based upon a difference of the religious individuality, which, whether it appears as a national characteristic or in the individual, possesses an intrinsic right to self-preservation and continuance; in the latter case, the higher stage must conserve perfectly what is good in the lower, just as, on the other hand, a general obligation would rest upon the latter to pass over into the higher. Perhaps neither the one nor the other completely expresses the case; perhaps Protestantism, which is conscious of representing a higher stage of the religious spirit, has nevertheless only a partial right to be held as completely realizing it, inasmuch as, whilst representing what is indeed a higher stage and therefore one to be entered on by the whole of Christendom, it represents it in an individual manner, so that possibly upon the same stage other forms of the Christian spirit may yet show themselves,—

Christian peculiarities, which are now perhaps hidden in the other churches amidst the dross, may at some future time come forth, as soon as the disfiguring element is removed and the stage of evangelical life is reached; and such an event would be of benefit even to the Protestant Church, which is indeed at present preserved against certain dangers by the Roman Catholic Church as by a warning example, but is also easily driven involuntarily into a certain onesidedness, and may by the very existence of the Roman Catholic Church, within any part of whose boundaries it must shrink from entering, be hindered in the free development of itself, especially in respect of the sides positively Christian but lying nearer to [Roman] Catholicism. In presence of such different individualities belonging to the evangelical stage, we could scarcely speak any longer of a plurality of evangelical churches, for no healthy individuality will maintain an exclusive attitude towards others in respect of their true nature, but rather one of recognition and love, in giving and taking,—in a word, that of one member in relation to the whole and to the other constituent parts.

Protestantism seeks indeed its ultimate foundation in the nature of Christianity, as it is handed down to us in a documentary form in the Holy Scriptures. But it dare not decline the task of justifying its separate existence and its peculiar nature *historically, i.e.* of showing by a historical review that a necessity for its appearance had arisen both in a negative and a positive respect, that it appeared when the fulness of the time was come, and now still asserts its indispensable place in Christendom.

That Protestantism does not consist in a chaos of tendencies of every possible kind, not in a confused mass of accidental opinions, and is not dependent on the positive element against which it on each occasion protests, but may, in spite of its many internal differences, be represented as a homogeneous formation, indicative of one principle,—this indeed can only be made fully evident by a historical account of Protestant Theology. Provisionally, it may be sufficient to remember, that in the European family of nations the name Protestantism denotes, since the sixteenth century, the whole offspring of the Reformation, and embraces all those who are rooted in the soil of the Reformation. The Protestants have, it is true, received their name in the first instance from that Diet of Spires (1529), at which those evangelical States, which upon the ground of the right furnished by the former resolutions of the Diet had begun in their lands a reformation according to the Word of God, were required by the majority of States, acting under the approbation of the Emperor, to institute a counter-reformation. In opposition to this demand the evangelical States entered their protestation of right, upon the good ground of their German and Christian rights and duties, and not upon the ground of anarchical caprice or love of liberty. They wished to preserve evangelical liberty, and to allow no human and separating medium to stand between believers and Christ; but they wished also to have that liberty controlled by evangelical truth and love, and by the regulations to which these might have given rise. Those who stood and spoke thus at Spires were termed Protesters, or the Protestant States of the Empire, and from this place—where the Reformation showed itself for the first time as a conscious and compact historical movement, even as it attained in the following year at Augsburg to a determinate and pregnant Confession before the Emperor and Empire, and one conservative of all the Catholic elements of Christianity—the name spread over Protestant countries, in which it lost its reference to the relations of German right, but preserved its true meaning of a free and candid testimony to scriptural and evangelical truth, in opposition to all perversions of it; hence we dare not allow this name of honour, which our fathers won and bore with self-sacrificing courage, to be taken from us or become distasteful to us, seeing that all depends simply upon our asserting it in its historical significance, according to which the protest against injustice and error had its root and power in positive truth, in the advancement of the Kingdom of God, and thus also of the Fatherland.

The great work of the Reformation, whose fruit is the historical formation denoted by the name of Protestantism, the constructing of an evangelical Christendom or comprehensive Church beside the Greek and the Roman Catholic Churches, took place, it is true, historically in several acts, but has nevertheless also its unity, and this not merely through essential contemporaneousness and the affinity of the nations which formed its theatre, still less through the leading and typical position of one country or of one person. On the contrary, eminent though the position of Germany, Wittenberg, Luther, and Calvin was, still there were essentially similar inward motives and instincts which urged the Reformation movement simultaneously in many countries of Christian Europe in a great degree independent of each other. It is not individuals who have accomplished this work; the most influential of the Reformers only desired to be instruments in their own humble place for the work of God, and, without any previous plans of reformation, have almost against their will, in any case contrarily to their expectation, been borne onwards through faithfulness in that which is little to the most comprehensive thoughts of reform. There was a more universal and divine design which was to be accomplished to a degree far beyond the thoughts of men; the Christian Church was to enter a new stage in the appropriation of salvation and in the development of Christianity. This one divine design is therefore, in spite of the manifold differences and divisions within the circle of Protestantism, the uniting power for all who are truly grafted into the great Reformation movement of the sixteenth century; they constitute and exhibit in the midst of the rest of Christendom one family of homogeneous type, whose parent seat is the German nation.

It is true that Protestantism thus acknowledges itself beforehand to be a special particular movement within the sphere of universal Christendom. But if it has hitherto been the German race, with its different nations, which has been entrusted with the gift of the Reformation, and with that work in the history of the world which is to carry on and render fruitful the work of the Reformation, there in no way follows from its [Protestantism] thus acknowledging itself a mere many-membered part of the Church, that it seeks only to confess to a part of Christian truth, or must, or will, exclude anything whatever which is able to prove itself truly Christian. It desires the whole Christian truth, even although it is as unsuccessful in perfectly appropriating it as any man in the course of history; but what it seeks to maintain as a possession already existing, is a new aspect of this whole Christian truth, a more perfect appropriation of the same in thought, will, and feeling,—viz. the *personal*, which it has discerned to be the aim of Christianity in its innermost tendency. Hence, in spite of its particularistic appearance,—the conquering of which is not dependent upon itself alone, since it is rather forced upon it from without,—it necessarily makes this claim,

Introduction. 5

that the essential of that for which it contends is designed for all, and all for it; for this essential is the common matter of Christianity (which also boasts an outward universality or catholicity), but that common matter *in personal application and in a personal direction;* and this latter, so far as it has an intrinsic right to, although it does not yet enjoy, a universal recognition in Christendom, possesses at least an intrinsic catholicity. However much that is perishable may cling to the appearance of Protestantism, the *evangelical stage,* which constitutes its essence, must be defended by Protestantism, if it is not to surrender its own existence, as the universal aim and common duty of Christians. Compared with the other two great Church parties of Christendom, Protestantism will neither rest content with a mere intellectual appropriation of Christianity, whether in a speculative form, or in a recollective form that faces a traditional doctrine, nor with a mere subjection of the will to a dogmatic or even practical Church law. Christianity is for it power, light, and life, which must be appropriated and worked out by the whole person in the believing heart, and it [Protestantism] lives in the confidence that the Church of Christ has thereby begun to gain a new and higher stage, which must come in after a normal fashion, and can therefore in itself be so much the less termed the cause of the division of the Western Church, that the higher stage is higher only in so far as it preserves in itself space for the tested and solid matter of earlier stages, and as the earlier stages contain in themselves the germs which in it grow to development; so that the earlier stage cannot turn itself against, nor cut itself off from, the essential element of Protestantism, without doing violence to itself and damaging the germs of its own future.

It cannot be the province of science, and would little accord with the dignity of history, to be subservient to denominational ambition and to human self-exaltation. It becomes us, however, to retain a vivid and grateful sense of the deeds of God towards our nation, that we may be found all the more fit and willing instruments for the purposes in reference to the whole of Christendom upon earth which God will accomplish by means of the evangelical Church. The countries of the Reformation are the theatre of the greatest work of God which has taken place since the days of the Apostles in the innermost province of the spirit, in religion, and of whose blessing so many races and nations are already partakers. Our German Fatherland, in particular, has been the most prominent scene of this work of God, and the Reformation, with its healthful and quickening influences, averting death and corruption, has been of benefit to the whole people, even to that part of it which has hitherto held itself aloof, and is seeking to enjoy the fruits without receiving, as it were, into their home the tree which bears them.

The new light which was thrown in the sixteenth century, and in harmony with primitive Christianity, upon the way to true peace and to the salvation of the soul, shot its rays in an unexpected manner over all Christian doctrines, and disclosed a whole new world of ideas and perceptions; but at the same time presented a whole *row of new problems*, whose common element consisted in this, that it was necessary, from the newly won point of view, to seize all the various matters in their central point, and to place them both in thought and treatment in the light of one great connection. For every movement of the souls of men which is deeper than ordinary, brings nearer to one another the spheres which are externally separate, and gives us to know in their common root the internal connection of things which are otherwise distinct. The solution of these problems, which related to the whole moral, religious, theoretical, and practical life of the individual and of communities in heaven and on earth, could not fail to be in many instances very different and antagonistic; and that created to the superficial observer the appearance as if the working of the Reformation were a chaos, the destruction of all unity. Where, however, the Protestant principle but remained and worked as a common possession, there the "clashing of minds against each other," and the shivering of unsatisfactory forms by the strokes of conflict, brought to light the noble and pure gold of truth, which accommodates itself to and enriches the whole. But where a breach was made with the Protestant principle itself, and use was made only of the formal enfranchisement of minds by the Reformation, there a history of the life of the Protestant Church and theology is no longer to be discerned, though possibly a history of their sufferings (for the Protestant Church is as little to blame as the Roman Church, and even less than it, for the appearance of Voltairianism, or of the degrading Humanism of Italy); in the end, however, such appearances as these, which cannot be shown

Introduction.

to be positive momenta or developments of the principle, must yet, if they do not exert a purifying influence, stand before us as great lessons or monuments to demonstrate the final impracticability of the errors which swerve from evangelical truth.

It is not possible, however, to place the historical movement of evangelical theology in the right light, or to understand it in relation to its starting-point and goal, if we do not first of all obtain for ourselves a faithful picture of the Reformation and of its aspirations. For what the creative period of the Reformation furnished in primitive strength, clear and ripe in its fundamental thought rather than finished and thoroughly connected in its development, to this the seventeenth century brings the enclosing walls and the analysis of formal logic, the eighteenth century, however, the breaking-up by negative criticism, while the *nineteenth* century is endeavouring, more consciously than any previous period, to make itself master of things in their principle, and of the principle in its fruitfulness and power, and to carry on the analysis to synthesis in a newer and higher form.

We shall therefore, by way of introduction, first of all consider the hidden work of preparation for the Reformation, and search in it for that quietly moving Hand, which was still keeping in the secret of divine silence what it proposed to accomplish, till, after the most manifold processes of purification by exclusion and by assimilation, the Reformation principle became internally ripe, and broke with conquering power from its shell. We shall then have to see how the purifying waters, gathering from every quarter, burst forth with mighty power here and there, especially however at the heathful fountain at Wittenberg, to pour a new life over Germany, nay, over a great part of Christendom. It is not only somewhat remarkable, but somewhat symbolical, and of the force of a model as to its manner, how the Reformation principle prepared for itself a place in the souls of the Reformers, gradually overmastered them, and created them its depositaries and defenders; how they at first dreamed not of its infinite meaning, still less deemed themselves worthy of being made the means for the accomplishment of so great a work; how, nevertheless, their godly believing heart became strong through the truth known and embraced, and the meekness, timid at first, and even trembling, was perfected in the manly courage which forgets itself and its own weakness in the concerns of God, and will sacrifice itself to these. We forget not, that no single man and no single people is clothed with the pure Christianity itself; that, on the contrary, all that is individual and national suffers from certain onesided defects; but it is not on that account the less becoming to hold in honour the common heritage of the evangelical Church of the Reformation period, that which our fathers sought, wrought, suffered, for which they fought as for the treasure of their soul and the Palladium of the German nation and its future, ever anew to revive the sense of its value, and to preserve faithfully for ourselves in true remembrance, and so also for the whole of Christendom, what was won by our fathers, the precious possession which the Greek and Romish confessions still want, but need.

But evangelical truth is no dead treasure, but a living fructifying principle. This has in a broad and general way been recognized and acted on by the Evangelical Church in its history, extending over more than three centuries. This fruitfulness of the Protestant principle, and the special forms it has assumed in work and conflict upon the different fields of action, it will be incumbent on us to exhibit in the following books, that thus the wealth of Christianity may become apparent to us, in the extent to which that wealth can be displayed in the evangelical stage of its appropriation.

The countries outside of Germany, especially the Reformed, have, upon the whole, hitherto sought to exhibit the Protestant principle rather in its realistic aspect, that of the practical moral life: Germany has hitherto seized rather the ideal side of Protestantism, and, alongside of the Cultus, has developed the Protestant view of the world rather in a speculative and scientific manner. It may have some connection with this circumstance, that here, too, Protestantism, even as a religious principle, has most thoroughly and purely shown itself a religious, world-stirring power, that here true *freedom* and *authority* have been brought most radically into *religious harmony*. And again, because the inner world of mind has here developed itself most independently and most richly, here in an especial manner is the seat of *Protestant Theology*, and that with ever-increasing ascendancy down to the most recent times. There is probably no branch of the whole Protestant Church amongst the different nations on this and that side of the Channel, and of the Sounds,

Introduction.

and even of the Atlantic, but must own that the strength of scientific Protestantism, both in exegetical, historical, and systematical Theology, rests in Germany. Whilst we are conscious that, because this is the peculiar gift of the German mind, the history of German Protestant Theology possesses a more universal importance for Protestantism in general, it is at the same time only fitting to connect with this knowledge the confession of our weakness and shortcomings in comparison with other countries, in respect of the practical and moral application of the Protestant principle,—a need for being supplemented and an imperfection which are not removed by the fact, that the more recent Theology, in accordance with the ethical impulse which pervades it, has with an insight into this want found the inward transition from the life of thought to the whole world of practice, and has seen that all the benefits and excellences which are manifested in the different provinces of evangelical Christendom, and which have their root in the evangelical principle, are designed for interchange, and for appropriation in accordance with the individual basis, and must therefore be also mutually studied. But such a contemplation extends beyond the limits of our enterprise, which refers to the history, not of the Protestant Church, but of its Theology.

On the other hand, Evangelical Christians are responsible for the proof of their claim, as that has been described above in general outlines. It may contribute essentially to the clearness and certainty of the religious and ecclesiastical, as well as of the theological, self-consciousness of Evangelical Christians, if historical evidence is adduced to show that Protestantism, this vital and pregnant formation, is, in reference to its origin and past, a thoroughly justifiable manifestation, based on good Christian and historical grounds, and presenting itself with a good Christian conscience; further, that it has hitherto in all its movements and in its antitheses preserved the steadiness or continuity of a historical and growing formation; and finally, that there are entrusted to it, and henceforth to it alone, not merely for itself, but also for Christendom, certain clearly recognizable duties and aims.

There is a difficulty in the way of depicting with the proposed comprehensiveness the history of Protestant Theology as a homogeneous formation, namely, the difference of the two evangelical

Confessions, which have obtained a firm footing even in Germany. Let us look more closely at the situation of affairs in general, and especially in Germany, leaving out of account the territory of the Greek Church in the East. Roman Catholicism and Protestantism are distributed in Europe and America in such a manner that the North of Europe and America, especially the North of Germany, belongs in general to the latter, but the South to the former. The difference between the Lutheran and the Reformed Confessions forms, on the other hand, a cross-division. We see in the territory of the Evangelical Catholic Church a West, composed of Scotland, England, Holland, and France, as far as Switzerland, which is in a preponderating degree Reformed, and an East, in a preponderating degree Lutheran, reaching from Würtemberg and Bavaria in the South through Central and Northern Germany to Denmark, Sweden, Norway, and the Russian Baltic provinces. To the Reformed West, North America also belongs by an overwhelming preponderance. Again, there are to be found in these two principal Protestant groups connecting links of different kinds; outside of Germany, in Hungary, where the two Evangelical Confessions are nearly equally balanced, and also in Alsace; an inward bond of union between the two Evangelical Confessions is further formed, on the one hand, by Reformed Switzerland in virtue of its nationality and intercourse with Germany, and on the other hand, by the Anglican Church in virtue of the Lutheranism which in many respects characterizes it. But such connecting links between the two Churches are to be found most of all in Germany,—thus, on the Lutheran side, Würtemberg, whilst in nearly the whole of Germany there is to be found only a modified Reformed creed, which is secretly friendly to the Lutheran Confession,—so in Baden and the Palatinate, in Hesse and Rhineland, in Westphalia and East Friesland.

This condition of affairs renders it possible to bring within the compass of an undivided contemplation the history of the Protestant Theology of Germany, naturally not without taking into account its reciprocal relations with foreign lands. The peoples and races, which came under the influence of the Reformation, have, especially in Germany, even where they were subsequently divided into two confessions and existed separately, nevertheless derived from the common origin of the one great Reformation movement a certain family resemblance of a negative and positive kind, a rich common property, by the power of which the great Reformation work was in general accomplished, so that they at first seemed to themselves and to others to form one Church party. Even granting that differences, which afterwards appeared in definite and divisive form, existed from the very first in germ, it is quite consistent with that admission that the Lutheran and the Reformed Confessions may be regarded as different developments of the one and the same Protestant principle, in which this principle has begun to work out its strength and fulness, and which when brought to a mutual exchange will be of service to the whole. There is, besides, the fact, that even during their separate existence, when they were wont to advance only in lines parallel to one another, the Evangelical Confessions have yet discovered with especial clearness at the crises of their development—this all the more, the more important these crises have been—their inward relationship to one another on account of the fundamental family resemblance, whether this relationship was manifested rather in the form of variance or antithesis, or more in a pacificatory spirit and with the desire to effect an understanding.

Another difficulty in the way of our undertaking has reference to the relation of theology to the Church. It is not worth the while to speak of the history of a thing, unless there has not only been movement in general, but the movement has begotten something really new, has begotten progress, and is thus at the same time the development of the original germ, in which the primitive power of the thing was enclosed. Now, it may be said, the Church's summary of doctrine was already in 1530, in 1580, and in 1619, settled and closed; the results of later theological labour, however valuable may be the matter they contain, have not yet obtained canonical sanction; and not only so, but the evangelical Church is in a great measure without even the forms for such a sanction, by which the early Church, through the erection as it were of boundary stones, ratified the progress in different directions attained by the common conviction of the Church. Besides this, the later theological movements, especially since the eighteenth century, diverge so far from one another that we may well be diffident of retaining the thread of an ecclesiastical development.

But the evidence that the thread has never been broken is possible. How else were it to be explained that the evangelical Church of the nineteenth century has again become so vividly conscious of its connection with the Reformation, not only where an artificially contrived, so to say improvised, return to the Reformation time has been attempted, but also where the never wholly extinct but revivified recollection of it has again united the spirit inwardly and firmly, organically and in the way of growth, with the Reformation?

It will therefore only be necessary that we should recognize the connection, which even the eighteenth century, in many respects unconsciously, has with the Reformation time, and should incorporate it into the body of the History of Protestant Theology. Thus, then, in order to speak of a development of the system of doctrine, there is no necessity for councils nor for the formal fixing of the dogma by a positive canon. The opposite is proved by the three first centuries of the Christian Church (to which the three first centuries of the Protestant Church bear so manifold a resemblance), in which, without œcumenical synods, the progress of dogma was for centuries as rapid as it was sure and constant. Never, however, was dogma created, or constituted truth, by the sanction of the Church in a juridical, canonical form; but, on the contrary, because it had in its substance established itself in the common faith, there followed the declarative sanction and establishment, which in itself adds nothing to the truth, but only seeks to ensure its acceptation by investing it with the form of external authority. But it is precisely the latter which is of lesser importance to the Evangelical Church, since it allows no infallibility to ecclesiastical authority. If the progress achieved seems to be thus less surely established for that Church, it is thus also that the free, real appropriation of the truth is, where space is allowed it as in the Evangelical Church, the more clearly proved to be the power which moulds and captivates the minds of men, without chaining them to the erroneous and only seemingly progressive along with the true, or transforming the errors of the past into an obligatory heritage, a sacred hereditary evil without the *beneficium inventarii*.

We cannot accordingly adduce any utterance of an ecclesiastical tribunal in support of what has been achieved since the symbols were completed, nor would we even desire to prove its achievement in this way. But even as such external proofs of evangelical truth are denied us, so we have no need of them. At the same time we do not despise external authorities. Everything, however, depends upon our grasping firmly and clearly the Protestant principle in its purity, and wielding it as the regulative and judicial, and also relatively as the debarring and refutative principle.

Finally, in order not to occasion confusion and distraction through the copiousness of the matter pertaining to the individual sciences of Protestant Theology and to their productions, it will be necessary to narrate the history of Protestant Theology in such a manner that it shall be at the same time, and above all, a History of the Protestant Principle.

BOOK I.

THE PRIMITIVE PERIOD OF PROTESTANTISM.

FIRST DIVISION.

The Preparation of the Evangelical Principle in a Negative and in a Positive Aspect.

SECTION I.

THE NEGATIVE SIDE OF THE PREPARATION.

CHAPTER I.

THE PRE-REFORMATION CHURCH IN GENERAL.

THE Catholic Church of the middle ages, which embraced the whole of Western Christendom, and even the Papacy, rendered important services to humanity in its day. It educated and disciplined the wild strength of the nations which now bear the destinies of the world, and it thereby, in a way in which the Oriental Church cannot boast to have done in its sphere, laid a foundation for more modern European humanity. It guided the youth of these nations, and communicated to them the primary elements of civilization, and it even contributed materially to the founding of the mediæval states. For it habituated the nations, by means of a highly refined canonical law and church regulations, to legal order, imparted a divine sacredness to their statutes and their rulers, and accustomed them, in the stead of a vagrant profession of arms, to settled habits and the labours of peace; it brought these unspoiled but unpolished nations to recognize something higher than might and force, outward lordship and honour; it elevated their warlike ambition into a chivalrous virtue, and prevailed on them to bow the proud neck to powers greater than the strength of man and horse. It was also a great matter, that, in claiming for the Church the homage of the pious and courageous mind of these nations, it instilled into them the idea of universality, of the oneness of humanity in Christ, of the connection of all with one whole, and that, in opposing an all-embracing spiritual kingdom to the division of races and the enmity of nations, it broke their untamed, natural and particularistic self-will. In the middle ages, indeed, down to the overthrow of the Hohenstaufen, this idea of a universal kingdom sought a political fulfilment in the Empire, the successor to the Roman dominion. But evidently with less inherent right than that by which the unity of humanity is represented in the form of a universal Church, because the political life of races, in which national, geographical, and historical conditions necessarily play so great a part, is injured and retarded by a universal political empire, just in proportion as the latter aims at unity,—if indeed the issue must not be the oppression of all nationalities by what must ever be the onesided nationality of the ruling party. The postulate even of a federative political state must still in any case be the pre-existence of an agreement in the morals of religious faith. No wonder that the popular faith placed the spiritual empire of the Papacy in the middle ages, so far as its rights and honours were concerned, above the political, and entertained less fears of it than of the latter in their bearing upon national independence. It may be also further said, that in its conception of Christianity the Western Roman Church exhibits progress in one respect, in comparison with the Greek confession. For in the Oriental Church Christianity is in an overweening measure restricted to a pure doctrine (ὀρθοδοξία, πίστις ὀρθόδοξος), and to the enlightenment which it confers. It is an after effect of the Grecian cast of mind that in it the intellectual, the life of thought, is especially stimulated, piety and morality being regarded as the natural and necessary consequence of correct thinking. That is the Greek form of Determinism.[1] This intellectualism was, in the flourishing period of the Oriental Church, rather of a speculative and spontaneous, productive nature, as the works of an Irenæus, Origen, Athanasius, and of the Cappadocian Fathers show; and with this personal activity there was also connected at that time a more intense personal piety, certainly inclining somewhat onesidedly to the contemplative character, as is seen from the characteristic facts of Greek monachism and of its literary productions. At a later

[1] "Determinismus" is the technical name for a theory of the way in which the religious and moral action of man is determined.—*Tr.*

date, however, the speculative and productive impulse of the Greek Church vanishes; the intellectual tendency remains and manifests itself, in the case of some, in a formal employment of the understanding and in dialectics, which, without theological reproductiveness, but in a simply scholastic manner, defend, refine, and fence in more and more the dogmas (Trinity, Christology) established at the œcumenical councils; whilst the rest, who form the general mass, exhibit the intellectual tendency merely in a receptive or passive manner, inasmuch as they no longer look for salvation in the knowledge of Christian truth, but in the appropriation through the memory of traditional formulæ of doctrine, which become more and more but dead mysteries, and even, as it usually happens, lose their original meaning and spirit, and occasion grossness of conception and superstitious and parasitical imaginations.

To this intellectual tendency towards objective truth (the Three-one God, the Logos, the divine and human nature in Christ and their union), and the delusion it nourished concerning the magical power of pure doctrine as a means for the protection and blessing of the whole man, there was united a moral security and religious torpidity, which were maintained by the kindred delusion that the knowledge of the truth, even its mere reception as a matter of memory, brings with it the Christian salvation, that sin is essentially only a want of knowledge or error. Christ is thus reduced to a mere revealer of the true doctrine concerning God, and concerning the past and future. Guilt and reconciliation through Christ, as also sanctification, received too little consideration, both in life and doctrine. Thus the Church became a school, and soon a mere community confessing the formulæ of faith, which was not even in a position to kindle a living missionary zeal. No wonder that when the Church thus confined itself to the mental province of conception or knowledge, the worldly mind retained its power, and the old Grecian world was not in reality renewed from within. At the Byzantine court a kind of Christian varnish was necessary to veil the working of falsehood and deceit, of avarice and ambition, of intrigue and corruption. If the Emperor only held fast by pure doctrine, or even did nothing more than uphold it with the arm of force, he was the "divine" and "most divine" Emperor, before whom even those cringed in servility and self-debasement whose duty it was to be the defenders of the Church and of the Word of God. He who recognizes the perniciousness of the Byzantine mixture of Church and State, which served to secularize the Church and its office-bearers, and to lead the State to forget in its ecclesiastical drapery its proper duties, the care of right and justice, must at least acknowledge this benefit in the Osman rule, that the Greek confession has now, in its antagonism to the unbelieving head of the Empire, had imposed upon it, even although it be by pressure from without, a greater ecclesiastical and religious independence and veracity; and from this religious basis the renovation of Greece, now begun, has derived its strength.

The WESTERN Church exhibited from an early period, since Tertullian, Cyprian, Hilary, Ambrose, and Augustine, a more practical tendency; it sought for Christianity an other than ideal existence. The doctrinal heritage of the Greek Church, to the matter of which it contributed little, it appropriated without occupying itself theologically with it to any extent; on the other hand, it sought to convert the ideas of the East into reality. It possessed a severe moral earnestness, which, in the above-named Latin Fathers, directed even the theological studies of the Church to the anthropological questions as to the freedom of man in relation to grace, the primitive condition and fall of man, natural depravity and the means of deliverance from the power of sin, which is not broken through mere instruction. It conceived of Christianity not as a mere matter of knowledge or of confession, as a *fides historica*, but as an affair of the will, as *assensus*, and that practically in subjection to the Church, and thus it describes an essentially higher stage of the penetration of the Gospel into the spirit of man,—namely, the passage of the Gospel from the intellect into the will. In this manner, the ethics of Christianity receive a higher significance, and Christianity is transformed from a mere science and divine theory into a divine rule of life for all nations. It is difficult to say whether it was that the necessities of the barbaric nations which were won to the Western Church called forth and developed this tendency towards moral discipline and the moral regulation of life, or whether it was rather the already existing tendency towards Christian morality and towards its ecclesiastical supremacy which led to the subjection of these nations to the Latin Church.

However that may be, it is certain that this Church, by the severe training to which it subjected these nations of modern times, has deserved well of them. But it is also not less certain, that the Western Church became more and more decidedly inclined to identify its canon law in process of development with the divine law, and to confound the supremacy of the Church and of its rulers over the nations with the supremacy of God over the hearts and even within the souls of men.

This leads us to that which rendered a reformation of the mediæval Church necessary. For however readily Protestant science recognizes all that has just been explained, there still remains the crucial question,—What is in general, in the middle ages, the nature and tendency of the Church system, with the papacy at its head, which united under it the Western nations? What is the mediæval doctrinal concept of the Gospel? And what, in accordance with the principles resulting from it, was the prevalent form of the ecclesiastical and Christian life?[1] Let us accordingly consider in this chapter the *idea* prevalent in the middle ages *regarding the one universal Church.*

Christianity has no interest in that merely negative universality which pre-Christian philosophical systems, especially the Stoic, had already proposed, and which consists only in abstraction from the existing differences in humanity; nor in that merely external universality which the Roman Empire partly achieved by force, and which consists in the annihilation of nationalities, in the subjection of all under one common external

[1] Cf. amongst the earlier literature, Walch, in *Luthers Werken,* V. xv. p. 4 ff.: *Von der Nothwendigkeit der Reformation,* 1745, which adduces a great number of writings connected with it, *e.g.* of Joh. Aurifaber, Joh. Mathesius, Fried. Myconius, Val. Ernst Löscher, *vollständige Reformationsacten,* Sleidanus, *de statu relig. et reipubl. Carolo V. Cæsare Commentarii,* 1555. Sam. v. Puffendorff's *Politische Betrachtung der geistlichen Monarchie des Stuhls zu Rom;* H. v. d. Hardt, *Magnum œcumenicum Concilium Constantiense* and *Historia literar. Reformat.,* but especially the testimonies of Catholic theologians to the necessity of a Reform, *e.g.* B. von Ch. Gerson, Nic. von Clemangis, Petrus de Alliaco, Erasmus, &c. Of more recent times: Veit Ludw. v. Seckendorff, *Historia Lutheranismi,* 1692. Salig, *vollständige Historie der Augsburger Confession und deren Apologie,* Halle, 1730, ff. 4 Thl. Planck, *Geschichte der Entstehung, der Veränderung, und der Bildung unseres Protestantischen Lehrbegriffes bis zur Einführung der Concordienformel.* 6 Bde. 1791-1800. Marheineke, *Geschichte der Reformation,* 4 Thle. 1831-34. L. Ranke, *Geschichte der Deutschen in der Zeit der Reformation,* 6 Thle., 1839. Neudecker, *Reformationsgeschichte,* 1843. Holzhausen, *Geschichte der Protestantismus,* 1847, f.

law. Instead of such merely formal, superficial, as well as barren uniformity, Christianity aims at a pregnant, many-membered unity of mankind. The world must become a living temple of God, humanity "the body of Christ with many members." Its bond is not to be external, mere might or law, but internal, the Holy Spirit, who, dwelling in the heart by faith, places all in immediate communion with Christ, the Head. The new higher life which the Spirit of Christ imparts is a life of redemption from all the spiritual evils which burden mankind not yet in Christ; it is the deliverance of the heart from the oppressive feeling of guilt, or reconciliation and peace with God; it is the deliverance of the will from the power of sin, or a life of holiness and love; and finally, it is the deliverance of the mind from darkness and error in divine things and a life of light through divine illumination.

How, then, does the Papal Church of the middle ages stand in general to this simple outline of the Gospel, which embraces however all the wants of the soul?

Seeing that the carrying out of a statutory and harmonious rule of life for the nations is her highest aim, she has assumed into this her aim, and therefore into her theory, the principle of authority, power and lordship, in such a way that she no longer subordinates herself as a means to the spiritual renovation of the nations, but the perversion takes place, that that authority and lordship is treated as its own end and highest good,—of which perversion it is only the reverse side, that the spiritual blessings which the Church administers, Christian knowledge, and the power of sanctification and reconciliation, are transformed into instruments of ecclesiastical power, and even of hierarchical rule. We shall consider this in detail, and only make the preliminary remark with reference to the significance of this perversion, that the error of the hierarchy might seem to be an error only in a secondary matter, inasmuch as the question concerning power and rule is a subordinate one for him who knows the inner nature of Christianity; and it is precisely the more superficial opposition to the Romish Church which is wont to give the chief prominence to this aspect of it. If, however, a secondary matter is made the principal matter, the doing so is no longer a secondary matter, but leads to the subversion of the truth. Further, the theory of the hierarchy and its growth to priestly domination is not a mere external matter, else it might be regarded without disquietude, but its principle pierces deep and destructive into the inner nature of Christianity; it corrupts the theory of the Church itself as well as of Christianity. The former, because when it comes to the bare question of authority and power in the Church, the natural consequence is that the Church must divide itself into two classes, the ruling or the order of the priests and the lay community, whose principal value for the theory of the Church consists in this, that it is ruled; for in so far as that lay community were made the end, in so far would the hierarchy become a means animated by a love which would establish, or at least strive for, equality. There occurs, however, here a falsification of Christianity, since the properly religious impulse is both in the clergy and in the laity diverted from its Christian aim, the renewal of the personality and the communion of the Spirit, and offered a visionary satisfaction by means of the wielding of or through obedience to the statutory ecclesiastical rules of life. The impetus towards such a hierarchy germinates so early as the time in which the Greek Church still possessed the ascendancy; it is found in the form of a pretendedly divine *authority over doctrine*. But in the Latin Church the germ of hierarchy unfolded itself in the direction of the sphere of volition, and hence first in full power. Here the clergy regards itself as the proper Church. In Christ's name, and even in His stead, the hierarchy assigns to itself the administration of the office of Christ upon earth, not only of the office of infallible teacher or the prophetical office, but also of the reconciling or priestly office, as well as royal power. This is the triple crown which the papacy claims, and of the three it is the kingly office, to which, as centre, everything else, even the prophetic and priestly office, is subservient.

With regard, first of all, to the benefit of RECONCILIATION, the consequence of the hierarchical ideas is that the unclerical masses in themselves are without the means of reconciliation, without any participation in it, and without immediate fellowship with God, whilst the Church on the other hand, comprehended in the clergy, is furnished with an endless variety of means and powers of reconciliation. The clergy has the power of reconciliation in its own hand, and stands over against the people as a judge in God's stead, who can retain or remit sins, and can attach absolution to conditions which it imposes as Lawgiver in God's stead. Thus no one can be reconciled with God unless he is first of all united and reconciled with the Church. But such subjection to the law and judgment of the priest does not yield the satisfaction of the desire for *immediate* communion of the heart with God, and the certainty of the forgiveness of sins is in no way assured by the absolution of the priests, for the efficacy of this absolution depends upon circumstances of the existence of which there can never be perfect certainty,—*e.g.*, whether the priest is in reality a *rité* ordained priest—a question which can never be satisfactorily answered, since it reaches back through the whole chain of ordaining bishops to the Apostles. Further, whether the priest has administered the sacrament with the intention of doing what the Church wills? whether everything had been confessed that was to be confessed?—an endless inquiry for the conscientious, and many other such questions. Whilst the enjoyment of the gracious Gospel is thus spoiled for the sincere Christian, the frivolous finds contentment in absolution. Both are through the Church's sacrament of confession placed under the power of the clergy. But the heart never comes into immediate conscious fellowship with God Himself. The people are restricted by the priests to the outer court. It is only the office and impersonal institution which boasts the immediate enjoyment of divine powers. As regards his own moral person, as distinct from his office, the cleric is not in the slightest degree better off than the layman; he can just as little rejoice in his personal forgiveness and fellowship with God. Thus the benefit which the Church dispenses, because it is not a benefit of personal fellowship with God, but rather, as it were, only of a material kind, has become an impersonal matter. It is mysterious influences and powers connected with the province of the Church, and with the clergy, which are made to constitute the riches of Christianity; and so piety, robbed of its personal end, attaches itself to the visible altar and to other sensible things,—pictures, relics, and holy water, concerning which the hope is cherished that they at least establish for the moment a *rapport* with the expiatory influences of the Christian salvation, or drive away powers of evil.

Since, on the other hand, it goes against even the dullest conscience to seek salvation with perfect confidence in such external magical grace, dependent too upon accidental circumstances, how natural is it, that for the attainment of the forgiveness of sins and divine grace, confidence is also placed in meritorious performances in the way of doing or suffering, to which as good works an atoning power is made to belong. But this leads us to a second point, the relation of the Church to SANCTIFICATION.

That holiness essentially belongs to the idea of the Christian Church, is certainly firmly maintained; but in opposition to Novatianism, and especially to Donatism, the idea of the holiness of the Church became more and more dissociated from the moral holiness of the individual person, and more and more inclined to this form, that the Church possesses inalienable holiness by means of its sacraments,—in the last instance, through that sacrament of sacraments, ordination. The ordained and ordaining clergy is the point of earthly Christendom with which the Holy Spirit is inseparably connected, and from which He can never withdraw. The race of men possessed of the Holy Spirit is thus in all times to be seen in the clergy, who administer also the powers of consecration and the gifts of grace. That ordination renders the ordained good men, is not indeed asserted, but nevertheless the office is made to enjoy inalienably the possession of the Holy Spirit, and mankind as connected with the clergy by obedience is connected with the Holy Spirit, and is therefore called holy Christendom. But here we have again (so to speak) a material instead of an ethical personal holiness. It rests upon the divine origin of the hierarchical institution, upon its sacramental consecration and investiture with the treasures of grace, as well as upon its holy authority. How darkening and even misleading for the moral consciousness of the clergy must have been this entailing of holiness through an external manipulation! What wonder if the hierarchy went astray after ends very different from the realization of holiness in the world,—the ends, much more, of power and authority? The constitution of the world which would please God was regarded by the hierarchy as consisting in this, that the world should be subject to it and to the Church's rules of life, and perform certain works connected with the Church.

But whilst the ethics of the public ecclesiastical body aim in this way at subduing the world to the sovereignty of the Church, that could not satisfy the more sincere, those anxious about their personal salvation. Over against this public system of ethics there stands a private system, which turns aside from and flees the world, aiming at nothing but the salvation of the soul in retirement from active life and from the exhibition of the unity and splendour of the Catholic Church. But however opposed these two are, they both suffer from the same fault, which prevents the union of the true in both. The conquest of the world by the Church was enjoined by love, but when the object in view was the extension of the authority of the Church and not the good of the soul, the effort to conquer the world for Christ degenerated into a far more worldly shape, and was defiled by ecclesiastical egotism. But not less is that anxiety for one's own soul, which forgets the mission of Christian love in the world, not a pure fear of God and love to Him, but a love of God marred by the spiritual selfishness of the subject. Accordingly, these two great opposite tendencies of the mediæval Church are one in this, that the conception they have of the conquest of the world is, like themselves, external. Whilst the Church acts as if the world were won for Christ in so far as it is subject to the law of the Church, monasticism acts as if the world were conquered when the subject retires from the possessions and occupations of the world, *i.e.* of human society, but also from its sufferings, preparing for itself, instead of them, self-chosen sufferings, and so exhibiting a pattern to the world. On the other hand, what is inseparably connected as faith and love, personal and corporative consciousness, concern for one's own soul and concern for the community, are in both separated from one another. There the attention to works destroys the fixing of the mind on God, here the religious instinct effaces the moral task appointed in the world. Thus the whole ethical system of the middle ages rends asunder what has its significance only in its intimate internal connection, for the proof of purity in intercourse with the world is that the inward freedom from the world, the having as if one had not, the renunciation of the world, is not wanting, without which a collected self-assertion of the Christian disposition is not possible. And the proof of the purity of that love which turns in renunciation of the world towards God is, whether it makes a gift of the love of God also to the world, whether it is animated by a love to one's neighbour. That therefore which, when interpenetrating itself in a right manner, would form an exhibition of Christian ethics, is parted into two sickly tendencies; and even the knowledge which would necessarily impel the two to interpenetration, namely, that the moral must be essentially and inwardly one and the same whole, was obscured partly by the conception of the so-called "higher perfection" not necessary for all, and partly by the conception of the Church in its mediæval configuration as the *corpus mysticum* of Christ. For, according to the standpoint of the middle ages, there takes place by means of the Church this mystical body, a completion and vicarious representation of one member by another even in an ethical point of view, so that, if the Church were blamed for cherishing monasticism and in it an impure ethics, consisting in flight from the world, it composedly points to its exterior aspect, by no means exhibiting a flight from the world, its subjugation of the world, its government by means of its extensive institutions; and when it is reproached with its tendency to defilement with the world, it points to monasticism and its holiness in retirement from the world. In the later mediæval period we find an effort made in the direction of a union of these two ethical factors, inasmuch as monasticism, especially the preaching division of the begging orders, placed itself more and more at the service of the Church, and the Church sought to clericalize monasticism, whilst the clergy on the other hand had for a long time been increasingly subjected to certain monastic rules. Still, what was false in both tendencies was not by this means effaced; their endeavour to unite, however, is to be ranked amongst the signs already apparent, that mediæval piety must by an inward necessity strive to reach beyond itself, beyond its dualism.

But how, finally, does the mediæval Church stand related to the third blessing of the Gospel, to TRUTH?

It has been already mentioned how the Church, especially the episcopate, was already regarded in the Oriental Church as the infallible repository of Christian truth, with divine authority in doctrine. The right of expounding the Holy Scriptures passed over more and more to the bishops, and it became a received axiom, that although individual bishops or even provincial synods might err, still the utterances of an œcumenical synod are infallible, because the whole of Christendom, which is supposed to be represented in the episcopate, can never fall away and err. But the setting up of such a doctrinal regency exercises a great influence even upon the inner Christian life, upon the formation of a personal conviction. For how natural was it now, in answer to the question, "Why one ought to believe?" to point to the formal divine authority of the Church, instead of preaching repentance and faith, after the manner of the Gospel, which at its entrance into the heathen world could appeal to no already recognized authority of Church or Scriptures, and of trusting for the rest to the innate power of the Gospel, and attributing to it the power of convincing the souls that are longing after salvation?

The Occident, again, in which the idea of the one Church as the race of men governed by the Christian law of life forms the central point, has, in accordance therewith, developed (as already indicated) new phases of the hierarchical principle. This law, in order to cope with the wants and questions which are ever afresh coming to the surface, required a continuous legislative activity, and no less the administration of the law. The organ for both is found in the hierarchy. Everything, even the Gospel, is now viewed from the standpoint of the law. Is the question asked, "Why the doctrine which the Church teaches is to be believed?" the answer is, "Because the Church is the pillar and ground of the truth." Is the proof demanded for such an authority on the part of the Church—*i.e.* on the part of the clergy culminating in the episcopate—the last answer, after perhaps much circumlocution, is, "The Church must be believed, because it ascribes infallibility to itself;" that is, the question is given back as an answer, or the doubt forbidden. Thus the command of the Church and obedience to it takes the place of the self-evidencing power of evangelical truth, and of the divine certainty which it produces. Nor is it to be thought that the clergy at least participate in this personal assurance, and that it is only wanting to the people, who are, as it were, in nonage. On the contrary, the clergy has here no essential advantage; for to allow to the truth the power of self-attestation, which is acknowledged not to belong to the Church, is to place the truth above the Church, and would also imply a relative independence of the subject who had access to the truth, which would destroy the whole fabric of external authority. Another connection between truth and the spirit of man than that effected through the authority of the Church the official Church does not know, although in all ages individuals have attained assurance of the truth of Christian truth through inward experience.

The Mediæval Church a Spiritual Kingdom. 29

What has been said bears evidence to an infringement by the hierarchy, as such, upon the Christian blessing of illumination. But a further deterioration was caused by the Romish development of the hierarchy. Since each individual bishop may err, and synods are not at hand to give a new answer to the new questions of every age, the question arises, Where is the infallible Church, so that one may find and listen to it? It must be recognizable and visible: it must, continued the argument of the middle ages, have a fixed seat upon earth, not a merely momentary one, like the assemblies of bishops. Therefore the Church of Rome, with the successor of Peter, the prince of the Apostles, is appointed the visible seat and citadel of the truth. Here the true Church enjoys an imperishable visibility; from this chair the Holy Spirit never departs; he who abides by obedience in connection with it and its decisions cannot fall from the truth. This crowning of the hierarchical pyramid was, however, the necessary result of the general fundamental tendency mentioned at the beginning. For if the Church is regarded principally as a spiritual *kingdom*, then the unity of the Church inevitably requires, that the royal power of Christ which it perpetuates should be exercised in the most perfect form—*i.e.* one characterized by organic unity, in the form of a spiritual monarchy. Is the most vital matter that of government and of obedience to the ordinances of the Church—not the communion of members in the Holy Ghost with the living Head of the Church, then the power remains best undivided in one hand. Hence it was the irresistible tendency—so to speak, the natural impulse—of the now degraded ecclesiasticism, which cared only for an evident formal and spiritually barren unity, to accomplish its own doom, and to witness the embodiment of that idea of the unity of the universal Church in one sensibly visible and definite place and see. Thus ends, after it had asserted itself for the last time at the reforming synods of the fifteenth century, the great idea of the catholicity, of the universality of the Church, which acquiesces in the independence of all the branches of the Church, because in all the one universal Church lives. At the close of the development it stands there, narrowed and transformed into a sensible particularity, which claims to be the true essence of the Catholic Church, and seeks to deprive everything external to itself of personal independent life. The Romish Church—this single one—is held to be identical with the Church in general, to be the principial power of the whole; this single member claims to be the universal. The faith became prevalent that Rome is the hinge and head, the foundation and rule, and even the principle of all churches (Roma cardo et caput omnium ecclesiarum, fundamentum et forma, a qua omnis ecclesiæ principium sumpserunt).

The mediæval idea of the Church and of the hierarchy culminating in the papacy, conceived by the greatest of the popes, Gregory VII. (1073-1085), Alexander III. (1159-1181), and Innocent III. (1198-1216), and to nearly its whole extent carried out by them, had, in order to this being done completely, two works to accomplish:—

1. To lead the papacy beyond the *collegiate nature* of the episcopate on to an absolute monarchy.

2. To achieve the so-called independence of the Church over against the *State*.

With regard to the former, the papacy had grown out of the episcopate, and was at every new papal election anew dependent on it. But, as has been already remarked, the endeavour was not unsuccessful, to hold forth the papacy, this product of episcopal development, much more now as the principle of all the ordinances of the Church, as the source even of episcopal power, as if it were an immortal entity, supporting as it were itself and everything else, dependent only upon the law of its own life. The means by which this was accomplished it belongs to Church history to relate more particularly. As the chief momenta in the process of setting aside dependence upon the episcopate and the synods, there are four which may be named:

(1.) The pseudo-Isidorian decretals, executed according to recent investigations between 847 and 853 in the province of Rheims, had—if it was not (as Hinschius thinks) their direct design—yet at any rate (as even Weizsäcker allows) this result, that by their help, as pretended papal decrees, the power of bishops and patriarchs was broken, especially by Gregory VII.

(2.) The choice of a pope was transferred by Gregory VII. to a standing college of cardinals appointed by the pope, and there was thus withdrawn from the episcopate its influence upon the papal election. Upon this followed—

(3.) The attempt, virtually to ascribe to himself, along with this college of cardinals, the privy council of the pope, the power and the rights of œcumenical synods, in that synods were held in Rome itself.

The first Romish-œcumenical Lateran Council took place under Calixtus II., 1123. Free œcumenical councils were for centuries together no longer held. [See App., note A.]

(4.) The national Churches with their episcopate were from the time of Gregory VII. held in check by the system of papal *legates*, as well as by the *exemption* of important portions of the Church as convents, chapters, and abbeys, from the government of the respective bishops. The Dominicans and Franciscans especially were placed immediately under papal rule, as it were in immediate contact with the ecclesiastical monarchy [similarly to the relation of the imperial cities to the German empire as distinguished from the countries in which they were situated]. These orders formed the war-equipped organ of the pope, and mediated for him a kind of universal presence for the carrying out of his will. The *priests*, too, were, in consequence of the celibacy enforced by Gregory VII., the more weaned from natural and national interests, and the more closely bound to the ecclesiastical system. Thus it came now to be said in behalf of the popes, the bishops are called to association in the cure, but not to a supreme power (in partem solicitudinis non in plenitudinem potestatis). The essential co-ordination of bishops, which had stood fast for ages, inasmuch as the bishop of Rome passed only for the first amongst equals, was changed into a subordination, and it was denied by the curia [or papal court—von dem curialistischen System] that the episcopate derives its power equally with the pope immediately from Christ. The one Church is thus no longer an union of co-ordinate free communities, of confederate episcopal sees, but an absolute spiritual monarchy, in which the bishops stand like an aristocracy as counsellors at the side of the pope. And these claims of the pope the nations recognized, although the bishops did not do so, but rather—though finally in vain—made the utmost efforts to subject the pope to the reforming synods.

The *second* requisite is the *liberation* of the *Papacy* from *State authority*.

The claim of the State, especially of the Empire, to represent in its own fashion the Christian universal monarchy, still threatened the Romish hierarchy with another collegiateship, especially as the Romish Church assumed increasingly the shape of a visible kingdom and the forms of civil government. As the State life branches out into different ministries, so the Church had also its finances, taxes, and spiritual commerce (indulgence, jubilees, Peter's pence, tithes, annates, &c.); it had a hierarchy of officials, and an extensive governing organization distinguished from that of the state by its claim to a divine origin, a spiritual administration of justice invested with the power of punishing disobedience and heresy, and even provided, in the confessional, where the clergy officiated as judges, with power over the gates of heaven and hell. There was also an army at the service of this spiritual state in the spiritual orders and monks; the legates were its diplomatic agents. But the more the objective Church developed itself in this way into a system of external power with divine pretensions, the less became the possibility of avoiding conflicts with the State, of which the Church by its present nature and theory as it were itself furnished the State with a justification. For if it comes ultimately to be a question of might and supremacy, the Church must submit to the fate, which belongs to one state in another, or which one state may encounter at the hands of a neighbour. The Old Testament theocracy, besides, which the Church had taught the nations to regard as a model, had a king and not a priest at its head, so that the Christian Emperor might, according to this, regard himself as the successor of David. The hierarchy, on the other hand, could plead for itself that all nations had been given by Christ to no Emperor but to the Church; that it had to represent the higher, the spiritual; that the emperor could only adduce as his title the succession in an originally heathen old Roman empire, to which the higher sanctity first came through the acknowledged papal coronation. The principal momenta in this conflict between Church and State are the following:—

The first was the effort to at least emancipate the Church from the State. This is the significance of the investiture controversy, which reaches from Gregory VII. to Henry V. († 1122). But the mere co-ordination satisfied neither party. As the house of the Hohenstaufen ardently cherished its memories of the rights of the Empire under Charles the Great and Otho I., and felt itself strong enough to enforce these claims, so also was the Hildebrandine idea of the Church and the papacy far removed from stopping short at a mere dualism of the highest powers. Innocent III. established firmly this idea in respect of the temporal power, and impressed it so deeply upon the Christian community that it continued to work long after his death. In the firmament of the universal Church are two high dignities set by God, the higher for the government of souls, the lower for the government of bodies, the papal authority and the royal power, related to one another as sun and moon; and similar to those also in this respect that the latter derives its splendour from the former. Peter is the vicar of Him to whom belongeth the earth and the fulness thereof. The Lord has given over to the government of Peter not only the whole Church but the whole earth. To this divine call of the papacy even to temporal rule is to be added also the pretended ignobleness of the origin of kingly power; it was extorted in the Old Testament only by human wilfulness, instituted *per extorsionem humanam*; its origin for the most part is craft or force; participation in divine authority it can obtain only by the consecrating act of the Church; there can be only one supreme source of power upon earth. Since the world has been given over by Christ to the Church, it cannot be a second time immediately given over to another by Christ. Although Peter did not forthwith enter upon this sole supremacy, he is nevertheless entering on it now in virtue of imprescriptible divine right. And in fact the papacy succeeded in the thirteenth century in overthrowing the imperial house of the Hohenstaufen, and in taking the house of Hapsburg into its service.

But the papacy could not maintain itself upon this dizzy height—the climax of its power was the beginning of its fall. The victory over the Empire gave the papacy still more decidedly a worldly tendency, the character of a temporal kingdom, which was now exposed to all the dangers of such a kingdom, and to all the disturbances of worldly passions internally and externally.

Philip IV. the Fair, of France, succeeded, by relying upon the third estate, in withdrawing himself from the yoke of Pope Boniface VIII., and even in humbling him, and accomplishing the transference of the papal chair to Avignon, under the protection and power of France. At the same time there was developed the system of the Gallican Liberties, an ecclesiastical model upon an episcopal principle. The Babylonian captivity at Avignon (1309-1377), injured however the independence and impartiality of the papacy, which seemed to have become the instrument of the ascendancy of one nation over another. And when, under Gregory XI., the papacy sought to withdraw itself from its imprisonment, and France, on the other hand, would not let go any of its power over the papacy, but designed rather to make use of it to secure the succession to the empire, there arose the schism of 1378, a double papacy, which rendered its own idea illusory, and served rather to turn confidence again towards the universal Church and its representation in councils. In the fifteenth century emerges again the memory of the old basis upon which the papacy first raised itself to absolute supremacy of power. The Gallican Church was particularly active in the attempt to place the representation of supreme ecclesiastical unity and power in the assembled episcopate of the independent national churches. But the great Councils of Pisa, 1409, of Constance, 1414, and Basle, 1431, were wrecked upon the internal contradiction of desiring a hierarchical form of unity for the Church, and yet combating the highest manifestation of this unity and power in the papacy; of desiring a council—not a permanent one, however—above the pope, and yet granting to the pope in ordinary the highest rank in virtue of divine authority; of maintaining, and even strengthening, by a corresponding theory of the Church, the hierarchy, and yet declining the consequences which impel to an absolute monarchy. The reformation of the Church in general was, however, wrecked upon the preponderating attention given to the constitution of the Church and the question of ecclesiastical power. The contradiction was maintained of spurning a reformation of doctrine, whilst nevertheless gross errors in the doctrinal theory of the Church were the protection and strength, and even in part the origin, of the evils which were contemned as destructive. Thus the so-called Reforming Synods quickened but did not satisfy the need of reform. Out of the struggle of the fifteenth century between the "universal" and the Romish Church, the latter emerged victorious on account of its clear objects and decided action. And all the more was the former system of general oppression now undisturbedly and boldly continued by the papal power in the sovereignty it had achieved, the care of morality and religion in the most lamentable manner neglected, and all public reformation, so long contended for, brought to a stand-

Dualism in Mediæval Doctrine.

still. Æneas Sylvius, as Pope Pius II. (A.D. 1458-1464), after a dissolute life, retracted his former views[1] and wished to annul the liberties of the Gallican and German Churches. "*In ecclesia militante, quæ instar triumphantis se habet,* Unus est omnium moderator et arbiter Jesu Christi Vicarius, a quo tanquam capite omnis in *subjecta* membra potestas et auctoritas derivatur, quæ a Christo Domino Deo nostro sine medio in ipsum influit." This vicar is the *locum tenens* of Christ. The system was so perverted, that whoever involved himself with its machinery, even although with the purpose of reforming it, was inevitably carried away by it. In addition to this there was the abuse which a succession of popes in the times immediately preceding the Reformation made of their position by their personal licentiousness and covetousness, their intolerance and profanity, whereby the disposition of the most pious nations was alienated from the dominant Church. Even Möhler acknowledges that before the Reformation the papal chair was occupied by men whom hell has devoured.

CHAPTER II.

THE DEVELOPMENT OF CHURCH DOCTRINE IN RESPECT OF ITS FORM AND SUBJECT-MATTER.

WE shall confine ourselves with respect to the prevalent doctrine of the middle ages to a principjal consideration of it, *i.e.* to a consideration, in its formal aspect, of its principles of knowledge, and with respect to its subject-matter, of the fundamental view pervading the dogma and determining its particulars.

The same dualism, which asserts itself in the Church system between the ruling and the subject parties (Chap. I.), formally presents itself *in its ideal aspect* in the conflict between *faith* and *knowledge* in the time of the Schoolmen. The Church dogma, which claims for itself unlimited authority, cannot or will not be reconciled with personal certainty and conviction, as appears most of all in the last sceptical period of scholasticism. But in that the subject is thus rendered blindly and passively subject to the Church dogma, as to a law which neither requires nor allows any other form of attestation than that given in the divine authority

[1] Cf. G. Voigt, *Enea Sylvio de' Piccolomini, &c. und sein Zeitalter,* Berlin, 1856.

of the Church, there is formed an antagonism between the intelligent spirit longing for assurance and the dark power of tradition standing over against it. This abject submission is called faith, neither bearing certainty in itself, nor yet suited to form the principle of Christian knowledge. This dualism the older scholasticism sought to overcome, the later to conceal, until finally it dared to assert it as an axiom and to make absolute ignorance the basis of ecclesiastical positivity.

Anselm of Canterbury[1] places faith, *i.e.* the reception of the objective Church doctrine, as the first element, with the design of letting knowledge follow through religious experience as the second; he does not yet dream of the possibility of a contradiction between this experience together with the knowledge communicated by it and the doctrine of the Church, just as he does not yet inquire whether that reception must take place intelligently and as a recognized duty, or blindly. For he starts from the standpoint of the piety, unweakened and undisturbed by doubt, of a man yet in the nonage of Christianity, but who from his youth up has belonged to the Church and has maintained this piety in his moral behaviour,—without reflecting upon a case where this piety cannot be in existence, as in the case of the man who is not a Christian, or is no longer in existence, as in the case of the doubter; he only gives prominence admirably to this, that historical faith must be furnished through personal experience with certainty and paired with knowledge, whereby the representation given and possessed of the object of faith preserves its right of being in a position to inspire the certainty of its own truth, whilst it may have been accepted only in deference to authority. *Abelard*, on the other hand, regards it as necessary above all to *know* what is to be believed, even because, as his treatise "Yes and No" (*Sic et non*) shows with great prodigality of learning, the faith of the Church is in many important points uncertain and even discordant; on general grounds, however, because only that is to be believed which is known to be true. Hence he changes the formula of Anselm, "I believe that I may know" (*Credo ut intelligam*), into the other, "I know that I may believe" (*Intelligo ut credam*). But a faith, which accepts only that which has been proved true, is nothing more than the sense of the evidence for what has been proved, that feeling of certainty,

---

[1] Hasse, *Anselm von Canterbury*, vol. ii. 34, 1852.

which of itself accompanies the normal process of knowledge, and which has as yet, so far as itself is concerned, nothing to do with the religious feeling and life. The feeling of certainty or evidence ought, according to Anselm, to be effected through a moral religious experience, according to Abelard in a purely intellectual way. Abelard thus leaves for that experience and for the will no essential place in the obtaining of personal certainty of the truth of Christianity (which according to him is of an intellectual, not of a religious kind). According to his principles, Christian truth must be capable of demonstration by the reason; and Christianity accordingly must belong to the sphere of universal reason, in which case it might be dispensed with. Hence his repudiation by the Church is not to be wondered at. Only it must not be overlooked that this repudiation leaves the question untouched,—How can others than those in nonage enter in a moral way into a blind subjection to the subject-matter of Church doctrine on the ground of the authority of the Church? Even that which Anselm had granted with regard to the value of a relatively independent knowledge, acquired through personal experience, succeeding times seem to have forgotten; the Church dogma did not wish to expose itself to a trial, whether it could not through experience render the soul certain of its own truth. For how then, if it did not attest its own certainty, but rather challenged criticism? Then the whole matter would be at an end.

No wonder that the later scholasticism retired more and more decidedly upon the Church as the sole supreme authority, even although it did not omit to explain details of the Church doctrine, to define it more closely or reconcile it in thought to the soul, as was done especially by *Thomas Aquinas*. Scholasticism in its most flourishing period felt itself so directly one with the Church, that it became the chief support of the whole ecclesiastical structure, in that it arranged, divided, and harmonized the collected matter of Church dogmas, but did no more. Theology, it was said, is the positive science, and boasts supernatural sources; it is the Domina, whom philosophy serves as handmaid. But the very restriction this involved of the use of reason to a purely formal exercise upon positive dogmas entailed peculiar dangers. By its passion for dialectics, scholasticism lost itself in subtleties and endless hair-splittings; a cold frivolous reason often treated the holiest objects in a spirit which proclaimed the absence of all inward participation in them. Thus it broke at length with the actual life, and this diverged away from it partly into mysticism, partly into scepticism, so that, especially about 1500, it existed only for its own amusement. *Duns Scotus* exhibits the last attempt to support the most absolute Church positivism, in assigning to it as a speculative basis the supreme omnipotence and absolute freedom of God, and denying that there was anything in itself true and good, since, on the contrary, only that must pass for true and good which God in fact will have to be regarded thus, of which matter of fact the Church possesses authentic information, and is to be believed the more unconditionally that there cannot be any certainty upon objective grounds of what is in itself true and good. This placing, however, of an unlimited faith in authority upon the basis of caprice as the supreme principle which ultimately governs everything, is already in its very nature absolute scepticism, doubt of the fixedness and necessity of truth in general, and of the possibility of knowing it; it is further a confession that the Church doctrine is not at one with the spirit, but is rather for it something external and accidental; *i.e.* it is the admission that the body of Church doctrine is antecedently foreign to the spirit, even although it be accompanied by the assertion that the relation cannot and ought not to be other than dualistic. But for all that, in this voluntary and abject service of the thinking spirit the consciousness of the subject finally gathered strength in its attitude towards the Church, which was thus ultimately indebted to it for the proof of the indispensableness of its own positive authority. A blow which, aimed at the possibility of knowing any truth, falls like a beheading of the spirit, will secure to the heart repose from all doubts, and will secure to the doctrine of the Church by anticipation, and in every case, the privilege of being in the right.

Since the Church knew neither how to guide this nascent consciousness, nor how to appease this need of truth and certainty, there was awakened in those faithful to the Church an indifference to the substantial truth of the dogma in itself, seeing it was not supposed to carry with it its own power of conviction and consequent worth, but be indebted for them to the authority of the Church; in others, however, doubts were aroused as to the Church doctrine. Knowledge, says *Occam*, deals only with what is seen:

what lies beyond is only for faith. There is no philosophy of the divine; theology, however, which alone has the knowledge of the divine, rests only upon the authority of the Church. But even in theology there is no unity nor necessity. All the commands of God are arbitrary, even the commandment of love to God. Occam delights in isolating free absolute omnipotence from love and wisdom, and so emphasizing it that all fixed notions are brought into uncertainty; that the supernatural world not only transcends all conception, but contradicts all conceptions, sporting, as it were, with the whole natural and logical world. All this he carries out with what seems to us a frivolous pleasure. He finds it probable, for example, according to the Church doctrine of the communication of divine attributes to the human nature of Christ, that the head of Christ may be also his hand, and his hand also his eye. Whether it was in honest submission to the authority of the Church or in irony that he drew these consequences from the principle of pure authority, is disputed. However that may be, even the existence of God is for him and his school only probable. Probability began to eat away even the moral consciousness of many. The sickliness and gradual decay of science was the symptom of a deeper distemper in the life of the Church, which was divided against itself, and only in the rise of a new learning and view of life could there be found for science the reconciliation which it needed. Hemmed in by the course of development hitherto, which piled up the products of what was by no means a normal process into blank walls, a point was now reached when enlightened progress seemed no longer possible, when one could neither go backwards nor forwards. "The force of a sense, which sought the new without being able to give it shape, drove all parties to an extremity."[1] The end of the middle ages exhibits therefore the ruin not only of the moral life of the clergy, of the papal court, and of the monkhood, but also of the life of consciousness; the dualism between the dogma based on authority and the spirit, which had existed from the beginning, being concealed, but not overcome, broke forth more and more openly in a thousand symptoms, especially in Italy, the seat of the papacy, where the heathen nature, softened by the culture of the beautiful, especially of the forms of the antique world, or, more correctly, awakened as it

[1] Hein. Ritter, *Geschichte der Chr. Phil.* Thl. 4, 1845, p. 603.

were galvanically to the resemblance of a new and splendid life, seated itself upon the throne, and began to treat Christianity as a profitable fable suited for the common people.

Of what kind the new, that which should arrest the corruption, must be, may in general be gathered from what has been already said. It was necessary that the Gospel, which had once already proved the preserving salt for the world where putrefaction had begun, should again penetrate in its original purity, power, and leavening influence into the hearts and life of the people. It was necessary for theology that Christian saving truth should maintain the surety of its foundation, and through betaking itself again to its sources should come forth in its original independent splendour, in order to put an end to the merely formal action of dialectics which had been forsaken by an ethical and religious spirit, and were therefore indifferent and sceptical; but it was also necessary that that saving truth should not remain a mere external authority ultimately dependent again upon the Church, but that the right way should be pointed out, how it implants itself in the innermost knowledge and will of the heart, that thereby the awakened subjectivity may be filled with the ethically religious unadulterated substance, by which it may not only recover health, but also attain to the higher stage of self-conscious evangelical liberty.

That all this was necessary, if the now wavering confidence in Christianity was to be restored and the decay now beginning was to be averted, will appear still more clearly if we turn our attention to the *subject-matter of the doctrine* which had been reared upon the basis of the divine authority of the Romish Church. For here, too, the same *dualism* exhibits itself to us in another aspect as the leading characteristic. There is both an unwillingness to give up God and an impossibility of doing so, and yet by the doctrine of the vicegerency of the Church, of the deputed representation of God and Christ, an anthropocentrical standpoint is taken up, which manifests itself especially macrocosmically in the form of the great moral personality of the Church, and hides beneath this veil, but cannot escape, the guilt of affecting and penetrating the life of the individual.

The mediæval doctrine suffers from the *dualism* of a *magical* and of a *Pelagianizing conception of grace and freedom*, of the divine and of the human,—both founded in thinking of the relation of the divine and the human not as that of essential and internal connection, but only after the manner of the relation of the tangent to the circle,—which was a necessary consequence of the legal standpoint. This appears already in the doctrine discussed above of the hierarchy and synods, so far as participation in the Holy Ghost is accepted as sacramentally assured to the dignitary, whilst his moral personality is not affected by it, but may be utterly profane. Similarly, the individual believer continues cut off from the knowledge of the truth and immediate intercourse with God, and is directed principally only to the connection with the office and the institution.

With regard to the more concrete matter of the dogma, the prevalent doctrine of the middle ages with regard to the *original condition* of man does not suffer righteousness and holiness to be regarded as belonging to the idea of his proper nature in virtue of its appointed constitution, but these are conferred on him only as an added gift (*donum superadditum*). It is thus declared, that moral perfection is not the perfection demanded by the constitution of his created nature, or a perfected realization of this itself, but only an additional gift accidental to the idea of man, and magically imposed upon him from without by grace. If the constitution of man in itself stands thus in a relation of indifference towards good and bad, no injury is inflicted on it by *sin;* and *redemption* does not require to attach itself to the possibility of good still constantly existing in man, *i.e.* to his living receptivity, but may become externally the property of man (as is supposed to be the case in baptism), just as magically as the supernatural gift became the property of the first man in his original condition as an accidental addition to his nature.

The prevalent doctrine of sin, accordingly, regarded the natural man not as wicked in itself, not in the essential infringement of its idea and of its spiritual nature. The carnal desires which rise in man (*concupiscentia*) are not regarded as sinful in themselves, but we are only considered to stand in need of salvation, because we have inherited debt [Schuld] from Adam (*debitum*, not *culpa*), and have suffered in consequence a weakening of the will. Thus the evil from which we are to be redeemed, is only a defilement externally contracted, a burden imposed from without, whereby our freedom itself is not essentially touched. If Adam had a *donum superadditum*, his posterity have, as a punishment for his having lost it, a *malum superadditum*. If, however, the wickedness of the person, who has and retains freedom of choice (*liberum arbitrium*), is thus entirely external, then on the other hand help can come in a merely external way, without any participation of the inward personality itself in an inward regeneration, and in a complete conversion of the tendency of the will, being necessary, *i.e.* it may come in a *magical* way. It is taught, that the baptized person (let it be remembered that baptism had now become practically infant baptism), is not only free from debt but also from sin, so that he must now be in a condition to remain sinless from the restoration to him of his proper freedom.

It is true that all fall again after baptism, and the restored sinlessness vanishes again like a beautiful dream, but still not without leaving new obligations behind. For, so proceeds the theory, salvation is no longer of such easy purchase as in baptism, but is only possible through the *sacrament of penance*, through penitence, confession, and satisfaction. This way of salvation prescribed by the Church, imposes on the one hand performances upon man, by which he is not only to expiate his punishment, but may also merit something for himself (thus, for example, even penitence is a good work, procuring *meritum congrui*), and in this aspect it is supposed that there is still an integrity of his powers, and a strength for good in man, in spite of his guilty fall from baptismal grace,—wherein, certainly, a *Pelagian* element cannot be denied; nevertheless, on the other hand, grace is communicated to man through the Church in virtue of an act performed by it (*ex opere operato*), without any antecedent or subsequent profounder inward process, accordingly in a *magical* manner, just as also in order to faith there belongs only an historical acceptance and credence, and alongside of faith there may exist mortal sin.

This leads us to what was to become the kernel of the controversy, the relation of divine *grace* to human *freedom*. Grace is so defined, that if and so far as it works, human freedom is suspended or excluded; and freedom is so conceived, that if and so far as it works, merit, whether of congruity (*ex congruo*), or even of worthiness (*ex condigno*), may take the place of grace. But a grace, which so far as it reaches, binds, or excludes freedom, instead of employing it for the communication of itself, is magical; and a freedom which, so far as it is there, thrusts grace aside, and stands in its own strength, is conceived after a Pelagian fashion. Properly these two, conceived in such mutual exclusiveness, must flee one another; the one must be sacrificed to the other. Only, either the moral or the religious interests would suffer from this logical consistency. And so a compromise is attempted. Since they are so conceived that they cannot be represented as working simultaneously, they are allowed to appear in alternate action in the process of salvation, and to share it with one another; as if it were not precisely in the union of the divine and human that salvation lay; as if anything were accomplished by a grace which does not require or establish freedom; or as if it were a gain for the freedom of man and not rather a loss, if it had to stand upon itself, to centre in itself, instead of finding true strength and happiness in fellowship with God and sacrificing love. The scholastic systems of Thomas and of Duns Scotus, which, at least by means of the influences which issued from them, governed the common public doctrine from the fourteenth to the sixteenth centuries, are both such combinations of 'grace and freedom as have been described, with the emphasis laid upon grace by Thomas, and upon freedom by Scotus. We cannot here prosecute the inquiry, how these elements mingle in the two governing systems, how the Thomist system, although it emphasizes grace, yet lets it be so entirely given over to the Church, and chained to it, that the Church appears as the Vicar of God, and grace serves precisely to lay the basis of a false independence on the part of Christian humanity over against God,—which is the fundamental essence of Pelagianism; or how the Scotist system, whilst starting from the freedom of man, yet wins room for the magical element, inasmuch as that which certainly escapes the power of the individual man for his own redemption, does not escape the true humankind, the Church, since God has surrendered to it the divine powers of salvation, or absolute power of absolution and beatification, so that it has now power over God Himself in the holy sacrifice of the mass, in absolution, and in indulgence. If the self-redemption of the individual is accordingly not directly asserted by Scotus—this, as it were subjective Pelagianism, was long proscribed, because it too manifestly stripped Christianity of value—he, on the other hand, held fast by a self-redemption of Christian humanity, or an objective Pelagianism; and as this seemed to minister to the glorifying of the Church, and of its saints, with their inexhaustible treasure of might and grace, it was certain of the most enthusiastic applause, and this thrusting back of God and of Christ, as well as of communion with God, behind communion with the Church, was regarded as peculiarly pious, as exalted above the ordinary form of piety, which would not thus direct the ardour of its devotion towards Mary and the saints.

That is now the anthropocentrical apotheosis of the Church, slightly veiled by making the saints, with Mary at the head, and angels to form the ideal and heavenly portion of it. But the heavenly ideal Church is conceived as so narrowly bound together with the earthly Romish Church in the unity of the *Corpus mysticum Christi*, that the earthly congregation has power over the heavenly by prayer for its intercession and by sacrifice, even as on the other hand Mary, together with the saints, exercises a determining influence upon the Father and the Son. This deification, however, was brought about by the *connection* and *mingling* of *magical* and *Pelagian* elements, of *unbelief* and *superstition*. A strong current of *unbelief* especially is recognizable in it. Instead of seeking by constant dependence upon God, and by a perpetually renewed dedication to Christ, to draw power and life every moment out of the fulness of the living God, the religious slothfulness of the natural mind has given in to the proud inclination of the human heart, as far as possible to stand upon, and centre in, itself, to feel itself satisfied and rich without a perpetual dependence upon God. This inclination is the irreligious root of all Pelagianism and unbelief, of all the imagination of being full of divine powers in one's self, without a perpetual dependence upon the free grace and gift of God. But whilst the Pelagianism of the natural man trusts, in forgetfulness of God, to its own unaided powers, it assumes in the middle ages a subtler form, inasmuch as the religious slothfulness and unbelief veils itself in *superstition*. In this the constant spiritual wrestling and struggle for the renewal of immediate fellowship with God is paralyzed, and even represented as unnecessary, by the superstitious supposition, that God has irrevocably and unreservedly poured out once for all upon the Church, that is to say upon the Romish Church, His treasures of grace, confined this inexhaustible supply exclusively to it and its priesthood, and so given it, through the medium of certain words and acts, power over God, made it even the Vicar of God. Thus has the Romish Church come to occupy for the period of the present world the place of God; we cannot come into communion with Him, but only with the divine governing system of the world, with the treasures of grace which have been made over to it, that it may dispose of them freely as of its own.

Thus it may now appear as an *alter Deus*, since God and Christ have retired into the distance, to a transcendental region, to come forth again only at the end of all things, to the judgment of the world. It is traced indeed to the immeasurable love of God, that God has for the period of the present world, as it were, surrendered to the Church for its benefit the dispensation of His grace. But since it is of the nature of love that it has to do, not only with impersonal gifts, but with fellowship with the beloved object, and since he who truly loves offers himself as the best gift for the intercourse of love, that seemingly excessive endowment of the Church on the part of God would still be a refusal of what is best, in reality a separation from Him, the maintenance of religion in a lower form, of a merely mediate fellowship with God: and if, as the Romish Church does not dare to deny, that earthly hierarchical organism, which in this world forms the basis of faith, nay, is itself the fundamental dogma, shall in the world to come have no significance, but even pass away, then that is almost an admission that the world to come will, in so far as that basis is concerned, bring a new and a different religion than the Christian religion of the present world, and is also a failure to see that Christianity is now already the absolute perfect religion, because by it we can have even now participation in eternal life and in immediate fellowship with God.

Superstition creates for itself, in forgetfulness of what is truly and vitally divine (*i.e.* upon the basis of unbelief), surrogates or substitutes for the divine in the world, in things, institutions, and persons, which are arbitrarily invested with a sacred halo. But that can nowhere and at no time happen without the true divinity having withdrawn itself from man, and having been superseded by a phantom of the divine, into which man changes the true (Rom. i. 20, ff.). The true divinity is free and omnipresent, but also carries on its saving operation historically by word and sacrament. The divinity which is claimed by the official Romish Church of the middle ages is chained to the priest and his action, and occupies a passive relation to this dignitary, who has it in his power, and has, as judicial arbiter, the disposal of absolutions binding even before God, and presents Christ as a sacrifice which he, the priest, has made; this divinity is not universally operative wherever the preaching of the Gospel sounds (Rom. x. 7), but is restricted in time and place, and ultimately to one spot on earth, the seat of the Pope, and even to a sinful and mortal man. And the Church does not conduct, and take knowledge of, itself as the organ of the ever-working Christ, but in virtue of its assumed appointment to Christ's place, it invests its operations apart from, and even possibly against, Christ, with the pretensions of operations conducted in the authority of Christ, which avails once for all. The consequence of this is, that the forgotten dependence upon God changes into a bondage of men under men. For the grace, conceived as magical, with which the Church is supposed to be furnished, can only work in a way destructive of the personality, set itself in the place of man—in a second act of false substitution, and thus prove the negation of the human. Consciousness and will, this human element in man, do not come into consideration in relation to the magical operation of grace. The substitutions of the middle ages are not productive, but are of a character directed against freedom and personality. The sacraments work *ex opere operato;* the minimum of an act of human freedom, the not interposing a bar (*non ponere obicem*), is enough for them. Low mass works in the distance without the knowledge of those for whom it is said—works even in the world beneath. The Church undertakes the case of individual souls, even of the departed, before God. But what would be thus attained, even in the best case, by Christian grace? No rich world of personal spirits bearing the divine image; the very sphere, therefore, which manifests its peculiar might and creative power, is lost. Even although the system of the church may succeed in repressing the old man into momentary latency,—in exorcising as it were the hostile powers; still it is only playing the while upon the surface of human nature; the inward part remains what it was.

Want of an Ethical Idea of God. 47

At the basis of the dualism we have pointed out in the Romish doctrine of salvation there lies ultimately an immoral *idea of God*. An excessively physical conception of God determines the conception of grace; for that divinity, which has power over itself to favour impersonality and thus to withdraw from morality its basis, possesses in its spirit and in its manner of working the nature of a physical power. A grace that is hostile to freedom and repressive of personality could not grow out of true love. Love desires the personal, desires living holy objects with free powers of motion, desires its objects as its own end.[1] This physical element in the conception of God shows itself also in the materialistic representation of the sanctifying influence of sensible things, wherein emanatistic, that is again physical, representations co-operate, and of the communication of divine powers to individual things, pictures, places, &c., to which they are passively linked, and so are supposed to win a separate existence, similarly to the heathen divisions and hypostatizings of divinity. But alongside of the profuse goodness—not conceived as purely moral—which is poured out upon the Church, there is certainly also much said of the transcendent and exalted nature of God in itself. He is the Majestic One, the Unapproachable, the Sinner-consuming, the Holy One and the Just. Christ Himself is, according to the view of the middle ages, the stern Judge; the God-man is, as it were, lost in God. The Church, on the other hand, the empirical, but especially the heavenly represented by Mary and the saints, exhibits the gracious love which moves the Son and even the Father. With this majestic God, who is in His essence unknown to mankind, communion is not possible; He is void of love in Himself, else He would not require that love and pity should first be excited in Him from without by the saints; He is in His exalted position only just and holy, but righteousness and goodness come not in God to mutual interpenetration in holy love, and even the grace to which God is moved by Mary has the appearance rather of caprice and partiality.

[1] [Will ihre Gegenstände als—Selbstzweck.]

CHAPTER III.

THE LIFE OF THE CHURCH OF THE MIDDLE AGES IN ITS CONCRETE OPPOSITES.

THE dualism, which we have marked hitherto, shows itself also in the *moral and religious constitution* of the mediæval Church life. The most significant phenomena belonging to this department are: the increasing worldliness of the Church and alongside of it monasticism, the requirement of strict obedience to the Church and alongside of it a moral laxity which penetrated even into the sanctuary, a rigorous penitential discipline and alongside of it indulgences, the asserted vicegerency of God and investiture with divine power, and alongside of it impotency to pacify the inward pain and unrest even of the simplest and most needy hearts. Its economy of salvation became rather a systematized arrangement for keeping the individual in uncertainty about his salvation (cf. above, Ch. I.). The result accordingly could only be, that the Church in its mediæval form was no longer able to satisfy the higher wants awakened in the better portion of mankind. The practical correlative of the dualism we have marked was that the subject in whom it was concentrated (let one think *e.g.* of the Flagellants,[1] of the system of pilgrimages, &c.), turning now to its one side and now to its other, tossed hither and thither by this constant change, passing from contrition to frivolity, and from frivolity to contrition, lost at last all heart and character, drifted anchorless and broken to the abyss of inward emptiness and spiritual death, continuing the while perhaps the dead machinery of religious performances, from which the doubting, nay unbelieving heart had been alienated. The masses followed the law of gravity, *i.e.* they followed tradition, and the usages prescribed by devotion to the Church; the centres of intelligence, and Rome above all, were eaten up by unbelief. Whilst an obtuse people changed the prayer, which the Lord gave in order that we might not prate as the heathen do, into a Paternoster, and prayed its rosary, and ran after the vendors of indulgences, and undertook pilgrimages and money payments, and even severe mortifications for the appeasing of inward disquiet, there were not wanting in Rome those who said,

---

[1] Who went about in bands, scourging themselves publicly.—*Tr.*

True Reconciliation wanting in the Middle Ages. 49

' This fable of Christ has brought us great gain,' or those who, when they heard of Melancthon's faith in eternal life and the judgment, declared they would esteem him a more modest man if he did not believe such things.[1] Even a Bellarmine acknowledges: Some years before the Lutheran and Calvinist heresy arose there was no strictness in spiritual courts, no chastity in manners, no reverence in presence of what was sacred, no scholarship, in short, almost no religion. There had already spread, even amongst the people, ridicule or the bitterest hatred of everything that was called monk and pope.

But all this is in its innermost principle embraced when, turning back to the beginning (Ch. I.), we say: The life of the mediæval Church had no *reconciliation*,[2] and did not know where to find it. The key of Peter opened indeed the treasures of the nations, but not the treasures of heavenly peace. Whilst the key to these was lost, an interdict was laid upon those who sought or found it elsewhere. The Church system of penance, with its expiatory performances and its indulgences, was devised for the pacification or silencing of frivolous and temporarily alarmed sinners, but at the price of leaving the conscientious without comfort, because without the certainty of the forgiveness of sins. The confessional became for them a stall of martyrdom and a conscience-rack, because they could never know whether they had not confessed too little, and the absolution was consequently valueless. Let it be added, that the deliverance from purgatory and the entrance into heaven was made dependent upon the power and number of the petitions and masses for the soul, which were to be bought with money; and the natural consequence was, that amongst the intelligent, who knew well that the present differences of rich and poor dare not influence the world to come, confidence in venal priestly grace gave place to a contempt, which, in the absence of anything better, fell only too frequently into frivolity and unbelief.

[1] Herzog, *Œcolampad.*, Basle, 1837, 1843, 2 vols.
[2] That is, was without the blessing of being consciously reconciled to God. See p. 24. – *Tr.*

SECTION II.

THE POSITIVE PREPARATION FOR THE REFORMATION.

IT would be unjust to the middle ages to stop short at the gloomy picture of the Church before the Reformation, as we have till now been painting it. And the Reformation itself also would lose its historical basis and connection, if, in order to furnish a triumphant justification of it, we were to see nothing but darkness before it. Its legitimacy consisted not merely in the fact that before it matters were in an evil state, but also in the fact, that everything noble which previously made way for itself stands to it, as it were, in unconscious and secret alliance; that the best efforts of the middle ages have a light shed on them from it as the centre, and were indeed gathered up in it; in a word, that it is the rich and natural fruit of the noblest conservative sap of the mediæval life, and the solution of the problem for the multiform dualism in its midst. Only by it are we able to lay our hands upon all that is truly great in the middle ages, and are in a position to recognize the organic connection of the evangelical with the ancient Church, and even with the primitive apostolic period; whilst, were it a new church, connected by no vital links with primitive times, it would, even in consequence of this anti-historical position, awaken the suspicion that human caprice had the principal share in it, and that it was a meteor, portentous indeed for the Romish Church, but which, as it had abruptly appeared, might perhaps as suddenly vanish,— without that inward blissful power and permanence by which the portentous appearance might rather be changed, even for the Romish Church, into an object of joyful thanksgiving (Heb. xii. 7-11). If the Church of the Reformation is to deserve the name of evangelical, which has been accorded to it in history, the pure stream of the Gospel, which can never since Christ have been wholly obscured amongst mankind, must have found in it a new channel, not in order to the withdrawal thenceforward of what is evangelical from the Catholic Church, but in order to preserve it *for* her as well as against her corruptive action. Amongst these positive, preservative, and progressive powers of the middle ages, the following are to be especially distinguished: *first*, mysticism and the mystical theology; *secondly*, the return to the Holy Scriptures, and Biblical science; *thirdly*, the education of the people. These three factors, however, are not all present at once, and even where they are found together they seem at first coy of one another. It is their conjunction which first gives to the principle of the Reformation its inward ripeness, its truly ecclesiastical and church-regenerating power and form. Only after these were amalgamated in it, had this principle outgrown all attacks, for it united in solemn league all the powers truly capable of life. Amongst the momenta we have named, we must without doubt begin with that one, which occupies here the place which the budding axillary leaf occupies in the plant, that which by its deepest inwardness possesses the most plastic susceptibility for the reception even of the outward in its innermost substance,—with that element, which furnishes the hope of the most thorough conquest of the mediæval dualism, and which, though long entangled with that dualism, bears most clearly in itself the principle of true personality. We begin then with the mysticism of the middle ages, and observe how its wants and onesided aspects are gradually obliterated by the working-in of other factors,—nay, how with a clear practical eye which distinguishes between form and essence, it more and more enriches and purifies itself, for the education of the people, with scriptural knowledge and scientific thought, as well as with a true church spirit and interest.

CHAPTER I.

THE MYSTICISM OF THE MIDDLE AGES.

WHATEVER judgment one may form of mysticism in general,[1] its nature and worth, it is only the want of religious or moral education which would lead one to dispute, that the great mysticism

[1] *Literature of the Mysticism of the Middle Ages:* cf. Pfeiffer, *Deutsche Mystiker des 14ten Jahrhunderts*, 2 Bde. 1845. 57. H. Suso's *Leben und Schriften, u.s.w.*, ed. Diepenbrock, ed. 3, 1854. Tauler's *Predigten*, Basle, 1521. J. Ruysbroek, *Vier Schriften in niederdeutscher Sprache*, Hannover, 1848. *Mystische und ascetische Bibliothek, vorzüglich des Mittelalters*, Köln, 1849-57. Gottfr. Arnold, *Historia Theologiæ Mysticæ*, Fcf. 1702 ff. and his *Kirchen- und Ketzer-historie*. Helfferich, *Die Christliche Mystik in ihrer Entwickelung u. in ihrem Denken*, 2 Thle. Hamburg, 1842. Görres, *Die Christliche Mystik*, 1836.

of the middle ages, especially the German, was animated by an aspiration, which points in the direction of true religious experience, of the personal indwelling of God. It walks in the light of eternity and learns to look at the things of this world in this light, even although it may all the while remain the child of its own time. But the consequence of this for us is, that we cannot, with some recent writers, regard it only as a kind of philosophy, or as the preliminary stage of a modern speculative mode of thought, which fell with its time,—a stage, however, which retires in obscure idealism into itself, to find in itself all truth and reality. Since in such anthropologism as this there can be no talk whatever of a true religious fellowship of the subject with the personal God and of God with him, whilst the whole essence of mysticism lies in such real fellowship with God, mysticism would, according to this conception of its essence, be a self-deception, a lower stage of philosophic knowledge, vanishing like the stars of night, when the sun of a higher philosophy arises.

The religious element must be regarded as the original principle, as the life-germ of mysticism; but it may assume a more *intellectual* or a more *ethical* tendency, which must, since each by itself is onesided, be in their further progress completed by one another. The internal progress of mysticism arises, we may say, from this, that the intellectual and the ethical factors seek to form an union upon the permanent underlying religious basis. If, however, in the phenomena of mysticism the original element is of a religious kind, the question arises,—is the religious element itself the same in the mystic as in every pious man, or does religion assume in him a peculiar form?

Piety is concerned in general about fellowship with God; it longs for attestations of and vital relations with God. But here two tendencies are possible. *Either* man keeps by holy things which are objectively knowable or tangible, in which God is believed to be present, and through which a *rapport* with God is

---

Böhringer, *Die Kirchengeschichte in Biographien*, 1855 ff. Hamberger, *Stimmen aus dem Heiligthum der Christlichen Mystik und Theosophie.* Treatises: Martensen, *Meister Eckhart*, Hamburg, 1842. Schmidt, *Meister Eckhart, Studien und Kritiken*, 1839, S. 663 ff. Schmidt, *Rudelbachs und Bährings Monographien über J. Tauler.* Ullmann, *Reformatoren vor der Reformation*, i. ii. 1841. [Translated in Clark's *Foreign Theological Library*.] Engelhardt, *Richard v. St. Victor und Ruysbrock*, 1838. Liebner, *Hugo v. St. Victor*, 1832. Reifenrath, *Die Deutsche Theologie des Frankfurter Gottesfreundes*, 1863.

thought to be effected; not necessarily in such a way, that by the mere outward participation in them there is participation in God, or that man is satisfied with participation in these holy things, but at least in such a way that it is only in connection with these holy things that man can be blessed with communion with God. *Or*, on the other hand, man resolves in the power of a more lively religious impulse not to stop short at what is merely tangible, accessible to the senses, not even, it may be, merely at God's revelation, so far as it is only a *work* of God, and not God Himself, but strives to become a partaker of the living God Himself,—that which cannot take place without passing beyond the empirical,—not without the negation, that is, of its sufficiency,—not without the transcendent critical momentum of living faith as opposed to external empiricism.

The first tendency is not straightway to be termed superstitious. The historical and empirical, which avails in God's hand for the revelation of an inward connection, is of the greatest importance for religion. For man himself is an historical finite being, and requires, in order to participation in the infinite God, that He should become apprehensible to him, and should, through certain external media, draw near to him, set him in movement, and furnish him with helps to lay hold of, by which he may climb to communion with God. These media are not the divinity itself, but prepare for it in the midst of the finite world consecrated abodes, pledges of the Divine presence, a *Templum* in the ancient sense of the word, or a *Sacramentum*. In this innate tendency of all true piety towards the historical, towards a divinity revealed in finite form, lies one of the chief signs of our being created unto Christ. Nevertheless, the external contact with these holy things, which, belonging as they do to the world of sense, convey the impression of reality, can never satisfy the need of the heart to have the certainty of the real Divinity and to enjoy His communion. It does not satisfy the pure religious instinct. It is not enough that contemplation, or conception and memory—in short, the outer court of the spirit—is opened for, and becomes filled by, the divinity revealed in time and space. It is necessary that the spirit itself should be unlocked in its centre for the religious object, and that this should penetrate into the depths of the spirit. Only in this way is the external templum made alive for us, inasmuch as there is now discovered in the external form the inward significance, as it were, and the inward essence, and we are made sensible, by means of, or in, the external form, of an act of fellowship on the part of the living God drawing near to us. Where this process does not reach its goal, where religious sloth changes what is meant only for a means and channel into the end, and into that itself with which man must be united,—there the stopping short at a mere historical faith (*fides historica*) must run into superstition, which submits to be satisfied in the world, out of which it capriciously constructs its holy things. This is the case with heathendom, and with unbelieving Judaism, neither of which for that reason has any mysticism. For magical representations of the operations of these holy things, whether they be divine institutions or human, do not deserve the name of mysticism.

There is, on the other hand, nothing more characteristic of the mysticism, which is so in reality, than that it will not stop short at the "means," but seeks communion with God Himself, contact of the soul with Him, *i.e.* real religion. The sensible tangibleness of divine ordinances does not satisfy it; it seeks the spiritual certainty of God, its salvation, through the present living God, not merely through past actions which may have become mere symbols of His presence; it seeks that the soul may, above all, rejoice in its God.

But even it is certainly not safe against corruptions. If the first tendency led to religious materialism, this leads to spiritualism. If the religious process took place in us in a purely immanent manner without intercourse with the external and historical, there would be a great danger of this process degenerating into merely subjective emotions, without reaching the goal of union with the objective God. Nay, there might be deceitfully mingled with those subjective feelings, those which express, without possessing, union with God. The merely imaginary possession of communion with God is, without historical correctives, so much the more difficult to rectify, since in the purely internal province that which is only human emotion is not easy to distinguish from that which springs from the Spirit of God. In addition to this, mysticism, like piety, is essentially dependent upon the idea of God and man existing at the time, upon the degree of the consciousness of God. True union with God is not possible, where the intellectual and moral attributes of God have no truth for piety, where God appears to the infinite yearning of man almost exclusively as the Infinite Being and Life. Nor is it possible thus to provide for the deepest needs of the soul. From this it is evident, that mysticism has a long way to its goal. On the other hand, however, it not seldom refuses to go this way, which, moreover, leads through history. For it is its nature not to consent to keep hanging on to the external, however holy it may be,—hence it often gives itself too little concern about history, and accounts it rather its highest honour to pass behind revelation, behind the world of means, as it terms it, into the foundation or mystery, as if the highest and deepest lay in the incomprehensible, the indefinite, or as if definiteness were only limitation and loss. But it is precisely the moral nature of God which can reveal itself only in definite acts, for love is love only as loving, or through acts of love. Hence, when mysticism pretends that it is necessary to abstract itself from the divine acts of revelation, even from that made in Christ, in order to find access, beyond and above the individual and limited, into a higher, into the infinite nature of God, this abstraction from love as loving is an abstraction from living love itself; so that mysticism is always in danger of sinking into a divinity, which, as infinite, absorbs everything into itself, rather than loves, for love sets before it as its end the existence and continuance of another. If therefore mysticism desires to rise above the standpoint of the merely physical categories of God, and so above the dualism, or swaying, between revelation and mystery, it must effect a mediation, and that of course out of its own internal nature, with the world of those objective acts of God, which form the matter of Church faith, of the *fides historica*. And that takes place in that the conception of God becomes for it more definitely moral in its form. The more it seeks union with God as wise and holy Love, the more is the inclination awakened in it to grasp this love in the act of loving, in the revelation of its love. And thus it acquires the faculty of seeing in the world of means or of revelation not merely an interposed and separating symbol, emblem, and husk, but in the means also the mediation, the mediating power, in the Way also the Truth and the Life, in the Mediator also the End, in the Son the Father, *i.e.* in the historical Christ the manifested personal love of God (John xiv. 9). It has thus by inward progress achieved a vital union with what is true in the first tendency, which lies nearer to the crowd. In its perfection it has become in general identical with intense Christian piety. Accordingly, this at least is settled, that the inner life-pulse of true piety lies in what constitutes the essence of mysticism. It stands, indeed, in need of being educated and filled by the elements which are to be found upon the first side, the historical Church, with its ordinances, the Word and sacraments. But all this knowledge and all these benefits, which are deposited in the individual soul by the educating Church, remain like dead coals, scattered about, unless the Spirit of Life from above kindles the desire for immediate fellowship with God,— unless that flame from the heavenly sanctuary itself, which unites, purifies, and ennobles all, is kindled upon the altar of the heart. And then only does the life of Christian piety reach its full power, inasmuch as it is now no longer the mere outward man, but also not merely the soul, but, in the language of the Psalmist, body and soul [heart and flesh], which rejoice in the living God.

In the old *Greek* mysticism, whose chief representative is the Areopagite,[1] the intellectual side of the susceptibility for God is disclosed, but in such a way, that the highest splendour of piety is the losing of one's self in the contemplation of God, who is thought of as an infinite ocean of light, dazzling with the brilliancy of its radiance, for the finite mind equivalent to darkness; here, accordingly, personality is lost. In such a contemplation of divine darkness the senses perish, and the mind is stupefied. For what is sought to be contemplated is only the Infinite Existence, which wants all definiteness. This Infinite Existence is indeed thought of and insisted on as the highest, as the proper divine majesty, which fills with holy awe, but there is not therein contemplated that Eye of love, which tenderly cherishes and maintains in itself the finite person.

In *Latin* mysticism, whose chief representatives are to be found in the school of St. Victor, there rises already, alongside of an essentially similar idea of God, the ethical factor upon the *human side*. Here it is already a more personal and inward fellowship with God which is treated of,—the soul desires to taste God, to have a savoury knowledge of God (*sapida Dei notitia*), to enjoy Him in the feeling of spiritual life. In this

[1] The pseudo-Dionysius. The writings which were ascribed to Dionysius first appeared in the beginning of the sixth century.—*Tr.*

there is awakened a powerful movement of the personality, as also in making union with God an act of freedom, a mounting up, nay an ecstatic soaring above one's self, an *excessus* out of one's self. God is not properly thought of as active, as morally energetic, but rather as only the object and matter of spiritual enjoyment, or as the quiescent highest good, as the ocean of blessedness and goodness. The activity, nay the unrest, falls upon the human side, which seeks to win participation in God by moral effort in accordance with the laws of a spiritual methodism [*Methodik*], which becomes more and more developed.

Finally, *German* mysticism apparently allows subjectivity to retire again into the background; in reality, however, the momenta of evangelical faith advance in it, step by step, into definite shape. In opposition to the unrest of that mystical methodism, "divine resignation" now appears as the highest element. The "suffering" of the divine act now takes the place of human effort and desire to enjoy God. Thus the idea of *God* is quickened,—from His loving act the prepared soul expects blessed union and the sense of it. The preparation consists just in being resigned to God, in the being emptied, or free, of all that is one's own, that the Lord may fill it, whether with willingness to suffer [be passive] and the blessedness of suffering, as thinks *Heinrich Suso*, or with the vision of the glory of the exalted Son of God, which forms the fundamental trait in the mysticism of *Ruysbroeck*. Divine resignation is not merely effected by the emptying out of the representative and the creatural, in order to prepare room for God; it demands also the emptying out of the egoism [*Ichheit*] by conflict with self-regard [*Eigenheit*], and thus places the sphere of the desire for a higher personal righteousness in the apparent renunciation of egoism. What is here the real intention, although still in obscurity, is the *moral* reduction of one's self to nothing, or estimation of one's self as nothing. But in order to accomplish that emptying out of the creatural from the world of means, the mystic amour [*Minne*] seeks to turn from everything external, even from the historical, from Church and sacraments, in which it sees only symbols for the excitement of the mystic consciousness, that it may gain the knowledge of itself by means of the objective. The consciousness of God does not yet seek to unite with the consciousness of the world, but always regards itself as disturbed by the latter; hence the connection with the historical revelation is only a loose one. Christ, although much is spoken about Him, remains only God, or the Christ *for us* vanishes in the Christ *in us*. Even so the working of divine resignation assumes, not rarely, a pantheistic form; so that the perfected mystic thinks of himself as a personal manifestation of God, in whose thinking and willing God thinks, wills, and personally exists. So it is with the most speculative, the daring *Eckardt;* and even the *Deutsche Theologey*[1] is not altogether free from such sentences (cf. *e.g.* cap. 55). True, the pious spirit of mysticism is not wanting in the consciousness of these dangers; even Ruysbroeck, the "Doctor ecstaticus," frequently warns against them, and Suso represents them under the figure of a tempting and lawless spirit, which visits the friend of God, and seeks to draw him into the ways of false liberty, of efflorescent reason. Only it was easier to warn against the false issue, than clearly to point out and tread in the right way.

Higher in this respect stands *Tauler*, the mighty preacher of repentance. Resignation unto God, self-abnegation so as to lose one's self in the upholding of all things by God [das Sichselbstentwerden in sein Nichtssinken], is for him too the fundamental requirement, in order to God being ever born anew in man. And this perpetual incarnation of God is for him at the same time a deification of man. But he does not, as Suso for example, drive repentance back into monastic forms; poverty, vigils, fasts, scourgings, are for him not good works in themselves, but only means; they are "to be directed to their end." There are not holier and less holy orders; to all alike applies the requirement of weanedness from the creature, that God only may be loved; spiritual poverty is demanded of all, the same inward riches are promised to all. This is further unfolded in the excellent little work of Thomas à Kempis († 1471) upon following Christ (*De Imitatione Christi*). In it mysticism acquires through its ethical direction a more generally intelligible form. The above-mentioned treatise, *Ein Deutsche Theologey*, goes

[1] This "noble little book," as Luther calls it, was first published by Luther himself. The author, however, is unknown. It seems to have been composed about the end of the fourteenth century, and an old MS. speaks of the author as one of the "Friends of God," a priest and custos in the House of the Teutonic Knights at Hamburg, and a man "who lived before his time." The work has been translated into English by Miss Winkworth.—*Tr.*

further, however, in the working out of the conception of God, so that this conception is connected essentially with revelation. God (the revealed) is to be distinguished from Divinity. The divine glory does not consist in His hidden nature, or in this, that He is the undefined, infinite Being. The book desires a living, self-discovering God. We have here a great revolution, in that the defined is rated more highly than the undefined infinitude. The *Deutsche Theologey* has already escaped the spell of this infinitude, to which ordinary mysticism (as well as superficial thought) holds as the highest. To God, as Divinity, it says, belongs neither will nor knowledge, neither this nor that. But to God, as God, belongs, that He discloses, knows, and loves Himself, and reveals Himself first of all to Himself in Himself. In this way the *Deutsche Theologey* succeeds in attaching itself again to the Christian doctrine of the Trinity. God is for it not merely absolutely simple [*einfach*] in Himself, but disclosed in and for Himself, conscious free Love in Himself. And with this, the creation of the world is in the most intimate manner connected. Without the creature, God, although not simply Divinity, is still only existent [*ein Wesen*], not operative [*ein Wirken*]; but God will not merely be God in existence, but also formally and actually, and that is He in the creature in which He works and exercises what He is. In the world He is, and works as in something which is His own : in man He makes use of His own, and informs Himself of the same,—in him accordingly He has His conscious and suitable organ. Thus the world is no longer a mere nothing, not an evil thing; but since it is of worth for God Himself, it is confirmed in God. And so the consciousness of God and of the world must also be reconcilable, nay, must belong to one another. In us, indeed, the left eye looks upon the temporal, and the right upon the eternal; the two will not unite themselves into one vision, but when the one opens, the other shuts. This, however, is not in itself necessary. In Christ both eyes have been united: Christ, however, is our pattern. Hence, this treatise regards no sort of hatred of the world as justifiable. The world is there in order that God may work in it through man. Thus it is lawful to meddle with it, only it must not be misused. The position which is taken up with reference to the history of revelation, is connected with this more friendly position to the outer world. Christ as man is the pattern of resignation to the work of God in us, and conversely, God has found His working in perfection in Christ. Even Christ's passion is invested with this significance, that God, in whom there can be neither suffering nor grief, so far as He Himself is concerned, does yet, when He is man, that is in a deified humanity, endure grief and suffering on account of sin, and would willingly be sacrificed in order that He might thereby expiate one man's sins.

And yet the mysticism of the *Deutsche Theologey* has many deficiencies. God and the world are not distinguished with sufficient definiteness, for the goodness in God is not yet distinctly conceived as ethical, which also carries righteousness in itself. This is especially seen in that guilt is no longer spoken of, nor the penal deserts of the wicked; in that Christ is for it not yet the mediator, but the pattern of resignation, and of that love that suffers *with* the sin of the world; which Suso also depicts affectingly and poetically, but almost more mariologically than christologically. Since the virtue of divine resignation is never perfect, whilst the communication of grace is conditioned by it, it never attains to the lasting possession of peace, and the quiet and certain growth of the new personality that is reconciled to God; but, instead of this, the *Deutsche Theologey* stops short at all sorts of righteousness of spiritual works,—at endeavours to adapt one's self for grace by divine resignation, which, when, and so far as, it is there, becomes a partaker of divine grace and blessedness,—whereby peace is evidently made dependent upon the measure of the virtue. There is in general a great deal said in mysticism about self-abnegation and emptying, but almost nothing of the positive and free laying hold of grace, and little of the negative condition of laying hold of it, the renunciation of confidence in one's own righteousness, even in that of mysticism. By springing over this connecting link of *Faith*, the transition is immediately effected from divine resignation to deification, to the mystic enjoyment of God. Humility is, indeed, powerfully preached as a being empty of the creature; but even where it acquires a more strictly ethical nature, and the renunciation of everything selfish becomes more definitively its spirit, it adheres all the more to the thought: first, purification from everything ungodly, then fellowship with God. But this implied that, before perfect sanctification, no fellowship with

Mysticism conducted back to History. 61

God is possible, and thus it can never be attained on earth God must, however, be able to have fellowship with the sinner, else he is lost,—at all events with the sinner who, without being holy, yet knows his guilt, and the deservedness of punishment. Nay, we must even say that humility itself is only pure and true, where the soul knows itself deserving of punishment, its separation from God by unexpiated guilt,—where, consequently, giving honour to the righteousness of God, it seeks above all reconciliation, and does not dream at once of deification. The anticipatory character of mysticism, then, is punished by a perpetual swaying between exultation in mystic bliss, in momentary ecstasies, and the being without comfort; it has not yet found the condition of being, even in the foolishness of a perpetual consciousness of sin, yet full of abiding comfort, because the sting of sin, the guilt, is known as expiated in that fellowship with the Mediator, which possesses the mastery over sin. This, however, is the essential function of Christian faith, to grasp the expiation of guilt in spite of the (constantly combated) continuance of sinfulness. This distinguishing of guilt and sin, of the destruction of guilt without immediate destruction of sin, is yet unknown to mysticism, together with the Church of its time; now it dreams of an effusion of blessedness which is at the same time the destruction of all sin, deification; and now, when it cannot deny the continuance of sin, it is not conscious of enjoying the expiation of guilt, reconciliation and peace with God. Still, in the emphasizing of the divine sufferings of Christ, the suffering of His love, as the New Testament depicts it, on account of our sin, a path has been struck which was followed out by other pioneers of the Reformation, especially by *John Wessel*, in whom (see below), in place of divine resignation on the one hand and the mystic contemplation or sensation of God on the other, *evangelical faith* in the Mediator begins to show itself. If the proper conclusion of the mystic process lies in the atonement of guilt through Christ, who is also the pledge of victory over sin, then the mystic is even thereby made open in general to the world of history as the scene of the acts of God, and therefore to the records of this history, the Holy Scriptures, and to the Church which preaches Christ, and an inward shyness to which mysticism, as such, never overcame. As the mystic love to God now becomes love to the Father of Jesus Christ and to Christ, so also the same love to Christ cannot but become the love of Him in the brethren. And thus the mystic, without giving up his inwardness, but rather through gaining in true depth and inwardness, is restored to the world. The mystic strength now manifests itself also in a positive, even though inwardly free, relation to human interests, especially to the Church. This then is the union of mystic solitariness and of fellowship.

But when, after this inward career, the mystic turns himself again to the Church, he occupies a different position from formerly, when he was standing in unembarrassed union with it in simple historical faith. The return to the Church cannot be a blind uncritical return, else new slavery, separation from God through human interposition, new mechanism, would carry off the whole gain of the past. And the mediæval Church and its life was by no means so constituted, as not to excite criticism from the standpoint of these new acquisitions.

But according to what rule should criticism be applied to the Church, and love to it be shown in the effort at its amelioration? According to the rule of mystic subjectivity? But if this appeals to the Spirit of God, so also does the Church, which, if the question is one of human authority, can claim more authority than the individual. It is evident that either amelioration, which is not possible without criticism, is itself an impossibility, and we must abide by the authority of the Church, which sanctions its own corruptions, or there must be an authority, independent of both parties and superior to them, to which both must submit themselves. Since both lay claim to Christianity, the decision, where there is a falling away from Christianity, must evidently be determined by a comparison with the *primitive Christianity recorded* in the Holy Scriptures. This must be the rule of decision in the controversy between the Church and the pious subject. If mysticism accordingly is to be of some worth to the Church, it must receive a more objective character by adopting the *character of Scripturalness;* it must however, in order to be able to win and champion the true understanding of the Holy Scriptures, first of all open communications with the Scriptures, and not shun the toil of a thorough understanding of them; it must, before it seeks to regulate the Church according to the Scriptures, itself assume more of a canonical nature. The Holy Scriptures are to be understood according to their true sense as gathered from the whole,—else caprice and allegory may find in them the warrant for everything imaginable, even for a Romish Church. Mysticism must therefore first allow itself to be disciplined by the Holy Scriptures,—which will also promote its own inward strengthening and certainty, because in that case this is based not merely upon subjective impressions, but upon the immutable objective testimony, free from all subjectivity, of historical Christianity concerning itself.

CHAPTER II.

THE BIBLICAL FACTOR IN THE PREPARATION OF THE REFORMATION.

To the renewal of the Church by the Word of Scripture contribute in a moderate degree the *Waldensians*, with their far-reaching influence, and then the *Wycliffites* and the *Hussites*. The more these movements gained in depth and retired from a more superficial combating of the Catholic Church, the more friendly did they become to mysticism, and gained by it in inwardness and freedom; just as, conversely, mysticism, being regulated by them and by their knowledge of the Scriptures, grew in enlightenment and in simple practical sense,—both, however, in a lively sense of need of atonement for guilt and of redemption from sin, as well as in single-minded love to primitive Christianity, as the standard for the condition of the Church.

The *Biblical Principle* was first of all to grow strong in its independence, influenced neither by the Church nor by mysticism, and to go its own way, in order, when the time was come, to debouch into the common stream and contribute its quota to the Principle of the Reformation. The representatives of the biblical tendency had also a purifying process to undergo before they could acquire the mastery of the deeper matter of the Scripture, and thus become also capable of that inwardness, of which mysticism was from its very birth the champion. Temperate natures, of a practical and empiric turn, far removed from all speculation and religious originality, but honest, simple, and candid, were selected to be the first to re-establish the connection with historical primitive Christianity, and to diffuse the taste for it. The first in this rank are the *Waldensians*, so well-informed in the Bible, that their simple teachers had large portions of the Holy Scriptures verbally committed to memory. Their services of worship were a kind of Bible lecture [with short devotional exercises], aided by translations into the native dialect; and whoever was informed in the Bible considered himself entitled to preach. The laity went forth, as of old the Christians in the apostolic age, to preach the Word of God in the popular tongue.

They clung chiefly to the New Testament, and in it principally to the Gospels, this basis of canonical Christianity. The apostolic doctrinal ideas, especially the Pauline, were still unfamiliar to them. From the Gospels they derived their fundamental doctrine of "evangelical perfection in apostolical discipleship or poverty;" for their exegetical maxims were still very imperfect,—they proceeded now almost literally, and now in an allegorizing manner, as they also for their part held fast by the fourfold sense of Scripture of the middle ages. There was combined, however, with the dependence upon the Holy Scripture, which they sought after, a manifold interweaving of Romish dogmatics,—not indeed of their magical and conspicuously hierarchical elements; these were contrary to their sober spirit and sense of practical morality, as were also the unevangelical splendour of divine worship and its mechanical nature, and the doctrine of purgatory, by which this world is depreciated and the power of redemption translated almost entirely into the world to come. But they continued in harmony with those aspects of the Romish system, which are favourable, even though after a legal manner, to this earnest moral spirit, and which do homage to the righteousness of works. The requirement of poverty in following after Christ, and the idea of Christian perfection, which they cherished, bear the character of legality. Atonement and regeneration did not occupy with them an essential position, and they appear to have had no idea of justifying faith. In general they had little interest for dogma, and their opposition, as in the case of the so-called Reforming Synods, applied rather to the practical life alone,—certainly in an anti-hierarchical direction, which occasioned their persecution, but also dispersed their adherents over many lands. There was formed in England, and in the Netherlands, under the roof of the old Church, a kind of Waldensian Church, with bishops and presbyteries; they sought to gather together holy apostolic congregations with strict discipline of manners. These had, however, a Donatist odour; in order to the efficient administration of their office they demanded of the priests personal holiness. [See App. note B.]

The striving after conformity to Scripture was brought into connection with the *scientific factor* through John Wycliffe († 1384). In 1380, he translated the Holy Scriptures into English, and intentionally set them up as the sole authority in opposition to the principle of Church tradition, and to all bulls and popes. In this way he applies a sharp criticism to many dogmas, especially to the sacraments. He denies the transformation of the bread, and the sacramental character of confirmation and ordination: he also controverts Pelagianism, though certainly it is by force of a doctrine of absolute predestination, which drives him again to a negative conception of evil. Of a cool and sensible tendency, he stands aloof from all mysticism; and although he is not without a religious vein, which finds in particular a negative expression in the combating of all deification of the world and the Church, and in the rejection of all self-wrought merit, as well as of all dependence upon any intermediate authority between God and the soul, still immediate access to God has rather for him the meaning, simply, of free access to the Holy Scriptures and to the knowledge of God's commands. There is in him a powerful moral factor, and it is placed in a religious light by this, that man, according to him, is called to promote the glory of God through obedience. To the Church belong, according to him, the *Prædestinati*,[1] who only love God. He thus sets up a distinction between the visible and the invisible Church, but since he fails to give any statement of the essential marks of the Church, he restricts the proper conception of it only to the Church invisible. But in this way the historical Church also is for him no longer an independent entity: it falls into the hands of the State, to which he even ascribes the right of deciding, whether and in what it is a delinquent, and of wielding over it a punitive discipline. There is in his ideas of reform a strong State and national element, which soon entangled them with political tendencies. The ideal which floats before him, that the Church should lose its independence in the State, is a foreshadowing of what we afterwards find befalling the Anglican Church. The earlier history of England contributed to this, its shameful dependence upon the Romish See, by which a proportionately more powerful national reaction was excited in

---

[1] The *Prædestinati* are here distinguished by Wycliffe from the *Præsciti*, those foreknown as they who should perish.—*Tr*.

favour of civil and political freedom. The principal efforts of Wycliffe, too, are directed to the social political side, certainly in an earnest spirit, and one which aims at the amelioration of morals in the whole community; but the deeper religious spirit is wanting in his ideas of reform. The religious element does not attain to an independent development with him, but continues in onesided dependence upon the moral and the civil; and he exhibits little conception of the truth, that peace with God is much rather the condition, than the fruit, of true morality. He does not yet know the nature of justification, and does not yet understand the free grace of God, but sees in God rather the righteous Lawgiver, Governor, and Judge, than Holy Love. [See App. note C.]

But in his school, out of which *John Huss* rises with marked independence of position, the union established by Wycliffe between the biblical tendency and learning and science, incorporated the religious element with itself more definitely than ever, and began to assume a friendly attitude towards mysticism. Wycliffe has so little favour for mysticism, that he assails the contemplative life in general as sloth and laziness. He knows well that our good works do not suffice, and will strike down all pride with his predestination; he points the sinner finally to the comfort of reconciliation in Christ; but since Christ did not die for all, and His salvation only benefits the predestinated, and no one finally can tell whether he is elect, it is evident that he has no clear and certain knowledge of peace with God through the Atonement, and accordingly there only remains for him to require, that man should live in obedience to God's commands as if he were elect.

In *Huss*, on the other hand, appears the more powerful religious interest, especially in his doctrine of faith. "It is not enough to believe in a God (that He is) or to believe God (what He has said and commanded); rather must one believe *in God*,—believing, love Him,—believing, enter into Him and depend upon Him, become incorporated amongst His members." He seeks immediate fellowship with God, not mere connection with God's law and commandment. And that is not merely his endeavour or his hope; on the contrary, faith is for him the frame of heart, by which eternal life is begun in us. He considers contrition,—not however as a good work, deserving grace in a strict sense,—to be the sign of election, which is besides conditioned for him by the foreknowledge of God. In him the point of view of Augustine is again achieved, in which a high position is reserved for grace. Still, Huss does not advance beyond Augustine in so far as grace, justifying grace as well as sanctifying grace, is still regarded by him as immediate, and the relative independence of justification as distinguished from sanctification has not yet become clear to him, whilst he also adheres to the *Consilia Evangelica* [see App. note D.], and does not reject Transubstantiation and the sacrament of ordination, but seeks only to have the power and the divine authority of the priesthood limited. The power of the keys he allows to be conveyed to the whole Church, not to pope and cardinals. These are not the body of the universal Church, but a part, and the pope is not its head, but Christ, else those who make the popes might limit the Lord Christ. He also warns against the identification of the external church with the Church: it is one thing to be *of* the Church (*de Ecclesia*), another thing to be in it. His *followers*, who went at first to fanatical lengths, gained in intrinsic quality through the reverses they encountered, and purified and perfected their opposition to the Church. They did so not merely in the doctrine of indulgences, but also in the rejection of all the sacraments except baptism and the Lord's Supper, as well as of purgatory. They demanded the possession in their mother tongue of the Holy Scriptures, to which the highest reverence is due, and finally the Hussites (at least the later of them) said, that the doctrine of justification was the principal doctrine, upon the knowledge of which it depends whether any one belongs to the Church. They united themselves more closely with the Bohemian Waldenses, so that these also received a fresh quickening, so that in the year 1457 there were formed out of the Calixtines and the Waldenses [see App. note E.], the Brethren of the Law of Christ, who also called themselves the Union of Brethren, and who deliberately separated themselves from the Church on account of doctrine, and spread themselves chiefly in Moravia. These are the so-called Bohemian or Moravian Brethren, whose deputation Luther received with so much honour, and who were afterwards to come through Zinzendorf into still closer connection with the Evangelical Church.

Thus the biblical and moral movement, exhibited chiefly in the Waldenses, underwent a process of purification, in which they, coming into contact with different elements, advanced by the help of the Scripture from a Donatist position of enmity towards the Church to a Church spirit, from what was rather only negative and legal polemics against the customs and constitution of the Church to a purer knowledge of the faith. The Holy Scripture continued always to be their ultimate authority; there they strengthened their reformatory power, which had already manifested itself even in the matter of organization, in the regulation of congregations under elders, and in the connection of the congregations by bishops. This biblical movement—which spread, especially during the fourteenth and fifteenth centuries, from the South of France and Piedmont, through Switzerland, along the Rhine, to the Netherlands and England, and in its eastern current over Bohemia, Poland, and Moravia—contributed mightily to the diffusion throughout Christendom of the principle—as an incontrovertible and operative axiom—that the Church must submit to be tested by the Holy Scriptures. It no less gave the impulse to the numerous translations of the Scriptures into the vulgar tongue, which took place in the same century. [See App. note F.] Chief agents in this movement, as well as resulting from it, were more especially those popular and beneficent Netherlandish Brotherhoods, *The Brethren of Social Life*,[1] founded by *Gerhard Groot* († 1384), developed by Florentius Radewins; which lived together without oath or compulsion in community of goods, and in spiritual but not monastic societies, with a view to mutual edification, especially in the knowledge of Scripture, but also in order to diligent labour at their trades, and principally at the instruction of the people. They disseminated a scriptural religious education, even amongst the higher classes, harboured science, and even let mysticism find a place amongst them. They kept themselves free at the same time from a hostile relation to the Church, and in them the old fanatical Beghard and Beguine Societies rise again in a purified form. Previously to the Reformation, there is nowhere else accomplished to such an extent as in them the interpenetration of the elements of reformatory strength. The principle of the Reformation, which had been now so long active in the Church, is already, as it draws near to maturity, attempting its new formations beneath the roof of the old Church organization—there in the form of an orderly and purer church constitution, here in the form of free association.

[1] Also called the Brethren of the Common Lot, and the Brethren of Goodwill. See Ullmann's *Reformers before the Reformation.—Tr.*

CHAPTER III.

THE CHRISTIAN EDUCATION OF THE PEOPLE AND CHRISTIAN SCIENCE.

WHILST theoretical and ethical mysticism on the one hand, and scripturalism on the other were already beginning to amalgamate, whilst not only was the authority of the Scripture principle gaining strength in Christendom, but there were also falling away, more and more, the husks which held in confinement the germinating knowledge of the significance of the atonement, and of immediate access to God through faith in free grace in Christ, the mind turned not merely in the direction of depth, but also in the direction of width and breadth, and created in Germany a higher national Christian culture, to which the revival of the classic sciences essentially contributed. The nascent more liberal culture, deriving its strength from the classic antiquities, or the spreading might of *Humanism*,[1] assumed in many cases, and especially in Italy, a worldly and even frivolous form, and one reproductive of heathenism, and accordingly required in like manner to undergo first of all a purifying process. But it, too, was in the first instance to acquire strength independently in itself, in order thereafter, and only then, to enter into amalgamation with the other factors, especially those already treated of. Thus Humanism not only helped mightily in the emancipation of minds, and rendered the ground soft and susceptible for the Reformation, but it also in its own time contributed to it an important positive gift, most of all in that land which was to be the birthplace of the Reformation. The Reformation principle moved onwards to its maturity through such men as *Johann Goch, Johann von Wesel, Hieronynnus Savonarolo*, and especially *Johann Wessel*, in whom, though in different measure, mysticism and scripturalism are allied with science; and thus the Reformation principle grows to the form of a clear and intelligible doctrine capable of being universally communicated. Let us look at that somewhat more closely.

In contrast to monasticism, in so many respects lazy and

---

[1] I am not aware that this term has a place in our theological nomenclature but it is a literal translation of the German (Humanismus), and is perhaps the best that can be used to describe the culture of the humane letters, viewed as a movement and element in the history of this period.—*Tr.*

ignorant, with its mechanical devotions, the above-mentioned brotherhoods, extending in large numbers throughout Holland and Lower Germany, had made the most favourable impression upon the people by their simple and natural piety, by the circulation of good writings, but especially by their educational institutions, amongst which the school at Deventer won for itself the best name. Many eminent men, who were the pioneers of the Reformation, owed to them their education, as Johann Wessel, Erasmus, Hermann Busch, Agricola, Lange, Hegius. The desire to teach was met in a remarkable manner by the desire of the people to learn; there were teachers who had 800 to 1000 scholars. But this first received a more definite direction and a higher significance through the revival of classic literature. The Grecian Empire, even in its overthrow in the year 1453, scattered far and wide, like an old falling pine, seed which fell upon a receptive soil. The art of printing had just been discovered, which was to provide the new ideas with wings. And the ruin of scholasticism, which was just being accomplished, prepared the way at the same time for those new ideas, which were struggling towards formation amongst fermenting humanity. There are few parts in the province of earthly history where it is so strikingly evident how, without any concert, that which is most remote works irresistibly together with great and new designs as in a secret covenant, joined only by the Hand of Providence. There is an internal linking together of the inventions and discoveries following one upon another about the same time, and which, taking place in totally different provinces, appear externally independent of one another, but, being arranged with reference to one another, meet together in one common purpose. And it is only the Reformation which furnishes not merely the key to the understanding of their contemporaneous occurrence, but also the consecration of the same to the true blessing of humanity. It is true that the invention of powder and of the printing-press, as well as the discovery of America and the revival of classical antiquity, had for their common result the abolition of the barbarity and violence of mediæval chivalry, enlargement of view, the strengthening of the burgher community, and in all these respects the increase of culture; but all that co-operated to a true and lasting blessing only when it became the instrument, defence, and weapon of the

Reformation. The barbarity of chivalry was broken indeed by the new weapons, but a good part of the power of the people was even thereby subjected to an absolutism of royal might. Spain, which was most immediately concerned in the discovery of the new world, sucked in in its treasures a sweet poison, which wrought at first like a mighty life-charm, but soon with fatal effect. And in Italy, the vestibule of the newly arising arts and sciences, the press and classic antiquity aided indeed the formal cultivation of the mind; but because humanism, as far as the bulk of it was concerned, did not there find its ultimate goal in a religious awakening, rude forms and superstition gave place readily to a finer taste and to elegance. But there also culture became only too frequently a means of painting over unbelief and frivolity, of nourishing the intellectual desire of enjoyment and a refined egoism, and of implanting in men the dream of wealth and of a glorious existence, even without religion, in a life lived by one's own strength. These deceitful tendencies and errors preyed upon the noblest energies of the national life, and even turned them in the unnatural direction of attempting artificial renovations whilst there was spiritual slavery. The result was the speedy exhaustion of the power of production, and, as is shown by the history of the Renaissance in Italy and France since Louis XIV., the gradual disappearance even of the taste for science, art, and humane learning. It was otherwise with the German races on both sides of the sea, especially however in Germany, because here the revival of the sciences found its highest end in becoming one of the most blessed instruments of the Reformation.

In the middle ages—to begin with the steps of progress in the understanding of the Scriptures—a theologian seldom understood Greek and Hebrew; Latin and the Vulgate sufficed. But when it came to the thorough measuring of the Romish Church by the canonical standard, the means of an accurate historical understanding of the Holy Scriptures, as well as their circulation, necessarily acquired a decisive influence. In connection with the Old Testament, *Johann Reuchlin* is deserving of mention, as the founder of a more thorough grammatical study of the Hebrew language; and in connection with the New Testament, *Desiderius Erasmus*, who devoted his eminent acquaintance with the classical languages specially to the study of the Holy Scriptures in editions of the New Testament, criticism, exegesis, and paraphrase, and formed a large school of men destined to enter into a still more positive relationship to the Reformation than he himself occupied.

Linguistic culture, however, brought in itself no Reformation. The Erasmic spirit manifested more of the power of the virtuoso in bursting the fetters of barbarism, and in scourging superstition and ignorance, than in positive construction.

Hence a still more immediate importance is to be attached to the band of men—working for the most part in the universities which were numerously founded in the fifteenth century—who sought to bring the Reformation principle, which had been hitherto operating rather in secrecy, and the treasures of a deeper religious life to the open light of science and into the shape of formulated and purified doctrine. Amongst these men, whom we must here remember with honour, mysticism began to make the progress beyond itself which was still required. The better theology of the fifteenth century approached nearer and nearer to the decisive point, which was to be the watchword of the Reformation, to justification by faith, and did so by applying scriptural knowledge and scientific power to the wants of the deeper religious spirit, and thus acquiring a more penetrating understanding of the proper nature of Christianity, and of the person and work of Christ, as well as of faith in Him. These men show, on the other hand, with what difficulty and how slowly the pure concept of Christian faith disentangled itself from mediæval ideas, how so many errors were only gradually and imperfectly overcome by them, how deficiencies seemingly small nevertheless crippled again the whole reformatory power of the new learning, how often, finally, the very excessiveness of the opposition to Romish errors became implicated again in the principle of these errors; and hence it is only through them that we can receive a vivid impression of the difficulty and greatness of the work which is in question. *Johann von Goch* (properly Pupper, from Goch near Cleves, † 1475) and *Johann von Wesel* († 1481) manifest already the tendency towards a new theology. Johann von Goch treated anthropology and soteriology in the spirit of Augustine. But if the indeterminateness and impersonality of the Augustinian word *Grace* had furnished an impulse to the (as it were) material conception of it and to a magical sacerdotal dispensation of it, Johann von Goch now set in its place the

Holy Spirit, in order to secure in this way the immediateness of the vital relations between God and man, and at the same time the freedom of grace over against man: he combats not the less the Thomist doctrines of a merit according to adaptation and worthiness: he holds fast the prevenient character of grace, which is out of all proportion to our works of love. Only Christ has for him pure merit, and thereon rests our salvation. But if he is asked, on the other hand, how our justification takes place, even he is still standing upon the ground of Augustine and mysticism, and even in principle of the Romish Church, in that he regards the justifying power as lying properly in the God-given human love, in infused righteousness, *i.e.* in holiness (*justitia infusa*). His language seems unimpeachable, when he declares the justifying element to be *that* love, which is no created thing, but is God Himself, and has become in Christ our property; that is to say, the love which becomes ours through the dwelling of God in us. When he says: the life of salvation consists in this, that the Divine love flows infinitely and perpetually into us, and even so the created will flows eternally and perpetually back in the fulness of love to God,—it sounds in its generality beautiful and good; it is also true as a description of the Christian life in its continuance, after it has been born. But when we have to do with the conscious beginning, the foundation of this new life, where the question concerning the separation from God by guilt and sin and concerning reconciliation must stand in the forefront, there is in the foregoing nothing said as to this, *i.e.* as to the way of salvation, or rather, there is said what is false. For if we apply the language concerning the life of salvation, to which belongs the fulness of our love to God as well as the love of God to us, to the beginning of that life, it follows, as he himself also acknowledges, that faith is justifying, that it effects reconciliation, only as formed, *i.e.* as operative in love (*Fides caritate formata*). The consciousness of reconciliation can never, however, be reached in this way, nor the certainty of the forgiveness of sins. No matter although love is always to be thought of as infused by God, if participation in salvation, *i.e.* if peace, is to spring up in us only from the actual presence of this love, we dare not be assured of our reconciliation, since even he who is born again may never rest content with himself, until we have sanctification completed in us; for the effect is not before the cause. Then indeed sanctification could never be attained. For how could the love, whose fruit is to be reconciliation and blessedness, ever be kindled in us under the pressure of unreconciled guilt? That we cannot give it to ourselves, is evident to Goch, but not so clear is the cause of it, which lies not merely in finiteness, but in sin, ay, in guilt. How can the fear of God as the holy Judge, the unfilial fear of Him, be a condition suitable for the infusion of divine love? Only a magical transformation would be able straightway to change the fleeing from God, and fear of Him, into love. Psychological necessity, as well as the ethical character of Christianity, rather demands that recalling grace should first meet the fugitive with the loving message of forgiveness, which appeals to his hidden or developed longing, and that the message of free forgiveness should be believingly appropriated by the longing soul. And only now, after the consciousness of guilt is destroyed and a new consciousness has been won, is a turning-point in the inner life not only possible, but accomplished; and the consciousness of being loved by God, which we have received through becoming aware of His forgiveness, kindles in us responsive love; whereas a distinct consciousness of divine childhood never could be attained, if it were to become ours only through the infusion of holiness, since we could never know when and in how rich measure this infusion takes place. If, finally, we look to Christ, the Atoning One, what essential significance is left to him, if grace can immediately infuse love, which, so far as it is divine, justifies us? It is not an adventitious circumstance that *Johann von Goch* thinks of grace as based, not in Christ, but in the Holy Ghost, and does not insist upon a connection between faith and the historical Redeemer. This defect, which is inherited from mysticism, may be theologically expressed thus: The Divine Love is thought of indeed as prevenient and fruitful, but still as without holy righteousness, and therefore not purely ethically, not in a way distinct from physical goodness, else it could not thus be magically infused without any further step. Only when the right and honour due to it are accorded to the idea of righteousness, upon which the conceptions of freedom and the law, of guilt and punishment rest, are the personality and the necessity of the personal process recognized in their proper rights. And now the consciousness of deep separation from God through sin and guilt may become the basis of quite as conscious and voluntary a union with God, in which the personality finds its restoration and perfection. But the contrary view of an infusion of righteousness before the effacing of guilt is so connected with a Pelagian under-estimate of sin and guilt, as well as with magical views of divine saving operations and a physical conception of Divine goodness, that that mediæval union of the Pelagian and the magical is even here not yet properly dissolved. Still this inward representation of morality as love of God, which is itself divine and is alone the heart-infused justifying power, necessarily estranged from the [Roman] Catholic system of works, and in particular weaned every better conscience from the Church system of indulgences.

The struggle against *indulgences* was being waged for a long time before the Reformation. It was so especially in the University of Erfurt by *Jacob von Jüterbock*, the teacher of Wessel, then by *Johann von Wesel* (1400-1481, Professor in Erfurt about 1450, afterwards in Mayence and Worms) in several treatises. His attacks upon the hierarchy and indulgences led him into the hands of the court of the Inquisition, by which he, in a state of exhaustion and illness, allowed himself to be forced to recant; nevertheless, he died in prison. Like Gayler of Kaysersperg, he conducted his polemics in part with courage and wit, but it did not endure under persecution. In his view, too, infused righteousness still occupies an important place, whilst he distinguishes between the forgiveness of sins and salvation. Both are imparted only by God, the former through the priest; without there being any necessity for ecclesiastical penances, it is communicated by the declaration of the Church to the truly penitent. When any one is as far as possible prepared by means of penitence, God infuses righteousness into him; and only those who have this become partakers of salvation. Thus, evidently in the interests of opposition to the hierarchy, salvation is separated from the forgiveness of sins, but the significance of the latter is thereby weakened. If it were thought of as the love of God meeting us in reconciliation, salvation could not be wanting in the new-won fellowship of love with God; if it is wanting, the forgiveness of sins can only have reference to isolated instances, to the blotting out of sins that have been confessed, not of the condition of guilt in general. And even the assurance of this blotting out is effected, according to him, not through faith, but only through contrition, which betrays a feeble interest for the assurance of salvation. Just as little does he accord to faith a place in the infusion of righteousness; and since it is only from the latter that the certainty of salvation is to result, there are introduced all the evils already spoken of as arising from the confounding of *justificatio* with infused grace. A purifying work was carried on also either through treatise or preaching by Felix Hemmerlin, a canon in Zurich, who died about 1460; *Johannes Busch*, of Zwoll, 1420 [✝ 1479]; Johann Trithemius, ✝ 1516; Sebastian Brandt, ✝ 1520, and Johann Gayler of Kaysersperg, ✝ 1510.

A higher position belongs to *Hieronymus Savonarola*, ✝ 1498. Although his earlier years are characterized by a blending of political and ecclesiastical efforts at reform, he not merely exercised an anti-hierarchical influence, and purified manners and gave animation to the study of the Scriptures in his Order, but he also in his last days, in which he became quiet and ripe, gained deep glances into the nature of the Gospel, as is shown especially in his "Triumph of the Cross." He derived salvation neither from human merit, nor even from infused righteousness, whether as a condition, or as operative, but only from the cross of Christ, and thus laid great weight upon the certainty, which he calls the sealing, of the state of grace.

But the most distinguished who yet remains to be named, a man of high scientific culture, as versed in scholasticism as in the classic tongues and in Hebrew, is *Johann Wessel*, of Gröningen (1419 to 1489), a man animated by an inward mysticism of living freshness, and all this in connection with the Holy Scriptures. In Paris, where he taught, the name of "light of the world" (*Lux mundi*) was given to him. Luther said of him, "If I had read Wessel first, mine adversaries might have imagined that Luther had taken everything from Wessel; so that our spirits are in harmony, and there springs up thence to me a special joy and strength" (*Luthers Werke von Walch*, xiv. 220). He calls him a rare and lofty spirit, who proved himself to be truly taught of God. What specially distinguishes him is, that at last *faith* becomes, according to him, the central point. In the view of mysticism, believing appeared to be too little to conduct to salvation; it sought to effect the transition to God by contemplation or love in addition to repentance, according as its tendency was more theoretical or ethical. Johann Wessel sees how it is involved in our sin that we cannot in this way begin the process of salvation, but only by faith;

but he no longer takes faith to be a mere opinion or holding as true, a mere historical faith, but his mysticism enters into it as a component element. It is, according to him, in general, confidence, undoubtedly a moral act, in which lies trust and the being sure with regard to the good will of another. Specifically, however, the Christian faith is, according to him, the laying hold of the whole Christ, who is, in his view, the Atoning One, as well as the Sanctifier and the Dispenser of salvation. Faith is, according to him, not productive, like love, but also not merely passive and lifeless, like the mere submission to be determined by the authority and magic of the Church, or like mystic resignation, but it is an act of the will, yet of the will desiring to be the subject of the act of God in Christ,—an overcoming this of the Pelagian and the magical through the union of the true elements in both. He no longer allows the division, according to which the forgiveness of sins falls to the merit of Christ, but the gaining of salvation takes place through our love, even although that love be infused; but in his view Christ carries in himself the inexhaustible power of the whole of salvation; He does not operate, however, in a magical manner, but is only taken hold of by *faith*, by which every one of His gifts is gained possession of in its order. Since the benefits of redemption, sanctification, and full salvation, are not to be had outside of Christ nor without faith, Wessel obtains in this way with faith in Christ a specific difference between the natural and the spiritual life, a turning-point.[1] He too is the first to admit into its proper place the righteousness of God, which in mysticism generally remains absorbed in the divine love, whilst in the Church system it rather alternates with the divine love, than interpenetrates it. Wessel discusses the requirements of Righteousness, the honour of God, and the guilt of man in all their significance; Christ, however, is mediator not merely between God and man, but between the just God and God desiring to show mercy: in Him we behold, says he, not merely the reconciled God, but also the reconciling God, inasmuch as God, become Man, Himself performs, effects, and calls forth what His righteousness requires. It is, according to him, possible for God to look upon us as righteous and satisfying the law, in that he sees in Christ the surety of our fulfilment of the law, and us

[1] Ullmann, *Reformers before the Reformation*, ii. 458, 472, ff.

as believers united with him. The believer is assured of his righteousness, not through his virtue, but through real fellowship with Christ.

But such a doctrine regarding faith transforms also the idea of the *Church*, for now all belong to the Church, who are united to Christ in faith, hope, and love, whether they are under the pope and the Romish Church, or in a schismatic community. Through this view of faith, he comes also to the *universal priesthood*, which he expressly distinguishes from the priesthood of rank, the special priesthood provided for the sake of order, in and alongside of which, however, the universal priesthood must continue. He will not allow the so often misused image of the clergy as shepherds and the congregation as a flock to be carried out beyond the evangelical measure. The flock, he cries, is one that has reason and liberty; the shepherd may not simply exact obedience; there are cases in which the flock must care for itself. With regard to the authority of the Church he teaches: We believe in the Gospel for God's sake, in the pope and the Church for the Gospel's sake, but not in Christ on account of the Church. The well-known utterance of Augustine, "I would not have believed the Gospel if regard for the Church had not moved me," he interprets so as to make faith in the Gospel arise through the ministration of the Church, but not so as to place the consideration due to the Church higher than the Gospel. If the majority is against us, it must awaken doubt in us, but only the Gospel can decide. Many of the popes have erred fundamentally and fatally. If the pope does not build up, oppose him, for he stands under the Gospel, and has authority only as its champion. He exists only for the sake of order, and is without dogmatic significance. And yet Wessel did not wield the Scripture principle onesidedly, legally, and literalistically; on the contrary, he maintained in their respective places the Holy Spirit and the pure tradition preserved by Him, where it is to be found, as well as faith. "The Scriptures," he says, "are not equal to Christ, are not the whole Word of God; we have in nature and in the Scriptures only an abbreviated Word of God, an excerpt on account of our weakness; and although all is already given in Christ, still the Word of God is aye growing in His kingdom unto perfection." In the Lord's Supper he sees the whole God-man present, but not *merely* in it, and the bodily reception profits nothing without faith, but only injures. In the sacrament of penance he rejects the necessity for the confessional and the satisfaction by means of works, but derives contrition from a divine gift, for true penitence arises only from a knowledge of the divine love. "The true purgatory outside of us is the Gospel of Christ, which purifies the loving one with the more pain, the more purified he already is. But the true purgatory within us is the flame of divine love and godly sorrow. The dead do not stand under the rod of the lictor, but under the discipline of the Father, who instructs them and rejoices in their daily progress."

Let us now take another glance backwards. The necessity for a reformation of the Church in its head and members was recognized for centuries with increasing universality, and the series of Reforming Synods in the fifteenth century was not wanting in noble and important men, such as Peter d'Ailly (Cameracensis), † 1425, Johann Charlier Gerson, † 1429, Nicolaus de Clemangis, † sometime before 1440. If anything could be done by means of councils, those of the fifteenth century, favoured as they were by the weakness of the papacy, might have done it. But they were of no use, for they confined themselves to combating the symptoms of evil; they reduced reform to a question of power as between the pope and a universal Council; at the very most, they laboured for the improvement of the morals of the clergy, and especially of the papal court. For them, also, the hierarchical constitution was, in its episcopal form, an irremoveable dogma, and so the $\pi\rho\hat{\omega}\tau\text{o}\nu\ \psi\epsilon\hat{\upsilon}\delta\text{o}\varsigma$ was shared in by them; tradition remained the supreme source and authority; and so little was the consciousness of the necessity of dogmatic reforms awakened in them, that it was with the approval of the pious doctors that Huss was burnt on the 6th of July, 1415, and Jerome of Prague on the 30th May, 1416. So that the Church would have made no essential gain, even although the councils with their episcopal system had been victorious. The national element, as involving local sovereignty, would have become more powerful, and the unity of the Church would have been dissolved for the benefit of a popedom of a civil nature [*Cæsareopapie*]. That help was still less to be expected from the papacy than from councils, was shown by experience, especially by that of the last century before the Reformation, in which time the papacy, become secure after the Reforming Synods, saw at its head men who disgraced the Holy See with scandals of every sort,[1] brought the whole Reformation to a standstill, and instead introduced the Inquisition (in Spain in 1480 under Sixtus IV., in Germany in 1484), the prosecution of witches (under Innocent VIII.), and the censorship of literature (in Germany in 1503 under Alexander VI.).

If then, accordingly, neither pope nor councils would nor could give help, whence was help to come? There remained only the people with their princes,—a road to reform which might indeed bring about an ecclesiastical schism, and even in Germany a political one. The independence of the princes of the Empire over against the sovereign head of the Empire had been upon the increase long before the Reformation, to the detriment of the unity and strength of the Empire. If the Emperor had favoured the interests of Reformation, he would have had the best part of the people so entirely upon his side that, supported by their love and power, he might perhaps have been able to put a stop to the dissolution of the power of the Empire which had been begun by the princes. This the Hapsburgers, with more of a Spanish than of a German spirit, disdained to do. And only now did the increasing independence of the princes undertake with a good conscience the task that fell to it of preparing an asylum for the Reformation, when the power of the Empire should be opposed to it. Those who laboured to frustrate the accomplishment of a uniform reformation, so confessedly necessary, set themselves thereby in antagonism to that, through which the whole nation required to enter in united spiritual power into a new epoch.

As for the Church itself, Episcopacy began about the beginning of the sixteenth century to lose more and more its confidence even in itself; France, with its Gallican liberties, became humbler, and changed its Pragmatic Sanction of 1438 into a Concordat; the proud Sorbonne of Paris, with her twenty-one doctors, which had so long carried aloft the torch of science, lowered it; and Leo X. was able in 1517 to close the Lateran Council in triumph, because the papacy had proved victorious over every opposition, and seemed to stand more firmly than ever.

---

[1] Cf. Stephanus *Infessura Diariam Romanæ urbis*; Gieseler's *Kirchengeschichte*, ii. 4, p. 149, ff. [Translated in Clark's *Foreign Theological Library*.]

SECOND DIVISION.

The Reformation in its Initial Unity and Principial Basis, 1517-1525.

SECTION I.

THE LUTHERAN REFORMATION.

CHAPTER I.

THE PERSONAL DEVELOPMENT OF LUTHER TILL 1517.

THE personality of Luther is one of those great historical figures in which whole nations recognize their own type, " their intensified self,"[1] in which the germ of a new moral and religious perception is as it were embodied. It is, however, not so much his natural individuality which has given him his significance for the history of the world; on the contrary, it had many points that were undeniably harsh, narrow, and weak; indeed, his natural personality, with its contradictions and self-tortures, was consuming itself away, was in process of dissolution, and had become a chaos, until the creative breath of the pure Gospel, with its words of comfort and peace, brought the self-destructive conflict within him to a blessed issue, and gathered his powers harmoniously together around the central point of a new personality. He wished not to be esteemed a saint; but the significance as a type, and for the history of the world, which he possesses for the German mind, and far beyond the confines of Germany, has been obtained by him, because he was a man who lived through, and brought to a blissful termination, the inward struggles for peace and for immediate fellowship with God,—life questions which must stir the soul of every earnest

[1] ["*ihr potenzirtes Selbst*"]. Cf. Döllinger, *Kirche und Kirchenthum, Papstthum u. Kirchenstaat*, 1861, p. 386, f.

and thoughtful man. After he had lived through the struggle and the victory in his inmost soul, he communicated his experiences to the heart of his people with eloquent artlessness, and so won for himself the position of a skilful and trustworthy guide in the things which concern the everlasting salvation of the soul. He is certainly a champion of the national spirit of the Germans, whose image still exercises a magic power in both higher and lower circles; but as it is not his natural individuality, so also it is not his word as a mere doctrine, through which he has become so permanently influential, but it is all that which constituted him the type of a scholar of the Apostles, and a pattern, we do not say of the Christian life in general, but of a Christianity which is conscious and personal, and which has attained to manhood; above all, it was the bodying forth of his knowledge of the Christian salvation in a personality pure and free in God. For in his *faith* lies the secret of his strength, and the work of his life in its external aspect has for its object to disclose once more to the independent discernment of every individual the majesty and the power of the Gospel, and to lead even the simplest Christian to an experience of salvation as immediate and original, as that was, which had lifted him out of a world of death into life, out of hell into salvation.

The typical significance, which belongs to Luther's Christian piety, renders it necessary to recall to mind, how for a long period of his life there was no appearance of his being animated by the thought of bettering others or the world, but all the aspirations of his spirit, all the longing and wrestling of his soul, had for their only aim, to be at peace and in harmony with himself. But whilst his whole concern was still about the salvation of his soul, he soon learned that inward content and harmony could only come to him by his becoming a partaker of peace with God, and of the forgiveness of sins. Seeing that the Church presented itself as the guide to God, he entered (not without violating his filial duties) upon the course to which the Church directed so quick a religious instinct as his, and amid the paths, of which its ethics offered him the choice, he chose that which involved most self-sacrifice, and which should most surely conduct him to the goal and to the highest stage of perfection. He took the monastic vow. He not only willingly undertook the most menial services, but he also imposed upon himself, in extremest measure, the mortifications and penances, to which the Church ascribed special merit before God, and therefore power to secure His favour. "True it is," says he afterwards of his monastic life, " I was a pious monk, and observed the discipline of my Order more strictly than I can tell. If ever a monk came to Heaven through a monkish life, I would have come thither; all my cloister companions who knew me will bear me this testimony." And again: " If ever there was one who, before the Gospel dawned, held in high esteem the precepts of the Fathers and of the Pope, and was most sincerely zealous concerning them, I was especially so with all my heart; with fastings, vigils, prayers, and other exercises, I have tortured and wearied my body far more than all those, who are now my most bitter enemies and persecutors. Our adversaries do not believe that we could subject ourselves so willingly to such murderous treatment, in order only to bring our hearts and consciences to rest and peace before God, and yet could never find this peace in such abominable darkness." Now, what was the cause of such unappeasable disquietude, which would neither suffer itself to be hushed by the accumulated merits of his ascetic practices, nor by such language as: God does not desire of us perfection, but limits His requirements to the measure of our weakness, nor finally by the grants from the Church of indulgences and such like ? The cause lies, above all, in this, that it was not enough for him to stand before man as blameless and pious, nor even to be at peace with the Church; his innermost need had reference to God Himself, and according to this he estimated with a tender conscience his worth and inner condition. Before God, he ever found himself, no matter what works he extorted from himself, to be unclean and a sinner. His need of communion with God was not that indefinite need felt by the mystics before him. From their attempts to merge themselves in God, and to become one spirit with God, he was deterred by the profound consciousness of the Divine holiness, and of his own sinfulness, which made an immediate union with God appear to him impossible, and to attempt it sacrilege. In God he saw only the stern Avenger, who visits sinners with the pains of hell; such texts of Scripture as " Deliver me in Thy righteousness" filled him with terror, because he saw himself, before a just God, threatened only with condemnation and death. Whilst this conception of God drove him to the belief that he must seek to make atonement to Him by the mortification of the body, he experienced nevertheless the fruitlessness of these efforts, and wrote bewailingly to Dr Staupitz, "O my sin, my sin, my sin!" The comfort which this friend gave him, "Thou wilt become sinless, and hast now no proper sin," made no impression on his awakened conscience. He had yet to gain a deeper insight into his sin, to overcome the imagination which he, misled by the injunctions of the Church, still nourished and cherished, namely, that the matter in hand was the annulling of this or that particular sin, and not that a change of the whole inward man, and of its relation to God, was necessary, as well as the corresponding idea that he, to whom there as yet belonged only the power of sighing after the true life, could perform the works of this new life, or confer it on himself. This imagination was shaken by the words of a father, whose name is unknown, and to whom he bemoaned his distress of soul. He pointed him to the gracious forgiveness of sins in the Apostolic Creed, and showed him that he must also believe *in reference to himself* that the God of mercy has, through the sacrifice and blood of His obedient Son, procured for him the forgiveness of all his sins, and allowed it to be proclaimed in the word of absolution; that man is justified by faith without the works of the law (Rom. iii. 28). He began to understand, by means of the doctrine of the Gospel concerning the prevenient grace of God the Father, how that he, so long as he would owe his title to the Father's House to his own performances or merits, was ensnared in an unfilial and legal spirit, utterly foreign to the House of the heavenly Father, and wanted the joy of free and pure love as well as of true humility. He began to perceive, "That the righteousness of God is His mercy, through which He esteems and holds us for righteous." He was now rescued from the tortures, by which he had so long been consumed.

But it was at first only the personal *experience* of salvation by faith, of which he became possessed; the *knowledge* of the significance and of the bearing of this fact of the divine peace which he enjoyed, was still wanting to him, as well as the *scientific form* in which to express it. He had as yet no presentiment of the fact that there lay in it the germ of a totally different system of the economy of salvation, than the ecclesiastical. He was not hindered by it from continuing, as professor at Wittenberg, to propound the system which he had taught since his appointment to that office in 1508; besides, he was the less able to realize himself in contradiction with the doctrine of the Church, that the way to this experience had been shown to him within the pale of the Church itself, and the latter (as is shown also by the example of John Wessel) had not yet, before the Council of Trent, excluded its members from this experience. And what is still more, so little did he understand the universal and fundamental bearing of the principle of faith, that even after its attainment he persevered, according to the former custom, in the pretendedly meritorious practices of the Church. Although more recent researches render it doubtful if he, upon the occasion of his visit to Rome, in 1510, ascended upon his knees the staircase of Pilate, it is nevertheless certain that he greeted holy Rome with an ardent devotion, sought blessing for himself by making the circuit of all the places of pilgrimage, and attributed to the mass such a power for the salvation of the dead, that it was to him at that time "a sheer vexation that his father and mother were still alive; for he would gladly have delivered them out of purgatory by his masses in the Holy City." It is still further certain, that the frivolity and depravity of the clergy at Rome, and all that he there saw of the pageantry and merely mechanical labour of worship, rendered it more and more evident to him, that the power of salvation could not lie in all the outward works of the Church. The text, "The just shall live *by faith*," which was at several important moments of his life ever afresh recalled to memory, compelled him to compare with it the experiences he had made upon his journey to Rome, and to measure these by that text. He returned cooled in his enthusiasm for the Rome of those days, but without having as yet inwardly broken with it, or even become conscious of a divergence from the ways of the Church.

Soon after his return he became, in 1512, Doctor of Theology, and took the oath, which so often comforted him afterwards in his hours of conflict: I swear that I will defend evangelical truth according to my ability (*Juro me veritatem evangelicam pro virili defensurum*). Adhering—according to the custom of his Order, and still more closely than it—to the doctrine of Augustine, he now, as teacher of theology, zealously impugned the freedom of the human will for good, emphasized the doctrine of natural depravity, and, as he himself diligently studied and expounded the Holy Scriptures, so also he recommended everywhere the reading of the Bible, and pointed back from the Schoolmen, with their human precepts, to the original Gospel; and all this in the conviction that he was labouring the while in harmony with the spirit of the Romish Church, and in its behalf. But his eyes were soon to be opened on this point.

CHAPTER II.

DEVELOPMENT OF THE PURGATIVE AND CRITICAL SIDE OF THE REFORMATION PRINCIPLE IN LUTHER. 1517-1522.

LUTHER did not thrust himself forward as a reformer; but, in fulfilment of his calling, under compulsion of conscience, and in defence of the Christian economy of salvation, he became, upon the occasion of Tetzel's indulgences, the antagonist of a theory of repentance and salvation, which he held to be disallowed by the Church itself, and to be a mere accidental abuse of what he himself admitted and practised, without any embarrassment from the experience of faith to which he had attained. The struggle against *indulgences*—into which the Pelagian errors of the Church, and those which sanctioned a purely magical operation, had twisted themselves as it were into a knot—conducted him, however, still deeper into the relations of the Christian doctrine of salvation, and showed him, step by step, its incompatibility with the Romish doctrine, even in points which, as harmless, he had hitherto allowed to remain unraised. He would not destroy the outward unity of the Church; but when the Church, as represented in its dignitaries, accorded its protection to indulgences, the necessity of rejecting indulgences, which had been already impressed upon him by conscience, led him perforce to doubt the infallibility of the pope and of the Romish Church.

It was in the course of his calling that Luther came into contact with Tetzel, the shameless trader in indulgences, when, in the year 1517, several persons appeared at his confessional,—confessed their sins, indeed, but gave him to understand that they would not abstain from the sins which they confessed. The Doctor would not absolve them,—the penitents appealed to the pope's letter and Tetzel's indulgence. Luther answered, in refusing them absolution, "Except ye repent, ye shall all likewise perish." They went to Tetzel to give information against Luther; and he, in his indignation, reviled Luther from the pulpit, and also wrote a short instruction for the priests, for the purpose of recommending indulgences. Luther, in order that he might not be obliged to violate his conscience by the recognition of Tetzel's indulgences, addressed himself to the higher ecclesiastical authorities, to four bishops, with a request to put a stop to the disorder. The answers which came in were contemptuously or evasively worded. Luther now, on the 4th of September, published, in German, a sermon on indulgences, and, on the 31st of October, nailed the Ninety-five Theses to the door of the Schloss-Kirche at Wittenberg.

These contain much that is obscure, and even contradictory; which arose from the fact, that he still associated with the evangelical knowledge he had acquired an adherence to the Romish Church and its spiritual laws. He not only demands the mortification of the flesh as the external test of the genuineness of the internal repentance (Thes. 3); he also declares that God pardons the guilt of no one, whom He does not subject in the most complete and willing submission to the priest, His vicegerent (Thes. 7, 61, 38). The forgiveness of the pope is for him a declaration of the Divine forgiveness; who speaks against the truth of the papal pardon, let him be accursed (Thes. 71). According to his protestation at the close, he will submit himself to the Church. But there are two intimately connected points in which the light shines already clearly forth: *first*, repentance, which he transfers from the purgatory of the next world, over which the priest has no power, into this world: from mechanical and external exercises of penance, into the inwardness "of a right despair of one's self," and extends over the whole Christian life, as a disposition consisting in being without hope from one's self, instead of setting it in the particular acts of the sacrament of repentance. The *second* is the knowledge that the proper and true treasure of churches is the Gospel of the glory and grace of God (Thes. 62); and in intimate connection with this is the stress which he lays upon assurance of Divine grace (Thes. 16, 36). To the pope he allows the right of imposing and remitting penalties in this world, but so that neither priest nor pope can take away the most trivial daily sin, so far as its guilt is concerned, or do more than declare and confirm what may be given of God (Thes. 6, 36, 37). The canonical punishments, which the pope may at his pleasure impose upon, or remit to, the living (Thes. 5), must not be confounded with the Divine punishments, —a confusion which has involuntarily arisen, partly from the Divine authority of the papacy, and was partly implied in the extension of the punishments of purgatory to a period immeasurably remote. "This tare, that the canonical penances have been changed into the repentance of purgatory, has been sown whilst the bishops slept" (Thes. 11). These canonical penances belong only to the external world, to the ecclesiastical economy, in which Luther accords undiminished sway to the authority of the pope. But those sentences concerning true repentance and the true treasure of the Church are fundamentally destructive of indulgences, and deprive them of all value, inasmuch as they contribute nothing to the proper forgiveness of sins before God in this world and the next, and would prove it even better to endure the wholesome punishments of the Church than to mitigate them by the payment of money, which might be given to the poor (Thes. 43, 40).

It was the language, nay, the cry, of an oppressed conscience which was perceptible in these Theses,—of a conscience, which sought nothing for the man himself, and was even ready and willing to endure every external hardship, but was resolved to maintain itself inviolate and unspotted, let the cost be what it might. Such language finds echo in the hearts of men: "It was as if the angels ran as messengers" to carry the Theses through Europe. It was certain to make a deep impression, especially upon the consciences of the German people, as it announced a resistance of an unusual kind,—a power, which was quiet and humble, but at rest in itself and indomitable; ay, and the firm point, from which, as a centre, the Romish Church was to be shattered to its very foundations.

The struggle itself, which at its commencement bore throughout a purely defensive character, passed through *three stages*, by which the Reformation had to make room for itself.

At first the struggle against indulgences was conducted by Luther upon the supposition, that the highest dignitaries, the pope at least, would condemn them. Luther, whilst maintaining his position in firm and powerful language against the defenders of indulgences, especially Sylvester Prierias and J. Eck of Ingolstadt (even inferring that the result for the opposite side upon this question of indulgences would be excommunication and its power, which he recognized as regulating the outward fellowship of the Church, but as void of any influence over inward connection with Christ), turns devotedly to Rome with his revised theses, and a detailed explanation of them to guard them against misunderstandings, and promises obedience to the pope in the accompanying document.[1] But Rome—which must be allowed to have acted at first with moderation, restrained, doubtless, less by her feeling of shame for what had taken place, than by the admonitions to circumspectness, which emanated from men like Erasmus, perhaps also from the Elector of Saxony, as well as led by the gentle manner peculiar to Leo X., to whom the tone and demeanour of a Tetzel, Sylvester Prierias, or even of an Eck might seem too vicious—nevertheless gave no signs of condemning anything of what had taken place, or of characterizing it as an abuse. Instead of to Rome, Luther was summoned to Augsburg, to appear before Cardinal Cajetan, who demanded, in the name of the pope, the retractation of his doctrine of the necessity of faith in order to the enjoyment of sacraments, the retractation of his attacks upon indulgences, and submission to the papal court, which reprobated his doctrine. Firmly maintaining the necessity of faith, he had no other reply to give to him than that he regarded the sentence of canonical law, which based indulgences upon the merit of Christ and of the saints, as the doctrine of man, and the Holy Scriptures as of higher authority than the pope. He left Augsburg, since there was a talk of his imprisonment, with an appeal *a papa male [non bene] informato ad papam melius informandum*. But even from this position he was ousted by the papal bull of 9th November, 1518, sanctioning the doctrine of indulgences, in which the pope arrogated to himself, as vicar of Christ, and in virtue of his right of disposal over the stock of merit of Christ and of the saints, not only the right of dispensation from the penalties of the Church in this world, but also of the dispensation from temporal punishment (*i.e.* the punishment belonging to time in the other

[1] *Luthers Werke von Walch*, xv. 496.

world up till the day of judgment), which is imposed in accordance with Divine justice.

Since the situation had now become so far clear on the side of Rome, it could not long be doubtful what Luther's *second* step must be. For this the clumsy defenders of indulgences had also in their manner sufficiently provided. For when the Dominican Prierias, in the "conference" which he held with Luther, laid down his premises in these four axioms:[1] (1) the Romish Church is virtually (*virtualiter*) the Universal Church; the cardinals represent the Romish Church, and the pope is *virtualiter* the College of Cardinals, as the head of the Church; (2) the Pope, when he decides *ex cathedra*, cannot err; (3) whoever does not abide by the doctrine of the Romish Church, and of the Pope, as the infallible rule of faith, from which even the Holy Scriptures derive their power and authority, is a heretic; (4) the Romish Church or the pope teaches not only by words, but also by deeds, whether in matters of faith or life; he is therefore a heretic who thinks evil of the deeds of the Church: and when the same Prierias recommends indulgences by saying that there is absolutely no certainty of the personal forgiveness of sins, and so it is better to do too much than too little,—speeches of this kind challenged not alone such a man as Luther to critical reflections concerning the validity of the papal authority, which in the hands of its defenders assumed with such logical consistency the air of setting itself up above everything, of condemning Scripture, faith, and conscience to silence, and of reducing the whole duty of Christendom to a blind obedience, and a ready recognition of everything that the pope teaches or does. This was an absolutism such as no tyrant ever endeavoured to exercise; for none ever asserted such a blind and servile obedience to be the only virtue well-pleasing to God, to be the duty of conscience. Whilst such speeches encountered opposition and ridicule amongst the German people especially, they contributed, in the case of Luther, whose disposition demanded the possession of assurance in himself, or certainty in the truth, to turn his thoughts more and more definitely to the question concerning the foundation of Christian truth, and to the most rigid investigation, not so much of *what* we have to believe, as chiefly of *why* we must believe something, which the Christian Church teaches. We saw

[1] *Luthers Werke*, xviii. 81, ff.

above how the germ of a consistent standpoint, finished in itself, might be held to be already provided in his personal piety; but with this he still held the subjection to established authorities to be quite compatible, without asking himself, whether the admission of an external authority in faith was not detrimental, both to the authority of the Holy Scriptures and to the immunity of saving faith. It was necessary that, if the Scriptures and faith were to attain to the importance due to them as principles, they should not only be both exalted to a high place, but should, each in its own manner, occupy the exclusive and royal position, which, in its sphere, nothing dare compare itself with, or presume to rival. As there is one God, one world, and one Mediator, Jesus Christ, even so is there one supreme source of knowledge and rule of faith, and one manner of appropriating the Gospel.

It was through such opponents as Prierias, in general however through the stress laid by his opponents upon the formal, divine right of the ruling Church, that Luther was driven to the exclusion in doctrine and in principle, and not merely in practice, of false, or at best secondary, authorities, which have to await their rule and measure at a higher court.

But even after it had become perfectly clear to him that the Pope could not only err, but also, according to all accounts, was now erring and abusing his power for the defence of error, he was still far from being able with equal ease to take the third step, and to treat the *authority of the Church* as an authority which could be contradicted in certain cases. Here, too, at first avoiding a decision, he clung to the hoped-for possibility, that the Church could not, in the councils which represented it in its totality, approve and ratify error. He appealed, in December, 1518, to a future General Christian Council, upon the ground that the power of the Pope does not hold against, nor above, but for the Scriptures and the majesty of truth, and in subjection to them, and that he has received no power to destroy the sheep and to lead them into error. He would need better grounds to convince him, namely, the hearing of the voice of the Bride; for it is for him still she who hears certainly the voice of the Bridegroom. He would be her "scholar, not her adversary."[1] This position

---

[1] *Briefe an C. Cajetan*, 17 u. 18 Oct. 1518. De Wette, *Luthers Briefe*, i. 162, 164.

seemed quite tenable, inasmuch as there might easily be adduced from ecclesiastical tradition evidences, ecclesiastically uncontradicted, in support of what was Luther's most precious experience. But, on the one hand, the Romish Church could not allow that it possessed a double and contradictory tradition, but it insisted upon an authority, which should decide what forms part of the true ecclesiastical tradition and how the Fathers and the Holy Scriptures are to be interpreted with ecclesiastical correctness, and it appealed to old canonical precepts, and to decrees of synods, which accept the divine authority of Councils for doctrine and life. On the other hand, also, Luther could not abide by the admission of the infallibility of the Church, out of which (since it could not come to a verbal expression without some organ) the infallibility of some organ, which should speak in its name and represent it, would follow, if it were not to remain a mere illusory predicate.

At first the appeal to a General Council was followed by an armistice; indeed the negotiations of Miltiz with Luther assumed the appearance, as if the latter would retrace some of his steps, and draw nearer again to Rome. He condescended to every precaution, which should help to confine the strife which had been kindled within the narrowest limits, and to prevent fresh fuel from being added to the flame. In a special treatise he openly declares, that he would not separate from the Romish Church, and would recognize its power as the highest upon earth. He consents to let the recognized Romish doctrine of the intercession of the saints, of purgatory, of good works, such as fasting and prayer, remain; in a word, he agrees to ignore, and, as it were, confine within embankments, the wide fundamental bearing of the strife, which is not yet clear to himself, and to treat the whole as a dispute regarding a single point. He consents that this matter should stand still for the future—he will let it bleed to death, and, whilst he acknowledges that he has showed great heat and bitterness, will write no more about it.[1]

Luther was now in great straits. Not merely because his temporal ruler, high as that ruler prized him, desired the utmost submission, whilst he on his part felt the greatest reluctance to entangle the Elector in his affairs, or to render him co-respon-

---

[1] *Unterricht auf etliche Artikel der Heiligen Fürbitte, gute Werke, Fasten, Beten, römischer Kirchengewalt,* xv. 843.

sible: not merely because emigration to France was laid upon his heart: it was his piety towards the Church, which brought him, even in the face of so mild a defender as Miltiz, into the greatest inward distress. "As I had overcome through the Scriptures," says he later, "many arguments which lay in my way, so have I finally, through the grace of Christ, overcome with great anxiety, difficulty, and toil, this one, that the Church should be obeyed. For I regarded the Church of the Pope for the true Church with much greater earnestness and true reverence, and that from the heart, than do those shameful calumniators and perverters, who now talk haughtily against me. If I had despised the Pope, as those, who praise him so much, now despise him, I would have been afraid that the earth would in that hour have opened and swallowed me, like Korah and his company."

At the same time he yields nothing with regard to that one remaining point of dispute concerning indulgences; he not only declines most distinctly to recant, but would also refrain from polemics till the matter should be decided, for effecting which three German bishops, whom he names, should take action. His attacks upon indulgences should accordingly rank beforehand as equally justifiable with the opposite view, until a German court of arbitration might otherwise decide. We see, further, that he leaves to the Roman See its power, because nothing depends on it so far as salvation is concerned, because the power of the Church refers only to external matters, and in the recognition of the doctrines mentioned he has no intention of giving up the principle, that Christ is over all, and that the command of God is to be esteemed more highly than that of the Church.[1]

This yielding temper and readiness to acknowledge faults, which had occurred on his own side, was an act of great self-restraint, especially as he knew well how he had become already the idol of the German people, and as he also regarded the whole of his public conduct hitherto most decidedly, as is evident from many utterances of this period,[2] from a German national point of view, and, in connection with the revived, stirring, intellectual life of the German nation in general, as part of the emancipation of the German mind from the Italian.

Was it not at this moment imminent, as was scarcely ever

[1] *Luthers Werke von Walch*, xv. 845.   [2] De Wette, i. 145.

afterwards possible, that the Romish Church should reform the abuse of indulgences, but without proceeding beyond this point in the work of reformation? And what then?—Luther had meanwhile, until the results of the negotiations of Miltiz were pronounced upon in Rome, time enough to take the question into consideration, whether, provided the excessive abuses of indulgence were reprobated by the Church, all that was indispensable would be given? He could scarcely help seeing that, despite the best desire to regard indulgences as a separate and open question, this was nevertheless rendered impossible, not only by the number of the advocates of indulgences, but also by papal sanctions formerly given them, which had been renewed in the most recent bull; finally, because Luther's religious need, aiming at a divine certainty of the forgiveness of sins, and filled with a sense of the holiness of God, could not allow to a man the divine right to remit or retain sin. In this, however, the Romish idea of priesthood was assailed in its central point. But the clearing of the situation by means of the already mentioned new *third* step was not long to be delayed.

From the false position into which Luther had been brought by Miltiz, he was to be freed by the haste and blind zeal of Eck, a man to whom there cannot be denied a just perception of the inward significance and bearing of the first attacks of Luther. Luther's Theses were the cry of a distressed conscience. Eck, accustomed to logical inferences, was the man whose heresy-hunting inclinations were fitted to set forth conclusions, which Luther's piety towards the Church would rather have concealed from himself, as conclusions that were unavoidable, unless he should give up his sentences regarding the sources of knowledge of Christian truth and concerning the authority of the Church.

The armistice agreed upon with Miltiz was broken by Eck, not in itself by the *disputation* agreed upon long before with Carlstadt, which took place at Leipzig (27th June to 16th July, 1519), but by Eck's attacks upon Luther previously to it, at which Luther was much irritated.[1] The papal approbation of Miltiz's conditions was still wanting. At the disputation itself, in which he now also took part, Luther impugned the essential

---

[1] *Akten der Disput. bei Löscher, vollständige Reformationsakta und documenta (über 1517-19).* Leipzig, 1720, 3 Bde. iii. 215, ff. 292, ff. Cf. also Th. Wiedemann, *Dr. J. Eck*, 1865, p. 75, ff.

connection of the papacy with the Church upon the ground of the New Testament; the former was a more recent historical formation. Eck appealed to the passages of the New Testament concerning Peter, which he applied to the pope as the follower of Peter. When Luther rejected this interpretation as unnatural, Eck, not shunning the *petitio principii*, went off to the self-testimony of the Romish Church, by whose authority even the understanding of Scripture should be regulated. It was a dogma, that only the Romish Church is the true Church; that was declared at Constance against Wycliffe and Huss. Would Luther join himself to the heresy of Huss? The critical moment was now come, when Luther must either deny known truth, or confess it in spite of council and pope. He confessed that even true Christian propositions were condemned at Constance, and therein he had asserted the *fallibility of councils*, and assailed their authority. Eck made a great noise about the admission he had wrung from Luther, and hastened to Rome to urge there the conclusion of the suit against him. It is possible that the Romish Court would have remained inclined to greater forbearance, had Luther maintained the—for him—far more favourable position of appeal to the decision of the Church. But what would it have availed, to have appealed to the Holy Scriptures against indulgences and the divine authority of the pope, who was anew sanctioning them, two points already clearly discerned by him, if the Church had the right to be the canon of interpretation? Luther was, at Leipzig, to come to see, that the Gospel bore its truth in itself, and could not through the contradiction of councils be turned into untruth. But he certainly rendered himself thereby externally more defenceless; for the rejection of the divine authority of pope and council would necessarily appear in the highest degree dangerous to every one, who regarded the Holy Scriptures as dark and uncertain, and had, no conception of the inward self-evidencing character of the truth; it would also appear to him to expose everything to caprice.

The pope found that now, after the election of Charles V., and the declarations of the uniyersities of Paris, Cologne, and Lorraine against Luther's cause, whilst only Erfurt was for him, the matter was in such a shape as to enable him to give utterance on his part to the decisive word, the *ban* of excommunication of Luther, and of the truth he maintained. The bull *Exurge Domine* of 15th June, 1520, rejects forty-one propositions of Luther as destructive, offensive, or heretical. Luther exalted faith in opposition to all sacraments and works, rejected the supposition that the sacraments of the New Testament justify *ex opere operato*. He denied the doctrines of purgatory and of the freedom of the will, placed the councils above the pope, and taught men to despise the ban of the Church. He demanded communion in both kinds for the laity. In the bull of excommunication his books were proscribed and ordered to be burned, he himself was summoned to recant within sixty days, Lutheran teachers were sentenced to imprisonment and exile, and upon the places where they might sojourn an interdict was imposed. Thus was Luther, with his party, forcibly expelled from the Church, over which the pope had power. It was not that he separated himself from this Church, instead of manifesting to it and in its internal need the fidelity which he had just recognized to be still his duty, but the Romish Church did then separate itself from the voice of Christian conscience, whose spokesman Luther had become for the German nation. It thrust out the man who would not forsake it; it would not or could not endure any longer the testimony of evangelical truth. Luther—who, before the bull was published throughout Germany, had suffered himself to be prevailed upon to address one more epistle to the pope, 6th September, 1520, but, with a presentiment of what was coming, spoke with lofty candour—did, in order that none of the blame of the separation might attach to him, renew, 17th November, 1520, after the publication of the bull of excommunication had begun, his appeal to a general Christian Council,[1] which still reserved for him at least the significance of a judicial court of appeal,[2] inasmuch as its fallibility did not yet in itself imply the *necessity* of error; and he at the same time published his treatise "Against the Bull of Antichrist." Rome had now come into this position, that it could neither any longer refute nor would hear the truth. It sought its last resort in wantonness and in force. He faithfully warns every man, as much as is in his power, to take care of himself. "Let him forget me, let every man know that he can do me no service in despising the bull, and no injury in honouring it. By God's grace I am free, and dare, and will, neither comfort nor distress myself with any of these

[1] *Luthers Werke von Walch*, xv. 935.   [2] *Ibid.* xv. 1783.

things. I know well where my comfort and boast lies, which will stand sure to me before men and devils. I will do my part; each man will answer for himself at his dying day, or at the last judgment." He was already meditating also a formal abandonment of Rome by a solemn act, the burning of the bull of excommunication (which took place on the 10th December 1520). If Rome cherished the hope of getting rid, now as formerly, of troublesome witnesses for the truth by imprisonment and death, for once fire and sword must renounce their power;—for this the participation of the German nation in Luther's work had already provided. He himself,—since he had given utterance at the Leipzig disputation to that fatal expression concerning the errors even of councils, and had declared the necessity for the reformation of the Church, in doctrine also, and not merely in discipline and life,—felt himself now, as it were, in a new world of evangelical freedom; and there streamed in upon him, in a manner which astonished himself, ideas of reform of a grandeur and in a fulness which rendered the next years inwardly the most productive and rich of his life. He was himself astonished at the light which the knowledge acquired upon one point sheds for him upon a world of errors. Since that one point of the free grace of God in Christ, which is to be appropriated by faith, could freely assert itself as a principle of universal significance, he had found in it the key, which was ever opening to him new treasures in the Gospel. Thrust out of Rome with his party, he had to turn his attention to the preparation and procuring of a new Church home. His soul, so long held in monastic and Romish durance, broadened and stretched itself out at once toward all that was great and worthy of being incorporated into the purified life of a German national Church. To this is owing especially his position from this time towards humanism,—towards the German nation, its Christian nobility and its political commonwealth. Of humanism, with which Luther entered into friendly relations especially by means of *Melanchthon*, as well as of the university of Wittenberg, which became the headquarters of the Reformation, we shall afterwards speak. We shall dwell first of all on the writings in which Luther laid down his reformatory ideas,—classic monuments of the Reformation in themselves, but also for ever memorable on account of their results. For it is the Reformation proclaimed in these writings, and no other, which the German nation has accepted. These are the three principal writings of Luther: *To His Imperial Majesty and the Christian nobility of the German nation on the improvement of the Christian condition; On the Babylonian captivity;* and *On the freedom of a Christian man;*[1] to which is also to be added the first edition of the *Loci theologici* of Melanchthon.

The first of these writings of Luther is pervaded by the consciousness, that in his cause he occupies the position at once of a Christian and of a son of the German nation, which he addresses in inspired and telling language. The occasion was the covenant of fellowship which the chivalrous humanist, *Ulrich von Hutten,* Franz von Sickingen, the bravest knight of the time, Sylvester von Schauenburg, and others, offered him at the very time when the bolt of excommunication was forged at Rome, as was universally known, at the instigation of John Eck. Not only has the tone of this writing, and of that on the Babylonian captivity, been declared too violent, but their matter also to be revolutionary. But the Reformation, as depicted in these three writings for the German nation, and accepted by it, turns back to the ideas, which contain the principle of true primitive Christian order. He who rejects the universal priesthood of believers disclaims for himself all right in the Reformation, and has to ascribe it to himself, if in this department, the genetic point of the Reformation, he feels strange, and has not found the home of his Church life. He who laments that the episcopal organization and its authority were here violated, may either bring against the episcopate of that time the accusation, that it lent a guilty support to Rome, instead of resisting it, in the matter of indulgences; that it rather sought its own ends under the shadow of the Papal See, than showed itself mindful of the Reforming Synods and of its duties, by taking the Reformation into its own hands; or he may bring this accusation against himself, that in his concern for the external unity and order, he has lost a due sense of the essential matter, and the inward corruption of the Church has become to him a thing of indifference, or a thing better than its rejuvenated, though combated and struggling, life. How in all the world could there be hope of improvement by means of the episcopate and its assemblies, in the position which the episcopate, even that of Germany, occupied, after it had accepted,

---

[1] *Luthers Werke von Walch,* xv. 1940, xix. 4, ff. 1206, ff.

without any remonstrance, the new papal bull upon indulgences? As what may be termed an outline of the Reformation is contained in the three writings we have named, we will state their leading thoughts.

The first is designed to be a cry for help, "if God would give some one the spirit to reach out his hand to the suffering nation." The Romanists, he begins, have carried three walls round themselves, so that no one may reform them, and thereby the whole of Christendom is horribly fallen. In the first place, since compulsion has been put on them by worldly power, they have said that worldly power has no authority against them. In the second place, when it has been tried to rebuke them with the Holy Scriptures, they have met that with the contention, it belongs to no one but the Pope to expound Scripture. In the third place, when they have been threatened with a council, they have pretended that no one but the Pope can call a council. So that they have secretly stolen from us three rods, that they may not be chastised, and have gotten themselves within the safe defence of these walls to carry on all sort of knavery and wickedness. The councils they have enfeebled, and given the Pope full power over everything ordered by a council, so that it is all one whether there are many councils or none. Now, may God help us, and give us one of those trumpets, by which the walls of Jericho were thrown down, that we may blow down also those walls of straw and paper!

And now he charges at the *first* wall, the Romish distinction between the rights of the laity and of the clergy in the Church, wherein he develops, for the first time, the Protestant idea of the independent Christian State upon the basis of the idea of the universal Christian priesthood.

All Christians, he says, are truly possessed of spiritual rank, and there is among them no difference except upon account of office only. Ordination, unction, tonsure, make no one a spiritual man, but, on the contrary, we are consecrated as priests altogether through baptism; as St. Peter says, "Ye are a royal priesthood." But he is far from giving in this the signal for a dissolution of the organization of the Church, for he continues: Although we are all priests, yet it is not seemly in any one to thrust himself forward (of his own accord) and exercise this office; just because all have the same power, no individual may bring himself forward to discharge this office without the consent and choice of the congregation. But priestly ordination is no part thereof. A congregation of Christians in a wilderness may choose a minister for itself.[1] The priest is an officer; "because he holds office, he precedes; but if he is deposed, he is a citizen or peasant, like the rest. Here, however, they have invented *characteres indelebiles*." In this he rejected the Romish sacrament of sacraments, priestly ordination, which confers the power for the effective administration of the sacraments. Inasmuch as spiritual and civil now describes for him no other difference than what exists on account of office and work, he comes, in the application of it, upon the relation of Church and State. He looks upon them as the two sides, and as co-ordinate sides with equal rights, of the one Christian national life, which stands before his eyes as their higher unity. He will not make the State the highest unity, investing it, as it were, also with ecclesiastical functions; he will not exchange the sole dominion of the Church for a sole dominion of the State; the organism of a Christian nation stands before his eyes as a unity, but with distinguishable functions, and that in such a way that he takes it for granted that all members of the nation belong vitally and actively to both sides. But what he has particularly to bring forward as certainly a new perception, is, that the State (the magistracy) is in its own way [ordained] by the grace of God, like the Church, and may not be treated with contempt as a worldly, earthly thing.

Christ has not two kinds of bodies, one civil, the other spiritual; one Head is over the whole, and it has one body: every member however has his office, and is to be a priest therein. Priesthood, accordingly, can and ought to be exercised in the so-called worldly daily calling, even in business, so that there are many kinds of works, all in one congregation, for the furtherance of body and soul, even as the members of the body all serve one another. The officers of the Church have to administer word and sacrament, the civil magistracy bears the sword for the protection and punishment even of the clergy, and it is a false doctrine that the civil magistracy cannot punish the clergy. The magistracy ought rather to concern itself for the Church and its necessities, for it is unnatural, not to say unchristian, that one member should not help the other nor guard it against destruction:

[1] Cf. also Luther's *Briefe an die Christen zu Prag*. See below.

indeed, the nobler the member is, the more the others should help it. Therefore the office of the magistracy, which is ordained of God, should be wielded free and unhindered through the whole body of Christendom, without respect of persons; it reaches to pope, bishops, priests, monks, nuns, or whatever any one may be, let them threaten or excommunicate as they like. Whoever is guilty, let him suffer; whatever clerical law says to the contrary is simply an invention of Romish presumption. "Accordingly, I think that this first paper wall lies prostrate, since civil authority has become a member of the Christian body."

The second wall is still worse and weaker, namely, that they will be the only masters of Scripture, and call the Pope infallible. However much he may err, he can no longer be convicted from the Scriptures. But for what then would the Holy Scriptures still be necessary or useful? Let us burn them, and be content with the ignorant gentlemen at Rome, who are possessed by the Holy Ghost, who nevertheless will take possession only of pious hearts! The Scripture does not teach that he is to be believed who simply occupies the chief place, but he who has something better revealed to him (1 Cor. xiv. 30). And as all Christians are to be taught of God (John vi. 45; Isa. liv. 13), it may happen that some poor man has the right understanding, and that the Pope and his party are wicked, and not true Christians, nor taught of God. And has not the Pope fallen into many errors? Who would help Christendom when the Pope errs, if more credence were not given to another who has the Scriptures on his side, than to the Pope? There are Christians among us who have the right faith, the Spirit and mind of Christ; why should they be rejected and the Pope believed? Then we must no longer pray, "I believe in the Holy Catholic Church," but "I believe in the Pope at Rome," which would be nothing else than a devilish error. Besides, we are all priests, and have one faith, one Gospel, and the same sacrament. How then should we not also have power to taste and to judge, what would be right or wrong in faith? (1 Cor. ii. 15; 2 Cor. iv. 13.) Therefore we should be courageous and free, and not let the spirit of liberty (2 Cor. iii. 17) be frightened away by invented words of the popes, but throughout judge afresh everything that they do or allow, according to our believing understanding of the Scriptures, and compel them to follow the better, and not merely their own, understanding. "A believing understanding of the Scriptures," therefore, is, in his view, the standard of all things, not mere private judgment, not the subjective understanding, which, on the contrary, he expressly rebukes. He demands rather an authentication and proving of everything subjective by the objective and in itself *clear* word of Scripture; indeed, he respects also the common judgment of the Church, especially of the old Fathers, but certainly allows no such dependence upon popes and bishops, as if they had for certain, or even alone, the Holy Spirit.

The third wall, also, the assertion that only the Pope may call a council, is without foundation, as the old councils show; Christian princes too can, and now at present should, call a free Christian council, since they are now also fellow-priests, co-spiritual, with like power in all things. Every citizen of the spiritual city of Christ should extinguish whatever fire of offence may anywhere break out, whether in the government of the Pope, or wherever it may be. There is no power in the Church, except for improvement. Does the Pope seek to exercise power and prevent a free Christian council, we must not regard him nor his power, and if he excommunicate and thunder, we must just despise it and excommunicate him in turn. And if even signs should happen in his favour and against the civil power, we must just see in them lying wonders, though it should rain and hail wonders and plagues. The keys are given to the whole congregation, and not to Peter only. He then makes for a future free Christian council propositions of reformation, affecting partly doctrine and partly church order. He proposes to do away with canonical law, so far as it gives sovereignty and opulency to the clergy, to restore the Emperor to his former rights in respect of the Church, to abolish the kissing of the foot, the begging orders, and the bestowal of German fiefs on creatures sent from Rome, to remove the obligation of celibacy, and to put an end to pilgrimages. But, in particular, he demands the *reformation* of the whole *system of schools and education, from the common school to the university.* He will have the Bible placed in the centre, and the scholastic sentences done away with. Christendom has sinned grievously against the Hussites; they deserve recognition, and to be provided with a bishop. Let them think as they like regarding the manner of the presence of Christ in the Supper, the determining point is that they accept the reality of that presence.

In this treatise Luther by no means sold himself to the standpoint of the nobility. He had no pleasure in a rising on their part against the Emperor in the interests of their rank, nor in ways of force and revolution; on the contrary, this treatise, which calls with powerful trumpet-tone to Christian duty, is directed as much to the Emperor as the Christian nobility of the German nation. Since the hope that the existing Church authorities would lend their aid—a hope which he had cherished until the contrary was proven—was shattered, he turns, in order that the movement may not wildly overflow its banks, as happened only too soon in the peasant rising, to the existing Christian magistracy, the princely power; not that they may rule and decide within the Church, but that, taking the reins into their own hand, they may call a free Christian council, and let this decide, in the hope that thus the truth might gain the victory, unity and order being at the same time preserved. This is not revolution, but a regard for the order of Christendom, upon the basis certainly of a Protestant view of the laity and the State. It is not to be denied that this aid to be rendered by the princes to the Church in its distress might have cost it dear, and perhaps brought new dangers, if the *imperial* power, recalling its past under the Carlovingians and the Othos, had, for the purpose of uniting the spiritual power with the civil,[1] placed itself at the head of the work of Reformation, and so at the head of the Church, and, what would then have been inevitable, had restored itself to its old sovereignty and power. But no one has yet been able to show, how in any other way, than by seeking the assistance of the princely power, an orderly Reformation and a real national Church could have been accomplished in opposition to the Church of the clergy. Necessity induced the princes to undertake those governing functions of the bishops which had been for some time neglected, but never did Luther accord to them a divine right to the government of the Church or in matters of faith. But certainly he considered the oppression of the Church by the power of the State to be an outward suffering, less fatal and dangerous than the inward destruction of the

---

[1] Cf. Giesebrecht, *Geschichte der deutschen Kaiserzeit*, 1860, i. 123, ff., 316, ff., 476, ff.

Church by the transformation of its essence into a legal hierarchy.

The *dogmatic side* of the project of Reformation is brought under consideration[1] in the treatise *On the Babylonian captivity*, October, 1520. There are treated in it already almost all those errors, from which the Evangelical Church has cast itself loose. The Romish doctrine of the sacraments forms the central point, and this doctrine he judges according to the standard of the evangelical principle of faith, which is at one with the Scriptures, and that in such a manner that the other doctrines also are always being again and again glanced at from the point of view of the sacraments.

To the idea of a *sacrament* there belongs a word of institution and promise united with a visible sign, as is already taught by Augustine; hence there are not seven, but only three sacraments, baptism, the Supper, and repentance; indeed, taken strictly, there are only two, because the outward sign is wanting in repentance.

The *Supper* is not a sacrifice, not a meritorious work, but a gift of God; hence receptive faith is here, as in general in the sacraments, the principal matter. In this he shows himself opposed to the *opus operatum*. He demurs also to the doctrine of Transubstantiation, only holding firmly by the presence of Christ, without being willing to give any expression as to the nature of the connection between Him and the elements. As the significance of the Supper is already found by him to lie in the believing *enjoyment* of it, not in the mass, nor in the ceremonial show, it was only natural that his doubt regarding the doctrine of Transubstantiation rose to a denial of it, after he saw how the worship of the host followed so naturally from that doctrine.[2]

Baptism is, according to him, not merely an emblem, but a beginning of the spiritual dying and resurrection of man, both of which are to be carried on all through life, so that the whole life is a progressive baptism which is perfected at the last day (§ 104).[3] The grace of baptism has an abiding validity, and cannot be annulled except by persistent unbelief. He praises it by saying how rich it makes a Christian man to know that he is

[1] *Luthers Werke von Walch*, xix. 4-153.

[2] Henry VIII., *Defensor fidei*, taking the field against this treatise of Luther's, contributed to bring it about, that the latter combated Transubstantiation as a superfluous miracle.

[3] *Luthers Werke von Walch*, xix. p. 64, ff.

baptized, not by a man, but by the Trinity itself through him who baptizes in its name. He says that it is thinking lightly of the power of baptism, as might indeed be thought with regard to its operation already in the very moment of the outward act, if the sacrament is regarded as "a rapid over-passing performance, and not as continuously enduring." For if it be allowed that grace is, be it even in richest fulness, imparted in baptism, but is afterwards thrust out by sin, so that baptism would accordingly be entirely annulled, then there must afterwards be another way of entering into heaven. Then indeed the whole series of [Roman] Catholic sacraments must come in as compensation for the loss of baptism, penance, confirmation, and extreme unction. "Thy baptism is never annulled, unless thou dost despair and will'st not come again to thy salvation." He sees also (§ 107) how, in this doctrine of the ever-abiding validity and power of baptism, the objective basis, the foundation-stone of Christian freedom, has been won; for the doctrine of the annulling of baptism, and therefore of freedom in God and of divine childhood, is assuredly the starting-point in the doctrine of Rome for setting, in the place of the prevenient grace of baptism, the saving ordinance of the later sacraments, in which there are imposed upon a man works of satisfaction, which keep him for ever in the distraction we have already described, and in inward dependence upon the Church, in legal bondage.—With reference to the question, how baptism can accomplish so much, he here also binds together in the closest manner the word of promise and the faith which lays hold of it; the *opus operatum* is here also rejected; baptism in itself profits no one, justifies no one without faith, not on the part of him baptizing, but of him baptized. He does not at present pay any more special attention to infant baptism, and accordingly he requires not baptism for future faith, but faith already before baptism. But he speaks with a want of clearness, and with inward uncertainty, of a slumbering faith of infants and of a vicarious faith of the god-parents. His doctrine of infant baptism only reached its final completion after the Anabaptist movement, which adopted his rejection of the *opus operatum* in such a manner as to deny any particular power to infant baptism, because faith was necessary even before baptism.

The consequence of his doctrine regarding baptism was a different position in regard to *vows;* the baptismal vow is the only one necessary, by which all other special vows are annulled; for everything Christian, to which we are in duty bound, is contained in the baptismal vow. It is no less a necessary consequence of this opinion with regard to baptism, that repentance and absolution are no new sacrament (no *baptismus iteratus*); but it is only a revival of the baptismal grace that is effected by them, when there is added to contrition, which he holds firmly, that faith through which baptismal grace is renewed to us. The *confessio*, as a confession of all particular sins, is impossible; works of satisfaction are to be utterly rejected. The four other sacraments have partly not signs together with a promise, partly at least not divine institution.

If the treatise *To His Imperial Majesty and the Christian nobility* had a warlike, and in part defiant, sound,—if the treatise *On the Babylonian captivity* exhibits the Reformation principle in its dogmatic fertility, as the former exhibited it in its power of ethical revolution,—if in both together that principle appears as one which in a narrower sense affects the history of the world, —the sermon *On the freedom of a Christian man* is pleasant, without polemics, full of inwardness and of the overflowing power of love to God and man. The Reformation principle is here displayed in its depth, its rich inwardness and religious originality. There is contained in this treatise, which is animated by the spirit of lofty peace, the noble wine of purest mysticism. It shows, how in this genuine mysticism the synthesis of the dogmatical and ethical factors with the religious is found, and how the fulness and inwardness of the original religious perception of Luther contains also a wealth of new impulses for the intellectual, and indeed the speculative, life of the Christian soul. The evangelical principle in relationship to faith and love has probably never been developed with such clearness, fulness, and depth.

"A Christian man," Luther begins here, "is a free lord over all things, and next a ministering servant of all things, and subject to every one; he is free through faith, and a servant through love."[1] He first discusses his *freedom*. "The soul should be free throughout and the body its servant." But how is it free? Not through anything external,—consecration, fasts, and the like; for piety and freedom are as little bodily and outward as

[1] *Luthers Werke von Walch*, xix. 1206, f.

sin and captivity. There is nothing else, in heaven or on earth, wherein the soul is pious and free, than the holy Gospel, the *Word of God* concerning Christ. The soul can want everything but the Word of God; without this nothing else will help it; in the Word it has enough food, joy, peace, light, skill, righteousness, wisdom, freedom, and everything good. Whilst mysticism said, " The soul can do without everything but God," Luther says, " The soul is in need of God revealing Himself in history in objective acts; *but God in revelation is God in the Word.*"

But now, what is the Word, and how can it effect freedom? In the Old and New Testaments, he answers, a distinction is to be drawn between law and promise. The laws prescribe good works, but they are not thereby performed; they point well, but they do not help; they teach well, but they give no strength. They are so ordained that man learns his impotence and despairs of himself. If anxiety befalls him, the other word comes to him —the divine promise—and says, " Wilt thou fulfil all the commandments, behold, believe in Christ, in whom I assign to thee all grace, righteousness, peace, freedom; dost thou believe, then thou hast; dost thou not believe, then thou hast not; so that it may all be of God, both the commandment and the fulfilling of the commandment." And because the Word of God is not in his view a dead letter, which could effect salvation by a kind of charm, a dull mechanical reception is not enough, according to him, for the soul becoming free; *faith* belongs to the Word. The doctrine of mysticism regarding the contemplation and love of God is brought by Luther, in his doctrine regarding faith, into a modest form, mindful of sin and dependent upon the history of revelation, —in a word, into connection with God as revealed in Christ.

In the Word, he says, thou shouldst hear nothing else than thy God speaking to thee. The life and work of Christ are not to be superficially preached or received as a mere history or chronicle; but, on the contrary, faith grows only, and is maintained, by its being said to me not merely that, but why, Christ is come, how He is to be made use of and enjoyed, and what He has brought and given to *me*. All the words of God are holy, true, righteous, peaceful, and full of all goodness. As the Word is, so will also the soul become through the Word, by attaching itself to it in a right faith. Even as iron becomes red-hot as fire from its union with fire, so do all the virtues of the Word become the property of the believing soul. So that in *faith in the Word* there is continued an imitation of the union of the divine and the human, as it originally existed in the person of Christ. In the word of proclamation regarding Himself, Christ, as it were, sues His bride; to this word the soul must trust itself: thus through word and trust, or faith, that union is accomplished, in which Christ betroths Himself as bridegroom to the soul, as it to Him; the result of which is marriage, so that Christ and the soul become one body. Thus the benefits, hap, mishap of each, and all things, are common. What Christ has is the property of the believing soul; what the soul has becomes the property of Christ. But Christ has every benefit and salvation, these become the property of the soul; the soul, however, has every sin and defect upon it, these become the property of Christ. And now there arises the joyful exchange and conflict: since Christ is God and man, and His piety is insuperable, eternal, and omnipotent, therefore, when He makes the sins of believing souls His own through their wedding-ring, *i.e.* faith, He does with them just as if He had committed the sins, and therefore these sins must be swallowed up and drowned in Him. For His insuperable righteousness is stronger than all sins. The soul, accordingly, is delivered and freed from all its sins purely through its marriage portion, that is, on account of faith, and gifted with the everlasting righteousness of Christ, its bridegroom. " Is not this now a joyful piece of work, when the rich, noble, pious bridegroom Christ takes the poor despised wicked harlot to wed, delivers her from all evil, and adorns her with every benefit? Thus it is not now possible for her sins to condemn her, for they lie now upon Christ, and are swallowed up in Him."

Thus the power and inwardness of his mysticism was able to render fusible the historical element, which is to the common mystic external and hard matter, because it [his mysticism], being animated by an ethical spirit, places the consciousness of sin and reconciliation in the centre, and has won for the latter an idea of substitution that is full of life and ethically sustained.

He then pictures the *dignities and honours to which Christ exalts believers through faith.* Christ is a king and priest, but spiritually. As Christ is the first-born, with the honour and dignity of that position, He shares it with all His Christians; so that they also must all, through faith, be kings and priests with Christ (1 Pet. ii. 9). The first is effected in such a way, that a Christian man is exalted by faith so high above all things, that he is spiritually a lord over them all. Not that we are in a bodily manner possessed of power over all things: bodily we must die and be subjected to many things; but nothing can injure the believer in respect of salvation, even death and suffering must subserve his best interests. This is indeed a high dignity and a true omnipotent lordship, a spiritual kingdom, since there is nothing so good nor so wicked, but it must subserve my good if I believe; and yet I have no need of it, but my faith is sufficient for me. Behold what a precious power is this that Christians have! Besides, we are priests, and that is something far more than to be a king, because priesthood makes us worthy to appear before God and pray for one another.

Who can compass in thought the honour and lofty position of a Christian man? By his kingdom he has power over all things, by his priesthood he has a power over God, for God does what he asks and seeks (Psa. xlv. 10). To these honours he comes only through faith, and through no work; and whenever any one thinks to become pious and free, to be saved or to be a Christian through good works, he loses faith together with all things. Faith on the other hand brings everything in overflowing measure (§ 29): for this much is justly ascribed to faith, that it fulfils all the commandments, and makes one pious without any other work, for it is the fulfilling of the one command, "Thou shalt honour thy God." The faith of the heart ascribes truth and everything good to God. No works, if the honour is not at the same time given to God, make one pious; but he, on the other hand, who fulfils the first and chief commandment, fulfils certainly and easily all other commandments; therefore is faith alone the righteousness of man and the fulfilling of all the commandments. We do not ask what is done, but we seek the doer, who honours God and doeth the works. This is none other than the faith of the heart; that is the chief matter and the whole essence of piety.

The Christian man is, according to Luther, made so free and placed so high by faith, that he requires nothing more for himself: we are sufficiently justified by faith; works are no longer necessary for the forgiveness of sins and salvation; indeed, it would be destructive of the freedom and chief righteousness of the inner man if any one were to seek to presume to be justified by works. The only point upon which everything still depends is this, that faith and joy shall grow until the end.

But if the Christian man occupies so free a position, and all other duties are as it were swallowed up in the one duty of faith, that seems to have an Antinomian sound, and it has occasioned the reproach, that Luther isolates the religious element, and sows a moral indifferentism. "The law is, according to Luther, distinguished from the Gospel, like hell from heaven, like night from day; in heaven it has no place, it has reference only to this bodily perishing existence; morality has, according to him, only a transitory worth, and piety is everything. This, however, must lead to a dualism between the inner and the outer life."[1] But the great thing with Luther is this, that he effects an intimate union between faith and good works, and secures the latter, just in this way, that before everything else he places reconciliation through faith independently of works, and then exhibits this very independence of justification from antecedent good works as the fruitful womb of good works. This is done in the second part of this treatise.

He proceeds: If then faith can make us sufficiently religious, why are good works commanded? we will seek to *be* good and do nothing. No, dear sir, he answers, not so; for although inwardly man is sufficiently justified by faith, he still continues in this bodily life, and must govern his own body and have intercourse with others in the body. And it is necessary that the body be obedient to the inner man by faith, and be made conformable to it. "The inner man is one with God, joyful and happy, on account of Christ, who has done so much for him, and his whole desire is that he in his turn may serve God freely in free love. But now he finds in his flesh a refractory will which seeks what pleases it; this faith will not tolerate, and throws itself lustily at its neck to suffocate it and to restrain it." Upon the ground, therefore, of the joy and salvation that lie in fellowship with Christ, out of which a grateful and pure responsive love rises of itself in the heart, Luther proceeds to the matter of sanctification, and first of all of the proper personality. Faith, by which the dualism between God and man is removed, acts by virtue of

[1] Möhler's *Symbolik. Ausg.* 6, p. 232, ff.

its inward tendency upon the unity and totality of the personality. Since the soul is pure by faith, it would gladly have all things pure in like manner, especially its own body, and every one to love and praise God along with it. Thus it happens that man cannot be idle; he must, even in order to compel his own body, practise many good works, and yet he is not pious and just before God by means of them, but he does them out of free love, freely, to please God: for the will of God is what he would like best of all to do, like Adam in Paradise, for through his faith he is again placed in Paradise. As Adam did not require to be first justified by works, and yet did not go idle, but had to plant, to till, and to keep Paradise, to please God, not in order to gain something in respect of God which he had not before, so it is commanded to the believer that he do not go idle, but all his works are freely performed to please God, not that he may become pious by them. But to the work of subduing the *flesh* and gaining the level of the Spirit, there is now to be added also this (§ 53), that love to God impels to *love* to *one's neighbour*. Man lives not only in his body, but also amongst other men upon earth, and must have to do with them; but here again, not in order to be saved thereby, but he is saved, and even from out of this state of salvation faith enters cordially into the work. The believer no longer requires works for himself in order to be saved, but precisely because he has enough for himself in his faith and is saved therein, he can and will serve his neighbour out of pure free love. Even as Christ (Phil. ii. 6, 7) had enough for Himself, and His life and work and suffering were not necessary to His becoming pious or being saved, and yet He regarded nothing but our highest good, and became a servant for our sake: so a Christian man, being complete and satisfied in faith, makes himself willingly, like Christ his Head, the servant of his neighbour, to help him, to live and deal with him, as God has dealt with him through Christ; and all this freely, not seeking anything therein but the good pleasure of God, and thinking accordingly, "Well, my God has given to me, an unworthy condemned man, without any merit, purely, freely, and of simple mercy, through and in Christ, a perfect wealth of all goodness and blessedness, so that I henceforth require nothing more than to believe that so it is. Why, I in my turn will render to such a Father, who has thus loaded me with His abundant benefits, freely, gladly, and without fee, whatever is well-pleasing to Him, and will also be a Christian to my neighbour, as Christ has been to me." This therefore is the sum of his doctrine. To the purity of the grace, which undertakes the cause not of the righteous but of sinners, and thus seems to disregard the law, because it is gracious to the unworthy, and gives bountifully to them, not simply in advance, in anticipation of future payment, but freely and for nothing— it is precisely to this prevenient love that it is given to kindle in us also a love which deserves to be called so, because it too loves freely, not for reward, not even for the reward of salvation.

Faith is therefore so far from giving their dismissal to the law and to good works, that on the contrary no good works can come to pass except through faith. "Where there is not faith, there is sin. Good pious works never make a good pious man, but a pious man does good works. For it is evident that the fruits do not bear the tree nor do trees grow upon the fruits, but the trees bear the fruit and the fruits grow upon the tree; the trees must be before the fruits. He who will do good works must therefore not begin with the works, but with the *person* who is to do the works. No one however makes the person good, but only faith, and no one makes it bad, but only unbelief. If then works make no person pious, but a pious person does good works, it is evident that only faith, out of pure grace through Christ and His Word, makes the person sufficiently pious and confers on it salvation." He then describes comprehensively the whole course of the life of love in its movement from God to God. "Accordingly the benefits of God must flow from one to another and be common, so that every one may be interested in his neighbour as if it were himself. They flow to us from Christ, who has undertaken our case as if He were what we are; from us they should flow to those who need them, so that I accordingly must interpose my faith and righteousness for my neighbour, to cover his sins, must take them upon myself, and not act otherwise than as if they were my own, even as Christ has done for us all. Behold, this is the nature of love when it is genuine; it is genuine, however, where faith is genuine." Love is therefore, according to him, the disposition to set one's self in the place of others; faith is, according to him, the reception of that love, whereby Christ has placed Himself in our room or of the substitution of Christ. " From all this follows the conclusion,"—it is thus he ends,—" that a Christian man does not live in himself but in Christ and his neighbour, in Christ through faith, in his neighbour through love. Through faith he passes above himself into God; out of God he passes again beneath himself through love, and yet abides always in God, and God in him" (John i. 51).

It is a noble and significant circumstance, that Luther appended this golden treatise to his last epistle to the Pope (6th Sept. 1520), as if gathering up and explaining in an evangelical way the best of what was scattered in the Church, and especially in mysticism, and as if with a request for a peaceful leave-taking and a more favourable disposition, and with the promise, however matters might turn out, of willingness to serve the Romish Church, even though their ways might be separate, by virtue of pure love which springs from faith. But it is in particular instructive and refreshing to notice the quiet collectedness of soul, the deep rest and clearness, which Luther maintained in the most threatening struggle, and in the near prospect of the bull of excommunication. This untroubled mirror of a childlike heart, in which the peace of heaven is reflected, stands in wonderful contrast to the storms which gathered around him, and is a proof that the confessor of the righteousness of faith had what he confessed, and was what he taught.

THE UNIVERSITY OF WITTENBERG; IN PARTICULAR, MELANCHTHON AND THE ALLIANCE OF THE REFORMATION WITH SCIENCE.

What a power the cause of Luther had in its earliest years become in Germany is shown in particular in the high school in the town of Wittenberg, which rose to the rank of the spiritual metropolis of rejuvenated Germany. All transactions hitherto consisted only in speech and counter-speech, not in deeds, excepting the bull of excommunication and Luther's consequent secession from Rome (10th Dec. 1520). No change had yet been made in the Church life, cultus, constitution, celibacy, monasticism; reverence for age, toleration for the weak, uncertainty with regard to the inward ripeness of the people, kept back from the positive amelioration of, and doing away, with what was old; and Luther, besides, was in his first beginnings far removed from far-reaching plans of a reformation, which should be linked with his name. But a spiritual power was already, in 1521, given in Wittenberg, the first firm centre for the renovated Church, for which the time had now come. Thousands of youths flocked from all parts of Germany, and even from far abroad, to receive the seed of the evangelical life and spirit, and to bear it forth in all directions. A new race of those, who had in future to lead the German nation in Church and State and school, had to be formed in this way. At the university, again, the kernel was composed of a number of pious, learned, and decided men, closely allied amongst themselves, fired with Luther's spirit, and united by the idea of the Reformation. Melanchthon, Jonas, Bugenhagen (Pomeranus), Andreas von Bodenstein, called Carlstadt, J. Agricola, called Eisleben, Amsdorf, the jurist Hieronymus Schurff, &c. We have in particular to dwell upon *Melanchthon*.

Even until after 1517, Luther was concerned, in quiet and faithful toil, only about the salvation of his own soul and of those entrusted to him. In this retirement, although not without an inclination to the classical studies, he stood at a distance from the striving of humanism, which led so frequently to a mere seeming satisfaction of the higher interests of life through beauty and brilliancy of speech and thought, and to a merely outward manifestation in religious and even moral superficiality. In like manner, philosophy, *i.e.* Aristotle and scholasticism, were hated by him, not merely on account of their formalism, but still more because Aristotelian scholasticism was considered by him to be the arsenal of the scientific artillery of Roman Catholicism. He exhorted indeed to the study of the Scriptures in order to banish scholasticism thereby, but it had for him rather an immediately religious purpose, that of awakening and nourishing faith. Luther had as yet no idea that in the principle of faith itself there lay a *new spiritual world*, and also a new theology and science, the development of which was indispensable, if the principle of faith was to become the foundation of a new Church formation. The process of Church reformation which had lasted through centuries had come inwardly to a conclusion in Luther's person; the inward invisible foundations of the Church, as they are to be laid in the soul of the individual through the Word and faith, had begun to be joined together harmoniously in him, and personally, as well as through inspired word, he gave testimony thereto and to the new divine life which he had tasted. But to organize this new matter, to arrange the life of a new community, this Luther did not dare. Neither the power for the construction of a system of theology, nor the gift of ecclesiastical organization (the innermost sanctuary, the cultus, excepted, in song, prayer, and sermon) belonged to him in any particular degree. He represented the fruitful creative principle for all the secondary formations in life and science, and the tender evangelical conscience, by which all these formations must submit to be measured.

The Reformation spirit, however, would have been soon shattered and evaporated, if it had not found its appropriate vessels in a new *science* and in a suitable *church order*.[1] Everything depended upon the Reformation idea being brought into a form free from subjectivity, and generally binding and intelligible, upon effacing the accidental and purely individual features which always cleave to the original expression of personal inward experiences and intuitions, upon the instructive exhibition of them in their secure and lucid kernel and in their inward connection. It was therefore a splendid divine providence which called from a distance to Luther's side the man who became his faithful and complementary fellow-labourer.

The great humanist *Melanchthon*, after he had received from Luther the baptism of the spirit, became the *Magister Germaniæ*, the second Reformer of Germany. The wonderful interposition of a higher hand is to be seen in the friendship, which united the man of inspired προφητεία with the man of διδασκαλία; "the miner's son, who drew forth the metal of faith out of the deep pit, and the armourer's son, who fashioned the metal for defence and defiance." What one individuality would not have compassed, was compassed by the Reformation pair, which worked as one power, and by which, in spite of later and subordinate differences between them, which never however destroyed the love and fidelity in the bottom of their hearts, only one German Reformation was effected. And this is none other than that which embraces both men, and which has won just through them both together its wide power of comprehension. If Luther was able to kindle, to rouse and elevate, and

[1] By this is to be understood forms of government, worship, &c. See note, p. 118.—*Tr.*

even ravish the heart, it was through Melanchthon's co-operation that the effect he produced received its abiding power, outlasting the change of moods; and thus what Luther gave was incorporated with the daily life, with quiet Christian enlightenment. In Melanchthon, Luther, the man of the people, had placed by his side the fine architectural and organizing spirit, who, being gifted with a delicate moral tact, a circumspect and dialectic mind, and a power of unadorned, but transparent and convincing representation, had the skill to give to the matter, born at first in the heart of Luther, an objective shape and the stamp of general validity, and was able even to set the specific substance of evangelical ideas in a vital relationship to the universally human. Melanchthon, by his clear formulating of the new found subject-matter of faith, and by his connected scientific unfolding of the principle of faith, brought Luther to the conscious perception, how there was contained in it a totality, a world of truths that held firmly and closely together, a new view of the world, which seems foolishness indeed to the natural reason, but is in itself, and for him who enters into it, divine power and divine wisdom, harmoniously according with the whole world of the first creation. It was so soon as in his inaugural address at Wittenberg, on the 29th August 1518, that Melanchthon unrolled the hopeful picture of an approaching new era, and showed how the newly discovered mines of antiquity subserve the study of the Scriptures; how every art and science would, through the refreshing return to the sources, blossom anew, in order to present their spices to an ennobled human existence; and finally, how through all the arts and sciences, and through the whole house of humanity, the precious ointment of the Gospel would penetrate like a heavenly odour. Such words could not fail to give Luther some idea as to how the *studia renascentia* stand in secret covenant with the anew-discovered Gospel, as well as that the latter could not be destined to remain a closed treasure in individual solitary souls, but that, without being itself lost, it was *appointed for the transfiguration of the human in every department*. The relations with the humanists *Reuchlin* and *Erasmus* were now on a friendly footing, as Luther's letters to both show; and this had not only the external result of the winning of confederates, but also this inward result, that the Reformation drew closer to the educated classes of the nation, opened its treasures to them also, and stood before them full of promise, without leading them back into new monastic barbarity, or to a mystic cloisteral life entombed within itself. Melanchthon, in particular, was the medium of extending the Reformation to the educated classes, to statesmen and learned men, who might easily have failed to recognize in Luther's sturdy language the matter that was of saving virtue for them; and so of extending it first to the whole nation. The true humanism, besides, as represented in particular by Melanchthon and Reuchlin, as it was an important critical medium for the coming controversies, through its labours directed towards the sources and [the ascertainment of] the original, was also a weapon and instrument for imparting the new matter clearly and distinctly in a suitable form, for alienating the mind from everything unnatural and preposterous, and for reawakening the simple taste for truth and greatness. In particular, however, and this is the point of widest importance in this joining-in of the best humanist efforts in the work of Reformation, it was only through it that the Reformation consciously found the true relation between the universally human and the Christian, between the first and second creation. A predisposition for all this existed already in Luther's healthy nature and piety; how else could he have been able so soon to lovingly embrace and reverence Melanchthon? But still it was a different matter, when a master of humanism, united with him in the ground of faith, exhibited personally before his eyes the picture of the union of humanism and the Gospel, of the Christian and the learned virtuoso, and thereby opened for him prospects altogether new, as is shown by a series of letters of this period, which look forward full of hope to the rising youth, and full of pride to a Germany, compared with Italy, approaching its regeneration.

For some time, Melanchthon allowed himself to be drawn in by Luther into animosity against Aristotle and philosophy in general; but soon (already towards the end of the third decade of the century) he came to entertain the hope, that Christianity might be exhibited as the true philosophy, as it is, and that the *studia renascentia* must also be the means of producing a new philosophy, which would no longer be, as he thought at first, merely Aristotle restored to the position of being rightly understood. Although he did not himself accomplish this, but only commented on Aristotelian writings, in particular his Ethics (from and after 1529), still he imparted to evangelical truth an instructive form and communicability, not merely for the heart, but also for intellectual thought. He is the dogmatic theologian of the Reformation; he is also its apologist, highly esteemed even by antagonists, and capable, by reason of his comprehensive education and elasticity, of transporting himself into them, in order to lay hold of the better elements in them. He was the learned and restless representative and solicitor of the Reformation in negotiations, colloquies, and even in the diets of the Empire; he was the wise chancellor and counsellor of the Reformation. By means of his [written] opinions [on points submitted to him], his journeys, his Church Orders,[1] and other institutional works, he became, not indeed the creative, but the organizing spirit of the Reformation of the Church. In the department of theology he has rendered most services to ethics, he being himself less of a religiously original and genial, than of an ethical nature, animated by the quiet flame of upright piety (he was called ἠθικός in a funeral oration), conscientious to the minutest particular, spending himself in labour for the Church and the education of its youth, possessing rare purity, and the nobility of a finely-organized nature; courageous at the same time, because always forgetful of himself in decisive moments, but still stronger in suffering for the Church. This character shows itself also in his dogmatic tendency. As little as he can be called, in comparison with Luther, original in his religious views, as independent and thoroughly formed is his ethical turn of mind, and it in increasing measure asserts its independence, even in opposition to Luther, in those points in which the doctrine of faith is conditioned by ethical principles,—so in the doctrines of liberty, of human guilt, of predestination; and in these points it is the Melanchthonic type which finally preponderated in the life and science, although less in the confessions, of the German Reformation. His principal dogmatic treatise, the *Loci communes*, which

---

[1] This phrase is used here and afterwards as the equivalent for *Kirchenordnungen*, the name given to the body of rules by which the doctrine, worship, government, discipline, and financial administration of the Church was regulated in each of the states of Germany after the Reformation. They generally consisted of two parts, the *credenda* and the *agenda*—the latter containing also minute instructions for the different officials. Being composed about the same time, and in a great measure by the same hands, the *Kirchenordnungen* of the different states had a close family resemblance to one another.— *Tr*.

grew out of lectures on the Epistle to the Romans (1520), in its first edition (1521), defended throughout Luther's standpoint, not merely in reference to faith, but also philosophy, scholasticism and predestination; but in its later editions, until 1559, became more and more pervaded by his ethical mode of contemplation; the first edition, however, preserves this advantage, that there is diffused over it a fresh breath of the religious spirit, and the treatise commends itself for ever by the lively utterance of evangelical conviction, as well as by its rich wealth of thought, to the love and gratitude especially of evangelical student youth.[1]

LUTHER IN WORMS, AND THE IMPULSE TO ACTS OF REFORMATION.

A new and mighty impulse was given to the work of Reformation by Luther's good confession before the Emperor and the Empire, which was followed by the commencement of attempts at practical reformation.

The eyes of all Germany were directed towards Wittenberg; from there the watchword summoning to the *deed* of reformation was looked for, from there the proceeding with a reformation of the Church, to which in hundreds and thousands of places men were ready to join themselves. But Luther, so bold in word and so forgetful of himself in personal dangers, always hesitated actually to begin the Reformation. He shrunk from interfering with the consciences of others by a general regulation. Even those fiery reformatory writings were only designed to be a programme, a setting up of a project of reformation; but when the Pope and the bishops refused to act, he would not take the initiative upon himself, for he did not find in his doctorate the call to reformatory action in place of the authorities hitherto existing; and, just because he was without a commission from the German nation and the organized Church, and, on the other hand, the issues involved in that reformatory step, which went forth from Wittenberg, were incomputably great and full of responsibility, he had addressed himself to his Imperial majesty and the Christian nobility, to undertake the cause of the wretched nation.

But he was to be, as it were, forced against his will to interfere also in the way of action, and to set his hand to the act of

[1] Cf. Rothe's *Gedächtnissrede auf Melanchthon*, 1860; Nitzsch, *Melanchthon;* and my speech, *Jahrbücher für deutsche Theologie*, 1860.

the reformation of the German people. To this the act of Romish violence, declining all reformation, which was at this very time accomplished against him in his unconditioned excommunication (3rd January 1521), must contribute essentially. The excommunication of the papal court would be a dead flash, if it were not transformed by the Diet of the Empire into the ban of outlawry. The papal court accordingly laboured with all its might to procure this ban. Luther was summoned from Wittenberg to Worms, where, on the 18th of April 1521, he made, before the Emperor and the Diet, that brave Christian confession of willingness to die and to sacrifice himself for the truth, content for himself, if he only kept pure his Christian conscience, which was captive to the Word of God. This testimony, indeed, was not able to ward off from him the ban (on the contrary, it was brought about not without the help of sinister methods by the legate Alexander). But it procured for him the esteem and love of more than one of the high-spirited German princes, and the outlaw was rescued by the increasing affection of his Prince and preserved in his " Patmos."

Whilst he now surveyed in retirement, but at the same time from a free and lofty point of view, the situation of affairs, he saw that nothing would be more beneficial, and was more necessary, for the inward progress of the evangelical spirit in the nation, than an intimate acquaintance with the Holy Scriptures. And so he devoted the greater part of his sojourn of nearly a year upon the Wartburg to the translation of the New Testament.

But whilst he was in his secret solitude, the movement did not stand still, but began, because a proper leader was wanting, to overflow its banks. A fire broke out in Wittenberg, which threatened the whole work of reformation, and yet that was only a feeble premonition of the frightful commotions of the next fourteen or fifteen years, which tore up the lowest depths of the German people. To these belong the fanatical outbreakings of different kinds, especially of *Anabaptism*, for which to this day the enemies of the Reformation seek to make it responsible. But these storms prove rather, on the one hand, how loose all the old moral bonds of society had become under the despotism of Rome, what a mass of corruption had collected, previously to the Reformation, in life, and in moral, as well as religious, ideas, without hindrance from the Romish Church system; and on the other hand, they prove again the remarkable working of Providence in the progress of the Reformation. For, falling in this ploughed-up and trembling German soil, the seed of the Reformation took root the more easily, and, after subduing its opponents,—who were so much the more dangerous because they arrayed themselves in the garb of confederacy, whilst in innermost principle they stood still upon the pre-Reformation stage, and even led back beyond it,—it was possible for the Reformation principle, which had now been strengthened and brought up on both sides to a pure definition by its struggle with what was false in the old and false in the new, to assert itself all the more unrestrictedly and purely. Opposition sects had never been wanting in the middle ages, but the church-forming and nation-reforming power was wanting, because the evangelical principle had neither appeared in its purity and constructive power, nor been able to set the nation in motion. But now it was no longer a mere sect-formation that was to branch off, but a purified *national church* which was to be accomplished and realized, at least amongst the German races. To this all these movements must conduce.

What would have resulted from the condition of the people, as it was then displayed, if the Reformation had not followed? The massiveness and vehemence of these movements is a plain sign that, without the work of the reformers, who, as in the first three years, would have liked best to have stopped short at doctrine and the inward purifying of public opinion, the people, in the absence of a purified church community, and being completely alienated from the Romish Church system, must have become the prey of a spiritual desolation, of an apostasy from Christianity, or at least of a chaotic system of sects. In this aspect of them, these events gave to the reformers—by whom stood the choicest portion of the people, together with some enlightened princes—a mighty impulse to seek the realization of a purer church formation. But these same movements were a principal means of correcting the public opinion with regard to its proper form. For the events here referred to are one in this, that they were fitted, as nothing else could be, to produce a common settled conviction as to how the Reformation was *not* to be carried out, if they were not either to fall back into the Romish Church, or to move forward into a condition of complete anarchy. Only under the pressure of the most bitter necessity does our race resolve upon bold and unanimous action in new creations; the necessity must first exist upon both sides, and the throes come in double intensity, in order that the *Evangelical Church formation* might be born.

CHAPTER III.

THE DEVELOPMENT AND LIMITATION OF THE EVANGELICAL PRINCIPLE IN ITS CHURCH FORMING ASPECTS, FROM 1522 TO 1536, IN CONFLICT WITH ANTAGONISTIC PARTIES.

HITHERTO the conflict had been necessary, and had been conducted, only against one side, the Romish Church. But in reality the Reformation, like the Gospel, stands in opposition to two extremes, though these again are in their innermost nature related to one another. So long as the opposition is realized only against one of the two, those who stand upon the other extreme, although severed quite as fundamentally from the truth, may assume the appearance of advocating the truth, and may even seemingly outrun the zeal of its true representatives. Hence arises the danger of false alliances with those who occupy an essentially similar position to the first antagonist. The principle of the Reformation, accordingly, if it was at the same time to be evangelical, could not escape directing its antagonism also against the side which was at first seemingly friendly, but was bound to it only by community of opposition. For it would not otherwise have overcome the old in its essence. It was thus that it not merely carried out a show, but gave effect to itself; and it was this faithfulness to itself, this act of faith, which, even in the midst of the unavoidable loss of many friends, first secured to it its future.

We have under this point of view to speak for a little of the excesses and caricatures of the Reformation movement, which with their false ideals of reform lay in the way of the formation of an Evangelical Church,—of the false mysticism of an ethical and theoretical kind which would not let go the evangelical principle, and sought to rob it of its ecclesiastical power. There fall under this head the fanatical movements of an *ethical* nature, which run their course in three principal acts, to wit, the *Carl-*

stadt disturbances, the peasant war under *Thomas Münzer* and *Metzler*, and the *Anabaptist* insurrection; then the *theoretical* mysticism of such men as *Gaspar Schwenckfeld, Sebastian Franck, Theobald Thamer, Michael Servede, Theophrastus Paracelsus*, and others; and finally the Antinomians. But besides clearing itself from these eccentrical movements, the Reformation principle had to separate itself equally from the *Moderatism* of Reform, represented especially by *Erasmus* and *George Wizel*, and to guard the novelty and purity of its essence against false accommodations, so that it might not, by exaggerating its antagonism to the fanatics, fall back upon the Roman Catholic standpoint in a more moderate form.

It is still, upon the whole, Luther's great mind which confronts these numerous and almost more difficult conflicts, and guides them to a victorious issue. Hitherto he had laid bare in their order the false foundations of the old ecclesiastical structure, and had applied the principle of evangelical faith to the critical confutation of the errors concerning the papacy, councils, priesthood, the doctrine of the sacraments, indulgences, the vow, purgatory, and the righteousness of works: he sought by evangelical doctrine to bring the Church to reform itself. Now, it was to be given to the outlawed and banished man to survey from the height of the Wartburg, with a free and far-reaching glance, the position in which he stood, to ponder with all circumspection the connections of things, to reflect upon the requirements of the people, to shape more definitely the picture of reform, and to take into consideration the means which belonged to it. There is no doubt that Luther, whilst in the Wartburg, was conscientiously busied in enlightening himself upon every side as to the true foundations of the Church, and in clearly marking them off, even in opposition to those, who were driven hither and thither by the spirit of an empty negative freedom. This is shown not only by his eagerness to render the Holy Scriptures accessible to the whole people, but is also proved in the clearest manner by the position which, upon his return to Wittenberg, he forthwith assumed towards the fanaticism then breaking out, and by his whole subsequent conduct. From an external point of view, he assumes now a different position. *Gottfried Arnold* regards it as a wavering of his high daring spirit,—Möhler and Döllinger as a logical inconsistency by which he condemns his past,—and even those who think they may reckon themselves as belonging to the Evangelical Church, consider—that he now rectified, and even substantially retracted, the revolutionary utterances of his earlier years, which were directed against the divine authority of episcopacy and ecclesiastical office, against the *opus operatum* and the godly veneration for the visible Church, and which maintained the universal priesthood of believers; in a word, that he now for the first time set forth the principle which is able to support a church. It has become customary in certain circles to speak of a distinction of two periods in Luther's life, as if at the commencement he was entangled in "subjectivity," and as if in the time of his Christian manhood he had rejected his first standpoint as an escapade, in order again to own allegiance to "objectivity."[1] Luther, however, whilst conscious of a distinction of periods as regards himself, even in the year 1545, is conscious of it in quite a different direction, namely, inasmuch as he at first, with great humility, left too many articles to the Pope, which he afterwards condemned as abominations.[2] In his controversy with the sectarians and fanatics he did not seek to retain certain remnants of a Romish nature, in order by means of these to operate against them, but out of the innermost core of the standpoint of faith assumed by him from the beginning, did he conduct the controversy against them too, as at the first against the Romish Church. Where has Luther ever confessed to a view of the Church, of which the basis was not justifying faith, born of word and sacrament by the Holy Spirit, but the institution of a divine office? Where has he withdrawn that view of the Church, which has passed even into the confessions, according to which it is above all the community of believers, who are gathered around the word and sacrament? Where has he recalled the criticism evolved from faith, which assailed the Romish doctrine of the sacraments, the *opus operatum* and the ecclesiastical office? If he had made any retractation in these matters, he would himself have recalled for his part the Reformation, and there would then have remained only the problem, how a division so unjustifiably begun could have been conscientiously continued. We shall soon see how the significance, which Luther attributed to the means of grace and to office, was in no way Roman Catholic

---

[1] Thus Leo, Kliefoth, Vorreiter.   [2] *Luthers Werke von Walch*, xiv. 465.

in its nature, and was in nowise borrowed at the expense of justification by faith, but was rather directly owing to the principle of faith; that at a later period he was as little conscious of any breach with his first outset in the Reformation, as is the German nation, which as a purified Church has turned, not to a Luther who had afterwards condemned his first reforming years as revolutionary, but to a Luther who conserved that outset, and in many particulars rectified but also enriched it. The power, as well as the source of his polemics, against the Romish Church lay for him, even in his supremely critical period, always in the new *position*. But this same positive element also induced his opposition to the fanatics. As both extremes were from his standpoint equally repugnant, he asserted his position in its contrast to them both; and his fundamental idea stood its test just in this, that it was equally opposed to the two extremes of a false objectivity and subjectivity, and proved equal to them both. Hence, in a purely historical aspect, the matter stands thus: only in the rarest cases is it granted, in the different departments of life, to one and the same mind, to add to the works of war and conflict those of peace, to the work of criticizing and destroying the old and outlived the creative production of the new. But it was granted to the mind of Luther; and if anything, it is confessedly this, which marks him out in the eyes of the Church as a favoured instrument of the Lord, who had certainly not without ground, and in order to the purifying of his natural fire, withdrawn him into solitude.

I. *The Fanatics of a practical sort; in particular, the false ethical Mysticism.*[1]

The ideas disseminated from Wittenberg had kindled the flame; the mind was alienated from the existing worship and constitution. In Wittenberg, in Saxony, and in the South German free cities, public opinion was pressing to a decision. In fact, too, an arrest could not be made at a mere reformation of doctrine; this itself aimed at a revolution of life and worship. How could the mass be still performed in the old manner, with adoration of the host, with offertory prayers [see App. note G], as low mass, and with reference to purgatory, when the belief in the transforma-

---

[1] Cornelius, *Bericht über das Münstersche, Wiedertäuferreich*, 1853. Erbkam, *Geschichte der protestantischen Secten im Zeitalter der Reformation*, 1848.

tion, in the *opus operatum*, and in the sacrificial significance of this sacrament had been rejected ? Or, to say nothing of indulgences, how was the administration of conventual obligation and of celibacy still admissible, when these vows were, in the sight of God, and as a matter of equity, not binding ? The situation was thus exceedingly uneasy ; the new was not there, and the continuance of the old was ever becoming more plainly irreconcilable with internal truth of worship. The Elector might have taken reform into his own hands, with the help of thoroughly intelligent advice ; he even procured a formal opinion from the Faculty and from the Augustine Order, but both shrunk from decided innovations, and so the Elector suffered the old to continue. There now arose, however, a great stir amongst monks, preachers, students, and citizens. Thirteen Augustinian monks, in response to the fiery summons of Gabriel Didymus, laid aside the cowl; Jacob Seideler in Meissen, and Feldkirch in Kemberg married; and, at Christmas of 1521, *Carlstadt* celebrated the Holy Supper, against the will of the Elector, according to the new rite in both kinds, in the parish church of Wittenberg. Although his mistake was thus more of a formal kind, still, inasmuch as he set himself at the head of the movement in Luther's absence, he had undertaken a work to which he was not equal, and which uplifted him to a dizzy height; and because he himself did not stand on sufficiently firm ground, he easily suffered himself to be drawn out of the right path by the waves, which began to rise higher and more wild.

Andreas Bodenstein von Carlstadt, from 1510 Professor of Theology, was no ordinary mind, but one composed of extraordinary opposites, which never attained to unity during his public life ; not without a disposition to depth, but of too restless a nature to devote himself wholly to any matter so as to become master of it, or bring it into a clear shape, in or out of himself. As a Thomist, he was long buried in scholasticism, but he was also much occupied with Scotist philosophy ; a great reader, with a touch of the polyhistorian, intent on uniting theology and jurisprudence, in his dialectics a formal logician. He was thus at first a vehement opponent of Luther, but suffered himself to be infected by the universal opposition to scholasticism in Wittenberg, and from 1517 entered the lists alongside of Luther in favour of Augustinianism. He allowed himself to be influenced somewhat by the mysticism which Luther and Staupitz revived, and combated the attack made upon Luther by Eck in his *Obeliscis;* but for a considerable time he refrained from directly contesting indulgences and the papal primacy, and perhaps it had some connection with this, that at Leipsic he confined himself to the controverting of Pelagianism. He allowed himself to be then carried away to a very furious denial of the freedom of the will. He accepted, with Augustine, absolute dependence upon God; but he apprehended it rather physically than ethically. There is no very earnest conception of sin and guilt traceable in him; but only a lively, though rather indefinitely entertained, need of God, the satisfaction of which takes place, according to him, by means of the cross which God imposes in order to humiliation, upon which follows the infusion of grace. This he does not bring into any closer connection with Christ: the cross of Christ is for him, as for those mystics before the Reformation, most of all only a pattern for our spiritual suffering, to which he also reckons pain on account of others, and accordingly the love of one's neighbour, which is thus, according to him, not founded in justifying faith. He early manifested, indeed, a zealous antagonism to any magical operation through external and empirical means, in which grace was supposed to be confined; but because he deemed he could not attribute a real causality to anything creatural, he did not, in connection with his abstract predestinarianism, get rid of an *internal magic* in the province of the spirit. Grace, according to him, is imparted abruptly—in infusion without mediating causes. His doctrine of grace has an extremely loose connection with the doctrine of the means of grace.

He holds the *Holy Scriptures* indeed in high esteem as rule and standard, and places them above tradition, but he does not esteem them nor their power (*efficacia*) equally highly as a means of grace. He treats it as it were in a juridical manner, as a codex of law, even as he often calls the New Testament the new law. But that the question is not merely one of adjustment and external regulation, but one of a new life of regeneration through reconciliation and sanctification, this escapes his shallow moral consciousness. And accordingly he has no idea of passing beyond the stage of a merely legal relationship to the Holy Scriptures. The positive power of good he ascribes indeed to

God and not to man, but teaches so exclusive an operation of God in the annihilation of all human working, that according to him we are only impersonal [1] transition-points of good divine action, a new personal centre of life by means of the Spirit of Christ is never realized, and thus there is little said of the communication of grace, because power is wanting on the part of the subject to receive and appropriate the same. Since grace, or more properly the divine operation, has only to pass through us, there remains for *us*, according to him, only repentance, the continual painful contemplation of our sin, for *we* can do nothing but sin. Thus he holds fast by a perpetual retrospective sadness, but does not know that true repentance also looks forward, and that the being inwardly "bowed down" passes by faith in Christ into a "being raised up." He easily came afterwards to connect again with this self-tormenting repentance the Pelagianizing error, that it disposed for grace and rendered one worthy of it. Inasmuch as grace remains above and outside of man, and at most a gracious glance of God towards man becomes the portion of faith, he does not conceive of faith as an act which makes grace the property of man, but that spiritual dolour draws God to itself only in such a way, that He works through the man who feels it, or instead of him. Justification and sanctification, between which he makes no distinction, he apprehends after such a fashion, that even the infusion of the grace of sanctification does not properly sanctify man, but only denotes him as holy in the divine regard; it is in a certain measure a *sanctificatio forensis*. Hence the means of grace, according to him, effect nothing, but are only evidences and signs of something that is absent, to which they call attention, but only the attention of him who knows already what they signify. But all the more on that account do they become qualified to take the place of a *law*, for which he felt a necessity so long as he sought with correct tact a limit to the power of subjectivity, which he had not inwardly restrained,—a counterpoise, which he found in a legal appeal to the Holy Scriptures, even of the Old Testament, and that in a literal manner. By means of his treatise *Libellus de canonicis scripturis* (August, 1520) he, in eloquent words, contributed not a little to enforce the duty of universal acquaintance with the Scriptures, and thus to prepare the way for Luther's translation. He there advo-

[1] Or passive—*selbstlos.*—Tr.

cates with Luther the sufficiency, clearness, and universal accessibility of the Holy Scriptures, and only comes into opposition to Luther in so far as he, without naming him, impugns his freer judgment of the Epistle of James, as well as the principles which led to it. Whilst Luther in his ninety-five theses, and in his treatise on the *Babylonian Captivity*, treats justifying faith as an equally authoritative criterion for deciding the canonicity of any scripture, inasmuch as no Holy Scripture dare contradict this faith, and the latter accordingly possesses independence and truth in itself, Carlstadt, on the other hand, declaimed sharply against this, and demanded that that should be regarded as the obligatory Word of God, which has been once sanctioned as canonical by the Church. And yet even he, resting upon Jerome in opposition to the decision of the Romish Church, desired to let fall the canonicity of the Apocrypha of the Old Testament. And further, he did not see that, according to his acceptation, the Church became again the decisive and infallible court of appeal as to what was canonical, which easily secured to it by implication the exclusive right of interpretation. He cautions against the subjectivity which, instead of subordinating itself to the Holy Scriptures (*i.e.* to the canon of the Church), seeks to decide in the first place upon the canonicity of the Holy Scriptures.[1] He is accordingly entirely averse to a scientific criticism, and does not for a moment allow to justifying faith, that nothing dare contradict it, which seeks to pass for canonical. He is not conscious of a distinction between a criticism of faith and a criticism of unbelief or caprice, and he curtails the principle of faith, because he is not at home in it, and hence he has no knowledge of the inner law of life, of which faith can never cease its hold. And just as in relation to *criticism*, so also in relation to the *interpretation of the Holy Scriptures*, he does not allow to the believing subject his rights. The Church or the Pope ought not indeed to have the right of a normative interpretation of Scripture; he demands a self-interpretation of the Holy Scriptures, yet not through the intervention of a believing spiritual understanding, inwardly one with them, but he proceeds in relation to the Scriptures as if they were a codex of law, according to the rule of jurists in relation to their sources of law: *quod interpretatio non est extra materiam interpretatam.*

[1] Cf. Credner, *Zur Geschichte des Canons*, 1847, 291-412.

Everything depends, in his eyes, upon the external collocation and harmonizing of different passages, but he has no idea of the real unity of the Scriptures, the unity accessible to faith, by which they illumine their individual parts, and themselves decide what is to be apprehended literally and what figuratively: his juristic nature lays here again the chief accent upon the letter. With this is most intimately connected a very harsh theory of inspiration. In accordance with that dualism between the divine and the human, which corresponds to his legal standpoint, he will on no account suffer the human side of the sacred authors to pass as co-efficient for the Holy Scriptures; their character as the solid divine law would seem to him to be thereby altered. A human mouth would, in his opinion, be wholly unfit to speak God's Word. The divine, according to him, never becomes the property of man; consequently it could only be falsified by the human. The human, where it exists and works, is for him extra-divine, and even anti-divine; therefore the divine, if it is to work, must take the place of the human, and the latter become a purely passive vehicle through which the Word of God passes, as the melody through the organ.

The converse of this severe view of the Holy Scriptures is indeed, of inward necessity, the thrusting of them into the background, in so far as they are designed to be a *means of grace*. He does not find in them an inner side, only accessible to faith, in the outer, the letter; but the inner, which he conceives of as the will and law of God, is for him entirely merged in the outer, the letter, which accordingly possesses the right of regulating life with divine authority. He himself, however, does not find in this his religious satisfaction; he longs for an immediate relationship to God, which he hopes to obtain under mystical conditions. These conditions, as has been said, are not, according to him, to be realized through external means of grace, which must always carry in them something creatural and therefore, as he thinks, foreign to God, and on the other hand call for active effort; but they are to be realized through directly divine infusion. To him who has experienced it the Word of Scripture appears, in comparison with the living fellowship with God, only like a dead letter of the law, which has nothing to do with those inward raptures. In accordance with this view he says, even before the Leipzig disputation, that the letter of the Holy Scriptures (*i.e.* according to him the Holy Scriptures) does not secure true consolation, that it even serves for transgression, sin, and death. Whilst it is for him only law, and he has learned this much that the law killeth, he has yet a sufficient glimmering of a higher stage, to render the pure standpoint of law unbearable. But his mystic rapture does not know how to find the way back to the Holy Scriptures. It is no wonder that at a later period, after the failure of his attempts at legal reformation, the more he fortified himself in his mystic position, the more the Holy Scriptures seemed alien to him and to belong to a subordinate stage. In the year 1524, he set[1] the internal testimony of the Spirit in direct opposition to the external testimony of the Holy Scriptures: "for my part," he said, "I do not require the external testimony; I will have my testimony from the Spirit, from my inward man." "As the Apostles first of all had the Spirit, and after being sealed by Him preached Christ externally in Word and Scripture, so ought we to be like the Apostles." As if the Apostles had not seen and heard the Lord before Pentecost. According to him, conversion would be possible without any connection with the Scriptures and historical Christianity, by the sheer internal magic of grace, if Christianity is not even lowered by him to the mere purpose of bearing witness to what we already have and are. At any rate, according to him, the Holy Scriptures come, so to speak, upon the stage only when the inward work of the Spirit is already accomplished; their objective testimony is not interwoven and incorporated into the growing life of faith; it does not assume for the latter a definite shape, so as to ensure soundness to faith, the consciousness of the objectivity of its matter; but the Holy Scriptures continue to be for him only the normal rule for Christians, the source of authorization for his practical reforms, but in the way of verbal interpretation.

Of such an interpretation he made use now in Luther's absence. Seeing that he does not find in faith the centre of a conscious new and free personality, but that union with God, so far as his knowledge of it extends, is only the dissolution of the human personality in God in pure passivity, there are also wanting to him the proper inward power of judgment on the part of the new personality, a true understanding of Scripture, and an in-

[1] *Luthers Werke von Walch*, xx. 2893.

ward guiding-star in the work of reformation. All the more did he seek the rule for reformation only outside of himself, and found it above all in the Holy Scriptures as a law. "What is not contained in them is to be done away with," without more ado,—what they, even the Old Testament, may forbid. Accordingly he sounds the summons to the destruction of images, for they contradict the decalogue, and are idolatry. With regard to property, there must be no beggar amongst Christians. Indeed, in general, he seeks to supplant the civil law by the law of Moses. The Lord's Supper he would like best to celebrate with twelve, as it was at the first. Every bishop must marry. There is no necessity for a learned education; even the Apostles were unlearned men. He aimed at the introduction of a new theocracy, and the Christian, in his opinion, has to apply all his energies to its establishment, even though it be by force; for the law of God must prevail, it is a matter of indifference whether it is expressed in the Old Testament or by Christ. For even Christ is for him only "the bearer of the Father's Word, through whom God has spoken, as also through the prophets." He had so little understanding of the more protracted process of the transformation of the outward through the growing inner life, that he was content if only the appearance corresponded to the law, as he understood it. Accordingly, for the purpose of suppressing the sacrament of penance, he granted to every one free access to the bread and cup, without requiring preparation or confession, and he laid it down as a commandment to make use of Christian freedom, to marry, and to introduce a theocracy. Thus, under the name of freedom from the traditions of Rome, there was only created again a yoke, which was a Judaistic sidepiece of the former, and the principle of legality anew set fast, whereby the Reformation would have been in its essence annihilated. Indeed, by his above-mentioned distinction between the Spirit and the Scriptures, he soon lost for his reforms the firm basis of Scripture as the canon of reformation. He was so much the less able to combat the possibility of new revelations of the divine will, since an infusion of grace, not effected by the means of grace, played with him so important a part, and since he did not see in Christianity a revelation which had attained to unity and completeness, nor saw in the Scriptures the record of this revelation. He had thus no ground upon which to ascribe authority or inspiration to the canonical Scriptures in an exclusive sense. The new and great age might seem to require new revelations, through whose prohibitions and commands what remained indeterminate and uncertain in the law of the Scriptures should become fixed. These new prohibitions, then, had to refer to definite external works, and might, since he was accustomed to resile from the criticism of whatever claimed to be revelation, likewise demand that a purely passive position be assumed in reference to them. Besides, as we have seen, every standard of criticism had slipped from him.

When, therefore, the so-called *Inspired* or *heavenly prophets* from Zwickau appeared in Wittenberg in the end of the year 1521, with their new inward revelations, with a new and pretendedly divine law, which required the overthrow of the whole existing condition of things, and since they invested certain sudden subjective impulses with the character of unconditional religious requirements, Carlstadt was defenceless against them, and even attracted towards them. The temptation found in him a perfectly kindred inclination, whilst the Scriptures now lost for him even the dignity of being the all-sufficient norm, the all-sufficient law for the ordering of questions of reform. These prophets were *Nicolaus Storch* and *Marcus Thomä*, two weavers, Marcus Stübner and Martin Cellarius, afterwards professor in Basle, together with *Thomas Münzer*. Rejected of Zwickau, they sought to obtain the decision of the university in favour of their inspirations and plans of reform. Very different men from Luther were necessary—men of a loftier spirit. What good could it do to keep so closely to Scripture? It was ineffectual for true instruction: only that man was instructed who was illumined by the Holy Ghost. God held with them reliable intercourse, and said to them what they should do and preach. Storch, their leader, chose to himself twelve apostles and seventy-two disciples, and, under the pretence of a divine commission, exercised over them despotic power. Reformation and Christian liberty were to be introduced by mighty judgments from God, the day of the Lord was at hand, the present temporal and wicked rulers were to be destroyed, the saints and righteous were to be put in their place,—in connection with which they did not forget a princely position for themselves. A purification by blood would come: only the righteous would survive in the

Church. Ridiculed at first in Wittenberg, by and by they made an impression even upon *Melanchthon*, especially on account of their attacks upon *infant baptism*, which was against reason, as well as against the word and purpose of Christ. They hit here, in the view of Melanchthon, upon a "weak point;" for whilst he had a sure and direct feeling of its great importance, still the Reformation principle of personality and the Reformation antagonism to the magical *opus operatum* seemed here to come into direct collision with the doctrine of the means of grace, since infants are not yet free intelligent persons. But still more than Melanchthon did *Carlstadt*, who already passed with the people for another Elias, concern himself with them. He did not, indeed, give himself to them entirely, but still in sufficient strength. When they said that the vital point was not the external means of grace nor instruction, but the sudden operation of the Spirit, he agreed with them; when they sought, instead of daily repentance, a sudden spiritual uplifting by ecstatic rapture, he was the less disinclined to this, that it seemed to him small and humiliating for his inner life to bow to anything external, as word and sacrament, and that they themselves stated a method whereby to attain to the hearing of the heavenly voice.[1] Only he who has passed through the stages of purification, amazement, weariness, and emptying of the creature by perfect mortification, is righteous, is filled with the Holy Ghost, so that he can do, know, and will all things. It is in their position a contemptible thing still to speak of sin; they dream of themselves as above the Apostles and above the law, as pure from sin. Carlstadt did not go so far; but still he set the Holy Spirit in opposition to science, and said to the students that they should rather go home and work in the fields; science was of no avail, but the Spirit, and it was said, "In the sweat of thy brow shalt thou eat bread;" upon which two hundred betook themselves home. He himself, too, laid aside the title of doctor, because it was said, "Be not called rabbi," gave himself the name of "Neighbour Andrew," and for a while engaged in agricultural pursuits. There was no necessity for a special ministerial order; all are equal and free before God. Every one might engage in preaching alongside of his handicraft, if he was only inspired. This contempt for the office of preacher was very naturally

[1] *Luthers Werke von Walch*, iii. 2264, x. 1778.

shared by the Inspired. It is evident that Carlstadt was just upon the point of dissolving the whole organization of the Church and its ordinances, and the Reformation would have thus lost itself in the sand.

The *religious* liberty mania extends its fibres visibly into the peasant rising; *Thomas Münzer* was, in 1525, the head of the peasants in Middle Germany, as *Schübler*, the chancellor of the Hohenlohes, was in Southern Germany. The mode of religious thought most prevalent amongst the insurrectionary peasants was the Anabaptist; the preaching of Christian liberty had touched them, but only stirred their carnal nature; they desired to know nothing of true repentance, but only of judgment, in their dark hatred against nobles and rulers,—a hatred begotten indeed by long oppression. They sought to draw from the principle of the Reformation only a divine sanction for their desire of temporal freedom. Even Carlstadt suffered himself to be afterwards drawn into a more and more ambiguous connection with the camp of the peasants in Franconia, where he was during the peasant rising there; but at a later period he publicly disclaimed the revolutionary impulses and secret leagues of *Thomas Münzer*.[1] Let us consider this at somewhat greater length.

The doctrine of salvation as held by the *earlier Anabaptists*.[2] In Wittenberg there was, said Thomas Münzer, clandestinely taught a fictitious faith, which was far too easy. There it was said, God will take care of everything, I will simply believe. That is a poisonous faith. The beginning of true faith takes place amid the deepest trembling and terror, and quaking in presence of the condemnation of God. In this fear of God the Holy Ghost finds for itself a place and overshadows the man. Whoever attains to faith in another way is frivolous, and has placed a new patch in an old beggar's garment. If these desperate scribes are asked the ground of their firm faith, of which they boast, and the proper root of an undeceivable faith, they point to the *Scriptures*. But that is not enough. The Scriptures give testimony, but not, as they imagine, faith;

---

[1] It might also be mentioned that Carlstadt afterwards materially modified many of the views above described, especially in the closing years of his life, as professor at Basle.—*Tr.*

[2] Seidemann, *Thomas Münzer.* Förstemann, *neues Urkundebuch zur Geschichte der evang. Kirchenreformation,* 1842. Cornelius, see ref. Göbel, *Geschichte des christlichen Lebens,* vol. i. 140, ff. Erbkam, see ref.

the truth must be brought in its completeness to the light, after it has slumbered so long; whoever is taught of God is to be believed, not simply on the ground of the Scriptures. Münzer accordingly sees in all dependence upon the Holy Scriptures only a dependence upon external authority, similar to the [Roman] Catholic. He places Luther still upon the [Roman] Catholic side, and in evangelical faith he sees a laxity in respect of the majestic and righteous God, before whom we must tremble in order to be disposed for His illumination. On the other hand, he himself makes the crowd dependent upon those who pretend to be illumined, as if they were the priests and organs of the divine will. He ascribes to these illumined ones such a position that, if they had never, their whole life long, seen nor heard anything of the Bible, they might yet through the teaching of the Spirit possess a true faith, even as those who wrote the Scriptures, and be certain that they were not in this faith counterfeiting the devil and their own nature, but really obtained it from God. In the midst of unbelievers, and without any books, the Holy Ghost could teach the true faith. The Wittenbergians say, one must begin with the Scriptures, they bring faith; but no certain reason can be given to the godless why they are to receive and not reject the Scriptures than simply this, that they come down from antiquity and are received by many men. But that is the argument of the Jew and the Turk. True faith requires a clearer light than the Word; it follows only the incitement of the Spirit. The Spirit, however, is received by hoping and waiting for illumination. The heart of the elect is continually impelled to its source by the power of the Highest. Man in himself is from all eternity adapted for God; but if besides he takes the Holy Spirit to be his teacher, then faith comes. We must all, then, undergo this experience—that we carnal, earthly men, are to become gods through the incarnation of Christ, completely transformed into God, that the earthly life circles into the heavenly. The scribes despise what is poor; often though the Eternal Word has mounted into the chosen men at our Nazareth of Christendom. We tremble, too, like the mother of God, at the greeting, when God will deify us through the incarnation of His Son (in us). In the empty, passive soul, in the broken-spirited, the power of God possesses its effect; there the ground of the soul is completely irradiated and clarified by the Light of the world, which is the unfictitious, true Son of God, Jesus Christ.[1] Christ is accordingly for him not the historical Christ, but the Eternal Word, being ever formed in this and that elected man. With atonement and sanctification we have here nothing to do. *Münzer* believes that everything is gotten by his deification; what is still wanting is only the lordship over the external world. Similar pantheistic views were also disseminated otherwise amongst the Anabaptists, *e.g.* in the case of *David Joris*, who gave himself out for a new and the royal incarnation of the Word;[2] the Münzerian Anabaptists, however, struck a coin with the inscription, *Verbum caro factum habitavit in nobis*. They regarded themselves as a new incarnation of God, and a new formation of the world was to begin with them.

Münzer is besides zealously opposed to the opinion that revelation is concluded in the Scriptures. If this deplorable Christendom is to be judged, then must the Church wait and pray for a new John, a preacher rich in grace; he must come in the spirit and power of Elias, and bring everything into the proper train with supreme zeal and might. "On the other hand, the doctrine of the Wittenbergians will have absolutely nothing to do with this work." He thus sets up his *chiliastic* views in opposition to them as a pseudo-Messias. God will found a new kingdom, composed purely of saints. Everything which seems to him to belong to the setting up of this holy kingdom he demands, and is ready to accomplish by force. Whoever withstands him is a rebel against God. His most prominent principles in reference to the restoration of the true kingdom of God are these: The cause of there being so little faith lies in the reception of those void of grace into Christendom. Therefore infant baptism is to be rejected, and the unholy removed out of the Church. Only holy *ministers* can administer word and sacrament; they must be as certain of their faith as the sacred authors. *Marriage* with unbelievers is no marriage, and allows of divorce. Among the saints all *goods* are *common;* he speaks and acts also, as if they alone had the true right to property, and nothing was due to unbelievers but judgment. In reference to the *State* and civil *rulers*, he required the princes to join themselves to his covenant or to be slain: for he was chosen and inspired to set up

[1] Erbkam, 241, see ref.
[2] Cf. Niedner's *Zeitschrift für historische Theologie*, 1864.

the kingdom of God upon earth. Having joined him, they have to help in the destruction of those who are not elect. The kingdom of God cannot come without division and separation; this seems the most impossible of all things, of which no man will hear, except as being at the end of the days through the angels; by the angels, however, are to be understood the messengers of God; the time of judgment is now. It may also easily be known who is elect. The civil rulers, who do not belong to the elect, have no authority; if any one serves them even where they are not Christian, and accordingly do not serve the will of God, he is seeking to serve two masters, he is creating an idol. God suffers this not; judgment is coming; the godless are to be hurled from their seat, and the humble exalted. In his exposition of Luke i. he says: God has, in His displeasure, given lords and princes to the world, and He will take them away again in His anger. This is the explanation of the nature of civil rulers. God will pluck out tyrants by the root; therefore are they so hardened. These thoughts of destruction may be summed up in this, that he seeks to annihilate all the principles of human order which belong to the first creation, in order to set in its place a second creation, pretendedly divine, but in reality murderous.

This malady of Anabaptism and fanaticism had, in the third and fourth decades, spread like a burning fever through all Germany; from Schwabia and Switzerland, along the Rhine to Holland and Friesland,—from Bavaria, Middle Germany, Westphalia, and Saxony, as far as Holstein. All the different anti-ecclesiastical tendencies, which, for the most part, with a dualistic colouring, had secretly pervaded the life of the people in the middle ages, got vent after the reform excitement issued from Wittenberg, and obtained a wider extension under the new movement; they even appropriated the name of Reformation and of Christian liberty as their common watchword. But it is the duty of the historian, by searching them to their bases, to try whether they are the offspring of the spirit of the Reformation, or of the pre-Reformation spirit. If indeed we listen to their language, then they stand so entirely upon the ground of the Reformation, that they only seek the more logical and emphatic carrying out of its ideas, and stand upon the shoulders of the Wittenbergians. But it is precisely these ideas of the Reformation that are entirely wanting to them, and hence also their hostility to the existing circumstances of the Church has quite a different meaning and spirit, and different methods and aims, from those of the Reformation. If we look to their positive proposals, and church ideals, these are essentially the growth of a pre-Reformation soil; and what they are looking to is not so much an internal reformation of Christendom and a higher condition of the Church, as a spiritual kingdom in opposition to the Romish Church, and essentially related to the mediæval ideal of the Church by its contemptuous estimate of the State and of temporal rulers. Even their doctrine concerning the sources of the knowledge of the truth presents analogies, in the thrusting of the Holy Scriptures into the background, and in the high esteem of ecstatic raptures and immediate revelations.

In *Anabaptism* and its fanaticism there burst again into life that enthusiastic subjective principle, which breaks loose from the Scriptures, and so from primitive Christianity in its objective form, and which had since the period of Montanism only passed into a chrysalis condition under the hierarchy. [See App. note H.] The Anabaptists are indeed amongst themselves very different. Some are rather of a passive nature, and approach, in their appearance, to certain monastic orders, such as the God-resigned, praying Baptists, who did almost nothing but pray, and made praying their work; the secluded spiritual Baptists, who could not see laughter nor mirth without sighing, and who, after the fashion of the monastic orders, laid down definite rules with regard to clothes, walking, and standing; so too the ecstatic and the silent brethren. Others are urged rather by practical impulses, whether it be to introduce by force the holy kingdom or to employ themselves in teaching, as the apostolic brethren, who preached repentance, evangelized, forsook wife and children, and, after the fashion of the begging orders, let themselves be nourished by others. Others, again, the so-called free brethren, are Antinomians: after having received true baptism (anabaptism) it is impossible to sin any more; community of goods and wives belongs to the holy kingdom; nothing external is of any importance, God looks upon the heart, hence one may even deny the truth under persecution. Still all these tendencies have also a common family likeness. Besides the above-described elevation, after an enthusiastic fashion, of the Spirit or the internal Word of God above the Holy Scriptures, they have a *church ideal* which is essentially impregnated by Romish ideas. Their doctrine of *faith* in relation to works is also anything but the Reformation doctrine; it rather occupies essentially the Romish standpoint. Man becomes pious before God not by faith without works, but by the infusion of love and holiness (which must certainly evidence itself according to their views in a sort of communism). Further, just as the Romish Church suffers from a onesided impulse towards manifestation and exhibition in a visible form,—just as in the capricious anticipation of perfection it possesses a chiliastic trait, in this, namely, that it regards the present as already an embodiment of the perfect kingdom of God, or thinks it is already standing in the period of perfection, even so does the Anabaptism of that period appropriate the chiliastic passion for manifestation, which carnalizes the view and brings it into connection with the legality of the Romish system. The distinction made between the Church visible and invisible, which is of such importance for the standpoint of the Reformation, is quite as unacceptable to the Anabaptists as it is to Roman Catholicism. And finally, it stands in connection with the immediately foregoing, that they both occupy a kindred position towards the State. Whilst both aim in the most decided manner at the State form of community for what they call the Church, they both regard the State in itself as profane in its nature, and as having no proper independent moral significance.

The Anabaptists forbid Christians to take offices of civil authority, oaths, or military service, although they do not disdain the means of external compulsion, which only become the State, for the purpose of carrying out their theory. The ground of this inimical position towards the State does not lie chiefly in the experience of persecution at its hands; but principally in the sharp antithesis of the divine and the human into which they had fallen, and from which, though certainly in lesser measure, the Romish doctrine also suffers. They would that only the exclusively divine will should prevail, in whatever form it may make itself known. They are thus the enemy of all natural human ordinances, and would have them supplanted by theocratical; but they do not perceive that they would thereby change religion into a moral law, and reject the free ethical movement of life, of which the spirit of the Gospel is the soul. In a word, there lurked amongst the Anabaptists an opposition State in the form of a theocracy, based upon a prophetical office; and on this account they appear in rivalry against the State, as well as against the Romish Church, whose formal and material principle in many respects resembles their own.

But as they broke with the State, so also did they break with the national life. The kingdom of God, which they have in view, does not trouble itself about the differences of nations. Where the Spirit of God erects it by His inspiration and calling, there the nucleus of a visible temporal kingdom has been founded. There is here manifested certainly a decided difference from the Romish system, inasmuch as they have become the prey of a subjectivity sealed by nothing, and will know as little of external authority as of magically working sacraments, ay, and inasmuch as their abrupt ecstatic mode finds it impossible to conceive of nature as a medium for the mental and spiritual, but is only able to take up an antagonistic position to nature and to history, which was embodied in their doctrine of infant baptism and in their docetic Christology, whilst in the Romish Church the originally enthusiastic element was allayed and transposed by a powerful spirit of community into settled ordinances, by which the communication of the Spirit should be securely continued from member to member. But even in this last respect there is evident a common fundamental tendency, inasmuch as both, instead of letting the first creation be glorified by the process of a gradual introduction of spiritual life, would rather set a second and spiritual creation, foreign to the first, in its place. There is probably also no doubt, that if the phenomenon of Anabaptism had been able to secure for itself a longer existence, it must have struck out the same paths, as the old Montanism, when it began to embody itself in a church. But the fanaticism of Anabaptism did not possess a sufficient spiritual store for long duration. It was, as has been shown, like other mediæval sects, essentially bound up with pre-Reformation principles and views. What of the Reformation it appropriated was the idea of freedom from human authority by means of fellowship with God; but, since it did not realize this fellowship by means of atonement and the earnestness of sanctification by faith, it wanted internal moderation and the guiding star; the idea of evangelical liberty, which only stirred its ear as it were from afar, awoke for it only the passions of the unrenewed heart and those negative destructive endeavours, which were void of any power of creating *new and healthy* formations.

II. *Dogmatic confutation of the fanatics of the species of false ethical mysticism.*

Luther overcame the fanatical movements that accompanied the Reformation practically as well as theoretically, but was also driven by them to bring the evangelical conception of the Church in its fundamental elements into a surer form, and to exhibit definitely the internal connection of the evangelical principle of faith on the one hand, and of the Word and sacraments on the other. Thus the transition was found from the individual faith of the Christian personality to the Church. This likewise entailed upon him the development of his doctrine concerning the office of the ministry and concerning the relation between Church and State.

When he heard upon the Wartburg of the fire which had broken out in Wittenberg, without submitting to any farther delay, he returned thither in March 1522, and preached, for eight days in succession, upon the questions in controversy with such power that he restored order. In doing so, he with his own peculiar power united wisdom and mildness, and declared himself, even as he was opposed to the violent action of the fanatics, to be also opposed to violent regulations against them, so long as they would confine their movements to the field of thought and teaching, and not pass over to action. "By the Word the heavens and the earth were created; the same Word must do the work here also; by the Word the world is overcome; therefore I will preach, speak, write it, but compel or drive by force will I no man." His conception of the Church, although starting from adult believers, takes from the first a national direction, which renders possible a national Church, inasmuch as he vindicates for the Church not merely, as the fanatics would have it, an exhibitive, but also a pedagogic, side, and in this step even takes the Apostle Paul for a pattern. "Let help be given to the weak; let the strong use their liberty without offending the weak; I can drag no man to the Gospel by the hair of his head, I cannot drive any man to heaven. It must be faith which gives God the glory; love however uses liberty for its neighbour's benefit. The Word alone is omnipotent and takes prisoners the hearts; where these are taken, there must the work (of Romish abuses) fall away of itself."

Nevertheless he now soon began, indulgently following up the old, to set up an evangelical order of service (*formula missæ et communionis*, 1523, with previous intimation on the part of communicants, and the right of debarring by the bishop, also communion in both kinds); as well as an evangelical hymn-book, 1524, the melodies of which he helped to arrange,—in a maturer form, 1526, in the *Deutsche Messe*,[1] and including also Latin hymns. He also practically maintained the invalidity of the monastic vow, and of the celibacy of the clergy, and concluded, under a sense of duty, and also for the purpose of evidencing by the force of example the firmness of his moral conviction, the bond of marriage with Catharina von Bora, 3d June, 1525. He did it "in believing defiance of his enemies, without the passion of love, in order to bear witness to the honour in which he himself taught that marriage should be held." In every matter justifying faith was his standard of right; he always felt himself uncertain, until he had found a decision drawn clearly out of this principle. Thus, for example, he wavered for some time with regard to the binding nature of vows, because they were certainly voluntarily undertaken, until he took into view their connection with the desire for salvation, and was able now to characterize them as impious and godless, as sins against the first commandment. Even so in reference to the reformation of the mass; he would not do away with the cultus of the sacrifice of the mass, until the perception became firmly rooted that the true sacrifice of Christians is the living and spiritual, whilst the Romish sacrifice of the mass is to be regarded as idolatry. For this purpose he wrote *On the Abuse of the Mass*.

As a permanent memorial of the results of evangelical knowledge acquired in these controversies with the fanatical and Anabaptist movement, he wrote several treatises, especially the important work, *In Opposition to the Heavenly Prophets concerning Images and the Sacrament*.[2] He has here luminously ex-

[1] A liturgy in the German language, regulating the manner of celebrating the Sacrament of the Supper, as well as other parts of Divine service.—*Tr.*
[2] *Luthers Werke von Walch*, xx. 186, f.

hibited the foundations of the evangelical conception of the Church as the medium between two extremes, the Romish and the fanatical, and maintained, in place of a breach with the past, the historical character and continuity of the Christian Church, which has never become extinct, though it has often been concealed, in Christendom, even as also not everything which comes from the Papists is bad,—without however, on the other hand, finding this continuity of the Church in the apostolic succession, ordination, and hierarchy. For the true stem of the Church is for him persons, namely, its living members, the believers, who hold in honour God's Word and sacrament, through which the Holy Spirit works as His means. The fanatics grant the working of the Holy Spirit, but deny the external continuity between the past and the present, because they condemn the traditional means of grace. Thus Luther is brought to enter upon a searching discussion of the doctrine of the *means of grace*, wherein everything depends in his view upon setting clearly forth the internal relation between them and faith, as well as in general the relation of the external to the internal in the work of salvation.[1]

God, he says, has of His great goodness again given us the pure Gospel, the noble, precious treasure of salvation; because the devil cannot smother it by force, he will do it by false prophets. God however deals with us in two ways, outwardly and inwardly. Outwardly by the oral words of the Gospel and the corporeal signs in the sacraments, inwardly by the Holy Ghost and faith together with other gifts. All that, however, takes place after *this* order, that the outward things are to and must precede, and the inward come afterwards and *by means of* the outward; that God accordingly has resolved to give no one the inward things save through the outward, not to give the Spirit and faith save through external signs and words.

"But the factious spirit reverses this order, and brings forward an absurd one out of its own pure wantonness. First of all, what God has ordained outwardly for the spirit inwardly,—ah! how contemptuously does it cast that to the wind, and will at once right into the spirit." "Shall a handful of water indeed make one pure from sin? The Spirit, the Spirit, the Spirit must do it inwardly. Shall bread and wine help me? No, the

---

[1] *Luthers Werke von Walch*, xx. 271.

flesh of Christ must be eaten spiritually;" so that he who does not know the devil might think that with such splendid words they have five holy spirits in them. If they are asked, How do I come into the possession of such a sublime spirit? they point thee not to the outward Gospel but to Utopia, tell thee to stand for a tedious length of time and wait for the heavenly voice, till God Himself speaks with thee. Seest thou there the devil, the enemy of divine order, how he makes thy mouth gape at the words, 'Spirit, spirit, spirit,' and yet the while is tearing away the bridges, plank, road, ladder, and everything by which the Spirit is to come to thee, namely, the external ordinances of God in sensible baptism and word and sign, and is seeking to teach thee, not how the Spirit is to come to thee, but how thou art to come to the Spirit, that thou mayest learn to career upon the clouds and ride upon the wind, and not be still saying, 'how? where? when? what?' but mayest thyself experience it, as they do."

"Again. As they imagine a spirit of their own, so do they also point to external ordinances, about which God has neither given any command nor prohibition; such as, that one should have no pictures, churches, or altars, should wear grey clothes, endure no injustice, slay godless princes, and practise much external humility and attitudes, which their own fancy has created, and which God does not respect. Whoever acts otherwise in these respects, than they, is an ambiguous papist and scribe; but whoever does as they, has already leapt into the Spirit, and is a man taught of the Spirit. Even thus, what God inwardly ordains, such as faith, that they apply to external works," and then he describes the method of their ascetic mysticism. His final judgment is, "What God ordains concerning inward faith and spirit, of that they make a purely human work (legal ordinances); again, what God ordains concerning external words and sign, of that they make an inward spirit, and set the mortification of the flesh before faith, and even before the Word; accordingly, as is the manner of the devil, they move outwards where God will move inwards, and inwards where God will outwards. Faith does not come by works, not even by the work of the mortification of the flesh, but by the hearing of the Gospel. In the same Word comes the Spirit, and gives faith where and to whom He will; afterwards proceeds the mortification and the cross and the work of love."

In accordance with these principles he is against the rejection of *pictures*.[1] Even the Scripture has pictures. "Hence I may for the sake of memory and a better understanding, paint them upon the wall, even as they do no harm in the Holy Scriptures. In like manner I must also make myself pictures of Christ in my heart; whether I will or not, when I contemplate the sufferings of Christ, there projects itself in my heart the picture of a man hanging upon the Cross. Now, if it is no sin that I have the picture in my heart, why should it be sin if I have it in the eye, especially when the heart is of more importance than the eye?" This question decides the relation of Protestantism to art. The poetic, genial, and ideal feeling of Luther will as little dispense with the divine gift of painting as of music, but will rather see them employed in the interests of religion.[2]

It might seem to contradict the inwardness of the Protestant spirit, its desire after a personal certainty of salvation and immediate communion with God, to lay great weight upon anything outward whatsoever, and accordingly even upon the Holy Scriptures and sacraments. But just because Protestant piety seeks after the communion of love with the objective God Himself, and this can be a vital communion only when it evidences

---

[1] And images. *Bilder* includes both: what follows is to be read accordingly.—*Tr.*

[2] Thus far Calvin is of the same mind, *Institut. christ. rel.* l. i. c. xi. § 12. But the question remains untouched in the above, which Calvin answers in the negative: whether God Himself may be represented? and then: whether pictures, as *e.g.* of Christ, may really be used in connection with worship? For the negative speak the facts, that no picture corresponds to the infinite substance of the object of religious veneration, whilst the habit of representing this object to one's self under the aspect of the outward picture easily induces a contraction and even falsification of it,—to say nothing of the danger that the habit of reverencing the object in its picture may soon undermine the Christian sobriety which distinguishes between the picture and the thing, or may even furnish occasion for superstitious conceptions of a mysterious connection of the living object with its picture. The question of pictures has besides in another aspect a wide bearing, namely: what is the relation between the Old Testament, in which images are forbidden, and the New? [As regards Calvin's agreement with Luther, all he says is, that painting and sculpture are gifts of God, which are to be used in a pure and lawful manner. He says again, that they are bestowed by God for His glory and our good. Besides denying that it is lawful to attempt to depict God, he deems it more unbecoming the sacredness of churches than he can well express, to admit into them any other images than those living symbols which the Lord has consecrated by His Word,—meaning Baptism and the Lord's Supper, with the other ceremonies.—*Tr.*]

itself in deeds of love, there is innate in this piety an objective impulse, and even an impulse towards history. Since it has to do with a good conscience before God and the forgiveness of sins in earnestness and not merely in the shape of formal absolution, it cannot find nourishment for itself in its own fancies about God or in its own feelings, but must long after the testimony of God in a form independent from the person, and with the guarantee of sure objectivity. Whilst the *Word of God in the Holy Scriptures* is thus established as the means of grace in general, grace assumes in the *sacraments*, on the other hand, a form having reference still more immediately to the individual person, as living in a specific time and space. It is an expression of Luther's in reference to this, as frequent as it is singularly descriptive, that God "deals with us" (*mit uns handle*) through the means of grace.

The saving work of Christ, and the reconciliation of the world by Him, presents itself indeed to Luther as objectively closed and accomplished, with universal reference to mankind, and thus it might seem that there was no necessity for a farther historical act of God towards and for the individual, but that the utmost that was necessary was that faith should *subjectively* presentiate the past, as if it had only taken place to-day and for it. It might farther be thought that, since Luther teaches an absolute and eternal election, the soul only required to be enlightened as to its being included in the number of the elect, or the faith that it was included, in order to its becoming possessed of the certainty of salvation. But both objections forget, that it does not satisfy the vital religious need, as it expresses itself in Luther, to *know* of a divine decree of salvation, whether concerning the individual person or concerning the past, even although eternally valid, work of atonement, but the soul of the pious longs after the living God, and hence requires not merely past history or eternal decrees, but also deeds of love on the part of God, which, as it were, renew their youth, the present glance of love and greeting from above. To this is to be added, that Luther by no means conceives of the universality of grace, as if it stood in the power of every one to turn grace towards, and to apply it to, himself. Much rather, although the counsel of Divine love is universal, there nevertheless consists with it in a, for us, mysterious manner an election of individuals (see below), whilst the non-elect do not attain to faith. And even if this election had reference only to the earlier or later date of the calling, justification, and sanctification (which however in his view is not the case), this would itself already imply that no one could take salvation to himself, but that it came to him historically when and where it pleased God. But the idea of having it without God having given it, would be a foolish and vain delusion. Thus—even apart from the question, how then the knowledge of individual election is possible without a communicative act on the part of God—there follows only the more necessarily from the doctrine of election an historical attestation, reaching to the individual, of the counsel of divine grace. This attestation, however, must now farther be linked to the act of redemption once accomplished in Christ. Were the saving act of God, which is necessary for the individual, and which lays hold of him in the present, out of connection with the saving act of God in Christ, then the latter would not be the beginning [principle] of a new history of the salvation of mankind, but the saving act would have as it were to begin afresh with every momentum, and Christ with His saving work would be buried. Even the Romish doctrine, embodied in the mass, has for its religious motive the necessity of not being bound to something altogether past, but of enjoying the present saving act of God; only, this is separated from Christ's historical work of salvation as one of continuous vital efficacy; the objective sufficiency of the latter is disputed; and a daily repeated offering of Christ is set in the place of the one eternal but living sacrifice, stretching in its efficacy over all ages, and ever remaining new.

Now, this continuity between the present saving act necessary for the individual and the historical saving work of Christ is effected, on the one hand, by Christ, in that He as exalted Lord, in whom the efficient will of redemption, after He had offered the sacrifice of His life, continues in living energy upon the ground of His earthly work of atonement, now seeks the diffusion throughout mankind of the blessing won by Him. His salvation is to be applied to the individual, and to this end there serves now, on the other hand, the testimony continually borne to Him in the Church, and the administration of the sacraments instituted by Him. Both word and sacrament refer back to His historical life and work—are, indeed, authentic institutions, *after-operations* of this life. But in their course through the world He accompanies them with His Spirit, with His *perpetual operation*, which is, on the one hand, a new, loving and saving act towards the individual; but is, on the other hand, only the application, maintenance, and rendering fruitful of what is already concluded in His historical work, the incorporation of the individual into the fellowship of His love, but by means of the historical revelation of His love as instituting fellowship with man.

These are the fundamental thoughts by which Luther connects faith principally with the Word (mediately also with the sacrament).[1] The means of grace are thus for him not something dead and merely external, but the means adapted to our need, by which grace itself continues in living movement, and gains as it were the elasticity and assimilative power, as well as the means, for retaining its identity amid eternal rejuvenescence, and its continuity with the saving act of Christ. And as far as specially concerns the sacraments, these, addressing themselves to the separate persons, are still more decidedly an individual application of grace than the Word. So little do they contradict the peculiar nature of the Protestant faith, that, on the contrary, inasmuch as grace assumes a special form by presenting itself for acceptance to the particular individual, there belongs to faith the possibility and the right, and even the duty, of becoming personal faith (*fides specialis*).[2] What he had said already in the *Resolutiones* to his Theses points in the same direction. Penitence is not of itself transformed into certainty of salvation, but the sure and earnestly-intended salvation must be offered us from outside, in order that faith may confidently lay hold of it, and then, by this laying hold, will the objective earnest gift of salvation become the property of the person and be rendered certain to him. There lies already in this a distinction between *fides* as appropriating trust (*fiducia*) and the fruit of this trust, the assurance of faith (*certitudo salutis*). (See below.)

The faith, accordingly, which lays hold of one's own salvation, is by the *doctrine concerning the Word as a means of grace* more nearly defined thus: It is the apperception of Christ's eternal

---

[1] *Luthers Werke von Walch*, xviii. 2060, 2136.

[2] *Ibid.* ii. 1538, f., i. 1906, xiii. 2504, xvi. 2810, f., *von den Concilien und Kirchen*, in the year 1539.

counsel of redemption, entering into the particularity of time and space for our benefit by means of the Word. The Word, however, is the vehicle, by which appropriating faith becomes conscious of the love of Christ as intending the particular person.

This is probably the ground of the high esteem which Luther has for absolution as applicable to the individual, and accordingly for *private confession,* in connection with which the interest by no means attaches to the confession of sins being made in private, or even in its entering into particulars, but to the private *absolution.* For there most of all the Word clothes itself in a form addressed to the particular person. Neither does the emphasis lie for him upon the *priest* pronouncing the absolution; the right of declaring the forgiveness of sins is not entrusted to a particular order, but to the Church, to be orderly administered. Wherever, then, it is purely announced and reaches the individual, there it takes place by the administration of Christ, there Christ's counsel of grace comes, as it were, into immediate personal contact with man. Hence it may briefly be said: Luther lays the foundation-stone of an evangelical doctrine of the means of grace, in that he conceives of the Word of God, after a lively manner, as a speech of God continually sounding through the world, as it were ever proceeding anew out of His mouth—conceives of it, as it were, sacramentally, but without anything magical. The mere empty doctrine transforms itself for him into deed, into a dealing of God in Christ with man, which continues throughout time, and forms and governs the history of religious life.

How much more does the evangelical doctrine of the means of grace thus already contain than the Romish, with all its pomp of miracles and magic! How the requirements of the whole man, outer and inner, are cared for in it; how both the bodily senses of sight and hearing, as well as that which is perceptible by the senses, are drawn into the service of faith, so that faith, instead of consisting in a merely internal, subjective, deceitful process, passes beyond itself and fastens upon an objectivity independent of the subject, principally upon the Word, but not so as to lose itself in this, or blindly to submit itself to it as an external law, but so as to absorb into itself the matter of the Word, to experience its spiritual power, and to become, by means of the spiritual but receptive act of faith, strengthened,

Luther on Faith and the Sacraments in 1518. 151

founded upon God, and yet at the same time united with the objective world, the world of history!

The basis, which Luther in this manner obtained for the objective Word of God, comprehended in the Scriptures, from nothing else than the personal movement of faith towards certainty, proved besides of explicit advantage for the conception taken of the *sacraments*.

At first, indeed, he assumes towards them a looser position, for the most urgent point with him is jealously to secure the evangelical faith against the Romish conception of the sacraments.[1] If the righteousness of works, which followed particularly from the doctrine of works of satisfaction, threatened directly the free grace of God, and—provided the works were to be the product of faith—only indirectly threatened faith, the magical *opus operatum* of the Romish doctrine of the sacraments touched evangelical faith directly and fatally, because grace thereby assumed a shape or manner of working, for which faith in the narrower sense was superfluous or a matter of indifference, and whereby contact with the mere surface of man was declared to be sufficient for salvation. Hence Luther, in the year 1518, declares the leading principle to be:[2] Whatever may be the case with the sacraments, faith must maintain its rights and honours. He applies it both thus: that without faith no blessing can come to a man from the sacrament, nay:[3] the sacraments do not effect the grace which they signify; not the sacrament, but faith in it justifies; it purifies not because it takes place, but because it is believed (*non sacramentum, sed fides sacramenti justificat; abluit sacramentum non quia fit, sed quia creditur*); and also thus, that he teaches that faith may also receive apart from the sacrament the same thing as in the sacrament, namely, the forgiveness of sins (through faith in the *Word*). "The just shall live by faith and not by works." He turns this saying also against the Romish conception of the sacrament with its *opus operatum*. He never doubted, indeed, that the sacraments bring a blessing, but he stands upon this: There belongs to the sacrament a work of the working God and of receiving man (*opus operantis Dei et accipientis hominis*); for the Almighty God Himself can work

---

[1] *On the Babylonian Captivity.* See above.
[2] *Disputatio pro veritate inquirenda,* last corollary.
[3] In his *Asteriscis* against Eck, 1518.

nothing good in man unless he believes. In the year 1520:[1] In order that the receiving may be blessed, man must bring to it faith, which accordingly does not first come into existence by means of the sacrament, but is effected in general by the preaching of the Word. There was in this, indeed, so much attributed to the Word and faith, that the sure independent significance of the sacraments for faith might become questionable.

What, then, is the position which he finds for the sacraments?

In general, it may be anticipated that the basis of the significance of the external Word for faith will serve him as a prototype for the fitting in of the sacraments also into the economy of salvation. Let us consider in detail his development in reference to the doctrine of the sacraments, from and after 1518. First of all, the *sacrament of the holy Supper*, and we shall be convinced, in considering it, that it is again only the practical interest, the regard to the salvation of the soul, which opens up to him, step by step, the way to the understanding of the matter.

In 1518, he starts from the question, how may one worthily prepare himself for the enjoyment of the holy Supper?[2] He has here nothing to do immediately with theories about the relation of the elements to Christ's body and blood, but with the way to the blessing of the sacrament. In the place of the Romish requirement of freedom from mortal sins in order to a worthy partaking, he desires faith; for "all sins, which are commited in a state of unbelief, are mortal sins." As little does he require a definite measure of accurate dogmatic knowledge concerning the holy Supper. The true preparation is a soul hungering for God's righteousness and grace, and a firm joyful faith.[3] And to this he adheres even at a later period, as *e.g.* the Little Catechism shows.[4] With regard to the benefits which are procured in the holy Supper, these are for him no other than those which are also presented in the Word of God; the forgiveness of sins, life, righteousness, and salvation.

The *second* stage of his doctrinal development, marked by his treatise of the year 1519,[5] concerning the worshipful sacrament of the holy body of Christ and regarding the Fraternities, dis-

[1] *Luthers Werke von Walch*, xix. 1265, f. 1293.
[2] *Von der würdigen Bereitung zum hochheil. Sacr.* xii. 1746-61.
[3] *Luthers Werke von Walch*, xix. 1276, 1301.   [4] *Catech. min*, 382, 10.
[5] *Luthers Werke von Walch*, xix. 522-555. [In this sermon the Communion of the body of Christ is opposed to the Roman Catholic Fraternities.—*Tr.*]

cusses more precisely, what is the proper use, that is, the profit of the sacrament? In it the Lord's Supper is regarded by him as the sacrament of the unity and love (*unitas et charitas*) of the spiritual body of Christ. In order to understand this remarkable and witty[1] writing, which however can only appeal to one portion of the exegetical treasury (namely 1 Cor. x. 16), we must keep in mind that, in 1519, no change had been made in the cultus, nor accordingly in the mass, nor even any breach in the doctrine of transubstantiation, doubts of which are first raised in the treatise on the *Babylonian Captivity*. It is manifest, on the other hand, how harsh is the collision between the sacrifice of the mass, this principal element in the Romish sacrament of the Supper, and the principle of faith.

The above-mentioned writing of the year 1519, contains the attempt to regenerate the Romish mass, as it were, from the heart outwards, by a new casting of it without denying the miracle of transubstantiation, and to shape it conformably to the principle of faith. In this attempt, the ideas, which he expounds more clearly in the following year in his treatise upon the *Freedom of a Christian man*, render him material service. Faith, he says, has and knows the *unio mystica* between the head and the members, and this faith impels also to the communion of love with the brethren. The essence of Christianity consists in this, that Christ, the Head, forms with all the saints and with us one mystical body; believers become through Him a community (*communio*). In the holy Supper there is presented for our contemplation the threefold communion, which constitutes the essence of this spiritual body, namely, first of all, the communion of the head with the members. For by means of the elevation (*elevatio*) of the transformed elements, and the offering (*oblatio*) is represented (his meaning is, not for God, after the manner of a sacrifice, but for us) how *Christ* offers Himself (not the priest Christ), how He out of love transforms Himself into the likeness of man, taking upon Himself their sin and suffering. Thus the mass is the representation of the perfect incarnation of Christ through the representation of His suffering. The transformation of the bread into the body of Christ has for its purpose, to create again, in order to translate it into the present, that the former offering of which was the proof of His vicarious love, which lightly esteemed

---

[1] *Geistvoll*. Witty, in the old sense of the term, is our best equivalent.—*Tr*.

His natural body for the sake of the spiritual body. *In the second place*, there is also represented in it the communion of the members with Him through faith, to wit: how upon the ground of the sacrifice of Christ for us, and His presentation to us for our enjoyment, believers are changed into the likeness of Christ, and enter into fellowship with Christ, by which they are transformed and joined into the spiritual body of Christ. This is symbolized on the one hand by the changing of the bread into the body of Christ, *i.e.* of men into Him. For it is we who are signified by the bread, this unity of many grains, and the wine, this unity of many berries. But on the other hand, also, by the enjoyment of the elements of the sacrament; for there is no more intimate union than that of food which is changed into the body. There is thus a double change, a double transformation, which takes place before our eyes in the mass, the transformation of Christ into us and our misery, in virtue of His *love*, and our transformation into Him by *faith*. Thus the Romish doctrine of transubstantiation is elevated to an ethical significance; the holy Supper shows us how Christ translates Himself into us, we ourselves into Him; the sacrifice of the mass, however, is in this manner transformed into an objective representation of His death of love, for us, not for God; a representation, which Christ certainly effects by means of His presence, but whose substance only contains for the believing eye the same as the living Word. But finally, in the *third* place, the holy Supper also exhibits the communion of love of the members amongst themselves, so that the quickening of *unitas et charitas* is with right described as the whole result of this festival of a symbolical nature. The meaning and significance of this objective procedure is accordingly for him of a merely symbolical nature, even although the apparatus for this symbolical representation is purchased by the miracle of transubstantiation.

With this conception, in which the relation between means and end was so perverted, Luther naturally could not long rest content, especially as the Word had already succeeded in controlling this representation. Luther is here manifestly standing nearer than ever to the Zwinglian doctrine of the sacrament, which also bears a preponderatingly ethical character. He has, in conceiving of the holy Supper as the sacrament of love founded upon faith, struck a chord, which has been more recently too much forgotten, and which belongs to the dogmatical matter to which he at a later period continues to adhere. Every thing, the procedure, the earthly elements and the invisible, which is present to faith, is for him here the sign of the rich and manifold *communio*, which takes place in the spiritual body to the increase of the *unio et charitas*. It would be for him the degradation of faith, and of the finished completeness of the Christianity which is given to faith, if something should be given in the sacrament which could not be received apart from it. Believe, and thou hast enjoyed the sacrament, he says with Augustine, even as he afterwards in general maintains, that the sacraments cannot be without the Word, whilst the Word, if it is believed, saves and offers to us the whole Christ, even His flesh.[1]

But certainly the dogmatical aspect of the holy Supper falls for him very much into the background. He afterwards confesses regarding this time,[2] that nothing would then have been more welcome to him than if some one had taught him that in the sacrament there was simply bread; he had at that time endured a hard conflict, wrestled with and overcome himself, because he had seen that he would have been able to have given the papacy a mighty whack. It is true that even here he holds firmly to the presence, even to the present operation of Christ; the holy Supper, although in comparison with the Word it confers no different gift, is for him even now a sure sign, appointed by God, that he, who has received it according to the will of God, possesses citizenship in the city of God. It is for him, and that through the presence of Christ, letter and seal, manuscript and stamp for the assurance of faith, which ought to exercise and entice itself in the sacrament to pierce beyond the visible, even the body and blood of Christ, into the spiritual body, which is the principal matter. But the unevenness of his standpoint at that time is not to be mistaken, an unevenness which consists in seeking to hold fast the miracle of transubstantiation for the purpose of a mere symbolical representation, which representation, including the presence of Christ, must no doubt assume the form of a pledge of the *unio mystica* by faith, and of a means for quickening love. Farther, there cleaves to this symbolism

---

[1] *That the Words of Christ, "This is my Body" still stand fast*, 1427, *Werke*, xx. 950, ff.

[2] *Briefe*, ii. 577.

the fault, that the body of Christ, present by means of the transformation of the elements, remains invisible, whilst a certifying seal and sign seems to require to belong somehow to the visible world.[1] Evidently it would be more logical to find the sensible element, which is to form the symbol, only in the Word and the elements, but to regard the presence of Christ as rendered certain in the word of promise, which is connected with the elements, —a standpoint, which was first maintained in the *Syngramma Suevicum*.

Luther soon came[2] to the consciousness of that first unevenness, and that in pursuance of the interests of the religious need. If hitherto the sacrifice of the mass was the principal matter, and the *communio* relegated to the background, that writing of the year 1519 was the transition to the application, on the contrary, of the sacrifice of the mass itself to the exhibition of the *communio* of Christ with us and of us with Christ. But what can the mere objective exhibition of the past sacrifice of Christ's love, or even of His present counsel of love, be worth in comparison with this [*communio* itself], if, as is much more the case, Christ does by a new act of love unto and in the soul give Himself to be the property of faith? When this latter conception of the holy Supper has been attained, then is the lesser contained in the greater, the merely objective representation falls away as a mere preliminary to the true participation, everything sinks before the reality of the communion of life with Christ, as in comparison but worthless, symbolical husks.

In the *third stage* of the development of his doctrine of the Supper, dating from the year 1520, the fundamental thought consequently is, that the purpose of the institution is not to be found in the offering of Christ, not even as a mere objective representation, nor in the adoration of the sacrament,[3] but that the presence of Christ in the holy Supper, as well as its institution, has for its object personal *participation*.

This appears[4] at once in the sermon on the New Testament, *i.e.* on the mass, 1520, and on the worthy receiving of the true

---

[1] Yet compare, *über unsichtbare Zeichen*, Erlanger edition, xxx. 337 (*grosses Bekenntniss vom Abendmahl*).

[2] *Luthers Werke von Walch*, xix. 41.

[3] *Vom Anbeten des Sacraments*, 1523. *Ibid.* xix. 1593. *Briefe*, ii. 435. Here he first expressly disputes the denial of the corporeal presence.

[4] *Luthers Werke von Walch*, xix. 1265-1304, July 1520.

and holy body of Christ, 1521;[1] in the same year, "On the abuse of the mass," to the Augustinians at Wittenberg.[2] He now, especially in the first-named writing, enters upon the right way for deducing from the Scriptures the meaning and purpose of the Supper. Going back to the words of institution, he finds that there is nothing in the text about the sacrifice of the mass, but certainly and only of participation, "Take, eat, and drink."[3] Whilst the transfiguration of the Supper into a priestly sacrifice, through the magic of priestly power, must be opposed to the principle of faith, for faith is directed to the reception and not to the offering of Christ; he, in holding to the words of Scripture, unexpectedly finds in the holy Supper a point of contact for faith. The Holy Scriptures point to a benefit (*beneficium*), and not an obligatory performance (*officium*); the holy Supper corresponds to the nature of the new covenant, the covenant of grace, in that the words "take, eat, drink," point to a gift; it claims to be a testament of promise, namely of the forgiveness of sins, and this is certainly intended to be the object of faith. Thus everything assumes a harmonious shape. The emphasis is to be laid upon the word or testament of promise; it is said, " for you, for the forgiveness of sins." The words are the testament, the signs are the sacrament; the testament is of far greater consequence than the sacrament, the words than the signs. Man may be saved without the sacrament, but not without the testament. I can daily enjoy the mass (the holy Supper) in faith. The choice of the sacrament is the testament.[4] By the sign or seal, however, he understands not merely the external elements, but also the present body and blood of Christ. Christ, as it were, deposits His body and blood, by which the forgiveness of sins was gained, in the holy Supper, as if he would say, "As certainly as I have died, as certainly do ye enter upon the inheritance which comes to you in consequence of my death, if ye believe." For a testament denotes a sure, irrevocable will. Upon the word of promise He has hung the noblest of all signs and seals. It is indeed external, but yet it includes and denotes a spiritual thing, His body and blood underneath the signs; for everything must be living which is in this testament. Hence Christ does not give a dead writing and seal, but living words, and His body and

---

[1] *Luthers Werke von Walch*, xii. 1762-71, in the year 1521.
[2] *Ibid.* xix. 1304-1437.   [3] *Ibid.* xix. 1285.   [4] *Ibid.* xix. 1280.

blood, that we may be drawn by means of the outward into the spiritual. But the tasting (participation) is brought by faith, which confides in the testament.[1]

We see, accordingly, that Luther, in pursuance of the principle of faith, came nearer to the holy Supper, in that he sees in it a word of God, but one holding vital intercourse or dealing with us as individuals. The signs, and even the body and blood of Christ, do not give something specially contained in them, which is not to be had otherwise; but they are only the sealing form, the pledge of the gift, by which the substance of the blessing, which lies in the word of promise even in connection with the holy Supper, may become the sooner fixed and be the more certain. *But the substance itself is the forgiveness of sins.* The body and blood of Christ are not properly in themselves regarded as the gift, which is the object of the holy Supper, but they are only the means of assurance, divine and holy pledges of the proper gift, namely, of the forgiveness of sins, with which life and salvation are connected. This, then, is the doctrine to which Luther continued essentially to adhere, and which has become peculiar to the Lutheran Church. The holy Supper is, according to this form of doctrine, a promise of the forgiveness of sins confirmed by signs or seal, wherein not merely bread and wine, but even and emphatically the present body and blood of Christ, form the pledge; and this in such a way that faith receives the same matter both in and outside of the sacrament, the forgiveness of sins, only in the holy Supper with special external certification by means of the God-given pledge. To this the Lutheran confessions adhere. Apol. 201: *Idem effectus est verbi et ritus*, after Augustine's language; *Sacramentum esse verbum visibile, quia—ritus est quasi pictura verbi, idem significans quod verbum, quare idem est utriusque effectus.*

The fact cannot well be overlooked, that in this conception there still remains something of the mode of representation in the year 1519. For the presence of Christ's body and blood is both times only a sign, but not the proper *saving gift* itself, with which the Supper has to do; and the gracious presence has

[1] *Luthers Werke von Walch*, xix. 1974-1278. Similarly also in the year 1525, x. 2658. "Far more depends upon words or the promise than upon the signs; for we can do without the signs, but we cannot dispense with the words; for faith cannot exist without the Divine Word. God's words are His letter, His signs are the stamp and seal of the letter."

the significance of a pledge for something else than itself, namely, the forgiveness of sins. There is progress in this, that Luther now considers the main stress to fall upon the receiving, nay, participation of this pledge, which stands in the closest connection with the benefit of salvation procured by Christ's body and blood, and upon the absorbing of it into the innermost heart. But the difference from the Swiss doctrine, in so far only as the latter confesses also to the reception of a divine gift in the sacrament, does not so much concern the saving gift itself as only the invisible pledge of the same, namely, Christ's body and blood alongside of the Word and elements; whilst the Swiss abide by the significance of the Word and elements as pledges. For the Lutheran theology, however, there still remains the difficulty, how can a non-sensible emblem or pledge give more certainty than a sensible?

Is then, further, Christ's body and blood inseparably connected with the elements for all partakers, and the forgiveness of sins absolutely and inseparably attached to Christ's body and blood? Then he who partook of the holy elements might of course be absolutely *certain* of the forgiveness of sins.[1] But that could not and would not be said, for faith alone receives the blessing, *i.e.* the forgiveness of sins, whilst unbelief dissolves the sacramental *unio* between the elements of bread and wine, together with the body of Christ, and the forgiveness of sins (the unbelieving partakers *Christum ut Salvatorem a se repellunt*, *F. C.* 601, 16). But if it is so, the presence of Christ's body and blood evidently furnishes no stronger assurance of the forgiveness of sins than the Word of Christ, which is united to the elements, and in this way becomes a pledge. *Faith* belongs as much to the sacrament as to the Word, if the promise of the forgiveness of sins, which is connected with it, is not to be rendered precarious. If, accordingly, the presence of Christ's body and blood in the holy Supper add nothing new to the *certification* of the gift, the question becomes necessary, whether then the body and blood of Christ may not perhaps be regarded as the *gift* in the holy Supper, instead of as a mere *means* of certifying the gift of the forgiveness of sins?

Since even without the presence of Christ's body and blood there may be contained in the Supper the seal and pledge of

[1] Dieckhoff, *das heilige Abendmahl*, i. 1854, p. 383, 422.

the forgiveness of sins, as well as the imparting of it (which certainly follows already from the fact, that otherwise Luther must deny to the Word the power of imparting it), Luther's insisting upon this presence would be puzzling, if we were not to suppose that in his religious feeling communion with the body and blood of Christ appeared to him nevertheless to be in itself a saving benefit. He even uses literally the expression, that we are thereby nourished unto eternal life and incorporated into Christ; and the absence of this side of the matter would be, in fact, irreconcilable with the mysticism of his faith. Still, it is only seldom that our resurrection is placed by him in connection with the holy Supper. The reason why Luther did not dare, with more definite development of doctrine, to assign to the body and blood of Christ another significance than that of guarantees, and to account them the proper substance of the gift, was probably the fear that, if the holy Supper imparted, in comparison with the Word, an additional special gift besides the forgiveness of sins, the finished unity and completeness of the Gospel might suffer; hence he, as do also the Confessions, would prefer to attribute also to the Word the communication of Christ's flesh and blood, than furnish the Supper alone with this gift.

Even Melanchthon, in the first edition of his *Loci*, 1521, treats the sacrament as a guarantee or sign, and that without any more minute exposition of the relation between Christ's body and blood and the elements. The sacrament, according to all this, continues to be apprehended by Luther as a promise under the general point of view of the Word of God. It is a Word of God to us made visible, whereby God deals with us. In the administration of word and sacrament, the objective grace enters upon its realization, and is individualized or specialized so as to meet the requirements of faith.

As to what still farther concerns the relation of Christ's body and blood to the elements, in 1519 he characterized it as false subtlety to rack one's brains about it. In the year 1520: Even without transubstantiation the real presence of Christ's body and blood is possible, in that bread remains bread but is appropriated by Christ.[1] This view, propounded by Ignatius, Irenæus, Ruprecht von Deutz, and Pierre d'Ailly, received the name of *Impanatio*, also *Consubstantiatio*,—with no more right than if one were to re-

---

[1] *Luthers Werke von Walch*, xix. 535. Similarly *Captiv. Babyl.*

gard the utterance of Ignatius, the gospels are the σὰρξ Χριστοῦ, as a doctrine of incarnation. At a later period, in the conflict with Zwingle, about 1527, he inclines to the view of Gabriel Biel, who held the co-subsistence [*ein Nebeneinander*] of the elements and of the body of Christ, but in close connection. In this he also allows a synecdoche; the part is set for the whole, or the containing (*continens*), the bread for the contained (*pro contento*), as cradle and child.

For the rest, Luther does not think of Christ as ascending and descending for the Supper. This he can dispense with, since he regards Christ as exalted, even according to His humanity, to the right hand of God. Further, Christ is present, according to him, in the Supper with His *glorified* body, and no emphasis is to be laid upon the passage where, in order to make sure the real presence, he charges Melanchthon, as to his negotiations with Bucer, to maintain that we, in the Holy Supper, *dentibus Christum laceramus*. For that is only said by him παρὰ συνεκδόχην. Christ's body is now, according to him, exalted to heaven and glorified, nay, of a spiritual and divine nature, according to its essence, even from the beginning.[1] Christ fills everything; in the Word also He is certainly everywhere. But the reason why the presence of Christ, who is exalted to the right hand of God, is conceivable in the Holy Supper, is dependent upon his view of the person of Christ, which we shall afterwards consider. Quite as erroneous would be the opinion, that Luther does not conceive of the whole Christ as present, but only His body, on the ground that it is certainly the latter that possesses for him the most immediate significance as a pledge, and that Luther even sometimes emphasizes Christ's body apart from His soul and person.[2] For even in the writing addressed to the Bohemians, 1523, he only censures the hypercritical inquiry, how the soul and spirit of Christ, Divinity and Trinity, are in the sacrament? but he also says, that Christ is never separated from His body and blood.[3] A separation of the body of Christ from His person would be also in contradiction with the fundamental idea of his Christology.[4] Further, Luther does not teach that the sacramental *unio* has a miraculous effect

[1] Compare *Luthers Werke von Walch*, xx. 1090. Köstlin's *Luthers Lehre*, ii. 162, 512. *F. Conc.* 604, 42.
[2] Dieckhoff, as cited, 405. Köstlin, ii. 109, f., 514, f., 162.
[3] *Vom Anbeten des Sacrament*, xix. 1616.
[4] Compare *F. Conc.* 607, 611, § 32.

upon the elements themselves, altering them physically; rather do they remain what they were, and hence there is no other miracle to be spoken of than Christ's miraculous love communicating itself to us. A change in the elements would lead again to transubstantiation. The connection of Christ with the elements is accordingly not mutual, as if the elements now held Him fast or bound Him passively to themselves, but it is the will of the love of Christ by which they become means of grace. Finally, he always adhered to this, that the unbelievers receive no blessing, and if he nevertheless allows that the unworthy partakers receive Christ's body and blood, it is only because he does not regard the body and blood as itself a saving gift, but only as the pledge thereof. If, accordingly, one would so shape the doctrine of the Supper that the body and blood of Christ become the saving gift, then, in order not to let the saving gift become the portion of the unworthy, he must suffer the declaration to fall, that even the unworthy partake of Christ's body and blood. For it was never his meaning, to ascribe to the body and blood of Christ any other than a salutary effect.

Let us now turn to his doctrine regarding *holy baptism*.[1] Here also, in the first stage of his doctrinal development with respect to baptism in general, he particularly emphasizes faith, which he even assumes into the sacrament as constitutive. The sign, the immersion, and the rising again from the water, signifies the drowning of the old man and the rising of the new,[2] not, however, as an immediate effect of the external act in the moment of baptism, but the baptism denotes what ought to be a continuous dying and resurrection until the death of this body. He very early guards himself against a magical over-estimation of the immediate effect of the baptismal act. Sin remains even after baptism, conflict and struggle only rightly begin afterwards. If one thinks with the Romish Church, that baptism forthwith renders the man perfect, he implants security against sin, and, when sin and guilt nevertheless disturb us afterwards, doubt of the divine power of baptism. "The spiritual birth takes its rise

---

[1] Of the year 1518: *Sermon vom Sacrament der Taufe, Luthers Werke von Walch*, x. 2592-2611; *De Circumcisione*, xix. 1720, f. Of the year 1520: *Theologische Abhandlung von der Taufe des Gesetzes, Johannis und Christi*, x. 2612, f.; vii. 980, f.; *Predigt von der heiligen Taufe*, 1535, *Luthers Werke von Walch*, x. 2512, ff.

[2] *Ibid.* x. 2593.

indeed in baptism, proceeds and increases; but only in the last day is its significance fulfilled; only in death are we rightly lifted out of baptism by the angels into eternal life."[1] Still, baptism is not a mere sign, not a mere summoning of us to conversion. The sign is a sign of God, a word of God to the baptized one, which is at the same time deed, in that God becomes one with him in a gracious and comforting covenant.[2] Thus, in 1518, he conceives of baptism, as in 1519 of the holy Supper, as a *covenant*, and indeed as a new covenant. The covenant is mutual, not merely imperative, like the old.[3] On the part of man, there is a desire to die unto sin,—to be made a new creature on the last day. God accepts the desire, and from that moment begins, on His part, to make thee a new creature in baptism, and to pour out His grace to mortify nature and sin, and to prepare for the resurrection. Further, in baptism thou bindest thyself to continue after this manner, and to mortify sin more and more even unto death. On the other hand, God binds Himself to thee, not to impute the sins which are in thy nature after baptism; even a fall shall not hurt thee, if thou enterest again into the covenant, and risest again. For by virtue of the sacrament and the covenanting the sins are already no more[4] (that is to say, before God, in an eternal manner). Baptism, however, as the sign of God, informs us of this eternal manner. Thus sin is wholly forgiven in baptism, not that it is not there, but that it is not imputed. Everything, however, still depends upon this, that it is firmly believed that the sacrament does not merely signify death and resurrection, but certainly commences both,—effects, and places us in, the covenant with God, in virtue of which we, although still sinful, are pure and guiltless before God, and able to fight against sin. For baptism extends its influence through the whole life, even to the last day. This, then, is the fundamental understanding of Luther, which he never again gave up, that baptism is not something isolated and passing away, although the external act "soon takes place," but that in the particular moment of time and space the eternally faithful saving counsel of God concerning the individual baptized comes to its historical revelation,—the preventing gracious will of God, in which the new man, as it were, has his pre-existence, since nothing can

[1] *Sermon vom Sacrament der Taufe*, x. 2596. [2] *Ibid.* x. 2598, ff.
[3] x. 2599, ff. [4] x. 2600, 2602.

come into existence [*werden*] if it does not already in a certain sense exist [*ist*]. This gracious will the believer lays hold of as holding good for him specially and as sure, and only to be rendered fruitless by persistent unbelief.

Thus holy baptism receives an infinitely higher significance than in the Romish doctrine; for whilst the power of forthwith wholly abolishing sin is indeed denied to it, it is nevertheless as a covenant of grace, in spite of sin, the abiding basis of holy childhood, which must first be laid before the moral work of overcoming evil can proceed. Since a return can always be made to this baptismal covenant by means of repentance, it contains all the power which the Romish doctrine distributes along a series of other sacraments—confirmation, absolution, and extreme unction. Baptism contains even more than the two former, by means of the continuance, guaranteed by it, of prevenient grace. And whilst the *extrema unctio*, whose substance most resembles it otherwise, only sanctifies for death, baptism sanctifies the life subsequent to itself to a life of holiness, in which it becomes a fruitful principle, whilst, according to the Romish doctrine, baptismal grace is almost, in fact only, there in order to disappear again, at the same time burdening men, who universally fall again into sin, with the greater guilt.

More difficult, however, than the doctrine of baptism in general was *that of infant baptism*. There is scarcely anything so constant amongst the fanatical parties of this time as the attacks upon infant baptism, *i.e.* the regular ecclesiastical administration of baptism in general. It was not expressly commanded in Scripture; again, it also stood in contradiction to the principle of faith. For, since children could not believe, it led unavoidably, if it was to have any effect, to a magical *opus operatum*. If baptism even without faith was a truly valid sacrament, then there was a breach of the sentence otherwise so strongly emphasized by Luther, that the blessing of the sacrament could only become the property of man by personal faith. We saw what a deep impression the tenets of the heavenly prophets made upon Melanchthon.[1] The appeal to the custom of the Church and to the sentence of Augustine, that original sin renders the sacrament necessary also for children, could not

[1] *Corp. reform.* i. 514, 534. De Wette, *Briefe*, ii. 124-128, of the 13th January of the year 1522, to Melanchthon.

satisfy him, so long as the lawfulness of infant baptism, and that indeed in virtue of the principle of faith, was not demonstrated. Luther clearly discerned the dangerous bearing of the Anabaptist tenets, the dissolution of the idea of a national Church, and of the union of the principle of Christianity with the family, and the threatening of the whole pedagogic aspect of the earthly Church. He sees that Anabaptism, in seeking an earthly Church composed purely of the regenerate, aims at a separation of the leaven from the lump to be operated on by it, a separation which must be as dangerous for the spiritual health of the "saints" as for the increase of the kingdom of God upon earth. But how then does he doctrinally combat this tendency? The following alternative illustrates his difficulty: If faith is not yet present for the reception of the sacrament, how can the latter give that blessing as an external act, since the man is not yet personally accessory to it by means of the believing reception of it?[1] Contrariwise, if faith must be presupposed in order to baptism, and the latter effects its blessing, according to the universal canon of evangelical doctrine, only through the mediation of faith, there is indeed no threatening of *external* magic, but, apart from the question whether unconscious children can already receive baptism with real faith, this question arises, whence is this faith *before* baptism to originate? Certainly by means of the Holy Ghost, but He works through the means of grace; "faith cometh by preaching" (Romans x. 17); the internal springing up of faith apart from the means of grace would accordingly be spiritualistic, and lead to an *internal* magic of grace, to a very doubtful kinship to the Anabaptist doctrine of the dispensableness of the external means of grace. The Romish Church does not come here into straits: it lays no weight upon the personal reception of salvation, but appeals to the *corpus mysticum* of the Church, whose faith serves vicariously upon its own prayer for the benefit of the child.[2] Luther cannot make use of this for the decisive point. At first, indeed, he says,—The little children, who do not understand the promise of God, and so have

[1] Hence he said in the writing to the Bohemian Waldensians, 1523, xix. 1625, "It would be better to baptize no child anywhere than to baptize without faith."
[2] *De Captiv. Bab.*, xix. 87, 88; similarly in the year 1523, xix. 1625: The young children are, through the faith and prayer of the Church, purified from unbelief and the devil, and gifted with faith and accordingly baptized; also xii 1757-58; on the other hand, compare the following note.

not baptismal faith, are helped out by the faith of others, of those who bring them to baptism. Upon the prayer of the believing Church presenting the child, God, to whom all things are possible, changes the little child by means of faith infused, purifies and renews it, and thus it still holds, both that the baptism is not in vain, as well as that the sacraments work only in virtue of faith, but without faith do absolutely nothing, in accordance with the sentence already expressed, *non sacramentum, sed fides sacramenti justificat*. Still, however, the faith of the petitioning church is not regarded by him as a substitution in the sense of a compensation, but as an occasion for the springing up of faith in the child itself, in favour of which he appeals especially to the power of prayer.[1] Hence he could, even already in the treatise upon the Babylonian captivity, hold, even in respect of infant baptism, to the general sentence,—Where God's promise is, there each one stands for himself, and faith is demanded of each; each one also will give account for himself, and bear his own burden; I cannot receive the sacrament or hear the gospel for another, I cannot believe for another.[2]

This standpoint is liturgically expressed in Luther's *Instruction as to the way of administering Baptism*, 1521, and in his *Taufbüchlein*, 1523.[3] There the formula still sounds similarly to the Romish; take the sign of the holy cross; receive the faith of the holy commandments, whilst the baptismal method of 1523 points out the place for the prayer of the congregation, "that God would pour out His grace upon His servant (the child to be baptized), that he might become worthy of coming to the grace of baptism." The exorcism, still very minute in 1523, appears much shortened, and only in the way of being indicated in the baptismal formula of the year 1524.[4] The godparents however come forward as the substitutionary mouthpiece of the child to be baptized, who through them prays for the gift of baptism, and even before baptism confesses faith in the apostolic creed.

This representation, however, according to which children come to the baptismal act already believing in virtue of the prayers of the congregation, for whose sake faith is infused, has

---

[1] "The faith of another is of no avail for salvation, except in the way of helping to personal faith," xi. 2040-42, 2277 and 673.
[2] *Ibid.*, xix. 52, 53.   [3] x. 2622, f. 2624.   [4] x. 2632, f.

in it much that is discordant. For the faith of the Church, even when conceived as working faith in the baptized one, is still by no means the personal faith of the baptized, and the baptism which takes place on the ground of this faith of the Church is still, for all that is said to the contrary, not essentially anything else than baptism upon the ground of the future faith of the child,—which he rejects.[1] Further, how is faith to arise in the child, if to faith belongs preaching, and yet the understanding of the preaching is not yet possible to the child ? In reference to this, he in 1519 (in his *Commentary on the Epistle to the Galatians*[2]) pointed to the omnipotence of the Holy Spirit, unto whom nothing is deaf, to the Word of God spoken on the occasion of the baptismal act, which outwardly strikes upon the ear, whilst the Holy Spirit may work inwardly, and finally to the greater susceptibility of children for the Word, since they are not, like adults, so often antagonistic and encased in alien elements. But this means that through baptism itself, as a proclamation, is faith first effected, whilst he had required faith *before* baptism: hence he afterwards resiles from this position. But again, what sort of *effect* would be left to baptism as a sacrament, if the prayers of the Church produce a faith, which already renews and transforms and confesses the apostolic creed *with the forgiveness of sins?* In order to escape all these difficulties, and in order to avoid inadmissible anticipations, a double faith would require to be maintained, a faith before baptism which is nothing more than natural *susceptibility* for God and His Spirit, and a faith which consciously and personally appropriates baptismal grace. In fact, Luther sometimes compares the faith of children before baptism to the faith of adults in sleep,[3] conceives of it accordingly not as an act, but as a condition (*fides habitualis*), as a latent power of reception which is by baptism set in activity. But this expedient threatens to deprive faith of its evangelical stamp and to degrade it to the [Roman] Catholic *obicem non ponere*. Even a mere condition of being *willing* to receive grace we cannot conceive of in the case of the unconscious child. If, moreover, the right of infant baptism is founded upon the praying, faith-working faith of the Church or godparents, then the vali-

---

[1] *Ibid.*, xix. 1625, of the year 1523.
[2] Erlanger edition of Luther's Works, *opp. lat.* iii. 258.
[3] *Luthers Werke von Walch*, xi. 678, § 39.

dity of the sacrament would be dependent upon their intention, which may be be awanting and is accordingly uncertain,—to say nothing of this, that a power of internal magic would belong to this prayer, if it were able immediately in the moment of baptism, without any co-operation of the child, certainly to produce faith in it. If, however, it is said that that faith necessary for baptism is only the universal susceptibility for Christian salvation, as it already exists in every man by nature, then we would have a faith which all men have, even in their natural condition. But fortunately, in Matthew xxviii., faith is not required before baptism, so as to make baptism before faith invalid, but in Mark xvi. faith is only required for baptism, so that the latter may work salvation.

Upon this point Luther's representation fastens in its *third stage*, in which his doctrine of infant baptism reaches its completion.

The difficulties not yet solved led him, in the year 1528, in opposition to the still clamant opposition of the Anabaptists, who laid such stress upon faith before baptism, that they did not baptize where they did not discern faith, and even declared baptism without faith on the part of the baptized one to be invalid, to new and comprehensive investigations in the letter to two parish ministers upon Anabaptism, and in the Large Catechism, to which is to be added his sermon on holy baptism, 1535.[1] He still held indeed to this, that it could not be proved that the children have no faith. The Church may hope, that its prayer regarding the faith of the children is effectual. We bring the children hither in the hope that God gives them faith to receive the blessing of the sacrament. But whilst he had hitherto tacitly taken it for granted that baptism without faith is unjustifiable and inadmissible, and even that faith is co-constitutive of a rightly administered baptism, according to the sentence: *non sacramentum sed fides sacramenti justificat;* he now goes back to the divine institution of baptism, and its divine validity resting thereupon, whence results the relative independence in its essence of baptism from faith. After, as before, he holds to this, that its blessing reaches the *person* only through faith.

[1] *Ibid.*, xvii. 2643, ff., especially 2667, § 53, ff.; x. 2513-43, especially 2536-2582.

It is again the return to the Holy Scriptures which dispels for him the darkness more and more. In that he now bases baptism principally upon the commandment and ordinance of God, and will not treat it as a human work, nor base it upon our faith and our worthiness, as if it were not enough that God orders it thus; as if, on the contrary, the work of God must first be strengthened by faith, and as if this work of God could not be of any avail until our faith comes to its aid,—the chief difficulty of infant baptism has vanished for him. He now sees that it is not faith which makes the sacrament, but that this is rather there as the object of faith, which it must sooner or later lay hold of; and this is followed up by the distinction between the *essence* of baptism (to which no human operation belongs, but only an element and the Word of God) and its *power*, between its *vaildity* and its *beneficial effect*.[1] The latter he continues to regard as dependent upon faith, not that it deserves it, but appropriates it. On the other hand, the validity of baptism stands fast for him, whether faith is already there or not. My faith does not make baptism, but appropriates it; it is not dependent upon our faith, but on the Word of God. Baptism is a divine revelation, nay, a dealing of the present Lord with and towards the child of a prevenient character, hence also valid in itself upon God's side as a presentation of grace and reception into divine childhood, as independently of the presence of faith in the child itself as of faith on the part of the priest, the godparents, or the Church. He teaches accordingly: The Anabaptists say:[2] " Thou wast baptized when thou wast yet a child and hadst not believed; therefore thy baptism is nothing." But that means: If thou dost not believe, God's word and sacrament is nothing; but if thou believest, it is something; those who do not believe receive only water, and therefore must be baptized again when they begin to believe. We must rather however make a proper distinction against these erring spirits, that it is one thing to receive the proper *baptism*, and another thing to get its proper influence and use. We may not despise baptism nor repudiate it, although it is received and given without faith.[3] To build baptism upon personal faith, or the faith of him who baptizes, is to build upon sand, is to devolve a work which belongs to the Divine Majesty upon a creature;

---

[1] *Cat. maj.*, 545, § 47-53; xvii. 2667.
[2] *Ibid.*, x. 2525, of the year 1535.   [3] x. 2577.

not only does it make baptism uncertain, as is the baptism of the Anabaptists, who say that only believers are to be baptized, and yet never know whether the baptized one does believe, but it is also forbidden and condemned.[1] Thus so little stress lies for him now upon the question, whether faith is already in the child, that he will hand over the question, whether children believe, to the doctors, and only demands the firm maintenance of the truth, that the Lord calls children to Himself, and will have them baptized. Has baptism taken place without faith, it is not on that account to be repeated, but rather it remains valid, and it is then to be said: hast thou not yet believed, then believe now.[2] He thus regards the decisive weight as falling only upon this, that personal faith, whenever it may arise, is built upon the basis of baptism, in which objective grace specializes or individualizes itself, and does not spring up upon the ground of human imagination and assumption of salvation, but of the prevenient grace of God, which is objectively presented and revealed in the sacrament of baptism. He distinguishes himself from the Waldensians, who only allow the promise of future grace to come to the baptized infant in baptism, and who baptize upon the ground of future faith, but does so at present only in such a way, that he allows the effect of baptism to commence in the child already in the baptismal act, correspondingly to the measure of lively susceptibility,[3] without, however, seeking to define how far this extends,—a matter which had become to him of secondary importance, since in any case it remains true that the baptismal blessing is so rich, that only the complete life of the Christian can completely appropriate and manifest it.

Luther's doctrine of the sacraments had now reached its perfection. If consequently the requirement of faith *before* reception is only definitely made in connection with the holy Supper,

[1] *Ibid.*, x. 2584. *Cat. maj.* 544-48.
[2] *Cat. maj.* 545, f.
[3] This susceptibility, indeed, he terms faith, but upon the occasion of the Wittenberg Concord, he expresses himself more definitely upon the point thus (1537): "It must not be thought that the children have understood (the Word): but there are the movements and inclinations to believe the Lord Christ and to love God, in some measure similar to the movements of those who otherwise have faith and love; and it is in this way that we desire to be understood when we say that the children have personal faith," xvii. 2557, f. This is very similar to Calvin's *fides seminalis*, *Instt.* iv. cap. 16, § 19, 20, and very different from the *fides specialis*, the necessity of which in addition is jealously guarded.

that fact is intimately allied with this, that in baptism, as the act of reception into the kingdom of God, the prevenient grace of God must have its place. For the rest, in the case of both sacraments, the validity is quite as independent of faith, as the appropriation of the real blessing is dependent upon it, so that the opposition to the *opus operatum* is maintained. In reference to the connection between divine grace and the external sign by means of the Word, Luther often speaks as if by the power of the Word the water of baptism was interpenetrated by a divine essence and became another thing, mighty to accomplish an unutterable effect, mighty to beget pure and holy men, thoroughly heavenly and divine; nay, he even says that Christ's crimson blood is mingled with the white water, so we are dipped even into the blood of Christ.[1] This approximates to the Thomist view, according to which God Himself has set a spiritual power in the water, whereby it has power to wash away sin. But that Luther will not have us understand these passages doctrinally, but figuratively and rhetorically, is a conclusion we may draw from his Schmalkaldic Articles,[2] where this Thomist view, and the magical operation of the external element, is expressly rejected. Neither was it adopted by the Church. But certainly, on the other hand, Luther does not think of the relation between grace and the water as so loose that the will of God simply assists upon the occasion of baptism by man in water, but baptism, *i.e.* the form of baptism, the sign and the action is, in his view, a word, or a deed of God; hence he names baptism also the Word of God connected with immersion, the bath set in the Word of God.[3]

To draw a farther parallel between the sacraments and the Word, there is offered to unbelief in both the very same as to faith, not merely something external, but also something inward and spiritual. But the unbeliever does not receive it into the inward parts, but refuses it, although he received word and sign even as the believer.

Luther holds fast, in general, to the necessity of baptism in order to salvation, but in reference to the children of Christians who have died unbaptized, he says: the holy and merciful God will think kindly upon them. What He will do with them,

---
[1] x. 2538; vii. 1018-22.   [2] A. S. iii. 5, p. 325.
[3] [The idea is—as a jewel is set in gold, or a picture in a frame.—*Tr.*]

The Ethical side of the Controversy.

He has revealed to no one, that baptism may not be despised, but has reserved to His own mercy; God does wrong to no man.[1] In general, and not as applicable merely to the children of Christians, he says: God has not bound Himself to the sacraments so as not to be able to do otherwise, without the sacrament. So I hope, that the good and gracious God has something good in view for those who, not by any guilt of their own, are unbaptized.[2]

III. *The Ethical side of the controversy with the fanatics. The office of the ministry and Church order.*

Even as Luther, in opposition to Carlstadt and the fanatics, maintains the Word of God and the two Sacraments to be essential means of grace or the treasure which the Church is to distribute, so also does he, in virtue of the principle of faith, take up the defence of the *regular office of the ministry* in the Church, and affirms it against the opposite errors. For as certainly as God has given to the Church the treasures of grace in the Word and Sacrament, as certainly does He desire their orderly use and their application. The Church, he tells the Anabaptists, has received divine *plenary power* to distribute the Gospel and the sacraments, and not less the *duty* of caring by means of both for the extension of the salvation designed to be universal. Let right and duty, however, be united in thought, and there arises the idea of *office*. The Church has received from God the office of preaching and of the administration of the sacraments, together with the promise that God will be present with His Spirit, and change the actions of the Church in His name into divine actions by means of the Church. Now, if the Church has received this plenary power and duty in order to be exercised, it is also its duty and right to care for the maintenance of these functions, and to devolve them upon individuals. Ordination signifies nothing else than as if the bishop instead of, or in personation of, the whole Church should take out of the multitude one out of those who have all equal power, and command him to administer this same power for the others.[3] That for this there should be selected particular persons, namely, those who are aptly qualified, is in no contradiction to the principle of faith

[1] xxii. 872. [2] xxi. 1443.
[3] *An den Christlichen Adel*. See above, x. 296, ff.

and the universal priesthood, "for precisely where something belongs to all together, not every one, who considers himself taught of God, is at liberty to take upon himself this office, no one is at liberty to thrust himself forward and take upon himself that which belongs to us all." But he does not suffer his antagonism to the sacrament of episcopal ordination to be weakened by his opposition to the fanatics.[1] The individual *persons* do not require to establish any *immediately* divine call to the public office of the ministry, neither by means of sacramental ordination nor by the immediate call of the Spirit. In the place of both he sets the *regular* call (*rite vocari*) by the congregation, to whom the office has been entrusted, or by those constitutionally entrusted with the counsels of the congregation. In so far, then, as the installation of persons into office is effected through human intervention, errors may be made and unworthy persons called. Nevertheless the regular call by means of man is to be regarded as the divine will and call, as in the case of every delegated office.[2] "He who will come out as a minister must show a regular call, or else a miracle; wherever there is no stand made upon the call (*vocatio*), there would be left in the end no more a church." He declares to the Anabaptists; "Whoever comes without a call, is a crawling fellow and an assassin, ay, a messenger of the devil. For the Holy Ghost does not crawl, but flies down openly from heaven. The serpents crawl, the doves fly. By the regular call the devil may be made timid. I would not take the wealth of the world in exchange for my doctorship, by which I am regularly called."[3]

What, then, is Luther's position in reference to the question, whether the immediate divine commission to the Church is only to care in general for the maintenance of the *functions* of the office? or, whether also the manner according to which the exercise of the office is devolved permanently, *e.g.* for life, upon

---

[1] Compare, *That a Christian congregation has the right and power of judging all doctrine and of calling teachers*, x. 1795, ff. *Sendschreiben an Rath und Gemeine der Stadt Prag*, x. 1814, in the year 1523, and x. 1861, f.; v. 1505, f.

[2] x. 1861; xix. 1622, f. of the year 1523; compare *de certitudine vocat. den Commentar z. Galat. Erlanger Ausgabe*, i. 31, 32.

[3] xx. 2074, ff, *von den Schleichern u. Winkelpredigern*, 1531, and *Auslegung des 82. Psalms*, 1530; v. 1026, ff.

particular office-bearers, is divinely instituted?[1] Höfling only allows a mediate open command of God to set apart particular servants in word. It may certainly be adduced against this view that Luther says: Christ has appointed some with a special command to be overseers of the Church; it is divine order and institution,[2] that in every town there should be bishops, or at least one.[3] But, on the other hand, he bases the right and duty of administering the Word of God generally upon the priesthood of all believers,[4] and for the proof of the administration of the office of the Church by particular separated men, he points[5] partly to the variety in the Christian graces, which he regards as the work and appointment of Christ; partly to the necessity that everything should take place regularly and honourably, even as also in other respects natural differences of age and sex, and the like, are not negatived or ignored by Christian order; and finally to this, that by means of this orderly ecclesiastical separation of particular men, the Word of God can be sounded everywhere freely, openly, certainly, and without adulteration, even as Christ desires it.[6] Hence it may without doubt be said, that Luther does not regard the appointment of permanent preachers as dogmatically necessary; but, on the other hand, it is not merely what is dogmatically necessary which he regards as divine, but also that which in given circumstances is morally necessary.—But even, granting that Luther's views were in favour of the immediately divine institution of a special office of the ministry, in favour of allowing an immediate command to the Church to devolve its office upon permanent office-bearers, still that would not by any means be "to speak of an original dualism in the Church, implanted in the congregation, which

[1] Höfling, *Kirchenverfassung.* Köstlin, *Luthers Lehre von der Kirche,* 1853. Pfisterer, *Luthers Lehre von der Beichte,* 1857.

[2] xiii. 2717, § 38.

[3] xix. 1334; xx. 2084.

[4] Cf. Köstlin, *Luthers Theologie,* ii. 126-135 (on the powers of the universal priesthood). In cases of necessity all Christians may exercise all the functions of the clergy, x. 1857, f.; xi. 1507; but order requires the devolving of the office upon particular persons, to support which 1 Cor. xiv. 16, 30 is made use of.

[5] v. 1505. Degrees in the spiritual office are not *juris divini,* xvii. 1442, f.; xvi. 2792.

[6] iii. 2566; x. 488, 1897, f., of the year 1543; xi. 1262; xii. 711; xiii. 1283; xvi. 2793; xvii. 1442.

(dualism) is the proper root and basis of the Church."¹ For the Church he regards in every case as that which devolves the office, and which is consequently presupposed by it, and only Christ's office precedes the Church. The latter, however, has certainly along with its birth also the divine power and obligation of office. The congregation, as an unity, not as a dualism, commits the office to individuals, and this first occasions their *difference* from the others, but no *dualism*.² Luther seeks that the congregations, even in matters concerning the administration of the means of grace, should not be reduced to a passive and merely submissive position in respect of the office-bearers; he will not have freedom destroyed by order.³ He ascribes to the congregation the right and duty of proving and watching over the doctrine and official administration of the office-bearers.⁴ The difference, accordingly, between office-bearers and non-official members is only secondary and derivative, founded in the unity which the congregation forms. For its manifold task in respect of the world, it must decree a plurality of offices; which it, the unity, devolves upon different individual members, that it may become master of the chaos. To the congregation there further belongs the right and duty of reformation. Where there is no other way, it must itself do away with errors of a radically destructive nature, even apart from, ay, and in opposition to, the existing officials; and must alter the ecclesiastical order brought down by it from the past, when this is directed against the foundations upon which the whole congregation is supported. Accordingly those have Luther not for them, but against them, who say that every ecclesiastical action which takes place without and against the will of the office-bearers is unwarranted or void of blessing. Where, then, would be the Reformation itself? This becomes more particularly evident when we consider Luther's doctrine of *the keys and of the power of the keys*.

The power of the keys⁵ includes, according to the Romish idea,

---

¹ Against Klieforth, Löhe, &c.   Cf. Pfisterer, see above, 131, ff.   Köstlin, *Luthers Lehre von der Kirche*, 77, ff.

² v. 1503. Least of all does the congregation first take its rise through the office of the Church, but originally only through the office of Christ.

³ x. 303; cf. p. 174, note 4.   ⁴ xi. 1886.

⁵ *Sermon vom Bann*, 1519, and *Disputation vom Bann*, 1521, xix. 1099 and 1121; *von der Beichte*, 1520; xix. 918; *Kirchenpostille vom Tag Pauli u. Petri*, 1524, xi. 3070; *von den Schlüsseln*, 1530, xix. 1121-90; *von der Beichte an Sic-*

the plenary power of absolution and excommunication, and that in virtue of judicial authority. Church government also, and the right of imposing laws, that is to say, legislation and administration, are reckoned as belonging to it in addition to the judicial office. Luther excludes from the power of the keys the judicial element, government and legislation; but extends it on the other hand so that it is regarded by him as the power to teach and apply the Gospel. The keys are entrusted properly, not to an order, but to the congregation; for it exists perpetually upon earth, and in it the Divine Spirit undoubtedly dwells; it is only of it that one is sure that it has the keys. In accordance with that energetic conception of the Word of God, he regards all preaching of the pure Gospel as already a dealing of God with man; the regularly called servant of the Church receives the keys entrusted to it, in order to use them in a regular manner in the name and by commission of the Church, and to dispense the Gospel to individuals, by which accordingly a dealing of God takes place with the individual. It is by no means his meaning that all preaching (absolution is included under it) has been devolved upon the public office of preacher or restricted to it. Not only does he say, in his earlier years:[1] "This power of forgiving sins is nothing else than that the priest, and even if it be necessary every Christian man, may say to another, 'Thy sins are forgiven thee;' and in this any Christian does quite as much as the priest, even although it were a woman or child, young or old;" but also in 1537[2] he says: "This right and liberty (of rebuking sins and preaching forgiveness) is possessed wherever two or three are gathered together in His name, that they may announce and assure to one another consolation and the forgiveness of sins. God accordingly pours out upon Christians much more abundantly, and fills every corner for them full of the forgiveness of sins, that they may find it at home in the house, in the field, in the garden, and wherever one meets another." And in the year 1538: Every brother may rebuke his neighbour, and

---

kingen, xix. 1015, f.; *von der Kraft des Bannes*, in the year 1518, xix. 1088; *Gutachten an den Nürnberger Rath de Wette*, iv. 482; *Artikel von der Christlichen Kirchengewalt*, xix. 1190,

[1] Köstlin, *Luthers Theologie*, ii. 520-524, ff.

[2] *Predigt über das Evangelium Matthäi*, xviii. 19, f.; xi. 1042, f. and of the year 1530. xix. 1085, f. Cf. Köstlin, *Luthers Lehre von der Kirche*, p. 29, and *Luthers Theologie*, ii. 524, f.

that is the wielding of the keys. The keys belong to the Church, to the Christian people; only he will not have the public office of the ministry thereby brought into contempt, or confusion occasioned.[1] Although confession is no privilege of the priest, nor his absolution any different in effect from that of a layman, which must be reserved for cases of necessity; still, for the sake of order, one should keep by the regular ministerial office, and confession should be conserved as a Church ordinance especially before the sacrament of the altar, although it is not a compulsory ordinance, does not constitute a sacrament, and no ultimately authoritative judicial sentence is connected with it. Whoever is in spiritual distress ought not to take his stand upon his internal experience, nor seek to continue alone, nor wait for immediate divine illumination; but should keep by the congregation, to which, along with the Word of God, absolution is entrusted, in such a way that He will deal through it.[2] Where the word announcing the forgiveness of sins is uttered by the congregation, to which it has been given, or in its name, there is real absolution, —grace is presented and conferred. But absolution itself he does not regard as a mere impotent wishing for one the forgiveness of sins, still less as the mere assurance that, if a man repent, his sins are forgiven him; but it is the free presentation of grace to the individual as meant in earnest by God, in order that man may lay hold of it in penitent faith. For the object, in which faith is to be placed, must first of all be presented to faith. Hence he desires to see the absolution unconditionally expressed, as valid on the side of God, not because or provided one believes already before absolution, but in order that he may believe.[3] But it is of course understood that "whoever does not accept it has nothing" so that the *possession* of absolution is indeed limited by faith. *Who* is in possession of justifying faith, which no one sees, that must indeed remain uncertain; hence we cannot speak of a judicial act concerning the possession of the forgiveness of sins. But the keys of the kingdom of heaven are not on that account uncertain or slipping keys, but fitting keys, even although the ungodly

---

[1] viii. 445-448; in the year 1536, vi. 2119, *A. Sm.* 345, 24; in the year 1539, xvi. 2791; in the year 1545, xvii. 1345.
[2] x. 16.
[3] xix. 1172-1176; xxi. 424, f.; xiii. 2074; cf. Köstlin, *Luthers Theologie*, i. 523, cf. i. 218, ii. 435. De Wette, *Briefe*, iv. 482.

should make grace of none effect.¹ Here, too, he points out how the doctrine of the papists, though seeming more, offers less. Their key seeks to be judicial, but it misses; for they do not say, "I certainly absolve thee, only believe," but, "Art thou penitent and pious? then I absolve thee; if not, I absolve thee not;" notwithstanding that one can never be adequately penitent.² Thou hast just so much as thou believest.³ If a man believes without repentance he only increases his sin; and since the Church is under the obligation of guarding against this, it becomes its duty to condition its ordinary absolution upon its being able to assume that the man is sorry for his sin, and does not lay hold of grace of mere wantonness, but is in the regular way of the acceptance of salvation and understands the nature of absolution, namely, that it is only there for the purpose of being laid hold of by penitent faith.⁴ Therefore, although the confessional is not commanded, the Church must require the confession of sins before it can proceed to absolution. But a long register of sins is no part of the confession; the desire for the forgiveness of sins is already a confession of sins.⁵ It is at the same time good, but optional, to mention by name sins which are specially burdensome.⁶ Auricular confession is still rejected;⁷ absolution may not be made dependent upon the number of special sins a man may have confessed. Felt need under sin is the only lawful motive for the dispensation of the forgiveness of sins; hence the requirement of the confession of sins is only fitting. If it is falsely made, the Church does not err in its absolution; the offer of it was sincere, but now it works out judgment. Man may lie to God and make a mock at Him. If Luther, as is well known, set great store by private confession, he regarded it as valuable because in certain situations in life it may help the heart the more easily to appropriate the forgiveness of sins. Properly considered, he finds a greater value in private absolution than in private confession. Even the hearing of confession, which he requires, is not intended to discover how the confessor stands before God, whether he has repentance and faith or is a hypo-

---

[1] xix. 1144, f. 1155, 1177, of the year 1530; x. 1493; xiii. 2080, 2084; xii. 2402; xi. 804, 849.
[2] xi. 1050; xix. 1153, 982; xiii. 1194, 1196, 2074, 2788.
[3] x. 1486; xiii. 2087; xv. 1813.   [4] xi. 985, f.   [5] x. 1487.
[6] xi. 806, f.; xvii. 2449.   [7] xx. 947. Köstlin, as cited, ii. 529.

crite, "on that point the priest *must* be uncertain, and nothing depends on his knowing it."[1] The hearing has much rather a pedagogic significance; it is an act of pastoral care, of the application of law and Gospel, especially for the ignorant, and a means for the guidance of perplexed consciences: and again, it is to give him who absolves the certainty that he may pronounce the absolution without sin on his part and without injury to the confessor.[2] Further, high as Luther places absolution, still he does not properly regard it as a sacrament; it is only the Word, which here operates with individual application after a sacramental manner, but upon the ground of the universality of grace, and especially of the still effective power of baptism. What is given in absolution is given also in the preaching of the Gospel. In it, too, Christ "deals" with us.

But in the case of violent and impenitent sinners, to whom absolution is not to be imparted, *i.e.* upon occasion of the exercise of *excommunication*, does not the Church appear to accomplish a judicial act? Certainly in the declaration, that absolution and the Holy Supper are withheld, there is contained a judicial sentence; and upon the lesser excommunication there may even follow exclusion from the congregation; but this sentence may only apply to public acts,[3] so that properly nothing new is expressed in the ecclesiastical sentence in itself, but it is only declared to the sinner out of God's Word that by his sin he is separated from God and given over to Satan. "I do not bind thee, but thou hast bound thyself with thy sin." There is here, accordingly, no judgment passed upon the inward reality: "one may be in a state of excommunication in the sight of God, and not of men; whoever hears and does not believe, but inwardly resists, the Gospel, falls under secret excommunication in the sight of God."[4] Conversely, one may be excommunicated of men and yet not of God, whether that he is no longer so, in that he has repented, or never has been so, in that the excommunication was not properly administered.[5] At the same time, the binding key is by no means a key that misses; when excommunication is not properly used, there it was rather not the right key. Hence excommunication, taken exactly, is only a "threatening" with divine inclemency, not collative or exhibitive

---

[1] xvii. 2449; x. 1485.   [2] x. 2765.   [3] xvi. 2790; xix. 1069.
[4] xix. 1102; xxii. 967, f.   [5] xix. 1098, 1107, 1120. De Wette, iv. 482.

like absolution; it is not the imposition of the loss of salvation, but is a testimony that the soul is bereft of it.[1] The purpose of such divine threatening, however, is, as respects believers, their maintenance in a penitent frame. It is a wholesome means of chastisement, a motherly punishment on the part of the Church. As respects unbelievers, it does the work of the law, but in favour of the Gospel;[2] it is to declare to them that their inward excommunication before God is recognized from their manifest sins. This declaration is certainly not ineffective, but renders the situation still more decisive, and indeed the lesser excommunication is, in the presence of God, the severest.[3] But since the sentence of the Church is only then the sentence of God, when excommunication has been made proper use of, it is quite intelligible that Luther should speak much less of the keys as binding than as loosing. Before excommunication takes place, he will have the sin first of all rebuked in a brotherly manner, and the sinner finally convicted publicly before the congregation. He desires accordingly to have *church discipline*, and in the epistle to the Bohemian and Moravian brethren, he complains bitterly that amongst his own people he cannot make good morals or discipline current: "Church discipline would be a right Christian work, but I alone dare not establish it."[4] "I would gladly institute it," he says in his *Tischreden*,[5] "but it is not yet time; in order to excommunication, there must be finehearted, cheerful, intelligent pastors." "It is still green with us, and ripens slowly," he says to the Bohemian brethren, "but pray for us that God may give us good help."[6] He regards excommunication as properly belonging to the nature of every Christian congregation; where sin is forgiven or punished publicly or specially, know thou that the people of God are there.[7] The holy Supper, especially, must be guarded from unworthy, *i.e.* manifest sinners;[8] we dare not make ourselves partakers of

---

[1] At a later period (cf. Köstlin, ii. 53) Luther seems to think of the binding key as also collative. But even where it is properly used, it itself only collates *threatening*, for no definite decision is thereby made as to damnation.

[2] xix. 1184, 1093, 1127; xiii. 1183; of the year 1518, xix. 1091.

[3] De Wette, iv. 462. *Luthers Werke von Walch*, xix. 1107.

[4] Cf. Köstlin, as cited, ii. 560, ff. *Luthers Werke von Walch*, xvi. 2785; xx. 57, 58.

[5] *Luthers Werke von Walch*, xxii. 975, 962.   [6] *Ibid.* xix. 1630.

[7] xvi. 2789. *Von den Concilien*, &c.   [8] x. 2765. De Wette, iv. 462.

the sins of others. But since whoever may be excommunicated must first of all be publicly convicted before the congregation, there is due also to the congregation, and that the congregation of the place, a voice in the matter; for it concerns the souls belonging to the congregation, and therefore the congregation should be furnished with judges.[1] He advises the calling in of two counsellors; he has also, in the preface to the *Deutsche Messe*, thrown out the thought, that a good Church discipline might begin in the circle of those who resolved to be Christians in earnest, and to engage themselves to take cognizance of, rebuke, better, expel or excommunicate those who did not conduct themselves in a Christian manner. He naturally desires, however, to exclude all civil consequences from excommunication and Church discipline.

To the congregation he concedes in general participation in Church action, even as he holds immovably to the truth that Christ has consecrated us (believers) all priests.[2] He would rather not have the name priest for the public office at all, but calls them "ministers of the Word." The congregation has no power whatever to hand over the office of preaching and the keys, which are entrusted to it, once for all to a particular order, which should alone bear the responsibility. It is its right and duty, in the case of need, again to interfere; it is always its duty to care for the maintenance of pure preaching. Of an "office of the means of grace," which first renders the Word and sacrament effectual, there is no trace in Luther; and such an office is contrary to the principle of faith, because it creates a new condition of salvation, and one opposed to the formal principle or the Word of God, because it denies to it, as well as to the sacrament, the possession of inherent power. Luther had also an appreciation of the *diaconate*,[3] and rejoiced at every symptom of it, but it, too,

---

[1] xix. 1182; xxii. 964. Köstlin, as cited, ii. 561, ff.

[2] See pages 108, ff. 174. Köstlin, as cited, ii. 539, ff. 547; i. 261, 327. Luther intends that the participation of the congregation should be understood of the choice of a bishop and of legislation as well as of excommunication.

[3] He says, "it is not an office for reading the Gospel and the Epistle, as is at present customary, but for distributing the goods of the Church to the poor. After the office of the ministry, there is no higher office in the Church than this administration." (*Luthers Werke von Walch*, b. xiii. p. 2464.) Accordingly the oldest (many before 1530) Lutheran Church Orders (see p. 118), contain instructions for the institution of the diaconate.—*Tr.*

he did not introduce. For the rest, he regards all ecclesiastical order, not as having in itself an absolute worth, but as merely a means in order to lead to faith. He abjures tyrannical oppression by means of human ordinances, and as distinctly as he leaves the congregation free to provide itself with ordinances according to its need, so absolutely does he prohibit the setting up of any farther conditions of salvation than the means of grace, objectively, and faith, subjectively. The other ethical points, which were attacked by the fanatics of the practical kind spoken of, and their defence on the side of the Reformation, will be treated of in their connection afterwards (Chapter III.).

IV. *The false theoretical mysticism.*

As the evangelical principle, in the conflicts with Carlstadt, the heavenly prophets, and the Anabaptists, had to set clear its position in reference to a false pre-Reformation mysticism of a practical kind, so also in reference to a theoretical. The representative of this false mysticism, which was however still esteemed Christian, is *Schwenckfeld von Ossing.* In Ludwig Hetzer, Johann Denk, Johann Campanus, Michael Servetus, Theophrastus Paracelsus, Theobald Thamer, Sebastian Franck, &c., there is already opposed to the Reformation a school of thought, which degenerated more or less into naturalism, and which gave itself little concern about the evangelical reformation of the doctrines concerning the natural powers of man and concerning sin, concerning the way of salvation, and especially faith, but on the contrary, laid hands upon and sought to render less objectionable to the natural reason, or altogether denied, the objective dogmas handed down from the early Church concerning the Triune God and the divinity and humanity of Christ.

1. *The Christian side of the theoretical mysticism.*

Caspar Schwenckfeld[1] manifests indeed a strong practical tendency, and formed small congregations which maintained themselves for a considerable time; but still he is properly not a church reformer, although he desired to be so, but the noblest representative of theoretical mysticism in the Reformation age.

---

[1] *Schwenckfelds Werke, gesammelt,* 1564, iv. fol. Hahn, *Schw. sententia de Jesu Christi persona,* 1845. Erbkam, *Geschichte der protestantischen Sekten,* Hamburg and Gotha, 1848, pp. 357-475.

He assumes a peculiar position in reference to the controversy between the Swiss and Luther, related to both, and unwelcome to both. For that wherein he is related to both has reference to that whereby they are most of all opposed to one another. There is united in him that which each blames most of all in the other, and he seeks to bring that to a harmonious issue which most of all operated to their mutual repulsion and separation. Thus he presents to both in a living way the problem of a mutual understanding, which might prove the more effective from his seeking to reach what was characteristic in the one tendency from what was characteristic of the other, not as it were by taking the edge off the points, but in the sharpening of them by an attempt at their inward confirmation.

Together with the Swiss he seeks a looser connection than Luther does between the means of grace, as well as everything external, and divine grace: he will in no manner recognize heavenly grace as bound to visible elements. He even goes on this point as far essentially as Carlstadt. That which is the vital matter in Christianity cannot be given through any creature, corporeal word, Scripture, or sacrament, but only through the almighty, eternal Word, which proceeds from the mouth of God. That which is external he regards as only the representation, testimony, doctrine, remembrancer of God; all creatures are only representations of God, and cannot bring God into the soul nor produce faith; still less is God chained to them. But in the proof of this, he diverges essentially from the Swiss. For he does not reject the operation of the means of grace, because Divine Omnipotence might be endangered by an efficacy on the part of creatural means of grace, or the Divine Majesty by linking grace to a creatural thing. His propositions are based much rather upon his view of the relation between the first and second creation, and even farther back in his sharp separation of the might of God, and its province, from the *nature* of God, of which he conceives as substantial radiant love. Everything creatural is constituted through the mere operation of Divine might; it is outside of the Divine, because God's nature, *i.e.* His righteousness, holiness, love, and grace, is not in it; consequently, God's nature cannot be communicated in the material or written Word, or in the elements of the sacraments, which are certainly derived from what is outside of the Divine. Man, too, as a creature, is outside of the Divine, without the indwelling of God, and since he has besides fallen into sin, there is the more need for a second creation, a new birth, which was already indeed in contemplation at the first creation, but for which the latter could do nothing. Accordingly, the ground of Schwenckfeld's denial of an efficacy on the part of the means of grace is not that too little, but that too much, is thereby attributed to Divine might. The ethical condition, for which man is foreordained, the indwelling of God in His proper, *i.e.* His ethical nature, cannot be traced back to mere Divine might and its province. It is also evident from this, that his negative position towards the means of grace is in no way intended to assert the dispensableness of grace or the perfection of the natural man; he rather regards the creation of man as in the first instance imperfect, especially since sin has entered, until a second act of God, His almighty love and grace, makes man perfect. Even *Flacius* does not satisfy him; he calls him a Pelagian, because, according to him, man may be helped by a mere creature, Scripture, preaching, and so on. He regards the idea of man as realized only when he has God's ethical nature for his own. This is not intended by him in a pantheistic sense; God is not for him, as for so many mystics, simply an abyss which threatens to absorb the human personality, but in the very innermost an ethical substance, hence personality; and the human personality is also hidden in the Divine. Certainly, however, it is the desire for immediate fellowship with God, which alienates Schwenckfeld from the creatural means, all the more that these, as lifeless, cannot, according to him, have in themselves or impart to us the nature of God. He thinks that on this point he can prop himself upon the authority of Luther as he was at the outset, but he accuses the Lutherans of having cast off the mysticism which gave them birth, and of bowing down again to an ecclesiasticism, which must only restore the old form of impersonal piety and of bondage to the letter.

Whilst *Schwenckfeld*, however, has, in reference to the efficacy of the external means of grace, and accordingly in reference to the manner or way of the origin of faith, a view which approximates to the Swiss, he stands nevertheless nearer to the Lutherans in respect of the *matter of faith*. He will not enter into a relationship with the unlimited, undefined Divine of the mystics, or only with the Holy Ghost, as Carlstadt, but with God in His living revelation. This he finds in the humanity of the God-man, and therefore the innermost movement of his piety is turned towards the person of Christ, which he beholds "in the radiant splendour of mystic illumination, in a new glory." It is the truth, *i.e.* the perfection of humanity and the unity and completeness of Christ, the glorified Redeemer, upon which his eye is fixed above all, because it is first from the glorified Lord that that communication of the divine nature, of a higher spiritually corporeal[1] nature proceeds, which is our new birth and completion.

He holds fast by the true and eternal reality of this humanity, even of its body, and will not, as Andreas Osiander, have it conceived of as a mere vehicle in order to suffer, or as a mere means of revelation, but as an essential part of the inheritance of salvation itself. Hence he insists upon a truly human development [*Werden*] of Christ, a growth of the Son of Man into the divine nature of the Son of God, who at first had united himself with him only according to His person, apart from His nature. But this man becomes for him God, deified, "the high-born, august man, and reigning king of grace," who may no more be called a creature, but is removed into the Trinity, even according to His humanity. Even in the same way he will, in complete accordance with the Church, allow to the suffering of Christ its atoning significance; but he reminds us that we cannot separate between Christ's person and merit. For, on the contrary, his chief activity is self-communication, *communicatio sui, non idiomatum;* he inculcates, that Christ by His passion has also won for us the sending of the Holy Spirit, and does not seek to be known merely in His first estate but also in His second, in which He has the power and the will to glorify us, and to make us partakers of the divine nature.

But he maintains also the *unity* and *completeness* of Christ as distinctly as the true *humanity*. He is much dissatisfied with the prevailing scholastic Christology, which brought the two natures as essentially separate together, only in the unity of the person, and admitted at most a nominal communication of attributes. Hence and in a similar way he blames the Swiss also for leaving the two natures disunited; as separate and independent existences they necessarily lead to two persons, to two Sons. He

---

[1] = *geistleiblich.— Tr.*

shares accordingly in the labours of Luther in reference to the perfect, living unity in Christ. Luther even seeks to carry this unity into the concrete natures. Still, Schwenckfeld is not satisfied even with Luther; for [says Schwenckfeld] since he speaks of a communication of *properties*, he repudiates an union of both natures in essence. The essence of both always forms for Luther a division in the person of Christ. The real communication of properties is impossible alongside of essential difference of natures, even as it itself acquiesces in a division of the one Christ, although it be of a very fine character.

He does not, however, favour those pantheistic views which were being disseminated from Italy, and which identify the human nature in itself and in its immediateness with the divine, in virtue of a new Ebionitism: and in like manner, conversely, he will not obtain the unity which he seeks by changing, like the Anabaptists *Melchior Hoffmann*, and *Corvinus*, the corporeal birth of Christ, through the assumption of a heavenly humanity,[1] into a mere semblance. His attempt at a solution is rather as follows, and is intimately connected with his doctrine concerning God.

Man, he says, is not merely a created thing, something having the origin and nature of our flesh. To man belongs also, in the proper idea of him, the indwelling of God, participation in the divine nature, which could not indeed be given by the first creation, but was nevertheless from the beginning decreed to man. But whilst the second act of our genesis, through which our idea was first realized, could not follow immediately upon the first,—since our nature, as created by mere omnipotence, is a stranger to God, and our sin sets us in antagonism to God,—that second act is to be accomplished through Christ. But how could Christ effect this and yet become true man? If He derived His body only from the created Adamite nature, he stood so far only in the position of a stranger to God, and could not impart to us the higher life, the divine nature. In order to His possessing a living susceptibility for the indwelling of the Son of God, and yet being the Son of Mary, He required to receive something which raised Him

---

[1] *I.e.* of a heavenly humanity during the existence of the Logos on earth. The Logos, according to Hoffman, did not assume the flesh descended from Adam, which was under the curse, but *became* flesh, embodied itself in a heavenly humanity, and in this heavenly humanity suffered on the cross.—*Tr.*

up out of the Adamite nature, and which was suited to the Logos, as the susceptibility for being filled. This became His by means of the believing conception of Mary. It is the beginning of a higher humanity, endowed with a capacity for the Son of God, which Christ received of the Virgin, who, by means of her faith, became possessed of a birth from God, divine substance begotten of God, and imparted this to Christ. This substance is the proper body of Jesus, His true humanity. Schwenckfeld must indeed allow, besides this spiritual corporeity, which is of God through Mary, also an earthly body, out of the earthly elements of Mary, out of the creatural world, in order not to become Docetic, like the Anabaptists. In what manner he conceived of the internal relations of this double corporeity is not clear. Only so much is clear, that he does not find the true humanity in this elementary body; the latter he regards as belonging only to the estate of humiliation and suffering; it no longer exists in the perfected, glorified Lord, there all inequality is overcome.

He thus obtains the following doctrine of the person of Christ, in which it is claimed that the unity of the person is conserved as well as the truthfulness of the humanity. The true and permanent element of His humanity is the vital susceptibility, which is capable of increase, for the indwelling of God the Son. The substratum of this susceptibility is, in his view, not merely a corporeity but also a human soul. Christ possesses this susceptibility together with the earthly, suffering body from the Virgin, and thus truly belongs to our race. With this germ of humanity, however, the Son of God has, from the beginning, allied Himself, so that Christ is ever God-man: but if the Son of God had at the first brought not only His person but also His divine *nature* (properties) into humanity, if the child Jesus had, according to His humanity, forthwith taken part in the divine omnipotence, omnipresence, and omniscience, and performed all divine works, the humanity would have become a mere semblance. Hence regard must be paid to the "increase of this man into God," and in the interest of a true growth [*Werden*] of the humanity he first assumed a gradual appropriation of the divine nature through Jesus, and then most carefully developed the doctrine of a *twofold state of Christ*. By right (*auctoritative*) He was from the beginning the perfect Son of God; also, according to His true humanity, *Filius Dei naturalis*. But in reality His humanity had first to grow up into the Son of God, had actually to appropriate the fulness of His nature, until both, the humanity (the susceptibility) and the divinity (as its satisfaction) lost their inequality, and, after the conquest and expulsion of everything transient from the epoch of the resurrection, nothing which stood outside of the divine essence, nothing merely creatural dwelt any longer in Christ, although the humanity, however, was not in this way destroyed, for it continues still as a fulfilled susceptibility, in possession of the divine as its own. Since His ascension, He imparts to believers His spiritual corporeal essence (His divine nature) wherein our holiness and resurrection is secured —imparts it also in the holy Supper, but not in it alone.

The acuteness and connection of these thoughts cannot be disputed; they contain several suggestive points of view, which have afterwards been turned to account. But the distinction, weighty in itself, between the moral nature of God and His omnipotence, is in His doctrine regarding the first and second creation so sharply applied, that the two stand toward each other in an alien, unconnected, and dualistic position.[1] This is repeated again in the relation between Christ's spiritually corporeal nature out of Mary, and His earthly body. The appeal to the faith of Mary and the divine substance in her only conceals the utter want of connection between the first and the second creation, but does not take it away. The problem is only removed from Christ back to Mary, if the first creation in its substance is alien to the divine nature, and wanting in susceptibility for it. The same abrupt miracle, too, must be repeated in every case of regeneration.

Further, the aversion from the world of the first creation, the hostility to nature, which lies in Schwenckfeld's tendency to abstract inwardness, can only admit of faith and the possession of salvation being realized in the way of inward magic. Since he overlooks the participation of the natural man in the divine in the form of the law which addresses itself to the will, it only remains for him, who will nevertheless maintain the inwardness and freedom of the Spirit, to regard the sanctification and perfection of man as consisting in a spiritually corporeal *nature*, which,

---

[1] Luther also speaks often of a second and separate element in God. But— which is characteristic of his ethical sense—it is, in his view, righteousness (self-assertion) which stands over against love (self-communication), and not omnipotence.

because it comes into man in an unethical, *i.e.* magical way, abjures the ethical character, and does not allow of the actual appropriation of the divine by man. This possession is rather for him who has it a mere accident; it even comes, properly speaking, to quite a different subject than the creatural man. With Schwenckfeld, accordingly, in like manner as with *Theophrastus Paracelsus*, the ethical process is obscured through a mysticism of nature, and the glorified, deified corporeity is in his eyes essential holiness. Although there may be in all this the right idea that the ethical does not consist wholly in acts, but has also an ontological side, still he has stopped short at the standpoint of physics or of an unethical, although loftier, substantiality, and even therein appears the ethical weakness of his mysticism, which makes too little mention of law, sin, and the will, and rather derives salvation, the transformation into the nature of Christ, from the spiritual contemplation of His glory.

2. *The naturalistic side of theoretical mysticism.*

There is still manifested in the Christology of Schwenckfeld a positive and inwardly religious tendency. But others allowed themselves—which was more logical—to be led, through the relegation to an inferior position of the external means of grace, in which they were at one with him, to the rejection of the historical revelation, of which we would have no sure record apart from the Scriptures, and to the refashioning of the Christian doctrine of God, to which in its essentials Schwenckfeld held fast. In this class we name first *Michael Servetus*, born 1509, died on the 27th October 1553, whom we might call the Latin Schwenckfeld, had he only possessed the deep piety of the latter.[1]

Animated by the most various elements of culture belonging to that time, Humanism, the revived Platonism, a mystic natural philosophy after the manner of Theophrastus Paracelsus, for a long time secretary to the Emperor on account of his juristic learning, but also in contact with the Reformers through his theological proclivities, Servetus hoped by means of his mystic pantheistic natural philosophy to enlighten Christendom regarding its deepest errors, especially the Trinity and its Christology, and to discover to it the truths which were intended under these doctrines, but which had been falsified. The Church doctrine of the Trinity, in

[1] M. Servetus, *Restitutio Christianismi; De trinitatis erroribus.*

which he sees a division of the One indivisible divine essence, he regarded as forming, along with infant baptism and the hierarchy, the fundamental cause of the corruption. On it lies the guilt of the unbelief of the Mohammedans, the ridicule of the Jews, and the doubt of so many in Christendom. Unitarianism is based upon both the Old and New Testaments, and was firmly maintained by the pre-Constantine Church. The truth is, that there are no personal differences in God, but only self-dispositions[1] of the One God, which however are eternal. The *Logos* is not in itself personal, but it is the Word of God, *i.e.* the ideal image of the world present to God. The idea of Jesus Christ forms from the very beginning the centre in this image of the world; it is the beginning, middle, and end of all other *modi* or original images [types] in God; it is however also the ideal revelation of the Father Himself in the centre of His nature. Whilst therefore the Logos, which is identical with the complete image of the world, is, though including in itself all self-revelation on the part of God, yet in itself impersonal, it acquires in the realization of the idea of Christ real human personality in time, because it here finds in its concentration a historical manifestation. This is the begetting of the Son. In that ideal image of the world the divine breath or the Holy Spirit is contained in an eternal manner, and this breath is the soul of Christ,—the original place, from which all communication of the Spirit proceeds. But even Christ's bodily nature he regards as a divine substance, and he rejects the doctrine of two natures. His pantheism sees in a certain sense a divine substance in everything; still he teaches a miraculous birth and conception of Christ. The formative principle, which occupies the place of the male factor, is in his view the original light out of the *divine* substance itself, which was revealed as early as Exod. 13, 21, f. Since the substance out of Mary, also in itself divine, was formed by this divine principle of light, there arises a corporeal organ, capable of the reception of that soul, and Christ is capable of personally manifesting the centre of the image of the world, the concentrated Logos. He must first however submit to a truly human development, which closes with His resurrection, and there parts with

---

[1] These self-dispositions are, according to him, not necessary but arbitrary. God disposes Himself to two modes of revelation, a mode of manifestation in the Word, and a mode of communication in the Spirit.—*Tr.*

everything corruptible. Christ is thus for him the man miraculously born, who manifests really in a historical process [*Werden*] the ideal image of the world and thereby the nature of the Father. There is no mention of an indwelling of God in Christ, since it is much rather the case that His humanity in respect both of body and soul is in itself of a divine substance. Since however everything is in his eyes divine, though in different degrees, he weakens the distinction between nature and grace; the deeper ground of this lies in the neglect of the ethical side of Christianity.[1] He takes it to be a metaphysical doctrine, and thinks himself able to set up a better in opposition to it, but he leaves out of view sin and atonement, as well as in general the historical work of Christ.

In a similar manner, also, *Denk*, who died in Basle in 1528, regarded the world as the great Word of God, and individuals as the letters of the word. Christ is for him the highest blossom and summit of the world, wherein all the rays of the word are gathered in intensest strength. Still he considers Him a mere creature, like us, not an atoning One, but a forerunner and example. He drew into this circle of thought, where the divinity and atonement of Christ as well as the Trinity are denied, *Ludwig Hetzer*, who had at first, starting from Anabaptist mysticism and spiritualism, but in divine resignation of a predestinarian kind, awaited salvation by the act of God. Under the influence of Denk, he now set righteousness of life in the place of justifying faith, denied the causality of Christ in salvation, and united this with his doctrine of eternal election in such a way that the divine decree was regarded by him as independent of Christ. Whilst Denk however maintained an universal restoration, Hetzer rejected it. *Johann Campanus*, who appeared along with Servetus in Wittenberg about 1530, seeks to have the Father and Son conceived of as a pair [$\sigma\nu\zeta\nu\gamma\iota\alpha$]; they form together, according to him, after the analogy of a marriage, a higher conjunct person; for after the creation it is not Adam nor Eve separately who is called the image of God, but both together as a unity. The Holy Ghost again he regarded as the operation of this conjunct unity. There is in him accordingly a disposition

---

[1] Faith is, according to him, the one comprehensive act required of man; but he thinks of faith as a mere intellectual belief that Jesus is the Son of God. He considers the belief of this point to involve the belief of the whole theory.—*Tr.*

towards Tritheism, which afterwards manifested itself more distinctly in Valentin Gentilis, Bernh. Occhino, &c.,[1] but always, where logically developed, ended in Tetradism, or in this, that over and above the three absolute personalities an unity is assumed, which necessarily stands above them, and leads accordingly to Subordinationism and Unitarianism. *David Joris*, of Delft, born 1501, set up a doctrine of the Trinity of a Sabellian type. The immanent Trinity and the incarnation of God is contradictory to His essence. God can only dwell and move in a man. That however has taken place in various forms, in stages, which correspond to the trinity of body, soul, and spirit, or to childhood, youth, and manhood;[2] namely, in Moses, then in Jesus, the type of the Christ. The third stage, that of the Christ, he seems in connection with chiliastic ideas to have reserved for himself. Christ (*i.e.* David Joris) will bring in perfection and set up the kingdom.

Finally, *Theobald Thamer*, † 1569, resigns himself to Naturalism, and most unreservedly of all, *Sebastian Franck*, of Donauwörth. *Thamer* is more rationalistic than mystic. Christ is, according to him, the Son of God, as a man perfect through divine power (the Holy Ghost), and for us pattern and teacher. To follow after his example justifies.[3] *Seb. Franck* attaches himself to the pantheistic utterances of the mystics, like Eckard, Tauler, and *die deutsche Theologey*, but his tendency was rather towards the external, and a certain power of popular address is not to be denied in him. He was possessed of extensive learning, humanistic culture, wit and satire, and used these gifts, after the fashion of so many in the sixteenth century, to lash the existing state of matters. But since he was wanting in positive internal steadfastness, and in the power and desire of origination, he was for the most part a peevish critic of all the principal tendencies of the time, to none of which could he reconcile himself,

---

[1] Trechsel, *die prot. Antitrinitarier vor Faustus Socinus*, 1839.

[2] In these stages faith, hope, and love respectively predominate. Joris sometimes speaks of the first stage as that of Adam, and of the third commonly as that of Elias or David. He represents regeneration as including three corresponding stages in the individual. — *Tr.*

[3] Cf. Neander, *Theob. Thamer, Repräsentant und Vorgänger modcrner Geistesrichtung*, 1842. Salig, *Historie der Augsburger Confession*, iii. 199, ff. [There is also an element of pantheism in Thamer's rationalism. "The conscience, which is Divinity and is Christ Himself, who now dwells in our hearts, understands and judges what is good and bad." It is the first and best source of evidence regarding God. After it, and before the Scriptures, comes creation.—*Tr.*]

and his outward restless life became a reflection of his inward state. He also attacked Luther and his party, because they, forsaking the paths of the old mysticism, form an ecclesiastical association, and limit freedom by the Holy Scriptures and a Church doctrine, but especially by connection with the State. On friendly terms with many Anabaptists, he demanded full religious liberty for all, condemned all State persecutions on account of religion, and said much that was worthy of being laid to heart concerning the close connection of the Church with princes, and which Luther was driven by necessity to approve, when the bishops withdrew, and the power of the nobility on the other hand and of the people was broken in consequence of the suppressed rising, and neither consequently could be induced to take part in the conduct of the Church. "If the prince," says he, "chooses to be evangelical, it rains Christians. If he is succeeded by a Nero—God help us!—they all disappear, and Herr Omnes vanishes like the flies in winter." His principal works are, *Chronik oder Zeitbuch*, 1531; *Kosmographie oder Weltbuch*, 1534; *Paradoxa*, 1559; *Das verbütschirte, mit sieben Siegeln verschlossene Buch*, 1539.

With regard to the holy *Scriptures* he says that it is not properly they, but their divine sense and spirit which constitutes the Word of God. The Scriptures are only the shell, cradle, sheath, lantern, outer court, letter, veil and surrounding of the Word of God, which is the kernel, infant, sword, light, sanctuary, spirit and life, fulness and reality. God has also purposely furnished the Scriptures with contradictions, in order that we may be impelled deeper into the Scriptures, and out of them back again to Him and into the Spirit. He speaks of a conflict in the Scriptures; they are as it were divided and sundered into two camps. But what is contradictory in the letter is harmonious in the Spirit. Where the Spirit is, he proceeds, there is liberty; the Spirit is not bound to the creature nor to the Scriptures, but only to itself. No less, however, does every individual conscience require the living Word of God; the Scriptures do not satisfy a conscience in distress. And every individual must have from God a special word to himself; the general word, which is addressed to all, does not satisfy. He has here touched upon the thoroughly evangelical thought of the personal certainty of salvation on the part of every individual. But he does not reach the self-individualization of grace, because he does not properly attain to the conception of grace, but substitutes for it a mystically coloured, pantheistic doctrine of the nature of God and man, of a natural, only not forthwith actual, divinity of man. God is, according to him, the simple, unnamed and impersonal, inconceivable essence, the essence of all essences, the Is of all being [*aller Ist Ist*]. Without feeling and without will, the all-sufficient divine substance reposes in itself, without movement in itself. Only in us does God become moveable, will, changeable, in short a man. Thus, then, we are the actuality of God, our nature is divine; every one is a word of God and a particular word: man is, as it were, the formative principle, God is only the matter for man. He deals lightly with sin. He does not seek to make God the author of it; but since God is, according to him, the essence and potentiality of all things, he can only regard sin as a restrictive defect, or as a semblance. His view is that God takes upon Himself all human affections in becoming incarnate in us. He is now in such a manner in us, and in such a manner partaker of evil, that the sin of man occasions Him suffering and more sorrow than His own agony and death in Christ. Where there is only at the basis a will towards God and displeasure at sin, there God has certainly become man. Such a man experiences, that it (evil) is not his, and takes it as little to himself as if it were not. Herein accordingly consists, in his view, the justification of man, that after his inner divine essence he has no pleasure in evil, but only experiences in reference to it suffering and pain, but at the same time thinks of this his inner essence as uncontaminated by evil and inaccessible to it. The new birth is thus reduced to a mere process of knowing that the essence of man is divine, and in the contemplation of this essence the reality may, nay, must, be disregarded. The divine, unchanging, and constant *essence* of man is thus made to assume the place of the Mediator who is always reconciling the *reality* of man.[1] Only, taken strictly, there remains nothing to reconcile; even the earnest resolve of the man upon the reality of a holy moral life is disregarded. Man's need

---

[1] The historical Christ is lost in that divine essence, which is in all men. He is only the prophet of what was already written in the heart. His death only inaugurated the consciousness of that reconciliation which in itself existed eternally. Hence the language used in the above sentence.—*Tr.*

of reconciliation is only changed into a necessity that he, coming to the true knowledge, should lay aside error, just as if the vital point were still something else than the knowledge of the divine essence of man, and what is to be destroyed were no more sin, but the delusion that it is a matter to be taken in earnest, and not much rather a mere semblance or something indifferent in comparison with the divine essence of man.

V. *The Reformation in opposition to the false theoretical mysticism.*

Luther and Melanchthon, in reforming the old anthropological and soteriological form of doctrine, felt, not without good reason, objections against dragging into the turmoil the objective church doctrines of God and of the Holy Trinity, as well as of the person of Christ. They did not dispute the lawfulness nor the necessity of a progress of doctrine even in this respect; but as they did not find a true reformation of these doctrines amongst the men just mentioned, so neither did they themselves subscribe the summons to reformation upon these points. Hence *Melanchthon*, after having preliminarily and designedly placed these doctrines in the background as unknowable, and in their exacter definitions unfruitful for the life of faith, continued rather to adhere to the traditional form of them. "These mysteries," he had said at the first in his *Loci*, "are better reverenced than inquired into." The investigations in the Church hitherto had not effected much, but had rather obscured the benefaction of Christ. When the antitrinitarian movements broke out, and Joachim Camerarius desired his verdict regarding Servetus, he described him[1] in general as undecided, obscured, full of complete misapprehension in the question of justification, and the slave of his own imagination. But in respect of the Divine Triad, he, Melanchthon, had long expected the breaking out of such movements. Good God! he concludes, what tragedies will be excited amongst our posterity by the question, whether the Logos and the Spirit are hypostases? He himself, convinced that the investigation of the conception and of the differences of the hypostases was of little use, seeks rather to fall back upon the holy Scriptures, and with them to hold fast to the worship of Christ, which affords so much consolation.

[1] *Corp. Reformatorum*, ii. 629, of 9th February 1533.

He repeats the same views in a letter to *J. Brenz*,[1] with the addition that the scholastic doctrine of two natures in the person of Christ has much against it. Instead of the doctrine of Servetus, which makes the Logos only an action of the Father, and instead of the scholastic, which with its two natures in Christ does not make out the unity of His person, we must rather receive it, that the essential Son of God (*filius Dei naturalis*) has undergone humiliation. He seems here to have regarded the humanity as the form of the self-humiliation of the Son. But from this view, which was current amongst the Anabaptists of the Reformation period, he soon again fell, doubtless in consequence of the recognition of its new and greater difficulties, and afterwards in his *Loci* attached himself strongly to the scholastic form of the *Communicatio idiomatum*. Nevertheless, at a later period, he attempted in the *Loci* a speculative construction of the doctrine of the Trinity. He regards it as representing the eternal necessary process of the divine self-consciousness, in which God, whose thoughts are realities, eternally sets Himself over against Himself, but also again unites with Himself.

But Luther finds[2] the name and development of the doctrine of the Trinity to be anything but perfect. But since he knows no better mode of expression, he contents himself with that hitherto in use, and occasionally expresses himself very favourably regarding the Athanasian Creed.[3] In the Catechism he confines himself to the economical Trinity: he regards God the Father, Son and Holy Spirit as corresponding respectively to creation together with providence, redemption and sanctification. In the exposition of the Johannic prologue he frequently applies man's way of speaking with himself to the illustration of the self-division in God; he has also in other ways sought analogies for the Trinity in nature. The trace of it is imprinted on everything that lives; even in God we are to accept a beginning, middle, and end.[4] The flower provides a reflection of it. Its form and substance reflects God the Father in His omnipotence; its odour represents to us the Eternal Wisdom or the Son of God, its special power and efficacy the power of the Holy Ghost.[5]

Justly, however, were the questions regarding the appropria-

[1] *Corp. Reformatorum*, ii. 660, July, 1533.
[2] *Luthers Werke von Walch*, xi. 1549; xiii. 2631.
[3] *Ibid.* xiii. 1523, ff.; vi. 2313, f.   [4] xii. 851.   [5] xxii. 372, f.

tion of salvation of the first importance for the Reformers, and they full of these questions. The reform of the œcumenical foundations was thought of in the period of the Reformation only by those who regarded the Reformation merely as a theoretical or moral undertaking, not as one of practical religion. The Reformation itself was with good reason restricted to its immediate province. And, besides, a regeneration of the objective dogmas can be successfully accomplished only upon the basis of the evangelical principle of faith. The Church accordingly had first to be firmly grounded in this, in order to express clearly on every side what is therein contained. Had this taken place, then a more perfect conception of God could not indeed long be wanting. Out of the living experience of faith must arise a purer knowledge of God, which would then seek also its scientific expression, and must new-shape the mediæval conception of God. For by the middle ages on their legal side God was regarded too much only as the Righteous One and the Judge, on their magical side however as an unethical goodness. As certainly as the evangelical principle of faith now triumphs over the legal Pelagian doctrine and the magical, as certainly must it contain the basis of a higher conception of God, one which truly unites righteousness and love. This principle, accordingly, had, before everything else, to be set fast as the postulate of all further reform, and to be protected against those who would evade or reject it. In the meantime, however, those aspects of the traditional dogma were adhered to, which lay nearest to the principle of faith, and for the Trinity those revelations of God were appealed to which are mentioned in the Little Catechism;[1] and amongst these it is especially the revelation given in Christ, to which in itself, and in its relation to word and sacrament, Luther applies his mind.

In fact, Luther made a very significant progress in Christology, and that very early, long before the dispute with Zwingli, and in connection with his observations regarding revelation in general, as also with the principle of faith. He sees two things in Christ, the perfection of the revelation and the perfection of man; he re-

[1] The reference is to the division of the Apostolic Creed according to the revelations of God in creation, redemption, and sanctification. It is, however, in the Large Catechism that Luther connects this division of the Creed with the Three Persons of the Trinity.—*Tr.*

gards Him as by nature the original type of that union between God and man, which is by faith in Him imitatively accomplished through the Holy Ghost. He is for him the Son of God and Son of man, who, by means of His death and resurrection, wins out from amongst sinners a family of children of God, whose Head He is. It is an erroneous view which represents Luther as seeing in Christ only the present God, and in His humanity, accordingly, only the veil of God, the impersonal organ of revelation. In what is merely material [*dinglich*] God could not, as Luther well knew, perfectly reveal Himself. He rather regards it as of importance, that we should recognize how *humanity* is in Christ elevated and glorified. Revelation itself has, according to him, first found its goal in the bringing forth of the perfect man, who is the Son of Man. Since he lays as much stress upon the full but true reality of the humanity in Christ as upon the divine side, as much upon the knowledge of the exaltation of humanity as of the condescension of God, he insists as much upon the formula, " Man has become God in Christ," as upon that other, " God is in Christ become man." Still he does not look upon the believer as annihilated in respect of his person, but represents him as a personality full of life, full even of God. The second characteristic of his Christology appears in him still more strongly and powerfully. He seeks to see in Christ the bringing of the divine and human into perfect union; this stands vitally connected with the deepest interests of his faith. In this the truth and reality of His humanity must not suffer alongside of the divinity; that stands fast in his eyes as an axiom. But certainly at a later period, upon occasion of the controversy concerning the Supper, he declared without diffidence what the unity seemed to him logically to acquire, in a form which would not leave the full reality of the humanity of Jesus quite uninjured.

For the unity of the person of Christ, in which God and man are united, he finds a basis by remoulding the conception regarding God and man according to the standard of the principle of faith. Under the old conception of God, the " old wisdom," wherein majesty, might, and infinitude passed for the highest and innermost essence in God, it must have appeared unbefitting that God should not only act upon a man, or accept and bear a man, so to speak, as His revelation and figure, but should make humanity His own and impute it to Himself as Himself to it. But, says Luther, God is not content with the glory of being the Creator of all creatures, like us also the Jews and Turks praise and celebrate Him. He seeks also to be known in what He is inwardly. His glory is His love, which seeks the lowly and the poor. *This is the new wisdom.*[1] God's good pleasure in the incarnation consists in this, that therein He pours out His nature, reveals His heart. And He resolved upon this even when sin was nowhere in existence. Not less,[2] in "the old language," does creature signify something which is infinitely separated from the highest divinity, so that the two are directly opposed to one another. But in the new language or wisdom humanity signifies something different, unutterably nearly connected with Divinity, and we must learn to give utterance to the new wisdom as it were in new tongues.[3] The new wisdom accordingly gives first the true conception of man, according to which he in himself, *i.e.* by nature, is not a complete whole, at least does not correspond to the idea for which God destined him; but it belongs to His idea, and in so far also to the *truth* of his nature, that he should enjoy participation in God through the communion of God with him. It belongs, however, to the *old wisdom* to represent God and man, according to their relative conceptions, as mutually exclusive. In this way every doctrine of transformation, whether of God into man or the reverse, is for him excluded. For if the one set itself in the place of the other, there would be renewed precisely the old exclusiveness of the two conceptions. In this sense, then—which however includes the essential connection of the two into one whole—he adheres to the doctrine of the two natures, and that in their completeness, so that he does not speak of the humanity of Christ as impersonal.

There can be no difficulty in acknowledging this *idea* of the nature of the God-man, according to which the Son of God is at the same time man, and the Son of Man at the same time the Son of God; but in this it is only the perfect or exalted God-man who is thought of. How, then, does Luther look upon the historical Christ, on whom religious interest is already fastened by the connection between justification and atonement? Here Luther

---

[1] *Luthers Werke von Walch*, vii. 1826-43; x. 1372, 1402.
[2] *Ibid.* i. 35; ii. 584; vii. 1424, 1498, 1544-55.   [3] ii. 582; x. 1372.

holds firmly by this, that the Son of God was from the beginning inseparably connected with this man, so that the Son of God also regarded as His own everything which this man did and suffered, and the Son of Man did nothing apart from unity with the Son of God. But, on the other hand, he also saw that if the humanity of Christ already had, knew, and did upon earth everything which the eternal Son of God has, knows, and does, and were accordingly already almighty and blessed, omniscient, omnipresent and all-governing, the truth of His human weakness and of His suffering, of His human growth and learning, could no longer stand. Hence Luther admitted for the earthly period a limitation of the participation of the human nature in the Divine attributes (and herein accorded its due to a true thought of Schwenckfeld and Servetus), and thus distinguished a *double state* in him,—the state of humiliation and the state of exaltation. He casts aside earnestly and decidedly all mythical representations, which the Church legends wound round the child Jesus to the cost of His true humanity. He will look upon Him as lying helpless upon His mother's breast, as playing innocently like other children; but will not think of Him as speaking in infancy, nor as teaching and working miracles in boyhood. He maintains a true bodily, mental, and spiritual development of Jesus. The words, "'He increased in age[1] and wisdom, and in favour with God and man,' ought to be understood in the simplest possible manner. If He was at all time full of the Spirit and grace, the Spirit did not at all times move Him, but awakened Him now to this, now to that. If He was in Him from the beginning of His conception, still even as His body grew and His reason increased in a natural manner as in other men, so also the Spirit sunk into Him more and more, and moved Him the more, the more late the period; so that it is no jugglery when Luke says He waxed strong in the Spirit, but as the words give a distinct utterance, so also it proceeded in the simplest manner, that He truly became the older the bigger, the bigger the wiser, the wiser the stronger in the Spirit and the fuller of wisdom before God and in Himself and before the people."[2] Attempts have been made to weaken the significance of this remarkable passage, with its clear free

---

[1] The German Bible gives a correcter translation here than the English version, "stature."—*Tr.*

[2] *Luthers Werke von Walch*, vii. 1498, ff.; xi. 389, ff.

insight, by observing that Luther speaks of a gradual sinking of the Holy Spirit, but not of the Logos, into the humanity of Christ. That, however, makes no difference as to the vital point. For Luther will not say that Jesus had not yet the Holy Spirit perfectly, but was nevertheless through the Logos and the union with Him omniscient and omnipotent and absolutely perfect, even according to His humanity, from the very beginning; but it is precisely this which he is concerned to deny in the interests of the thorough reality of His humanity. In like manner, in another place:[1] "The humanity of Christ, like any other holy natural man, did not always think, speak, will, observe all things, even as some would make of Him an omnipotent man and unwisely mix the two natures with one another, but in such a way as God conducted Him and brought them before Him." He takes his stand upon this, that Christ required to learn obedience and to endure true conflicts and temptations in His sufferings; Christ had to be viewed here as a man engaged in a struggle, in which divinity concealed itself, "withheld"[2] itself, *i.e.* its influence upon the humanity, or the actual union with it. Without such a real process in the struggle the merit of His passion and work would have been abridged. For he regards it as settled, that Christ has in a real historical manner effected or *procured* salvation; he regards Him as the historical cause of salvation, not merely the symbol or messenger of salvation.

If, as has been already indicated, there is much which is said by him afterwards, in connection with the doctrine of the Supper, which does not accord with these weighty Christological utterances, it is still to be doubted whether the former, as *e.g.* the assertion of an absolutely perfect *unio* from the very beginning, was regarded by him as a dogma, or was only essayed as a *basis* for that which he regarded as the vital point in the holy Supper. In the latter case, another basis would only have been welcome to him and in accordance with his mind, provided a suitable one could have been found, and one alongside of which the Christological utterances above mentioned, and never given up by him, could have been maintained. It is deserving of prominence, as especially meritorious, that Luther did not, like the old Church Christo-

---

[1] *Kirchenpostille, Predigt am dritten Christtag über Hebr.* i. 1, ff, *Erlanger Ausgabe*, vii. 185.
[2] *Luthers Werke von Walch*, v. 327-331.

logers, seek the union of the divine and human principally in the province of the person, of the Ego, as if this were a vacant point,—a method which always leads irresistibly either to the impersonality of the human nature or to a double personality, a double Ego. He rather looks entirely away from the Ego as a particular entity or substance which might have come into consideration; what he concerns himself with is the union of the natures with their attributes, or in their living actuality, to which self-consciousness and will also belong; he showed, however, with regard to these natures, that they do not exclude one another, but have internal and mutual connection. The Ego he regards as an act or function of the nature. It is true that all this, in which are contained so many grand and new perceptions, is not developed by him dialectically and in consecutive exposition, by which alone what is here new would, in its distinction from the old Christology, have become to himself a confirmed and sure possession. Still we are historically entitled, when concerned with the depicting of what is peculiar to him, to lay more stress upon those new and great thoughts, than upon the reminiscences of the old, which are to be found in him now and again.

VI. *The controversy with Erasmus*, 1525.[1]

The German Reformation had to maintain an exclusive attitude, not only towards the impure form of ethical and theoretical mysticism, but also in opposition to the hybrid Erasmian Reformation, in order to conserve the principle of the Reformation in its pure and new nature, and in distinction from Humanism.

Erasmus was at first well-affected to the Reformation, especially as long as it was occupied in combating the monastic body, which was as ignorant as it was arrogant; he was also on very friendly terms with the German Reformers, and especially with the Swiss, and played the part of their patron in high circles. He meditated a reformation, however, by means of education and science. He had a natural antipathy to all bold external steps, to any disturbance of harmony and peace by passionate movements. The Reformation he did not regard as a matter of conscience, but of noetic illumination; and wherever he penetrated with his school, this Erasmian Reformation assumed a certain

[1] Compare pp. 122, 123.

middle temperature, which was indeed far removed from all extremes, but was without any staminal life. He would not have bemoaned the destruction of monasticism, nor even of the papacy, but would gladly have set in their place a hierarchy of the learned. "Let others affect martyrdom, I do not deem myself worthy of that honour. (*Affectent alii martyrium, ego me non arbitror hoc honore dignum.*) Discord is so hateful to me, that even the truth displeases me, which is the occasion of dispeace. (*Mihi adeo invisa est discordia, ut veritas etiam displiceat seditiosa.*)[1] Erasmus is to be found wherever there is evangelical peace." From tumultuous movements he fears returning barbarism. He seeks to exercise a calming influence upon Pope and Emperor in favour of the Reformation; only he keeps himself back from it. Instead of the burning of Luther's books, he demands their refutation. Theologians must teach, not compel and proscribe; an amendment of the Church was necessary, only Luther had gone too far, and so landed in error. The matter might be determined by a tribunal composed of recognizedly pious and learned men and esteemed princes, or by means of a general council. For years he withstood, under this way of thinking, the summonses from the catholic and evangelical sides to enter into the lists.

These summonses became more and more decided from the evangelical side, and were felt by him to be more and more difficult. He seemed to the evangelicals to belong by necessity to the Reformation party as much as Reuchlin, to be almost even more alienated than the Reformers from everything that was superstitious in the Romish Church, which made him a most desirable co-operator in the exegetical department. But inasmuch as the principle of his critical activity in opposition to superstition was not religious faith, he remained in his innermost being a stranger to that which formed the soul of the Reformation, and after it, as before, adhered rather to the fundamental views of [Roman] Catholicism, after abstraction of that which does not abide enlightenment. When Luther saw that Erasmus was remaining in suspense, he wrote regarding him: Erasmus has accomplished that to which he was appointed, the reintroduction of the classical studies. But he does not go forward to the higher sphere which belongs to piety. He is well able to point

[1] *Erasmi epist.*, ed. Basil, p. 449; cf. Niedner, *Kirchengeschichte*, 629.

out the bad, but not the good; he is wanting in spiritual understanding; hence he should let alone the exposition of Scripture of which he is not capable. He even writes to him himself in graceful recognition of his philological merits and splendid scientific gifts, but adds:[1] The cause has attained a magnitude which has long outstripped thy measure. (*Magnitudo causæ modulum tuum dudum egressa est.*) Old as he was, he might honourably be a spectator of the tragedy, and keep from writing against him; he was quite ready to do the same towards him. Erasmus answered that he would, in writing against him, do more service to the Gospel than many of the fools who were writing for him; and he now composed the tractate, *Diatribe de libero arbitrio*, which Luther met with the treatise, *De servo arbitrio*.[2] Erasmus answered with his *Hyperaspistes adversus Lutheri servum arbitrium*.[3]

The point of attack was well chosen, fitted to conceal his own weakness, which consisted in placing religious faith behind morally good works after a Pelagian fashion, as well as to hit the weak side of his opponent, inasmuch as the question of the freedom of the will, having been little agitated since the Leipzig discussion in 1521, had not yet attained a doctrinal shape, well weighed upon every side. Erasmus might hope for some success amongst the learned and the princes in erecting a dam against the Reformation, when he obliged it to exhibit itself as denying freedom, whilst it laid claim to freedom in opposition to Rome. At an earlier period, too, not a little observation had been excited, of which epistolary evidences are still to hand, when

[1] *Luthers Werke von Walch*, xviii. 1958-1962; De Wette, ii. 493; *Luthers Brief an Erasmus*, April 1524.

[2] *Luthers Werke von Walch*, xviii. 2049-2483 of the year 1525. Haberkorn, Zentgraf, and Seb. Schmid, in the seventeenth century, Walch in the eighteenth century, and Rudelbach in our day, sought to justify and explain Luther's controversial treatise against Erasmus by the standard of later orthodoxy. Besides the Gnesio-Lutherans, there stands opposed to them, as early as in the sixteenth century, especially Chyträus (Gieseler, *Kirchengeschichte*, ii. 1). Cf. Jul. Müller, *Lutheri De predestin. et lib. arb. doctrina*, Gott. 1832; *Union*, 1854, p. 274; Schweizer, *protestantische Centraldogmen*, i. 1854; Lütkens, *Luthers Predestinationslehre*, Dorpat, 1858, following, and even going beyond Jul. Müller and Schweizer. Lütkens is combated by Harnack, *Luthers Theologie*, i. 70, 149, ff., 1862; Philippi, in Dieckhoff's *theol. Zeitschrift*, 1860, ii. 161, ff; Franck, *Theologie der Concordienformel*, i. 119, ff. The most intelligent and objective exposition is to be found in Köstlin, *Luthers Theologie*, ii. 32-52, 307-331.

[3] *Erasmi Opera*, ed. Ludg. Batav., vol. ix. x.

Wise Choice of the Point of Attack on Luther. 205

the news spread that in Wittenberg the freedom of the human will had been given up. On the other hand, a searching controversy had not yet been entered on with regard to this point, since even in the middle ages a Laurentius Valla, a Thomas Bradwardinus,[1] and others, had ventured to adhere closely to Augustine. It was also perfectly evident that the Reformation had not a fatalist or stoical denial of freedom in view, but that it was only intent upon the maintenance of the absolute dependence of man upon God as the necessary postulate of all humility, and upon keeping pure the need for God, in opposition to the Pelagian method of centering man in himself. Luther must certainly have perceived in Pelagianism the hideous caricature of the Protestant principle of the freedom of the Christian man, the perversion of the material principle, even as he had to combat in Enthusiasm the antagonism to the formal principle, and the caricature of evangelical freedom on the side of knowledge. Luther justly saw in Pelagianism the ultimate reason why Humanism as a whole could not attain to a religious decision of conscience in favour of the Reformation, but continued inwardly allied to the Romish Church, which was then quite content that the free independence of man and the merit of works should be asserted over against God, if only dependence upon the Church was not at the same time denied.

Erasmus threw himself in his pamphlet[2] upon what is certainly a harsh utterance of Luther in his *Assertiones*, according to which man would have absolutely no moral freedom of will. (Male dixi, quod liberum arbitrium ante gratiam sit res de solo titulo, sed simpliciter debui dicere: liberum arbitrium est figmentum in rebus seu titulus sine re, quia nulli est in manu quidpiam cogitare mali aut boni, sed omnia, ut Wyclefi articulus Constantiæ damnatus recte docet, de necessitate absoluta eveniunt.) Erasmus prefixes some remarks regarding the dogmatic source of proof.

The Scriptures are not enough; everything depends upon the right exposition of the Scriptures. Is it said, science and the wisdom of the world are of no avail, of what avail then is ignorance? It is said that the majority does not make the matter right. But neither does the minority. The exposition of

---
[1] Cf. Lechler, *Thomas Bradwardinus*, Lips. 1862.
[2] *Diatribe*, in Walch, xviii. 1962, ff.

the Scriptures cannot be left in the hands of an individual, for whereby is it to be known that he is in possession of the Spirit? It thus remains most probable that the true exposition of Scripture lies in the Church. But the Church finds the freedom of man taught in the Scriptures. It will be seen how all idea of the assurance of faith, the material principle, escapes Erasmus. If neither the Scriptures be plain nor the truth endued with the power of attesting itself to the spirit, then indeed it is quite logical to rest content with external authority. But this Erasmian faith in Church authority is in its innermost nature sceptical, because it is despair of the knowableness of truth as such; this is sharply held up to him in Luther's answer. His book is an uncertain book, like to an eel. A sceptical submission to the Church is a novel humility and holiness. What is liker to wretchedness and damnation than uncertainty, especially in a point so weighty and so nearly touching the majesty and grace of God.

Erasmus defines freedom as the power of the human will, in virtue of which it rests with it to turn itself to that which leads to eternal blessedness, or to turn itself away from it. He does not mean thereby simply the susceptibility for the truly good, but also the power of producing the good out of itself, and without leaving any essential place for Christian grace in order to salvation, whilst Luther seeks to think of God as the origin of everything that is good, but will not the less on that account render man responsible for what is evil.

Hence Erasmus says simply: man has two arms, one for good, the other for evil; Luther cuts off his right arm, and leaves him only the left. But if not only the evil, but also the good, is there for us to know, why not also for the will? And this he then follows up with all the grounds and consequences, which are always, even by the more recent Lutheran theology, insisted on in opposition to the doctrine of absolute election. Without free will in his sense of it, sin would be, according to Erasmus, no more sin, and imputation, the righteousness of punishment, and the aim of all exhortations, warnings, and commands would be done away with. Luther would exalt the merit of Christ, and let grace shine in the highest light, but for that purpose he makes God the author of evil, and cruel, inasmuch as He lays up grace for the believers, who, however, have not become so by their own act, but wrath for the unbelievers whom He has made. Hence it is to be said, God begins the good work by means of the impulse of grace, but then there is to be attributed to the human will some degree of power, although the reward at the end is purely matter of grace.

It is well known that in every age, in which the splendour and freshness of Christianity rose before mankind with new clearness, there is to be observed the most powerful emphasizing of absolute dependence upon God, and a return particularly to the Pauline exhibition of doctrine. It was thus with Augustine, it was thus at the commencement of the Reformation, with all the Reformers of the first rank, it was thus also in our own century, especially with Schleiermacher. Even a doctrine of magical grace is more acceptable to piety than a mode of thought which lets man centre in himself and places him in self-sufficient independence of God. For the latter is directly irreligious, since it sets man in the place of God. Hence it was Pelagianism, which the Reformation, taught by the corruptions of the Church in the middle ages, treats as the fundamental enemy of Christianity, and even of all religion, an enemy which is above everything to be rooted out. It aimed in the first instance at what was religious, not at what was moral. And yet the denial, at first universal, of the freedom of the will in spiritual things (*liberum arbitrium in spiritualibus*) was not the object it had in view, but only a postulate which seemed indispensable. There was no desire to deny the freedom of the will in civil matters (*liberum arbitrium in civilibus*), whereby is understood what is commonly called the province of moral works (of *justitia civilis*), but only to exclude all reasonings from this starting-point, which would involve freedom also in spiritual things for self-redemption. All freedom in respect of God was declared against, because the admission of it seemed also to entail a *liberum arbitrium in spiritualibus* and to deny the absolute need of redemption.

Luther starts from this fact in religious experience, that the greatest saints have in their temptations quite forgotten the freedom of the will, even when they taught it otherwise.[1] I will confess for myself, he says, that I would not desire to have a free will left me, wherewith I might strive after salvation, even

[1] Luther, *de servo arbitrio*, § 152. *Luthers Werke von Walch*, xviii. 2139.

although there were no doubt and no temptation. For I would be (with my freedom of choice) as one that beats the air and never certain of my salvation. But since God has taken my salvation out of my free will and placed it in His free will, I am certain that He is faithful and cannot belie His promise. And inasmuch as the counsel of God was formed, before we were in existence, he deduces from election the independence of our salvation from our own merit and also from the law. What an anxious life would it be, if we could only comfort ourselves with the assurance of grace when we fulfilled the law ! for who does that ? But grace is promised before the law, that is to say, preveniently, and that is the will of God. The doctrine of election, accordingly, he regards as the objective complement of the personal assurance of salvation, and the latter as only perfect when it rests upon the counsel of grace having reference to one person, and which is eternal, unchangeable, and omnipotently decisive. And who can deny, that the pious man will not consent to thank himself for anything good, but knows that it all comes from above? (James i. 17.) The pious consciousness indeed attributes what is evil to man; and that Luther would by no means discourage.

The question, however, certainly arises, whether the system of doctrine here attempted by Luther does not issue in puzzles and contradictions, which are not only disturbing for the moral consciousness, but also for a religious contemplation of the world?

Luther in this treatise repudiated *all* freedom on the part of man over against God. He calls necessity indeed an ill-advised, unsuitable, unpleasant word, because it indicates a compulsion, which is contrary to the will and leaves no place for the cause, which is impelled (*i.e.* the secondary cause).[1] But although he attributes to man a real will, which is not a mere seeming causality, he nevertheless regards God as the all-determining causality, and the free will as a divine title, a lofty expression, which only befits God.[2] Neither the human nor the divine will does anything by compulsion, but by inclination.[3] Manichæism and stoical fatalism are repugnant to him. But in free will lies a divine power, which no creature has in itself, and no one ought to bear this name, but the Divine Majesty.[4] In support of the statement that man does even that to which God determines

---

[1]. *Luthers Werke von Walch*, xviii. 2085, § 59. [2] *Ibid.* § 13, p. 2126.
[3] *Ibid.* § 442. [4] *Ibid.* § 135, p. 2129.

him, by personal inclination, he says, God moves every power according to its nature. It might thus be thought that the nature, which every one has, must, on that account, be not originally determined by God, but only that after man had, without the co-operation of God, received a constitution, *e.g.* an evil one, God impels and moves him, like every other creature, to develop and manifest himself according to his own proper nature. But he goes further. He falls back upon the eternal divine foreknowledge and the omnipotent divine power, and deduces therefrom, that even as we were not created by ourselves, so neither are we able to do anything of ourselves alone, but everything is done by His almighty power. He does not accordingly stop short at a theological basis for the absence of freedom, but goes on to the metaphysical.[1]

Now, as has been said, he regards the proof of the absence of freedom in man as a means and support in proof of the necessity of grace and redemption. But it is precisely to this purpose that the proof adduced by no means corresponds. All power of self-redemption, indeed, is stricken down by it; but if God decrees and decides everything according to His power, how is it then with guilt and sin, this which is presupposed by atonement and redemption, seeing that what is not punishable requires no atonement? God's supreme and absolute power and His free good pleasure would certainly be able to justify and sanctify even without Christ and without faith. That absolute freedom of God, to which the supreme place is given, only allows a capricious and accidental significance to the historical economy of salvation. Hence he does not stop short at a metaphysical denial of freedom on account of the Divine omnipotence and foresight, and from this point he proves superior to Erasmus. The

[1] § 433-437, p. 2315, ff. "Since He foresaw from eternity that we should be even thus, and has made us in consequence in every respect according as His foresight appointed, and at this very moment makes, impels, and governs us according thereto, say, good friend, what can we in any way call or imagine to be free in us? For this reason are God's eternal foresight and our free will directly opposed to one another, like fire and water. Either God fails in His foresight and errs in His working, which is impossible, or we must do and suffer ourselves to be done with, as His eternal foresight and working intend." § 437, "God is an Almighty God, not only in respect of power, but also in respect of effectual operation, else were he a God to be mocked." § 434, "Yes, these two things, omnipotent power and eternal foresight, fundamentally destroy free-will, so that not a hair of it even is left."

natural corruption of man, his impotence in spiritual things on account of sin, he regards as completing his doctrine of man's need of help. Man is not free, not only because God is Almighty, but especially because he is the slave of sin.[1] The law stands immutably firm; man however is in contradiction with it through sin and guilt. This brings him into antagonism within himself, nay, into bondage; especially, the law condemns him as he is. Erasmus indeed makes an easy matter of it; he imputes sin to the flesh, so that the spirit may be at the same time good and pure. But then the best part of us would have no need of Christ; Christ would only redeem the meanest, grossest part. But no! man is wicked as a whole, in his completeness. Man has not *of himself* the least spark[2] of divine life in himself, only the receptivity for the divine operation, which he also calls passivity[3] (*aptitudo, dispositiva qualitas*). He only ascribes to man the capability of *being led* to eternal life. He here falls back upon the whole structure of the Epistle to the Romans, according to which all men since Adam are subject to sin and death. If to this there be added his doctrine of omnipotence, above stated, the latter co-operates with the consequences of Adam's sin in such a way that man is absolutely void of freedom in divine things. It is the impulsive moving power for every operation of the creature according to its nature. The nature of man, however, has through Adam's fall become sinful; God accordingly impels man according to his present nature.[4] The working of God on Pharaoh finds him already wicked, and only brings out what is latent. "If wickedness takes place, the fault is in the wicked tools which God does not allow to stand idle." God indeed preserves the wicked, but He does not create within them a new element of wickedness. The rider of a lame horse does not create the lameness. But since man is turned away from what is good, the unlimited eternal working of God makes it so that he must now err and sin, until the Spirit of God changes him. For God has certainly reserved to Himself a higher working, transcending nature and the law of its present life.[5]

[1] § 510-521. [2] § 559-569. [3] § 128, p. 2125, ff.
[4] Cf. Julius Müller, *das göttliche Recht der Union*, 1854, p. 274, ff., and his above-mentioned treatise, v. p. 204, note 2.
[5] § 400, p. 2294.

Doctrine of the Origin of Natural Corruption. 211

But if God's almighty working is modified by natural depravity, if this, and not God, is the cause of wickedness being wrought according to the constitution of man, then the whole stress falls upon the question, "How does the case stand with *Adam and the origin of sin?*" Is it not again the omnipotence of God which is the cause of Adam's fall? Or is Adam's fall his own free act? Luther teaches[1] that he was created pure by God; that he stood there in freedom, whilst we are not free; he had a noble position, although one still in need of confirmation, and not yet participatory in eternal life. This then would be the Augustinian infralapsarian doctrine.[2] It would also be in accordance therewith that he does not speak of any decree to impel man to sin, and that he points to the devil as the cause of temptation.[3] But the question regarding the origin of sin would be thereby only thrust further back, and the above utterances regarding Divine omnipotence do not admit freedom as the cause of Adam's fall, when, at the same time, they do not compel God to be made the positive cause of evil, inasmuch as the fall would be explicable by the mere withholding of the power of withstanding the temptation necessary to confirmation. And that is in reality his doctrine. He reminds us that with the law a new commandment came to Adam, to the observance of which there would have belonged a higher spiritual power than that which was his at first. His power, since he was pure, would have sufficed for the task hitherto imposed on him; but the new task he could not discharge without a new gift of God. This God gave not. He must learn how impotent (*impotens*) he was without grace. Hence he was left to himself, forsaken of God (*sibi relictus et desertus a Deo*).[4] Divine omnipotence, according to him, does not suffer anything accidental, even as the Divine foresight embraces everything. And thus, according to Luther's mind, there is not to be understood by Adam's freedom before the fall the power of good and evil; he saw no boon in freedom to evil, and the power of good he can never ascribe to man of himself; but he regards it [the freedom before the fall] as denoting freedom from sin, or the as yet certainly imperfect parti-

[1] *Luthers Werke von Walch*, xi. 3077.
[2] Cf. the above note; viii. 405, i. 110, 115, 423; cf. xviii. 2292, § 398 (Adam).
[3] xi. 3077.
[4] Köstlin, as cited, i. 244; ii. 44, ff. *Luthers Werke von Walch*, xviii. 2292, § 398.

cipation in Divine freedom, which he had through grace.[1] The consciousness of sin and guilt is nevertheless for Luther so directly vivid, that the denial of freedom of choice occasions him no fears regarding it; and he only allows that theoretical process of thought to play, as it were, upon the surface of the consciousness of guilt.

The Reformed doctors, too, did not advance beyond Luther in respect of the possibility of uniting a view of the Divine omnipotence, which denied freedom, with sin and guilt;[2] and it thus only remains for us to see *what position Luther takes up in reference to a series of questions* which his doctrine forces into view. In a certain measure, says he, one may speak of a free will on the part of man in respect of what is under him,[3] although this, at the same time, is ruled only through God's will, and the most Christian way would be to dismiss the word "free will" altogether.[4] But if we have no free will whatever in spiritual things, what significance have the Divine admonitions, threatenings, &c.?[5] Erasmus deduces the ability from the command; Luther finds its significance in this, that by the law we discern our impotence. God says, "Do it, if thou canst; let us see if thou canst; although, at the same time, thou mayest through grace."[6] In this way, certainly, he does not need to strip the law of its spiritual reference, in order to preserve some significance in the admonition.—
But if man in his present position is driven to set forth the evil —which in itself dwells in him not as a dead inheritance handed down from Adam, but as his own evil, to which he consents— why, then, does God preserve evil and not bring His working to an end, that so evil might cease? Or why has He not annihilated the mediate cause, the Deceiver of man, but preserves him by His power? Is not such a will on the part of His omnipotence in contradiction to the will expressed by His law? He answers, that would mean that God should cease to be God and good, in order that the godless might not become more wicked. God deals quite differently: He increases the power of evil, but He does so in order to lead, through the revelation of the evil, to a

---

[1] xi. 3077.   [2] Cf. the subsequent Division.   [3] § 135, p. 2129.
[4] Similarly Melanchthon in his *Locis* of 1521, where he calls it philosophical and untheological to speak of a free will. Cf. Galle, *Charakteristik Melanchthons als Theolog.*, Halle, 1845. Schmidt, *Ph. Melanchthons Leben*, 1864, p. 64, ff.
[5] § 309, ff. p. 2237.   [6] § 300, p. 2232; § 327, p. 2249, ff.

a crisis, to the longing for salvation, and so to the overcoming of the evil. For those who believe He creates anew.¹

The problem might thereby be said to be solved, if all men attained to salvation. But since Luther adheres firmly to the presupposition that a portion is lost, since in general he places the decision of the eternal destiny in this life, since he, further, like Augustine, does not place the faith, which obtains salvation, in the freedom of man, there results the new problem, *How can God suffer some to be lost, and save the others?*² seeing that the latter resemble the former in sinfulness and impotence, and can only be saved by means of a miracle of grace. He answers principally by pointing out the factiousness and selfishness of the reason in such argumentations; since, if one looks at the justice of the thing, it is in itself quite as astonishing that, when all are unrighteous, some are rewarded, as that, when all deserve it, some are punished. Why is it not rather said that, since the condemnation of the unrighteous is just, the salvation even of a single unrighteous man is unjust?

As the problem of the salvation of some in spite of justice is solved by means of Christian grace, so may also the remaining problem, How is it that a portion is excluded from salvation? This much is already evident, that there is no unrighteousness in the punishment of some, since God would not be unrighteous if He punished all, as no one has a right to grace.—But the inequality of the final destiny, considered in connection with the original equality of sin and of dependence upon God, remains nevertheless after this manner a problem, which would only disappear if it could be admitted that the destination of all at their creation was not the same, that men do not belong to one and the same stock. The Gospel, however, treats mankind as one; the law obtains for all, for all the promise of salvation, if they believe. He himself asks, whether God, who so highly magnifies His pure goodness in the Gospel, does not contradict Himself and His Word, when He nevertheless finds pleasure in the torment of the damned?³ " At this many people have taken offence in all times; these thoughts gave great offence to himself, so as to drive him into deepest despair, until he learned how useful is despair, and how close at its heels is grace. Instead of seeking to vindicate God with acute and lofty art, one must learn that

¹ § 398, 435.   ² § 435, p. 2316.   ³ § 435, p. 2316, cf. § 297-303.

there is a difference between the *revealed* and the *secret* will of God.[1] He lets His law and grace be proclaimed to all, but the secret will ordains who and how many are to be partakers of grace. (In this he certainly endangers the certainty of the Word of grace, and has to put a forced meaning upon passages like Matt. xxiii. 37; 1 Tim. ii. 4.) God and God's Word are not the same; God has revealed Himself in the Word, but He has not wholly bound Himself to the Word. He moves in transcendent freedom."—But if God moves in freedom above the law as above the Gospel which He allows to be proclaimed, if the two have not an essential connection with God, it seems as if neither were intended in perfect earnestness, but as if only that were contained in them which He desires to have proclaimed, whilst He reserves it to Himself to carry out in reality, instead of a grace proclaimed to be of universal validity, one which is only limited. The revealed will seems thus to come into contradiction with the secret, which alone decides the actual result. Luther, however, does not allow that there is a contradiction, but rather summons us to *believe* that the contradiction is only seeming. We are manifestly directed to the revealed will; it is neither commanded nor lawful to inquire into the secret. We are directed to Christ; He has come to make our salvation perfectly certain to us; He is the mirror in which we have to seek and to contemplate our salvation; he is the Book of Life.[2] In spite of those utterances regarding the all-transcending freedom of God, he holds to it that in Christ the heart of God is truly opened to us, and the innermost nature of God (love) revealed. The purpose of redemption in general is not merely proclaimed, so as if God were not in earnest about it; but God's nature is, as it were, in-set in the Word of Christ and in the sacraments. But Luther does not consider that in this purpose of redemption in general, which gave Christ, an act of love took place, which communicates faith to all and thus actually imparts to all the salvation in Christ, which in itself is sufficient for all.[3] By this distinc-

---

[1] § 303-307. [2] *Luther's Werke*, ii. 257, f. 261.
[3] Many, as *e.g.* Franck, *die Lehre der Concordienformel*, 1858, say that Luther's doctrine of the means of grace brought him ultimately to place predestination in the background, and to seek the cause of the damnation of some only in their unbelief,—which is refuted by what is said above, and could only have had a meaning, if he had ascribed to men liberty to assume this or that position to grace. But in opposition to this stands the fact that he (*Art. Smalc.* p. 318), in the year 1537,

tion he seeks to avert the danger of rendering the revealed will of God uncertain by reason of the secret will. The will revealed in the law remains, in fact, unshaken for all; but the purpose of grace, which is expressed in general terms, is nevertheless only realized in a portion, without there being greater guilt on the part of those who are lost; and the effect of this upon the offer of grace in the means of grace must be, that its acceptance does not take place with the certain confidence that God will vouchsafe His Spirit for the opening up of the requisite susceptibility. It seems to be the case (and this holds, too, of the Calvinist doctrine) that by the *decretum absol. particulare*,—not exactly that the *offer* which takes place in the means of grace is rendered uncertain, and the relation of the heavenly gifts to the elements is loosened; but since the offer can only be made in order to be received, and the power of receiving, or faith, is to depend exclusively upon God, who does not vouchsafe it to all, it may always in the end be said, that it cannot be God's earnest purpose, in offering grace to all to make all partakers of the same, and the result is quite the same as if the grace did not lie in the means of grace as such, but only united itself with them for those to whom faith is appointed. The point upon which everything depends cannot be merely the power of salvation *resident* in the means of grace; the principal point is, whether they possess *operative efficacy* for salvation for all, and that, since there is no *liberum arbitrium* in man, of an irresistible character, alike for all—which Luther denies, inasmuch as he falls back upon the saying, God gives faith and the Holy Spirit where and to whom He will.

Since, accordingly, Luther's proof of human necessitousness by means of the denial of freedom threatens both the conception

---

denies that man has freedom to do the good and to abandon the evil, and the reverse. He said further (cf. Julius Müller, *das Verhältniss der Wirksamkeit des heiligen Geistes*, &c., *Studien und Kritiken*, 1856, ii. p. 337), at a late period in his life, in reviewing his writings, that he oftentimes desired, like another Saturn, to swallow all his children; amongst the very few exceptions which he makes, he names his book, *De servo arbitrio*. In the commentary on Genesis, which belongs to his latest period, he unites the universality of the promise in the Word with the conversion of only a portion of the hearers, without referring to liberty, so as to say that the external Word alone effects nothing, else all would believe to whom it comes; much rather must the Holy Spirit also work in the heart. He makes no mention of any difference in the doctrine of the Swiss in the article *de servo arbitrio*, neither in his earlier nor in his later controversial writings. On this point he knows himself to be essentially one with them.

of guilt (and hence again the necessity of salvation), to which he so distinctly adheres, and the doctrine of the means of grace otherwise maintained by him both before and after, it may confidently be said that those utterances which absolutely repudiate liberty appear in the whole system as heterogeneous, and by anticipation doomed to expulsion. There may also be noticed as characteristic features of Luther's doctrine of predestination, that it will not renounce the *universality of the purpose of divine love*, little as he is able to vindicate it, and that he also admits the *possibility of apostasy* on the part of those who have obtained grace, wherein the factor of human freedom might again unconsciously assert itself, as in his above-mentioned postulate, that the conception of sin and guilt must remain for him uninjured. It is not clear, how complete apostasy is possible in the case of one chosen to salvation, without the breaking up of Luther's conception of election, and the more logical development of this point is to be found in Calvin, who attributes to all the elect also the gift of perseverance (*donum perseverantiæ*).

On the whole, Luther has also the feeling that he has not completely mastered the difficulties of the problem; he is sure and clear so long as his glance rests in the luminous world of salvation, but around this world there is extended a darkness in respect of sin in the still unbelieving world within and without Christendom. Here, in respect of those still standing outside of grace, his statement is still tentative and even not free from contradictions. According to his doctrine of Omnipotence, he must make God, either by His doing or forbearing, the origin of evil, which he nevertheless will not do. But the strength and kernel of his treatise is not to be sought in this, but rather in that wherein he stays himself upon the Apostle Paul, as his spiritual father. As Paul in the Epistle to the Romans describes the great periods of human history and the process of faith, and shows how sin in mankind is co-ordinated with grace, how upon the knowledge of sin and guilt there should follow righteousness by faith in Christ, from the righteousness of faith peace, and from this free love, the liberation from the bondage and threatenings of the law, as he then (ch. viii.-xi.) soars above time and adoringly engrosses himself in the Divine Counsel, which marches without wavering through all the stages from the calling to the glory of the justified, in order then in the joyous con-

Superiority to Erasmus. 217

sciousness of a personality hid in God to break into that lofty song of triumph (Rom. viii. 32, ff.): so Luther also,—after he had in the indulgence controversy summoned to true repentance, and then unfolded with growing clearness the faith that justifies, and discovered therein peace, the power of sanctification, and the life of salvation,—after he had, further, out of the inward freedom felt by the Christian, proclaimed in the subsequent writings (in that, too, against Erasmus), his freedom from the traditions of men and from the law,—finally reposes in the contemplation of the Divine foreknowledge of God, and has thus given to the doctrine of true freedom, which is as much opposed to caprice as to slavery, its ultimate basis in the immutability of God and His counsel. Everything, even the temporary power of sin, has for him converged into a divine harmony, so long as he looks only at believers.—Erasmus makes man at first richer than Luther does, but yet how far is Luther's conception of freedom ultimately superior to that of Erasmus, who views the highest and best element of freedom as reached in freedom of choice, and who accordingly must logically teach an everlasting possibility of falling, and makes perfection eternally insecure! Luther's conception of freedom leads to godlike real freedom by grace; for this it would be no excellence, but only a defect, to be still enveloped in choice and uncertainty. Here too, accordingly, as in the Christology, it is the goal of the idea which is to be perfectly realized, which Luther has most clearly apprehended, although he has been less successful in describing completely and surely the stages by which the goal is reached, and the factors of the process. The conception of freedom entertained by Erasmus, with its eternal twofold possibility and with its uncertainty in respect of salvation, cannot appear to him to be one to be envied, and he cannot see that any loss is sustained, if man, by the power of God-given love, like God by virtue of His free proper love, cannot in future do otherwise than will what is good.

If Luther believed that in the way towards that goal he dared not interweave the freedom of choice as a momentum into the process of salvation, because he feared that if once admitted it would lead inevitably to the acceptance of meritorious works and to a denial that everything good is to be derived from God, —the Church of the German Reformation has not upon this point adhered to Luther, but there is to be observed at an early stage a reaction, principally amongst the laity, against the complete denial of freedom. It is also officially expressed in the first public confession of the Augustana. *Melanchthon* and the other theologians were guided by the consciousness that they had not to state Luther's doctrine of predestination as the common confession of the Evangelicals. Hence, as Melanchthon writes[1] to Brenz, this question was purposely passed over in silence in the confession, the *liberum arbitrium in civilibus* was taught, whilst in reference to spiritual things the secondary causes were specially emphasized, without, however, omitting to declare that word and sacrament only possess the efficacy for salvation, potentially resident in them, when and where God is willing to co-operate by means of His Spirit.[2]

The feeling of German Evangelical Christendom, that this matter had been unfairly dealt with, was at a later period more and more distinctly expressed by Melanchthon, the second chief German Reformer. And even so it has never come to pass that the doctrine of absolute predestination has been looked upon in the German Evangelical Church as the only orthodox doctrine, or the opposite doctrine rejected by the Church as unevangelical. Melanchthon, whose nature was in a supreme measure ethical, and who was thus complementary of Luther, always sought increasingly, in his commentaries and in the later editions of his *Glaubenslehre*, to secure a place for the moral freedom of choice in man, and especially in Adam, whereby the above-mentioned dangers of Luther's doctrine might be averted. And the most expressive memorial of the mode of thought prevalent in Germany regarding this point of doctrine is that, whilst the formula of union is in other respects unfavourable to Melanchthonianism, and is even designed to suppress it, it adheres upon this point to his fundamental tendency, although it does not follow his

---

[1] *Corp. Reformatorum*, ii. 547.

[2] *Conf. Aug.* v. Hence it is a calumny against Melanchthon, when this silence regarding the doctrine of predestination in the *Conf. Aug.* is branded as a dishonourable act, whilst, conversely, the Confession would have been an untruth, *i.e.* not a confession of the common evangelical faith, which it is designed to be, if that doctrine had been there put forward as an article of faith. To this it is to be added, that Melanchthon even in 1530 by no means laid on it the same stress as in his *Loci* of 1521. Luther also allowed a *lib. arb.* in relation to worldly matters (*in civilibus*). Cf. Galle, *Melanchthon*, as quoted before.

development of doctrine in its particulars, and seeks to provide for the freedom of choice its indispensable place.[1]

It only remains to be noticed as the final result of the conflict between Erasmus and Luther (as with Hutten), that the attempt

[1] So early as in the Saxon Articles of Visitation of 1527, Melanchthon emphasized in the strongest manner the ethical side alongside of the directly religious, and laid a stress upon the law and repentance, which drew upon him accusations of Antinomianism (Joh. Agricola), whereupon Luther took up Melanchthon's side decidedly, and in his Catechisms gave its proper place to ethical matter, especially to the Decalogue. It was thus already declared that the path of evangelical doctrine regarding the freedom of the will and the law would hold midway between Erasmus and Antinomianism. Melanchthon however was always carrying out his ethical religious standpoint more sharply and independently. In the edition of the *Loci* of 1533 he already declared himself against the denial of accident in relation to God, and calls the denial of freedom stoicism; he proves from antiquity that the conscience remained and spoke, and was even a propelling factor. He acknowledges that the idea of guilt would suffer, if, whether by reason of the divine omnipotence or original sin, every moral factor on the side of the will were denied. We have, according to him, to hold to the universal promise, and not to rack our brains about election, and although the mercy of God is the cause of election, we, regarding the matter from beneath, may nevertheless say, those are surely elect who lay hold upon grace. In justification there is a certain causality even in the recipient, although not worthiness. In the year 1535 (*Corp. Reform.* xxi. 331, ff. 373, ff.), in combating Laurentius Valla, he insists on separating the question regarding human powers from the question regarding the Absolute Counsel, which excludes all chance. He does not deny the spiritual incapacity of the will, but this is strengthened by the Word, to which it can cleave. He thus arrives at his typical doctrine of the three co-operative causes of salvation, the Word, the Holy Spirit, and the Will, which does not remain idle, but struggles against its weakness, but that in such a way that God's call and helpful impulse precedes the will, which merits nothing, but is only related instrumentally to salvation. Finally, from 1543 (xxi. 552, ff.), he says: There are not in God *contrariæ voluntates*, since His promise is earnestly intended for all; if, however, some are lost, the cause is not in God but only in men, who receive grace differently. The cause of the distinction, *discriminis*, lies in the different method of treatment which is possible to believers as to others. Man may pray for help and reject grace. This he calls free will, as the power of laying hold of grace (*liberum arbitrium* as *facultas applicandi sese ad gratiam*). Grace disposes man, and he must freely consent to it. Melanchthon, too, will here by no means (as Franck, *Concordienformel*, i. 134, declares) ascribe to free will a meritorious causality (*causa meritoria*). *Fides* remains for him ὄργανον ληπτικόν, the instrumental procuring of the possession of salvation, not of merit. He also holds fast the absolute need of salvation (xxi. 652, 655). The power of deciding for good, he always derives from God, from grace communicating itself through the Word, which grace is thought of as, according to nature, antecedent, and as dispelling the effect of original sin. Only in this one point is Melanchthon's doctrine not brought to a logical conclusion, that he does not make original sin and the tendency it produces to unbelief to be sooner or later counterbalanced in all men by prevenient grace. In its matter Melanchthon's doctrine of free will cannot be

was henceforth abandoned, to bring the Evangelical Reformation and the [Roman] Catholic amelioration of science and of the school nearer to one another.[1]

CHAPTER IV.

EXHIBITION OF THE EVANGELICAL PRINCIPLE IN THE FORMATION OF THE CHURCH.

DURING the first struggles, which we have considered in the former chapter, the evangelical principle was strengthening and exercising its church-forming power, inasmuch as its pure essence was, in opposition to the divergences on both sides, set forth with growing clearness and consciousness in a shape which forms a strong foundation for a renewed Church. Luther clearly discerned, and succeeded in exhibiting, in the most pregnant manner, *justification only by faith in Christ,* and the *sole divine authority of the Holy Scriptures, i.e.* the so-called *material and formal sides of the evangelical principle,* each in its independent worth and title, but both also in their inward inseparable connection. In none of his writings, indeed, is there to be found a comprehensive and connected scientific exposition of this principle of the Reformation. We even once and again find utterances, which in setting forth only one side, do not seem to accord with others which, with as much vehemence, insist only upon the other side. Still it is not difficult to apprehend his true meaning, if one only does not stop short at the particular momentum, as if it were the whole. Does he give more prominence now to the one side, and now to the other, now rather to the relative independence of the material momentum, now rather to that of the formal, then a statement, to be faithful, will have to exhibit in full strength this relative independence of each in order, but will

---

essentially found fault with; nor is it in its true design affected by the utterances of the *F. C.* He has not the slightest desire to diminish grace or magnify man's independence of God, but only to conserve the conception of guilt and the moral character of the process of salvation ; and he desires accordingly that the work of conversion should proceed in the form of proper personal consciousness and volition, which cannot be denied without injuring a fundamental feature of the Reformation, its regard to the personality.

[1] Cf. Niedner, *Kirchengeschichte,* 630.

then have also to inquire, what he has accomplished doctrinally for the internal union of the two, which must have taken place in his own conscious life of faith?

For this end, and before we enter more minutely upon these three points, let us place before our mind, in brief outline, the progress of his inward development, and of the doctrinal expression of his experience in the faith.

We saw above (p. 84, ff.), that faith, together with its experience of salvation, was already found in him, before he had a fully-formed doctrine of the Holy Scriptures, or knew what he should include in the canon, or how to expound it. The decision was wrought when he was laid hold of by that word of the monk, which directed him to the article of the apostolic symbol concerning the forgiveness of sins,—a word, accordingly, which, as regards its matter, was a Scriptural divine utterance, but as regards its form, was a proclamation by the Church. He was thus at first led to the light and peace, not through the reading of the Holy Scriptures, but just as little in an unhistorical and purely subjective way, but rather through the living utterance of the Church, although not in such a way that it was the authority of the Church which lent to the utterance its highest pacifying credentials and certainty; in his case, moreover, the postulate was not awanting, that that utterance of the symbol regarding the forgiveness of sins, the subject matter, accordingly, which effected his salvation, be purely Christian and Scriptural: but neither was he brought to rest by the authority of the Scriptures, in which, previously to his experience in the faith, he had no living belief, although it is not to be denied that his development in the faith only reached a firm and clear conclusion, after he had become more intimate with the Holy Scriptures, especially with the Epistles to the Romans and the Galatians. *The Apostolic and prophetic writings only came to be regarded by him as the decisive rule and judge, after the saving matter, which the Church still had in common with the Scriptures, had approved itself to his heart by its own inherent power.* Before the decisive turning-point of his life, the Scriptures only influenced him as a *means of grace*, similar to preaching, but not as a divine *rule*, recognized by him as independent.

In order, however, clearly to understand the growth of the whole Reformation principle in his consciousness in regard to both the sides which it includes, we must cast a glance into the period immediately before he came out as a Reformer. When he was engaged in acquiring, by internal labour, a conscious knowledge of the treasures of his experience in the faith, and in giving to them a doctrinal shape, he found himself attracted most of all by the noblest representatives of mysticism, the *Deutsche Theologey* and Tauler, and employed their language and circle of ideas for his exposition, but still so that his individuality and a stronger ethical tendency is already apparent in him. In this period, before 1517, he gains the most important *anthropological and theological postulates for the evangelical principle of faith*.[1]

To his sense of God, allied in its vividness to mysticism, the world appears in every momentum appointed and supported by God, and dependence on Him, as well as connection of life with Him, perennial. He is thereby led, in opposition to Pelagianism and Deism, to preserve humility as the basis of all piety, and also to exclude all false surrogates for God, the false substitutes for God, and accordingly whatever is magical. We need God Himself; nothing creatural, no medium of revelation which is not at the same time Himself, can satisfy the susceptibility and necessity of our nature. So much do we need God, that we only have our true existence in God; we are in untruth if we have an existence for ourselves outside of God; if we, bent back or "curved" into ourselves, would, as it were, shut ourselves up anthropocentrically and self-sufficiently into a circle reposing in itself. Man must again become "nothing;" God must accomplish everything in him. He does not mean by this a pantheistic mingling of God and man,[2] but he regards union with God as belonging to the *essential nature* of man; hence he demands the giving up, the putting to death of that false egoism [*Ichheit*], its annihilation by means of repentance, because that egoism excludes us from the true good which belongs to our essential nature, and banishes us into our own poverty, into the nothing, which appears to us wealth. But as we may not seek the highest

[1] Ernst Val. Löscher, *vollständige Reformationsakten*, 1720, 2 Thle.; *Luthers Werke von Walch*, xii. 2144-2337; Dieckhoff, *deutsche Zeitschrift*, 1853; Harries, *deutsche Jahrbücher*, 1861, vi. 714, 805.

[2] Löscher, i. 241: *non quod in Verbum substantiale mutemur,—nos non Deus efficimur*, but rather as *appetitus et appetibile, amor et amatum unum sunt—non substantialiter*.

good in ourselves, so also not through ourselves, by our own means. In opposition to the pelagianizing mysticism, with its doctrine of stages and method of spiritual ascents, he will have us come to God through God; God must be not merely the goal and the blessing, but also means, mediator, and guide, to the goal: as the Good He must grant us His love, else there is no salvation for us. By means of the consciousness of sin and guilt he passes beyond the mediæval mysticism, with its calm resignation to God, and its passive waiting, in short, the mystic repentance, which is a merely negative behaviour and a sort of expiation; and in the place of that calm resignation, and even of the feeling of forsakenness by God, with which the spiritual joy of the mystic alternates, he sets the fear of God under a feeling of sin and guilt,—a misery, accordingly, which is not merely æsthetic, but of ethical mood, and which also stands in need of quite a different cure from what the mystic raptures offer it. The cure of despair, under a sense of the righteousness of God and one's own unworthiness, redemption from the state of bondage therein implied, cannot consist in grace, *i.e.* love to God, being suddenly infused into us in place of fear; for that would be to deny the rightfulness and the necessity of fear, which have their foundation in our guilt over against God. Fear must rather continue, because founded in truth, but, if it is to become well with us, it must (we will see immediately by what means) become filial fear (*timor filialis*). It must come to this (however it be reached), that fear and love be no more severed, but both unitedly directed towards God, so that love is incorporated with fear as confidence, and fear with love as reverence, as holy dread of everything displeasing to God. It may be difficult to attain to this; but this we must abide by, that hope endures amid quaking and faith amid trembling, as grace amid our sin.

Thus grace is not in the first instance the production or merit of holiness, nor of infused love; but the union of these widely different things, fear of God on account of sin, and the resigning one's self to fellowship with God, is contained in *faith*, which at this period he also oftentimes calls hope. Grace, however, must be offered freely and preveniently, in order that faith may lay hold of it, and by gradual growth overcome sin, until by means of love grown perfect all slavish fear is cast out. There is no other victory than our faith, which lays hold of the present Christ, to whom everything is easy of conquest.[1] Bodily exercises may be profitable, and even necessary at the outset; afterwards they hamper the progress from slavish to filial fear. The most important thing is, to be day and night occupied with the Gospel.

Since, then, the power of uniting fear and love lies only in faith, and faith again presupposes an object as to be, and capable of being, laid hold of, the antecedent apprehensible revelation of the love of God, we are conducted thus to the *second* postulate of his doctrine regarding faith, the theological, where he again forms a connection in a peculiar fashion with mysticism. There comes up here for consideration before everything else Luther's *doctrine of revelation*, whose tendency is to represent God in His living character and in His apprehensibility by us.[2] God is not to his view as He was to the earlier mystics, merely the unconditioned infinite existence, which is everywhere, but can never be apprehended. It belongs much rather to God's eternal living nature, to formulate Himself in a movement, by which he determines Himself within Himself; through this movement there proceeds in God the Eternal Word of God; through this determinateness, which God's infinitude assumes, and whereby it becomes apprehensible, God enters into a relation to the world, especially to the spiritual world, and to the communion of life with Himself; for through that eternal movement and self-determination within Himself, God becomes accessible and self-communicative; as on the other hand our nature possesses, and even is, an original susceptibility for God, which is not lost even by sin. It is, as it were, the matter which longs to obtain form through God; it seeks through God to obtain possession of God, and can do so where he gives, or offers, Himself. This eternal formulating of God *within Himself* cannot, however, satisfy us; God is invisible and incapable of being apprehended by man in His present sinful condition, which is entirely subject to what is visible. God must accordingly make Himself visible, apprehensible, as it were cosmical, in order that we may obtain possession of Him. This has taken place in the incarnation: God has not merely in Christ assumed flesh as a cloak; Christ is not merely the means or sign of the absent God revealing Himself, it might be, through His doctrine, but in Christ we lay hold of God. For His humanity belongs to the Word, as God belongs to the humanity;

---

[1] Löscher, as cited, i. 230, *an den Probst in Lizka*.
[2] i. 231, f., *Weihnachtspredigt*, 1515.

the Word is not changed into flesh (humanity), but it also does not merely possess and support the flesh; the Word became flesh, in order that flesh might become the Word, the revelation of God, and in the Son we have the Father. The power and essence, which belong to the internal Word in God, the Word in the Trinity, in His eternal mode, dwell also in His temporal or cosmical mode, in the Word become flesh; this is only a second act in the self-modification of God, one which draws nearer to the creature. No less, in fine, does the Scripture, the Word concerning the incarnate Word, bear in itself the power and essence of the same, and can lodge itself in those who yearn thereafter, make them partakers of the substance of all Divine blessings, and even transform them into children of God, into brothers of the First-born Son, and deify them. If the faith which grasps the Word does not yet possess the whole actual power of the Divine life, it nevertheless possesses in hope the whole treasures of its wealth extending into infinitude.

By means of this doctrine regarding the Word of God, as rendering itself apprehensible and historical, Luther made it theologically possible, in spite of his complete antagonism to Pelagianism, to advance beyond the mere mystic absorption in the infinitude of God, to a faith which is neither mere passivity and idle quietism, essence, nor mere doing, but passivity and action in one another, namely, an active taking and a consenting to be determined by God. And as his yearning for fellowship with God is pervaded by a deep conviction of sin and guilt, and so by a feeling of the fear of God and of separation from God, in like manner does the perfect revelation, in which God draws near to faith, possess a correspondingly ethical character, in which righteousness and love are united. The manifestation of Christ, His life, sufferings and death, has the most direct reference to sin and guilt, and takes away the fear of God by the confirmation of its propriety, and of the deservedness of punishment in the enduring of misery, and the bearing of Divine wrath on account of it; so that faith, in order to be persuaded of its union to, and reconciliation with, God in childlike fear, does not now require to withdraw their due from the righteousness of God and the just fear of Him.

But even with these premises, the result was not by any means a clear and sure description of the *nature of saving faith*.

Owing to the connection with Augustine and mysticism, justification and sanctification, or love, were not at first (in the *Resolutiones* of his 95 Theses) definitely distinguished by him from one another, but the consciousness of reconciliation was made to result partly from the good already planted in us, and partly from faith in Christ's word of promise. He held that there was, even before priestly absolution, the beginning of a Divine infusion of grace, which, inasmuch as it produces what is good in man, is a proof that God has already forgiven. Even the desire for the remission of guilt is the effect of grace, and is a communication [or infusion], which upon its side only operates in the man, whom God has already forgiven.[1] This communication of grace and good impulses he calls already the beginning of justification, or of being made righteous by God. Everything indeed continues thus to be dependent upon grace, as with Augustine; even forgiveness on the part of God is conceived of as preceding the communication, and not first conditioned or effected by those better movements; but the consciousness of forgiveness is made dependent on that communication; and since man is not yet by that communication rendered conscious nor certain of his justification, there is required in addition priestly absolution and faith, not so much in the person or office of the priest, but in Christ's word of promise, the proclamation of which exercises faith, and even awakens it by the very offer, which is objectively real and true, even when it is not made effectual by faith. Faith and repentance, without which faith is psychologically impossible, is not meritorious; it does not procure the offer, which is much rather prevenient and free; but whilst everything Pelagian is abhorrent to him, no less abhorrent is the magical doctrine that one may obtain objective salvation without faith, if he only does not interpose any hindrance. He regards the sacrament as the objective presentation of salvation, valid upon God's part even previously to faith; but he says quite as distinctly that it is faith only, and not the sacrament, which justifies, because the appropriation of what is presented in the sacrament only takes place through faith. It is this *possession* of offered grace which he then calls the actual *justificatio* of man, and he also includes in it *inward transformation and regeneration*, which began even before faith in the communication of grace, in order to produce the feeling of guilt and the desire for assurance of salvation,

[1] Köstlin, as cited, i. 218, ff.

which is finally satisfied by faith in the absolution of the priest.

This statement, inasmuch as it at least does not sufficiently separate between the *consciousness* of justification and sanctification, and even places the infusion of good antecedently to the faith which appropriates justification, suffers from one defect, which does not allow the full and joyful certainty of salvation to be realized.

Since sanctification is never perfect, but only progressive in Christians, so long as justification is not more distinctly distinguished from it, it must share the same fate as sanctification; that is to say, justification is in like manner present only in a partial, and never in a perfect or certain manner, so long as sanctification is not perfected, but is rather still struggling and fluctuating.

Hence Luther's further development necessarily proceeds beyond Augustine, so that grace may in its free prevenient nature enter clearly into the sphere of human consciousness. Let us dwell awhile upon this stage of his matured knowledge of the faith, and depict according to it the evangelical principle in the distinctiveness and mutual connection of its two sides.

A. *The natural side of the evangelical principle by itself, or in its relative independence.*

Grace, as regenerating, love-producing, and sanctifying, can only be communicated step by step, in accordance with the laws of a spiritual process [*Werdens*]; according to its nature, also, it can form a gift only in such a manner as to effect at the same time a change in man. The prevenient character of free grace towards sinners can, accordingly, be manifested, in the first instance, not in the grace of sanctification, but only in justification, provided, namely, that this does not include a forgiveness of sins which is merely partial, and conditioned by present or future love. If Luther had already, in the *Resolutiones*, set by itself the Divine forgiveness, or His, so to speak, inward reconciliation with the sinner, and made this the foundation or presupposition in the Divine Being of the communication of grace and the whole process of salvation, he afterwards conceived of this forgiveness more definitely as the first subject-matter of the communication of grace or of *justificatio*; and makes the free and full forgiveness of sins to be before everything else presented as an objective gift, as a discovery of the gracious counsel of the love of God, who within Himself, before His inward tribunal, has for Christ's sake forgiven man,—presented to him, not because he repents and believes, but in order that he may believe. For that which is to be laid hold of must precede the believing apprehension thereof. The revelation of this gracious counsel of God, by virtue of which He offers to enemies and sinners to be reconciled with them, and the greeting of love as to His own children, takes place in general in the preaching of the Gospel, but specially for the particular individual in baptism and in absolution, which effects the renewal of baptismal grace; as well as in the holy Supper. This reconciliation of God with mankind and with individuals through Christ, by means of whose imputed righteousness God can deal with sinners as children, forms the perpetual basis of His whole conduct towards men, of the whole process of salvation, and of all the fulness of grace which God has designed for men, and which He can impart gradually according to the progressive stages of sanctification. The inward reconciliation of the fatherly heart of God in itself with sinners must be and remain the first thing: but as it does not exhaust the counsel of Divine grace, it cannot remain a mere internal thought or a mere internal movement in God, but the counsel of Divine grace must be revealed in order to bring the world to the enjoyment of the life of reconciliation, to love and salvation.

The *historical* process of salvation in man must itself reflect and exhibit this internal relation of the momenta in God. Hence it is not the amelioration of man, or the work of regeneration and sanctification, which begins the saving process. In order that man may stand open in childlike susceptibility to the communication of sanctifying grace, there must first of all be removed upon his side the fear of, and the aversion to God, on account of the sin and guilt which separate him from God, so that the fundamental relationship may be rightly ordered and transformed from a relationship of enmity and alienation into the normal relationship of childlike confidence. Therefore it is that the process of salvation begins with the preaching of the prevenient and free grace of the complete forgiveness of sins, whereby God on His part offers Himself to men as His children, that they may believe in this reconciliation which avails them, and may in faith find life and salvation.

As, however, the counsel of love in God is not exhausted in the forgiveness of sins and guilt, but God as Father has designed for His children, after the restoration of the normal fundamental relationship, the fulness of graces reaching into eternity; so also it belongs to faith, which lays hold of this pure and perfect Divine counsel of reconciliation, to appropriate, but in a progressive manner, that fulness of graces, and to hold it as a personal possession. That the first-fruits of the gifts of the Spirit become also the portion of man, even along with the appropriation of the forgiveness of sins by faith, is very evident from the consideration, that (what is certainly much more prominent in Luther than in Melanchthon) faith in the forgiveness of sins is not mere faith in an impersonal merit (*meritum*) of Christ, but—as is exhibited with particular beauty in the treatise on the freedom of the Christian—confiding resignation to the living Christ as Reconciler. In Him faith lays hold of the God-given, personified reconciliation. It is His high-priestly love, full of substitutionary intention and power, to whose application to itself faith has to respond by means of confiding resignation. But once entered into fellowship with the living Reconciler, faith is wedded to the whole Christ; so that by virtue of this union not merely the reconciliation and the forgiveness of sins procured by Christ, but also all His benefits and gifts, become common to man, although only in a gradual and progressive manner. Hence Luther, like the better dogmatic theologians of a later date, holds by the view, that in justifying faith—*i.e.* the faith which appropriates justification—love is also involved, and good works are present at least in principle. Hence the believer does not remain as before; not only is the manner of contemplation changed upon the side of God, as it is upon the side of man, into one which imputes the merit of Christ, but in faith there is also a new life made the property of man. Faith is a new tree of life, on which the fruits of love and wisdom of necessity grow. Since a new condition of life is thus implied in the forgiveness of sins, or *justificatio*, which is appropriated by faith, it is not to be wondered at that, *e.g.* in the Apology of the *Conf. Aug.*, faith is called regenerating as well as justifying, and *justificatio* is even termed *renovatio* and *regeneratio*, whilst the *Form. Con.* seeks to draw a sharper separation in conception between what it does not regard as separate in fact. This, however, became afterwards too frequently an objective separation of what is internally united. But no less clear is this other consideration, that since the life of love continues always imperfect and militant, and since even faith and its childlike confidence is often little and weak, though it must ever be growing, the peace and joy of the inner man cannot all through life be ultimately based upon personal perfection in any reference whatsoever, nor in general upon the goodness of any subjective disposition whatsoever, but must always go back again to the ground of that free prevenient forgiveness in the heart of God, in the forum within God. The only blessing of grace which we, so long as we are growing Christians, possess in fulness and completeness is the forgiveness of sins, or reconciliation for Christ's sake, or the fact, that God on His part maintains immovably the fundamental fatherly relationship to us, inasmuch as He looks upon us in Christ, so long as we have not despised fellowship with Christ by unbelief and unwillingness to repent. On the other hand, this forgiveness, even as it is offered in all earnestness before faith exists, continues sure even to the faith which is weak; even a trembling hand of faith is still a hand. Since, further, the covenant relationship to God is, by means of the forgiveness of sins, transformed and ordered aright; and this relationship is that which, amid all the changes in the inner life of the Christian, ever remains the same, the consequence, as respects the relationship of the righteousness of faith to the righteousness of life, or to the love which is ever remaining imperfect, is that the consciousness of peace and even joy in God is perfectly consistent with a consciousness of sin, which not only does not disappear, but even becomes more intense, inasmuch as fellowship with Christ by faith and the faithfulness of Christ covers and completely atones for our imperfection and sin before God, as well as constitutes the pledge of our real perfection.

By faith man becomes *personally a partaker* of the grace of God, and, before all, of the forgiveness of sins. It is indeed an act of man, but it is an act induced or wrought by means of the love of God revealed in Christ, and of the Holy Spirit proceeding from Him. If man has performed the act of trustful resignation and acceptance, the subject-matter of that which has been received becomes a sure and conscious possession. There is a difference between receiving faith and faith as it exists in a state of grace, between the trustful reception (*fiducia*) and the assurance of salvation (*certitudo salutis*). Faith, when it is instituted, receives the blessing of divine assurance,—in the first instance, the assurance of being personally reconciled through resignation to Christ, but, along with this, also the divine assurance of the worthiness of Christ as Redeemer, and of the truth of the message of Christian salvation. Divine truth itself has now, by having approved itself a power of God, become present in the spirit, and faith is rendered conscious of this by the witness of the Holy Ghost. It is not in the first instance a theoretical truth, a dogma, as, for example, the inspiration of the Scriptures, which is made known to faith, nor is it personal goodness nor the transformation which is certainly the effect of faith, nor, finally, is it a *new relationship of our life to God;* but, on the contrary, receiving faith, after it has grown up, is a becoming conscious of being known and loved by God, of a new *relationship of the life of God to us*, a knowledge of being personally redeemed in Christ, or of the personal direction which the love of God takes towards the sinner. God's thought and speech, however, is creative; His testimony is productive, and entails the witness of our heart, that we are His children, and does so in such a way, that we are not wanting in the consciousness, that what our heart testifies is the result and testimony of the Spirit, and not the imagination of the flesh.

At all times Luther laid the greatest stress upon this certainty of salvation, and of the divine truth of Christianity. The grand original certainty, on which all other certainty depends, is the justification of the sinner for the sake of Christ, appropriated by faith; this is only expressed objectively, when it is said, that in his view Christ as Redeemer is the original certainty, in resignation to whom faith finds perfect satisfaction, and knows that it is standing in the truth. It thus stands fast, that for him the great original certainty which attests all other truths, as it is not the authority of the Church, so also is not the authority of the canon of the Holy Scriptures handed down by the Church. It is rather the *subject-matter of the Word of God*, which, however different may be its forms of expression, is able to attest itself to the hearts of men as the Word of God by itself and its divine power. As Luther himself did not arrive at faith and the assurance of salvation by the direct reading of the Holy Scriptures, nor on account of their authority, he could not assign to the formal authority of the canon the position, that *it* is first of all to be believed, but it is the *subject-matter* of the Christian evangel, which captivates him, as a lively need for it was awakened in him, and whose divine self-evidencing power he experiences, after he confidingly entrusted himself to it.

It is true that, when such was the genesis of his faith, the Holy Scriptures co-operated at least unconsciously as a *means of grace*. Without the presupposition, that the historical truth of the testimony of the Church regarding Christ is in general guaranteed (the ultimate guarantee, however, is simply the documentary record of the New Testament), he could not have accomplished the act of faith in the historical Christ. Without the historical testimony regarding Christ, the object of faith, as it is historically revealed, would be wanting to it. But although historical faith presupposes this testimony in general as trustworthy, it is not yet true saving faith, nor is this esteeming the testimony historically true to be considered true assurance. The Gospel as mere historical truth would be something past and dead, like a mere doctrinal system of eternal truths, without life and without reference to the living person. It is the nature of the Gospel, that is truly known and apprehended only when the historical Christ is at the same time embraced as the present, as well as the eternally abiding, and accordingly also future, Christ, —although past, still livingly active to-day, and pointing forward into the depths of an eternity, whose vital energies repose in Him. If the subject-matter of the historical Gospel is thus recognized and apprehended according to its internal nature as historically real and at the same time eternal, then the resting-place of eternal peace and divine life has been found ; and as little as the sun requires a proof by means of some other light, that it is light and diffuses warmth, as little can the faith which has become possessor of the inward presence of truth and of its power, stand in need of some additional assurance of the same.

But let us consider more minutely how this new-formed thing, faith in justification before God through Christ, proves its distinctiveness and relative independence in respect of the Holy Scriptures. Whilst faith and the Holy Scriptures are not, as regards their subject-matter, or at least ought not to be, essentially different—for it is just the essential matter of the Scriptures which is the matter of Christian faith—faith, on the other hand, owes its distinctiveness and relative independence in relation to the Holy Scriptures to the *assurance of salvation and assurance of Christian truth* which belongs to it,—an assurance which is obtained not by way of subjective mysticism or natural reason, but by the intervention of faith as confiding trust (*fiducia*) in the objective Gospel which is to be received. The constitution of our natural reason being what it is,[1] faith is accomplished only by the same being taken captive to the obedience of the faith. What is to be taken captive in it is its pride and self-sufficiency, and despising of what is humble and without appearance, although divine power and wisdom is there ;—in reality, accordingly the unreasonable in the empirical reason ; and what takes it captive is the nascent true reason, which is seeking God and His fellowship, salvation and the certainty of salvation, which can and ought to become despair of one's own person, as well as a trustful laying hold of objective Christianity.

How highly Luther estimates this assurance is evident from numerous passages. When Christ summons us[2] to be on our guard against false prophets, he recognizes in this the right of all Christians, not of the Pope and Councils, to judge of doctrine. He cries to the Pope, " Thou hast determined conclusions with the Councils ; I have the deciding of whether I will accept them or not. Why so ? Thou wilt not stand for me and answer, when I must die, but I must see how I am placed as to being certain of my affairs." Then, turning to the Christian, he continues, " Thou must be as certain of the matter, that it is the Word of God, as thou art certain that thou livest, and even more certain, for on this alone must thy conscience rest. And even if all men came, ay, even the angels and all the world, and determined something : if *thou* canst not form nor conclude the decision, thou art lost. For thou must not place thy decision upon the Pope or any other ; thou must thyself accordingly be so skilful, that thou canst say, ' God says this, not that ; this is right, that is wrong,' else it is not possible to endure. Dost thou stand upon Pope and *Concilia ?* then the devil may at once knock a hole in thee, and insinuate, ' How, if it were false ? how, if they have erred ?' Then thou art laid low at once ; therefore thou must bring conscience into play, that thou mayest boldly and defiantly say,

[1] *Luthers Werke von Walch*, i. 162 ; vi. 181 ; vii. 1425 ; xi. 389, 1625, 2051, 2739 ; xii. 426, 923-27, 1529.
[2] *Ibid.*, xi. 1887.

'That is God's Word; on that will I risk body and life, and a hundred thousand necks, if I had them.'" He demands that the spirit should not come to rest before Christ has in His truth evidenced Himself to it, to its own innermost experience and knowledge; and although he does not let the Holy Spirit work without the intervention of the Word, which preaches Christ, still he sees also that the Holy Scriptures themselves do not seek to hold men fast by themselves alone, but point them to the living Lord Himself, of whom they testify; and that, as they do not demand that the individual be made sure by means of the authority of the Church, so neither by means of their own formal authority; but that faith, begotten by the Holy Ghost and the Gospel, or the "Word" (*i.e.* the subject-matter of Scripture), is an independent structure, a new creation, which occupies a certain independent attitude towards the canon of the Holy Scriptures. This is irrefragably evident from his explanations of historical faith, and from his position to the standpoint of the Waldensians, who assign to the Holy Scriptures the very same position which Catholicism assigns to the Church, namely, that of a merely legal authority. Luther does not impugn historical faith as the first form in which the Gospel is received; he does not dispute that Christian education should take into its service the piety which, upon the morally enforced authority of others, receives what is not yet known to be true. The natural man must first become Christian; Christianity, because it is not yet in him, must approach him in the first instance as the requirement of a higher condition of life. But the Romish Church seeks to stop short at this form of obedience, which is, above all, obedience to the Church. Christ is to be believed in on account of the authority of the Church, not the Church on account of the self-evidencing authority belonging to Christ. It thus, in the first place, denies to man immediate communion with Christ, and, in the second place, it in fact places itself above Christ, and even describes everything as impiety which advances beyond the standpoint of obedience to itself, to an independent knowledge of the truth itself, of the exclusive redemptive merit of Christ, and of the certain forgiveness of sins. More akin to Catholicism, as appears at the first glance, is the standpoint of the Waldensians, which believes in Christ on account of the Holy Scriptures, and in which faith, cut off by the Scriptures from immediate communion with Christ, would be delivered over to the legal standpoint. Even the Scripture is not Christ, though it operates only by means of the Holy Spirit, where and when He will. Luther had tasted the personal assurance of reconciliation through Christ, and to this verification of Christian *truth*, through assurance of *salvation* in Christ, man must come by the act of God the Holy Ghost, which even the Holy Scriptures cannot supplant, although they may be a medium for this act of God. "The Romanists say,[1] 'Yes, but how can we know what is God's Word and what is true or false? we must learn it from the Pope and the Councils.' Very well, let them decree and say what they will, still say I, Thou canst not rest thy confidence thereon, nor satisfy thy conscience; thou must thyself decide; thy neck is at stake, thy life is at stake. Therefore must God say to thee in thine heart, 'This is God's Word,' else it is undecided."

"God suffered (he continues) the same word to be preached by the apostles, and suffers it to be preached still. But though the archangel Gabriel should say it to me from heaven, that does not help me: I must have *God's* Word, I will hear what God says. The Word may indeed be preached to me, but no one can give it me into my heart except God alone, who must speak in the heart, else there is no result; for if He keeps silence, then it has not been spoken. Therefore no one shall turn me from the Word which *God* teaches me, and that must I know as certainly as that three and two make five, that an ell is longer than a half. That is certain, and though all the world speak to the contrary, still I know that it is not otherwise. Who decides me there? No man, but only the truth, which is so perfectly certain, that nobody can deny it." He thus places the attainable assurance of Christian truth on exactly the same footing as the knowledge of the so-called eternal truths,[2] and hence it is a significant circumstance that he also terms Christian assurance "conscience,"

---

[1] *Luthers Werke von Walch*, xi. 1888.
[2] *Luthers Werke von Walch*, xix. 128, 129. "Our understanding assuredly and without deceit declares that three and seven are ten, and yet cannot show any reason why that is true or why it cannot be denied to be true; that is to say, it is itself made subject, inasmuch as it is rather judged by the truth, than judges it. Such an understanding there is also in the Church, to judge doctrines by the illumination of the Spirit.—Even as amongst philosophers no one decides regarding common notions, but all the others are judged by these, so is it amongst us with the mind of the Spirit, which judges all things and yet is judged of no man (1 Cor. ii. 15)."

which is so much the more apt on account of the moral nature
of the matter believed. Faith he considers to be the conscience[1]
in Christian potency. "Confirmation is especially necessary in
Christian doctrine, for I ought to be certain of what I am to hold
from God, or rather, of what He holds from me. It has been an
abominable error in the Papist doctrine, whereby they have
settled it amongst the people, that they should be doubtful of
the forgiveness of sins and the grace of God.[2] They have said,
'Thou oughtest to know that thou art a sinner, and such a sinner
as can by no means be certain of his salvation.' If the Papacy
had had no sin and error besides, even this would have been an
abominable blindness and error, that they have taught that we
should always go hither and thither in doubt, waver, be uncertain, and doubt of our salvation, for such uncertainty robs me
of my baptism and of the grace of God (Ps. li. 12; 1 Cor. ix. 26;
Heb. xii. 12; 2 Peter i. 10; Rom. xiv. 23). We must therefore
learn that God is no uncertain, ambiguous, or changeable God,
with many meanings, and like an uncertain reed; but has only
one meaning, and is perfectly certain, when He says, 'I baptize
thee in the name of the Father, and of the Son, and of the Holy
Ghost—I absolve thee and acquit thee.' God sends to Christians even the Spirit, whom Christ has, who is also a child, that
they may at the same time cry with Him, 'Abba, dear Father'
(Rom. viii. 15; Gal. iv. 1-8).[3] This cry, however, is felt by one
when his conscience, without any wavering or doubt, firmly expects and is certain that not only are his sins forgiven him, but
also that he is the child of God, sure of salvation, and may, with
a joyful and assured heart, in all confidence name and call upon
God as his dear father. It must be certain of this as that not
even its own life can be as certain, and it would sooner suffer all
manner of deaths, and even hell itself, than let this be taken
from it or doubt it. There may indeed be a conflict occasioned
by man feeling and fearing that he is not a child, and is sensible
of God as his angry and stern Judge. But in the struggle, childlike confidence must finally triumph, though with trembling
or quaking, else all is lost. When Cain hears that, he will bless
himself hand and foot, and say with great humility, 'What!
God guard me from abominable heresy and presumption!

---

[1] *Luthers Werke*, xi. 1887; ii. 2343; ix. 805; xviii. 2060.
[2] ii. 1985-87.   [3] xii. 322, 323.

Should I, a poor sinner, be so proud and say I am God's child? No, no; I will humble myself and acknowledge myself a poor sinner,' &c. Let such go, and beware of them as the greatest enemies of the Christian faith and thy salvation! We know well that we are poor sinners; but it avails not here to look at what we are and do, but at what Christ is, and has done, and is doing, for us. We do not speak of our nature, but of the grace of God, which is as much more than we as the heaven is higher than the earth. Does it seem a great matter for thee to be the child of God, beloved? Let it not appear a small matter to thee that the Son of God has come, born of a woman, made under the law, that thou mightest become such a child. Everything is great which God works, therefore be very joyful and courageous, ye undismayed spirits, who are afraid of nothing and able for everything. Cain's way of it is poor, and simply creates dismayed anxious hearts, which are of no use, neither for suffering nor working, and are afraid of the leaf of a tree (Lev. xxvi. 36).[1] There is therefore such a thing as personal assurance; we may feel the crying of the Spirit in the heart, for it is at the same time the cry of the heart itself, and the Spirit cries with all power, *i.e.* with the whole, and a full heart, so that the whole lives and moves in this confidence (Rom. viii. 16, 26). Dost thou not feel the cry? then cease not in intercession until God hears thee; for thou art Cain, and it is not well with thee. Thou must not, indeed, wish that this cry should be heard alone and pure in thee; thy sin also cries and establishes despair in thy conscience. But the Spirit of Christ should and must drown that cry, *i.e.* create a confidence stronger than the despair (1 John iii. 19-22). Thus this crying of the Spirit is nothing else than a mighty, strong, unwavering, trustful looking with the whole heart to God as a beloved Father by us as His dear children. And by the childlike spirit there are described [2] the power of the kingdom of Christ, and the proper work, and the true and lofty worship, which are wrought in the believer by the Holy Spirit, to wit, the hearty calling upon God, and the consolation whereby the heart is delivered from terror and the fear of sin, and is made satisfied. Where the faith of Christ is, there the Holy Spirit works in the heart this consolation and sure, child-

---

[1] *Luthers Werke von Walch*, xii. 324 and 1045 (on Rom. viii. 12-17).
[2] xii. 1044.

like confidence. The witness of the Holy Spirit is just this, that by His operation our heart is possessed of consolation, confidence, and childlike prayer. It is not of ourselves, nor by the law, that we are able to esteem ourselves the children of God; but it is the witness of the Holy Spirit, who in our weakness testifies to this [1] in face of the law and of the feeling of our unworthiness, and makes us certain of it. This testimony takes place, accordingly, in such a way that we also feel and are sensible of the power of the Holy Spirit as He works in us through the word, and our experience accords with the word or preaching; for this thou must always feel to be the case with thee, when thou in need and anxiety receivest comfort from the Gospel, and overcomest doubt and alarm, that thy heart can firmly conclude that thou hast a gracious God."[2]

His meaning, however, is not, as might be supposed from some isolated expressions, that we are simply to resolve or decree by ourselves that we are God's children, and that the assurance of salvation rests only on the strength of the resolution to consider ourselves as God's children. As little as he places this assurance of salvation outside of ourselves in the sure objective word, or the sure sacramental signs of grace, so little does he consider this assurance a merely subjective human work. He rather regards this *subjective* assurance as an effect of the *objective* Spirit,

---

[1] *Luthers Werke von Walch*, xii. 1046.

[2] *Ibid.* viii. 1030-1033, he says: At the Apostolic Council there was a danger of them all stumbling, if these three men had not stood bravely firm. God has not promised the Holy Spirit to any council, but to the hearts of Christians. Even James was not able to remain perfectly pure, and Peter stumbled (Gal ii.). Hence every one must see to himself that he is certain and sure of the right doctrine, and not rest upon the expositions and conclusions of other people. If not, the Holy Spirit will soon let thee get a slap. If thou art to be saved, thou must be for thyself so sure of the word of grace, that if all men spake otherwise, and all angels said No, thou canst nevertheless stand alone and say, "Still I know that this word is right." Those who are against us think that where the greatest crowd lights, thither we should after them. Meet them with the question, Why here (Acts xv.) in the great matter of Christian faith, all the best Christians fell into error, excepting three persons?—Hence I have said that every Christian must be so certain as to feel in his heart what is right or not (John x.). The sheep must be certain of the voice of its shepherd, and shut eyes and ears, and resolve to listen not to how great, and many, and pious, and wise people these are. If it does not do this, and will first hear what has been finally decided, it is already seduced from the Shepherd. God allows thee to strengthen thy faith by the concurrence of pious people who hold it along with thee; accept it, but do not trust to it.

accomplished by means of the objective Gospel, but an effect different from the testimony contained in the Gospel, although coinciding with it, for the spirit of the child recognizes itself again in the Gospel.[1] If there were no witness of the Spirit created within us, whereby our self-consciousness is made to bear testimony to our divine childhood, our Ego and the testimony of Scripture would remain severed, the Scripture would be to us only a law, and we would be without the new consciousness. But, on the other hand, he censures also *false security*, the counterfeit of the divine assurance of salvation, the *securitas* instead of the *certitudo*, in those proud spirits who despise the Scriptures.[2] They despise the Word by which God gives strength and comfort. Accordingly the *royal way* to acquire the consciousness of childhood is this, that the faith of the man who is in distress on account of his sin, and moved by doubt of salvation, be in the first instance a receiving faith. What is received is the Gospel (which presents and offers to faith its object, above all the forgiveness of sins), with which the Holy Spirit connects Himself, in order, by persuading and drawing men to the Father, to effect the reception when and where He will. Receiving faith is therefore not yet sure, but only trusting faith, it may even be with trembling. But it is the work of the Holy Spirit to render the matter received also powerfully and actively operative, and even a personal possession, and to bestow upon receiving faith the assurance of salvation, peace, and joy in the consciousness of personal justification, and to generate a new conscious creature. Thus salvation reaches its goal in the independent formation of the new man, who knows of his own salvation and of Christ as Redeemer no longer merely from hearsay, or on the authority of others, nor merely on account of the authority of the Scriptures, nor merely by means of his own judgment, but from his *personal experience*, the result of the objective Holy Spirit and of the saving power of the Word which brings Christ to us, whereby what was preliminarily a trustful and hopeful receiving is made a blessed assurance, an independent knowledge of Christ, His majesty, and His merit. And only now does there take place the *proper attestation* of the Holy Scriptures, of their SUBJECT-MATTER, to our hearts, a divine assurance of the truth of that matter, kindled by God through the illumina-

[1] *Luthers Werke von Walch*, xii. 435, § 95.   [2] xii. 938.

tion of His Spirit, and infinitely higher than a faith in the Scriptures, which is only the acceptation of the ecclesiastical canon, and confidence in the correctness of the decision of the Church regarding the Scriptures.

It holds true of *receiving* faith, when he says, it is a hearty, simple trust in Christ; it gives due honour to God, it is the fulfilling of the fundamental command to practise no idolatry,[1] it is even in germ the fulfilling of all the commands of God, it is the true service of God, and the true sacrifice.[2] With regard to faith, which *has received* in trust, he says, it is continually in a condition of improvement; it is already pious and blessed, and pleases God so well, because it derives its splendour from Christ; as Christ pleases God, so believers please God; for the soul becomes again through Christ the image of God,[3] like the Word on which it depends. Receiving faith procures deliverance from guilt and the law, regeneration, salvation from punishment, sin, and death.[4] Thus faith is accordingly justifying,[5] but not properly in itself on account of its own power or virtue, but on account of him who now belongs and is imputed to it, even Christ.[6] It is not the power of the receiving confidence which is the ground of justification, but even a weak faith is faith, if it embraces in trembling the substance which possesses justifying power. Accordingly he does not regard justification and regeneration as consisting in the feeling and sense of salvation; but even when we have not such feelings, there may be assurance in reliance upon Christ.[7]

The assurance, which faith obtains through the Holy Ghost and the mediation of the Word, is not, however, *confined by Luther to the assurance of the forgiveness of sins*, although he regards this as forming the basis of all Christian knowledge, but by means of it the whole spiritual life obtains firmness and solidity. Speech and action, meditation and teaching, everything must take place in divine assurance.[8] No one should say anything as a preacher, unless he is sure that he speaks it as the

---

[1] xiii. 2454; iv. 1068, f.; viii. 2040, cf. *Apologie*, p. 70, ed. Hase.
[2] xi. 945, 1018, ff.; 2040.   [3] i. 622; x. 2220, ff.; xi. 1555, 1526.
[4] xi. 853, ff.; 1569, ff.
[5] i. 1140, ff; vi. 2315, ff.; xii. 644, ff.; 2089; xvi. 1432.
[6] viii. 1729; xii. 319.
[7] vi. 715. ff,; cf. Köstlin, as cited, ii. 467, ff.; 508.
[8] ix. 804, upon 1 Peter. iv. 11.

Faith and the Exposition of Scripture. 241

Word of God. "We must stand in such certainty of God's speaking and working in us, that our faith can say, 'What I have spoken and done, that has God done and spoken,' so that I am ready to die for it, else, if I am not certain of my affair, it stands upon sand, whilst God has ordained that our conscience must stand upon the solid rock." True faith, he says, has a very quick sight;[1] a blind and yet clear knowledge,[2] it judges all things, and, because it alone has a true knowledge of God and alone penetrates into the secrets of the kingdom of God,[3] it makes dark the light of reason.[4] It is a clear mirror of, and a perpetual looking at, Christ.[5] Faith delivers from being in tutelage under teachers, for believers should themselves have judicial power; faith is master, judge, and rule of all doctrine and prophecy.[6]

He requires, accordingly, divine personal assurance, by means of the Holy Ghost, so decidedly that we, according to him, ought not to be satisfied even although an apostle says anything (*cf.* Gal. i. 8); the matter of the Word stands security for itself, and is not dependent on the respect paid to any creature whatsoever. Hence results the position, which Luther ascribes to *faith in relation to the holy Scriptures.*

In the *first* place, faith and it alone *expounds* the holy Scriptures. In no way, indeed, did Luther desire a spiritual exposition in *opposition* to a grammatical; on the contrary, the keenness and singleness of his scientific glance is manifested in the fact that, like Calvin, he condemns the prevailing fourfold Scripture-sense of Scholasticism. The truly good *theologus* is not begotten by means of the literal sense (*sensus litteralis*), nor by means of the allegorical, anagogical, and tropological, although he himself proceeds not infrequently to an allegorical treatment of the Scriptures for purposes of edification. The Holy Spirit is the simplest of all writers and speakers; hence, too, His words cannot have anything more than the simplest possible meaning,[7] which we call the Scriptural or literal sense of the language.[8] Whoever seeks another meaning, than the strict meaning of the words, he calls a roving spirit and chamois-hunter. Hence it was for him a fundamental necessity, to direct the greater attention to the culti-

[1] xi. 3083; xii. 12.   [2] iii. 323.   [3] viii. 2066.
[4] viii. 2353, ff.; x. 19.   [5] xii. 579; viii. 2353.
[6] xxii. 268, ff.   [7] xviii. 1602.   [8] i. 2075, ff.; xii. 1111.

vation of the languages. It is again the principle of faith, which unites with grammar and philology, in order to have security against the falsification of the matter to be received. At the same time, however, it is still spiritual matter, to which expression is given in the element of the letter; therefore the Scripture can only be understood by a mind and spirit allied to it. What is necessary for salvation is intelligible to all who are spiritually disposed, and the dissimilarity in education and philological skill of exposition is by means of this perspicuity (*perspicuitas*) of the Scriptures essentially reduced again to an equality. But more is seen by the faith already established; the spiritual is perceived by spiritual men.[1] Faith is as it were the eye, for which the Scripture seeks, in order to mirror itself therein, and the mouth, in order to give utterance to its subject-matter. The believing man is the organ which the holy Scriptures create for themselves in order to expound themselves through the same. In faith, as a living mirror, there is implied an understanding of the matter of Scripture, as truth; hence there is more than a mere dead reflecting of the rays, which fall from the Scriptures upon the spirit; there is possible to faith an intelligent reproduction of the Word, which is not a mere dead echo of the Scriptures, but conscious and free, whilst faithful. But as little may the expositor explain the holy Scriptures according to the rule of any human summary of doctrine whatsoever, whether it be called apostolic symbolism, or *regula, analogia fidei*, or Church doctrine. Whoever asserts that such a rule, furnished by men, is necessary in order to a correct interpretation of the Scriptures, denies the *perspicuitas scripturæ sacræ*. There is rather to be received only an *analogia scripturæ sacræ, i.e.* Scripture cannot contradict Scripture; but out of the really canonical portions of the Codex there is formed by the believing investigator of Scripture an unity, an homoiogeneous whole, and this is the analogy of faith (*analogia fidei*), by which also the common faith of the Church is to be measured. The opposite would be a forcing down of the Scriptures beneath the Church, whilst it is the Word of God, which makes the Church, and not the reverse.[2]

In the *second* place, the relative independence of faith in relation to the holy Scriptures is more distinctly prominent in this,

---

[1] iii. 21; ix. 857, ff.; 1391; x. 451; xi. 256; xii. 1109.
[2] xix. 128, ff.; 1319; xx. 1257, 2096.

that, after faith has been awakened by the Spirit through the Word, it has the right, and on it devolves the duty, of *unfolding and applying* the knowledge it has acquired, in doing which the vital point is the correct deduction from true faith, not the capacity of what is derived for being verbally authenticated in the Scriptures. Even Christian preaching, hymnology, and art operate as the word of God, but must always submit to be measured by the canonical word of Scripture.

But, in the *third* place, the relative independence of faith in respect of the Scriptures comes into prominence most clearly of all in the *critical authority*, which Luther ascribes to faith in reference to the canon, and which he wielded in ample measure. It has been mentioned above that he denies the canonicity of the Epistle of James, without however regarding it as spurious, and to this view he adhered. He occupied at least a similar position to the Epistle to the Hebrews and to the Apocalypse, although he afterwards (1545) passed a somewhat more favourable judgment on the latter. He even says of a proof led by the Apostle Paul in Galatians, that it is too weak to hold. It gives him no trouble to allow, that in external matters not only Stephen, but even the sacred authors, contain inaccuracies. So far as the Old Testament is concerned, its authority does not appear to him invalidated by the admission,[1] that several of these writings have passed through revising hands; what would it matter, he asks, in reference to the Pentateuch, if Moses did not himself write it? and in reference to the prophets he says, they studied Moses and one another; thus were their books originated, inasmuch as they wrote out their thoughts inspired by the Holy Spirit. If, therefore, these good and faithful teachers and searchers of the Scriptures sometimes built much hay, stubble, and wood along with the rest, and not pure gold, silver, and precious stones, still the foundation abides, the fire of the day shall consume the former, for in this manner do we treat the writings of Augustine, &c. In the Old Testament he gives a particularly high place to Genesis; it is the fountain, from which under the inspiration of the Holy Ghost all the later prophets flowed;[2] amongst the historical books, the Books of Kings are far more to be believed

---

[1] Cf. Herzog, *theol. Realencyclop.* viii. 609; Köstlin, *Luthers Theol.* ii. 262, 276, ff.; Erl. ed. viii. 23; lxiii. 970.
[2] *Luthers Werke von Walch,* xiv. 172, ff.

than the Books of Chronicles; Ecclesiastes is forged and does not come from Solomon, is slipshod, &c. Even the Book Esther he does not regard as canonical; he would that the Books of the Maccabees did not exist, for they are too Jewish and have much heathen rudeness.

The canon has been formed by the Church; it may have erred in the adoption of a book; and faith dare not without more ado or blindly accept anything as canonical upon the decision of the Church, but it has first to take the proof. Therefore, the Apocrypha of the Old Testament, although the Church received them as canonical, are ejected from the canon. And even in reference to the New Testament, the series of writings received by him is determined by his critical judgment, and no small portion of them receives a secondary, duetero-canonical position, which continued, so long as the critical consciousness had not expired, as far as into the seventeenth century.[1]

This testing by means of faith may also lead to the result, that the one Scripture obtains a greater value than the other and exhibits a higher degree of inspiration, wherein his view of inspiration betrays itself in the plainest manner to be historical and full of vitality. For the above shows that he acknowledges in the Scriptures not only what is divine, but also what is human, and even what is only human. *There is thus most indubitably admitted by the German Reformer a difference between the Word of God and the holy Scriptures, not merely in reference to the form, but also in reference to the subject-matter.* In the New Testament, he calls the Gospel of John the alone and tender chief Gospel, far to be preferred to the other three, whilst the Epistles of Paul and Peter also stand far above these. In short, the Gospel and First Epistle of John, the Epistles of Paul, especially those to the Romans, Ephesians, and Galatians, and the First Epistle of Peter, these are the books which exhibit Christ and teach all that it is necessary and saving for thee to know.

Entertaining such a view of the Holy Scriptures, he is able to say:[2] Therefore, if any one should press thee with expressions, which speak of works, and which thou canst not bring into concord with the others, thou oughtst to say, since Christ Himself is the treasure whereby I am bought and redeemed, I care not

---

[1] Bleek, *Einleit. ins N. T.* 1862, *Vorbemerkungen*.
[2] *Luthers Werke von Walch*, viii. 2138, ff. *Comm. z. Galat.*, Erl. ed. i. 387.

the slightest jot for all the expressions of Scripture, to set up by them the righteousness of works and to lay down the righteousness of faith. For I have on my side the Master and the Lord of the Scripture, to whom I will keep, and I know he will not lie nor deceive me,—and let them go on in their hostile cry, that the Scriptures contradict themselves! *At the same time it is impossible* that the Scriptures should contradict themselves, save only that the unintelligent, coarse, and hardened hypocrites imagine it. Therefore thou mayest see how thou makest the expressions to agree, of which thou sayest that they do not coincide; I keep by Him who is Lord and Master of the Scriptures. Hear thou well, he continues, thou art almost a bully with the Scriptures, which are nevertheless under Christ as a servant, and for this end thou bringest out of them what is not altogether the best portion. For this I do not care in the slightest; boast away of the servant, I, however, glory in Christ, who is the true Lord and Sovereign of the Scriptures, who has by His death and resurrection merited and procured for me righteousness and salvation; Him have I, and by Him I abide.

But alongside of these bold utterances he asserts quite as distinctly

B. *The essential independence of the holy Scriptures in respect of faith and the Church.*

The necessity of this independent position of the Scriptures is evident to him in the first place particularly from history. The Romish Church had furnished a warning example of how easily oral tradition becomes impure, and how then the faith, which still continues to believe in the operation of the Holy Spirit in the Church, must only serve to conceal and justify error, inasmuch as it engenders violent treatment of the holy Scriptures, as if they, instead of interpreting themselves, had to draw their light from the Church. These dangers of subjective caprice, which are not diminished but rather increased by the fact that a great, collective person, the Church, is set in the place of the true objectivity and of God, were discerned by Luther at the very time when the subjectivity, in which the spirit is carried away, clothed itself in a Protestant garb. He discerned in the clearest manner the essential identity of the fanatical or enthusiastic and of the Romish error; *Papatus simpliciter est merus enthusiasmus.* He regards the holy Scriptures as necessary in order to ensure the true Christian objective matter, on which the Church as well as the individual is dependent, in so far as either desires to be Christian; and in order to exclude caprice even from their exposition, he demands this grammatical exposition on the part of faith, conducted according to the objective and universal laws of language. It is thus, in the second place, particularly remarkable, that he discerns the reason of the necessity of the holy Scriptures, not merely in the sin and weakness of man, but even in the essence of faith, which is not yet sight, but holds to the historical revelation of God. All true regeneration he regards as effected and conditioned by the word, sacrament, and Christian communion; these all, however, are works of the manifested Christ, and by means of them alone regeneration stands in connection with the historical manifestation of Christ. The union of the divine and human, which exists in the person of Christ, has remained a historical self-continuing power in the Word of Christ. Not that this comes in the place of the constant working of Christ, but He acts through His word, and the sensible historical presence of the person of Christ, lost since His ascension, has provided for itself in the visible word and sacrament a sensible memorial and succedaneum. It is thus he is to be understood, when he says, that the holy Scriptures are the $\sigma\grave{\alpha}\rho\xi$ $X\rho\iota\sigma\tau o\hat{v}$, when he fears a dissolution of the Christology, whether in a Docetic or Ebionite manner, from that doctrine regarding the internal word which shows itself indifferent towards the external word. He says, that it is only through these historical works of Christ that we can after so many centuries lay hold upon the historical Christ Himself, that therefore whoever despises the documentary records of Christ and the sacrament, destroys in fact the foundations of the Church and the knowableness of Christ,—which must result in the evaporation of Christianity. According to this aspect of it, he calls the Word of Scripture the true star, which of a truth points to Christ,[1] the swaddling-clothes or the cradle in which Jesus was laid,[2] and says; In the mouth of the apostles lies the death and resurrection of Christ together with heaven and eternal life; Christ has laid it there. Our Lord Jesus Christ has in-laid the forgiveness

---

[1] *Luthers Werke von Walch,* xiii. 313.   [2] xxii. 87, ff.

of sins in the Word;[1] it is the enclosing of the Eternal Word, whereby it comes near to man (see above, p. 224, ff.). And with regard to the internal connection between the Word and the thing of which it testifies, he says:[2] With us Faith and the Word are not without the thing. He finds the connection of the Eternal Word and the Word of Scripture to be dissolved by the fanatics, and the abiding revelation of the Eternal Word to be thereby endangered for mankind; in the Word, which is brought nigh to men externally, he sees grace to have assumed the form of particularity and finiteness, in order to deal with men and elevate them into the divine life. He sees in this enclosing as in the presentation of the Word a gracious, divine act, and is therefore indignant when he hears the preaching of the Gospel called an empty echo and sound, or when a so-called inner Word is opposed to the outward in such a way as if the former contained a subject-matter different from the latter, or as if it worked independently of the outward, instead of through it. The outward Word is not merely a sound, but has a *meaning*. It is in his view, however, not merely the *sign* of a meaning, but the *expression* of nigh and present grace, as it were the historical body, which grace has assumed in accordance with its historical nature, and thus, in virtue of its meaning or subject-matter, the Scripture possesses also *power* (*efficacia*) in itself. God speaks through the Word, He says,[3] the Word of God is the instrument, whereby God begins justification. It is the will and purpose of God not to speak to men otherwise than through the instrumentality of the external Word.[4] He holds fast indeed the distinction of the creative, essential, living Word of God from the Word in the Scriptures, and convincingly excludes a magical operation of the outward Word by the reminder that the Word of Scripture does not operate creatively in all. But the creative Word will not operate without the outward instrument. That he at the same time attributes clearness (*perspicuitas, semet ipsam interpretandi facultas*) in all matters necessary to salvation, has been already remarked upon (under A.). It is his opinion, still further, that the Word of God is not *in the holy Scriptures alone*, as little as that there is in the Church canon nothing else than the Word of God. The first thing is the

[1] xiii. 1188, ff.; 1198.   [2] xvii. 1908.   [3] xxii. 92, ff.
[4] xxii. 92. Köstlin, as cited, ii. 252, 286, ff.

essential Word (Λόγος), so equal to God, that the whole Godhead is in this Word; the speaker of this Word is God. The essential Word, however, is also itself a speaking Word; all creatures are simply living signs of the Word of God.[1] Still, the divine speech in the world is various. It is always a revelation, but it is a different matter whether God in His speech reveals only His *might* or holiness, or also *grace* and *truth*. Only the latter is a revelation of God in the fuller sense, for God is, as the German name signifies, the Good One. Therefore it is only in the essential Word become flesh that there has been given the revelation of God after His heart, the Word, as it were, out of the *innermost depths of His heart*. The holy Scriptures, however, are the testimony of this perfect revelation, and thus they *bring* to us the Word of God. *But still* the Word of God is *not resolved into the holy Scriptures*. Christ remains the essential Word, working through the Holy Spirit, and the Word of the Scriptures should lead to Him. But Luther will see the Word of God even in the thoughts and spiritual works of faith (see above, p. 240, on 1 Peter iv.). What the believer speaks and does by the Spirit of Christ, is a Word of God, still more than what the creature is and brings forth; for what is born of the Spirit is Spirit. Hence in many places he calls preaching, which nevertheless takes place by means of men and not merely in words of Scripture, pure doctrine, the sacred hymns and prayers of the Church, also words of God. He is on that account able to allow so high and free a position to Christian science, art, and preaching, and if a later period was forgetful of this eternal self-renovation and rejuvenescence, this fructification of the Word in the spirit of believers, and so took up a lifeless conception of the holy Scriptures as a mere law, Luther, on the contrary, would not by his doctrine regarding the Scriptures hinder the pure current of the Holy Spirit in the Church, this true tradition.

On the other hand, however, he certainly regards *the holy Scriptures as the only source of knowledge* of what constitutes the pure original proclamation of the Apostles of Christ, the only rule and norm of what is Christian. He desires, therefore,[2] that everything be tried by the Word of God in the Scriptures; and although he ascribes to faith a proper knowledge and assurance

[1] xi. 217; xxii. 871. [2] xxii. 87, ff.

of the truth, still he will have what is derived and developed from faith subjected to the standard of the holy Scriptures.[1]

Faith, indeed, exercises criticism regarding the canon, but Luther does not mean that it is able to make something the Word of God, which is it not, nor that it can take away from what is the Word of God this sacred character; but faith has only to assist the Holy Scriptures, which are so indeed, in obtaining the recognition of the unique character of their worth and authority. The question certainly suggests itself, how Luther can make these allowances to criticism, these distinctions in the worth of the holy Scriptures, and yet hold fast unlimited confidence in them, and even make them the rule for faith, which should nevertheless have the right and duty of judging regarding their canonicity? This leads us to the third point.

C. *The internal connection of the Scriptures and faith, without detracting from their relative independence.*

There is not indeed to be found in Luther any connected and distinct express systematic doctrine on this point; but still both sides of the evangelical principle are, through the tact born of a sound knowledge of the faith, regarded by him as internally allied.

The Word and faith, faith and the Word, are that which Luther always conjoins in decisive moments, and where the ultimate principle is being treated of.[2] But how, then, are these two things to be admitted together, that faith in its integrity is dependent on the holy Scriptures, and that it nevertheless stands over against them in such independence, that it must itself have a word to say regarding the canonicity of a writing? If faith in the Scriptures, and not merely faith in the preached Gospel, is necessary in order to the assurance of faith, how does the assurance of faith harmonize with the critical investigations regarding the holy Scriptures, which are still to be left open? must not the assurance of faith be suspended through the uncertainties which arise in respect of particular writings of the canon, which are dependent upon historico-critical investigations, and not upon faith? must not the faith which seeks to support itself

---

[1] *Artic. Smalc. Verbum Dei condat articulos fidei et preterea nemo, ne angelus quidem,* p. 308.

[2] vi. 2371; viii. 2655; xvii. 1908; xx. 1017, 1138, 1157, 1189, 1385.

on Scripture be moved and shaken, or even feel itself suspended in thin air, from the fact that no writing may be excepted from critical investigations ? Is not, further, the universal priesthood of believers necessarily infringed upon by this principle regarding the Scriptures, inasmuch as faith is either made dependent on learned researches, which are only the concern of a few, or else is blindly directed to the canon set up by the Church, that is to say, upon the authority of the Church ? On the one hand, there is demanded of faith, as Christian faith, resignation to the Scriptures as entitled to authority; on the other hand, if it is to judge regarding them, it must, it seems, place itself above them. First of all, there is here to be set aside the idea that the human mind in general, and not rather *faith*, is capable of dogmatically deciding whether a writing may pass as canonical. There certainly seems to be here the danger of reasoning in a circle. In order to attain in a moral way to faith in the Scriptures, a certain *knowledge of the truth* must go before; on the other hand, faith, out of which springs the knowledge of Christian truth, seems to involve a subjection to the Scriptures, which leaves no more room for criticism. In order to a solution, we will have to inquire whether the Holy Scriptures, which indeed are so, may not in virtue of their subject-matter possess for the faith, which is yet to be created, a significance as means of grace and invitation to faith, without being already an authoritative norm, in such a manner as for the faith which is actually instituted: further, how the recognition of a norm harmonizes with the internal freedom of faith.

In general, it is to be premised, that faith and the Scriptures are not, in the view of Luther, disparate things, which hinder or even exclude one another; they are rather, according to him, internally connected; both have a like origin in the same Holy Spirit, who proceeds from Christ; how can there be discordance or enmity between them ?

More particularly, however, the process of reconciliation between the Word and faith is this; according to Luther, three factors co-operate for the salvation of man, and only by means of their co-operation does there arise the living formation of the new personality. These factors are: the Holy Spirit, the Word, faith. Their result, salvation, is not effected by the Word of the Church, or of the holy Scriptures, in itself without the Holy

Ghost; God is not changed into the Word, but broods over it a, His medium, and makes the Word operative. He does n t work, however, without the medium of the Word, neither by external nor by internal magic. In the Word there is presented what it is to be believed, and there is thus room left for faith, it is even expected. But even the subjective reception does not in itself constitute salvation, but salvation is bestowed on the faith which lays hold of it, and thence results the assurance of salvation; the Word presents the object of faith, and by the power of the Holy Ghost draws man on to be willing penitently to receive it. When he has received it, the Holy Spirit suffers peace and the assurance of salvation to spring forth from the matter appropriated. We are thus furnished with Luther's doctrine regarding the internal relation between the Scriptures and faith. The *holy Scriptures point through themselves to faith*, the production of which they seek to subserve as means of grace; for their subject-matter, the truth, they seek to obtain also a new form of existence in man, as believed; and they require faith for their preservation, critical determination, and exposition. *Faith again points through its very idea to the holy Scriptures* and their authority. Let us contemplate both.

First: The *holy Scriptures* demand, according to Luther, not merely the mnemonic or intellectual, but impersonal acceptance (*fides historica* and *assensus*); they seek from man an individual affirmative judgment of their worth by means of the personal experience of faith, which is only possible when faith resigns and opens itself to them in perfect confidence. They demand trustful reception, a personal act, the believing application to the personality of the salvation proclaimed by them, whereby they may produce the assurance of faith by the power of the subject-matter received. In order to this confiding resignation, whose fruit, and whose alone, is the experience of salvation and the assurance of faith, there is not requisite any blind, and therefore morally doubtful, resignation and subjection. As little, too, is that kind of assurance regarding the subject-matter or the authority of the holy Scriptures as yet possible, which is effected by means of the *appropriated* matter. Full divine assurance rather belongs only to the faith which *has* laid hold of Christ. But still there may, by the power of preparatory grace and the attractive effect of the subject-matter of Scripture (supposed or proved to be historically credible), that is to say, by the operation, even although it be mediate, of the holy Scriptures as a means of grace, be formed an assurance of the duty of believing, which is equal to every other religious or moral assurance of this stage, and is even superior to them, in so far as there is discerned the dependence of all salutary progress upon the fulfilment of the duty of believing.[1]

But with the new consciousness, which the saving experience of faith brings along with it, there is given completely that eye, to which the holy Scripture opens itself up, after man has been opened for it. Only now is man able to appreciate and understand its greatness and fulness in free liking and submission; only now can faith as an instrument accomplish for it what it requires. Since faith has an eye for what is Christian, and can distinguish what is against Christ and what is for Him, its right of criticizing the Church canon cannot be contested; if a writing did not contain Christ, if it is without this centre, it would not be holy Scripture. The deciding principle as to whether a writing is to pass for canonical, lies, in a dogmatic aspect, according to Luther, as is well known, in this, whether it is occupied with Christ. He recognizes it accordingly to be the province of faith to exercise criticism, not from caprice, but upon objective dogmatical grounds, and this apart from historical investigations regarding genuineness and integrity. He does not here advance to the point, that the holy Scripture may not contain anything, which is not contained in the consciousness of faith; if it might not contain anything more, nor purify empirical, imperfect faith, it would no longer maintain any authority; faith would be the standard of the holy Scriptures and of all truth, that is, absolutely its own standard, autonomic. But however much the holy Scriptures may contain for the enriching and purifying of the believing consciousness, the holy Scriptures may not contradict faith in that which constitutes it, and of which it possesses Divine assurance; for faith, so far as it goes, is, as well as the Scriptures, the work of the Holy Ghost. The critical right of faith is thus reduced to this negative form, that nothing which contradicts saving faith can have canonical authority; Christianity, it is allowed, does not contradict the universal conscience,

[1] This, however, may also take place, according to Luther, through Scriptural preaching, &c. In it, too, the Scriptures are operative, see p. 253.

but unites itself to it; faith, however, is in the view of Luther, as we have seen, the Christian conscience. Since, further, faith on its side, as we shall immediately see, is in unison with the records of the holy Scriptures, a canonical writing in contradiction with faith would be also in contradiction with the Scriptures, namely, with other portions of the canon, which have in themselves something which that wants, namely, the power of serving to beget faith and the accordance with what is for faith divinely sure. It is thus evident that *Luther's criticism of the canon by faith becomes properly criticism of the holy Scriptures by themselves*, and is only a measuring of them by themselves through the medium of the believing individual, who does not stand above the Scriptures, but may only declare the actual fact, purify the canon from what is heterogeneous, and restore it to equality with itself, to harmony in the richness of its component parts. Luther thus obtains a *canon in the canon by means of the material principle : The centre of the holy Scriptures, Christ, is the standard of canonicity ; corresponding to the self-interpretation of the holy Scriptures is their self-criticism.*

Secondly. In like manner, however, as the holy Scriptures require faith, and even therein the formation of a " Bible in the heart,"—to use the expression of one (Cl. Harms), who most of all recent thinkers exhibits traits of Luther's mind,—does *faith in its very idea point to the holy Scriptures*, for its *origin* as well as for its *maintenance?* Although faith may be awakened by the Word of God even in the form of oral preaching, still all evangelical preaching must, even though unconsciously, be based upon the apostolic testimony, in so far as it is only by the Holy Scriptures that the Christianity of what is preached, its accordance with the primitive apostolic testimony, may be measured.[1] Even saving faith itself, it is admitted, would not be Christian saving faith, were it not animated by the sure presupposition, that the preaching, which it followed, was at the same time the apostolic word and a testimony of true facts, and did not rest upon the imagination of men.[2] The trial as to whether harmony with the Scriptures exists must, in case of need, be capable of being made at any moment, that so every individual may compare his faith and the preaching with the holy Scriptures. The consciousness of this harmony of faith and of the preaching, which

[1] ii. 287. [2] xi. 1633.

awakens faith, with the holy Scriptures belongs to the keenness of the Protestant consciousness; hence Luther will have the Bible given into the hands of the laity. For him, indeed, who has yet to come to faith in Christ, and has not yet experienced Him as his Redeemer, the authority of the holy Scriptures cannot yet be really sure, for an authority resting upon the recommendation of the Church is only an external authority. But still they will operate as a means of grace, that so faith may be produced in him who draws closer to them. Indeed, since faith cannot spring up without something in which it believes, and this object, as we have just seen, is only assured by the holy Scriptures, and the possible appeal to them alone furnishes to us, with certainty, and in a historical manner, the contents of apostolic faith, and accordingly Christ Himself, there follows the indispensableness of the holy Scriptures in order to the Church being able to awaken faith by means of her testimony. Her preaching must venture to assume and be able to prove upon record its scriptural character.

When faith in what forms the subject-matter of evangelical preaching and the kernel of the Holy Scriptures has, however, been *instituted*, the latter acquire a new position and the value of the greatest treasure on account of this subject-matter, which has evidenced itself experimentally to the spirit and been recognized by it as truth, spirit, and life · they are now recognized on their own account as an *authority*, for which they have not to thank men, but themselves,[1] and faith is only the eye for their divine subject-matter. Faith traces now what is spoken by the Spirit, and imputes *inspiration* to the holy men who composed them. But Luther is not of the opinion that the words of Scripture have been dictated to them by the Holy Spirit, but there is produced by the Holy Spirit and His illumination that *knowledge* of the Christian salvation and the economy thereof which was imparted to the apostles as chosen instruments, and especially to the sacred authors (p. 243); and so divine truth assumed already a human form, and the knowledge of God [owned by God] became the innermost personal knowledge of [*i.e.* in] man. This union of the divine and human—which, in respect of *perception*, is not limited exclusively to the moral and religious stage of the sacred authors—is certainly perpetuated during the writing;

[1] iv. 1425; vii. 1786; xii. 926.

for its Origin and Maintenance. 255

but in this human and not divine act the sacred authors received the historical matter not by the illumination of the Spirit, but in a historical manner; but they sifted it, arranged it, and set in the true divine light by the power of the illumining Spirit working in them, and according to the measure of this power.[1] Further, according to Luther, the excellence of the holy Scripture is not to be founded on the fact that it only has Spirit; for its value and power consists in his view even in this, that it, by its testimony, is continually begetting spirit. As there is one faith and one baptism in the apostles and those who believe through them, so it is also one Spirit, and not a twofold, who illumines them and Christendom. This however does not, according to him, destroy, but renders discernible, the normative authority of the holy Scriptures.

If, then, it is precisely faith only which is able to appreciate the exalted nature of the holy Scriptures, both now stand firm; the apostolic Word, and through it the prophetical, is regulative and authoritative for faith as nothing else is; for faith seeks to be Christian and one with the apostolical; and yet the recognition of this authority does not again bring one under the law, but the authority has become internal and the recognition free; faith unites with the Scriptures as that which constitutes faith true, and which by its exalted nature forms for faith, in virtue of personal knowledge and experience, the rule and impulse of a healthy growth. *The means which served to generate faith, the Word and Sacrament, do not become useless after it is generated. What has been born must grow,* faith must increase, and that in conflict with the old man. Growth takes place through nourishment, nourishment requires the same means which called it into being. Further,[2] faith is indeed rich, for it really possesses Christ, and so the totality; and all development in wisdom, in Christian knowledge and in holy living, is only the unfolding of what it already possesses in principle (see p. 240, f.); Christianity is a unity, and hence the development of faith is perpetual and inward, not as if additions to it were necessary from without, and its perfection needed to be of a composite character. But *what is in principle already the possession of faith* is not yet on that account actually developed, is not yet its distinct and conscious possession, for there still remains for the believer the possibility

[1] Cf. Köstlin, ii. 278, ff.; cf. *Comment. zu Galat.*, Erl. ed. 26, 100.
[2] xi. 1526.

of error, and even of a cluster of errors. Since the Scriptures, on the other hand, contain an endless wealth, on which Christendom may live until perfection, especially in the historical picture of Christ which they exhibit to the eye; it is they, the holy Scriptures, which by their treasures both act as a perpetual enticement to faith to develop itself more and more, and point out the way for a healthy normal development of faith, and preserve it from the false paths which offer themselves, again and again, at every point of the development of the inward life, and which are to be avoided. *Faith,* therefore, *requires the holy Scriptures for its maintenance and development,* as a sure *rule* and *standard* whereby to try its purity and Christian soundness. Not in spite of, but in virtue of what it already has, does faith enter into the school of Christ and the apostles. What these further give to it, it has so to unite with what it as faith already possesses, that that gift from the holy Scriptures becomes only the development of what already exists in it in germ. *The process of union between faith and the Word of God must therefore be continuous* in a religious, intellectual, and moral view of it; here the principle always holds: The vital point is "that we equalize the Scriptures and the (Christian) conscience,"[1] that is, bring them to the same level, so as to attain the full indubitable assurance which consists in the union of the personal, the subjective, and of the objective holy Scriptures.

If, therefore, Luther does not give an explicit answer to all the questions which here suggest themselves, so much is clear, that the assurance and joy of faith is not, in his view, suspended by leaving criticism in the exercise of its rights. On the contrary, the holy Scriptures do not, in his opinion, lose in value or authority by his emphasizing of faith, but rather gain, since they now become an inward authority, which cannot be abandoned by faith, whilst it, through its close connection with the holy

---

[1] xi. 1888, 1526: "Those who have once laid hold of the Shepherd, cleave with all confidence to him and hear no other doctrine, for they have very fine ears, and are almost expert to know and distinguish from all others the voice of the Shepherd. For they have now the experience of their conscience and the testimony of the Holy Spirit in their heart." xi. 1636: "We must grasp the right and simple understanding of the Word, that we may base our conscience on it, that we may not waver and shake, and may be armed with clear and certain Scripture. By uncertain understanding of the Scriptures, the devil gets us on his fork and tosses us hither and thither like a withered leaf."

Scriptures, grows in self-assurance, because, knowing itself at one with what corresponds to it objectively and is independent of, and even superior to, but yet harmonious with it, it gains also for itself an inward objectivity. This question especially remains, however, still undisposed of: whether, if criticism may without limitation doubt all the holy Scriptures, the significance of the holy Scriptures for the origin and maintenance of faith is not again placed in question, so that it cannot form an integrally constitutive factor for the life of faith itself? This and similar points could only come to be disposed of through the formation of a scientific criticism, inasmuch as it must thus be made evident that there are inner laws and limits by which historical criticism is bound, as it could not itself any longer subsist without historical sources. For the want of such a science as this, which by an internal standard judges and overcomes possible excesses, there was sought indeed for a while in the following century a compensation, which does not accord with the Protestant principle.

Let us close by casting a glance at the practical reach and fertility of the Reformation principle which has been exhibited. The result of the union of the principle of faith with the holy Scriptures was, according to Luther, first of all the *universal priesthood* of believers, wherein, as we saw, there lay already a rejection of the Romish doctrine of the priesthood and of the sacrament of *ordination*, the [Roman] Catholic basis of all the sacraments. By the immediateness of the relationship to God in faith there was also excluded all creatural or human lordship over faith, and accordingly, confidence in the *saints*, and the worship of them: the mediatorship of a heavenly *hierarchy*, as well as of the earthly. A material mediatorship, however, by means of the *Romish sacraments*, or other holy performances, was of necessity condemned by the principle of faith, because a working *ex opere operato* would render unnecessary the faith by which grace is procured. Especially, however, was the *sacrament of repentance*, which is practically of such deep influence, completely transformed, and even destroyed, by faith; its first momentum, oral confession, was undermined, partly because the true humility and penitence, which belongs to faith, recognizes the impossibility of confessing every individual sin, partly because it was too superficial a method to stop at particular works instead of proving faith and unbelief; the necessity of confession to the priest is, however, finally destroyed with his mediatorial position. Penances (*satisfactiones*) fell before the principle of faith, because grace was recognized as free, not as communicated on account of works, not even on account of works to be done in future. And finally, the judicial position of the priest in remitting or retaining sins yielded to the knowledge that God through the gospel, which the Church has certainly to administer in an orderly manner, offers and promises grace to man preveniently, without requiring in doing so a human vicariate, and making the validity of the offer thereby uncertain, or destroying the immediate character of the relationship. Even so it is faith, by which, as we saw above, particular *vows* are abrogated, inasmuch as everything is traced up to the one life-vow of perfect surrender to God in Christ.

Let us now turn to consider the *relation of the Reformation principle* to the different provinces of *thought*, and especially *morals*, in order to observe how it furnishes an entirely new position and new view of the world.

For *science*, first of all, the Reformation opened up a new and broad path, not merely negatively, by destroying the yoke of alien and external authority, but also positively. Faith, with its religious certainty, sets up, as it were, in the innermost centre of man, the original, the prototype of the certainty which science also ought to strive after, the equalization of knowing and being, the assumption of the latter into the former, and the rendering it transparently intelligible, the transferring of thought, which nevertheless stands apart from the objective reality, into the province of the real. And that archetype of certainty is the more fertile, since faith has become aware and certain of the central truth, upon which all other knowledge grows, and in which the whole world of knowledge is possessed, in reference to beginning and end, of a firm and luminous centre, so that, starting from it, a connected system of knowledge may be developed in union with the supreme, divine principle. With regard to *philosophy*,—there was given to it by the Reformation principle a mighty although not immediately operative impulse, and it cannot be termed an accidental circumstance that it was first in Germany after the Reformation that it achieved an independent and powerful development. For, whilst the Roman and Greek Churches in no way insist upon personal assurance, and hence stick fast in the world of mere external authority and empiricism, whereby the substance of Christianity itself does not succeed in being truly assimilated, the striving after perfect certainty of the truth, or after making it the personal property of man, and its innermost alliance with his self-consciousness, is, on the other hand, a genuinely Protestant characteristic. And besides this formal excellence, it is not to be forgotten how the principle of faith corroborates for the highest stage, for religious certainty, the harmony between the first and second creation, nay, becomes security for the rights of the former, and thereby guarantees the union of the man and the Christian. For evangelical faith unites itself to the conscience, the Gospel to the law; and it is not with another and new law that the former has to do, but with the satisfaction and fulfilment of the one old and eternal law. And as the moral law and the conscience are ratified in the Gospel, so also the laws of thought, logic, and the natural knowledge of God. In a word, the whole province of eternal truths is not despised, overleapt, or injured by evangelical faith, but forms the point of attachment for the purpose of conducting the consciousness to the higher stage of faith. This is in itself only the highest stage of self-consciousness, that in which the Ego knows itself in its full truth, or so as it is thought and willed by God, in restored union with God. If there is in faith, in the first instance, only religious experience, the knowledge of a personal state of grace before God, still there is immediately involved therein a knowledge of objective subject-matter, first (since it was only the believed preaching of Christ which brought that grace) a knowledge of *Christ* as Redeemer; not less a knowledge of God as the Father reconciled in Christ, and finally, since there is divine assurance in faith, a knowledge of God as operative and generative in the spirit of man, or of God as the Holy Ghost, so that faith shows itself, in virtue of its subject-matter, capable of forming (provided the scientific talent is already there), an objective Christian doctrine of God, and even a Christian philosophy.

This was anticipated even in the time of the Reformation.[1]

[1] Schwarz, *Thom. Venatorius, &c., Studien und Kritiken*, 1850, i.; cf. 1855, iv., 1853, i.

There is a knowledge, a fundamental knowledge, contained in Luther's faith, and he compares it in respect of immediate axiomatic evidence with the eternal truths (the κοιναί ἔννοιαι);[1] and in respect of the subject-matter, he feels the liveliest need of the union of the particular in principle, as is shown by his judgment regarding the so-called material principle,[2] which we will speedily become acquainted with (p. 261, f.). Strongly as the unregenerate reason is bidden hold its peace by Luther, when it, without being spiritual, would pass decisive judgment in the things of salvation, still he not only allows that throughout the whole civil province it gives light in arts and sciences, and founds equity and law for the peace and order of the world, but reason, when it is enlightened, is also the handmaid of faith, and learns and teaches that what seemed foolish is divine wisdom. *Melanchthon*, accordingly, wrote *Dialectics*, and a *philosophia moralis*, after an Aristotelian fashion, as well as became the creator of an evangelical *theology*.[3] His *Loci* exhibit already a connected dogmatical plan, which is formed out of the consciousness of faith, but in union with the Scriptures; it is the antagonism of sin and grace, which is unfolded in a fertile and connected manner. Although the subjective starting-point does not at the beginning entail the unfolding of the objective dogmas concerning God, the creation, and Christ, still the relation of man to God is based upon the presupposition that it is preceded by a relation of God to man; and that these relations or acts of God have also a connection with His nature, is a reservation understood, as is evidenced by the later editions of the *Loci*, and even by Melanchthon's attempts to construct a doctrine of the Trinity out of the divine self-consciousness.

But also for *historical science*, philology included, the Reformation was of the greatest importance, and here again Melanchthon's merits are supreme. That striving after true certainty did, in historical matters, instigate the falling back upon the ultimate grounds, the investigation of authorities, which was of importance, especially in the eyes of Melanchthon, from an early period, but was also pursued by Luther, and after him particularly by the *Magdeburg Centuriators*. This tendency was espe-

[1] *Luthers Werke von Walch*, xix. 129. See above, p. 235.
[2] *Artic. Smalc.* 305; cf. viii. 2655.
[3] *Glaubenslehre*, system of doctrine believed.—*Tr*.

cially beneficial to the study of the holy Scriptures, but Luther and Melanchthon are also one in recommending and ardently promoting *classical studies;* they recommended the founding of gymnasia. Melanchthon was very extensively consulted in the appointments to their staff, and he himself kept, for many a year, a *schola privata*, even as Luther, in like manner, desired diligent instruction in history, *mathematics* and *music*.[1] Melanchthon delivered lectures on universal history, as well as on many of the Roman and Greek classics. So highly did Luther esteem the laws of language, that he confessed that, whenever Melanchthon condemned any exposition, he yielded to this grammarian. In general, however, classical and oriental philology found within the evangelical Church a weighty and permanent point of support in the interest which peculiarly belongs to these studies by reason of the exposition of Scripture.

But there is still another point of importance for the modelling of science, to be considered in its connection with the Reformation principle. The Christian Church had set up or defined a whole series of dogmas, without their internal connection and their relative worth being intelligently apprehended, and much less, any distinction being made between the substance and form of the dogma. If the question, however, was started as to the foundation of these dogmas in their separate particularity, attention was turned only to their being contained in the holy Scriptures and ecclesiastical tradition, *i.e.* to the formal authority of the Scriptures or the Church. If they derive their confirmation, however, only from these authorities and not from their internal matter, then all dogmas are on an absolutely equal footing, in so far as they are only equally embraced by these formal authorities. In that case the dogmas are laws of faith, the Scriptures and tradition become a dogmatic and ethical code, whilst divergence even from the most insignificant dogma sanctioned is, equally with divergence from the most fundamental, a breach of those formal authorities which alone impart to every dogma its authority. The matter assumes an entirely different shape under the influence of the Reformation principle. Not only are the dogmas of the Church tried by the holy Scriptures, but even within the Scriptures everything is not of the same worth. Faith is the eye

[1] Koch, *Melanchthons Schola privata*, 1860. Schäfer, *Luthers Verdienste um das Schulwesen.* Raumer, *Geschichte der Pädagogik.*

formed by God, which, directed to the subject-matter of the Scriptures, recognizes in them indeed a homogeneous unity and totality, but also a membrated unity. And thus the Scriptures no longer appear to it merely an object of universal but indefinite reverence, but they are more definitely understood and applied, as being what they are, and as what in their particular parts they seek to be considered; what is in their head and heart is accordingly distinguished in them, just as in the body, from the remaining members, which are conditioned through the head and heart.

Faith, however, is not in its genesis to be forthwith and at once directed equally upon everything in the Scriptures, but it has to regard that which is the vital kernel and centre of the sacred Scriptures, or the light by which everything else is illumined, *i.e.* Christ. It has first of all to effect an union with this centre, that the rest may also gradually become clear and easy to it, according to the greater nearness or distance of the connection; but salvation does not lie in the reception of this more distant or derived matter in itself, but in faith in that vital centre. *Thus vital saving faith is also the scientifically important principle which determines the appreciation and systematic arrangement of the different portions of the contents of Scripture*, and it cannot any longer be said that for the pure doctrine of salvation all dogmatic sentences are of equal importance, everything is alike, that is to say, fundamental,—the inverted form of which would be, that that, which is alone the centre, shared this its unique position with everything else,—that Christ and faith were accordingly no longer the only centre of saving doctrine. So manifestly did the depth and thoroughness of his religious experience become for Luther the source of higher scientific requirements and render it possible for him to satisfy them. It is in fact apparent from many proofs how far Luther is beyond that legal equalization of all dogmas. It is apparent above all *from the unique position which he assigns to justifying faith in Christ.* To this and to nothing else does he ascribe everything which belongs properly to the principle of the whole. Whilst he confesses in the Schmalkaldic Articles (Pars iii.), that with regard to quite a number of doctrines and their proper understanding there might still be negotiation with pious and learned men of the Romish Church, or even inside of the Evangelical—

amongst which there are by no means merely insignificant doctrines to be found,—he says of justification by faith[1] that it is the article whereby the Church stands or falls. Everything was contained in it which he taught and urged against the world and the devil in his whole life (*articulus stantis et cadentis ecclesiæ. De hoc articulo cedere, aut aliquid contra illum largiri nemo piorum potest, etiamsi cœlum et terra et omnia corruant. Nam in hoc articulo sita sunt omnia, quæ contra diabolum et mundum universum in tota vita nostra testamur et agimus*). Further, Luther esteems those articles more highly, which the whole of Christendom has always held by, such as the apostolic symbol. He does not refuse a Christian character or the title of brethren to a community which preserves the centre, although other weighty doctrines may be obscured in it.[2] " A Christian, holy people is to be recognized wherever it has the holy Word of God, although this may have unequal way. Some have it quite pure, some not. Where God's word is still current, there are always believers to be found. Further:[3] I see that they preach and confess Christ as sent by the Father, that by His death He should reconcile us to Him and obtain mercy for us, so we are one in these matters, and hold them for dear brethren in Christ and members of the Christian Church, even as also under the Papacy this preaching was continued, and has saved many on their deathbed, when they cast everything away and trusted in Christ." He has similarly expressed himself with regard to the divergencies of the Waldensians in particular points of doctrine, —as well as in the celebrated letter to the Zurichers after the Wittenberg Concord of 1537.[4] The basis of all these views is that he regards none of the visible Christian communities, together with their respective confessions, as identical with the true Church; for it is not the true confession which in his eyes constitutes the Church, nor even word and sacrament, but to the Church there belong all believers, and only true faith can accomplish a true confession. And even if a church had a perfect confession, still there are always unbelievers and hypocrites outwardly con-

[1] *Artic. Smalc.* 305. To this agrees also the *F. C.* when it says, appealing to Luther, that if this one article remains uninjured, the purity of all doctrine is secured, because all heresies can be overcome by this. Cf. *F. C.* 683.
[2] *Von den Concilien u. Kirchen, Luthers Werke von Walch*, xvi. 2615, ff.
[3] viii. 486, ff.; zu Joh. xvi. 1, 2.
[4] *Luthers Werke*, xvii. 2594, ff., of 1st Dec. 1537; and 2617, f., of the year 1538.

nected with it, and on the other hand in every Christian community whatsoever there are to be found members of the true Church.

It is true that Luther did not always preserve the same view; as, for example, in his controversy with the Swiss. He himself, at another time, laid an extravagant stress upon the dogmatical form of the pure doctrine. We do not say, that he had already made the distinction between dogmatic form and substance. But unquestionably he consciously entertained the distinction between the principle and the inference, the foundation and the superstructure; it even belongs to the most essential features of the physiognomy of the Reformation. Here, too, that is not to be regarded as the most important and peculiar in which the effects of pre-Reformation views involuntarily display themselves, but what is to be held as belonging to the Reformation is the new, which he opposes to the old, even although he does not carry it out on all sides.

This Reformation principle, as it is enforced most purely of all by Luther, and as it is implanted in the Evangelical Church, opens also *for the moral sphere the possibility of a regeneration,* and even prepares the way for it from within.

THE PROVINCE OF CHRISTIAN MORALS UNDER THE POINT OF VIEW OF THE REFORMATION PRINCIPLE.

We have learned, especially from the treatise on the freedom of the Christian, how justifying faith is in its essence the fruitful principle of sanctification or of the Christian moral life. The disinterested purity of godlike love is enkindled by the overwhelming, freely and graciously pardoning love of God towards the sinner; its prevenient nature dissipates fear, but dissipates also the inclination to disown sin to Christ and to one's self, for that would be to disown the undeserved benefaction of Christ. Justification, indeed, as a divine act for the sake of Christ, precedes all inward changes for the better in man, and simply describes the reconciled paternal heart of God, the real counsel of reconciliation in God, as it were in its inward forum. The love or the new life of man has no place, whether as merit or even merely as condition, in presence of this active purpose of God, upon His part, to regard men as reconciled and justified for

Christ's sake. On the other hand, this new divine view of men, which takes place not on account of *their* connection with Christ in faith but in virtue of the fellowship of *Christ* with men, even whilst they are yet sinners, and which rests entirely on the undeserved and free grace of God, does not remain locked up in God nor an idle decision. The Gospel is rather the glad tidings thereof, and this revelation is mighty enough to bring with it a transformation in the whole inner world, which it effects by persuading the convicted conscience of the unworthy sinner to recognize the prevenient love-work of the suffering Mediator, and to respond to it with believing surrender. Since faith lays hold of Christ in the fulness of His self-communicating grace, as it is laid hold of by him, there is necessarily involved in such faith participation in the new life as well as in the blessedness of Christ,—without, however, the forgiveness of sins, *i.e.* the reconciliation of God with the sinner being in any way caused by this new life, or even by the surrender of man to Christ in faith, since, on the contrary, it is entirely through the fellowship of *Christ* with man that the forgiveness of sins and all salvation is procured and assured.

But just as sure as this objective validity of the forgiveness of sins offered on the part of God *before* faith, stands this second point, that this forgiveness, valid in itself, can only be *personally appropriated* and enjoyed *by means of* faith. It takes place before faith, and is proclaimed to those who do not yet believe, in order that they may believe. If they despise this message, in which innermost and utter love towards the unworthy is revealed, there is henceforth no more redemption for them; they abide in death and its inevitable development. They thus make void the gracious counsel which avails even for them, and are lost, not on account of their former sins in themselves, but because they let their sins mount to the point of rejecting the love of Christ, suffering for them. The believers, on the other hand, are so, only through receiving the Gospel as grace, as a prevenient manifestation of love towards sinners, hence with the knowledge and sense of their unworthiness, else in their reception of it they would not know what they had received, and would accordingly in fact not have received grace as such, although it availed for them. Whilst these considerations show that to the believing reception of grace there necessarily belongs repentance, that is to say, the beginning of a moral transformation, which is, however, produced by the offer of salvation,—the power of positive moral renewing unto that negative condition (unto repentance) lies in faith, which establishes communion with Christ and all His benefits, and in which honest repentance is perfected. But that which becomes the motive power of the new personal life and endeavour in holiness is the power of Christ, of which faith becomes a partaker, above all, by means of that knowledge and experience of the gift of love, which is not of a bit-by-bit character, nor dependent upon the performances and stages of inward growth, but is fully and completely available for man even now in all his imperfection. This is the experience of the inward witness of the Holy Ghost concerning the forgiveness of sins and peace with God, by virtue of which also our own heart may give us witness that we are the children of God. This is the joyous and blessed background of our present, growing, and yet always imperfect life, the eternal completion of our imperfection unto righteousness before God, if we only continue in the faith. This is the ideal anticipation of our perfection and the perpetual enjoyment of our personal regeneration—the lot even of our consciousness in time—that the ideal may be realized by actual and effectual communion with Christ.

Sanctification, or the moral ordering of the life of the Christian, is thus for Luther only the necessary outcome and manifestation of the power given in faith;—faith is the doer, love is the deed; faith corresponds to the divine nature in Christ (to the πνεῦμα), love to the human nature, even as he terms it also the incarnation of faith (*fides incarnata*). The progress on to love is thus so completely a necessity of the higher nature, similar to the necessity by which a good tree brings forth good fruit, that where this fruit fails, either faith is not there, or else an unhealthy hardening of the sap, a backward movement and breaking up of the begun work of God, must have taken place. Hence he does not shrink from treating the *new life of love which is being formed as an evidence of faith*, not merely for others, but even for one's own consciousness and assurance of salvation, naturally not in such a way as if we had to place our confidence upon the goodness of our always imperfect life of love, instead of upon Christ, but rather in such a way that we possess in the life of love in course of growth within us, similarly as in the sacraments, a pledge, which is strengthening to faith, of an abiding state of grace.¹

In what concerns the further development of *the world of morals*, Luther is certainly disposed just to hold to faith as the principle of sanctification; he exhibits it in all its fulness and power, and in its blessedness, out of which springs the desire and free impulse towards all that is good. *Melanchthon*, without denying this natural free impulse of faith, which seeks to become love, pays more regard to the way and to the means, which belong to the doing of what is good. Alongside of gratitude for the salvation received in Christ, as the abiding impulse to the performance of the divine will, he pays regard also to the moral understanding or wisdom, by means of which alone advance is made, beyond the mere good will in general, to the willing of that particular good which is next in order, and by means of which, further, the Christian first attains to a not merely abrupt or impulsive exertion of grateful faith, but to an orderly modelling of the moral life. Melanchthon sees clearly that this orderly modelling does not come of itself by means of faith, which indeed has respect to God, and not to the world,—that there is much rather necessary the acquisition of a systematic moral knowledge of ourselves and of the world. Hence for Melanchthon, the man of science, *ethics* possessed an altogether special interest; he laid a great stress upon the law for the moral understanding, even in the regenerate, and so, on the one hand, drew upon the ancient ethics, especially Aristotle, and, on the other hand, turned to account at their right value the ethics of the Old Testament, and treated the Book of Proverbs with special delight. And since the proper moral treatment of earthly things and relations is conditioned by their constitution and laws of life, he searched through the world of the first creation, physics, psychology, jurisprudence, as sources partly of the preliminary bases of ethics, and partly of moral knowledge itself. But he always brought everything again under the view-point of faith, because it is only thus that religion, which is the centre of ethics, can remain the soul of the whole human life, the ill-founded antagonism between morality and religion be removed, and the fountains of power be maintained open for the fulfilment of what is recognized to be good. Luther, who often speaks—*e.g.* in the Preface

¹ For the passages, cf. Köstlin, ii. 458, ff.

to the Epistle to the Romans—as if faith of itself, without further help, hit by a sure instinct upon what is morally correct, knew well, on the other hand, what a valuable possession was his in the ethical genius of Melanchthon; with as much sagacity as bravery he defended him against those who held that faith was endangered, if it was not exclusively everything (v. afterwards, Agricola); for he knew well that faith would cease to possess the virtue of a principle just where it was no longer the principle of something. "Faith alone justifies, but faith does not continue alone." (*Fides sola justificat, sed fides non est solitaria.*)

Besides, although it was not done in a scientifically systematic manner, Luther, as we have already seen in part, recognized the *moral communities* in their good divine order, in their natural foundation, and in their harmony with the life of faith, and with a sound tact, as well as with a sense of the organic inter-dependence of powers, earnestly pointed every man to his calling, "to his lesson," and, in his "Haustafel"[1] apportioned the "lessons" in a concise and popular manner.

Let us look, then, at the *moral communities* individually, according to their relation to the Reformation principle. He distinguishes *wedlock, family, and State* from the kingdom of heaven, which is spiritual and eternal, whilst these are earthly, visible, and temporal. Still they are not on that account to be characterized as profane; on the contrary, there is in all their arrangements a divine and holy appointment; in all, the divine appointment is waging war against the devil: thus all derive their title from God, and are of divine institution.[2] Together with the Church, they form the true hierarchy, and he names as the three true holy orders: (1.) the *Church*, with the distinction between hearers and teachers; (2.) the *State*, the union of authorities and subjects; (3.) the *household*, which embraces parents and children, masters and servants.[3]

With regard, first of all, to *marriage*,[4] Luther has purified the conception of it from all that contempt of what is natural, which

[1] A section of the Little Catechism, containing the duties of the different members of society and of the household.—*Tr.*
[2] *Luthers Werke*, vi. 3316, ff. A.D. 1528.
[3] viii. 1086. Cf. *von Concil. u. Kirchen*, 1539.
[4] *Luthers Werke*, xix. 896, ff.; viii. 1069, ff.; x. 693, ff.; iii. 64; ii. 776. Cf. Köstlin, ii. 482, ff. Nitzsch, *Vertheid. d. luth. Lehre v. Ehestand. Stud. u. Krit.* 1846, 3.

had crept into it in [Roman] Catholicism, partly through the recognition of celibacy, as if it were a more highly virtuous condition, partly through the doctrine that marriage only became a moral alliance through a special sacramental act of God, which rid it of its profane character. This good and holy natural basis of marriage[1] impels him also to repudiate the artificial character of the Romish doctrine in reference to prohibited degrees, and to investigate the appointments of the Old Testament law of marriage. As the divine purpose in the institution of marriage he specifies first of all the procuring of offspring (*procreatio sobolis*), which is a most noble work of God (*plenissimum admirationis*). But although, for the sake of this purpose, he regards marriage as marriage even in the case of wicked pairs, he forthwith adds education to procreation as constituting the purpose of marriage. The children are educated for State and Church; marriage is the fountain of the State (*fons reipublicæ*), and serves towards the extension of the Church (*paratio ecclesiæ*). Still he always sees something of sin in lust, and hence a gift of God, though a very rare one, in true chastity and virginity; but he regards marriage as even in this respect a beneficial institution, restraining the sinful outbreaks of lust, and on the other hand as forming, by means of the cross in the household, an exercise in prayer and faith.

Although he thus regards marriage, because in itself independent of the moral worth of the pair, and valid even where one of them is unbelieving, as in its constitutive essence merely a civil matter, pertaining to *justitia civilis*, and in this sense an external thing; still upon this basis marriage ought to be conducted and shaped after a moral and Christian manner; and even the entrance into it ought to be sanctified by the Word of God and faith. In 1522 he described marriage as possible even with heathen and Jews, namely, in so far as it is only the fundamental essence of the relationship which falls at the time within the scope of his argument. Although, therefore, he does not insist on the benediction of the Church as indispensable to the validity of marriage, he nevertheless desires that it should be exhibited as a public condition of life. He regards it, even apart from Christianity, as a not merely physical, but moral, relationship, a holy order even without the

[1] viii. 1086, A.D. 1523.

sacrament, an inseparable connection which can be severed before death only by sin. But since he does not hold it to be a sacrament, he does not absolutely interdict divorce, but strikes out a path which takes account of the hardness of the heart, inasmuch as he considers wicked desertion (*desertio malitiosa*), to which also the *denegatio debiti* is to be added, as a sufficient ground of divorce, as well as the πορνεία.

Faith transforms the *family* into a " church at home," in which the father is the priest, whilst instruction and training in conformity with the principle of faith must have their goal in Christian competency or full age [*die christliche Mündigung*]. In this way the work of the particular individual is rated still more highly than by means of infant baptism, which was still retained, but is common to all Christians. The instruction of the female sex is also most urgently recommended. In 1525 he addressed a treatise to the Councillors of every town in Germany, "That they ought to institute and maintain Christian schools." He was anxious for a school-system, and one section of the articles of visitation for the Electorate of Saxony is occupied with schools. In this Luther had expressly in view schools for the German people, whilst Melanchthon, and still more the prevalent humanism, chiefly aimed at learned schools alone.

So far as *art* is concerned, Luther prized highly all the arts, not merely in the interest of the Church, but also of intellectual culture in general, and he did not allow his vivid fresh sense of this gift of God to be hampered by the narrowness of an unpoetical mind, or one intent only upon what is useful, nor by a gloomy view of the world, which sees in it only vanity, and, on account of its being stained by sin, is averse from the whole province of the beautiful. By the composition of spiritual songs and music, especially choral music, he fostered art, and that, too, in a productive manner, and raised congregational singing to a principal place in the evangelical cultus. In like manner, Luther loved to cultivate fellowship with friends in free and fresh intercourse, on which occasions his talk was not wanting in the spice of national wit and graphic expression.

Luther's fundamental view regarding the relation of the life of faith to what is outward accords independence to all civil departments, and it is the *State* in particular which has reached its independence and a higher dignity through the principles of the

Reformation. Whilst he withdrew the authorities from ecclesiastical tutelage, and always brings into emphatic prominence the difference between Church and State,—the former having to do with spiritual heavenly things and the conscience, the government of which God has reserved to Himself, whilst the State has to do with earthly temporal things,—he did not on that account regard the latter as a department of a secular and human nature, as a work of mere craft and power; but he saw equally in the State, in its own place, a holy divine ordinance. But the rights of the State do not extend to the conscience nor the internal affairs of the Church. "Body, gold, and property God has given over to the Emperor; the heart, however, is the greatest and the best thing in man, and that God has reserved for Himself." The Church ought not to govern the State, as little ought the State to govern the Church; the two governments ought not, until the end of the world, to be intermixed, as happened in Old Testament times, if the Gospel and the true faith can in any other way be maintained.[1] "He who is a preacher must let civil government alone, that he may not occasion confusion and disorder; for we ought to govern the Church with the word, or the spoken sword, and bear the rod of the mouth, which alone touches the conscience. The civil authority, on the other hand, has no other sword than the sword of the fist and a wooden rod by which the body is stricken."[2] "The end of the Church is everlasting peace, the end of politics is temporal peace." (*Finis ecclesiæ est pax æterna, finis politiæ est pax mundi.*) Hence in things referring to God and the salvation of the soul,[3] civil rulers have not to give laws to the soul, but have, on the other hand, an unlimited right to require obedience in things relating to the body and to property.[4] Hence in the case of the insurrectionary peasants he maintained, in the most decided manner, the divine right of the civil authorities in opposition to the rioters. At first he sought to appease the peasants,[5] especially as the Schwabian and Franconian peasants did not in their resolutions fly beyond the word of God, but adopted amongst their articles a demand for evangelical preaching; he drew attention, however,

[1] *Briefe von de Wette*, iv. 105. *Luthers Werke*, iv. 2890; xiii. 207, 210.
[2] Similarly the *Augustana*, pp. 38, 39, ed. Hase. [3] xiii. 210.
[4] *Luthers Werke*, x. 426. *Von weltl. Obrigkeit*, 1523.
[5] xvi. 58. *Ermahnung zum Frieden auf die zwölf Artikel der Bauerschaft*, 1525.

to the difference between the freedom of a Christian, which can exist also in external slavery, and mere outward freedom, warned them against a strong-handed usurpation of the rights of rulers, and demanded of them rather to suffer, than to perpetrate, injustice. He allowed to them the right of choosing evangelical preachers, as well as the right of flight, if this right of choice were taken from them. At the same time he addressed himself in the strongest language to the princes and lords who oppressed the common people, and summoned them to desist. When the peasants, however, without hearkening to all this, made havoc with fire and sword, robbed and murdered, he summoned the princes in God's name to suppress by force this devilish procedure.[1] The Reformation principle, which has been so often termed disorganizing, and has even been confounded with the spirit of revolution, gave effect with a power previously unknown to the *divine right* of civil authority, and the duty binding upon the conscience of not resisting it even where it is wayward. It was so much the more enabled to do this, since by the Reformation there was restored to men that absolutely highest blessing, which renders men capable of dispensing with subordinate benefits, and enduring suffering in these departments.[2] The inward equality of men before God in the possession of the highest blessing, renders so much the more inexcusable every violent and illegal step towards the attainment of outward freedom.

But in speaking of the one side of the question he does not forget the other. This is manifest partly from what goes before, and partly and particularly in his attitude towards the question which afterwards emerged as to the right of an armed resistance to the Emperor, when he wished to suppress the Gospel and no longer allow the peaceful enjoyment of it. It is true it is only gradually that he entered in a more thorough manner into these questions; for a long time, especially so long as it was only his own person which was in question, he repudiated the protection of princes for the Gospel, and uttered powerful warnings against unbelief and fear, as well as against confidence in the arm of flesh.[3] But a more searching investigation about the time of the Schmalkaldic League, after 1530, made him sensible of a new side

---

[1] xvi. 90, ff. *Wider die räuberischen und mörderischen Bauern.*
[2] vii. 689-700.
[3] De Wette, iii. 561 (A.D. 1530); iv. 337 (A.D. 1532).

of the matter, whereby there was introduced the duty of a positive participation in State matters. The perception that the Gospel is not come in order to introduce any definite State constitution, but that the rightly existing laws of the State have authority from God, led him to the important axiom, "The Gospel does not suspend natural or positive law, but confirms it" (*Evangelium non tollit leges naturales aut positivas, sed affirmat*). In this was implied that persons in authority are not justified in demanding obedience in all and every particular, but only in their office and within the limits of the law on which their official right rests. Accordingly, temporal authorities have no right to require obedience to themselves in matters affecting the salvation of the soul, as, for example, to require apostacy from the Gospel. Further: "the civil magistrate is no werewolf, and does not exist in order to destroy land and people in insane tyranny; a werewolf may and ought to be rendered harmless." Finally, however, so far as the Emperor is concerned, if the laws of the Empire give him only a limited power, and the estates of the Empire have, according to existing imperial law, to protect land and people against unrighteous violence (concerning which the jurists have to decide as a fact of positive law), then the estates of the Empire form an essential part of the civil magistracy itself; and whilst Luther is far from approving even there an irregular resistance of individuals rising in opposition to the Emperor, still he declares that if the law of the Empire admits and even enjoins the opposition, then the theologian also must admit its legitimacy, although he always deemed it necessary notwithstanding to caution against a carnal confidence in compacts.[1] Hence in his *Warnung an die lieben Deutschen*, he declares, "Let there be rebellion only when one will himself be lord and appoint the law; defence of one's life is justifiable;" and in 1539, he says, "as the Gospel confirms the office of the civil magistracy, it confirms also natural and appointed laws." There is no doubt, that every father is bound to protect wife and child against open murder; and there is no difference between a private murderer and the Emperor, if the latter, going beyond

---

[1] Cf. Hortleder, *Handl. u. Ausschr. von Rechtmässigkeit u.s.w. des teutschen Kriegs*, Theil ii. Buch ii. cap. 9. *Luthers Werke*, Erl. Ausg. xxxv. 382. L. W. von *Walch*, x. 622-691.. Ratzeberger, *handschr. Gesch. über Luther u. seine Zeit*. ed. Neudecker, 1850.

his office, and particularly in a public manner or *notorie*, proposes injustice and violence. For open violence dissolves all the obligations subsisting *jure naturæ* between subjects and their rulers. At an even earlier date *Bugenhagen*, the Reformer of Denmark, and Melanchthon recognized these principles, since the Emperor, according to German law, is not absolute, but may, if he breaks the law, be deposed. Even imperial law, or the Emperor in his imperial rights, is in favour of the legality of an opposition on the part of the princes against the Emperor for the defence of their subjects and the Gospel, if the Emperor notoriously violate the law of the Empire.

What has been said implies that, according to Luther and the evangelical view, the civil magistrate, although he has not to decide in spiritual things (*spiritualia*), is yet in possession of a divine calling. He is, according to Luther, the servant of God, and has a relationship to everything good, because he has to maintain peace and order, and to give protection against evil, which is in its nature caprice. He regards his position as a Christian and honourable one, and because his work is good and well-pleasing to God, Luther condemns a negative attitude towards the State, such as the parties, who declined the oath and civil and military service, demanded of Christians, and on the contrary calls to participation in the State.[1]

But what follows, in connection with the declinature of the bishops to reform, goes still further. He requires of the civil magistrate, especially as a Christian, that as he protects and furthers everything good, so also the Gospel, only that he do not seek to wield authority over the heart. It is thus his right and duty to concern himself about the Church, and to care for outward order, repose, and peace within it. With his temporal civil service he is bound to serve God and His glory, even as he ought to know that he has his power from God. Hence it is his duty (and the fulfilment of it he calls the first virtue of princes[2]) to honour the Word of God above all things, and to further its teaching. The civil magistrate, whom he supposes like the subjects to be Christian, may and ought, according to him, to interfere, although not with the punishment of death, for the repression of the denial of the common Christian creed, or of the law;

[1] *Luthers Werke von Walch*, vii. 691-700.
[2] Exposition of Psalm lxxxii. A.D. 1530.

he ought not publicly to tolerate any offences, as, *e.g.* idolatrous masses, and picture-worship; at the most, he may tolerate them in secret, where they neither give offence nor offer temptation. Still even in this, effect is given above all to the position, that the civil magistrate is bound to avert faction, uproar, and public offence, because his office in general is to maintain order and peace; he does not, however, herein decide concerning the truth nor concerning Christian law. But since he has to administer the law in its minutest reference to the whole outward life, he may require obedience to everything which is of an outward worldly nature.[1]

This conducts us to the still more positive utterances regarding the admissibility of the functions of the civil magistrate in the Church, to Luther's doctrine regarding his *jus reformandi*. Since the bishops would not reform, and consequently a self-reorganization of the Church was not provided nor seemed forthwith attainable, the right was accorded to the civil magistrate, as Christian, to help from motives of Christian love to common arrangements, and the expression of the common will. For the civil magistrate constitutes the framework of general human order, and by it the Church too is encircled. Still, he always insists on the distinction of the spiritual functions themselves from those of the civil magistrate. He is not a bishop, for he does not preach, nor dare he force men into the faith with sword and fist. But it is one thing to preach, and another thing to place preachers and order evangelical preaching. As early as 1522, he demands of princes and lords to secure by the exercise of their power that nothing be pursued in opposition to the Gospel; if in the same district different doctrines are preached, if evangelical and Romish teachers dispute against each other, the civil magistrate ought, according to him,—since it is not good that in one parish the people should be exposed to contradictory preaching,—to hear both sides, and whatever side does not consist with the Scriptures, let it be ordered to be silent. But if the civil magistrate is summoned in this way to decide, it follows indeed as distinctly, that if the civil magistrate deems he is serving the glory of God by the suppression of evangelical doctrine, it is his right and duty to suppress it. And thus, according to these principles, which are manifestly not so thoroughly wrought

[1] De Wette, *Briefe*, iv. 107, A.D. 1530.

out[1] as his doctrine of salvation, the exercise of force is necessary in every territory where there are differences of religion, until one side is put down. For that different confessions, equally privileged by the State, are admissible in the same land and nation, is a view beyond the circle of ideas of that time. It was the great Elector who first practically carried out the view that the conscience belongs to God, not merely so far that no one may be forced to believing nor confessing, to which Luther restricts himself, but also so that attachment to a different confession does not entail civil loss.

As to what relates, on the other hand, to the *Church*, to which we now pass, he never withdraws the view, that it is not on any account to employ force, but is to labour only by the word; faith is a free thing, which is nothing helped, but only injured, by compulsion; it is the Word of God which is to struggle here; heresy is a spiritual thing, which no iron can hew nor fire burn.[2] At first Luther was not inclined towards the interference of the temporal power for the punishment of heretical teachers; as he comes from the Wartburg, he craves nothing from the Elector but that the office of the word be not hindered. "Let them (the Münzerites) only preach to their satisfaction and with vigour what they can and against whom they will, for there must be sects, and the Word of God must keep the field and fight. Let minds clash upon and hit one another,—if some the while are misled, let be—such is the way in the true course of war. We, who bear the Word of God, ought not to fight with the fist; it is a spiritual conflict." It is true however that he assigned more to the *State*, not merely from the point of view of order, but also from that of the glory of God, which it has to serve, so that a very indefinite and easily abused conception of its task was created. To this is to be added, that even the government of the Church fell to the lot of the civil magistrate, although only in cases of necessity, and thus these fine sentences regarding a spiritual conflict were rendered again for the most part illusory. This, however, was not his intention. To the last he was against a confounding of the civil and ecclesiastical; even the Christian civil magistrate had no spiritual calling; he wished the *adminis-*

---

[1] Cf. Köstlin, as cited, ii. 555, ff.; 488.
[2] De Wette, ii. 135, of A.D. 1522, 151, 549; iii. 51. *Von weltlicher Obrigkeit*, x. 426, f. Köstlin, i. 339; ii. 485, ff.

trationes et personas in civil and ecclesiastical matters to remain distinct.[1] He allows that the sovereign may act in a double capacity (*duplicem personam gerere*), and may in one of these stand at the head of the Church government, but into it the *aula, i.e.* the civil government of the sovereign, ought not to intrude. Practically, indeed, what was accepted of the theory of the *duplex persona* was simply the royal supremacy even in ecclesiastical affairs, but not the required independence of Church government over against the civil government; and the provisorial bishopric, founded on necessity, soon grew to be definitive, upon a territorial basis. Even Luther already was often troubled about the intrusions of the *aulici, i.e.* of the civil government, into ecclesiastical concerns.[2]

That Luther desired and founded a fixed *office of the ministry* has been shown (p. 172, ff.). But why did he not give himself any concern to develop a Church government, a Church organization in general, like the Waldenses or those of the Reformed Church, whilst he nevertheless perceived that the very idea of the thing required it? What we must regard as the reason is twofold: first of all, and principally, because he regarded the Church as consisting in a proper sense only of true believers (*vere credentes*); and these cannot be separated without falling into the errors of the Donatists, and therefore will not be organized. Even Church discipline could not furnish security against hypocritical members. But not even the exercise by the Church of Church discipline in the more limited antidonatist sense, such as he wished, seemed possible to Luther in his time; hence in order to secure the purity of the Gospel, he gladly assigned to the State a very wide care of morals.

If the Church is found in the *vere credentes*, then much of what belongs to the outward community of the Church is certainly not of the Church; and the right of calling the organization of this outward community the organization of the Church seems to be taken away, since not even the office-bearers are certainly believers. But, on the other hand, the outward com-

---

[1] De Wette, iv. 106, of A.D. 1530.
[2] De Wette, v. 591. If the *Aulici* are going to rule in the Church, the last will be worse than the first. p. 551; "The *Centauri et Harpyiæ aulicæ* will have nothing of Church discipline." p. 675; The Church government of the Court is a crab or a snail; cf. iii. 538, 551.

munity of the Church is still in a certain connection with the faith and with believers; believers are also visible persons, although their faith is invisible, and without the faith of believers the outward community would soon be in a perishing condition, whilst Luther holds firmly that the Church, even as the community of faith (*societas fidei*), has never died out. To this is to be added the possession of the means of grace, which are certainly outward, and are possessed even by the outward community of the Church, and the possession of which never continues altogether unfruitful, so that, taking all things together, Luther might have perceived even in the outward community of the Church, with all its difference from the proper idea of the Church, a community which recognized Christianity as its *norm*, a society inclined to Christianity and its idea, and might have deliberated upon its being ordered according to the rule of the Word of God, even as he did in reference to worship. Only, this outward community must certainly have assumed for the most part a pedagogic and legal character, from which Luther was then so much the more inclined to shrink, as the whole idea of the Church might thus have been easily resolved again into the purely legal. Besides this, Luther recognized the limits of his qualifications in reference to organization. Here accordingly he did not interfere in a decisive manner; although if one confined himself exclusively to the invisible side of the idea of the Church,—to that which has reference to persons, no organization at all, not even that of office and the ministry of the word, could be introduced. But the axiom, that the keys belong to the Church, was not meant by him to be an idle unpractical axiom. On the contrary, the keys are intrusted to the historical outward community of the Church, on account of the believers, who give to it the character of a Christian community.

We have therefore to attach all the greater importance to the circumstance that *Melanchthon* here completes Luther, and took a further and advantageous step. He, too, as the *C. A.* and the *Apologie* indicate, regarded the Church as strictly (*proprie*) the community of believers, who, being dispersed over the earth, are united to Christ by the Holy Spirit, and gathered around word and sacrament. And this definition was indispensable for reasons previously considered. But he lays far more emphasis upon the side of visibility in the conception of the Church, and invented for the outward community of the Church the expression "Church in the larger sense" (*ecclesia large dicta*) alongside of the *ecclesia proprie dicta*. He thus obtains an object to be subjected to ecclesiastical organization, and will by no means relegate everything that does not belong to the invisible Church to the State, or to the caprice of the subjects and to accident. That "Church in the larger sense," consisting of those who gather themselves around the word and sacrament, and so recognize the Gospel, though it should be in part hypocritically, to be the law of faith and life, cannot indeed claim to be the organization of the true believers. But it has this for its end and the idea of this for its principle, and has also in the believers who are in it, whoever they may be, an operative soul. Hence these may and must have an organization which subserves this end, and that organization will attain with ever increasing perfection to Church discipline, especially as this is already exercised in preaching. Melanchthon, to whom Luther left the principal charge of this department, possessed the talent for organization in a lofty degree. He became the regulative mind of the German Reformation, provided the outward church with Church Orders, interfered with Opinions full of wisdom, organized schools, and especially the spiritual education up to the trials of those who were to be ordained (*examen ordinandorum*), and so added to the ordinances of public worship introduced by Luther what was most necessary for the times. But these Church ordinances do not go the length of the *organization of congregations*. What stood in Melanchthon's way was that he was not a man of the people after the fashion of Luther. His starting-point is rather the Church as an unity, than the congregations, and partly in consequence of his historical taste for continuity, and partly in consequence of what may be called his aristocratic nature, he had a preference for episcopacy. There were attempts made in that direction, but these, after feeble beginnings, became, probably by means chiefly of the *aulici*, abortive. Only in the Scandinavian territories did this institution take root, but without exerting any reflex influence upon Germany, and without a constitution more full of life being thereby attained. Indeed, the Episcopate of these countries sank rather into a dependence upon the State similar to that of the Church government in Germany, where the consistories were introduced, in which the three estates (p. 268) were supposed to be represented, the clergy, the prince, and the laity.

The type of doctrine, which we have discovered in the foregoing discussion of principles, was in all essential points officially declared in the *Confessio Augustana*, 1530, to be the confession of the Protestant estates before the Emperor and the Empire; and was further explained in the *Apologia* appended to the confession. The large and little catechisms of Luther and the Schmalkaldic articles are essentially one in spirit with these writings of Melanchthon. These five works together exhibit the first formation of the Lutheran system of doctrine. We will sketch the construction of the most important of these writings, the *Augustana*, because, despite its peaceful and circumspect language, it already shows clearly how the Reformation doctrine of justification by faith is wielded as the formative principle of a new complete and harmonious system of doctrine.

The plan of the *C. A.* is this. The fourth article on justification by faith forms the centre of the whole, by which the adjustment of the whole is determined. There are prefixed to it in the three first articles its theological, anthropological, and christological postulates (*de Deo, de peccato originali, de filio Dei*). In it the stress is laid upon the conjunction of the free grace of God with faith, and then the Confession proceeds analytically to the doctrine of the *origin* of faith, together with its objective conditions, and to the doctrine of the *maintenance* of the faith that has been produced, and by both of these it is shown that the Christian community of the *Church* is not dissolved, but ensured, by means of evangelical doctrine.

First, faith *originates* through the service of the Church, which hands down to us word and sacrament, as well as through the Holy Ghost. Article v.

Secondly, faith, when it has been *produced*, brings forth the fruits of love. vi.

Thirdly, if this is the nature of faith in its origin and maintenance, evangelical faith in its very conception impels towards the *Church*, inasmuch as it partly presupposes it, and partly preserves it. Hence, from articles vii. to xvii. the Church is discoursed of at length. Its idea (vii.) is *principaliter* the community of the saints or of believers. It is imperishable, and is to be recognized by the right administration of word and sacrament, but preserves its unity amid the dissimilarity of human traditions. The reality (viii.) is in partial contradiction with its idea, because hypocrites and wicked men are mingled with it; but these do not make void the power and efficacy of word and sacrament. The *doctrine of the sacraments* is now brought forward in its particulars, positively and with a tacit criticism of the Roman Catholic doctrine. Articles ix. to xii. speak of Baptism, the Supper, Confession, and Repentance, and the relation of faith to the sacrament is exhibited in article xiii. in opposition to the *opus operatum*. Article xiv. affirms the evangelical idea of ordination as a regular call to the public administration of the means of grace, and thus secures the rights of ecclesiastical order against anarchy, but in such a way that the right of evangelical freedom must be kept intact over against the usages of the Church. It is again the principle of faith which decides regarding the necessity or dispensableness of the latter (xv.). Everything is to be expelled from tradition which is contrary to free grace, and fosters the delusion of meritorious works. The xvi. article proves the friendly relation of the evangelical doctrine to the *State* as a divine ordinance; it requires obedience and active participation in the life of the State; because love comes of faith. In fine, article xvii. treats of the perfection of the Church. The four articles which follow are occupied with warding off current objections. A searching refutation is given to the statements (*a*) that the Evangelicals in general deny the freedom of the will (xviii.), which they nevertheless allow for *justitia civilis;* (*b*) that they roll the origin of evil upon God (xix.); (*c*) that their doctrine hinders good works (xx.) or contemns the law. In like manner is (*d*) the imputed depreciation of the saints repudiated (xxi.). The xxii. article forms the transition to the abuses which are rejected on the part of the evangelicals. Seven points are here enumerated: the withholding of the cup, the celibacy of the priests, the offering of the mass, oral confession, regulations respecting food, the monastic vow, and several abuses of the episcopal and papal power at the expense of the Gospel and of the State.

SECTION II.

THE SWISS REFORMATION, AS FAR AS THE FORMATION OF ITS FIRST SYMBOLS, AND ITS RELATION TO THE GERMAN REFORMATION.

CHAPTER I.

THE FUNDAMENTAL REFORMATION IDEAS OF ZWINGLI.

INDEPENDENTLY from Luther, a similar Reformation movement was initiated in Switzerland by *Ulrich Zwingli* and his friends, the way being prepared for it in a peculiar manner by means of the freer civil development and the greater influence of Humanism. There were intimate relations between Switzerland and the free cities of the Empire in the south-west of Germany, which were very numerous, and the seats of a powerful burgher community, skilled in the arts and with an inclination towards Humanism. Hence these parts of Germany occupied a mediatory position in the relations between Luther and the Swiss. The southern part of *Swabia* in particular was at first, and until the controversy regarding the Supper, one with the Swiss, and in many respects determined by them.

There was at first no difference whatever observed on either side between the two Reformations. Their unity consisted not merely in a common antagonism to Rome, but also in an essential positive agreement upon those weightiest and fundamental tenets of the supreme authority of the holy Scriptures and the free grace of God in Christ. And this essential unity increased, after that the Swiss had to define their boundaries against the fanatical movements of a Hyperprotestantism, which appeared there not merely in the shape of Anabaptism, but also of antitrinitarian doctrines. But alongside of their common basis, and the antagonism to Pelagianism and a magical *opus operatum*, to spiritualism[1] and anarchical tendencies, there was certainly a *different* mental

[1] It is scarcely necessary to say that the word as used here refers to the fanatics of the Reformation period.—*Tr.*

tendency present, which expressed itself much more pointedly in the different method of combating the errors that have been named than in strictly dogmatic formulæ. This is seen in different ways. If the princely power and the nobility were the final authorities in North Germany, it was the free and powerful burgher community which occupied the place of pre-eminence in Upper Germany, Alsace, and German Switzerland, that community having its central points in the imperial cities of Augsburg, Ulm, and Strasburg, and the republican people who occupied this position in Switzerland. Civil freedom by itself indeed would not have produced the Reformation,—this is shown by the cantons which have continued [Roman] Catholic; but where civil freedom was conjoined with views enlarged by liberal education, there necessarily arose a taste and desire for reformation, although it was in the first instance only a reformation of the abuses of the Papal nunciatures, the offence of indulgences, and the superstitious aspects of mediæval Catholicism. Whatever this possessed that tended to bondage, or was contrary to sense, necessarily awakened an almost stronger antagonism in those quarters, where free self-consciousness was more alive than in the rest of Germany. This more powerful development of the natural personality had, however, another effect. The more general individual thought and personal self-consciousness was, the less was one individuality able to acquire the leadership of the whole movement; and it has continued to be generally characteristic of the Reformed Church,—it is connected both with its defects and excellences,—that it has at its head no man, standing forth in solitary prominence, who resembles the princely spirit of Luther. In the Reformed Church the reformation was rather the will and act of the people, but in the German reformation the hegemonic spirit of one man led everything, amid the free recognition of his contemporaries: this, however, in such a way, that the fiery spirit of this man was softened and purified by the prudence and the still power of the mildness of his incomparable friend. The Reformed Church, on the other hand, has, as it were, two stages of reformation, a less ripe and a riper; and only by means of both together did she become what—over against the Romish Church—she is, the twin sister of the Lutheran Church, which spread in the west of central Europe, from Geneva, through France, and along the Rhine to Holland, England, and

Scotland, and afterwards took possession also of the northern half of the new world. In the first of these two stages it is Zwingli who certainly occupies the first place; but alongside of him every canton has its own reformer, almost none of whom (some Zürichers excepted) bears his stamp in the way that so many fellow-workers of Luther in Germany are moulded by him. Hence, too, as the confessions of the Reformed Church show, Zwingli's mind and manner of doctrine, so far as his peculiarities are concerned, nowhere achieved (only Zürich again being partially excepted) a symbolic expression and currency.

Huldrich Zwingli was born on 1st January 1484, and received a humanist education in Vienna, and especially under Thomas Wyttenbach in Basle, and was already from 1512 labouring in Glaxus for the purification of manners and the removal of abuses, under a sense of patriotism. Called in 1517 to Einsiedeln, he had the best opportunities for gaining a deep insight into the corruption of the Church; for perceiving the effects of superstition in the crowd pouring round the black image of the Mother of God, and for combating the meritoriousness of the monastic life, pilgrimages, and the like. Called in December 1518 to the Minster at Zürich, he made it his first task to instruct the people more deeply in the knowledge of the Scriptures. He preached a series of sermons even during the week upon the New Testament; the sermon occupied the foremost place, instead of the mass. His manner of preaching—lucid, intelligible, and practically powerful—met with great applause, and he created for himself in the burgher community a well-prepared soil for the struggles which were soon to begin. *Bernhardin Samson*, the Swiss Tetzel, was now, in the course of his profitable indulgence circuit, on his way from the old cantons to Zürich, and Zwingli, who had already conflicted him in Einsiedeln, preached against indulgences with such success, that the Council in Zürich refused Samson admission into the town. As early as 1520 the Zürich Council issued a reformation order, according to which all parish ministers had to preach in uniform manner upon the New Testament, prove their doctrine from the Bible, and eschew all new and human inventions. But when thereafter the people sought to proceed at once from the reformation of doctrine to that of the cultus and church life, many no longer submitting to the injunctions to fast and the like, others planning a position of greater independence from the bishop and the Pope, others again striving for civil changes in consequence of the church reform, internal disorders began to threaten Zürich, in addition to the interference from without of the Bishop of Constance, Hugo von Landsberg, who was for the rest an educated man, and hitherto of a tolerably friendly disposition. Persecutions began, friends of Zwingli were deposed, his own life was endangered. The cause of Reformation was placed between two fires; on the one side were those friendly to Rome, and on the other anarchical and fanatical minds. The destruction of images, the doing away with the mass, and even with infant baptism, was recommended by *Ludwig Hetzer* and others. A great fermentation took possession of their spirits, and a destructive zeal against " idols " [*Götzen*]. In order to preserve the movement within the limits of an orderly progress, the government took the reins of church administration more and more into its own hands. The Council instituted a disputation in the Council Chamber, upon the 29th of January 1523, between the Reformation party and the [Roman] Catholics. The deputy of the latter, the Vicar-General of Constance, at first fought shy of the Scriptures, and when compelled to condescend upon them, a very decided impression was made upon the Council of his being worsted. The Council accordingly affirmed the right of evangelical preaching, and even began changes in the cultus, *e.g.* the introduction of the German tongue. Only the mass and images remained. Outward order, disturbed by the anarchists, was restored only by the imprisonment of their chiefs; and then a second disputation was held in Zürich in October 1523, in order to decide from the Word of God what is to be held respecting images. Conrad Schmidt, the honourable commander of Küssnacht,[1] demanded, like Luther, that this staff should not be torn out of the hand of the weak, so that they might not fall to the ground. Let the outward images stand for the simple, but set up beside them the strong staff, Jesus Christ, and thus of themselves they will no longer need images, and will lay hold of Christ. Whoever has the true image of Christ in the heart cannot be injured by the outward image.—Zwingli, with Sebastian Hoffmeister of Schaffhausen, would not, however, allow that images were sticks or staffs for the simple. Christians ought to

[1] Where there was a house of the Knights of St. John, whose commander Schmidt was.—*Tr.*

know better, and therefore such abuse ought not to be tolerated in them. If we were to defer the removal of abuses till they were no more cause of offence, and the victory over them had been achieved from within, there would never be anything to be gained by their removal. Accordingly, since even Schmidt summoned the Council to take the matter in hand in a Christian spirit, and boldly, the Council at once proceeded to issue a reformation mandate (1524), did away with the mass, together with images, and introduced the sermon and the supper in both kinds. At Easter, 1525, the first German celebration of the Supper took place in Zürich. No one, it was said, would be forced into faith, but the Council would take care, as became a Christian magistracy,[1] that only the Word of Christ would be proclaimed.

In a similar spirit the Reformation pressed its way, in part independently of Zwingli, in the other cantons. In *Basle* there were Caspar *Hedio* and *Kapito;* but only after Œcolampadius (Hausschein) came thither from Weinsberg (1523), did the Reformation movement advance with a more powerful tide. In 1524 he became Professor there, where also lived Erasmus, who, as well as Zwingli, was his friend. In the same year the Genevan *Farel* came to Basle, and won the Council for his cause. But since Basle was the seat of a bishop, and had intimate connections with Austria, the burgher community was divided, and the triumph of the Reformation was delayed till 1529. In *Bern*, Berthold *Haller* and Sebastian Mayer laboured successfully. The disputation in Baden in 1526 was indeed without any favourable result, but just so much the more triumphant for the Evangelicals was the disputation at Bern in 1527, where they were supported by Zwingli, Haller, Kolb, Capito, and Bucer. The following year the Reformation was set afoot in Bern.

For several years, however, the Reformation in Switzerland had to struggle against *fanatical,* and, in particular, *anabaptist* movements; the greater political freedom secured it against the attacks of [Roman] Catholicism. Zwingli was not merely preserved from this subjectivist form of reformation by his sobriety

---

[1] Cf. Hagenbach, *Vorlesungen über Wesen und Geschichte der Reformation*, 2 Thle. 1857, Aufl. 3. H. Bullinger, *Geschichte der Reform. v. 1519 bis 1631*, 3 Bde. Füssli, *Beiträge zur Erläuterung der Kirchen-Reformationsgeschichte des Schweizerlandes*, 1741, 5 Thle. J. Heinr. Hottinger, *hist. eccl.*, t. vi.-ix., 1665. J. J. Hottinger, *helv. Kirchengeschichte*, 1698, ff. Thl. 3.

and his practical ecclesiastical tact; he was also compelled to withstand these fanatical movements in virtue of his fundamental principle. Deep reverence for the majesty of God, to which everything is absolutely subject, is opposed to all human license; the earnest moral mind of Zwingli desires a rule for the human will, and this rule or the will of God he considers to be recorded in the *canonical scriptures*, which teach us how we are "to find rest in God," and are to "honour God." The holy Scriptures, inspired by God, stand before his eyes as a divine authority armed against all subjectivism and spiritualism. That authority, however, does not continue a mere outward law, but becomes "clear and sure" to the believer.

His position in reference to the *holy Scriptures* is made particularly clear by his own statements regarding his inward development. Zealously devoted to Humanism, he called himself a disciple of Plato and of the Stoics. Stirred, however, by a writing of Erasmus, he resolved to become a disciple of Christ. Philosophy and scholasticism did not free him from doubts nor suffer him to obtain assurance.[1] But in the Scriptures he found an enlightenment which brought his heart to rest. Hence he assigns to the Scriptures an unique position. "The Scriptures come from God, not from man; and even that God who enlightens will give thee to understand that the speech comes from God. The Word of God is to be held in the highest honour, and to no word is such faith to be accorded as to it. It cannot fail, it is bright, it teaches itself, it discloses itself, and illumines the soul with all salvation and grace, comforts it in God, humbles it, so that it loses and even forfeits itself and embraces God into itself.[2] In Him it lives, to Him it looks, despairs of any comfort from any creature, and God alone is its comfort and confidence: without Him it has no rest, in Him it rests alone. Ay, its blessedness begins even in this present time, not in its substantial form,

[1] *Zwinglii Opp. ed Schuler et Schulthess. Von der Klarheil und Gewüsse des Wortes Gottes* of the year 1522, i. 79 :—"When, seven or eight years ago, I began to give myself up wholly to the holy Scriptures, philosophy and theology would always keep suggesting quarrels to me. At last I came to this, that I thought, 'Thou must let all that lie, and learn the meaning of God purely out of His own simple Word.' Then I began to ask God for His light, and the Scriptures began to be much easier to me, although I am but lazy." Thus he "won an undeceived understanding, to which he would never have come in following the littleness of his own understanding."

[2] The same, p. 81.

but in the assurance of a comforting hope."¹ From this it is evident that it is wrong to think of *Zwingli* as if he had found rest and assurance in a philosophy, say that of Count Pico of Mirandola, or as if his primitive interest in life had been only of an intellectual, and not of a moral and religious kind; the consequence whereof would be that his reformation would only have been a kind of up-clearing. The truth, which he seeks and finds, is for him practical truth. God is indeed in his view, as in that of Count Pico, the true Being [*Sein*], but even on that account also the *supreme Good*, in whom alone the soul finds rest; He is, at the same time, according to him, intelligent Will; and he considers that it is in being animated by this Will of God, and in serving His glory, that we find the existence that is worthy of man, an existence which, from out of its rest in God, is lively and practically operative.

From that inward relationship which he establishes between God and the world, everything true in mankind is regarded by him as the work and revelation of God. Wherever religious truth is embraced in a scripture, there is holy scripture; but not all sacred authors are *infallible*, but only those through whom God has declared His Word without adulteration. These are the proper holy scriptures, those of the Spirit of God [*die "gottsgeistliche"*].[2] Still he frankly acknowledges inaccuracies in historical matters. It is not on account of the Church that we believe the holy Scriptures are inspired, but the Church has, in virtue of the Spirit dwelling in it, to exclude what is not genuine. To this class he assigns the Apocalypse, as well as the Apocrypha. The will or mind of the supreme Lord is expressed in the Scriptures, and therefore every earthly right and law must be fashioned according to the Scriptures; but this in such a way that it is not the particular case, but only the rule therein contained, irrespective of the circumstances of the time, which has an eternal significance.[3] Hence, although the Old Testament in itself and formally has, as the Word and Revelation of God, the same dignity as the New, still the ceremonial matter of it was only intended to have a local and temporal significance. As the Holy Scriptures are considered by him to be the *only*, so also are they the *sufficient, source* of the Word of God. Everything is sin which God has not taught through word or deed (*Peccatum est, quidquid*

[1] ii. 2, p. 20.   [2] The same.   [3] vii. 316 ; iii. 367.

Deus nec verbo nec facto docuit). According to this, every tradition which is not based upon the express words of Scripture ought to be rejected; and it would then be necessary, in respect of the cultus, and especially of infant baptism, to recur in every point to the forms of the apostolic times. But in the controversy with the Anabaptists he became much freer in this respect, although he always retained a dislike to the sensuous splendour and fulness of the cultus. At Marburg, in 1529, he recognized the article regarding tradition, according to which, whatever was not manifestly opposed to the Word of God continues permissible. But although he thus allowed that the holy Scriptures do not expressly regulate in practice every circumstance of the life of the Church, he still holds[1] with Luther that in matters of faith they are quite sufficient for salvation, and do not require to be completed by tradition. To be subject to them is not a slavish duty, but the precious right of recognizing only God the Lord and the absolute truth as obligatory. But the Scriptures must also be *expounded*. The Anabaptists are bold in the letter, but this does not reveal God without divine illumination. He who spoke the Word can alone know surely what He meant.[2] Hence the same Spirit, who is the source of the holy Scriptures, must also be their revealer and expounder. Still, this illumination only shows what is really expressed in the Word; the meaning of the holy Scriptures is simple; allegorical exposition is caprice. If one passage seems to contradict another, then the one scripture is to be weighed against the other, so that what is clear may illumine what is dark. Thus he, too, holds a self-interpretation of the Scriptures, but the analogy of faith, according to which the Scriptures are to be explained, is in his view not so much Christ or justification through faith in him, but the touchstone is, according to him, the honour of God; he lays down this sentence as the proper guide into [the understanding of] the Scriptures: *is spiritus ex deo est, qui illi solam gloriam tribuit*. This tends still more definitely to show that *the Scriptures are in his view chiefly the revelation or memorial of the Will of God*, certainly also of what the Will of God has done for us, but in particular of what He will have done by us.

In reference to the *power* and *efficacy* of the holy Scriptures, the outward letter cannot indeed, according to Zwingli, establish

---

[1] i. 194, 209.   [2] i. 231.

faith; in order to this there is required the inward illumination and drawing of the Spirit. This was also the teaching of Luther and the *Augustana* (Art. V.), in the interests of the liberty of God to work where He will. In the case of Zwingli, however, the motive is this, that there may not be ascribed to the letter, the creature, what is God's. At the same time, the letter is in his view of importance in opposition to a merely internal operation of the Spirit, such as the fanatics would have it. The Scriptures are necessary, that, for one thing, false doctrine may be recognized, tried, and refuted. He indeed who is born of the Spirit requires a book no longer, but the meaning must be thoroughly pointed out to the captious.[1] Still he adds that faith, although it is true, must be preserved by and upon the Scriptures, so that it may be known that it is not simply hypocritical nor a self-willed imagination.[2] Elsewhere, after saying that the Scripture entices or excites again to faith, he adds:[3] "Since I completely surrendered myself to the divine Word, I have directed all my doctrine to the end that the true and proper glory of God, His truth, and Christian life and peace be advanced." My care, he says afterwards, is this, that Christ, to whom we owe everything, may be glorified. To obey Christ, to know Christ and His benefaction, to love and really use them, is salvation; to care for the glory of God and for the salvation of souls is one and the same thing.

It may therefore be said that Zwingli's *material principle* is the glory of God, since he refers everything to that. This would be essentially different from Luther,—but not merely the *theo*logical expression of what Luther describes *anthropo*logically by justification by faith,—if he regarded the glory of God as lying only in His might and omnipotent perfection, and not also in the free grace and love of God, which sets man before it as its object, or if man had to promote the glory of God through moral performances according to the divine law, and not also through the reception of His free grace in the obedience of faith. That, however, is not the case. It is true that there is not to be observed in the case of Zwingli, as in the case of Luther and of Calvin, a sudden revolution or decisive turning-point of his inward life from internal discord to the joyful consciousness of reconciliation. He never stood in a living way and by a true membership

[1] ii. 2, p. 250. [2] ii. 2, p. 2; iii. 550. [3] ii. 1, p. 422.

within the Romish Church, and *e.g.* never believed in transubstantiation. Hence he had not the same inward struggles; he rather, starting from Humanism, advanced from the negative to the positive, inasmuch as he penetrated more and more deeply into the Scriptures. Increasing knowledge exerted upon him principally a morally purifying influence, and that in such a way that he soon came to regard evil as lying not in particular moral offences, but in a more universal circumstance, the want of love to God and of the fear of God. He very early perceived that religion, or faith, is the basis of works. Neither was there wanting in his case that need of salvation, which found its satisfaction and rest in God, the Father of Jesus Christ, whom the Scriptures proclaim to him. With all this it may be quite correct that, in the case of Zwingli, it is rather the wretchedness and misery of sin which comes into view, than its guilt and deserved punishment.[1] But it would be an error to suppose that Zwingli regarded God as eternally reconciled to evil, and Christ only as the revealer of the divine goodness, and not as reconciler, as destroyer of the guilt and as a satisfaction to punitive justice.[2] The object of saving faith is for him, as for Luther, reconciliation as procured by Christ. It has indeed been inferred that he was indifferent towards the historical Christ and His work, from his saying with reference to the heathen that they are saved: what they call wisdom, the Christians call faith. But the fact is that he sees, along with many of the Church fathers, an effect and revelation of the Logos in all truth previously to Christ, without, however, going so far as, with Justin, to call the wise men of antiquity, who lived according to the Logos, Christians. He says only that they are saved after death, in like manner as the Church also receives the same regarding the fathers of the Old Testament. In doing so, he could think of this salvation as effected and procured by Christ, and, at any rate, he thought of it as subsisting only in fellowship with Christ. And, besides, he regards Christ as, through the eternal council of reconciliation,

[1] Cf. Schneckenburger, *vergleichende Darstellung des luth. u. reform. Lehrbegriffs*, 1855.
[2] Zeller, and also Ritschl (*Jahrb. für deutsche Theol.*, 1860, p. 619) are in the right against A. Schweizer, *Gesch. der reform. Dogm.*, ii. 291, 356, 371, ff. This is evident from passages of Zwingli, such as i. 34, 75, 95, 261; ii. 1, 551. i. 76: "Place all thy comfort in the Lord Jesus Christ, and be sure that He who suffered for us is our reconciliation to all eternity."

not merely eternally sure, but also present for all times.[1] Thus those heathen are, according to him, saved only through Christ. He certainly does not say that they are first converted in the future state; he excludes conversion beyond the present state. He allows the fidelity which they have maintained in the present state towards the amount of true knowledge entrusted to them from the Logos, to stand in the place of faith. But there can scarcely be any doubt that he thinks of them as attaining in the future state to the knowledge and fellowship of Christ. In the case of the pious men of the Old Testament, the Church does not require, in order to their salvation, a more definite knowledge of Christ in the present state; this it could at most ascribe to the prophets. It is as incorrect to say that, according to Zwingli, Christian faith is a mere absolute feeling of dependence, and that necessitarianism takes the place of the material principle. On the contrary, as the righteousness of Christ the Reconciler belongs, according to him, to the subject-matter of faith,[2] he requires, in order to faith in its subjective aspect, self-denial, the renunciation of self-confidence and self-righteousness, and positively, in opposition to a merely historical faith, the *sure confidence*, whereby man relies upon the merits of Christ.[3] Faith is even, according to him, not a work, but a rest that comes from God, and security in the merit of Christ, the condition of being at one with God and of life in God. He also, as is undisputed, lays the greatest stress upon *personal assurance of salvation*. His fundamental sentence is: only in the supreme God Himself can we find truth, rest, and life. Nothing that is mediative or creatural, whether it be called church or letter of the Holy Scriptures and sacrament, can supersede this, or may separate us from it. That would be not only a lowering of our goal, but a robbery on the glory of God. Divine truth will not repose upon a testimony that is less than itself; it reposes upon itself, and bears witness to itself. Not less is his doctrine regarding faith in inward connection with practically operative love. Faith receives not only forgiving grace, but also Christ and the Holy Ghost.[4]

[1] viii. 20.   [2] i. 229, ff.   [3] i. 277.

[4] iii. 176 (*de vera et falsa religione*): *Justificatio* is nothing else than that man lays himself upon and resigns himself to the grace of God. i. 551: That the pious man lives, that is nothing else than that he has placed all his comfort in trust upon the Lord Jesus Christ. He lives now in Christ, and Christ in him. Such a believer needs no law. i. 555: The believer does not ask after a reward.—Even

Gathering up the whole, we find that there is between the two Reformations an essential agreement in owning to the normative solitary authority of the holy Scriptures, as well as to the free, reconciling, but also sanctifying, grace of God in Christ, and that the latter becomes the property of faith alone.

Still there is a *different colouring* in their apprehension of the evangelical principle. This difference between the two has been described diagnostically according to their different relationship to [Roman] Catholicism.[1] The opposition of Zwingli is directed rather against the heathen element in [Roman] Catholicism, against all deification of the creature, and hence he will ascribe to no creature saving power and effect, in order not to confound the divine and the human. And, in order that the glory may remain with God, he does not even come the length of fixing the new personality more distinctly as a proper free seat of life, but man continues to be regarded by him rather as a transition point for the divine act, whilst Luther, although denying human freedom, yet lays more emphasis upon personal sin and guilt, but conceives of the believer as a free causality, which is excited from an internal impulse and personal knowledge.[2] This, however, stands in connection with the process of their inward development. It is common to both, namely, that they speak with particular severity against that wherein they formerly lived, and sought above all to advance beyond that whose insufficiency they had most vividly experienced. Zwingli had experienced in particular the curse and unrest of false liberty and lust, that is to say, the principle of heathen sin, and so he fought with the greatest zeal in particular against everything heathen, which robs God of His glory and sets human caprice in the place of God ; Luther, however, had passed through the whole torment of

---

the hope of future blessedness is, according to him, not the motive, but the presence of the divine life, and the assurance of it, is, according to him, the impulsive power in Christians. iv. 63 ; i. 81.

[1] So first Herzog in Tholuck's *lit. Anz.*, 1840, No. 27. *Studien u. Krit.*, 1847, p. 953. Similarly Schweizer, *die Glaubensl. der evang. reform. K.*, 1844, vol. i. 7-52, and *Theol. Jahrb. v. Baur und Zeller*, 1848, i. p. 47, ff. ; 1856, i. p. 152. Cf. Hundeshagen, as cited, i. 304, ff. Thomas, *la Confession helvetique*, 1853, p. 118, ff.

[2] Luther has no *abstractly theological* necessitarianism, so that God determines man only as it were from without, but the determination is in his view psychically and physically mediated. See above, p. 208.

Romish legality, and so is in a position to praise free grace, freedom from the law. This view is not refuted, but confirmed by the circumstance, that Zwingli, even as a Reformer, thinks more highly of the classical antiquity than Luther, and that Luther is more conservative towards the Romish Church than Zwingli. For it is not the strictly heathen element, what was corrupt in heathenism, which Zwingli praised, when he held Socrates, Plato, and Aristotle in high estimation, but the purely human element in them, which was not yet overgrown by heathenism. And so, too, Luther was not conservative in respect of what was Pelagian and magical in the Church, but in respect of those treasures which he would assert as a true Christian inheritance, *e.g.* in the formation of dogmas, in the cultus, and in Christian manners. In what has been said, however, it is already implied that Zwingli did not live the law through as Luther did. We discern few traces in Zwingli of those terrors of conscience (*terrores conscientiæ*), of that ethical deepening of pre-Reformation mysticism to the consciousness of guilt, which we find in Luther's case. He became acquainted with sin, as Schenkel rightly perceives, not so much as a thing in antagonism to God and inclining towards what is demoniacal, but rather as something shameful, unworthy of man, bestial, and bringing misery along with it. A certain inclination towards an æsthetic contemplation of evil remained in him as the result of Humanism, because he did not so thoroughly pass through the stage of the law. In consequence of this, the conception of the redemption is somewhat differently coloured upon both sides, since Luther lets the chief emphasis fall upon the effacing of guilt, freedom from the bondage of the law, whilst Zwingli lets it fall upon the restoration, after the effacing of misery, of a worthy human existence in the individual and the people to the glory of God.[1] Whilst Luther's denial of freedom had a purely anti-Pelagian root, and had no connection with the narrowing of guilt and of the desert of condemnation, it is likely that, in the case of Zwingli, absolute predestinarianism exercised, with stricter logical sequence, an undue influence upon his conception of sin and guilt. The clearer knowledge of the law, which had previously wrought more distinctly in Luther so as to draw him to the reconciliation of Christ, was first pos-

---

[1] Cf. Hundeshagen, *Beiträge zur Kirchenverfassungsgeschichte und Kirchenpolitik, insbesondere des Protestantismus*, vol. i. 1864.

sessed by Zwingli by means of faith; hence he ascribes to the law a more important place inside of the state of faith. The Gospel is, according to him, intended more precisely to accomplish the right of the law to its fulfilment, and in this way the glory of God. Still, the glory of God is not considered by him to be the supreme principle after such a manner as if he thought God to be egoistically incommunicative, but God gives Himself to faith to be enjoyed by it. His pet passage was Matt. xi. 27. We can repose in no narrower good than God. God the supreme *good* is also the supreme *goodness (summa bonitas)*. That the world should enjoy Him and have portion in Him is His joy and glory; He delights to be enjoyed and possessed (*distrahi amat, possideri gaudet*). But just on that account, it is on the other hand the supreme task of man, who is in the image of God, that *God* should be his aim or his will. There is thus a reciprocity: man is the aim of God, God is the aim of man,—the former, however, in no such way as if God first found His reality ethically in man.[1] But certainly God and unredeemed man are not, in Zwingli's view, so far separated from one another as in Luther's, and there is thus introduced into his mode of thought a danger of the pantheistic element, since he did not previously to faith pass through a living experience of the righteousness of God and of the law, such as Luther did. This danger, however, is dissolved for him by his regarding God as personal Will, and by his according such an important place even after faith to the law of God, the obedience of man, and reverence of God.

The attestation of the divine life, which he received in faith, is placed by Zwingli in the foreground, before the inward and in particular religious self-education. Luther lingered rather in the inward sphere of the self-consciousness as renewed by God, in which man knows himself to be a child of God. It is accordingly rather the moral element in its absolute reference which he emphasizes, whilst Zwingli, on the other hand, lays stress rather upon man's being there to increase the glory of God upon earth, which is done by the fulfilment of His will and by a purifying conformation of life and of the community. It is here that the patriotic interest of Zwingli has its religious root. A living care for the community accompanied him through life and conducted him to death; he took with him the testimony that

[1] As Siegwart has it; *Ulr. Zwingli*, 1855, p. 229, ff.; cf. p. 57, ff. 69.

to the very last he had been an "honest confederate" ["*redlicher Eidgenosse*"].

The tendency towards exhibitive action in the moral relations of life does not however in any way lead to his appearing in restless officiousness; Zwingli, who desires action from out of repose in God, creates the impression of a firmly-grounded stable personality. But that tendency towards moral action is, in the case of Zwingli, more original than in the Lutheran reformation; hence, too, the greater rapidity and more vigorous measures which characterized his procedure in the Reformation. He does not so carefully and patiently require an inward process until what is erroneous falls away; he considers something good to be already accomplished, if the community is only no longer in evident contradiction with the word of God, or seems no longer to recognize by toleration what is contrary to Scripture. He has a deep feeling of the blot resting upon the community through tolerated sin, whilst Luther, who is more regardful of the separate personality, thinks that nothing worthy of being named has been attained, unless the inner being has been truly brought to faith, wherewith he considers the chief work effected.[1]

Zwingli ascribes to the Christian congregation the right and duty of excommunication and of discipline; but that in such a way that, soon after the appearance of the Anabaptists upon the

[1] Stahl, *das Lutherthum und die Union*, p. 61, &c., expresses it thus: In the Lutheran Church there is a tendency rather to contemplation, in the Reformed Church to legality. *Schneckenburger's* formula (cf. *Darst.* i. 158, f.) is more happy: In the Reformed Church the active momenta predominate, in the Lutheran the reposing consciousness as a state; hence in the former the science of morals was at an early date diligently cultivated. But I will not maintain the statements which Schneckenburger develops out of the foregoing, *e.g.* regarding the closer connection of the Reformed piety with the [Roman] Catholic, and especially regarding the dependence of the assurance of salvation in the case of the Reformed Church from sanctification and works (the 86th qu. of the *Heidelb. Cat.* finds a symbolic analogy in the *Apol.* 116), although I do not find *Güder's* attempt at improvement (the same, p. xxxviii.) to be exhaustive: "The Lutheran doctrine exhibits faith in its definiteness immediately after conversion, the Reformed in the definiteness of the subsequent stage of sanctification." For this leaves the question still untouched, whether the basis of sanctification is the same, and sanctification is not rather already mingled with justification. This only is correct that the wealth and inward independence of the life of faith is not done justice to by Zwingli, whilst he grasps more energetically the outward moral world. This has been accurately perceived and acknowledged by *Hundeshagen* (as cited, *e.g.* i. 332). Similarly Tholuck, *Das kirchliche Leben des* 17*ten Jahrhunderts*, in many passages.

scene, he makes over these functions to the civil magistrate, the civil and ecclesiastical community [*Volksgemeinde*] being, in his view, essentially one. Severe orders affecting morals were issued, a kind of office of censor was set up, but presbyteries, such as Œcolampadius wished, and Calvin afterwards carried out, were not introduced into Bern and Zürich. Basle, Strasburg, and the friendly towns of Swabia, did more for the constitution of the Church. Strasburg left church discipline in like manner to the civil magistrate, but introduced presbyteries.

Another difference in the colouring of the doctrine as to the principles has reference rather to the *formal* side. For one thing, Zwingli's doctrine of the internal word alongside of the external. We saw that he lays great stress upon immediate illumination and fellowship with God. Man must acquire the assurance of the truth immediately through the Holy Ghost.[1] If we trusted only to the external word without the witness of the Spirit in us, we would be relying again upon a creature, which cannot help us nor compensate for fellowship with God. As little may we, according to him, ascribe saving efficacy to the external word or to the sacraments. The living word is only to impel us to seek Christ, so that He through His Spirit may speak and work in us and give to us a sense of His comfort and His fellowship. This he calls the internal word, which lodges in the heart of believers (*quod in mentibus fidelium insidet*). It is the inward teacher (*internus doctor*),[2] with power to renew the inner being. When this inward teacher has wrought (*i.e.* has begun his work), then will we recollect with profit the letters, the outward words and signs. Their aim is to arouse us, to seek the truth inwardly. Words are signs, a spur, which drives, and does not run. It is by means of the inward word, too, that the outward first receives its assurance and confirmation. Even as election is free, so also the Spirit bloweth as He listeth, although the arrangement is that God does not give faith without hearing.[3]

Those sentences, also, which, distinguishing an inward from the outward word, attribute saving efficacy only to the former, are connected with the fundamental view we have previously

---

[1] *Opp.* i. 77, 81.
[2] i. 82, 79; ii. 2, p. 442. *Ausleg. der* 39 *Artikel*, i. 363. Similarly Œcolampadius in his *Antisyngramma*.
[3] iv. 184; viii. 179.

treated of, that salvation is exclusively in God, that is to say, with His abhorrence of all and every kind of deification. According to Luther, the inward word salvation, *Christ*, is set in the outward word and in the sacraments, in order to be thus brought nigh to us and outwardly offered for inward appropriation. *Zwingli*, as well as Œcolampadius, shrink from such doctrine as a deification of the outward word, and a dishonouring of Christ. The outward word is according to them only a sign, not a vehicle, of grace; it has not saving efficacy. The subject-matter, indeed, which is described or indicated by the signs, is for Zwingli essentially the same, but the connection between the outward and the inward is conceived of more loosely by the Swiss. And even when *Luther* allows, that no saving causality belongs to the outward word by itself, but only to the divine subject-matter which is bound together with the outward word, so that with the latter every one may receive the offer of grace or Christ,—not even this can be accepted by *Zwingli*, because it seemed to him to fetter the freedom of God and His grace by linking them to the outward signs, whilst it wore a very different aspect for Luther, who sees in it only the faithfulness of God to the free promise of the communication of inward grace with the outward sign, and a divine accommodation to the laws of the life of human nature, which requires external means for the reception of inward grace.

This fundamental sentence, that the creature can have no saving causality, and this independence of the inward word from the outward, is not applied by Zwingli to the historical human manifestation of Christ, but it is applied to the whole doctrine of the *means of grace*, and considered as the result of the axiom recognized by all evangelicals, that salvation is only in God Himself and in Christ.

It is, however, a very unfortunate as well as unjust description of this point, when Stahl speaks of an "antimysterious motive" in the whole formation of the Reformed Church, and even describes the antimysterious principle as the central dogma of the Reformed Church. A merely negative tenet cannot be the central dogma of a community. In that case, antimysterious would mean the denial of a mystery, which would seem to be only intended as a more modern substitute for "spiritualistic," or "rationalistic," as Rudelbach was fond of saying.

But if by mystery there is to be understood not natural mysteries, but divine, no one can deny that Zwingli, too, with his rest in God and union of the soul with Him in faith, knows the mystic element in true piety, although his living in it is less associated with phantasy and contemplation. His doctrine regarding the impotence and misery of man and the plenteous help of Christian grace, regarding absolute dependence, regarding divine election, is anything but rationalistic or Pelagian, and rather leaves too much than too little in mystery. It is in fact the Lutheran Church which has a more energetical conception of revelation, the discovery of God through word and sacrament, so that on this side it might sooner be said that Zwingli was too greatly mysterious. It is true that Luther accepted a more intimate connection of the divine with the creatural in the means of grace, than Zwingli did, and this is indeed a province of the mysterious, still we ought not to speak as if this one mystery were all mysteries, as if that man denied all connection between the divine and the creatural, who shrunk from attributing to the creatural a saving causality. We might sooner suppose that that looser connection of grace with the outward signs kept grace in a remote region, so that it is only shown and taught but not held out; and, starting from this point, we might come upon the distinction, that in the case of Zwingli the question is only one of doctrine, of an intellectual process, and in the Lutheran Church is one of the acts of God, of a real life-intercourse of God with man reaching through into the conditions of time. The consequence of this would be that, according to Zwingli, there would only be required the awakening of the powers already reposing in man, but not the communication of divine regenerating saving power. And that was the Pelagian error of the fanatics, who are still not unfrequently identified with Zwingli's doctrine, and according to whom the outward is only designed to remind us of the inward Word of God already resting in us by nature, *i.e.* to bring us to the consciousness of our true being. But, as has been shown, Zwingli held a communication of divine powers to man and a life-intercourse between God and him to be neither unnecessary nor impossible; so that the difference is not to be formulated, " There divine act, here divine doctrine," but only, " In Zwingli, a divine act, which proceeds alongside of the instructive and arousing outward means of grace; in Luther, a divine act through the mediation of the outward means of grace which bear and offer grace." That the objection brought by the Reformed party against the Lutheran view, that God is fettered to the outward signs, or even, that the outward signs are effective without God, and saving power is accordingly deputed to them, so that they magically lay hold of every one who comes into contact with them,—that this objection is as unjust as the other, has been shown above.

How far removed Zwingli was from a fanatical tendency, which certainly sought a point of attachment in him on account of the looser position of the outward to the inward, which rendered the outward completely empty, and which sought to treat it contemptuously as a mere husk, is seen in the clearest manner from the first conflict which he had with it.

CHAPTER II.

ZWINGLI'S CONFLICT WITH THE FANATICS, IN PARTICULAR WITH THE ANABAPTISTS.

ZWINGLI, too, like Luther, was admonished by the rising up of fanatical, in particular Anabaptist and Donatist movements, which came upon the scene from within and from without, to turn the edge of the Word of God even against seemingly zealous friends of the Reformation. Thus, besides *L. Hetzer*, against *Conrad Grebel*, Simon Stumpf, Felix Manz, *Balthasar Hubmaier*, *Thomas Münzer*, and others, who, beginning with a literalistic apprehension of the Scriptures as a codex for the restoration of a pure apostolic congregation, and despising the historical development of the Church, soon passed over to a spiritualistic depreciation of the Scriptures, and in particular turned against infant baptism.

Zwingli, as he himself afterwards confesses,[1] was also at first of the opinion, that it would be better, if children were first baptized at a seemly age when they could believe; for, like Luther, he thought at first that he was obliged to demand faith *before* baptism as indispensable, in opposition to external magic. But he did not wish, as he adds, to rush on so immodestly and

---

[1] ii. 1, p. 245.

presumptuously, as these new men, but sought a basis for this early baptism, although he could not ascribe to it as an external performance saving power and efficacy. Hence, he referred baptism entirely to the future,[1] it is according to him *a sign of the duty of repentance unto Christ and of the new life in faith*, the sensible acceptance of a life-vow, to which indeed consciousness and will seem just as requisite as they are to faith. Christian baptism was, according to him, not different from the baptism of John, and circumcision quite as good a sacrament as baptism.[2] When, thereafter, the Anabaptist theories passed into practice, he set himself more and more consciously in opposition to them. He did not indeed do so in the same way as *Calvin*, by a deeper apprehension of the sacrament on that side according to which it is an prevenient gift. On the contrary, it may be said,[3] that he sought to disarm the Anabaptists by trying to show that baptism had not the dogmatic importance which they attributed to it. But on the other hand, it is not merely external grounds which guide him in his conflict against them. On the contrary, he will have no Donatist Church, consisting purely of saints, which he saw to be the innermost tendency of the Anabaptist movement. It is his nature to have a lively sense for a public national Christianity, and he sees that the letting fall infant baptism would be as much as letting fall the national Church, would be to exchange a hitherto national Reformation of the Church for one more or less Donatist. For if infant baptism were given up, because faith was not yet there, then there only remained as the right time for it the moment when living faith and regeneration were certain. And then baptism would become the sign of the fellowship of the regenerate, the saints, who band themselves together as atoms out of the world. So that *what was perverted in Anabaptism was discovered by Zwingli not through a higher dogmatic conception of baptism, but from its ethical aspect*, inasmuch as, despite his doctrine of election, he had a lively consciousness of the task of the Church as one embracing the nations, and because everything of a separatist nature was antagonistic to him. And upon this there followed a new significance in infant baptism. It is according to him not merely a sign of the future duty of the baptized one, but also

---

[1] ii. 2, 242, 358.   [2] ii. 1, 357, ff.; iii. 232-234.
[3] Erbkam, as cited, p. 540.

a *symbolic act of the Church*, whereby it receives into the community of the people of God, into the covenant of grace, in like manner as that was effected in the Old Testament by circumcision. It is at the same time on the side of the Church a sign of duty, a sensible acceptance of the duty of conducting the children to grace. Hence infant baptism is proper for the children of Christians. They are God's, and belong, like the children of Israel, who had a right to circumcision, to the "people of God;" hence the sign of the covenant is to be imparted to them. He calls baptism also a sign of election, which is proper to all, who according to the view of men belong to the elect. This led, however, very easily to a return to the sacramental significance of baptism, for reception into the number of the people of God is a blessing, and assures of a share in the divine promises; the grace of the New Testament, too, cannot be narrower than that of the Old. That, according to him, the children of Christians are to be treated as elect, can never quite accord with his doctrine of election, and the kingdom of grace might be thereby placed under the law of birth, whilst he nevertheless otherwise holds firmly a doctrine of particular election inside of Christendom. But just as Luther alongside of his doctrine of election proclaims a universal grace, because he regards God as love, so Zwingli, in the interests of the Church, proceeds as if he knew of no particular election. It, this visible Church, is according to him the people of God, which is already there as a unity before individual believers by means of public institutions and ordinances,—the sphere wherein, and the organ whereby election and faith are realized; and it may be said that he founds his conception of the Church as little as Luther upon the separate regenerate subjectivities, but rather possesses in the ethical but dogmatically founded organism of the Church, as a popular institution, that objective sphere, which accomplishes for him what the more objective conception of word and sacrament accomplishes for Luther. At a later period[1] he drew still nearer to Luther, inasmuch as he ascribes to the sacrament a greater power of impelling one to seek justification, than he ascribes to the word by itself. He further calls baptism a testimony to the baptized one that his sins are washed away in the blood of Christ, and that righteousness and the forgiveness of sins are imparted to him of

---

[1] iii. 358, 563. *Baptismus initiatio ecclesiæ.*

pure grace, without work or merit. In this, baptism has become to him a *a pledge of the forgiveness of sins.*[1] In like manner, with reference to the Scriptures, he was secured against the standpoint of the fanatics, not merely by his ethics, but also by the dogmatic authority, which he imputed to it as the record of the will of God. The same reverence of the majesty of God, the same zeal for the glory of God in opposition to every creature, which hindered him from agreeing to Luther's doctrine of the condescension of God in word and sacrament, set him against those self-willed spiritualistic movements which despise the Scriptures. The Christian must serve the glory of God according to divine direction, not according to one's own fancy; hence the Word of God in Scripture forbids all caprice.

His Swiss fellow-workers rallied round him in this. After attempting moderate measures against the fanatics, which they rendered vain by their faithlessness to their word, and after several disputations with them, in particular on the 6th November 1526,[2] they were regarded as convicted, and the magistracy resorted to forcible measures against them.[3] Thus the Anabaptist element was excluded from the Swiss Reformation, but at the price of the Zürich Church falling into a state of constant dependence upon the State.

CHAPTER III.

RELATION OF THE SWISS AND GERMAN REFORMATIONS; THEIR HARMONY AT THE OUTSET, THEIR CONTROVERSY, AND PRELIMINARY PEACE.

1. *The original Harmony.*

THE original unity between the Swiss and German Reformations had, according to what has been said, not merely a negative, but also a positive ground, and reached far beyond the standpoint of Erasmus. But it was broken by the controversy on the Supper in 1526.

The politically independent position of Switzerland, as separated from the German Empire, whilst in relation to the Emperor

---

[1] Cf. Schenkel, *Wesen des Protestantismus*, 1847, ii. 400, ff.
[2] ii. 1, p. 345. Erbkam, as cited, 527.
[3] By inflicting imprisonment, fines, and even death by drowning.—*Tr.*

it facilitated the Reformation, nevertheless rendered it more difficult for it to grow together into one reformation with the German, and rendered the separation easier. But the commencement was harmonious and undisturbed. The cities of Upper Germany, from Strasburg to Ratisbon, from Nuremberg to Constance, took up a middle position between the evangelical North and South. The writings of Luther were eagerly read in Switzerland also— a book shop at Basle was occupied with the circulation of them. Zwingli himself first made himself acquainted with them after 1518. To the reproach of the Catholics, that he was a Lutheran, he replied by asserting his independence, accompanying the assertion with the warmest recognition of the merits of Luther. He had begun to preach the Gospel as early as 1516, and Luther's name continued unknown to him for two years after. It was through Paul that Luther and he had come, independently of one another, to the same knowledge. This free agreement was unpleasant for their opponents. But he preached the Word of Christ,—why not rather call him a Paulist or a Christian?[1] They passed, too, for one party, the Evangelical.

Along with the agreement between Zwingli and Luther in principle, there is certainly manifested an independence and separate peculiarity in the standpoint occupied. But the fundamental features were, as has been shown, common to both.

They are in common attached to the old Christian confessions

[1] With regard to Luther he says, *Opp.* i. *Uslegen und Gründ der Schlussreden*, p. 253, ff. : "In my opinion Luther is an admirable warrior of God, who searches the Scriptures with so much earnestness as there has been none upon earth for one thousand years. With the manly unmoved heart, with which he has attacked the Pope at Rome, there has never been one like to him so long as the Papacy has endured, all others unrebuked. But whose is this act? God's or Luther's? Ask Luther himself and he will certainly say to thee, God's.—I will bear no name but that of my Captain, Jesus Christ, whose trooper I am. Luther I esteem as high as any living. But I testify before God and all men that I have never written a letter to him, nor he to me." He refrained from establishing fellowship with him, because he wished thereby to show how uniform is the Spirit of God, since they, although at so great a distance from one another, are yet, without any arrangement, of one view. "Although I am not to be compared to him, for each does as much as he is able in God." Guericke, indeed, Rudelbach, and others, will not allow this independence of the two reformations from one another, which so distinctly indicates a higher necessity for the Reformation : according to them Calvin and Zwingli have taken everything good and true from Luther ; and since they owe everything to him, their divergence from him is regarded by these men as sin, and they alone bear the guilt of the separation, since they diverge from the God-sent Reformer.

regarding the Trinity and the Person of Christ, they both stand upon the evangelical principle on its formal and material sides, and they share the doctrine of divine election. They both reject the heathen and Judaistic elements in [Roman] Catholicism. And the opposition of the Reformed Church to the heathen element is only perfectly carried out, when it is directed not merely against the deification of the world, but also against Judaistic self-deification; and, in like manner, the anti-Pelagian Lutheran opposition between nature and grace, only when it is directed also against the magical element, against the transformation of divine grace into something physical or physically operative. Zwingli recognizes the former in principle, inasmuch as he regards faith as the renunciation of self-righteousness and self-confidence, whilst Luther, on the other hand, rejects the magical element, and may be said to see that the opposition to the Judaizing element would prove prejudicial even to grace and free love, if the law, that is to say the holiness and righteousness of God, were not maintained in their integrity. And as they both excluded the heathen and the Judaistic elements, so also the anarchical and Donatist. On both sides, further, is Christ placed in the midst as the only Mediator, with whom immediate life-communion, and consequently the assurance of salvation, is possible. In what concerns the ethical side, the State is on both sides no longer considered as profane, but as the ordinance of God appointed for the administration of justice, and hence for the protection of the Gospel. Both also thought alike with regard to Christian marriage, with regard to the care of the poor of the Church, and the right of the congregation to participate actively in the life of the Church; and if the Swiss Reformation was more distant towards art, especially in its application to divine service, it proved, on the other hand, more fruitful in the civil and social life; so that both Reformations appeared on the scene as if destined to be complementary to one another, like different individualities of one and the same family.

The conflict with the fanatical movements of Hyperprotestantism was adapted to bring both Reformations nearer to one another, even in the point in which at first a difference was most distinctly proclaimed, namely, the means of grace. In fact, too, the theologians of Switzerland took up the defence of the external word against Schwenckfeld, as Zwingli of infant baptism.

But the conflict with the fanatics had also another side, which led to a *controversy on the sacrament* between the Swiss and the Lutherans. In this controversy the difference lying at the basis came again to expression; it was apparent that by Zwingli the means of grace were rather apprehended ethically, or in the interests of the community, by Luther rather dogmatically. A personal element was also added, since *Carlstadt* met with a good reception in Switzerland, and sought to excite prejudice against Luther.

2. *The Controversy regarding the Supper.*

A remarkable normality of procedure, which is another proof of the essential similarity in kind of the two Reformations, is to be discerned in the circumstance, that when the question came to be one of the carrying out of an improved *church* order, there came up on both sides first the means of grace, the word of God, then baptism, then the Supper. Certainly the rich unity in dogma and the similarity of the law of life in both movements, renders it the more lamentable that the negotiations regarding the *holy Supper* led to a separation. For this controversy, by which the whole Reformation was soon agitated, did more than anything else to render the latter suspicious in the eyes of [Roman] Catholicism, and make it seem to it to be only a human, and not a divine work. The controversy between the Reformers seemed to prove that unanimity was only possible in unity under Rome. On the other hand, it must be acknowledged that when different fundamental views actually existed upon these questions, when it was not given to the Evangelicals on both sides to make themselves masters of the full truth at a stroke, and give expression to it with triumphant power, nothing could be gained by concealing the opposition, but the one standpoint was evidently to be set over against the other, so that a fruitful negotiation and final union might at least be attainable by this more protracted method. It is true that this furnishes no justification of the passionate nature of the conflict, or of the embitterment which led to a perpetuation of the division, and partly to incapacity to understand one another. But, on the other hand, the Evangelicals—in their twofold division, within which each confession maintained with greater emphasis that side which fell into the background in the other—rendered reciprocal assistance in the way of guarding and warning against going astray, and were even by means of the separation protected against the danger to which the Romish and Greek Church was exposed, —this namely, that an inbreaking malady might make itself master of the whole body of evangelical Christendom. The Divine Leader of the Church has known how to change that twofold division of the one evangelical Church, which arose out of human weakness and sin, into a strong dam against those sinful influences which are not wanting even in the history of the evangelical Church. Since, as we have seen, the one of the two Reformations is directed rather against what is heathen, the other rather against what is Judaistic (in which two are comprehended the principal possible forms of human sin), they are, seeing that both reject both in principle but have not an equally keen eye for both, secured by one another against falling back entirely into what is pre-Christian, whether it be what is heathen or what is Jewish, be it found within or without [Roman] Catholicism, and against retracting the Reformation either on the one side or the other. For in spite of their separation, which promoted their independent development, the two evangelical Confessions have never been able to rid themselves altogether of a great influence upon one another, so intimate is their relationship, and so great the power of the actual facts of the case, according to which there are to be found in their differences mutual complements, an impulse towards the recognition of which lies in the healthy elements of both.

What was peculiar in Zwingli's doctrine of the Supper begins first in 1524; until then he had been passing through several stages of the series in a manner similar to Luther. Let us linger here for a moment, for the purpose of showing how on this point the unity of the two Reformations was at first very great, and that when the Reformed Church afterwards confesses in its symbols to a richer conception of the Supper than Zwingli entertained after the end of 1524, it, in doing so, only turns back to the more positive reformatory outset of Zwingli, and to that standpoint, in a richer development of it, which Luther never found fault with, since his opposition applies to what was Zwingli's doctrine after 1524. And seeing that Zwingli towards the end of his life rather inclined again to the more positive views he held at the outset (which made it possible for him to approach so far towards Luther, as he did at Marburg in 1529), the chief object of the controversy presents itself only in the shape of an episode, and that so much the more as by means of the subsequent Calvinistic formation, which assimilated to itself nearly the whole territory of the Reformed Churches, the conception of the Supper which became symbolical in the Reformed Church was one which Luther did not dispute.

What is characteristic, then, in all the writings of Zwingli, previously to 1524,[1] is his opposition to the Supper as a sacrifice and mass. Although he considers Christianity to require self-sacrifice, still he never at this time makes the Supper to represent a human sacrifice, a human performance towards God, but he considers it as altogether a divine gift and institution, reposing upon the almighty and marvellously powerful will of the Lord Christ. In opposition to the *opus operatum*, he demands faith, which is in a condition so to celebrate the remembrance [*das "Wiedergedächtniss"*] of Christ, that Christ can communicate to it His blessing in the Supper. He exhorts to the examination of the "*ardor animi*" to be united with its "*sponsus Christi,*" and says, without any limitation, that no one is to seek to fish out anything out of his language, as if he in this matter ascribed anything to human action (*hac in re aliquid humanæ actioni tribuat*).[2] When he calls the Supper sometimes the body and blood of Christ, and sometimes, and more frequently, the remembrance of the death of Christ, and of all the benefits which it confers on us, the inference is not to be drawn from that circumstance, any more than from the word "Eucharist" of the early Church, that he considered the essence of the Supper to be the remembrance as a subjective performance. His only concern is to set aside in this way the idea of a sacrifice of the mass as a constantly repeated sacrifice of Christ, and to excite to the appropriation of that sacrifice, which happened once, and avails for ever, by means of the reminiscence of grace-*receiving* faith. He expressly calls attention to the similarity of his doctrine to that of Luther.

---

[1] Cf. Zwingli's 67 *Schlussreden für die erste Zürich. Disputat.*, 29 Jan. 1523, Art. xviii. xix., *Opp.* i. 154, and *Uslegen und Gründ der Schlussreden, Juli* 1523, i. 232-260. *Epichiresis* (*Entwurf eines Messkanons*) and *Apologia*, 1523, *Opp.* iii. 2, p. 83 ff., 177 ff., 121 ff. ; cf. i. 566. *Rathschlag von Bildern und Mess, ein Brief an Thom. Wyttenbach*, vii. 297-200, *Jun.* 1523. His *Erklärungen auf der zweiten Zür. Disput.*, Oct. 1523, i. 459, cf. 498. *Die kurze christenliche Ynleitung*, 1523, i. 541-565.

[2] iii. 115, 119.

The latter called it a testament, covenant, legacy, and described in this way its nature, essence, and property; for it was in fact a covenant of God with us for the forgiveness of sins, sealed by means of the outward signs. He (Zwingli) called it a memorial after the *use* to be made of it, for Christ had given it, had by the wine denoted His shed blood, and by the breaking of the bread the putting to death of His body, in order that this remembrancer (which he considered accordingly to be at once a memorial and a legacy) might strengthen us, inasmuch as He fed our souls with Himself. It was intended for faith to strengthen it, since a word of promise was connected with the sign. The New Testament was instituted by the blood of Christ upon the cross, and so the sacrament is an assurance, seal, and attestation to faith that this testament, and even Christ Himself, is *our* own. The dispute was not, whether the holy body and blood of Christ was eaten and drunken, for no Christian doubted that, but whether it was a sacrifice or a remembrance.[1] Thus mighty and at all times present was Christ. For He is an everlasting God, and His passion fruitful unto eternity.[2] He thus considers the Supper to be a remembrance instituted by Christ, at which He will be present, and whereby He, by means of His word of promise and the outward signs, will make the blessing of His death, whose inward power is eternal, to be actually effective in the Christian for the strengthening and assurance of faith. He adds to this the communion between the head and the members, the increase of the power of bearing the cross after Him, and the strengthening of love.[3] The consequence of this eating and drinking is that the brethren also by this recognize one another, because by our common devout eating we confess before all men that we are one body and one brotherhood.[4] That he thinks of Christ as present, is undeniable; he was at this feast host and banquet-food (*hospes et epulum*).[5] He certainly gives no proper explanation of the body and blood of Christ; he considers the strengthening power of the signs to lie in the word of promise. When Luther makes the body and blood of Christ the pledge of the forgiveness of sins, Zwingli is not satisfied with this, because he demands visibility for a pledge, and finds this in the elements with which the

---

[1] i. 242, 245.   [2] i. 242.   [3] i. 575.   [4] i. 576, ff.
[5] *Epichir.* iii. 115: *in hoc se in cibum præbuit, ut ejus alimento in virum perfectum plenæ ætatis suæ augesceremus.*

word of promise is connected.¹ Christ's invisible flesh seemed to Zwingli useless for this purpose (John vi. 63). He received, however, along with Luther, the *presence* of the body and blood of Christ, and in like manner saw the purpose of the Supper to lie in the certification of the forgiveness of sins as the fruit of the death of Christ. Only the manner in which this certification is effected, is differently conceived of by the two. What has been said may serve to prove, how the friends and opponents of Zwingli err, when, in order to make out the similarity of his doctrine at all periods, they set up the hypothesis, which only obtains a seeming support in Zwingli's own utterances, that at this earlier period he had concealed his true meaning and exercised self-accommodation. He simply says indefinitely that he had already at an earlier date entertained in part his subsequent ideas, but nothing from which one may infer a deceitful use of words. The supposition is also in itself unnatural, that he stood there from the beginning with a conviction finally made up, whilst in his case, as in Luther's, a process of development is what must *à priori* be considered probable. And such a process is shown in his writings, when read in the order of the series.

His *later mode of doctrine*, which diverges considerably from that previously maintained, has by some been traced up to the Dutch jurist *Hoën* (Honius), whose treatise on the holy Supper, A.D. 1523, came to Wittenberg along with Wessel's writings, but contains the view that the sacrament is an unity of sign and promise; the former is the pledge for the gift, which forms the subject-matter of the promise. Just as in the purchase of a field, the latter is really surrendered under the symbolic handing over [to the purchaser of a handful] of earth, so under the sacramental signs there is given the thing, the body and blood of Christ, Christ Himself, and with Him the forgiveness of sins.² The communication is a real one, but the *gift* is only " signified " by the outward signs. The *" est "* of institution is just so much as *significat*. The unbeliever may receive the bread, and even to him the present Christ offers Himself, but he does not enjoy the body and blood of Christ. This can happen only as the result of faith. It is evident that all this, with the exception of the exegetical basis, keeps almost entirely in the steps of Luther.

¹ i. 251; iii. 115.
² *Hoc, quod trado vobis, significat corpus meum, quod do vobis dando istud.*

More definitely than is the case with Luther, Hoën considers the body and blood of Christ to be in itself a gift, not merely a pledge for the forgiveness of sins. We may far rather accept in substance an influence from *Carlstadt* upon the later doctrine of Zwingli.

In 1521,[1] Carlstadt still taught similarly to Luther. During the absence of Luther, he, turning back to his unethical mysticism, lets the annulling of death and of the law be effected by the shed blood of Christ, and this victory over death and sin be communicated in the holy Supper.[2] The annulling of guilt is disregarded by him. In the eating of the body, there is not only certified to us (in principle) the resurrection of the flesh in glory, but the annulling of sin is also given to us through the annulling of mortality, an ethical effect through a physical, as is also to be found in Theophrastus Paracelsus, Schwenckfeld, Valentin Weigel, &c. Carlstadt, however, formed for himself a new doctrine of the Supper after 1523, when he left Wittenberg. He developed it chiefly in his *Dialogus* of 1524. Rightly perceiving that the annulling of sin must be a spiritual process, he proceeds now to the other extreme, and turns his attention exclusively to the words, which demand a *performance*, the remembrance of the Lord and the showing forth of His death, and is no longer able to adduce a motive for the real presence of Christ. We ought so to sink ourselves in the sacrificial death of Christ for us, that we become absorbed into His suffering and His resurrection, and by virtue of His sacrifice make the act of the Supper a holy self-sacrifice, the imperfection of which is supplemented and brought to perfection through faith in Him.[3] In order to contradict with proper effect the Romish doctrine of a renewed sacrifice of Christ unto the Father, he places in opposition to it his doctrine of self-sacrifice, in the remembrance and in the knowledge of Christ, without seeing what Luther soon perceived, that, in doing so, he recurred again essentially to the [Roman] Catholic standpoint, and changed the gift of God into a gift or sacrifice towards God on the part of man. Since the

---

[1] *Von dem Empfahn, Zeichen, und Zusag des heiligen Sakramentes des Fleisches und Blutes Christi von Carlstadt*, 1521. See above, p. 132.

[2] Carlstadt, *Von beiden Gestalten der heiligen Messe*. Jäger, *Andr. Bodenstein v. Carlstadt*, 1856, p. 256.

[3] Thus especially in his treatise, *Vom Priesterthum und Opfer*, 1524; cf. *Luthers Werke von Walch*, xx. 138, 378, 2852.

words of institution, "Take, eat, drink," do not indicate a giving, but a receiving, he extricated himself by completely separating the words having reference to the bread and wine from those having reference to the body and blood of Christ. The latter are supposed to have no reference whatever to an offering or receiving, but only the former. After He had given them bread and wine to partake of, Christ had said, pointing to Himself, "This is my body, which, and no other, is given for you." But since the Pauline account brings the elements too manifestly in connection with the body and blood of Christ in the words, "Drink, this is the cup of the New Testament in my blood," he seeks to connect the two again, but in such a way as not to lead to the conception of the taking of a gift, and seeks to exhibit the eating and drinking also as a performance [in which something is rendered]. As bitter herbs were to be eaten at the Passover, so also the eating was a bitter eating; it was to take place in remembrance of the death of Christ. The kernel of his view is, that in the Supper there is an exhibition of already existing faith; the elements are merely corporeal and cannot touch the inward man, but only the outward; the inward man, however, requires the inworking of the Holy Ghost apart from all means. In order to escape an outward magical operation of the elements, and to keep the process a spiritual one, he lapses into an inward magic, an abrupt, unmediated, overpowering working of the Holy Ghost, just as, in the conception of the sacrifice, he is more nearly allied to the Pelagianizing error, which he seeks to combat to the uttermost. In both together he only exhibits the idealistic mystical reflection of the magic and sacrifice of [Roman] Catholicism.

Zwingli himself, in his momentous letter to *Matthäus Alber*, November 1524, and to the people of Esslingen, in which he seeks to win both for himself, says, that Carlstadt's view did not displease him, only he wrote obscurely and violently. His exegetical basis, too, was not satisfactory. The "is" was to be taken for "signifies," in which accordingly he followed Hoën. Œcolampadius in Basle reminded us that the words of institution probably contained no ἐστί whatever, since they would have been spoken in Aramaic. The τοῦτο, referring to the signs, and connected with σῶμα and αἷμα as predicates, obliged us to take these predicates in the sense of "image of the body and blood," even as Christ is also figuratively called a rock (1 Cor. x. 4). The said letter to Alber, which Zwingli himself communicated also to others in many copies,[1] was received by Luther from Alber himself, who was on friendly terms with him. In this letter, the presence of Christ in the Supper, as well as the significance of the latter as a gift, was completely denied, and there was not even left to the outward signs the significance of visible pledges of grace. We are able to perceive how he reached this conclusion. Even at an earlier period, when he still considered the elements to be pledges of grace, he was unable to derive any meaning from the presence of the body and blood of Christ. There was next added, doubtless in consequence of Carlstadt's exhibition of Luther's views, the opinion that Luther favoured a religious materialism, and sought to strengthen faith and allow the communication of the forgiveness of sins by means of a "capernaitic" eating.[2] He was afraid of a relapse into the Popish *opus operatum* and magic.[3] He therefore devoted all his powers from that time to show that the presence of the body and blood of Christ was useless, since the body of Christ could effect nothing for the soul. He now sought also to show its impossibility, since the humanity of Christ as a creatural thing would then need to be thought of as omnipresent, and to be deified. In this, the difference already laid hold of a new dogma, the Christology. The presence of the *divinity* of Christ he did not deny, but he did not apply it so as to see a gift in the Supper. The reason thereof may be found in this, that he believed it needful to search out a *peculiar* significance for the Supper. This however could not well be found in the gift of the forgiveness of sins, to which Luther chiefly confined himself, if this, as all admitted, was to be had even outside of the Supper. Zwingli therefore thought it needful to give up in general the thought of a gift in the Supper; naturally without giving up on that account the antagonism to Pelagianism; he con-

---

[1] Zwingli, *Opp.* iii. 589.

[2] I have thought it best to preserve the original word in the translation, because the term—a novel one in this connection—seems to be employed in order to indicate—not simply a corporal and carnal eating, such as the Jews thought of, when they heard Christ's words at Capernaum (John vi. 51-53, 59), but also the fact that these words of Christ were largely made use of by the Swiss (*e.g.* in Zwingli's letter to M. Alber) in support of their distinctive views, whilst they imputed to the Lutherans the same erroneous ideas as the Jews exhibited and our Lord controverted in the Capernaum synagogue.—*Tr.*

[3] ii. i. 484.

tinues to maintain that faith receives the free gift of God. In order, then, to leave this sacred rite possessed of an independent and unassailable significance, and that precisely for believers, those who already participate in the forgiveness of sins, he turns to the *ethical significance* of the Supper upon the ground of the covenant of grace, in evident analogy with his doctrine of baptism (see above, p. 300). He now sees in it the exhibition of faith. He had already previously asserted this aspect of it, alongside of the dogmatic, as Luther also did, but Zwingli makes it now the chief matter in such a way, that the significance of the means of grace falls entirely into the background. The Supper he now considers to be the indispensable complement of baptism. As the latter is the divinely instituted act of the Church, whereby it in fulfilment of its duty mediates to the baptized one participation in the promises of the people of God; so there is in the feast of the Supper the grateful answer of the believer; and the common feast, which shows forth the death of Christ, brings the grateful faith in Christ to manifestation, and is a common confession and covenant vow, a self-dedication of believers to Christ (like our confirmation), and even thereby, the becoming visible of the invisible Church, the manifestation of the true body of Christ, of the congregation, which is a sacrifice well-pleasing unto God. Thus there takes place here a *conficere corpus Christi*, namely, of the congregation. Believers exhibit their faith and their love for one another upon the basis of the Christian salvation, and thus render themselves conscious of them. The communicating congregation is, on the one hand, a redeemed congregation, conscious of salvation, and on the other hand a congregation arming itself, by a quickening of the feeling of community, for the struggle against sin in particular and in general, for giving active effect to the moral religious life. It is evident that he thus considers the Supper not as a dispensable thing, as the Quakers do, and that he still continues to be essentially remote from Socinian doctrine, for it is Christian grace which still continues to be his basis. Upon this basis, however, he gives prominence in particular to the significance of the Supper for the *Church community*, whilst Luther,—and he was confirmed in doing so by his opposition to Zwingli,—sets forth rather its significance merely for the *individual subject*. The two are not excluded by one another, but during five years Zwingli purchased this significance of the Supper for the Church community at the expense of no longer accepting a self-communication of Christ in the Supper to individuals, and sinking its dogmatical significance entirely in the ethical. The course taken by the controversy, that soon broke out, was also not adapted to bring about a peaceful understanding.[1]

For a considerable time Luther restrained himself, even after Œcolampadius' treatise, which was answered briefly and feebly by *Bugenhagen* and then minutely by *Brenz*, with the *Swabians*, in the so-called Swabian Syngramma.[2] The leading thought of the Syngramma is a following up of Luther's doctrine of the Word already explained; God is the Word, and therein makes Himself apprehensible to the spirit, so that grace, which is eternal and irrespective of space, does therein approach us in order to communicate itself to us. Words are, in general, not merely signs of absent things, but, according to Aristotle, they bring a real science of the matter, and so the matter itself. Thus the words of Christ bring Christ along with them, and the words of institution also, according to His promise, bring body and blood, and that in such a way that bread and wine co-operate to this end, for they are themselves embraced by the word so as also to become a speaking word through the institution of Christ. The word accordingly does, as it were, extend itself in the sacrament, inasmuch as it takes the elements besides unto itself, and makes them too to be bearers of the spiritual benefits of the whole Christ, who draws near in them. But because these benefits are spiritual, they are for *faith;* the body and blood of Christ are food for the soul (*cibus animæ et fidei*). The connec-

---

[1] The principal passages regarding Zwingli's doctrine of the Supper after 1524, are: ii. 2, p. 1-223; iii. 145, ff.; 228, 239-272. *Subsidium seu Coronis de Eucharist*, 1525, p. 332. *Amica exegesis*, iii. 459. *Responsio ad Theob. Billicani et Urb. Rhegii epistolas*, iii. 646 (both men were at first for him). *De providentia Dei*, iv. 117; in the *Euch.* there takes place *memoria et gratiarum actio* for the death of Christ. Symbols and words only *proclaim* the death of Christ. Only the Holy Ghost imparts quickening. *Externæ res nihil ad fidem et remissionem afferunt. Cinglii fidei ratio ad Carolum V.* A.D. 1530; iv. 11-15. On the other hand, shortly before his death, in the *fidei chr. expositio*, iv. 56, ff., he inclines again to his earlier positive doctrine, inasmuch as he thinks of the Supper as a divine gift for the strengthening of faith. Œcolampadius never gave up this conception, not even in his writing; *De genuina verborum:* "*Hoc est corpus meum*" *expositione.* Cf. Pfaff, *Acta Eccles. Wirtemb.* p. 146.

[2] *Syngramma Suevicum*, in Pfaff, as cited, p. 153-97. *Luthers Werke von Walch*, xx. 667. *Bugenhagens Schrift*, xx. 648, ff.

tion between the body and the elements,—although not first formed *by means of* faith, as not by means of the power of the consecrating priest, nor existing only *for* believers, but on the contrary objectively, and therefore for all,—yet does not benefit the unbelieving. The body and blood of Christ is indeed offered to them, but the offering is one thing, and the receiving another. Though the enjoyment of the elements takes place through the mouth of the body, still if faith is wanting, *i.e.* the mouth which receives the body and blood of Christ, the heavenly gift is refused,[1] that is to say, the *unio sacramentalis* is dissolved again for unbelievers, though it was present even for them. For, as the Swabians still held even later, a fatal, condemning effect does not belong to the body of Christ (*proprius effectus carnis et sanguinis non est judicium sed vivificatio*, so that *judicium et mors* comes *non vitio et culpa carnis et sanguinis, sed vitio et culpa incredulitatis*).[2] At the same time they hold to the sentence, "Whosoever eateth the bread unworthily, eateth judgment unto himself" (1 Cor. xi. 27). When the word of institution is repeated, the gracious will of Christ, which instituted the sacrament, always actively perpetuates itself, and brings forth an union, which is a mystery analogous to the union of the two natures in Christ. The Swabians accordingly hold no oral partaking (*manducatio oralis*) of the body and blood of Christ, no partaking of the same by *unbelievers*; for them He is absent (*impiis absens est Deus et infidelibus, proinde nec illi Deum edunt h. e. non in Deum credunt*). The subject-matter however of the sacramental gift is not merely the forgiveness of sins, but also a *cibus animæ*. Inasmuch as the body and blood of Christ is in the first instance a strengthening for the soul, and so a spiritual gift, all materialism is antecedently excluded; and yet the presence of the real personality of Christ possesses, as a gift, an independent significance, and not merely that of a pledge of the forgiveness of sins.

Luther was greatly satisfied with the Syngramma, and took care of a German edition of it; to which he prefixed a very laudatory preface. This doctrine of the Syngramma is, in its

---

[1] *Repellitur*, according to the later expression of Brenz. Pfaff, as quoted, p. 35, 38; cf. *F. C.* 601, § 17.

[2] *Synod Stuttgard*, 1559; cf. Pfaff, *Acta et scripta publica Ecclesiæ Wirtembergicæ*, p. 338.

essentials, completely similar to that of Calvin, in what concerns the *manducatio oralis* and participation by unbelievers, as well as the earnest offer in the sacrament. Œcolampadius replied to the attacks of the Syngramma.[1] The word, he says, could not bring the body of Christ, else the bread must have become Christ. The eternal Word however was not designed to become bread, but man. The Swabians were in danger of introducing new gods. The offer of grace, and the inlaying of it into the word, he will not, like Zwingli, so think of, as if in what was outward grace itself was offered, as it were, in a concrete form. Not even Christ as a man was a form of divinity, Zwingli had said,[2] but of humanity. *Luther* now took up the matter in a public and impetuous treatise.

It was the nature of erring spirits to contradict themselves with a multitude of evasions, in order to escape the truth.[3] Hitherto he had spoken more of faith itself than of the object of faith, but now many would fain remove the latter. The devil was looking to the contents of the egg, and would leave us the shell, *i.e.* would take Christ's body and blood out of the bread and wine, so that there would only remain simple bread, such as the baker bakes.[4] Zwingli pursued the controversy, purposely in Latin;[5] Luther wrote in reply, in 1527, *That the words of Christ,* "*this is my body," still stand firm.*[6] Zwingli wrote in answer, now in German, *That the words of Christ, "this is my body," would eternally keep their old and alone meaning,*[7] upon which Luther issued his so-called large *Bekenntniss vom Abendmahl,* 1528.[8] The controversy grew hotter and hotter; they presupposed the worst of, and no longer understood one another. Only the Strasburgers sought a middle way between the controversialists, but they were too wanting in definiteness of view, and were held in too little respect to obtain a hearing. And at

[1] Œcolampadii *Antisyngramma.* Luthers Werke von Walch, xx. 727, ff. A.D. 1526.
[2] *Opp.* i. 57.
[3] *Sermon vom Sakrament des Leibes und Blutes Christi wider die Schwärmer,* xx. 915, A.D. 1526.
[4] Luthers Werke von Walch, xx. 917-932.
[5] *Exegesis Amica,* Luthers Werke von Walch, xx. 1386. Zw. opp. iii. 459; ii. 2, 1, ff.
[6] Luthers Werke von Walch, xx. 950.
[7] xx. 1407. Zwingli's *Werke,* ii. 2, p. 16-93.
[8] xx. 1118. Zwingli's Answer, ii. 2, p. 94-223

the disputation at Bern, 1528, the real presence of the body and blood of Christ was given up.

Let us consider the *dogmatic* grounds founded upon by the two parties. For that the exegetical were not what decided them, although they thought so, is palpable; and the Syngramma was right in only seeking to prove exegetically that one was not *obliged* to expound the words of institution in the Swiss sense. In the case of Luther, in particular, his clinging to the letter of the ἐστί stood in contrast to his, at other times, free view of the letter of the evangelical record,—a contrast which is explained out of the need of having, instead of going back upon the whole body of Scripture, a single crushing passage in proof of his dogmatical view; but a step, at the same time, which was certainly excessively fertile in results. For the distinction between the foundation and the superstructure was here for the first time practically denied, and bent in the direction of identifying faith and dogma.

The *chief grounds founded on by the Swiss*, resting in part upon misapprehension, are the following: there would be a perpetual miracle placed in the Supper, if we accepted more than the presence of the Logos in the Supper, more incomprehensible than the creating of the heaven and of the earth, and even than the incarnation of Christ itself. And just on this account there must be something definite in Scripture on this point. But the words of institution are not an imperative 'Become' [*Werde*], but an exposition of the signs. Sign and image, however, are not the thing.[1] It is evident that Luther's view was not distinguished from the Romish doctrine of transubstantiation, which accepts a miraculous change in the elements. Further, because there are many breads, we would have to accept many Christs; we would have one body in several places at once, and along with that, as long as the elements should remain, two bodies in one place.[2] Christ's body must then always be coming down from heaven, which would be against the article regarding the session of Christ at the right hand of the Father. He is much rather according to his humanity in heaven, and as a finite definite entity[3] retained within the same. The pious saints of

[1] xx. 724, 754, 771.   [2] xx. 784.

[3] The original term is *Grösse*, which corresponds to the mathematical term "quantity," but gives as much prominence to the notion of substance or matter as to the notion of measure or number, and is therefore difficult of translation. It is applied here, of course, to the human body of Christ.—*Tr.*

the Old Testament would then, because the body of Christ did not yet exist, not have had the full enjoyment of grace, like the Christians.[1] In truth, however, the presence of the body and blood of Christ in the sacrament would be useless, for the flesh profiteth nothing. And this whole representation served to dishonour Christ, for it led to a "Capernaitic"[2] eating, and to magical ideas, when Christ was thought of as chained to the elements after their consecration. He was and remained free. The worship of the elements, too, could scarcely be avoided, and it was against the honour of God to find one's comfort in what was creatural. We required immediate fellowship with God, and had it in the Holy Ghost in the heart. This external thing was separative, and therefore contradictory to the principle of faith, which tolerates no mediator between Christ and the soul.

On the Lutheran side it was rejoined, that whoever received with earnestness the greatest miracle, the incarnation in Mary, had no ground for doubting the presence of Christ in the Supper. In His love, Christ would come thus near to man; did He not even dwell in the heart of believers, and was nearer to us than we ourselves? It was denied that there was any intention of uniting the images or signs with the thing; and the controversy was fixed as being to this effect, the question was whether the image was the sign of a grace present, and to be had, in the Supper. In like manner, when it was declared to be offensive that the one Christ, who nevertheless sits on the right hand of God, should at the same time be present in many places, and be at the same time two bodies in one place, Christ and the elements, Luther was the first to protest against the *impanatio,* or the local confinement of the body of Christ to the particularity of place. The formula, " with or in the bread we receive the body," was only to describe the presence of the latter, not its confinement. Besides, both were possible, several bodies in one place and one body in several places. Christ passed through the sealed stone without damaging it, and through the closed door; His body in the Supper was a glorified body,[3] and Christ's heavenly body could be in many places, without any multiplication of His body being needful for this end. Luther comes here upon analogies which are the foundation of a *dynamic* presence. The voice is a weak and perishing thing, and yet it penetrates,

---

[1] xx. 760.   [2] See note p. 313.—*Tr.*   [3] xx. 921, § 15.

when I speak, into a hundred and a thousand ears and hearts at the same time, and each ear apprehends the whole and perfect voice and the whole word. So, too, the eye can fix upon a thousand grains of corn at the same time, and again a thousand eyes can be fixed upon one grain. Should not Christ with His glorified body be able to do more than we with the bodily eye and the voice?[1] In the large *Bekenntniss vom Abendmahl* he makes use of the image of the sun shining on a large lake; if hundreds upon hundreds stood round the lake, each one would have the image of the sun for himself at his place, and no one at the place of another. Every one sees the image for himself and not for another, and all see the same sun. It is evident from this comparison, how for Luther Christ stands there as the centre in the circle of humanity.—With regard to the objection drawn from the session at the right hand of God, Luther denies that Christ leaves the right hand of the Father in order to be with us. "The right hand of God is not a particular place, like a golden chair or the like;" we are not, it is remarked—not without ridicule, to think of Christ as shut up in heaven *quasi carcere*, but "the right hand of God is the almighty power of God, which can at the same time be nowhere (*i.e.* not confined to any space) and yet must be in all places. God as Creator and Preserver is in every creature, in their innermost and outermost, round and round, through and through, above and below, before and behind, so that nothing can be more present and more inward in any creature than God Himself with His power." Now it was Christ's humanity, and not merely His divinity, which was at the right hand of God, and therefore it is everywhere where the latter is, consequently also in the Supper, although not confined therein.[2]—This indeed proved too much, namely, that we can have Christ everywhere and in all things, and what then remained to the Supper? This is seen by Luther himself; and hence he adds,[3] "It is one thing for Him to be there, and another for Him to be there *for thee*; but He is there for thee then, when He puts His word to it, and says, Here art thou to find Me. Thou canst nowhere lay hold of the right hand of God, unless it binds itself for thy sake and points thee a place. This, however, it does, when it enters into the humanity of Christ and dwells in it. And although this humanity is now at the right hand of God,

---

[1] xx. 919-921.   [2] xx. 925-1002.   [3] xx. 1014, ff.

which is everywhere, still the Word is there which He bequeathed to thee, and speaks at the institution of the ordinance. By it thou canst be certain of His presence. Although He is everywhere, still it is not His will that I seek Him apart from the Word. Where the Word is, there thou layest hold of Him aright; otherwise thou settest up idolatry. In the sacrament He offers Himself, His body and blood, that He may be bodily received." This is no dishonour to Him, because He does not become passive in the hand of the priest; "for it is not the priest who does it, but Christ by means of man. *His honour is His goodness,* by virtue of which He does not suffer Himself to be content with being all about us, but He gives His own body to us for food, so that He may assure and comfort us with this pledge, that our body shall live for ever, because it participates, here upon earth, of an eternal and living food."[1] With respect to the pious men of the Old Testament, the Syngramma says that a retrospective operation of Christ upon them is to be supposed, so that they enjoyed just the same as Christians do,—by which indeed there would be established an eternal existence of the body of Christ, or else an enjoyment only of the fruits of His disposition of love, but at any rate a similarity of condition, which threatened the distinction between the Old Testament and the New, contrary to John viii. 56, Matt. xi. 11. Hence the later Lutherans fell from this, and placed a difference between the sacraments of the Old and New Testaments, and even doubted whether circumcision and the passover were to be regarded as sacraments.— When, finally, the Swiss said that the flesh profited nothing, Luther and his party demanded that a distinction be drawn between flesh and flesh. Christ's flesh was not like that, of which John iii. 5 speaks, but holy, and had brought us a new birth. It was not the old Adam, which is opposed to the Spirit, but Christ's flesh was the assumed good corporeal and earthly nature. It was now even incorruptible, and because God is in it, a spiritual flesh, living and giving life to all who eat it, in their body and soul.[2] The outward elements, however, were still profitable, to give us, as pledges of and the means of nourishing faith, the assurance of the inward invisible gift.[3] Christ's body and blood were to become mine, that I might be sure of the forgiveness of sins and

---

[1] xx. 1037; similarly also at Marburg, in accordance with the Syngramma.
[2] xx. 950, ff.; 1085, 1093.   [3] xx. 1037.

of eternal life.[1] It was not, as the fanatics thought,[2] that there could be nothing spiritual where there is anything bodily, but the contrary was true, that the Spirit cannot be with us otherwise than in bodily things, such as word, water, and in His saints upon earth. Mary had first to apprehend the *Word* of the angel, in order thereby to receive Him spiritually in faith, and then also bodily through faith.[3]

The different conception of the first creation in relation to the second, according to which Luther looks upon the former as a point of attachment for the latter, in such a way that its secondary causality is made use of for the kingdom of grace, and nature is susceptible and capable of exhibiting that kingdom and of serving to corporealize and presentiate it,—this conception necessarily runs through the whole doctrine of the means of grace, but it affects also the *Christology*.

Both Reformations assert the true humanity and the true divinity of Christ in the unity of the person, and that in such a way that, in opposition to the doctrine prevalent in [Roman] Catholicism, a sincere emphasis is laid upon the former. Since the unity of the person of Christ is not the sameness of its two sides, but the God-manhood of the one person is rather conditioned by the reality of the distinct sides, whilst the distinct sides, if they do not at the same time inwardly point back to one another, must divide the person, the problem arises how to develop the distinction between these two sides, as well as their unity, in equal measure, and to conduct them to one another. These two tasks have been apportioned between the two Reformations; the Swiss have treated predominantly only of the distinct sides, and Luther in the controversy upon the Supper has treated almost of the unity alone. Under the preponderating influence of the impulse derived from the doctrine of the Supper, the Christology was at present contemplated by Luther almost exclusively from the standpoint of the exaltation of Christ. The consequence of this is that the state of exaltation is too much carried back into the days of His flesh. The Swiss contemplate the Christology in a preponderating degree from the historical

---

[1] xx. 936, § 48.   [2] Cf. xx. 271.
[3] Cf. below, Calvin, according to whose representation the outward serves in like manner for the reception of Christ spiritually in faith, whence, however, an effect goes forth upon the corporeity of man.

Controversy regarding the Finitum and Infinitum. 323

standpoint, the state of humiliation, in which the distinction between the two sides came most sharply into prominence. Hence probably begins the development of the Christology into the *doctrine of the two estates*, which took place, however, in such a way, that each of the two Reformations treats with special preference of one of the two estates, whereby the other is curtailed, if not dissolved into a semblance, and that it is only out of both together that a real doctrine of the two estates is produced,—namely, when both are brought into a form, which leaves its full rights to each of the two sides.

A tendency runs through the mediæval Church to place the God-*man* in the background, by the evaporation of the humanity of Christ into a mere theophany, a mere garment, or else by such a deification of the humanity as made Christ again, as it were, only the Logos. And in opposition to this tendency, it was the common endeavour of the Reformation to bring the God-man again into the midst of the Christian and Church life, into full presence for faith. It is therefore to be regarded as an improvement and progress, even in the case of Zwingli, that in opposition to all Docetic semblance he powerfully asserted the truth of the humanity of Christ, and did not suffer the humanity to be buried beneath the divinity under the pretext of a higher representation of Christ. It belongs also to the distinction between the human and the divine, upon the maintenance of which he strongly insists,[1] that the humanity is conceived of as progressive [*werdende*], even as Luther also had emphatically expressed it previously.[2] In this the Reformed Church, too, remained faithful to Zwingli. But he conceived it requisite to include in the abiding and necessary distinction between the divine and human nature, that what is divine become in no way the property of the humanity. The essence of the humanity he considers to consist in being and remaining only finite. The divine power, wisdom, holiness, and the like, never belong to it, that is to say, neither the ethical nor the metaphysical attributes of God, but only human power, wisdom, holiness, and the like, in

---

[1] Zwinglii *Opp.* ii. 2, pp. 70, 71, 75, 180. Against the (modern) Kenotic view he says: *quod infinitum est, se ipsum contrahere non potest, quominus infinitum sit, ac rursus explicare, ut sit infinitum*, ii. 2, p. 73, 169.

[2] *Luthers Werke von Walch*, v. 327, 331; vii. 1498, ff. ; xi. 389 See above p. 200.

an exalted and intensified degree, which the later Reformed doctrine expresses by the *anointing* with the Holy Ghost. Still Zwingli was bent on maintaining the incarnation of the Logos, and the unity of the person, but was not able to make it clear, how, if nothing divine can become the property of humanity, and the reverse, only the divine Person is able to belong to the human nature. The humanity, if personal, seems as if it must here be thought of after the Nestorian manner; if impersonal, only as the garment of the Deity who walks in it. This seems to stand in contradiction with those utterances, which have made Zwingli suspected of pantheism. But these utterances accord perfectly well with the view, that it is impossible that the finite can have really divine attributes, that is to say, that no real *communicatio idiomatum* takes place.[1] Precisely in so far as God is, in his view, as in that of Pico of Mirandola, all Being [*alles Sein*], the infinite, unchangeable, absolutely simple reality, the things of the world can only be distinguished from God by their being only finite in all their parts and properties, only apportioned or divided Being [*getheiltes Sein*]. Each has only, as it were, a part of the infinite quantum of being, and thus it appears to be a bare contradiction, that the finite can in any way be infinite, for that would be saying that the part is the whole. The less Zwingli—following here his previous philosophical ideas, which in other respects he had left behind (see above, p. 287, ff.)—distinguishes the nature of man otherwise than quantitatively from God, the more obstinately, in order not to confound God and the world completely, must the negation, the limitation, be maintained to be that which constitutes the finitude. In connection with the reproach of pantheism it is not to be forgotten, that Augustine also, and Anselm and Thomas, speak in a similar way of all reality being included in God, nor is it to be forgotten that, along with that, Zwingli nevertheless (see above) teaches an absolutely free and self-conscious divine personality.[2]

The *Lutheran* view, upon its side, sees the essence of the finite not in a negation of the infinite, in the mere boundary

[1] Zwinglii *Opp.* ii. 2, p. 70; iii. 452, 525, ff.
[2] Against Rudelbach, *Reformation, Lutherthum, und Union,* p. 290, and Zeller, as cited. Cf. Schenkel, *Union,* p. 67. Cf. besides Sigwart, as cited, p. 69.

which may not be transcended, but in a positive element, namely, that of susceptibility for and need of God, that is to say, of the Infinite. But whilst God has the infinitude of fulness in and by means of Himself, man has originally only the infinitude of emptiness, which longs however to be filled. In this *intensively* infinite receptibility man possesses, according to the Lutheran standpoint, the possibility of, or natural basis for, being a little universe in himself, a microcosm and image of God, although it is only by means of the self-communication of God that this natural basis is changed into a reality. It is thus possible for man to become perfect, but it is by means of God, for whom he has a perfect receptibility. The difference between God and man is here on one side more profoundly conceived of, than the difference between the whole and the parts. The idea of the creation has more justice done to it. But at the same time this difference between God and the world is so defined, as to establish a mutual reference and connection between them, and introduce a life-intercourse between God and the creature. For the receptive need longs to be filled, even as the fulness of Divine Love delights to condescend to the lowly and enrich the poor.

His manner of conceiving the infinite and the finite exercised an influence also upon Zwingli's doctrine of the means of grace. Grace, he says,[1] is given by the Holy Ghost; the Spirit needs no conductor or vehicle, for He is Himself the power and the conveyance by which everything is carried. The drawing of God must do it. This takes place without means, is not itself a means, but is God Himself. "Word and sign as outward things are only spurs and goads to seek the inward Word or Light." In the case of the person of Christ, indeed, his Christian consciousness determined him to make the exception, that the man was taken into oneness with the person[2] of the Son of God, so that He might redeem us. At the same time, he not only guards against any transformation of the humanity, as well as of the divinity, in their nature (with which no fault could be found, provided that their nature were rightly conceived of), but he makes the causality that effects salvation to lie exclusively in the divinity of Christ, not in the humanity; and so, too, worship must be addressed to the Son of God to the exclusion of

---

[1] *Luthers Werke von Walch*, xx. 768-776.
[2] Zwinglii *Opp.* iii. 452; vi. 1, p. 331. In *Walch*, xx. 1497.

the latter. "The Word became flesh" does not signify, God has become man; He can become nothing, only man can. The meaning therefore is, man has become God,[1] or more strictly, since man is not changed into divinity, human nature has been taken upon Him by the Son of God. It is only a trope, an interchange of terms (*allöosis*),[2] when the whole person stands for one nature, or the one nature for the other. Each nature retained its properties, and operated according to its own manner in Christ. According to the Divine nature, he has power over all things and knows all things; according to the human side, he is subject to the Emperor and does not know all things.[3] Since the humanity of Christ continues a true creature, it cannot be infinite, for nothing that is made is infinite, *i.e.* unmeasured, unconceived, but only God alone. He was afraid that Luther's view would lead to Docetism, an evaporation of the humanity, and especially of the bodily organism of Christ, by means of unlimited extension. Hence he cries to Luther, "Marcion is breaking into your house" [*will dir in Garten*]; and in fact it is not to be denied, that Luther, who before the controversy on the Supper had so distinctly ascribed to Christ all the attributes that belong to true humanity, increase in wisdom and in favour with God and man, growth and learning, and had also denied of Him that He possessed during His life upon earth omnipotence, omniscience, and omnipresence, now let all this recede in the fancied interests of the Supper. In order to furnish a properly firm basis for the corporeal presence in the Supper, he went back, during the conflict with Zwingli, to the idea of the *unio* or the incarnation, without duly distinguishing the empirical becoming [*Werden*] upon earth from the full idea, which expresses the aim of the development of the God-man, and is accordingly absolutely realized only in the perfecting of Christ. From the idea of that *unio*, he rather deduces, that everything divine must from the beginning be proper also to the humanity of Christ, not first in His exaltation, but already in His conception and birth; the consequence whereof would be, that Christ, whilst He was in His mother's womb, was also in respect of His humanity present everywhere outside of it; that whilst He increased in wisdom, His humanity was at the same time already

---

[1] *Luthers Werke von Walch*, xx. 1497. [2] Zwinglii *Opp.* ii. 2, p. 66, ff.
[3] *Luthers Werke von Walch*, xx. 1493.

omniscient; that whilst He suffered upon the cross, His humanity also governed the world, being omnipresent—the very sentences, to which the later Lutherans, especially the Brenzian school, have given utterance. This must necessarily result either in a double humanity, a humanity omniscient, omnipresent, and the like, alongside of a humanity that is learning, is locally limited, and the like. Or else, since this would be not to confirm, but rend, the unity of the person of Christ, the limited growing learning humanity must be changed into a mere semblance. But although Zwingli's objection is in this well-founded, and has on its side Luther's own earlier Christology, Zwingli does not stop short here. He holds not merely the eternal duration of the lineaments of the humanity of Christ (which was also afterwards recognized in the *F. C.*, and which even Luther never sought to deny), but also the confining of Christ to a certain space in the heavens, and accordingly does not even allow to the exaltation of Christ this significance, that, because the *unio* of divinity and humanity is therein accomplished, Christ has the power of being present with His own, who form His body, without being hindered by the limits of space, but rather overcoming them by freedom in respect of space. Zwingli misunderstands Luther (see above, p. 198), in supposing him to design the dissolution of the humanity, so that only divinity should remain. So little is this the case, that it might far rather be said that, according to Zwingli, the Son of God only assumes an impersonal human nature as a garment void of personality [*selbstlos*] or an organon, whilst Luther establishes the humanity of Christ personally by means of the communication of the personality of the Logos, as well as of the divine attributes, and even afterwards, especially for the work of atonement, emphasizes in the strongest manner the humanity of Christ as the substitute of our humanity. But the two could not come to a mutual understanding; and it is owing to this, above all, that they never came to discuss the doctrine of God, and the relation of the infinite to the finite, independently,—this postulate of all Christology. This was reserved for a later time, in which philosophy has also a part to play. The consequence of this defect was that both sections, since they allowed themselves to be without a connected exhibition of the doctrine of the relation of God to man, formed their Christology, in accordance with the occasion of the Christological discussion, so as their theory of the Supper seemed to recommend. This however was itself improper, because, objectively regarded, the doctrine of the Supper must evidently be determined by means of the Christology, and what is dark or doubtful in the former has to seek its solution only in the latter, which is to be constructed not merely at odd occasions, but independently and out of its own proper interests, just as Luther's first Christological sketch possessed this more independent and free origin. Still it ought to be mentioned that Luther himself afterwards acknowledged that it was not necessary in the interests of the Supper, and might even be objectionable, to deduce, as a physically necessary and immediate consequence from the *unio*, such as it is from the beginning, an omnipresence of the body of Christ, which necessarily threatened His whole historical existence and the whole reality of His humanity. Hence he afterwards assigns to that going back upon the *unio*, as it was from the beginning, only the significance of an attempted medium of proof, not of an independent doctrinal tenet, and desires that the doctrine, which is the vital question, namely, the real presence of the whole God-man with His own, especially in the holy Supper, should not depend upon the adequacy of that medium of proof.[1] Since, on the other hand, Zwingli's Christology lays the chief emphasis upon the divinity in Christ, and he, too, considers it to be present in the Christian congregation, the difference between the two parties, even although the controversy was never adjusted, is not an absolute one, especially as Zwingli even accepts an indissoluble connection of the Logos with the humanity.

3. *The Preliminary Peace, or the Marburg Conference,* A.D. 1529, *and the Wittenberg Concord,* A.D. 1536.

The more passionate became the controversy amongst the Evangelicals, the more decidedly did the Catholics, with Charles V. at their head, believe that they would gain the upper hand. In 1526 the final act of the Diet of Spires had given to the Protestant princes the right of reformation in their own lands. The victories of the Emperor, and the schism amongst the Evangelicals, were of such consequence, that even the majority of the Estates at Spires, in 1529, revoked, under the auspices of the

---

[1] *Kurzes Bekenntniss vom heiligen Sakrament. Luthers Werke,* xx. 2195-2229, in the year 1544.

Emperor, the allowances formerly granted, and it only remained to the Evangelicals to stand forth from that time as the "Protestants" (20th and 25th April, 1529). Cause and reputation admonished more than ever to unity, and the farseeing *Philip the Magnanimous*, supported in particular by *Bucer* in Strasburg as middleman, brought about the Marburg conference in October 1529.[1] This is the most important union discussion between the two churches. They were represented by their leaders, Luther, Jonas, Melanchthon, Andreas Osiander, Stephanas Agricola, and Brenz, upon the one side, and Zwingli, Œcolampadius, Bucer, and Hedio, on the other. Zwingli could not, in spite of his urgent and moving entreaties, procure the recognition of his party as brethren in the faith, and the hope of union was already shattered. The Elector then urged that Luther should at least arrange together the articles in which they were at one, and might indicate what was still unadjusted. Luther agreed to this, but with the explanation that the Swiss would not accept what he would lay down. When, then, upon the 4th October, he laid before them his fifteen articles, they were, after a few alterations, signed by all present. In the first fourteen there was a complete unanimity. The Trinity, Christology, universality of original sin inherited from Adam as involving condemnation apart from Christ, were placed first; then, in the fifth to the eighth articles, there followed what was specifically Reformational: faith in the atonement of Christ justifies us; it is the work of God in us by the Holy Ghost when we hear the word of the Gospel; we are saved by this faith without merit or works of our own. The ninth article says, baptism is a sacrament instituted by God with a view to this faith, not a mere sign or watchword of Christians amongst themselves, but a sign and work of God, in which our faith is required and we are born again to life. The tenth article: faith produces love. The eleventh: confession is to be voluntary, but is a great benefit for doubting and troubled hearts on account of the comfort given by the Gospel, which is the true absolution. The twelfth: the civil magistrate is an ordinance of God. The thirteenth: traditions which are not contrary to the word of God, liberty is given to maintain or drop, but the weak are to be spared. The fourteenth: infant baptism is to be

---

[1] *Luthers Werke*, xvi. 181, ff.; xvii. 2357. Heppe, *die 15 Marburger Artikel*, 1848. Nitzsch, *Urkundenbuch der evang. Union*, Bonn, 1853.

approved of, since the children are thereby received into the grace of God and into Christendom. Finally, too, in the fifteenth article, regarding the Supper, they were at one in considering that the sacrifice of the mass was to be rejected, that both elements were necessary, and that the sacrament of the altar was a sacrament of the true body and blood of Christ, that the spiritual enjoyment of the body and blood of Christ was specially needful for every Christian, and finally that the sacrament and word were given by God, in order thereby to move weak consciences to faith and love through the Holy Ghost. "But although," so closes this important document, "we have not at this time come to an agreement, as to whether the true body and blood of Christ are corporeally in the bread and wine, still each party ought to manifest Christian love towards the other, as far as the conscience of each will allow, and both parties ought diligently to beseech Almighty God to affirm to us the right understanding by His Holy Spirit."

The conference indeed did not issue in a unity corresponding to the Consensus. Along with all liberality in matters of ceremony, it was thought on the Lutheran side that there must be absolute unity in dogma. The distinction was carried out between faith and works of the will, but not the distinction between faith and dogma, or works of Church thought. There would certainly have been, and continued to be, a not unimportant difference in the faith itself (and not merely in the dogmatic expression of it), if Zwingli and his party had still maintained the standpoint of his letter to Alber. But he manifested already an approximation again to his former doctrine regarding word and sacrament, so that alongside of the common Christian matter there was made manifest a rich evangelical consensus extending to word and sacrament, and at Marburg this consensus was formulated and formally recognized by the leaders of the Reformation on both sides.

That this reapproximation on the part of Zwingli does not rest upon mere momentary concession, or even accommodation, but upon conviction, is evident from the fact that even in other ways, as has been already indicated, Zwingli towards the end of his life expresses himself similarly. To this result Bucer may have co-operated, who always sought in the Supper a place for the presence of Christ.[1] Zwingli at last not merely confesses to a presence of Christ in the contemplation of faith, but the sacrament is in his view a memorial instituted by the Lord, and a pledge of His love, as the wedding-ring for the spouse; the elements indeed are to me only signs, but they are the symbol of the inward friendship of Christ (*indisjunctæ societatis et amicitiæ Christi*). The bread is thus holy bread; it is *sacramentaliter* the body of Christ; and whilst he formerly gave only an ethical significance to the sacrament, he now finds in it the expression of this truth, that as bread and wine strengthen and rejoice the life of man, so Christ alone renews, supports, and rejoices us. He even says, besides, that the sacraments strengthen faith (*opem et auxilium afferunt fidei*), and, as Luther says, The eye sees and the ear hears for the heart, so, according to Zwingli, the senses are in the sacrament taken into the service of faith, whilst, at other times, Satan tempts us through the senses. Sight, taste, and touch unite with the faith of the soul, and experience how kind the Lord is. And elsewhere[2] he says, When the bread and the wine are divided, is not the whole Christ brought near to the senses (*sensibiliter sensibus offertur*)? The Lord's Supper is glorious through His presence, and faith has not properly accomplished its contemplation, if the latter has not taken hold of the matter as certainly and indubitably as if it were externally presented to the senses. And Bullinger, his successor in the Zürich Reformation, expressed himself similarly.[3] He, with his friends, rejects indeed a capernaitic[4] eating, instead of a spiritual (*non carnaliter et crasse, sed spiritualiter et sacramentaliter*, is Christ enjoyed by faith). But Christ is truly present in the holy Supper, and it is His presence which first makes it the Supper of the Lord. (*Christum credimus vere esse in sacra cœna, imo non credimus esse Domini cœnam nisi Christus* ADSIT.) Has he promised to be pre-

[1] Cf. above, p. 315, note 1. *Zwingl. fidei chr. Expositio*, Opp. iv. 56. 68. Sigwart, as cited, has recognized this partly, but imperfectly. Further, *Zwingli fidei ratio*, 1530; Opp. iv. 11. 32. He holds indeed even now no *Assumptio* of the bread by Christ, nor a transformation, but yet the true presence of Christ in the Supper by the Holy Ghost. The Supper is *invisibilis gratiæ visibilis figura, factæ gratiæ signum*.

[2] Zwingli, Opp. iv. 32.

[3] iv. 73, in the Appendix *de Euchar. et Missa*, addressed to the Emperor, together with the *Abendmahlsagende* of Zürich, Bern, and Basle. Pestalozzi, *H. Bullinger*, 1858, p. 212, 519, ff.

[4] See p. 313, note 2.

sent where two or three are met in His name, how much more is He in His congregation!

We may not therefore, as is often done, characterize the conference at Marburg as resultless, even though later polemics have treated it as never existing. By this memorable act, in which they looked one another in the face, the impression was ineffaceably stamped upon the self-consciousness of both confessions in their inmost heart, that they together represented a large treasure of common evangelical truths, in addition to those common to all Christians. And when it is remembered that the Marburg articles became the basis of the Swabian, out of which grew the Augsburg Confession, it may be said: It is in correspondence with the Marburg conference, that the Reformed Church was afterwards able to assert its alliance to the Augsburg Confession.

After the Diet of Augsburg, the Evangelicals were declared to be enemies of the Empire, and were summoned by the victorious Emperor to submit themselves to the Pope. This admonished them still more urgently of the necessity of union. To this was added the perception, on the part of Melanchthon, that Christian antiquity did not, as he had hitherto thought, pronounce decisively against the figurative construction of the Supper.[1] Luther himself had sometimes a glimmering of the evil that resulted from the schism. He writes to Bucer,[2] "I wish that this schism were put an end to, even if I had to give my life for it three times over, because I see how necessary your fellowship is for us, and how much inconvenience this disunion has occasioned to the Gospel and still occasions, so that I am convinced that all the gates of hell, all the Papacy, the Turk, the whole world, the flesh, and whatever other evil thing there is, would not have been able to injure the Gospel so much, if we had remained at one." Hence he acted from that time more moderately, and, owing to this more peaceful disposition, Melanchthon introduced so early as 1531 some changes in the *Conf. Aug.*, so that the Swiss might be able to accept it. He omitted the words "under the form," which savoured to the Swiss of transubstantiation. He made

[1] Œcolampadius had convinced Melanchthon of this by his proofs from the history of doctrines; to this was added his natural love of peace, which Bucer fostered not a little.

[2] Marheinecke, *Geschichte der Reformation*, iii. 350. *Luthers Werke*, xxi. 334. xvii. 2395.

The Conference at Cassel, 1534. 333

still further alterations in 1533 and 1535, most of all, however, in 1540 (in the so-called *Editio variata*). Since the reception by unbelievers as well as by believers was more readily expressed in the "distributing" than in the "presenting," he put *exhibeantur* instead of *distribuantur*, and omitted *improbant secus docentes*. And no less was an inward approximation observable also at last upon the Swiss side. Evidence of it has been already given in the case of Zwingli; Œcolampadius acknowledged, in like manner, that the Supper was not merely a performance of faith, but brings a spiritual enjoyment to the believer; Bucer finally set forth, that as Christ was certainly present in the believer, so too he was in no way absent in the Supper; and this was not a mere remembrance, but rather, said he, in accordance with Zwingli's later formula, Christ is there *contemplatione fidei*, by which he meant, faith is, as it were, the eye which sees the present Christ.[1] This view of Bucer's was the ruling one in Strasburg after 1530, about the time that Calvin came thither, to whose view it forms the transition.

Philip of Hesse brought about a new conference at Cassel between Melanchthon and Bucer, 27th December 1534.[2] At this conference *Bucer* undertook that the Strasburg divines should teach according to the Augustana and its Apology, and should regard the Supper not merely as the sign of an absent thing, but should, on the contrary, although they would not receive a local inclusion and physical union of the body of Christ, maintain the presence of the body of Christ for believers. This was again essentially the standpoint of the Swabian Syngramma. Luther himself now proposed a *convention*, which took place at *Wittenberg* in 1536, and which issued in the so-called Wittenberg *Formula Concordiæ*.[3] Luther did not let himself be restrained from this by the fact, that Bucer did not confess to the enjoyment of the body and blood by unbelievers, even as the Syngramma also rejected it. At the Convention they were convinced of having cherished mutual misunderstandings. Bucer acknowledged that even Luther did not refuse every trope nor deny the perpetuation of the elements [as unchanged after consecration], nor fix their union with the body and blood of Christ so intimately, that what happened to the former befel also the latter, and he testified that injustice

[1] *Luthers Werke*, xvii. 2424.   [2] xvii. 2486, ff.
[3] xvii. 2516, ff, 2589; cf., p. 2395. Marheinecke, as cited, p. 373.

had been done on the other side to them, inasmuch as none of them present denied the presence of the body of Christ. They united in the formula: With the bread and the wine the body and blood of Christ are, by virtue of the institution of Christ, *vere et substantialiter* present, independently of the worthiness of the giver and receiver; the body and blood of Christ are truly offered even to the unworthy, and the unworthy receive it to their condemnation. This formula, on which Luther believed it necessary to insist, because it was only in the enjoyment by unbelievers that he saw the sure test for the reception of the real presence, could only be accepted by Bucer in a different sense from what it was by Luther, inasmuch as he would understand by the *indigni* not unbelievers, but the careless and slothful believers, who receive the body of Christ to their condemnation. It was thus only a semblance of union which was attained in respect of the *indigni*. That Luther, however, laid less stress upon this, is evident partly from the circumstance, that the formula, *indignos sumere ad judicium*, with which he contented himself, does not take the body of Christ immediately for its object, but stands by itself, so that it could be applied in case of need to the elements which all receive, and partly from this, that the difference which still remained could not escape his keen eye, but that still he did not on that account suspend the work of peace, but only upon his side would yield nothing of his conviction. They united in a similar manner in reference to *baptism*.[1] The promise was valid also for infants, and was to be appropriated to them through the ministration of the Church. Without regeneration there was even for infants no entrance into the kingdom of heaven. Infants indeed had no understanding, but the Holy Ghost exercised His power in them according to their measure, and thereby they pleased God. The way and manner of these operations was unknown, but it was certain that there were in them new and holy impulses, the inclination to believe in Christ and to love God, which was in a certain measure similar to those movements, which are otherwise possessed of faith and love. They also easily united in this, that private absolution was wholesome, but only general absolution necessary, as well as in this, that it is not the minister who makes the body and blood of Christ.

Bucer now turned to the Swiss, who had not yet adhered, and

[1] xvii. 2530, Art. 4.

asserted, over against them, that even a merely spiritual enjoyment on the part of believers was reconcilable with the formula agreed upon. Since they, however, did not trust him entirely, they wrote directly to Luther an honest, peaceful letter, A.D. 1536, inquiring whether it was true, what Bucer said, that even he held only a merely spiritual enjoyment? Meanwhile, however, they did not subscribe the formula; it was received only in Upper Germany, Hesse, and Osnabrück, and served to prepare the ground for a middle type of doctrine. Luther replied, on the 1st December, 1537, in a friendly manner, and in the spirit of the Schmalkaldic articles, which fall into the same year, and which draw a distinction in the value of the different articles of faith. We leave it in the hands of Divine Omnipotence, he says, *how* the body and blood of Christ are given to us in the Supper. Where we have not entirely come to an understanding in this, it is best that we be friendly towards one another, and always expect the best of one another, until the mire and troubled water settle.[1] From this it is evident how Luther regards it as indispensable, *that* the body and blood of Christ are given us in the Supper, but distinguishes from this the *How*, and the connection with the elements, and in doing so distinguishes from it the question regarding the enjoyment by unbelievers, as a question of subordinate worth. A surrender of his own view upon that point was not thereby accorded upon his side, nor was it demanded, whilst, on the other hand, the peace established between the two parties was recognized to be rightful, if there was agreement in the chief matter, in the *What*. The *Wittenberg Concordia* may therefore be regarded as a document, which shows beforehand that a standpoint in the doctrine of the Supper, such as afterwards became through Calvin the ruling one in the Reformed Churches, was acknowledged even by Luther himself to be one, with which brotherly communion was christianly lawful. And this historical judgment is not altered by the circumstance, that seven years afterwards Luther suddenly broke out again in his *Kleines Bekenntniss vom Abendmahl*, in violent ebullition against the Swiss, quite unexpectedly to all, except those who were envious of and hated Melanchthon, and who had goaded Luther on to this. The Swiss had never subscribed the Wittenberg Concordia on account of that ambiguous formula of

---

[1] xvii. 2597.

Bucer's, and there were not wanting among them those, who still adhered to the so-called Zwinglian doctrine of the Supper, a fact which was evidenced in literary productions.[1] It thus seemed to Luther that he had gained nothing by his former advances, but that a violation of his own standpoint had rather been transplanted into Germany (especially by Melanchthon, who in 1540 edited the *Variata*). Hence Luther was now intent upon the most decisive definition of his own doctrine in opposition to Spiritualism (Schwenckfeld, &c.) and to Zwingli. But even in this Luther did not turn against that type of doctrine, which afterwards became through Calvin the ruling one in the Reformed Church, and found acceptance even in Zürich itself as early as 1549 in the *Consensus Tigurinus*.[2]

Let us now, in closing, glance at the *public system of doctrine in the Reformed Church* at this period. As confessions of the first formation, there fall to be considered, not the writings of Zwingli, for not even his *Fidei ratio ad Carolum V.* was presented [formally to the Emperor] nor accounted symbolical, but the *Tetrapolitana* (of Strasburg, Constance, Memmingen, Lindau), presented in 1530 by Bucer,[3] the *Confessio Basileensis et Muelhusana*, A.D. 1532,[4] after the plan of Œcolampadius by Oswald Myconius, and the so-called *Helvetica I.*, A.D. 1536. They all recognize the formal principle, and even appropriate, excepting the Basle Confession, a special article to the Scriptures, the Helvetic treating of them with considerable minuteness and beauty. In like manner, they all confess to the material principle of the Reformation, to the absence of merit in works, and to the denial of free will in spiritual things, yet without becoming supralapsarian. At the same time, great stress was laid upon

---

[1] Most strongly in the *Bekenntniss der Züricher Prädicanten*, 1545 (the answer to Luther's *Kleines Bekenntniss vom Abendmahl*.

[2] Luther's distrust in the negotiations for peace, and in Melanchthon's steadfastness, explains (and it is to be judged of accordingly) the word, which Luther spoke (at least according to the German text of Walch, xvii. 2490) to Melanchthon on his departure, in 1534, for the Cassel Conference with Bucer; they might insist upon the recognition of this, that in the Supper the body of Christ was bitten with the teeth. This he himself had elsewhere rejected, xx. 1091, as it is also in the *F. C.*

[3] And Capito, at the Diet of Augsburg, to the vice-chancellor for transmission to the Emperor.—*Tr.*

[4] Though apparently commenced in 1532, it was not finished and adopted until 1534.—*Tr.*

good works, but not for justification. According to the *Tetrapolitana*, none is elected to life, without being also elected to conformity to the image of Christ (Art. IV.) The assurance of salvation is emphasized especially in the *Helv. I.*, 13. Of the remaining dogmas, the Trinity and the Christology were simply transferred from the old confessions. The Church is described, as on the Lutheran side, in the first instance according to its inward nature. There belong to it the elect or believers, who are known to God alone; yet there are marks by which it may be known, to which the *Tetrapolitana* reckons, in addition to word and sacrament, the fruits of the true Church, holy living, and the *Helv. I.* public discipline, and great stress is also laid upon the office of the ministry. In particular, however, there is still to be considered their *doctrine of the sacraments*. The *Tetrapolitana* emphasizes their ethical significance as confessions, whilst the others also regard them as signs of fellowship. But none of these three confessions will change the sacraments into a mere figure (*signa sine re*); for all of them they are also *signs of an invisible grace*. Baptism is a covenant of the promise of the Spirit of God, even for the children of the people of God, but faith is necessary. The Basle confession considers it as the offering of the washing away of sins, which is however accomplished by God alone; according to the *Helv. I.* it presents (*exhibet*) the laver of regeneration to the elect, to whom infants are to be benevolently reckoned, since they belong to the people of God.

With reference to the *Supper*, even the *Tetrapolitana* says, while declining idle questions, that believers receive the true body and blood of Christ for the true food of the soul, so that they live in Him and He in them. And the Basle confession, whilst it teaches, in addition to the confession of faith and the attestation of brotherly love, the offering (*oblatio*) of the true body and blood of Christ without transformation of the elements, seeing that Christ would give to souls to feed upon His flesh and drink His blood by means of true faith in Him, the crucified, adds as an effect of the Supper, besides the incorporation into the body of Christ, also the blessed resurrection by virtue of this communion with the Head (7, 8). Finally, the *Helv. I.* appropriates the formula, which was essentially that of the [*Augustana*] *Variata:* "There is presented in the Supper the body and blood of Christ, which serve for the nourishment of eternal life."

THIRD DIVISION.

The Development of the two Evangelical Systems of Doctrine until their symbolic settlement, or the period from the first formation of the Evangelical Confession, about 1530, until the second, 1580 and 1619.

SECTION I.

THE LUTHERAN CHURCH.

A SOLEMNLY recognized and common symbol was indeed procured for the Evangelicals in Germany by means of the Augsburg Confession (1530) and its Apology, but still an evangelical church was not thereby in any way firmly founded. On the contrary, the hope of a reconciliation was still cherished, and there even existed a readiness to submit to the bishops, if they would only allow the pure preaching of the Gospel and the administration of the sacraments, conformably to their institution. The fifty years down to the Formula of Concord (1580) form the period, in which the *relation to the Romish Church* was cleared up and explicated. To this conduced, upon the evangelical side, the necessity of establishing amongst themselves ecclesiastical order, since the General Council was always being waited for in vain. This order of their own was effected quite as much in accordance with the necessities of the evangelical spirit as under a cautious regard to what had been historically produced, so that after the first third of this period a church formation of a different kind from the Romish stood over against it. To give it up again for the sake of the bishops and outward unity soon became dogmatically impossible, namely, when the Romish opposition characterized this retractation and return under the bishops as necessary to salvation; whilst, on the other hand, if it had never come to this new configuration of the Church, very many of the customs and ordinances hitherto observed could have been retained, although in a different sense by the Evangelicals from what they had amongst the Roman Catholics. When new church usages and ordinances had been once introduced, the article of faith *C. A.* vii., which denied any dogmatical significance to church usages and ordinances, prevented the doing away with them from being imposed as a dogmatical necessity, a condition of things which came to light in the so-called *Adiaphorist controversies*. On the other side, the Council of Trent put into the form of dogma much which the Evangelicals would have consented to tolerate as an adiaphoron, and effected in general a dogmatic separation from the Reformation. Melanchthon, led not simply by the love of peace, and still less by personal fears, but by a mind which, from its historical education and lively sense of order, was averse from everything violent and tumultuous, only with great difficulty gave up the hope, that, if only evangelical doctrine were tolerated in the Church, and the Evangelicals would for the sake of unity be content to enter into the hitherto existing forms of the Church, the power of the Gospel working from within might make itself master of the whole body of the Church, and thus the breach in the Western Church be prevented. His purpose in this was not to sacrifice in the very slightest degree anything of the Gospel. But from his education he knew how, by going back to the first beginnings in the early Church, to procure in a judicious way for many Romish customs which had led to mechanism and superstition, a significance which indeed could scarcely be accessible to the mass. He had not, however, in this weighed the silent but mighty influence, which a world of customs, formulæ, and ordinances, born of a different religious view, must have involuntarily exercised upon the mind of the Evangelicals. He had not sufficiently considered the sufferings and the maiming which the evangelical spirit must experience, when it should be not merely robbed of a homogeneous embodiment in cultus and manners, and in so far limited, as it were, to an ideal existence in doctrine, but should be also enclosed, as it were, in a body alien to it. Finally, however, and principally, he had allowed himself to be deceived regarding the good will of the intellectual leaders of the Romish Church towards reformation, by the circumstance that men, like Contarini, Julius Pflug, Gropper, who really advanced half way towards the Reformation, were wilily put forward for a while to negotiate with the Evangelicals. It must be allowed to Luther that he had from the beginning a clearer view of this matter, as was shown in particular at the convention at Schmalkalden, and in his relations to the well-known subscription [*Unterschrift*] of Melanchthon regarding the eventual permissibility of the Papacy.[1] Luther's perception was sharpened by a more powerful grasp of the Reformation principle, and a more conscious feeling of the greatness of the distance between the fundamental religious views of the two sides,—a merit this, which did not indeed belong in like manner to the most zealous followers of Luther, who in their passionate procedure in the question regarding the Adiaphora soon after Luther's death, seem to have been led quite as much by hatred towards Melanchthon as by concern for the maintenance of the evangelical doctrine in its purity and power. No new dogmatic controversies with the *Romish* Church, worthy of being named, occurred besides in this period.

On the other hand, the *Evangelical* Church itself, especially in Germany, was moved in this period to its depths by party divisions, which indeed, as has probably been only too much traced out by Planck, were in many respects concurrent with human passion, but yet offer a more cheerful side for contemplation. First of all, a word regarding the outward aspect of the six principal controversies which fell in this period, and to all of which Melanchthon was in one way or another a party. The increasing respect in which Melanchthon was held, from whom a very large school issued (J. Camerarius, Paul Eber, P. Crell, Peucer, Pezel, Cruciger, Pfeffinger, Major, Menius, &c.), had already in

---

[1] In the Schmalkaldic articles, Luther expressed in the most unqualified terms his opposition to the institution, as well as to the character and conduct of the Papacy. Melanchthon, while holding that the Papacy was opposed to the design of Christ and the constitution of the Church, and that it had been a source of frightful evil (as his treatise, sanctioned by the Convention, and appended to the articles, shows), did not feel at liberty to cut off all hope of a reconciliation with Rome by declaring the Papacy to be absolutely inadmissible. Hence he alone of all who subscribed the Schmalkaldic articles, qualified his subscription,— adding, "With regard to the Pope, I hold that, if he would allow the Gospel, we ought, for the sake of peace and common unity with those who are, and in the future may be, under him, to allow to him *jure humano*, that superiority to the bishops, which he otherwise possesses." Luther's opinion upon this point was, that if the respect paid to the Pope had no divine but only a human basis, it could never be the means of effecting unity in the Church.—*Tr.*

the last years of Luther begun to excite, by way of reaction, the formation of an opposite party, *Agricola, Nicolaus von Amsdorf, Matthias Flacius, Gallus, Judex, Wigand*, and others, who, rallying more closely round Luther's name, opposed Melanchthon, and, without Luther's spirit, laboured to follow Luther's letter. Whilst one of the noblest elements in Luther was the large-heartedness (which qualified him for the place of Reformer), and the humility with which he recognized the peculiar gifts of others, and above all of Melanchthon, it was the endeavour of these narrow-hearted friends to limit Luther to himself, to forget the need for being completed felt even by this perhaps the greatest post-apostolic individuality, and also—in which however they did not succeed—to make himself forget it. They procured some separate expressions of dissatisfaction with Melanchthon, and as has been observed, a keener defence in his last years of what was distinctively his own. Still he did not break with Melanchthon, but held him dear and of worth in the bottom of his heart, nor did he cease to work personally together with him, *e.g.* at the improvement of the translation of the Bible. After Luther's death in 1546, Melanchthon might in a weak hour have felt himself freed from the ascendency of the princely, but also ruling, spirit of Luther, as from an oppressive weight, without it dawning on him how much the faithfulness of Luther's friendship, which was never violated, had covered him. Those followers of Luther, on the other hand, who had never been so united to him in friendship as Melanchthon was, and were still less of equal rank with those two men, deemed it after Luther's death to be their right and duty to play the part of Luther, but sought to assert their Lutheran character chiefly by emphasizing without judgment the extremest points of the doctrine of Luther, as well as by combating and excluding what was peculiar to Melanchthon. Occasion for doing so was indeed given them,—in addition to Melanchthon's conduct in the Adiaphorist controversy, which incited them to that most deserving and great work of Church history, the *Magdeburg Centuries*,—by the circumstance that the Melanchthonic type began after Luther's death, and through the Saxon *Corpus doctrinæ Philippicum*, to become the prevailing rule of doctrine. They therefore banded themselves more and more closely together into a party, whose common trait was principally only opposition to Melanchthon and his school, and to which, besides the above-named, men like *Joachim Mörlin, Irenäus, Tilemann Heshus, Westphal*, and others, attached themselves. But the inseparable inward mutual connection between Luther and Melanchthon, in order to compass in the way of reformation the German people, was shown in particular in this, that all the chiefs of this policy, with their outbidding of Luther in the exclusion of every Melanchthonianism, ran to an extreme, which itself brought about their fall,—a historical retribution, which was completed by the formation of a powerful third party, that of the *Swabian* and the *Lower Saxons*, with *Martin Chemnitz* and *J. Brenz* at their head. It was completed, although without an entire rehabilitation of Melanchthon, yet in this way, that the Formula of Concord, though predominantly Lutheran, yet kept the sickly onesidedness of those men at a distance from the Lutheran type of doctrine, and in the doctrine regarding the law, regarding free-will, regarding predestination and the appropriation of salvation, accorded no unimportant influence to the Melanchthonic type of doctrine.

By the treaty of Passau and the Ausburg religious peace of 1555, the " Interim," in which Melanchthon had allowed himself to be too deeply involved, and along with it the dangerous mixture of Roman Catholic forms of worship and constitution with Evangelical doctrine, from which the English Church suffers to this day, was avoided for the German Reformation; and the inward disturbances also, which had grown out of it, were, by Melanchthon's retractation of his compliance in the Adiaphoris, which had been carried by him too far, deprived of their chief significance.[1]

---

[1] Not indeed without this matter being incessantly discovered again to the disparagement of Melanchthon. When in more recent times those who claim to be the most faithful representatives of Lutherism* would wish to have those things which were introduced again by the "Interim," restored again in fact, this will, as nothing else easily could, give one an idea how the names and conceptions of historical things can be deranged, and how different such a modern Gnesio-Lutherism is from that of the sixteenth century. For it accepts as genuinely Lutheran very many things which Melanchthon, in contradiction to the Gnesio-Lutherans, regarded as permissible. May this change at least conduce to their learning to judge of Melanchthon historically and justly! For in the cultus and constitution he—like Calixt afterwards—treated Roman Catholicism more sparingly than his Gnesio-Lutheran opponents. The Melanchthonian *Menius* had in 1537 set up an idea of church *office* more nearly akin to the Roman Catholic view; in opposition

* The reference, I apprehend, is to that school, of which Löhe, Kliefoth, Zezschwitz, &c., are at present the extreme representatives.—*Tr.*

Methodical Course of these Controversies. 343

Of more importance for us are the doctrinal controversies within the Evangelical Church itself down to the *Formula Concordiæ*. Of the six chief controversies of this class, each two form a connected pair, and the Lutheran Church of this time was stirred by them to its very depths. These three pairs are; the *Antinomian* and the *Majorist* controversy, the *Osiandrian* and the *Stancarist*, the *Synergistic* and the *Flacian*. They present at the first glance a picture of the greatest confusion, especially because the parties cross one another to the most manifold degree. Thus the so-called Gnesio-Lutherans are partly with Melanchthon against Osiander, and partly against him on account of his peaceful attitude towards the Reformed Church; at the same time they also in turn stand for the most part upon the Reformed and Calvinistic side, inasmuch as they maintain in opposition to Melanchthon's doctrine of freedom, the doctrine of absolute predestination held at the commencement. In this there may be always seen a proof, that it was not a conscious spirit of faction, but interest in the cause, which decided each separate formation of parties. In like manner this coming up in pairs of mutually connected opposites, in each of which one momentum was exhibited onesidedly or carried to an extreme, is to be considered in the history of doctrines as the process, in which by means of conflict the mutually connected momenta of truth should lose the shape in which they were repulsive to one another, and should be combined into the fulness and ripeness of a more definite doctrinal form, and one sharpened by opposition. In this respect it may be said that these intricate controversies must promote the purer and fuller appropriation of the Reformation principle, that appropriation, as well as the unfolding of the Reformation doctrine, being at the first necessarily defective in each addition to the constantly increasing province of the Reformation. From these points of view some light is thrown upon the confusion of the strife. Irrespective of the points of incidence of human passions and accidental circumstances, it moves in its

---

to him *Flacius* maintained the genuinely Lutheran doctrine (Preger, *Flacius*, i. 400). In like manner Joh. *Frederus* contested the necessity of the laying on of hands, seeing that the legitimate vocation was sufficient, and he had right in the main. When the Lübeckian *Saliger* (*Beatus*) and *Fredeland* placed the *Unio sacr.* immediately after the consecration and *ante usum*, *Wigand*, Chemnitz, Chyträus, opposed them.

leading features regularly forward, for it embraces first in the *Antinomian* controversy, upon which follows on the other side the *Majorist*, the immediate *postulate* of the Gospel of free sin-pardoning grace, namely the law and its significance for the origin and maintenance of faith. An advance is thus made to the *objective side of the Gospel itself*, to the nearer determination of the objective matter of justifying faith, and the basis of the forgiveness of sins in the person and work of Christ; this in the *Osiandrian* and *Stancarist* controversies. Upon this there finally follows, thirdly, the discussion of the *subjective appropriation of the Gospel*, and hence of the relation between freedom and grace in the *Synergistic* and *Flacian* controversies, with which the circle of principial questions is complete. In all these questions it is ultimately a middle figure, excluding extremes, which acquires currency in the Church in the *Formula Concordiæ*, though not in every case equally satisfactorily. The extremes of the last controversy conduct to a more definite separation from the Reformed doctrine, which, without passing through these extremes, remains for a longer time unchanged under the influence of the powerful mind of Calvin.

FIRST DOCTRINAL ARTICLE.

The Antinomian and Majorist Controversies, 1527-1559.

These treat of the right relation of morality to religion according to the Reformation principle. The consciousness of the fulness of this principle, of the sufficient power of justification by faith alone, might lead, in the apparent enhancing of its importance, to a religious exclusiveness, to indifference towards morality, to a slothful and eudæmonistic resting in the enjoyment of reconciliation, and thereby to a falsification of the Reformation principle itself. The danger of the absorption of the moral interest into the centrality of a religious principle, idle in itself and unfruitful for sanctification, was averted by the rejection of the different forms and stages of Antinomianism from *Johann Agricola* on to *Nicholas von Amsdorf.* Against the former, the necessity of the law and of repentance *before* conscious faith, that is to say, the *ethical beginning* of faith, was in general established; and against the latter, the necessity of the law and good works *after* instituted faith, that is to say, the *ethical progress* of faith to sanctification, without, however, like *George Major*, deriving salvation from good works.[1]

The more the kernel of Christianity was perceived to lie in the free grace of the forgiveness of sins, in opposition to Romish penances and their legality, the greater became the likelihood of ascribing everything, even repentance, to the gospel,—of letting repentance itself grow first out of evangelical faith, so that the latter, with its subject-matter, might be really the whole, and Christianity abide in its absolute self-sufficiency, according to which it is constituted by nothing outside of or before it. In addition to this, it must always be doubtful, in the question regarding infant baptism, whether saving faith, for which an analogon, as we have seen, was thought to have been found in infants, must always be preceded by repentance. Further, Luther had, in opposition to the Judaistic standpoint, often spoken, in fact strongly enough, regarding the difference between the law and the gospel, "that they are as far apart from one another as heaven and earth," and even that conscience and the law in itself may, through the compulsion and the fear which follows it, be taken by hell to be its confederate. He had also, like Calvin afterwards, acknowledged that repentance in its perfection first proceeded from shame at the outraged love of God and Christ, and in so far from faith, even although it might not be personal (*fides specialis*). To this *Agricola* now held, and violently attacked Melanchthon, when he (see above, p. 219), in the Articles of Visitation of 1527,[2] assigned to the law and to repentance under the law a place before faith. He thus placed himself in opposition to the first attempt to arrange an orderly church, which was impossible without the recognition of the law. He

---

[1] *Luthers Werke von Walch*, xx. 2014. Förstemann, *Neues Urkundenbuch*, 1842. Schlüsselburg, *Catalogus hæreticorum*, tom. iv. Walch, *Religionsstreit in der luth. Kirche*, i. 118, 239, iv. 223. Planck, *Gesch. des protest. Lehrbegr.* ii. 399, v. 1. C. L. Nitzsch, *De Agricolæ Antinomismo*. Elwert, *De Antinomia Agricolæ Islebii*, Tur. 1836. K. J. Nitzsch, *Die Gesammterscheinungen des Antinomismus*, *Stud. u. Krit.* 1846, i. ii.

[2] That which appeared in 1527, and kindled the controversy, was the original Latin draft, published without Melanchthon's knowledge. The German edition, which varied but slightly from the former, was issued by Melanchthon and Luther in the following year. It was based on the experience acquired in the visitation of Saxony, and was designed for that country. It was the first, and might be called the parent, of many similar codes and Church Orders. (See Note p. 118.)—*Tr.*

thought that it threatened too much the unity and completeness of faith, if in any way anything good was acknowledged which did not spring out of faith as the *universum* of the Christian condition. The law of Moses was not necessary for doctrine, neither for the beginning, middle, nor end of justification. The gospel was all-sufficient through the Holy Ghost, which worked conversion by itself without the service of the law, inasmuch as it simply held forth the sacrifice and ransom-price of Christ. The law was scarcely to be called the word of God, and sin did not consist in the offence against the law but in the offence against Christ. The law belonged to the town-hall, not to the pulpit; it served only for outward order. God judged according to faith and unbelief, and therefore could not judge according to the law, else a double codex would be in force. The law did not even prepare the way for the gospel, but God must prepare the way by the gospel for the unbelief of despair. Amongst the followers of Agricola, these utterances were allied with frivolity and presumptuous assurance, especially as he sought a support for his doctrine in the total denial of the *liberum arbitrium*.

Luther, with whom he hoped to be at one in opposition to Melanchthon, seeing that he intended to assure the newness of the gospel and the opposite of everything Judaistic, stood firmly, however, upon Melanchthon's side. This was shown particularly in Luther's six disputations[1] against the destroyers of the law on the occasion of Agricola's second appearance in the field in 1536. Luther explains that faith without a previous operation of the law would be a *deus ex machina*, for if man was absolutely in need of salvation, grace must needs operate magically, supposing that it was without the point of attachment which is furnished in better knowledge and longing. The straining of the newness of the gospel was to form a Manichean conception of the pre-Christian condition,[2] so as to leave no longer any identity between the old and the new man. As a moral process *before* faith could not then be spoken of, so neither could a conflict with sin *after* faith, for the new man would be absolutely a different one from the old, already pure throughout, holy and

---

[1] The public disputations were, strictly speaking, only four in number. Then came a collection of theses against Agricola, and, lastly, a violent refutation of Agricola's defence of his views.—*Tr.*

[2] *Luthers Werke von Walch*, xx. 2056.

perfect. Luther farther points out that if the law were nothing then there would be no sin and guilt, and so punishment would be unjust, and the atoning work of Christ superfluous, nay meaningless. But such a denial of the law would be a relapse not into Judaism but into heathenism, and such an unethical doctrine of grace would lead to a "spiritual epicurism," to the dream of a love without righteousness. This would be simply to institute eternal impenitence and arrogance, and to cover over the plague and poison of sin.[1] Faith, besides, would thus become a good work, indeed, the only good work; and in so far as Agricola nevertheless requires a repentance on account of the offence against the Son, that is to say, a repentance that is the product of faith, in so far would he thereby bring us again under the law. On the contrary, however, the law was fulfilled by Christ and thereby blissfully abrogated; the gospel, accordingly, was the whole, not in the way of excluding the law, but in the way of carrying it in itself, whereby even the appearance of a change in the divine economy was removed. In these remarkable disputations Luther brought out more than anywhere else the ethical character of faith, and so conceived of it not as a separate article, as an act of the will or understanding depriving everything else of value, but as a principle that comprehends Christ in itself, and even thereby the fulfilling of the law, and that proves itself to be a principle by introducing a continuous spiritual dying.[2] After faith, too, the law has still, according to Luther, a place; sin, the knowledge of which is brought by the law, is not essentially removed by justification, but only upon the side of *guilt;* from this, and not from the *punishment,* we should first seek to be freed. If faith thus honours the law by being in the first instance concerned about satisfaction to righteousness, then it must desire also the fulfilling of the law. Agricola made a recantation in 1540.

Melanchthon upheld the law and the moral ideas more and more distinctly, and that in such a way as even to leave again a place for the *liberum arbitrium.* Still it was only after 1535, and the controversy with Cordatus, 1536, that this liberty and the new sanctified personality were brought by him into a closer connection with the work of redemption and salvation. New spiritual obedience was necessary in order to eternal life, because

---

[1] *Disput.* ii. 38; *Luthers Werke* as cited.   [2] *Disput.* iv. 20.

it must follow upon reconciliation with God. He did not let good works be the meritorious cause, but the negative condition (*conditio, causa sine quâ non*) of salvation.[1] Luther impugned Melanchthon's sentence, and he let it drop; but he continued to teach with more and more decision, that free-will too must be active for the work of conversion in the measure in which it, being made free by grace, can now do good works.[2] He never derived justification or salvation from human merit, but only sought to counteract a slothful passivity in the work of salvation. But when negotiations for agreement began with the Catholics at Ratisbon in 1540, and still more in connection with the "Interim," 1548, he allowed, that in those who should be saved there must be a begun obedience, which his Romish opponents did not limit, as he did, to the obedience of faith. Avowing agreement with him, *George Major* asserted, A.D. 1552, that works were necessary to *salvation*, though not to *justification*, since, as *Justus Menius* added, they belong to the *maintenance* of faith. Neither sought to conceive again of works as meritorious, but they could easily be understood as if they made justification to be conditioned by subsequent sanctification, whilst it can operate as the powerful principle of sanctification only when it is the work of free prevenient, unrestricted grace. And when they so distinguish between the forgiveness of sins and salvation, as to make good works the condition of the latter, though not of the former, they made it possible for the conception of the meritoriousness of works to find entrance again ultimately. Luther teaches, "where there is the forgiveness of sins, there is also life and salvation;" that distinction between the forgiveness of sins and salvation was foreign to him; in the present forgiveness of sins he saw already a positive element, the favour of the Father, the source of salvation. This Gallus, Wigand, Amsdorf, Flacius, made good. Luther indeed accepted the possibility of a falling away even in believers, naturally through unfaithfulness, from which it follows, that perseverance in the state of grace until the judgment was not yet implied in the true forgiveness of sins.

[1] *Melanchth. Loci*, 1535. *Opp.* xxi. 376, f. 432. *CR.* iii. 159-162; iv. 1037, of the year 1536. See above, p. 219, f. The *nova spiritualitas* was necessary *ad vitam eternam*. *Opp.* iii. 356.

[2] Whether the *Lib. arb.* co-operate as such, or only through prevenient grace, is a point on which he does not express himself distinctly; at any rate he does not consider it productive. Cf. Galle, *Melanchthon*, p. 319, ff.

But the relapse was necessarily regarded by him as a falling away from faith, and not merely as a defect in sanctification and good works. If faith is really there, it cannot refrain from bringing forth good works. Amongst the Majorists, on the other hand, it might assume the appearance as if true faith could be there without good works. Else they could have been content with requiring this faith as the essential thing for the state of grace, and have left to works the position of being the signs by which faith is known. They evidently did not trust entirely to faith that it would assuredly bring forth fruit wherever it was. This however is connected with a further point; they think with regard to the object of faith principally of the atoning death of Christ only, whilst Luther treats the resurrection of Christ as not less the object of faith, in that he considers the whole person of Christ, and therefore not merely His sin-effacing merit, but also His righteousness and holiness, to be the object of which faith lays hold. Thus Luther has no other faith than one which includes in itself also the principle of the new life. This is the place in which the importance of the active obedience in addition to the suffering is brought out (the *obedientia Christi activa* in addition to the *passiva*). *Melanchthon's* mode of doctrine held rather to the impersonal merit of Christ, and apprehended it preponderatingly as the effacing of guilt; *Luther* adheres rather to the view of the whole person of Christ. Thus in the School of Melanchthon the relation of the forgiveness of sins to sanctification, which was nevertheless necessary, might remain a more accidental and outward one, and a special motive might seem to be necessary so as to secure good works, namely the assertion of the dependence of salvation upon them.

Amsdorf, who was afraid of the all-sufficiency of faith being endangered, encountered *Majorism* in 1559, with the declaration that good works are injurious to salvation;[1] and Andreas *Musculus* said, that the law was probably useful for repentance before faith, but was useless for the regenerate. In this there began a new form of Antinomianism. The earlier form of it had yielded to the perception that a necessary significance belonged to the law *before* faith, since only in this way the relation between the first and second creations as one of mutual connec-

---

[1] Amsdorf; "*That the* propositio: *good works are injurious to salvation, be a right true Christian* propositio." 1559.

tion as well as of difference could be secured against overstraining; but this second form sought to make good the all-sufficiency of faith or of the religious sphere in an exclusive form, at least after faith existed. It sought a motive and a support in those utterances of Luther, which seemed to leave no place any longer to the law for believers, as if its requirements were already fulfilled of itself, as the tree bears fruit and the sun shines of itself. Amsdorf seems, for the rest, only to have meant the confidence in good works, which, however, he held to be almost inseparable from the striving after them.

The *Formula of Concord*[1] decided; good works are necessary because they are commanded and are our duty, as well as the expression of faith and gratitude; but for Christians they have no compulsory necessity and are not to be mixed up with the article upon justification. They effect neither this nor salvation, but are and remain the effects of justifying faith, but necessary effects. Works have an influence only upon the degree of blessedness. That the consciousness of the life of bliss, which flows from the normal development of the personality and is not conceivable without this, belongs also to salvation, finds indeed a place in this formula, but is not more closely considered on account of the [Roman] Catholic doctrine of works.—But with reference to the *law*, the formula of agreement recognizes in addition to the civil use of it (*usu politicus*), also a significance in it for the bringing forth of repentance (*usus pœdeuticus, elencticus*) and for faith an *usus normavus, didacticus*, in that it serves to develop the moral knowledge of the believer, but without its being at liberty to bring man again into bondage. The Old Testament and the New are not distinguished as law and gospel; even in the Old there is the promise, and in the New there is the law; but the law and the promise first reach their perfect form in the New Testament. The legal, *i.e.* the imperative, side even in the New Testament does not give salvation, but the law attains in the person of Christ the form which impels still more distinctly to the gospel. The point of view, on the other hand, according to which Christianity is the religion which carries all truth and therefore also the law in itself, and according to which the law is the reparing of the way, and therefore also the beginning of the appearance, of Christianity for the

[1] *Form. Conc.* 702, 591.

human spirit, is not yet attained in the formula of agreement. But rather, instead of this higher unity of the law and the gospel, which lies in the conception of Christianity as the perfect religion and is of higher importance for the final goal of the Christian, a halt is made at the law and the gospel as two essentially different economies, mutually connected, not in themselves, but only on account of sin, and even thereby at the appearance, as if according to the will of God the economy of the law would have been sufficient, if men had not fallen, and as if, therefore, a twofold determination of man had lain as possible in the counsel of God, a righteousness without the gospel, and one with it. The Pelagianizing consequences of accepting a possible righteousness before God, previously to natural depravity, by the pure freedom of the human will, were escaped by enhancing the original endowments of Adam, in that there was ascribed to him as a divine dowry, which rendered him well-pleasing to God, a natural perfect holiness and righteousness, which indeed passes over again involuntarily into mere innocence, integrity, and good inclination, and so into what the *Apologie* demands. For it is undeniable that this moral perfection still needed confirmation, that is to say, it had still to become one voluntarily willed and asserted.[1]

Of little permanent effect was the Antinomianism of *Poach* and *Otto*,[2] although it represents its most logical form. By faith, say they, we become God's children and gods, participating in the divine nature and in the divine name; what the Christian suffers and does is suffered and done not by him, but by Christ in him. As for the good works also which are done by Christians, it is nothing to them, but only to God. The carnal personality, to which the law comes and belongs, they so completely separate from the new, that they receive two complete men in the one man. But at the same time they will have the believer entirely absorbed into Christ, who takes the place of the new personality, and excludes all unfolding of the personality by this unproductive negative substitution. Perverted and unethical as this conception was, still it made a point against those who thought it to be possible, and even to be the original method, that perfect blessedness would have been attainable by the fulfilling of the law, and without the grace of the Holy Ghost which

[1] *Form. Conc.* 643. Cf. *Apol.* 51.
[2] Schlüsselburg, as cited, iv. 57.

first came in the Gospel. They indeed thought, on the other hand, that the merit of Christ was by no means the fulfilling of the law, that quite a different holiness was given in Christ and by Him than that which the law had demanded; that the righteousness of Christ was not of the law, but above and beyond it (*non ex lege, sed supra et extra legem*). Joachim Mörlin rightly replied, that Christ would then have done something different from that on account of the non-fulfilment of which we are accused by the law, and from that which the law required of us. But then what had been procured by Christ would be something with which we had nothing to do. It was much rather the case that the obedience required by God was none other than that rendered by Christ. Whoever therefore casts away our connection with the law casts away also our connection with Christ. The law and the Gospel agree completely together. The connection between the two was in this distinctly recognized, but still the positive and eternal pointing of the law towards the Gospel, without which the act of faith in Christ would be morally capricious,—that is to say, the perception that the law, rightly interpreted, requires faith in Christ, is not expressed. And as little is this other truth, that the original requirement of the law, which is directed to our personal holiness, finds its fulfilment only in the Gospel.

In the *Lutheran* Church, for the rest, antinomianism, as often as it afterwards reared its head again, attached itself to the all-sufficiency of faith, which there was a fear of prejudicing to some extent, whenever a high spiritual value was set upon anything which was not immediately faith itself again. In the *Reformed* Church, on the other hand, antinomianism attached itself, here and there, to an abstract doctrine of predestination, in such a manner that it was said, that because justification flowed absolutely from the grace and free choice of God, and God loves men only in Christ, therefore He neither hates one on account of his vices nor loves him on account of his holiness. Even without faith the elect were from eternity united with Christ, and faith was not the means of receiving Christ, but only the evidential mark that we have Christ. This conducts us back to the idea that the law in general, and even the acquirement of faith in Christ, is a capricious ordinance of the divine absolute sovereignty,—a view which is moreover by no means limited to the confessors of absolute predestination, but is also elsewhere widely spread, *e.g.*, amongst the Arminians and Socinians; and even in general the supposition that a twofold divine economy, a twofold idea of God regarding the perfect world, is conceivable, is intrinsically connected with it.

SECOND DOCTRINAL ARTICLE.
The Controversies regarding the Object of Faith. A. Osiander and F. Stancarus.[1]

Andreas Osiander forms a side-piece, after a certain fashion, of the antinomianism which makes faith the universum and will not let it be further explicated. In order to evade a doctrine of justification, which concentrates the whole Christian salvation into the imputation which takes place in the divine forum, he seeks an inward appropriation of Christ, more definitely of His divine nature, as the essential righteousness; but he is in no degree more successful in obtaining a productive substitution of Christ or an unfolding of the new personality, but keeps it as it were absorbed into Christ, by a kind of mystic Pantheism. His opponents however, especially *Franz Stancarus*, were quite as onesided in asserting the human nature of Christ, and the Melanchthonic school in asserting the solitary importance of the suffering obedience of Christ, at least for the procuring of salvation, and in making the annulling of punishment and guilt pass for salvation in general.

For Luther himself the object of faith is Christ in the totality of His person, not merely a particular work or suffering of Christ, still less the fruits thereof. Faith enters into a substantial mystical *unio* with the whole person. In that Christ, however, unites Himself to us in faith and dwells in us, we, in adopting Him, have adopted that One in whom obedience and suffering took place for us, and even thus do we receive with Christ also the effects of His life and suffering. We have thus in Him also our positive righteousness, and not merely the forgiveness of sins. This standpoint, characterized at once by unity and universality, which attaches itself in the closest manner to the noblest mysticism, and forms its perfection, is now in the present

---

[1] Planck, iv. 249, ff. Preger, *Flacius*, i. 205-297. The treatises on Osiander by Baur, Ritschl, Grau, Thomasius, *de obedientia Christi activa*, i. ii. The writings of Stancarus, see Salig, *Hist. d. Augsb. Conf.* ii. 714-947.

controversy dissolved into a contrast, in which the two sides separate from one another, each independently, until they are mutually excluded. There thus arose for the Formula of Concord the task of assaying such a form of doctrine as should, whilst recognizing the particular worth of each of the two sides, also comprehend their mutual inward connection.

There could scarcely be conceived a sharper contrast than that between *Melanchthon* and *Andreas Osiander;* the former of a historical and reflective, the latter of a speculative nature; the former intent simply upon what was commonly useful and necessary, the latter obscure, full of genius, but clumsy and full of idiosyncratic stubbornness. The Melanchthonic mode of doctrine—which lays the principal stress upon the merit and work of Christ, and in this upon His atoning death, so that according to it Christ is our righteousness, in so far as He has expiated our guilt by His suffering obedience—was afterwards driven by *Parsimonius* (Karg) in Ansbach, in the year 1563, to such an extent that he completely excluded the active obedience of Christ from His merit as it respects us, because He owed this on His own account. The law required only either fulfilment or punishment, but not both. If Christ's active obedience availed for us, then our obedience was no longer required. The *obedientia Christi activa* had accordingly no substitutionary significance.[1] As early as 1551, *Franz Stancarus*, giving a more definitely Christological application to the matter, said, in a similar manner, that Christ's merit, as it respects us, was a payment which He effected for us by the suffering of His humanity, and therefore the divinity did not come into consideration for the work of redemption, but only His humanity. For if the divinity of Christ came into the matter, then the contradiction arose, that it had at the same time to play the part of the afflicted portion and the part of mediator. Melanchthon now certainly declared himself[2] against this exaggeration of his views, which in the case of Stancarus went the length of caricature, but without advancing beyond that ascendency of the suffering obedience over the active, inasmuch as he had no idea of deriving sanctification in any way from the substitutionary life of Christ in us, but only of placing it under the point of view of restored human freedom.

[1] He recanted 1570. Heshus, Paul Eber, and others opposed him.
[2] Cf. *Opp.* viii. 133. Schlüsselb. *Catalog. Hæret.* ix. 163.

Andreas Osiander in Nuremberg, afterwards called by Duke Albert to Königsberg, belongs still to the Reformers, and stood, through his learning and intellect, in their foremost ranks; he was, through his speculative nature, coloured with mysticism, more nearly related to Luther than to Melanchthon, but without the noble and practical popularity of Luther. It was above all repugnant to him that the principal stress for salvation should fall upon an outward historical transaction, the suffering of Christ fifteen hundred years ago, and that it was always only the work and merit of Christ that were spoken of, and not the person of Christ, with which we should have communion. More frigid than ice, said he, is the doctrine that we are to be regarded as righteous only on account of the forgiveness of sins, and not also on account of the righteousness of Christ which dwells in us by faith. True righteousness must, according to him, be a positive thing. If righteousness consisted only in the ransoming, then we would be made righteous through the mere outward fact that Christ has paid the ransom price, just as when a slave has been ransomed from the Turks, his children are evidently and by nature free from slavery. Then in order to be assured of our justification, faith would scarcely be necessary as a religious act, but only the knowledge of the payment made by Christ for us, of the balance in our favour; we would not need to be, as it were, present at it, in order to become partakers of salvation. The Scriptures, however, set up a higher idea of righteousness; it was not merely freedom from punishment, but essential goodness, even as God (and here he falls back upon his celebrated doctrine of the Divine image) created us from the beginning to be righteous and good in our nature. For not even good works could make us righteous before God. But there is only one kind of goodness, not two kinds. The goodness, which abides before God, is only that which is in God, even God Himself and His nature, and if we would have a righteousness of the creature, that would become idolatry. Man is from the beginning created essentially in need of God in the most pregnant sense; divine nature belongs to his perfection, even as, on the other hand, goodness and righteousness, which is God, is essentially of a self-communicative nature. Even the law already indicates that the righteousness of God will not merely remain in God. Even the law, accordingly, when rightly viewed, requires that we should allow ourselves to be filled by essential righteousness, which is God. But this can only be communicated to us by the incarnation of God; if God did not enter into an equality with us, and come near to us in an apprehensible manner, presenting His righteousness, we in our finiteness could not lay hold of the essential righteousness which we require, even although there were no sin. Therefore the idea of man as it exists in God, the divine image, points already to the incarnation of the Son yet to come, which is the organ whereby we become partakers of His divine nature and power, as the branches in the vine. Through the mediation of the humanity, divinity comes into us (*Per humanitatem devenit in nos divinitas*). On account of sin having been introduced, Christ must certainly procure satisfaction by a suffering and active obedience; but even that obedience was of worth in itself only as an effect of His essential righteousness, for without divinity even the humanity of Christ would be only like a dry branch. The removal of the partition wall of our guilt must certainly precede the indwelling of God; He does not infuse His righteousness so long as we are still under wrath; only that does not yet help us to what is properly good; the thing is first given with the indwelling of Christ, when we live through the essential life of God, are glorified through His essential glory, and are inflamed through His essential love to love towards Him, and on His account towards our neighbour. We come to this through faith, by which we take Christ into our hearts and become members of Christ, in whom God dwells as in Christ, our Head. Faith, however, arises by our first hearing the *Word*. He conceives of the Word as furnished with manifold subject-matter, sufficing for each stage of faith through which we pass, by means of the Word, till we reach essential union with Christ. The word, in the first instance an outward voice and sound, has, for one thing, for its meaning and subject-matter, the forgiveness of sins for Christ's sake; enclosed in the outward word, it is offered to faith. But in this first inner word there lies infolded, germ-like, the second, the eternal Word. With the first, if we keep and understand it, we lay hold also of the essential Word, the divine nature of Christ. The inward thing, the secret of love in the humanity of Christ suffering for us, which we in the first instance lay hold of, is thus His divinity, and, conversely, the eternal real Word of God or the Son has clothed Himself in the human nature of Jesus, clothes Himself also in the outward word, and is present in it for us. The human word contains only the shadow, the divine Word contains the thing itself. God reflects Himself in the Son, whom He begets from eternity, and without whom "God would have been no God, because He would have perceived or known nothing, could not have lived without the Son."[1]

Osiander has been in many respects misunderstood; some, like *Chemnitz*, think that he romanizes, making justification dependent upon sanctification. But no one can call him pelagianizing. For righteousness he considers to be only the gift of the divine self-communication, and even works he considers to have, as outward, no worth in themselves. The divine nature of Christ he regards as our righteousness, not so far as it calls forth new movements or is operative; but it is in itself righteous, although, too, it cannot be idle. *Flacius* understood him more correctly, inasmuch as he sees that he makes everything depend upon habitual righteousness, upon the condition of holiness, and the quality of being,[2] not upon doing. But even Flacius is essentially in the wrong in opposition to him, for he holds that the righteousness which the law requires, and for which accordingly Christ needed to render substitutionary satisfaction, seeing that we had failed to fulfil it, is not a being, but a doing of good; that the law requires actual righteousness, not merely the inward ability to bring forth fruits, else the required righteousness would be a $\varphi v \sigma \iota \kappa \acute{o} v$. The obedience of man was a service due on the part of man towards God, creatural righteousness, not a gift of God, else there would be neither guilt nor merit. Hence even the essential righteousness of Christ could not help us, although this co-operated in the actual obedience of Christ, upon which, for the law of God, everything depends, and which, by means of substitution, necessarily benefits us. If everything depended only on the essential righteousness of Christ, righteousness would have been present already from the very birth of Christ; whilst he had rather to *procure* it, and this was to become our righteousness. Whilst it ought to be recognized that Flacius lays great weight upon the actuality of the person of Christ, whilst he also

[1] Andr. Osiander, *Ein gut Unterricht und getreuer Rathschlag aus heiliger Schrift*, 1524. *Von d. einigen Mittler J. Chr. u. Rechtfert. d. Glaubens*, 1551.
[2] Cf. Preger, *Flacius Illyr.* 1859. Bd. i. 222, ff.

exhibits admirably the inward inseparable unity of the *obedientia Christi activa* and *passiva*, still it is superficial in Flacius not to allow a reference of the law of God to the being, but only to the doing,—a view narrower even than that of the Old Testament, —or, for the same reason, not to allow the person of Christ to be our righteousness, but only His work, instead of seeing in the work the living actuality of the person. If this view were pursued, all the mysticism of faith would be dissolved, and the life-communion of man with God, viewed as a state, would, in a romanizing manner, be placed in the background by means of the active character of the actual fulfilling of the law. Flacius held indeed, in addition to the atonement, also the indwelling of God and Christ, but the latter can only preserve in his view an accidental importance. He must needs have been guarded against this error by the fact, that the law rejects not merely actual evil, but also an evil condition, natural depravity.

It is more to the point, upon this side of it, when *Melanchthon* objects to Andreas Osiander that he speaks as if the forgiveness of sins, which faith receives with the new life, were nothing particular. In fact it is not the forgiveness of sins which is for *Andreas Osiander* the turning-point of the inward life, but only the indwelling of God, "essential righteousness" (*justitia essentialis*). Melanchthon's *Opinion* further finds fault with Osiander for laying as much stress upon the indwelling of God, as if no one before him had taught anything of the new life of faith and the presence of God in believers. But, on the other hand, there can be no mistake that in the case of Melanchthon and his school, this inward self-communication of Christ, which plants the new life, was put behind the forgiveness of sins, and that the connection between the forgiveness of sins for the sake of the merit of Christ and the restored real freedom and holiness is not sufficiently evident. But when Melanchthon, in order to conceive the atoning work of Christ in its whole perfection, applies it also to sins of omission, when for the sake of the all-sufficiency of this merit he teaches that Christ has made satisfaction for all our sins of omission, past and future, there had still to be destroyed the appearance as if it were a matter of indifference and superfluity whether a holy life still followed upon our side.

Finally, a different judgment was given by the Swabians, who were called to Prussia by Duke Albert to adjust the controversy, *Brenz* and *Christoph Binder*, who came to the help of the much-assailed man with a view to opening the way for an understanding with him. They could justly point to misunderstandings arising from the ambiguity of the same formulas, even as on the other hand the actually existing community of doctrine was hidden by the variety of formulas. They said, both parties sought to derive reconciliation as well as sanctification from Christ through faith, only Osiander called holiness *justificatio, justitia essentialis*, and conversely, what the others meant by *justificatio*, he had in his ransom (*redemptio*). But still the difference in Osiander's way of speaking is connected with the circumstance, that he lays less weight upon the atonement, and therefore puts aside the word, which describes the oriflamme of the Reformation, for something else, namely regeneration (*renovatio*). Recognizing that the forgiveness of sins is the first momentum, he has nevertheless failed even more than his opponents to show its connection with the divine indwelling; he has not stated how one can be certain of being a partaker of the divine nature, and he thus loses for the consciousness the transition-point from the old to the new life, inasmuch as the change in being is transacted as it were behind the consciousness, whilst the new spiritual movements in faith, love, hope, are yet not so constant and pure that the new divine existence could thereby make itself known to the consciousness in a sure and uninterrupted manner. There is undeniably an ethical trait in Osiander, when he will neither rest content with an historical faith, nor with the mere knowledge, communicated through the outward word, of Christ's paying the ransom price for us, and the imputation of this merit. But with all his zeal against a merely imputed righteousness, in which God is to look upon men otherwise than they are in truth, he does not reach this point, that the essential divine righteousness becomes a truly human righteousness and man himself a righteous and holy causality. The new personality remains, in his view, absorbed into Christ, into His divine nature; Christ's substitution too is, according to his estimate, absorptive, in no way productive, even as he has not defined faith in any degree ethically. And with regard to the object of faith, he is quite right in this, that faith does not merely lay hold of Christ's ransom-price, does not merely rely upon His work, but attaches itself to His person, but then he himself clings not so much to the whole person of Christ as to His divine nature. The human nature is according to him only an impersonal means of presentation, the phenomenal form of the divine nature, no causality for the procuring of salvation through obedience and virtue. In this Flacius makes an important Christological point against him; in general, however, Osiander makes the ethical element lie only in the being, quite as onesidedly as Flacius only in the doing. What would a holy being, or a love be, which does not love? Love exists not without acting, although the act only reveals the nature. What would be left of an essential righteousness or a divine nature, which was conceived of without actual loving? Nothing further than the conception of a lofty, divinely noble existence, of a dignity, which remained idle, and called out Antinomian self-enjoyment.

The *Swabians* came too late; *Osiander* died suddenly in 1552, but the controversy lasted for ten years afterwards. His principal adherent, the court-preacher *Funck*, died upon the scaffold.[1] The *Corpus doctrinæ Pruthenium* proscribed his doctrine. The circumstance that on the side of the opponents, the subsequent apostate Staphylus, Stancarus, and Mörlin, there was, instead of a thorough explanation of their respective doctrine, above all an endeavour to depose Osiander,—that circumstance had this unfortunate effect, that many now sought to separate sharply from another, even in the description of the subjective process of salvation, the *Justificatio* and the *Renovatio*, which (as a subjective condition) were very closely linked together in the Augustana and Apology, as well as by Luther. And this was done by them even without the *Justificatio forensis* being treated as the basis of the free proclamation of salvation, and even of the whole subjective process of salvation, and therefore as at the same time the beginning whose terminus must be sanctification.[2] In this way, too, *fides* acquired a onesided regard to the historical merit of Christ, whilst it must be the initiation of a life-communion with the whole Christ. The *Form. Conc.* has only partly succeeded in obviating this misfortune.

But yet the idea of *fides*, which became supreme in the *Form. Conc.*, in which the Swabians, who had a more friendly disposi-

---

[1] In 1566, as an heretic and disturber of the peace.—*Tr.*

[2] The *justificatio* was placed behind the *Conversio Regeneratio*. See below.

tion towards Osiander had a prominent share, is by no means one which does away with the mysticism of faith. Esteemed theologians, too, like Justus Menius and Aepin of Hamburg expressly described the divine judicial utterance (*Justificatio forensis*) not as an empty declarative act, but as a *facere*, understanding by it a communication of the divine favour and grace, an introduction into divine childhood.[1] With respect to the work of Christ, the active obedience of Christ is given prominence to by the *Form. Conc.* in opposition to the Melanchthonic school, and the suffering in opposition to Osiander. The actual complete obedience of Christ, transferred to believers, makes them righteous before God. Faith itself lays hold, however, of the person of Christ, *certainly as it is revealed and exhibited in its work*.[2] By means of the substitution of Christ we are not merely free from guilt, but stand also as holy before God.[3] We are not indeed to know that we are righteous and holy by our having holiness already as our nature, but rather by means of the substitutionary righteousness of Christ, with which we are connected in faith.[4] But Christ, dwelling in us by faith is not idle; He produces also righteousness of life. Good works (*bona opera*) are always present at the same time *with* true faith, and do not merely follow it.[5] But they dare never be called our

---

[1] Thomasius, *De obedientia Christi activa*, ii. 25, 1846.

[2] *Form. Conc.* 585, 6. There is an *essentialis inhabitatio Christi et Trinitatis* not merely *operativa præsentia*.

[3] *Form. Conc.* as cited. In this it was not asserted to be necessary, as by Aepin, that Christ suffered punishment in hell. *F. C.* 788.

[4] The same, 584, 4. 585, 9.

[5] The question suggested in the Majorist controversy, whether *bona opera*, i.e. *bona motus*, must not be present already in true faith, although they do not justify, but only free grace does, is here answered in the affirmative; and even sec. 17 remained, especially in the theology of Jena, a recognized tenet; good works are present in faith (*bona opera præsentia in fide*). Cf. *C. F.* 586, 11. On the other hand, indeed the F. C. says even more frequently that *Regeneratio* or *Renovatio* only follows upon *Justificatio* (685, 18. 688, 28. 692, 41); which has a good meaning, if by *justificatio* is meant the divine pardon which is already presented in the Word, as well as if it be asked, which first comes within the sphere of *consciousness*. Objectively, however, or looking at the *reality*, faith according to *F. C.* enters at once into life-communion with the person of Christ, whereby it receives also a positive participation in His holiness. Later times have held more to the class of passages, in which the bond between *Justificatio* and sanctification appears to be looser. If the *Justificatio* as *forensis* has not its objective, fundamental position in God, *in foro Dei*, secured before faith, and if it is spoken of first within the subjective process of salvation, the consequence is that either justifi-

justification; this is in more exact dogmatical language to be distinguished from the *Renovatio* and regeneration (*Regeneratio*). The former is effected through the high-priestly total obedience of Christ; regeneration and sanctification point back to the kingly activity of Christ, the communication of the Holy Ghost.

In order to make the active obedience of Christ and His merit as it were disposable for the substitution in our room, the *Form. Conc.* deemed it necessary to say, that Christ, although God-man, did not owe obedience, for He was Lord of the law, even according to His humanity, in virtue of the communication to it of the divine predicates (*communicatio idiomatum*). But there lay in this an objectionable approximation to the doctrine of superfluous merit, as well as to the opinion, that what is good is without an inward necessity for the nature and will of God, inasmuch as God rather stands above the law (is *exlex*). The *Form. Conc.* thus came into contradiction with itself, since it has the wit to make good in other parts, in an admirable way, that the law is not something capricious, but its requirements are necessary according to the nature of God. Upon this point there still manifest themselves remnants of Romish views of the ethical, and a defect in the working out of ideas. If, in order that the obedience of Christ may have a substitutionary significance, it must be said that the God-man did not require to be holy for Himself, but in that He was so, obtained a disposable surplus, which He could distribute to believers, as he did not need it for Himself, then it must, as a logical consequence be said,—from which the *Form. Conc.* is very far removed,—that we do not need now to be obedient to the law, because He has already performed for us what is necessary. On the contrary, it is because the God-man was entirely what He should be, a perfected personality even in relation to the law, that He is capable of standing in the room of humanity in substitutionary love and self-communication, and of thus exercising a productive substitution.

This leads to the *Christological negotiations.* Melanchthon never shared the Christological views held by Luther in the time of the controversy on the Supper. The incarnation con-

---

cation or sanctification is prejudiced, whilst least of all does it come to be seen that the former is the principle of the latter; for within the subjective process the simultaneity of both is necessarily established, if faith is directed to Christ in His unity. See p. 359, and Book ii.

sists, according to him, in the adoption of the human nature into the *person* of the Logos, not however in the union (*Unio*) of the *nature* of the Logos with the *nature* of humanity in a real communication of the predicates of the former to the latter. The *communicatio idiomatum* is according to him only a dialectical or verbal one: the person of the Logos is the person of the whole Christ, and supports the humanity as its organon. Whether, if the nature and predicates of the Logos do not become proper to the humanity, the person of the Logos does not according to its infinite nature form an obstacle to the participation in it of the humanity, upon this question he does not enter more minutely. What would be left for the *Unio*, if neither the person nor the nature of the Logos has become proper to humanity? There would then only remain either a theophany, or a man who was in a peculiarly close manner connected with the Logos through the *will* of the latter.

Luther, on his side, as already shown, had indeed from the beginning emphasized the unity of the God-man, together with a real *communicatio idiomatum*, but also the true human *growth* [*Werden*] of Christ, especially previously to the controversy on the Supper. Nor was the latter afterwards retracted by him; on the contrary, he expressed himself in 1527 in a similar way to what he had formerly done.[1] But these two sides of the matter he never moulded into each other, and hence after his death they at once separated from one another again. Of these two parties the Melanchthonic—to which the Lower Saxons, with *Martin Chemnitz* at their head, also belong in respect of their Christology—held more to the earlier exposition of Luther, which sought a place for the growth of Christ, but did so in such a way as to deny the capacity of the human nature for divinity, which Luther never doubted; whilst the Swabian school, with *Brenz* and *Jacob Andreä* at their head, held firmly by this capacity of the human nature (*capacitas humanæ naturæ*) for the divine, and worked out the idea of it, but in doing so attached themselves to that form of Christological doctrine which Luther had asserted in the controversy on the Supper, but had never afterwards expounded on its own account.[2] The *Form. Conc.* sought, certainly prematurely, to adjust these differences also.

[1] Köstlin, as cited, ii. 390-402. Cf. *Erl. Ausg.* 47, 362.
[2] Köstlin, the same, 400.

Brenz rightly says that the idea of the God-man is not yet solved, if only a *presence* of the Son in Jesus is spoken of. Nor is it enough even that He is in Christ personally, for He is everywhere personally. Everything must depend upon what is common to the Man Jesus and to the Logos, and since Divinity can lose nothing and can receive nothing, everything rests upon what the *humanity* receives through and from the Logos, that is to say, upon the real *communicatio idiomatum*. This thing imparted by the Logos is called the *Majestas* of the humanity, under which all divine properties are embraced; and the many Christological writings of the Swabians treat, for more than fifty years from this date, of the *Majestas* of the human nature of Christ. Those properties (*idiomata*) however are not to be thought of as disjoined from the Divine nature, but their complex is the Divine nature itself. That is to say, the latter is according to one side of it communicable, and that is the *divinitas communicabilis*; everything in it is communicable, only not the self-existence (the *Aseity*), and this constitutes the eternal difference between God and the world.[1] The humanity of Christ, however, was one which truly grew; and the necessary counterpart of this is, as Luther formerly brought out distinctly, that the communication of God to Jesus was not to be forthwith placed as absolute already in the child, but that the Logos rather restricted His communication to the humanity, and His operation upon it, according to the measure and the stages of the capacity of the humanity and according to its laws. Even Christ's work of redemption demanded a not merely seeming humiliation, and Luther never ceased to emphasize this in the strongest manner, and especially the soul-suffering and the temptations of Christ,[2] without however ever going so far as a humiliation of the Logos Himself. But the Swabians taught, in opposition to *Bullinger* and *Theod. Beza*, that the humanity possessed, even in the very moment of its origin, the whole majesty and exaltation to the right hand of the Father, that the

---

[1] This communication of the Divine Majesty Luther had, for the sake of the Supper (see above, p. 322), established as absolutely complete from the act of incarnation (*Unio*), although he did not wish to deny thereby the true human growth of Christ. The Divine Majesty, in particular omnipresence, belongs to the humanity from the conception. This was now developed by the Swabians; but, on the other hand, they let the other side, and that which this requires, fall completely into the background.

[2] Köstlin, as cited, ii. 400, 401.

incarnation was already in itself the ascension, and this latter only an outward transaction which should show what already was. In His mother's womb the body of Christ was also already omnipresent; when He went anywhere, He was in His humanity properly there already; risen from the grave he was in His humanity still in the grave; whilst He hung upon the cross, he was also in Athens, and ruled omnipresently the world.[1] Thus the birth of Christ, His movements, His resurrection and ascension, became only an epideiktic action, a Docetism, which threatens to dissolve completely the condition of humiliation, the learning and growth. At the same time, in order to preserve the truthfulness of the sufferings of Christ, they would speak also of a growing, suffering, and exalted humanity of Christ alongside of one that was from the beginning omniscient, omnipotent, and omnipresent. Thus this very energetic striving after the unity of the Person of the God-man ended rather in a double humanity of Christ, a dualism, which renewed all the problems and absolutely rent asunder again the unity of the Person. Afterwards they sought to restore the unity in this way, that they posited an act of renunciation on the part of the humanity partaking of the Divine Majesty, whereby it was placed on an equality with vulgar humanity, nay, was itself humiliated. But in what period should this renunciation on the part of the humanity fall? Since the existence of the humanity in Mary begins with humiliation, a humiliation that was produced by renunciation on the part of humanity would lead back to an *Unio* in the pre-existent state of Christ, contrary to the *F. C.* 785, 85, to a pre-existent glorious humanity of Christ. But if Christ was really God-man in glory before the conception by Mary, then she is not truly His mother, but only the transition channel for Him, and His connection with our race is only a seeming one.—The solution of an act of renunciation on the part of Divinity of the possession or use of its attributes,[2]

[1] Cf. Dorner's *Gesch. der Christologie*, ii. 680. (Translation div. ii. vol. 2, p. 181.)

[2] The reference is to the κένωσις doctrine, propounded by Thomasius, professor at Erlangen. The ingenuity, speculative power, and dogmatic skill displayed in its construction cannot be denied, and it has been accepted in a greater or less degree by Hofmann, Delitzsch, Liebner, Oehler, and others. By none has it been so ably, and even keenly controverted, as by Dorner (see his *History of the Doctrine of the Person of Christ*, translated in *Clark's Library;* Division II. vol. iii. p. 331). A detailed reply to Dorner's critique is to be found in the second edition of Thomasius' *Dogmatik.—Tr*.

which might have been thought of, was considered by all without distinction, the Anabaptists perhaps excepted, to be a heathenish error. *F. C.* 612, 39; 773, 49; 781, 71.

This original Swabian Christology was opposed by *Martin Chemnitz* in his famous book, *De duabus Christi naturis*, 1570, though he did so gently and without naming the Swabians. He adopts the forgotten earlier tenet of Luther, with which Melanchthon also agreed, that the condition of humiliation and of growth must be a truth, and that accordingly it may not be said that the Logos absolutely completed the communication of Himself from the beginning of this man. On the contrary, he teaches that the *comm. idiom.* alway took place only as far as the laws of humanity and its separate successive stages allowed. The Logos maintained during the state of humiliation an attitude of repose, not communicating Himself absolutely to the humanity and operating in it, although not on that account giving up His operation in the world and His *Unio* with Jesus. But in general—and in this he diverged from Luther and approached more to the Wittenbergians, and even the Reformed theologians of that day— the *unio* might not, even for the estate of exaltation, be conceived of as so intimate as the Swabians would have it. The communication of the Divine nature and attributes might not lead to confusion, or to a Schwenkfeldian compromise (*exæquatio*), and therefore it must be said that the humanity could not receive the divine attributes in general to be in such a manner its own that they belonged to it *habitualiter, formaliter, subjective*. A real transference of the divine attributes to it did not take place; that would be an objectionable *communicatio physica, effusio;* but there was rather a co-existence and co-operation of the divine nature and the human, whereby the latter had its own excellences enhanced. The human nature in general was not *capax divinæ naturæ*. Whilst this is an agreement with the Reformed theologians, he immediately added to it what is indeed little in accordance with his other statements, as the Reformed theologians like Beza, Chandieu (Sadeel), and Danäus did not omit to discover, that the humanity of Jesus had nevertheless, by means of the contranatural and supernatural union (*Unio paraphysica et hyperphysica*), received, over and above, higher, we might say God-like attributes; and so the capability of being corporeally present in several places at once (*multipræsentia*) and the presence of Christ in the Supper according to His promises was thereby secured. But this omnipresence, or more properly multipresence of Christ, was in his view no physical necessity, but was only hypothetical, remaining subject to His will, and it was in no way, as the Swabians held, given immediately and absolutely in the *Unio.*

The negotiations between the Swabians and the Lower-Saxons issued in this compromise, that Chemnitz conceded a secret *possession* of the divine attributes on the part of the human nature from the moment of the *Unio,* whereby, if we consider that omnipresence and omniscience do not depend upon the will, but that they are essentially actual, there was conceded the Swabian doctrine of the omnipresence and omniscience of the humanity of Jesus from the beginning; whilst, on the other side, the Swabians allowed the actual possession on the part of the human nature to be again placed in question, inasmuch as they, in contradiction to their statement regarding the *capacitas humanæ naturæ* (*F. C.* 611, 34), allowed that the divine attributes are not merely above, but contrary to, human nature (*supra* and *contra naturam humanam, F. C.* 762, 4; 773, 50; 775, 54; 606, 28). Even the bond of aspiration on the part of the human nature after the divine would be thereby excluded, and the *Unio* could never become an inward one. The Swabians, on the other hand, got passages carried through, according to which an omnipresence of the body of Christ existed necessarily from the beginning in virtue of the *Unio,* being of itself given in that *Unio;* whilst other passages,[1] in deference to Chemnitz, go back upon the will of Christ. In the very nature of the case the passages of the second class were rendered illusory by those of the first. The Swabians, however, insisted in general, as in the matter of the omnipresence, upon this, that the humanity of Christ must from the beginning have made, although secretly, yet a complete *use* ($\chi\rho\hat{\eta}\sigma\iota s$) of the possession of the divine attributes, which possession alone Chemnitz would concede, whilst certainly a possession (for example) of omniscience without the exercise of it would be difficult to conceive.

This, then, is that which—to connect a further controversy at once with the foregoing—the *Tübingen Cryptists, Theodor Thumm, Lucas Osiander,* and others, made zealous use of in the

[1] *Form. Conc.* 608, 16.

controversy with the *Giessen Kenotists, Balthasar Menzer, and Justus Feuerborn* (which is an after-effect of the still remaining dissonances so laboriously concealed in the *Form. Conc.*). North Germany, where the necessary and absolute omnipresence of the body of Christ and the use of the divine prerogatives on the part of the humanity were never in general really received, had already previously witnessed a rehearsal of this controversy in the Helmstädt divines *Tilemann Heshus* and *Daniel Hoffmann*, who placed themselves in antagonism to the promoters of the *Form. Conc.*, partly in respect of their authority, partly of their signification, and in their turn taught the multipresence or hypothetical omnipresence of Chemnitz, which was obscured in the *Form. Conc.*, but at the same time the *possession* of all the divine attributes on the part of the humanity from its beginning.

To the *Giessen* divines belongs the praise of having sought to retain still some place for a true humanity, at least by their disputing the *use* of the divine attributes, which the human nature possessed from the beginning.[1] There followed the Saxon *Decisio*, which came out (A.D. 1624) full of assumption, originating in particular from *Matthias Hoë* of *Hoënegg*, which declares in the main for the Giessen Kenotists, but receives, even in the earthly life of Christ, a sporadic revelation of the Majesty through the humanity. The Kenoticism, which in spite of the *Form. Conc.* became prevalent in North Germany, supposes for the estate of humiliation a reservation of the operation of the Logos in Jesus, that is to say, seeing that a self-emptying of the Logos continues to be regarded as unworthy, a working by itself of the unchangeable Logos, so far as the humanity cannot yet, according to its law of life, make use of the possession which became its own through the *Unio* with the Logos. Hence the formula of the old Lutheran orthodoxy, that after the *Unio* the Logos was no longer outside of the humanity (*logos non extra carnem*), receives here a more restricted meaning than in the hands of the Tübingen divines, namely this, that the Logos, although always omnipresently operative (which the humanity was not, in spite of the possession of the Majesty), is personally connected only with the humanity of Christ,[2] and that in such a way, even as the most orthodox dogmatic theologians teach,

---

[1] From 1619; cf. my *Christology*, ii. 788. (Trans. div. ii. vol. 2, p. 293.)
[2] Cf. *Præsentia extima* and *intima* in *Ægid. Hunnius, de persona Chr.*

that His person is communicated also to the humanity and is become the person of the humanity, and the latter accordingly is made personal. This personal existence of the Logos in humanity makes Jesus accordingly the central locality of the operation of the Logos in the world in general.

In consequence of extravagances already mentioned in the doctrine of the Tübingen theologians, the Swabians lost in the seventeenth century the hegemony, which they had acquired in the second half of the sixteenth. Logically they must have reached, as has been shown, a heavenly humanity of Christ, a humanity which He had had before His birth, and which He had only transposed by self-privation into the estate of humiliation, or still more plainly a double humanity of Christ. Thus the way adopted by the Swabians, in order to preserve the unity, landed one on every side in shallows, where there was neither going forwards nor backwards; the whole mode of reckoning led irresistibly to these contradictions in the sum, and accordingly a perfectly new mode of reckoning was seen to be requisite. But the others, too, come no better speed, who are more concerned for the truth of the humanity and of the estate of humiliation. The premises of the Swabians (the Cryptists) regarding the absolute possession of the divine properties from the beginning of the human nature, were shared by the Kenotists, and they lagged behind the Swabians only in logical consistency. If the humanity was in possession of omniscience, how could it learn? If it was unchangeable, incapable of suffering like God, how could it grow and suffer? It is evident that a limitation of the *comm. idiom.* was absolutely requisite, if a real humanity was to be left, and also that it could not at once really receive all that of which it is, according to its idea, capable, but the measure of the divine self-communication must be determined according to the receptivity of each stage.

In spite of the discordances still left in the *Form. Conc.* with its premature decision (which was no decision) its doctrine secured all that was necessary to a complete system, namely, that the two natures remained unchanged according to their substance, and that the divine did not receive human attributes, for it is unchangeable and perfect. It would be *blasphemia* to say that the Logos himself was emptied, or that Jesus had even according to His divinity laid aside the power and majesty in order to receive it again in the estate of exaltation.[1] But still the union was inexpressibly inward, inasmuch as the humanity received, as communicated through the incarnation, everything that the Logos had, the nature, the person, and the attributes. This possession had been applied as the mediatorial work required; but there was requisite a co-operation of both natures, of each according to its kind. It was matter of comfort to us, that we needed not to behold in Christ bare Divinity, which would consume us, but that He through His humanity is and evermore remains accessible to us, and that, although God cannot suffer, still the sufferings of Jesus have also an at least mediate reference to the divine nature.

THIRD DOCTRINAL ARTICLE.

The Synergistic and Flacian Controversies regarding Anthropology aud Soteriology.[2]

At the outset *Melanchthon* (see above, p. 219, ff.) allowed himself to be carried away from *Luther*, in the interests of the absolute need of salvation, to a complete denial of free-will in a moral aspect (*liberum arbitrium*); but the more he comprehended this peculiarity of his own, the less was his highly-developed ethical judgment able to rest content with it. Led by his historical and church tact, as well as in the interests of the moral consciousness, he had already in the *Augustana* taught almost nothing regarding predestination, recognized the *liberum arbitrium* in civil matters, and laid the chief stress upon the absolute inability of man in *spiritual* matters. But this he kept separated from the doctrine of absolute predestination and from the metaphysical question, whether anything is accidental. He also maintained the universality of the promise of grace. All this is characteristic of the subsequent tendency of the Lutheran formation of doctrine.

These statements awakened no stir during Luther's lifetime. But after the Gnesio-Lutheran party of the so-called *Thuringian theologians*, Amsdorf, Flacius, Gallus, Wigand, &c., had been formed, whose number supplied the lack of a head of equal rank

[1] *Form. Conc.* 612, 39 ; 773, 49 ; 781, 71.
[2] Twesten, *Matth. Flacius Illyricus*, 1844. Salig. i. 648-651. Planck, iv. 553, f. ; v. 285. Schmid, *Zeitschr. f. Hist. Theol.* 1849. Preger, as cited, i. ii.

with Melanchthon, and who found a centre in the newly instituted University of *Jena*, the opposition to Melanchthon and the so-called *Meissen* theologians extended even to the soteriological question. Alongside of Flacius and Amsdorf in Jena there was the Melanchthonian *Victorin Strigel;* and there arose in that place a very violent controversy.

Already previously to this, *Pfeffinger*, a pupil of Melanchthon, had asserted that there is a certain cause in us, why some comply with the gospel, and others not.[1] *Flacius* and *Amsdorf* opposed him. "If the choice lies in man, to comply with the divine call or not, then there is naturally free-will for spiritual things (*liberum arbitrium in spiritualibus*), the doctrine of natural depravity is false, and man can of his own power prepare himself for grace. But man must much more by nature resist grace. If any one therefore is saved, it is a pure work of grace without the intervention of the *liberum arbitrium* at any point." The Jena theologians wrought upon their prince, Johann Friedrich, so as to procure the framing of a confutation of the tenets of Pfeffinger. Flacius succeeded in giving effect to his own doctrine instead of the view of Strigel, and when Strigel declared against it, he did penance for it in prison. The Flacian party abused their success in the most violent manner, *e.g.* by their ill-treatment of the pious and learned jurist, Wesenbeck, to such an extent that the University threatened to become deserted. Hence Johann Friedrich, in order to create peace, instituted a *colloquy at Weimar*, in 1560. Strigel and Flacius were pitted against one another. The former rejected, indeed, Pelagianism and Semi-pelagianism, but asserted that the *liberum arbitrium* was only restricted and injured but not altogether removed by original sin,—"sin has a confining effect upon it as the juice of darnel upon the magnet (*allium magneti illitum*);" if the restriction was only removed, the power for good revived again of itself. Natural depravity was no corruption of the substance, but only an accident attaching to the substance. Flacius replied, then sin would be a mere external addition, whereas it had laid hold of and penetrated the substance; regeneration too would be a mere liberation of already existing powers for good, and the new in Christianity would be no longer a real substance. Man was not merely seemingly dead, but like a

[1] Pfeffinger, *Proposit. de lib. arbitrio.* 1555. Planck, iv. 469, ff.; v. 1.

lifeless statue; in the reception of grace he occupied a purely passive attitude, nay of himself he resisted grace, and was converted while resisting it. Before a different and compliant will was given by God in place of the resisting will, man could do nothing else than reject grace. Strigel rejoined, if then natural depravity could not be called an accident attaching to the substance, was it itself a substance? Flacius at first declined the question as a philosophical one; but when pressed answered it in the affirmative. "Original sin is a substance, because otherwise holiness would not be a substance; the soul is by nature a mirror or image of Satan, it is original sin (*peccatum originale*), although not thus disfigured without the decree of God."[1] It was easy for Strigel to deduce from the absolute denial of freedom also the annihilation of the guilt of unbelief. Since, moreover, Strigel now condescended to a milder declaration of his doctrine—which was recognized as orthodox by the Swabians, Andreä, and Binder in 1562, and which was to the effect that the power of man for good was completely bound by original sin, and salvation did not stand within his own ability, that he was robbed of the divine image and maimed, but yet conversion took place in the form of will and consciousness, his *capacitas* being not merely *passiva* but a mode of acting (a *modus agendi*),—Strigel was acquitted, and the accusation was now directed against the accuser.

Flacius did not intend to teach what was properly Manichäism; he drew a distinction between two substantial forms in men, the physical and the theological; the former remained, only the latter was lost; he does not accordingly accept an evil matter or substance, but only an essential evil form cleaving to man; he also leaves to man what belongs to his physical nature unchanged in spite of original sin; and his meaning is properly only this twofold idea, that *holiness* belongs to the nature of man, *i.e.* to his idea essentially and not merely accidentally, and that therefore *sin* is to be looked upon not simply as a superficial power, but as one destructive of that ethical nature. This only served to make plain, how unsatisfactory are those abstract categories of substance and accident for the ethical province. But his restless,

---

[1] Flacius, Heshus, Amsdorf, and others were absolute predestinarians; man conducted himself *mere passive*, nay manifestly *repugnative* to converting grace. Spangenberg, Cölestin, Irenäus, and others, agreed with Flacius.

obstinate, inquisitorial nature, of which even the more modern attempts to rescue the honour of his name do not clear him, manifested itself even now, and brought about his fall. The fear of his doctrine being adulterated, united to a self-consciousness, which was not without foundation, but was overstrained, operated prejudicially to the very man who had sought to assign himself the position of orthodox judge of all others. He was deposed with forty-seven adherents, and died in 1575, in poverty.

The *Formula of Concord* decided both against the Semi-pelagianism, which allows the work of salvation to begin by means of good human powers of themselves, and also[1] against the opinion that whilst God indeed must begin the work, still man is only severely maimed and half-dead, so that, when the Holy Ghost has made the beginning through the Word and gift of grace, the human will can with its own natural powers aid its conversion somewhat, although only very little, can be a fellow-worker, follow up grace and believe the Gospel; in short, can with its own natural powers co-operate with the Holy Ghost in the carrying on and maintenance of the work of salvation. What is objected to, accordingly, is the so-called Synergism, or the opinion that man can alone with his natural powers effect one part of the work of salvation, whilst the other, certainly by far the greater, remains in the hands of grace. Thus Pfeffinger had, said, grace is related to what we work just so as if a handsome score were paid for one, but he himself could only contribute a farthing. In this, however, although the human good performance was thought of as the smallest, still the fundamental relation between grace and the powers of man was incorrectly defined. For the activity of man was not regarded as originally receptive, but was placed alongside of God as a productive causality, and the divine working was distinguished from the human only in degree; the matter was divided, although unequally, between the two, which is the [Roman] Catholic fundamental error. The Formula of Concord rightly opposes this by saying, there may not be any division of such a kind that anything whatever belongs exclusively to the human will and its goodness, and the Holy Ghost is excluded even only from a minimum, but the work of salvation is rather from its beginning to its completion possible only through the communicative grace of God. But it is not intended

[1] *Form. Conc.* 581, 11; 677, 77.

thereby to say, that the powers, which the Holy Ghost step by step sets free, awakens, or communicates (the *liberum arbitrium liberatum*), must not from that moment co-operate; they are indeed not powers of the natural man, but the Holy Ghost works in them. The whole work of salvation can and ought to proceed under the form of human will and consciousness, and even the working of the Holy Ghost does not exclude the human act. His action is rather one which induces the act; He makes the unwilling willing (*ex nolentibus facit volentes*). Conversion is accordingly, excepting the first impulse, in every part of it human and divine work at the same time.[1] The whole spirit of the Evangelical Confession was completely antagonistic to a magical process of salvation. When Melanchthon's three concurrent causalities in regeneration, *Spiritus Sanctus, verbum, hominis voluntas*, are reduced by the *Form. Conc.* to the first two, there is understood by causality the productive cause, but the mediatory is not excluded. This is made particularly plain by the rejection of Flacianism.[2] The *modus agendi*, it is now said, the form of the human will, is required for repentance and conversion; but in the regenerate themselves free-will co-operates with the Holy Ghost; in them it too becomes a productive causality.[3] Further, it may not be said, that the will of man before conversion (*conversio*) and in it resists the Holy Ghost, and that the latter is given to those who are stiff-neckedly striving against Him.[4] This can be reconciled with the doctrine in other places regarding original sin and the necessity of evil resistance only in this way: that previously to faith there is received a preparation by the Holy Ghost, which fetters that operation of original sin,—a prevenient grace. The result therefore would be, that grace removes not indeed the possibility, but the necessity, of resistance, and produces faith in those who do not exercise this still possible resistance.[5] This was afterwards explained by *Johann Musäus, Quenstedt, Hollaz*, as if inevitable good motions (*inevitabiles boni motus*) were first awakened in us by God and His means of grace, by which motions the possibility of faith along with the possibility of unbelief, that is to say, freedom of decision, is restored. But the *Form. Conc.* already rejects in general the metaphysical denial of the *liberum arbitrium*, as

---

[1] *Form. Conc.* 654, 581-83.   [2] *Ibid.* 654, ff.   [3] 582, ff.
[4] 580, 8.   [5] 580, 8, with which 621, 20, does not altogether agree.

well as the assertion that sin is the substance of man and conversion an annihilation of the substance of man. In spite of original sin, there were still sparks (*scintillulæ*) of good existent in man, only they were in themselves completely impotent. Unfortunately they are not expressly turned to account as points of attachment for the process of salvation. This leads us to the position which the Formula of Concord assumes to the *doctrine of predestination*.[1] The older form of doctrine, more nearly related to the Reformed theologians, was now symbolically altered in this bearing of it, chiefly through the influence of the Swabians, although a harmonious working out of it was not yet achieved. The doctrine of the absolute decree of rejection in respect of some (*decretum reprobationis*) was, after the overthrow of the Lutheran predestinarians, dismissed from the Formula of Concord, both in the form that a part was eternally predestinated to damnation on account of the unbelief originating from the free act of Adam, and in the Supralapsarian form, that the one part was ordained to eternal unbelief; it is rather said, as the merit of Christ is universal, so also is the tendency of grace. It is through personal guilt that unbelievers are lost.[2] The cause of unbelief and condemnation is not God, not a repulsive operation of the Gospel, not a particular calling (*vocatio particularis*),[3] not, finally, the want of *liberum arbitrium*,[4] but the evil will of man and of the devil,[5] and *this* evil will is not derived as necessary from original sin. The calling is general and sincere;[6] there is nothing wanting in it, and if man does not resist it, it produces faith.

But how does this emphasizing of the guilt of those who *are lost* accord with the doctrine of the *Form. Conc.* regarding the power of original sin? The following solution is attempted. The disposition of antagonism to God belongs indeed to all by nature equally, but yet it rests with man, who has still the

---

[1] *Form. Conc.* 579-583; 617-622; 797-823. In Strasburg in 1561 a controversy broke out between *Zanchi*, who in the same manner as Bucer and Martyr maintained predestination, and in particular the impossibility of the falling away of the believer, and *Marbach*, in which the *Tübingen* theologians (in opposition to those of Marburg, Heidelberg, and Zürich) declared distinctly for the possibility of falling from grace, even as Melanchthon in accord with Luther (De Wette, v. 40-44; *Corp. Ref.* v. 296-301) had asserted the possibility of a new fall of believers. From that time the sharper antithesis to *Calvin's* doctrine became more extended, whilst some Melanchthonians afterwards went over to him.

[2] *Form. Conc.* 618, 5; 881, 88; 882, 91.   [3] *Ibid.* 617-620.
[4] 580, 8; 677, 74.   [5] 617, 4; 621, 19; 799, 7.   [6] 618, 8; 621, 18.

liberum arbitrium in civilibus, to hear the Word of God or not. He who hears it is in the way of salvation, inasmuch as through the Word the Holy Ghost communicates Himself, and He changes the will and produces faith, whilst those who do not hear the Word, do not experience the power of the Holy Ghost. The willingness of the first to hear is as yet no *opus spirituale*, so that a spiritual work may not be derived out of the natural powers, but the unwillingness to hear involves damnable guilt. But it is not clear how so momentous a decision can be hung upon the act of the free will, such as is possible before the process of salvation. Without grace, it is elsewhere taught, free will exists only in civil things, but not in relation to the divine, and civil righteousness (*civilis justitia*) is treated of as essentially indifferent in a spiritual aspect. How then is damnable guilt or salvation to be derived from anything that is indifferent for the spiritual province, namely from a willingness to hear the Word that is as yet unspiritual, as for example, a willingness arising from curiosity or custom? And seeing that the natural knowledge of divine things is also denied, it seems to follow that those who despise the Word cannot possibly know what they do. To say nothing of this, that not all by any means can hear the Word.[1] The right working out of the doctrine is therefore to be sought, under condition of firmly maintaining the necessity of the outward Word to the originating of faith, in the line of recognizing that the *call* must really come *to all* sometime or other, in order that grace may really be offered to all, but that over and above the Holy Ghost must work *in all* through inward *preparation* the possibility of faith in spite of original sin. Only, the preference of some in particular election is thus excluded, if believers had been able to continue in a state of unbelief. This leads to the other side.

The *Form. Conc.* firmly maintains the *absoluta electio* to salvation of some, namely of believers, and calls this a comfortable doctrine, that furnishes support to the assurance of salvation.[2] It rejects the view that this election takes place in virtue of the divine foreknowledge of our faith, although there is no election irrespectively of faith and of Christ (*electio extra fidem et extra*

---

[1] Heshus, Th. Schnepf, and others, speak, in an infralapsarian manner, of a passing by of some, while others speak of a rejection.

[2] *Form. Conc.* 617-620 ; 798, 3.

Christum). Faith is no cause *electionis*.[1] It is here without doubt meritoriousness (*causa meritoria*) which is chiefly feared and rejected, and therefore the subjectively mediative cause, the receiving, is not here taken into account, alongside of which there must stand, if the preferring of some and the *predestinatio absoluta* are not to be recurred to, the possibility of not receiving. But if all come to salvation only in passing through the possibility of perseverance in unbelief and only through a free decision for faith, then the faith of those who are saved cannot be regarded as a work of the irresistible operation of grace which falls to the lot only of a part of men and is simply forced upon them, as the doctrine of absolute election requires it to be, but instead of the predetermination there must at this point be placed the divine foreknowledge. And this is the tendency, to which effect was given in the Lutheran Church (see below) in the seventeenth, and still more in the eighteenth century.

In the first instance, however, new controversies which soon broke out showed that on this point the decision, as given in the *Form. Conc.*, was still in no ways mature. Amongst the Lutherans a more decisive separation from Calvinism had been preparing since 1561. The discussion at Mömpelgart in 1586,[2] between Andreä and Beza, let this be seen in all its rigour. The Bernese *Sam. Huber*, who had fallen out with Beza and Calvinism, found reception in Würtemberg and afterwards in Saxony, and maintained about 1590 a *universalism of election* and justification, which he based upon the free grace of God and the all-sufficient merit of Christ.[3] Election did not take place on account of faith,—that seemed to him to be Pelagian; but certainly only faith came to the enjoyment of election, and unbelief was damnable. But faith itself was only possible if man had previously perceived that he was already elect.[4] If he rejects grace in unbelief, he excludes himself from salvation; it is not God,

[1] *Form. Conc.* 621, 20. The opinion is rejected: *quod etiam in nobis ipsis aliqua causa sit electionis divinæ.*

[2] *Acta colloq. Montis Belligart. Tub.*, 1581, p. 502-560.

[3] *Acta Huberiana*, P. i. ii., 1597. Huber: *dass Christ. Jesus gestorben sei für den Sünden des ganzen menschl. Geschl.* 1590. *Hist. Beschreibung des ganzen Streits zwischen Dr. Hunnen und Dr. Hubern von der Gnadenwahl*, 1597, and other writings.

[4] *Sendbrief an den ehrenvesten u. wohlweisen H. Burgermeister u. Rath der löbl. Stadt. Zürich*, 1598, cf. *Theses Huberianismo oppos.* Præs. Æg. Hunnio, 1597.

so that a double decree is in no way necessary. Against this it was justly objected that the word election was here inaccurately employed, not of the final certain issue; further, the Würtembergers said, election took place with an eye to faith and had salvation for its subject-matter. And thus the unity of will in God, upon which Huber laid great stress, was left intact. *Ægidius Hunn* especially, who was also a born Swabian and the most esteemed theologian immediately after the *Form. Conc.* at Wittenberg (previously in Marburg), whilst denying along with the *Form. Conc.* an universalism of election, restricts the unconditional character of the divine counsel of grace even for those who are saved. The *prævisa fides* he regards as constitutive for election.[1] The first cause of the particularity of the divine election the Lutherans must trace to unbelief and impenitence, as is done by *Hunn* and the Tübingian *Hafenreffer*. On the other hand, it is not acknowledged with the same definiteness that receiving faith is a concomitant *cause* of election, but the absoluteness of the decree of salvation for some is first broken only by this, that salvation is made sure only to those who will hear the gospel and do not again fall from grace. *Hunn*[2] sees perfectly that the outward hearing of the Word by itself does not better one, but that the inward hearing besides is necessary for that end; he thinks, however, that those who are *willing* to hear stand nearer to salvation than those who place obstructions in the way of it by unwillingness to hear, and that that explains the difference in their fate. If there is anything meant by this, then a spiritual significance is attributed to the works of the *justitia civilis*, and there is ascribed to man, irrespectively of the preparatory operations of the Holy Ghost, and in spite of original sin, a beginning of good motions, which is as great a divergence from the type of doctrine hitherto, as Synergism is. Hence, as above remarked, the later theologians have, more accurately, adopted for the called the general restoration of the possibility of a free decision by means of the Holy Ghost and the Word. The word *Electio*, however, was after the

---

[1] Æg. Hunnius, *Articul. de Providentia Dei et æt. Prædestin. seu Elect. filiorum Dei ad salut.* 1595, against Tossanus and Huber. Farther, *De providentia Dei tractatus, per Quæst. et Resp. explicatus*, p. 1-562, together with a *Rostocker Gutachten.*

[2] Ægid. Hunnius, as cited, and his treatise *de libero arbitrio*, 1598. Cf. Schweizer, *Centraldogmen*, i. 568, ff. Franck, *dei Concordienformel*, i. 113, ff.; vi. 121.

Huberian controversy applied to *persons*, to the *result of salvation* which should certainly be theirs (being placed under the *Voluntas Dei consequens*), and not applied to the gracious counsel of God for the general *offering* of salvation, *i.e.* to the *law* of the economy of salvation (*Voluntas Dei antecedens*).

Many as are the imperfections which cleave to the *Form. Conc.*, and little praiseworthy as were in part the means adopted for fabricating and carrying it out, still a sort of historical necessity lay at the basis of its construction. The Lutheran Church indeed possessed already alongside of the œcumenical its own common symbols, at least the Augustana and its Apology, but from their brevity and original design even the most highly esteemed of them could not contain any decision on the controversies which had subsequently arisen. And so gradually one province or important city of Germany after another sought to satisfy its instinct for unity of doctrine by a separate confession. The practical occasion was generally given by the doctrinal obligation of the clergy, or by the examination of those to be ordained, both of which had been set on foot in Saxony by Melanchthon, not without antagonism on the part of Andreas Osiander.[1] In the Church books of order, too, which were becoming more and more numerous, although connected by a family kinship, there was not unfrequently a special division included to contain the order of doctrine. In close connection with this stands the formation of the so-called *corpora doctrinæ*, into which approved doctrinal treatises, such as were held in particular esteem in the different countries, were adopted; above all the *Corp. doctrinæ Philippicum* or *Misnicum*, 1560 (containing after the œcumenical symbols only Melanchthonian writings, namely, *Conf. Aug. var.*, *Apolog.*, *Repetitio C. A.*, *Loci Theol.*, *Examen Ordinandorum*, *Resp. ad articulos Bavaricos*), and the similar *Pomeranum*, 1561; on the other side the more Lutheran, like the *Pruthenicum*, 1567 (containing the *Repetit. Corp. doctr. eccles.*, *C. A. Apol.*, *Art. Sm.*), and especially the *Thuringicum*, 1570; on the part of the Gnesio-Lutherans (*Conf. Aug.* of 1531,

[1] Even before 1540 the Augustana was obligatory in Wittenberg. [It was in the course of the controversy on the nature of justification, that Osiander, at that time minister in Nuremberg, attacked Melanchthon for imposing these obligations on the Saxon clergy.—*Tr.*]

Apol., Art. Sm., and the two catechisms of Luther, together with other local productions), which the *Julium* (of Braunschweig-Lüneburg) of 1576 resembles (only it has different appendices); the *Brandenburgicum*, of 1572; the *Confessio Saxonica* and *Würtembergica*, which were followed up by the Saxon articles of Visitation, the Danzig Notel, &c.[1] As long as Luther lived, a common authority was not wanting, and the endeavour of the Lutheran Church to exhibit a great unity, and especially a strong unity in doctrine, was satisfied sometimes by conventions of theologians, and sometimes by princes, the most important of whom set the highest value upon the interests of the Reformation or placed them in the forefront. But even the breach which had been made with the Reformed theologians,—a breach which reached over into Germany, inasmuch as the Elector of the Palatinate as well as Hesse, Bremen, Anhalt, and Friesland (in 1613 also the royal house of Brandenburg, and about 1700 that of the Electorate of Hanover), went over to the Reformed confession,—made a union of the evangelical princes in the affairs of the Reformation impossible; still more the breach between the theological tendencies inside of the Lutheran Church. Theological school and church were as yet in no way separated; the minutest theological controversies were, just as if they had been ecclesiastical and religious questions, carried into the congregations, under the presupposition that the idea of the Church required the complete accordance of all in all articles of doctrine and in all points of them. Only too frequently was the civil power carried away, by the immoderateness of theological parties, to violent measures against tendencies, which had to seek their union in the way of scientific negotiation. The extraordinary multiplicity of territories in Germany contributed still farther to enhance the difficulty of union, amid the many controversies which had broken out. Although, therefore, at first the most lively wish was entertained that the whole evangelical Church, and in the years after 1540 at least the whole Lutheran Church, should stand as a great unity in itself over against the [Roman] Catholics, and although all kinds of means were thought of for the realization of this wish, still even in the years after 1550 it was perceived to be certain that, in the first instance at least,

[1] For more minute information, see Köllner's *Symbolik*, 25.

Character of the Form. Conc. 381

each territory had to attend to its own interests.[1] But this in itself must, from the splitting up of Germany and the attitude of the imperial authority towards the Reformation, have had for its consequence an endless sectarian splitting up of the Lutheran Church, if there had not been introduced a weight which should counterbalance the prevailing particularism, and be in a position to hold the Lutherans together in unity and to preserve for the Lutheran Church, as well as for its doctrinal development, a larger church style. An impulse to this was given very specially by the formation, of which mention has been made, of territorial *corpora doctrinæ*, doctrinal books of order, and the like, in which considerable portions of the whole German Lutheran Church sought already a firm symbolic settlement, but necessarily in such a way, that they at the same time did more or less distinguish and define themselves off from the neighbouring Lutheran Churches, the chief stress being at the same time laid upon the distinctive feature, which referred to local requirements and controversies. Only two ways were possible, in order to bring the general Lutheran Church gradually to a verbal manifesto over against this particularism, and at least subordinate particularism to it; and these two ways were represented by the Lower Saxons and the Swabians. The latter, with *Jacob Andreä* now at their head, start from the idea of the one whole Lutheran Church, and seek to set up a common confession, decisive of internal controversies and furnished with theological and magisterial authority; whilst the Lower Saxons, with *Chemnitz* among them, were in the first instance concerned to bring their most important churches one by one into good condition in doctrine, cultus, and order of life, in the confidence that example, mutual counsel, and intercourse would themselves create or preserve the necessary amount of unity—a view which was evidently connected with the greatness and strength of the burgher community in the towns of Lower Saxony, and which, although animated by a Lutheran aim, possessed something of a republican cast. Chemnitz was at first little inclined for the undertaking of Andreä. At the same time, seeing that important princes like Duke *Julius of Brunswick* and Elector *Augustus of Saxony* had zealously interested themselves in the work of embracing the whole Lutheran Church in concord, and seeing, too, that Andreä could only achieve his end

[1] Brenz: Every fox must lurk in his own hole.

in the way of free negotiation with the separate national Churches, M. Chemnitz attached himself to the undertaking. To obtain a sure common starting-point, which was held to be obligatory upon all Lutherans, the *Augustana* and its apology were recurred to, with the expressed design of establishing its true meaning in opposition to misrepresentations, and of deciding according to it the controversies which had broken out. The work did not proceed without resorting to artificialities, and very much, especially what was peculiar to the *Form. Conc.* in the Christology, the Supper, and predestination, could not be shown to be in every part of it the necessary deduction from the *Augustana*. There is also assumed towards the Reformed theologians a far more exclusive attitude than in the older Lutheran confessions; and the Melanchthonian school (Philippists) received thereby a severe blow,—not indeed without their own fault, since they in the time of their ascendency—which procured for them the name of Cryptocalvinists—had been wanting in openness towards their thoroughly Lutheran princes. As far as the authority of the *Form. Conc.* reached, in those articles of doctrine in which Melanchthon approximated to the Reformed theologians, or was more friendly towards them, as in the Christology and Supper, his type of doctrine was proscribed. On the other side there can be no mistake, as we have repeatedly pointed out, that in the doctrines of free will, the law, original sin, and predestination, there was given by the *Form. Conc.* to the doctrinal development of the Church that direction which led, though only step by step, essentially to Melanchthon's form of doctrine.[1] This mode of doctrine penetrated afterwards—by means of Melanchthonians like Christoph. Petzel, Peucer, and Alb. Hardenberg—into the German Reformed Church, in which absolute predestinarianism did not succeed in taking root at first, and afterwards not lasting root. In like manner it is not to be denied that, although several decisions of the *Form. Conc.* were unsatisfactory and premature, still the work as a whole exhibits judiciousness and moderation; besides, every

---

[1] The predestination doctrine of the *F. C.* is no longer that of Luther nor of the Lutheran predestinarians. Cf. *F. C.* 617, ff. 797, ff. This reacts upon the conception of the *lib. arb.* Cf. *Form. Conc.* 580, 8; 581, 15: 582, 17, 18, 667, ff. So too the section *de tertio usu legis* corresponds to what Melanchthon held. Cf. above, p. 347, f.

effort was made to maintain the widest possible range of comprehension within the prescribed limits, and to render it acceptable to the different parties, and so, too, the esteem which it acquired is to be attributed not simply to the forcible measures adopted in connection with its introduction, but is due also for the most part to its intrinsic worth. The inclination, indeed, which dwelt from an early period in the Lutheran Church, to look for the soundness of the Church onesidedly in the doctrine, but not to distinguish between dogma and kerugma, between dogma and Christian faith, nor even between the confession of the congregation and the opinion of the school, found seal and expression in the *Form. Conc.*, which greatly furthered the German tendency towards contemplation, and even intellectualism, and thus formed the bridge which led over from the freshness of faith in the time of the Reformation to a new scholasticism upon evangelical territory. But even the *Reformed* Church was not spared a similar pathway. It, too,—and a more general law of Church-life is thereby discovered to us,—sought by a so-called *synodus generalis*, as we shall soon see, to gather itself together into a compact unity over against the Lutheran as well as the Romish confession, and to create in the *Dort decrees* a sort of work of concord for their internal difficulties. The danger, created by this coming to a *conclusion* on both sides, the danger of a stagnation of life, was however modified not merely by the fact that the two evangelical confessions stood side by side together, but chiefly by the circumstance that the *Form. Conc.* was not adopted in a large part of the lands of the Lutheran confession, as in Denmark, Holstein, Pomerania, Anhalt, Hesse, the Palatinate of Zweibrücken (Deuxponts), Brunswick, Nuremberg, &c.; the Dort articles on their part undergoing a similar experience. Yet those who did not adopt it could not be deprived of the character of Lutheran, seeing that they maintained their greater freedom upon the basis of the earlier confessions.

SECTION II.

THE REFORMED CHURCH OF THE SECOND SYMBOLIC FORMATION.

THE Reformed Church, orphaned by the death of Zwingli and Œcolampadius, received in *John Calvin*, great alike in mind and character, a firm centre and organizing soul for the doctrine and constitution of the Church. Geneva became through him the new Reformed metropolis instead of Zürich; and this community manifested a wonderful and far-conquering power.[1]

Calvin, like Melanchthon, gave himself up at first to Humanism. He exercised too upon the French language an influence similar to that of Luther upon the German. As he soon discerned how the French humanists were wanting in moral earnestness and religious ballast, how heathen and pantheistic conceptions prevailed amongst them, he set himself in opposition to them, and thus trained himself already for the mission which he was to fulfil against the Pantheists and Libertines of Geneva. A fruit of this time is his treatise *De psycho-pannychia*. Even in the choice of this theme his active energetic consciousness sought an expression, which was full of significance for that which afterwards became so central for him, the indissolubility of conscious communion with the Redeemer and the indefectibility of grace. In this treatise he taught that immortality was the rest of the soul in the Lord, and he supported this by the resurrection and especially by the holy Scriptures. As early as about 1532, in his twenty-third year, he had become acquainted with the Gospel, and published, as his first writing in defence of the Protestants, Seneca's treatise *De Clementia*, with a commentary. For Francis I. had already begun the persecutions of the Evangelicals, who were also called Lutherans in France. As Calvin was placed in greater danger in the measure in which he became

---

[1] Henry, *Calvins Leben;* Stähelin, *Calvins Leben*, 2 Bände, 1860, ff.; *Revue chrétienne*, 1854-57; Merle D'Aubigné, *Histoire de la Reform.;* the writings which appeared on occasion of the tricentenary of the death of Calvin, by Merle, Fritzsche, &c. Baum, Cunitz, and Reuss have begun to issue his works anew in a highly meritorious critical edition of them. (*J. Calvini Opera quæ supersunt omnia*, t. i.-vi., 1863 to 1867.)

better known, he went to Basle, where he published anonymously in 1535, in the French language, his *Institutio christianæ religionis*, with a preface, as a defence of the Evangelicals, in the form of a dedication to Francis. A Latin edition followed in 1536, with his name, and a revised edition in 1539 at Strasburg, under the anagram Alcuin. The last principal edition he prepared in 1559. Soon after his flight from France, the Princess Renée in Ferrara, sister-in-law of Francis I., received him, but after labouring there for the Gospel and its adherents, he was compelled to flee from Italy also. Upon this journey he came, in August 1536, to Geneva, where the Reformation had begun the year before through Viret and the fiery Farel, but was still greatly in need of confirmation through suitable regulations, and, for this end, of a judicious and wise hand. For the town was in great political and religious fermentation; Romish abuses were indeed done away with, but destructive caprice, united with religious and moral frivolity, threatened the whole work. Besides the Anabaptists, there were Libertines, who, following a naturalistic and pantheistic mode of thought, would recognize no law and no order. *Farel*, quickly perceiving the powerful and organizing mind of Calvin, desired him to remain in Geneva. He declined, as he wished to give himself to his studies. But when Farel, standing before him like a prophet, required obedience in the name of God, he submitted to be detained. He at once and with utmost energy adopted vigorous measures, especially in matters of Church discipline. The commotion in the town, however, was thereby increased to such an extent that even the authorities set themselves in opposition to him, and he had to leave Geneva again so soon as 1538. He betook himself by Basle to Strasburg, where he remained till 1541. Here he passed for a Lutheran, for the Wittenberg Concordia was concluded, and he subscribed the *Augustana* " in the sense of its author." But when Cardinal Sadolet, after Calvin's banishment from Geneva, deeming the opportunity favourable, used every effort to lead the town back to the Romish Church, the desire spread in Geneva for a leadership in Church matters in the power and spirit of Calvin, and his friends brought about his recall. He stipulated for the introduction of Church discipline, and now came back in 1541, conducted in triumph into the town, to remain in it to the end. By his labours until 1564 he so deeply impressed upon this town, religiously and politically, the seal of his powerful mind, that centuries have not been able to obliterate the traces of it. Geneva became the Athens of the Reformed Church; at the same time, a true missionary Church in [Roman] Catholic Christendom. In this little point, with its well-ordered Church, which was not without the "*nervus ecclesiæ*" (Church discipline), there was concentrated a muscular power, which worked out in all directions, snatched large provinces from the Romish Church, propagated the mind of Calvin in Holland, England, and Scotland, exercised a mighty influence upon Poland and Hungary, France and Germany, and became a nursery of Reformed piety, Church order, and learning.

The personal appearance of Calvin was that of an old Roman censor; he was of a fine make, pale, meagre, with an expression of deep earnestness and incisive sharpness. The Senate of Geneva said, after his death, that he was a majestic character. Loveable in social life, full of tender sympathy and friendly fidelity, indulgent and placable in all personal injuries, he was inflexibly severe when he saw the honour of God impugned in obstinacy or wickedness. Amongst his colleagues he had none who envied him, but many enthusiastic worshippers. French fire and practical intelligence seemed to have struck an alliance with German depth and judiciousness. If he was not of a speculative or intuitive mind, his understanding and his judgment were, on the other hand, so much the more piercing and keen; his memory was comprehensive; and he moved quite as easily in the world of ideas or of science as in the business of Church government. He is not indeed a man of the people, like Luther, but in his language more the man of learning; and his labours as a preacher and pastor cannot therefore be compared with those of Luther. On the other hand, his is more an architectural mind, and this in the department of science as well as in that of life. Both are for him one in their root, and his dogmatical structures, bold as they are in the logical consistency of their thought, yet always preserve for him at the same time an edifying character. Even when he daringly seeks to pierce into the divine mysteries of predestination, he is always led by the practical desire of subserving the holiness and majesty of God, and of finding for the heart an eternal anchorage, in which it can securely repose in the consciousness of election by free grace.

Attempt at the Union of Evangelical Confessions. 387

Amid all the affinity which subsists between Zwingli and Calvin in the doctrine of predestination, and in the emphasizing of the majesty and glory of God, there is still between the two a profound difference, which places Calvin nearer to the Lutheran confession, and, in what concerns the doctrine of predestination, in particular to Luther. A deeper consciousness of the holiness of God, a deeper feeling of sin and of its abominable and ungodly nature, gives also to his faith a more severe and more purely ethical tone, and conducts to a more complete agreement with Luther in the doctrine of *justification*. But even in the *formal principle*, Calvin modified the looser connection between the outward and inward Word held by Zwingli, and connected the two sides closer together. In reference therefore to the principle of the Reformation with its two sides, Calvin is, still more than Zwingli, of one mind and spirit with the German Lutheran Reformation; only that the formal principle is, according to him, the norm and source of dogma, whilst he does not treat faith, in the same way as Luther, as a source of knowledge for the dogmatical structure, that is to say, as the mediative principle of knowledge. But, on the other hand, he too holds firmly to the necessity of the inward witness of the Holy Ghost (*testimonium Spiritus Sancti internum*) and to the possibility, nay, necessity of the assurance of personal salvation, and this shapes itself for him into the consciousness of eternal election. When we consider what was Luther's position on occasion of the outbreaking of the controversy on the Supper, when he commended the Swabian Syngramma, it is scarcely to be thought that if Calvin had stood in Zwingli's place the controversy on the Supper would ever have arisen. But when the rupture had taken place, not even a Calvin was able to heal it. In this again we may discern a sign that the double form of the Reformation was determined in the counsel of God, even as, according to what we have already pointed out (p. 307), it necessarily subserved essentially the maintenance of the Reformation principle in its purity amid the kind of human development which it underwent. Calvin's endeavours to effect an union between the German and the Swiss Reformations, to which the nature of his mind and the leadings of his life seemed to call him, fell besides upon an unpropitious time. The religious communities on both sides, especially the German, were so much occupied with themselves, with the endeavour to become master of their own individuality, that the call to be mindful of what was common to them instead of their differences, or even the attempt to reconcile them, found little echo, nay, necessarily served to multiply the confusion. The greatly predominating tendency in Germany, which was encountered by Calvin, was to grasp, and confirm themselves wholly in, their own peculiarity, to give up nothing which might seem to be a gain, to thrust forward jealously even the hidden or supposed differences, in order thus to intensify their own self-consciousness. When such was their general disposition, mistrust would have stood in the way even of a more perfect doctrinal structure than that of Calvin, and one which everywhere exhibited what was true in the two sides in a higher unity than that of Calvin does, and the understanding for it have been locked up until this, their own self-consciousness, was purified. Hence the direction which was irresistibly taken was to live their different doctrines through, and to carry them out to their last consequences, and though not denying their common evangelical possession, to lessen it and to restrict as much as possible its authority or influence. This maiming of evangelical Catholicity brought forth, indeed, its bitter fruits and an alteration or even obscuration of the proper evangelical character. But only the actual incidence of these results could unlock again the susceptibility for what had been thrust into the background.

In what has been said there lies, even if we overlook the defects of the Calvinistic system of doctrine, a sufficient ground of explanation why Calvin, with his conscious endeavour to effect a union of all evangelicals and heal the breaches which had arisen, did not succeed in doing so, but became the occasion of a still more violent and lasting conflagration. As certainly as it may be said that Luther might have found some particulars perhaps, but nothing essential, to take exception to in Calvin's doctrine of the Supper and Predestination, if it had come before him about 1525, as little was Calvin's formula able to restore peace even immediately after Luther's death. After the *Consensus Tigurinus* of 1549, Calvin, who had been hitherto taken for a Lutheran, was with great grief set down as belonging to the Swiss side. His word was now of so much the less authority. It was not however by rebuke from without, but in the way of inward development and knowledge, even through its own loss, that the Lutheran

Church was to attain to that clearness which is able to distinguish the essence and kernel of the matter from what is subordinate, nay, to accomplish its self-purification in the power of this essence, and which is also the necessary pre-condition of union.

Let us first of all consider *Calvin's position* upon the *evangelical doctrine of principles*. The principal views of Calvin in reference to the *holy Scriptures* are these. It is not the Church which decides upon the truth; its authority especially does not determine the consideration due to the holy Scriptures, since the consideration due to the Church is rather based upon the holy Scriptures. The Scriptures possess the consideration which is theirs through the Holy Ghost, who working upon our hearts gives testimony to the *truth*. The assurance which they impart he calls a sense (*sensus*) arising out of a divine revelation. This testimony of the Holy Ghost is higher and stronger than any human judgment and means of proof; without it all other reasons are ineffectual. He thinks of this *testimonium* as resembling the sense of an axiomatic truth, in the case of which it is not reasons and probabilities that are first treated of, but at the same time it is not a blind, servile and superstitious submission to something unknown that takes place, but to which we adhere rather on account of immediate evidence, because we are well conscious that we are in possession of an inseparable truth, and because we indubitably feel the power and breath of God in the holy Scriptures, whereby we are drawn and incited consciously and willingly to obedience much more powerfully than through human will and human science. He is far from applying the *testimonium Spiritus Sancti* only to the form and origin of the holy Scriptures; it is the subject-matter of Scripture, or Christian truth, which makes upon him this impression of the divine breath, but certainly the form and the subject-matter of the holy Scriptures are so taken together by him, as if the testimony of the Holy Ghost to the subject-matter and its truth were also forthwith a testimony to the fact of inspiration.[1] He clearly

---

[1] *Instit.* i. 7, § 1-4. The question, whence do we know of the divine origin of the Scriptures, he answers by the counter question, whence do we learn to distinguish light from darkness, white from black, sweet from bitter? For (and in this he passes over immediately again to the subject-matter) the holy Scriptures do not give a less vivid feeling of their truth, than white and black things give of their colour.

recognizes this, that a mere refutation of opponents and of proofs that are merely addressed to the intellect are not as yet the right foundation; he calls that *testimonium* far preferable to all proofs; but still there may in his case be the appearance as if one might or must first be convinced of the divine origin, *i.e.* of the inspiration of the Scriptures, before he can stand in the Christian faith.[1] But since every one does not perceive of himself the divinity of the holy Scriptures, but only he in whom a light (that is to say the perception of the truth) is kindled through the Holy Ghost, so that he traces in the Scriptures the divine breath, faith in divine truth is made the condition, not the consequence of true faith in the inspiration of the holy Scriptures. It is evident at this point how Calvin did not perceive the relative independence of Christian truth from the form of Scripture in the same way as Luther, who is aware that truth may be exhibited in different forms, which cannot all claim canonicity. And with this is connected the circumstance, that Calvin does not allow to faith and believing science the same right of criticism as Luther does, although at the same time he by no means shares the Alexandrian theory of inspiration. The formal side of the Protestant principle retains with Calvin the ascendancy over the material; and with this is connected the fact that he sees in the holy Scriptures chiefly the revelation of the will of God, which He has prescribed to men through the sacred writers. The double form of the *Verbum Dei externum* and *internum*, held by Zwingli, gives place indeed in Calvin to a more inward connecting of the two sides; the Scriptures are according to him not merely the sign of an absent thing, but have in themselves divine matter and breath, which makes itself actively felt. But since he regards the holy Scriptures mainly as the revealed will of God, which also legally regulates the New Testament order of life, he has left less room for the free productions of the faith of the Church in legislation and dogma by means of the unfolding of the holy Scriptures, and he has looked upon the apostolic age as normative for all times, even for questions of church constitution; hence the churches which stood under his influence, especially the English and Scottish churches, describe their constitutions, which are indeed antagonistic, as a necessary divine ordinance. This justly

---

[1] *Instit.* i. 7, § 4 : *Non ante stabilitur doctrinæ fides, quam nobis indubie persuasum sit, autorem ejus (script. s.) esse Deum.*

seems objectionable to the Lutherans, because such dogmatizing of a particular form of constitution obscures even the principle of faith, if not through a new condition of salvation—namely, connection with the rightly constituted church—yet through the addition of a new criterion of the truth of the Church. There is here a disposition towards a legal tendency, which has been in part further developed in the Reformed churches. That a less free position is assigned to biblical criticism in the Reformed churches, is manifested very evidently in this, that several of their chief symbols enumerate the writings which form the canon, and so makes their inclusion in the holy Scriptures an article of faith, which is done by no Lutheran confession. This is the course taken in the *Anglicana*, vi., *Belgica*, ii.-iv.; cf. *Gallic.* ii.-v., *Helvet.* i. 2; ii. 1-5.[1]

With reference to the *material side of the Protestant principle*, Calvin regards sin as not merely sensuousness, disease, misery, as Zwingli does, but also as self-seeking and spiritual corruption; and it corresponds to this that he has a more austere idea of the righteousness and holiness of God. God can have no intercourse with sin, and so He must in disfavour turn His countenance away from the sinner. In like manner it is a necessity for God Himself that He does not forgive, without allowing justice to maintain its rights. Sin, too, is according to him not merely an alien guilt, because coming down from Adam, nor merely the error of ascendancy on the part of lower impulses, but a separation between us and God. From these premises, the forgiveness of sins or reconciliation must assume in his view a place similar to what it occupies in the Lutheran doctrine. Although his doctrine of predestination properly leaves no room for free guilt in our sin, still he proceeds, like Luther, as if free guilt were there; and his doctrine of predestination, in disclaiming here its proper consequences, makes as it were an atonement to the moral consciousness by this defect in systematic consistency. From the similarity of premises, then, there results an essential similarity of doctrine between Calvin and Luther in reference to *faith*, its *object* and its *effects*.

The *conception of faith* as a mere historical opinion and consent could not be more energetically rejected by Luther than it is by Calvin.[2] It is not abject faith; the intelligence is active in it;

[1] To which may be added the *Westminster Confession*, ch. i. sec. 2.—*Tr.*
[2] *Instit.* ii. 6, 4; iii. 2, 9, 8; 9, 13, 43.

nay more, the consent of faith is according to him matter of the heart and feeling more than of the intellect (*fidei assensio cordis est magis quam cerebri et affectus magis quam intelligentiæ*). *Fides* exists not without a pious movement of the heart; there even belongs to it an act of obedience. Accordingly, he considers intelligence, feeling, and will to participate in the act of *fides*, and that in such a way that the object of faith is apprehended by the intelligence, and presented to the will that it may make it the property of man in his innermost feeling. This inward embracing of it takes place in this way, that man renounces himself and passes out beyond himself in order to surrender himself to the object of faith.[1]

As the *object* of faith he designates in general the attributes of God, such as omnipotence, righteousness, holiness, and His acts, in particular, however, His promises. He says very happily, dismissing at the same time a doctrine of original sin which misunderstands itself, that without faith in God there cannot be fear of judgment nor desire for salvation. In so far faith in God is also the root of true repentance; but the design is that out of faith in God, the Almighty and Holy, there should spring faith in God, the Merciful. That takes place in this way, that faith in God becomes faith in Christ and His salvation. The objective cause of the necessity of faith in Christ in order to become a partaker of God as Merciful, lies in God Himself.[2] In Christ the love of God resides and rests (*residet et acquiescit patris amor*), out from Him it issues forth to us, and no one is loved by God outside of Christ. This love of God comes nigh to us in the word of Christ and in the sacraments.[3] What was in God incomprehensible and hidden, he says with Luther, *that* God was pleased to discover and make accessible to us in the Redeemer, as the sacraments might show to us. The deep secret original well of love, which would otherwise remain hidden from us, rises up in the Mediator for us; it is set before us as a flowing fountain, out of which we are to draw. Thus the person of Christ is for him the Divine Love itself, manifested and become apprehensible; and it is not merely the divine nature of Christ which effects salvation, but righteousness and the treasure of salvation resides for us in the humanity of Christ (*in Christi carne residat nobis justitia et salutis materia*).

[1] *Instit*. iii. 2, 14.   [2] *Ibid*. iii. 2, § 32; 3, § 9.
[3] *Ibid*. iii. 11, § 9.

Hence he places—in this, too, more resembling Luther—a close connection between Christ and the means of grace. Faith has an abiding connection with the word, and can be as little separated from it, as the rays from the sun from which they issue. Through the word the Holy Ghost lets us know Christ Himself, not merely in the intellect, but also in the will and consenting affection. What is presented, however, to us as to be believed by us, is not merely this, that the promises of grace are true only outside of us and not also in us, but the essential action of faith consists in this, that we, inwardly laying hold of the promises, make them our own (*cardo fidei in eo vertitur, ut eas (promissiones) intus amplectendo nostras faciamus*).[1] If this has taken place, which is possible only through the Holy Ghost, the word becomes like a seed, which strikes its roots in the innermost heart, and the fruit of this root is the state of faith and living communion with Christ.

The *effect* of the union of the believing subject with the believed object is, that in virtue of the union with the Head, into whose body we are joined, what is His becomes ours. Calvin here recalls the mysticism of Luther in the *Freedom of a Christian Man*, only with the reminder, that faith never penetrates our whole nature upon earth; hence the *unio mystica* has to pass through several stages. United with Christ, man knows himself to be, in the presence of God, and by His grace, His child; he has the assurance of salvation (*certitudo salutis*).[2] In faith there is an illumination of the understanding and also a confirmation of the heart, inasmuch as the Holy Ghost certifies divine childhood to it by His testimony. This is the sealing (*obsignatio*). And this matured faith is now defined as the sure and firm knowledge of the Divine complacency towards us, which, based upon the truth of the free promise in Christ, is sealed by the Holy Spirit to our spirit, as well as to our heart.[3] He is no less zealous than Luther in opposing the scholastic doctrine that we only possess a moral probability (*conjectura moralis*) of the grace of God towards us, according to the measure in which each one believes himself to be not unworthy of it.[4] It is clear from this, how far he is removed from deriving the assurance of salvation first from works, from the active manifestation of the new life, and so

[1] *Instit.* iii. 2, 6. [2] *Ibid.* iii. 2, § 33-36. Cf. with 14, § 8; ii. 3, § 8.
[3] iii. 2, § 7. [4] iii. 2, § 38.

falling back upon a circuitous way back into [Roman] Catholic doctrine,[1] which makes the assurance of salvation dependent upon works, and never lets it be actually realized amid the remaining imperfection of the present life.[2]

This conducts to the *relation of faith to justification and regeneration.* Faith lays hold of and possesses Christ, in whom is every blessing, reconciliation as well as sanctification of life. What we in our impotence need as the first thing is this, that God vouchsafes to embrace the sinner with His pure and free goodness, because Christ has washed away from us our impurity in the eye of God. It was not good works seen by God which determined Him to mercy, but our misery. Nor is it the intrinsic power of faith (*intrinseca virtus*), or the fact of its being the principle of holiness, which justifies us, in which case our righteousness would be always defective; but faith justifies only by means of its object, which it lays hold of; it is the *instrumentum*, which lays hold of *Christum extra nos*, who has as Mediator covered our sin before God. And so we obtain justification (*justificatio*) through the imputation of His merit, of His righteousness (and therefore too of the *obed. activa*), and through the forgiveness of sins.[3] This is the divine act of our acceptance, whereby God looks upon those received into grace as righteous (*in gratiam receptos pro justis habet*). *Osiander* indeed said that God could not justify *modo forensi*, by mere imputation, those who are still in reality unrighteous. But if our actual righteousness was requisite for *justificatio*, then we would never be wholly justified in this life. Justification must be not partial, but complete; a *portio justitiæ* could not pacify the conscience; our feeble moral advancements could never prepare for us rest, peace,

---

[1] *Instit.* iii. 11, § 16.

[2] Schneckenburger, in his comparative exhibition of the Lutheran and Reformed doctrine, has been guilty of greatly misrepresenting the Reformed doctrine upon this point. He succeeds to some appearance only from the fact, that he scarcely adduces the Reformed reformers or the Reformed confessions at all, but draws his principal proofs from the authors of the eighteenth century, in which century there are similar caricatures to be found even in the Lutheran Church. That the manifestations of the new life are a mark of true faith, not merely for others, but even for ourselves, and in so far form a momentum for the certainty of the consciousness of the state of grace, is taught also in Melanchthon's *Apology* and by Luther (see above, p. 296; Walch, xi. 1018); but they, like Calvin, are far from laying upon this the chief stress for the assurance of salvation.

[3] *Inst.* iii. 3, § 1; 11, § 7, 10, 21, 23; c. 2, § 39.

and spiritual joy. Hence another *modus justificationis* was necessary than that by means of sanctification, and he characterizes as thoughtless (a *nugamentum*) the opinion that a man is justified because he is a partaker of the Holy Ghost. It is rather the case that no such intercourse on the part of God with him takes place before the forgiveness of sins.

But certainly, he now adds, the real righteousness of life is not *separated* from the imputed righteousness (*a gratuita justitiæ imputatione non separatur realis ut ita loquar vitæ sanctitas*).[1] As he will not have *justificatio* and regeneration confounded, so too he resists their separation. The same Christ, who, being laid hold of by faith, imparts the forgiveness of sins and the consciousness of it, gives regeneration also as a second grace. He reckons thereto the feelings of spiritual joy which spring out of the forgiveness of sins, but he knows that these are somewhat fluctuating, and that to depend upon them would lead to a sort of spiritual eudæmonism.[2] On that account he rather admonishes faith that, instead of reflecting upon and enjoying itself, the task incumbent upon it was a continual spiritual dying and resurrection, *mortificatio et vivificatio*. In like manner does the Heidelberg Catechism deduce Christian gratitude from justification or the forgiveness of sins, and build upon this the whole doctrine of morals.

In what concerns the marks of regeneration, all the Reformed confessions are one with the Lutheran. Works do, as good fruits, prove the goodness of the tree to others, but also to the personal consciousness. But in the classical age of the Reformed Church the chief stress was not laid upon the assurance which resulted from the evidence of works, but upon the *Testimonium Spiritus Sancti internum*, or the God-given consciousness of divine childhood. There is accordingly, in reference to this central point of the evangelical Christian consciousness, only a psychological difference to be specified between the Lutheran mode and the Reformed mode, as in particular determined by Calvin, namely, that the Lutheran is more inclined to dwell upon the free grace of God, and the glory of it in adoring worship and contemplation, whilst the Reformed seeks rather to glorify God and thank Him through the will and deed—a difference which, instead of pointing to a necessary severance,

[1] *Instit.* iii. 3, § 1, c. 11.   [2] *Ibid.* iii, 3, § 3.

points rather to a beneficial completion of the two parts by one another, even as they both acknowledge one another in principle.

But does not the circumstance, that in the Calvinistic form of doctrine so great a stress is laid upon *eternal election*, conceal a deeper difference? Does not Calvin derive the assurance of salvation from the knowledge of eternal election, but Luther and the Lutheran Church from faith in Christ? We are thus led to a closer examination of *Calvin's doctrine of predestination*. It is not the power of faith which, according to Luther, makes one certain of and happy in salvation; but the power of the object laid hold of by faith, Christ and His faithfulness; and conversely Calvin does not postulate a knowledge of election in another way than through faith in Christ, even as there is in his view no election which does not include faith in it. Nay, it is not election which is in his view the proper and immediate object of faith, but Christ, even as the election did not take place *extra Christum*, but *in Christo*, and it is in no other way than through Christ that God has resolved to dispense grace to men. Hence Calvin, with Luther, calls Christ the mirror of our election.[1]

But although Calvin knows no *Electio extra Christum* and *extra fidem*, still he teaches a *Prædestinatio absoluta*, going back upon the absolute sovereignty of God, which is for some election (*Electio*), for others reprobation (*Reprobatio*).[2] The fruit of this doctrine was the humiliation of man to the very root, but also his exaltation into the eternal immovable assurance of salvation. No pious man dared to deny it altogether, but it was concealed by tenets which rendered it illusory, inasmuch as the prescience of God was made the cause of predestination. The right definition of it was:[3] the eternal counsel of God, wherein God deter-

---

[1] Rudelbach, *Reformation, Lutherthum, und Union*, has therefore not sufficiently acquainted himself with the Reformed doctrine, which he controverts, when, separating Calvin from Luther, he thinks that he can lay stress upon this, that Luther regarded Christ as the mirror of election. [The expression is taken from Augustine, as Calvin himself intimates. *Hoc prudenter animadvertit Augustinus, in ipso Ecclesiæ capite lucidissimum esse gratuitæ electionis speculum.—Inst.* iii. 22, 1. It is, however, endorsed and explained by Calvin, cf. *Inst.* iii. 24, 5: *Christus ergo speculum est in quo electionem nostram contemplari convenit, et sine fraude licet.* In proof of the statements made by Dr. Dorner, compare the *Inst.* iii. 24, 4 and 5.—*Tr.*]

[2] *Instit.* ii. c. 2-6; iii. 21-24; *De lib. arb. adv. Pigh.* 1543, *Opusc.* 216-351; *Consensus Pastorum Genevensium de æterna prædestinatione.*

[3] *Instit.* iii. 21, 7.

mined by Himself what He would have each one become; some
are ordained before to life, others to damnation (Æternum Dei
decretum, quo apud se constitutum habuit quid de unoquoque
homine fieri vellet. Non enim pari conditione errantur omnes,
sed aliis vita æterna aliis damnatio æterna præordinatur). Still
it was undeniable that not all who heard the word attained to
faith. Therefore it was to be said that God had, in virtue of
His immutable counsel, determined whom He would receive and
whom He would set apart for destruction. (Æterno et immu-
tabili consilio Deum semel constituisse, quos olim assumere vellet
in salutem, quos rursus exitio devovere.) Election was not
founded in a regard to human worthiness, but in God's free
mercy; for those who were appointed to damnation, the access
to life was cut off by the righteous judgment of God (quos vero
damnatione addicit, his justo quidem et irreprehensibili sed
incomprehensibili ejus judicio vitæ aditum præcludi).[1] An
Electio without a *Reprobatio* could not be received; the two are
in his view correlates. To elect is to select out of a number;
those passed by are *reprobi*. Hardening is in God's hand no less
than mercy. There are besides the elect such as God created to
destruction (*in vitæ contumeliam et mortis exitium*);[2] and that
wickedness might not be intruded as the cause of rejection, Paul
had said (Rom. ix. 11), "Before they had done good or evil."
Everything therefore ran up to the free will of God (*arbitrium*),
and a ground beyond that was not to be sought. That the
reprobates (*reprobi*) might come to their destiny, God robbed them
of the opportunity of hearing His word, or blinded and hardened
them by the preaching of it, for many became still blinder
through the light of Christ, and still deafer through His voice.
Why did God do this? It was said their wickedness deserved
it. Certainly, but our wickedness no less; we were not worthier
than our heathen ancestors, to whom Christ did not let the word
be preached. It must therefore be said, according to Romans ix.,
that they were given up to their wickedness because they were
raised up, according to God's righteous but unsearchable judgment, in order to show forth His glory through their condemnation. Was it asked, How then could those, who could do nothing
else than remain in this (inherited) wickedness, still receive damnation and judgment? and how this could be called righteous?

[1] *Instit.* iii. 24, § 1-12. [2] *Ibid.* iii. 23; 24, 12.

his answer is: Whatever God wills is to be deemed righteous, because He wills it; His will must be the cause of everything, else must something go before His will by which it would be bound. Hence it is ungodly to inquire after the cause of the Divine will. The highest law of righteousness is the Will of God (*summa justitiæ regula est Dei voluntas*). Dost thou ask, Why has God so willed this, which must be good because He has willed it? Thou seekest to pass out beyond the will of God, but there is nothing higher except for the godless, to whom God will answer. But although the will of God is free, and what He wills must be held by us to be good, still the free-will of God is not tyrannical and *exlex;* the *commentum absolutæ potentiæ* is profane and deserving of abhorrence. We do not imagine God outside the law, He is Himself the law. (*Non fingimus Deum exlegem, sibi ipse lex est.*) His will, pure from all error, is also the rule of highest perfection and the law of all laws. Thus we may not speak of a subordinate power, which God misuses in cruel sport, for before His judgment-seat we cannot answer for one of a thousand. As little as there is to be found in man a cause of election, as certainly is there in him a cause of damnation, and his destruction depends upon the predestination of God only in such a way that the ground and matter of it are to be found in himself.

Since this answer leads back to the guilt of man, the question is, whence does this arise, out of humanity or from God? God is justified as a punishing God, and His holiness discovered, when He is not the cause of sin. But since the universal sinfulness runs up to Adam, the cardinal question is: how is *Adam's fall* to be thought of in relation to God and His counsel? Here Calvin was somewhat undecided. On the one hand, he was not satisfied with a mere permission on the part of God; on the other hand, he seeks to devolve the guilt of the fall upon man. Man falls because Providence so orders it, but he falls through his own fault (*cadit homo Dei providentia sic ordinante, sed suo vitio cadit*). According to the latter formula, the transgression was not effected by God, but was only assumed into the general ordering (*ordinatio*) of the world as an element that existed for God [*eine für Gott gegebene Grösse*], inasmuch as nothing could at all events become actual, of which God had not decreed that it might attain to actuality. In support of this interpretation it may also be adduced, that Calvin never ceases to seek to maintain the idea of guilt and the *justitia Dei;* that he denies that Satan or the wicked do what is evil under compulsion by God, but rather do it voluntarily; and finally, that he, in the whole of the First Book, determines indeed, by the divine ordering of the world, the *result* of the actions, nay, even the *matter* of the *will*, of man, but in doing so only lets the decision extend to the *manner* in which the already existing evil is to give effect to itself, whilst he nowhere teaches an original effecting of evil by God, and in general does not let the *form* of the human will be disposed by God to evil, when this direction of it does not already exist. But certainly, on the other hand, the movement of his thoughts leads in a different direction; and it is probably in this that the reason is to be sought why, in the churches moulded by his influence, Supralapsarianism was able to win for itself the rights of citizenship alongside of Infralapsarianism. He is quite decided in not allowing Adam to be created with an evil principle, but pure and perfect,[1] and since he distinctly disputes the positive bringing forth of evil by God, he must, according to this side of it, go back for the origin of the fall upon Satan and man. But, on the other side, he says in the Third Book, that it is a frigid fancy (a *frigidum commentum*) that man prepared for himself his own fate by his *liberum arbitrium;* where then was the divine omnipotence? God had not created the noblest of His creatures for an uncertain aim. Nor could predestination, however it might be gone about, be got rid of in the case of posterity, for it could not happen through the mere order of nature that by the guilt of one man all fell into a lost condition. What hinders one then, he asks, from allowing in respect of one man, what he must, against his will, allow of the whole race? If the Scripture teaches that in the person of one man all have fallen under eternal death, and

[1] i. 15, 8: "Præclaris dotibus excelluit prima hominis conditio, ut ratio, intelligentia, etc., suppeterent non modo ad terrenæ vitæ gubernationem, sed quibus transcenderent usque ad Deum et æternam felicitatem.—In hac integritate libero arbitrio pollebat homo, quo si vellet, adipisci posset vitam æternam." Some falsely confuse this with predestination, whilst it is the nature of man that is treated of. "Potuit igitur Adam stare, si vellet, quando nonnisi propria voluntate cecidit : sed quia in utramque partem flexibilis erat ejus voluntas, nec data erat ad perseverandum constantia, ideo tam facile prolapsus est." The "donum perseverantiæ" however could not have been given him, else he could not have sinned. But cf. iii. 23, 8.

if this consequence cannot be ascribed to nature, then it must come out of the wonderful counsel of God, even as it is certain that whole nations with their children have been, through Adam's fall, actually involved in eternal death. A frightful [*schrecklich*] decree, certainly (*Decretum quidem horribile*,[1] *fateor*); but no one can deny that God foreknew the fall of Adam together with its effects, and foreknew it, because He had pre-ordained it. For He has allowed what could not have come actually to pass apart from His omnipotence, only because He has adopted or willed what He has allowed.[2] It is a greater honour for the omnipotence of God, to produce good even out of evil, than not to let the evil come into existence. A twofold activity on the part of God is to be traced in the case of the wicked; first of all, God forsakes them, whereby they harden to stone, and then He works, especially by means of Satan, for the determination of their (evil) will, suggests their projects, and incites, nay, intensifies their will. Thus the hardening of Pharaoh is the act of God. But since Calvin nowhere teaches distinctly a withdrawal of the Spirit of God of such a kind that, and thereby, a pious man, who depends on God, such as Adam originally was, becomes godless; it can always be said again, that the being forsaken by God presupposes the turning away from God, the forsaking of God by man, which was certainly foreknown by God and adopted into the government of the world. And when he derives the divine foreknowledge from pre-ordination, this, seeing that he does not express himself more minutely regarding the nature of this foreknowledge, may be understood in this way, that God draws His foreknowledge of the actual coming to pass of evil

---

[1] In a copy of an edition of the Institutes, published in 1590, which I picked up some time ago, there are written on the fly-leaf the following comments upon this word. "Dr. A. Clarke says that Calvin justly calls *decretum horribile*, the horrible decree of sovereign eternal irrespective reprobation. Ans. I. The phrase is applied by Calvin to God's permission of the fall of Adam. *Inst.* iii. 23, § 7. II. It is unfair to translate it, horrible decree. See Cicero, *Quinct. Horribile est causam capitis dicere, horribilius priore loco dicere.* It is a *solemn* thing, &c. See also Virgil, *Georg.* iii. 152. III. Dr. Clarke derives *Elohim* from *Alahu* (Arab.) *cum sacro horrore ac veneratione coluit.* Would it be fair to represent Dr. Clarke, in adopting this etymology, as teaching that God should always be worshipped with *horror?*"—*Tr.*

[2] iii. 23, 7, ff. In this a productive will for evil is certainly not asserted by Calvin, but only the embracing of evil also in the divine will regarding the system of the world.

from His pre-ordination, in so far as without His permissive adoption of the future realization of evil, the coming to pass of the reality of it, and therefore also the knowledge of this reality, would remain excluded.[1] Hence what can be set up as the distinct and clear doctrine of Calvin in this respect, is only this, that certainly, according to the counsel of God, the sin of Adam has passed over upon the whole race, whereby it deserves damnation, and that God resolved to elect and to save only a part, whilst in reference to the non-elect He did not stop short at the mere leaving of them in their condition, and the allowing of it, but, in His government of the world viewed as one whole, extends His activity to them also and assigns to them as it were a passive position, wherein they must subserve the purposes of God in the course of history as well as through their final destiny. This however does not essentially pass beyond the Infralapsarianism of Augustine. Nay, even the Lutheran doctrine of original sin and its effects stands essentially upon the same platform with this; it, too, has to answer the same problem: How does the idea of guilt consist with the universal and natural inheritance of evil? further, how does the arrangement accord with the goodness of God, and His government of the world, an arrangement which nevertheless would not be possible apart from Him, namely, that all the posterity of Adam are forthwith involved in the sin of Adam and its consequences? in particular, however, the arrangement that through this evil heritage so many nations, which do not hear the Gospel, go down to eternal damnation? So long as the Lutheran doctrine in this matter is not further worked out, it evidently teaches, in reference to the posterity of Adam, although struggling against it, an absolute predestination of some to damnation, and of all to sin and guilt descending from Adam.

The Lutheran doctrine certainly keeps steadfastly to the *universality* of the divine *promise*, although it knows that the merely particular fulfilment is not to be attributed only to the guilt of man, but yet involuntarily again makes the divine ordination,

---

[1] The justice of the punishment he deduces (ii. 4, 2) from this, that evil happens, although *servili*, yet *voluntaria, cupiditate*, even as the godless, too, cannot rid their hearts of the consciousness of guilt. ii. 5, 5, 4, 1; ii. 5, 1: "Nego peccatum ideo minus debere imputari, quod necessarium est; nego rursus evitabile esse, quia voluntarium sit. Pro servitute miserabiles sumus, pro voluntate inexcusabiles." Cf. Calvin's *Letters*, ed. J. Bonnet, i. 359.

which is independent of the guilt, responsible (*e.g.* in respect of the heathen) for that particularity. Calvin, on the other hand, proceeds to impugn the principal title of the promise to universality. As possessed of real efficacy—and everything depended upon this—the promise was not universal. It was indeed evident that not all were called, even as not all that were called attained to faith. But God had not promised that. God owes nothing to man; as little as the beasts may complain and ask why they were not rather created men, as little may the people murmur that He passes by one and chooses others. Even Jesus, too, the Head of the Church, is not the Son of God by means of His righteous life, but through the free choice of God. He has left some, nay, would have them, in sin and destruction, and has chosen others, because God has created everything (according to Solomon) on His own account, even the ungodly for the day of evil. In this, namely, that He has willed men to be born, who from their mother's womb are devoted to certain death, and through their destruction glorify His name,—in this He shows what all deserved, *i.e.* He reveals in them His righteousness, as in the elect His grace. Partiality therefore does not happen either on the one side or on the other. There is no law that could prevent Him from doing with His own what He will,—that prescribed to Him to exercise grace to none or to all.

Certainly we have thus a dualism of two classes of men, who have from the beginning an opposite destiny. Some are destined for the conscious free love of God, for proper personalities; others only for passive organs of the divine will. And this dualism penetrates also into the nature of God in so far as righteousness and love, if they were conceived of as really united in God, must actively demonstrate themselves in equal measure in men, who are essentially alike worthy by nature of condemnation. Above the two stands, according to Calvin, another power, which decides their operation, nay, the division of the revelation of them upon different subjects. He will not term this supreme sovereignty blind caprice, but will have it conceived of as wisdom which is for us incomprehensible. But inasmuch as he accepts a wisdom which stands above the moral nature of God, instead of letting the former be determined by the latter, he shows that it is not the moral nature of God which is, in his view, the highest thing, but the omnipotent Will, which is certainly presupposed to be wise. This dualism destroys at the same time the moral law. The same God, who forbids evil, ordains it; thus we have at the same time a double antagonistic divine will, the imperative (*præceptum*), and the efficacious or decisive (*voluntas*). There cannot be perfect earnestness in the former, if the efficacious will can decide against it in the case of the *reprobi*. Still, with all this, it is to be firmly maintained that Calvin will in no case allow the interests of religion and morality to be injured, but prefers to stop short in presence of the mystery or in inconsistency. The *præceptum* is not, in his view, affected by the *voluntas*; and as he will have *faith* in the righteousness and goodness of God held fast, even when we cannot solve the contradictions, so also *faith* in the objective certainty of the means of grace which offer salvation and the promise, although the secret will of God ordains only a particular realization of salvation. He does not allow his doctrine to develop itself freely, and constantly recommends one to keep by the approximate cause in reference to the damnation of the wicked, not to lose one's self in incomprehensibilities, but to hold to the revealed will of God and to Christ, the mirror of election. In reference to what concerns *election* itself, it is, according to him, not dependent in God upon faith; it does not first become valid and effective through faith, for faith much more comes from *Electio* (iii. 2, 11). Faith, too, according to him, does not come from the human knowledge of election, but the knowledge of election comes from faith; and he can thus make the distinct demand that we are not to inquire after the mysteries of the divine counsel *extra fidem*, but are to draw the assurance of election out of faith, which, where it exists, is the evidence of election. Another mark of election, which must not be wanting, is the calling. None is elected, who is not called; still all that are called are not elected. The Word and sacrament, as well as *fides*, are thus, instead of being threatened, only rendered so much the more secure by the doctrine of election. The means of grace have also some effect upon all. Beginnings of the communication of the Spirit are allotted even to the *reprobi*, but that indeed only in order ultimately to disappear again, or even to serve to harden them. There is therefore another gift of the Spirit destined for the elect, which they only receive, the gift of perseverance (*donum perseverantiæ*). And, accordingly, in the divine decree of election there is contained not merely the *vocatio gratuita*, but also the communication of the pledge of the future inheritance, that is to say, of the assurance of childhood through the testimony of the Holy Ghost (*arrhabo hæreditatis futuræ; quia scilicet eorum cordibus futuræ adoptionis certitudinem suo testimonio (Sp. s.) obsignat et stabilit*). As little as we are to fly above the clouds, but are rather to keep to the divine order, and are therefore to hold to the Word in the sobriety of faith, as distinctly must faith conceive of itself as the effect of election, and in so far go back upon it in order to give God the glory, so that the cause may not be thrust into the background by what is only the effect. The channel is not to hinder the source from receiving the glory due to it. In election lies also the *donum perseverantiæ*. For calling and faith would be little without this. There is an abiding communion with Christ, to whom is directed the look that seeks the reconciled Father, and in whom we are able to contemplate, as in a mirror, our election,[1] which has its cause neither in us, nor in God the Father apart from the Son. He it is, into whose body the Father hath decreed to join all the elect; we are in the Book of Life, if we are one with Christ, who leaves no sheep out of His fold.

But how does it agree with this, that there are always some falling away? There is, says he, also a seeming faith, and similarities on the part of those who are called but not elect to those who are elect. But one thing the former never had, the inward seal of election, the pledge of the future inheritance, which the latter have out of the word through faith. Genuine faith extends also to the future, and nothing is more contrary to it than doubt as to one's future fate. Even the elect indeed may fall, but not into unpardonable blasphemy (*irremissibilis blasphemia*); there remains in them a seed of election, whilst many, who had for some time a participation in the Holy Ghost and His illumination, are on account of their ingratitude forsaken again by God.

In the *doctrine of the sacraments* also, as in the doctrine of sin, guilt, and justification, Calvin has sought to draw nearer to Luther than Zwingli did. He has also effected the adhesion to his type of doctrine of the Reformed Confessions of the second formation, which are at the same time the most important, whilst

[1] *Instit.* ii. 17, 1 ; iii. 22, 1, 24, 5.

the doctrine held by Zwingli in the middle period of his life found reception in no symbol.

Calvin's fundamental thought follows up that which Zwingli taught at the outset and again at the close, namely that the sacraments are not bare signs nor merely a performance of gratitude or confession, but are a pledge and a seal of divine and present grace, and are in so far efficacious and mysterious. Entirely to this effect are the Heidelberg Catechism, the Helvetic Confession of the year 1566, the Gallic, Belgian, and Scotch Confessions.[1]

Baptism in particular[2] is according to Calvin not merely an emblem of our purification, but a pledge of divine grace, a divine sign of reception into the covenant of grace, which takes place by means of it. It is in his view also a seal of childhood. He considers it presumptuous to deny that even children believe; they may have a seed-like faith (a *fides seminalis*); the Lord may give to the little ones the first feelings and the enjoyment of the blessing which they are in future to enjoy in its fulness. Logically, he could properly see in baptism, and that on account of his doctrine of predestination, only a calling (*vocatio*), which could again be lost, and not in the case of all the actual adoption into the state of grace, only he does not bring this limitation to bear. And in like manner do the chief Reformed Confessions express themselves.[3]

In reference to the *Supper*, a reaction against the so-called

---

[1] *Cat. Heid.* Q. 65, 69, 73; *Helvet.* i. 19; *Gallic*, 34; *Belg.* 33; *Scot.* 21. [It is scarcely necessary to say that the *Confessio Scotica*, here cited, is that drawn up by Knox and his associates in 1560, and held as the Confession of the Scotch Church until the adoption of the Westminster Confession in 1647.—*Tr.*]

[2] *Instit.* iv. 15 (*Baptismus*), iv. 16, 1-5; 17, 18 (*Pædobaptismus*).

[3] *Cat. Heid.* Q. 69, 73; *Belg.* 34; *Scot.* 21: "Certo credimus, per Baptismum nos Jesu Christo inseri justitiæque ejus participes fieri." *Helvet.* i. 19: "Intus regeneramur, purificamur adeo per Spiritum S., foris autem accipimus obsignationem maximorum donorum in aqua." *Angl.* 27: "Baptism is not merely the sign of the *professio*, but signum regenerationis per quod tamquam per instrumentum recte baptismum suscipientes ecclesiæ inseruntur. Promissione—visibiliter obsignantur, fides confirmatur et vi divinæ invocationis gratio augetur." Here the sacramental effect is made dependent on faith. The English liturgy on the other hand says after the baptism of the infant, "Seeing now, dearly beloved brethren, that this child is regenerate and grafted into the body of Christ's Church, let us give thanks." There have arisen upon this point, especially in the most recent times, controversies regarding Baptismal Regeneration, by which, however, even Robert Wilberforce and Pusey only understand *Justificatio*. [See App. Note I.—*Tr.*]

Zwinglian doctrine of the Supper,—a reaction which issued from Strasburg and Basle—had early made itself manifest in Switzerland. Even the Zürich *Prædicantenordnung* of 1532 calls the sacraments high and holy mysteries, which must not be made of less account by reason of Popish abuses. There was certainly a wavering induced, as has been indicated, by Luther's smaller " Confession concerning the Supper." A certain patriotism held the Zürichers more closely connected with Zwingli, and in that locality his work was carried forward by a circle of grateful scholars, relatives, and friends (like Bullinger, Walther, and others). There was issued by them in Zürich, in 1545, as an answer to Luther, " The true confession of the servants of Christ" [*das wahrhaftige Bekenntniss der Diener Christi*], in which the presence of the body and blood of Christ in the Supper is summarily denied. But meanwhile Calvin had come upon the scene, and had become in the south-western part of Switzerland the representative of a mediatory movement. After his stay in Strasburg, subsequently to the Wittenberg Concord, he took a lively interest in the union of the confessions, and to this end wrote about 1540 the small but very important treatise *De cœna Domini*. He here assumes a very independent position towards Zwingli as well as towards Luther, but seeks to point out in each the truth which he represents, and to unite these elements into one. The purpose of the sacred procedure is the divine sealing of the promise of the body and blood, of the whole Christ, as food unto life eternal, that we may thank and praise Him and be incited to faith and love. It is the divine opening up of access unto Christ, the crucified and risen One, so that our sins may be blotted out, and we may be restored into heavenly and immortal life. In comparison with the Gospel, the Supper secures a fuller enjoyment and greater certainty. But how do these fruits become ours, and how does the Supper stand related to them ? His fundamental thought is this: Christ does not allow. Himself to be separated from the blessing which He has procured; His benefits do not apply to us, unless He Himself has come into closer relationship with us ; and His closer communion with us must be accompanied by the benefits which He has procured. On that account, the words of institution do not speak of the body of Christ apart from the fruits thereof, neither of the fruits apart from the body and blood, whereby they are procured. Therefore *Christ, His humanity also being included, is the matter and substance of the sacraments;* the graces and benefits of Christ are the power and *effect* of this substance. The substance must be conjoined with the effect, so that the effect may be based in a sure reality. The fruit would be nought, if Christ, the substance and basis of the whole matter, was not given to us in the Supper (*nisi in cœna S. Christus totius rei substantia et fundamentum nobis donetur*); the *cœna S.* is *communicatio Christi.* But Christ, His humanity included, is the source and matter of every benefit (*fons, origo, materia bonorum omnium*). Christ calls the bread and wine body and blood, because, as visible signs, they are at the same time instrumental means (*instrumenta*), whereby Christ dispenses to us His body and blood. Calvin thus evidently inclined to the Lutheran view in the *substance* of it. But in reference to the *proof*, he opposes Luther, and follows Zwingli rather in the explanation of the words of institution. The "is" must be taken in the sense of "signifies," but it does not follow from this that the Supper presents bare signs. This opinion is the fundamental error of Zwingli. The symbolic exhibition is at the same time a real presentation (*panis non modo representat sed etiam offert*); the signs are conjoined with the substance they denote (*signa veritati et substantiæ suæ conjuncta*). The security, however, for the conjunction of this substance with the elements is not a change in them nor a fettering of the body and blood of Christ to the elements (*inclusio, alligatio*), but the promissory will of Christ, and the act of Christ which, according to His promise, never fails.

This is the treatise, on account of which Luther, when he saw it, sent him his salutation, and even *Joachim Westphal* afterwards acknowledges that until 1549 he was looked upon by the Lutherans with the most friendly regard (*in deliciis*). He concludes: With one mouth therefore do we all confess, that we are truly made partakers of the substance of the body and blood of Christ (*uno igitur ore fatemur omnes, nos substantiæ corporis et sanguinis Christi vere fieri participes*). Calvin had thus carried the matter back essentially to the standpoint of the Swabian Syngramma, and even the new attack, made by Luther in the smaller Confession of 1544 (see p. 335), in no way applied to Calvin.

The favourable reception accorded to this treatise necessarily revived the hope entertained by Calvin, of being able, by means of his standpoint, to bring about a reconciliation; but he was forced also to perceive that the task, which in the first instance devolved upon him, was to bring back the Zürichers from the austerity of the standpoint which they had in 1545 again assumed, before any reconciliation with the Lutherans could be thought of. He complained, in letters to friends like Viret and Farel, of Zwingli's reservedness, called his view of the sacraments profane, and blamed the narrow-heartedness of the Zürichers, Walther, Bullinger, and others, who blazed into a passion when any one dared to prefer Luther to Zwingli, as if the Gospel perished when Zwingli lost. And yet no injustice was done to Zwingli in this, for if the two were compared, Luther stood far above him. He attempted now, in eager negotiation, to lead the Zürichers beyond Zwingli's doctrine of the Supper, by showing that one could repudiate everything in which they found just cause of offence, could receive also their explanation of the words of institution, and yet secure to the Supper the significance of a gift and of communion with the very person of Christ, which was present in the transaction. In order to this there was no necessity for an inclusion of Christ into the elements, nor for His descending from Heaven and ascending again, nor, again, of the real enjoyment of the body and blood of Christ on the side of unbelievers. As *Bullinger* had already sought to place the symbols of the Old and New Testaments upon a different footing by conceiving of the latter as exhibitive, those representations [of Calvin] found favourable entrance, and after a conference had been held in Zürich, the *Consensus Tigurinus* was brought about by Calvin and Farel in 1549. Its success, however, was obtained only in this way, that Calvin, in giving prominence to those divergencies from Luther—especially in connection with the words of institution,—which were common to him and the Zürichers, placed himself very decidedly and somewhat polemically upon the side of the Zurichers. Although these were more subordinate points in reference to the matter itself, still they came disproportionately into the foreground for Calvin's own standpoint; and to this was added, that although he did not keep his own view secret, but induced its recognition, still the positive working out of it remained brief and scanty. The sacraments are not empty signs (*tesseræ*), it is here said; without Christ they would be empty masks (*larvæ inanes*); they represent and are seals of the divine promise, namely, of our unity with Christ, of our incorporation into His body. Divine seals are true, and give what they promise. We distinguish between the sign and the thing denoted, but we do not separate them (Thes. 5, 6, 9); the elements are *organa* for the action (*actio*) of Christ through the Holy Ghost. But it is never the power of the elements, by means of which we are made partakers with Christ (Thesis 16), Although the power of the sacraments is effectual only for the elect, still this is not owing to any defect in the truth of the sacrament (*veritas sacramenti*), or to any defect in the counsel of grace to give the blessing to every one capable of receiving it; but it is owing to the want of faith, for this is the mouth which has the capacity for receiving the blessing which is offered, the spiritual enjoyment of Christ. But although unbelievers accordingly do not receive the blessing of the body and blood of Christ, still it is the sacramental presentation for all capable of receiving, and not the strength of faith, upon which the certainty of the presence of Christ rests. A local presence of Christ does not take place; Christ is in heaven, being restricted according to His humanity; consequently, whoever will receive the self-communication of that humanity must be exalted into heaven in faith through the Holy Ghost. Thus Christ feeds our souls by means of the power of the Holy Ghost through the enjoyment of His body and blood (*carnis suæ et sanguinis potione Spiritus Sancti virtute*). But in this he will not have Christ thought of passively as *alimentum*, but will keep everything placed under the point of view of the communicative act of Christ; hence he denies that there takes place any mingling or transfusion of substance (*aliqua substantiæ commixtio seu transfusio*), and he holds only, that we draw life from the flesh and blood of Christ, which were offered once for all. Still he will not, even now, think merely of the forgiveness of sins, or the operations of the Holy Ghost as the subject-matter of the blessing; but includes in it also an actual participation in the divine-human nature of Christ as a principle of power (of *vigor*) and of activity, and of this he made further use for the resurrection of our body. In this point, according to which communion with the divine-humanity of Christ appears as an independent benefit, the Zürichers followed him only with uncertain and lingering steps, even as the ambiguity of the formulæ adopted by them shows. They abode—in this agreeing with Luther—by the recognition of the forgiveness of sins as in particular the blessing of the Supper; only they did not look upon a reception of the body and blood of Christ, but upon the outward signs, as the sacramental pledge of the blessing.

Calvin had expected that the winning of the Zürichers to his own richer view must awaken joy in Germany, seeing that the real presence of the body and blood of Christ and the presentation of them were, in the mind of Luther, the chief matter. Calvin had also adopted into the *Consensus* the expressions of the *Aug.* of 1540,—which at that time was generally considered to be only a new improved edition, and was used officially in the Lutheran Church,—as a bridge for the restoration of peace between the two evangelical sections. Many Germans too, especially in Strasburg and Wittenberg, shared Calvin's hope. But he greatly deceived himself. *Joachim Westphal* in Hamburg,[1] the same who gave to Hamburg and other towns the only too effectual counsel to treat so cruelly the evangelical fugitives who had, under John Lasco, escaped from Bloody Mary in England,[2] attacked Calvin and the *Consensus Tigurinus* in the most violent manner, in several controversial writings from 1552 downwards. He holds that the bread is *substantialiter* the body of Christ; the

---

[1] *Joach. Westphali Farrago confusanearum et inter se dissidentium opinionum de Cœna Domini ex Sacramentariorum libris congesta*, 1552. Even Calvin he calls a *Sacramentarius*. Then, *Recta fides de Cœna Dom.*, 1553. *Collectanea sententiarum D. Aurelii Augustini de Cœna Dom.*, with a *Confutatio sacramentariorum*, 1555. *Fides D. Cyrilli Ep. Alex. de præsentia corporis*, &c. 1555. Calvin replied to him at first, 28th Nov. 1554, proudly and depreciatingly, in his *Defensio sanœ et orthodoxœ doctrinœ de Sacramentis*, for the justification of the *formula consensionis* in Switzerland; whereupon a reply was given in Westphal's *Adversus Sacramentarii cujusdam falsam criminationem justa defensio*, 1555. Calvin met him with his *Secunda defensio adv. Westphali calumnias*, 1556. *Calvin. Tractat. theolog.*, pp. 659-685. John Lasco, Bullinger, and Beza also wrote against Westphal. At last Calvin published his *Ultima admonitio ad Joach. Westphalum*, 1557. He replied again in many forms, and Brenz, Andreä, Timann, E. Schnepf, Er. Alber, Heshus, and others, adhered to him. Cf. *J. G. Walchii Bibliothec. theolog. selecta*, t. ii. 428, Jena, 1758. Stähelin, *J. Calvin*, ii. 122, 208, ff.

[2] The apology for Westphal by Mönckeberg (*Joach. Westphal and John Calvin*, 1565) does not gain its end. Westphal becomes self-accuser in the preface to the *Collectanea aus Augustin*, extols the unmerciful act as a good deed, and sets up Nebuchadnezzar as a pattern for such cases. Did they say they were condemned unheard, without a Synod, he answers, they were condemned at the holy Synods at Schmalkalden, in Würtemburg, nay, even in Ephesus.

Defence of Calvin against Westphal. 411

latter is everywhere, but irrespective of space (*extra locum*). He talks of the Swiss, but especially of Calvin, as heretics, talks also of diabolic blasphemies, of godless repudiation of Scripture, and the overthrow of all sacred things.[1] For a long time Calvin did not reply to these repeated attacks; only in the end of the year 1554, when he heard that Westphal was occupied in collecting signatures in the towns of Lower Germany, which should exhibit a Consensus of the Saxon Churches in opposition to the Swiss,[2] he wrote—not in the way of attacking the Lutheran Church, but in order as far as possible to anticipate misunderstandings—his exposition of the *Consensus Tigurinus*, dedicated to the principal cantons, in which he wrought out further the positive element in the *Consensus Tigurinus*, which Westphal had ignored or misrepresented. But as this utterance did not create peace, Calvin emitted two further treatises against Westphal, and in 1561 one against Tilemann Heshus.[3]

Calvin was able to ask Westphal, if in this Consensus he had changed his view, which had otherwise, as he himself (Westphal) acknowledged, found favour amongst the Lutherans? *i.e.* whether the Swiss had not approximated to his own and the Lutheran view? For Westphal himself confessed that Calvin's doctrine of the Supper had been long contained in his writings.[4] Westphal treated the Consensus as if it taught in the Supper bare signs, a theatrical pomp. Upon the faith which received Christ he threw suspicion as a mere imagination, and even so upon the receiving of the body and blood of Christ. But, asks Calvin, was then the dwelling of Christ in us a mere imagination? How earnest he is in holding a real receiving of the body and blood of Christ, is shown

---

[1] In the *Ep. nuncupatoria* to *Fides Cyrilli*, he says, p. 13, f.: "Nunc (according to Zwingli and Carlstadt) Diabolus denuo (præcipitii foveam) effodere et dilatare pergit per sacramentarios, qui ita ex baptismo et cœna Domini faciunt signa, *ut rem ipsam omnino tollant*. Ex cœna auferunt cibum corporis et potum sanguinis Christi, *relinquentes solum panem et vinum: adimunt etiam virtutem et efficaciam suam tum cœnæ Domini, tum baptismo.*"

[2] In 1557 Westphal accomplished the *Confess. fidei de Euchar. sacram.* on the part of the pastors of many of the Churches of Lower Saxony, as an answer to Calvin's *Secundo defensio*.

[3] Cf. p. 410. Against Heshus Calvin wrote the treatise, *De vera participatione carnis et sanguinis Christi*. In the *Tractat. th.*, pp. 723-743. Heshus disputed in Heidelberg with Klebitz regarding the Supper. Both were deposed, which was approved in a *Responsum* of Melanchthon.

[4] *Secunda Defensio*, p. 659.

by the following details:—The humanity (*caro*) of Christ is life-giving, not merely because salvation was once procured in it, but because even now that very body breathes life into us, inasmuch as we grow in holy unity with Christ, or in a word, because we have a common life with Him through the secret power of the Spirit, which is deposited in the body of Christ. For the life is miraculously infused out of the secret fountain of divinity into the body of Christ, in order to overflow thence into us.[1] When he spoke of spiritual enjoyment, then those persons murmured, as if the real enjoyment were dispelled. But if by the reality there was understood the truth as opposed to delusion or imagination, he would be quite pleased with this word, for what he was concerned about—that he testified—was the actual enjoyment of Christ. The body of Christ was life-giving, and no one upon their side denied its actual communication, only that it did not take place in a carnal way. Hence he still repudiates the physical descriptions *commixtio carnis, transfusio*, in so far as they, in contradiction to the pneumatic nature of Christ, make it something coarsely corporeal and passive; but he says: Like the sun, He pours over the lifegiving power of His flesh into us (*vivificum carnis suæ vigorem in nos transfundit, non secus ac vitali solis calore per radios vegetamur*). Remaining in heaven, He condescends to us by his power; He works from His own place, breathing life into us out of the substance of His body. The mediating principle, which brings us into fellowship with the powers of the body of Christ, is the Holy Spirit with His secret influence, which effects a spiritual elevation in men such as the *sursum corda* requires. For it is only faith which can receive Christ; *whoever teaches otherwise separates the Holy Spirit from Christ*. Not that the sacrament is changed by unbelief—that would make God dependent upon His creature;[2] but only faith *can* receive the blessing, which is in the first instance spiritual, although it has also through the mediation of faith a corporeal significance. The powers, which proceed from the body of Christ,

---

[1] *Secunda Defensio*, p. 657. He adds: "Nos sibi conjungens non modo vitam nobis instillat, sed unum quoque nobiscum efficitur." P. 650: "A carnis suæ substantia Christum vitam in nos spirare." Cf. the numerous passages which the American Dr. Nevin, formerly in Mercersburg, brings forward (*The Doctrine of the Reformed Church on the Lord's Supper*, 1850, p. 3-12).

[2] As cited, p. 656.

he seems accordingly to regard as a power of the Holy Ghost, who however is sent by Christ, nay, proceeds from His humanity, in order to unite with Himself. This union is in His view an elevation of the heart to heaven, but in this we are not to think of an ecstatic abandonment of the body.

Westphal's bustling activity struck the key-note in Germany of that distrust, with which from this time Calvin was, except by the school of Melanchthon, regarded on account of his connection with the Zürichers. The chief question in these controversies was no longer, as in the case of Luther against Zwingli, the subject-matter of the Supper, which must stand out suitably to the confession, but had reference to the mysterious *nature of the union* of grace or of Christ with the elements, and from this secondary question depends that concerning the enjoyment by unbelievers, as well as that concerning the ubiquity of the body of Christ. It now became the custom to look upon Calvin as essentially Zwinglian, but only as more dangerous, because he cunningly concealed his meaning under formulæ which sounded richer,—a historical injustice from which even the *Formula of Concord* is not free, seeing that it, though without naming Calvin, places his view essentially upon the same footing as the Zwinglian.

Still Calvin's more intermediate standpoint met in Germany not only with contradiction and misunderstanding, but also with ready acceptance. Melanchthon[1] counselled peace with the Reformed theologians in view of the terms of their present confessions, and abstinence from farther subtilties after the chief points had been secured. In Bremen the Reformed type of doctrine was by means of *Albert Hardenberg*, and under the Burgomaster Martin von Buren for a long time ascendant, and even after the fall of these men, the Reformed element still remained predominant. So, too, after much wavering, in the Palatinate, in a part of Hesse and in Anhalt. The Reformed Confession was consolidated in Germany by means of the *Heidelberg Catechism*[2] by *Zacharias Ursinus* and *Caspar Olevianus*, 1563.

[1] *Responsum Heidelbergense*, 1559.

[2] Special mention might also have been made of the *Confessia Helvetica II.*, A.D. 1564, of which Bullinger was the author. Of all the Confessions belonging to the second period of the Reformed Church, it was the only one which obtained more than a merely local or national recognition, being formally approved by the Scotch Church in 1566 and 1584, by the French Church, the Hungarian, and the

In general, however, there gradually arose, in Germany, over against the Lutheran, a Reformed Church, important more by reason of its outward position and spiritual wealth than for numbers, and nourished by a relatively large number of learned institutions and theological schools, such as Heidelberg, Marburg, Frankfort-on-the-Oder, and others. But the understanding which had been effected between Zürich and Geneva was still more fruitful of results for the Reformed churches outside of Germany. For now that that point of crystallization had been given, the power of the mind of Calvin drew the different Reformed churches into his sphere; his doctrine of the Supper in particular passed over into the chief Reformed confessions.[1] Those successes of Calvinism in and outside of Germany, *e.g.* those in the Palatinate, increased, however, the animosity in respect of the different creeds. The question of superior power, lying in the background, rendered nugatory beforehand every effect of the peace conference held at Maulbronn, 1564, between the Swabians, Brenz, and Andreä, and the theologians of the Palatinate, and at Mömpelgard, 1586, between Andreä and Beza.

Polish, as well as by the whole Reformed Church in Switzerland, and by the Palatinate. It was therefore as widely recognized as the Heidelberg Catechism, —although it does not seem to have maintained subsequently the same authority, —and may be taken as the representative symbol of that period of the Reformed Church.—*Tr.*

[1] The *Conf. Scotica* teaches an *unio cum corpore et sanguine Christi*, and thereby an enjoyment of the divine-human nature of Christ, which is brought into connection with the resurrection. In like manner, *Belg.* 35, *Gall.* 36, 37, *Helvet.* i. 21. And according to the Heidelberg Catechism, too, we are, through the Holy Ghost, placed in connection with the blessed body of Christ.

SECTION III.

THE REFORMED CHURCH FROM THE DEATH OF CALVIN TO THE SYNOD OF DORT.

THE chief theatre of the dogmatic labours of this period in the Reformed Church was *Holland*, where indeed a milder doctrine of predestination was by native theologians opposed in vain to the formation and church authority of the Belgian confession, and to the unconditioned particularity of grace, but where ultimately, after the exclusion of the Arminians, a certain middle type, which seeks to keep at a decided distance from supralapsarianism, became current in theology.

In Geneva, Calvin († 1564) left behind him a school which maintained and increased itself, especially through the college instituted in 1559, of which Beza became the head. The influence of Geneva upon Germany was in the first instance comparatively slight. Here there was a native Reformed theology of milder type, and on friendly terms with Melanchthon, the heads of which, however, being scattered at different points and exposed to different influences, did not achieve the unity of a compact movement as the Lutherans did. All the deeper, on that account, was the influence which Calvin exerted upon England, and especially, by means of John Knox, upon Scotland. But most immediate of all was the influence which the Geneva theological school—where Lambert Daneau, Ant. Chandieu (Sadeel), and others laboured along with Beza—exerted upon *France*, until the persecutions in that country, which reached their climax on the night of St. Bartholomew in 1572, caused a great interruption. The power of the French Reformed Church was now for a long time broken and shattered; their more important teachers betook themselves to foreign parts, especially to the universities of Holland, which were soon to attain a wonderfully flourishing condition, in connection with the magnificent burghal and state development of Holland. It was owing to these immigrations (*e.g.* there were twenty French doctors of theology at the same time in Holland) that the current of the indigenous Reformation of Holland, which had sprung from the Brethren of the Social Life and their schools, from Thomas à Kempis and Johann Wessel, and had been strengthened also through Lutheran influences, was overpowered, though not without obstinate resistance, in the decision of which in the end also political factors co-operated. The long struggle, in which little Holland wrestled with Philip II., required the most extreme straining of its energies on the part of Dutch Protestantism in order to preserve itself from certain destruction. To this severe strain accorded a mode of thought, which indeed casts man down in humility before the majesty of God, but also plants in him a spirit of independence and fearlessness before men, which, reposing upon the counsel of election, shrinks back from no danger. The Calvinist mode of thought, inasmuch as it unfurled the banner of the majesty and glory of God, towards which man places himself in the position of a willing instrument, inspired its faithful adherents with a mind courageous and confident of victory, a martyr spirit, and an invincible bravery,—virtues to which Calvinism owed a good portion of its power of conquest, and which constituted it the warring power of Protestantism. These political afflictions served accordingly to render the mind of the Dutch susceptible for the more severe Calvinistic doctrine, and to procure acceptance for the Belgian confession, which was composed by Guido de Bres, 1562, in the first instance as a private treatise, and whose purport is not indeed supralapsarian,[1] but otherwise severely predestinarian. It was however never without its opponents, who were strengthened partly through immigration from Germany, and partly and in particular through the relations with East Friesland, where *Johann von Lasco* had effected the introduction of a milder type of doctrine.[2] The defenders of a merely conditioned doctrine of predestination were *Clemens Martenson*, about 1554, and afterwards *Cornheert* and *Arnold Cornelii*, against *Martin Lydius* in Amsterdam. These men, with their numerous friends in Utrecht, Holland, and Friesland, demanded in 1586 a revision of the Belgian confession, which had been, as it were, imposed by force, whilst their opponents desired the annual subscription of that confession and of the Heidelberg Catechism.

[1] *Belgic artic.* xiii. xvi.   [2] Petrus Bartels, *Joh. a Lasco*, 1860.

But it was first through *Jacob Arminius* in Amsterdam that the division came the length of serious conflict. A talented man, of a clear head, and a scholar of Beza, he had at first, by commission of the Calvinist party, applied himself to the refutation of Cornheert; but the longer he occupied himself with the subject, the farther was he led away from Calvin. On entering upon his office in 1602 as professor in Leyden, he was publicly opposed by *Franz Gomarus*, and soon also by *Bogermann*. He sought to make election dependent upon faith, whilst they sought to enforce absolute predestination as the rule of faith, according to which the whole Scriptures are to be interpreted. This seemed to *Arminius* to be Popish, and he maintained that the holy Scriptures alone decided, but no truth was established for us previously to the Scriptures. He himself indeed was thereby caught in a delusion, for if his opponents placed the doctrine of an unconditioned divine decree as the material principle before the formal, he came to the Scriptures with the postulate of human freedom. The strict Calvinists were afraid that without the doctrine of predestination they would lose the principle which held their Church together, just as in the Lutheran Church the doctrine of justification is the bond which unites together all other doctrines.

The position of the two parties was in its ultimate issue this, that the one asserted the majesty and glory of God at the expense of man, who is viewed by them not as an end in himself, but only as a means to the glory of God, whilst Arminius and his party set up the well-being of man as the supreme end, but in doing so, make God only a means for man as the end. The former, indeed, would not annihilate man and render him worthless; for if man is a means for the glory of God, still there is properly something gained for God by means of man. Man is thus of some importance for God, especially as Calvinism summons him to make it his work to render himself a means for God in self-sacrifice and devotion to Him. Nay, starting from this point, one might be tempted to say: If the ethical element, which places others before it as an end, is the highest, then Calvinism transfers the highest element, the ethical, from the side of God to that of man (whilst Arminianism places it exclusively on the side of God), since, according to the Calvinists, God is supposed to have made everything only *propter se*, if it were not on the other hand to be confessed that this *propter se* is not to be taken in the egoistic sense, and that, on the contrary, the revelation of the *Misericordia* of God belongs also to the end He has in view, His *Misericordia* including—though this is not developed—man, or, at any rate, a part of mankind, as its end.

Arminianism, upon its part, thinks indeed of man as the end, but is quite unconcerned as to whether God is not rendered by it a mere means for men, nay, whether man is not thereby robbed of the highest element, of unselfish love to God as his end. At the same time, it is still essentially connected with Calvinism, inasmuch as it too, in order to preserve the transcendent majesty of God, lays a onesided emphasis upon His supreme sovereignty. Nay, in this point it exceeds Calvinism, for it will not—from which Calvinism differs (see p. 396, 402)—consider free divine sovereignty to be bound to any law in God, so that even the ethical receives a merely accidental position. Not because it is something good in itself is it, according to Arminius, willed by God; but that is good which God in fact wills and commands. The positive matter of fact is the source of the knowledge of what is good. Man is recognized as being in the image of God, not in the sense that he is essentially designed for the same good that God *is*, but for that which God *wills,* but might not have willed. If the ethical in general, the goodness as well as the righteousness of God, seems to be thus placed under His power, and to be in respect of it properly accidental, still it is for the most part only the holiness and righteousness of God amongst His ethical attributes which are thereby affected, for it remains in the view of Arminianism beyond all doubt that man and his well-being must be the end for the goodness of God. Man is designed for happiness, and the will and government of God contemplate this end. Thus it was no longer the glory of God, but the glorification of man, which was the supreme principle. This view was vehemently opposed by Calvinism, and with good right; for this theory, by dissolving the idea of a supreme principle in itself good, and the foundation of obligation, let loose those subjectivities which Calvinism confined and held together by the principle of the glory of God. In addition to this, the end ascribed by Arminianism to God, "the well-being of the world," does not disavow a savour of eudæmonism; and accordingly the love of God, which it would fain maintain, is rendered by it an unethical goodness. The reason of this lies in the neglect of the rights of that which is objectively in itself good and holy, in the will of God, as well as of man, *i.e.* in thrusting into the background the idea of divine righteousness. It is not the ethical in the world which is, according to Arminianism, the highest goal of the world for God, but the ethical only receives the position of a subservient means of happiness. There was nothing in God to prevent Him from giving other moral laws, if well-being had been thereby attainable; but now that God has given them, they are obligatory. The necessary co-ordination of well-being with morality, the essential destination of his nature for the latter, is not considered even in respect of man, but only the obligation to what God has once positively set up as good. Thus the power and the ethical nature of God are not wrought into one another; Arminianism has accustomed itself to regard the general weal as the highest good, which may perhaps be connected with its tendency towards the province of politics and law.

Arminianism had, especially in the seminary at Amsterdam, a διαδοχή of eminent theologians. After Arminius followed *Simon Episcopius* († 1643), author of the *Institutio relig. christ.*; then followed *Stephanus Curcellӓus* († 1659), *Arnold Pölenburg* († 1666), and *Pontanus* († 1698). In the eighteenth century they rose almost higher through *Philip v. Limborch* († 1711), *Adrian von Cattenburgh* till after 1730, *Jean Leclerc* (Clericus, born at Geneva, 1657, † 1736), *Wetstein* († 1754). Alongside of Episcopius, *Hugo Grotius* laboured in essentially the same spirit. Through its opposition to Predestinarianism, Arminianism possesses a certain similarity to the *Lutheran* doctrine, in the shape which the latter in the seventeenth century more and more assumed, but the similarity is rather a superficial one. The idea of God is intrinsically different in the two. In Arminianism there is not merely the absence of any mysticism, but there is wanting even the inwardness of the religious spirit, and the perception that the highest good lies in fellowship with God and the divine life. With its face towards subjectivity, it sees a security for freedom only in the limitation of the divine influence, or in man being placed in his own hands, though of course under the direction of the divine commands. In a word, it is the *Erasmian idea of freedom, which in substance emerges again in it.*

Whilst the evangelical material principle was firmly maintained, as has been shown, in Calvinism (inasmuch as the election in Christ to faith and salvation is, as it were, only the eternal act of justification by God—the act viewed as removed into the divine forum—for those who are made partakers of salvation); in Arminianism in general, on the other hand, the evangelical material principle, with its power as a bond of union, fell into the background, and so did the *Testimonium Spiritus Sancti*. Subjectivity, being now no longer inwardly restrained, begins to emancipate itself, and to recognize only an external limit in the formal principle or the holy Scriptures, which are placed in a sort of legal position. Faith, instead of resulting in a living fellowship with God and the possession of salvation, which is involved therein, is resolved into a receiving of the doctrines and commands of positive revelation; and the subjectivity sets itself to compensate for the loss of the demonstration of the Spirit and of power by proofs for the credibility of the revelation. In this way the reason, with its historical or other methods of proof, and the *fides humana* thereby produced, usurp the place of the *fides divina*. According to this, Arminianism, by its doctrine of the *liberum arbitrium*, allowed somewhat of a Pelagianizing element to enter into the doctrine of salvation and its appropriation; and it drew sanctification into the place even of justification, though this happened only step by step. Nay, in its subsequent course, and in accordance with the foregoing, it transformed even the objective basis of justification, the doctrine of God, of the Trinity, of the Person of Christ, and of the atonement. Let us consider these points severally.[1]

In opposition to all divine authority in the Church and tradition, Arminianism will only be bound by the *holy Scriptures*, and in so far the Reformed Church, with its more rapid development, exhibits in Arminianism a forerunner of the biblical supernaturalism, which first appears in the Lutheran Church in the eighteenth century. But there is shown in its case, that if the relatively independent material principle, with which the Scriptures are to be already approached, does not, by means of that living need of salvation which it includes, give security for the right meaning and spirit, the exegesis loses its sureness, since the subjectivity, which is not at once inwardly restrained and set free by the Christian spirit,

[1] Cf. Schneckenburger, *Lehrbegr. der kl. prot. Kirchenpart.* 1863, p. 2-26.

can easily insert into the Scriptures in reading them what it wants, as well as explain away from them what does not agree with it, and a self-delusion as to unity with the Scriptures is accordingly possible under the title of self-interpretation. That the Scriptures have alone to attest everything, is the postulate of Arminianism; but since it will not base the Scriptures upon the authority of the Church, and their claim to authority does not of itself stand sure as an axiom for all, it lays a substructure which is to support and attest the Scripture principle. But then, as has been said, it is ultimately not the Scriptures, but the *demonstrating reason,* which attests everything. With this end in view, *Hugo Grotius* already, who is still more inwardly than outwardly connected with the Arminians, constructed in his work, *De veritate religionis christianæ,* a sort of apologetics for the formal principle, and so did Episcopius.[1] The suspicion is not allowed against the New Testament authors, that they were not willing to communicate the truth as they might have done. Therefore what they say of miracles, of the resurrection of Christ, and so on, is true; and the divine origin of the Christian religion, which its founder asserted, is to be recognized. The attempt to supplement the empirical historical proof by a philosophic basis is made already by Arminius; and, in general, philosophic studies were zealously recommended by the Arminians.[2] But the same intellectual reason, which so altered the idea of faith that it sought to give a demonstration of it, had also the principal say in the exegesis, with very destructive results. The amount of labour expended by its apologetics upon miracles, inspiration, and so on, is out of proportion to the end which it is intended as a means to serve, the subject-matter which is found in the holy Scriptures. All the deeper ideas in Scripture are rendered superficial; regeneration becomes the incitement of the moral powers by precept and example; the operation of the Holy Ghost is necessary, but the Spirit as dwelling, operating, and creating in man is not necessary,—only His assistance; and this is applied also to the inspiration of the sacred writers. The obscurer passages are to be passed over; the clearer decide; all those, however, are obscure which allow more than one interpretation, and none of them

[1] *Episcopii Instit.*, lib. iv., § 1.
[2] *J. Arminii Opera, De certitudine theologica,* p. 56.

contains anything necessary for salvation. They thus secure themselves against being refuted from the Scriptures; but they also show that when they assign such a distinguished position to the Scriptures, apart from the material principle, it is more because of a dislike to the Church doctrine, against which these Scriptures serve them as a basis of operations, than from true reverence for them, and the desire to live and move in their element. And yet even they introduce, alongside of the doctrine of the *liberum arbitrium,* as another leading principle (a surrogate, as it were, for the material principle), according to which they explain the Scriptures, the maxim of practical utility, and the well-being of the world. Under this pretext was severed the life nerve of the so-called mysteries, which indeed were in a great measure perpetuated by the Evangelicals more as a doctrinal tradition, without being assimilated to the new perception of faith; and Episcopius, in particular, went the length of asserting the practical indifference even of the foremost doctrines, as, for example, the divine-humanity of Christ.

Let us now glance at the principal dogmatic points in order. First, at the doctrine of God. The two views which are united in the true idea of love, namely righteous self-assertion and self-communication, or: that God is His own end, but also at the same time man, inasmuch as he is the end of God Himself and that as His holy image, loving Him in return, and setting Him before himself as in turn his end,—these two views were, as we saw, divided between the two parties in Holland, so that the strict Calvinists held to the first view and the Arminians to the second. But just as the old Calvinism manifests in this a greater religious intensity, certainly at the cost of the ethical, to which Arminianism addresses itself just as onesidedly with a strong worldly tendency; so it may be regarded as the common doctrine of Arminianism that the ethical, which was reckoned by the orthodox to the nature of God, was by the Arminians placed in His mere action or will. Orthodoxy regards righteousness as unchangeable and eternally founded in the nature of God; thus Maresius, for example, works it out as a demonstration of the necessity of the atonement. The Arminians transform the wrath of God against evil into a kind of goodness which is prescribed by the Divine wisdom,—which must prove fatal for the doctrine of atonement. This is worked out much more comprehensively by *Conrad Vorstius* in Steinfurt, 1610. In alliance with Arminianism, he seeks to overturn the Calvinist view of the world with the doctrine of God for his fulcrum.[1] In order to procure more vivacity for the idea of God, this acute thinker, who gives utterance too to correct guesses, proceeds not only to let the action of God enter into space and time, but even to limit and render Him finite in His being, and to place space and time above God as if they were eternal primitive powers which bind Him.[2]

Arminianism modifies in like manner the *doctrine of the Trinity*. Arminius does not seek to alter it, nor does he expressly assert the subordination of the Son. But whilst Calvin had taught that the Son, although as Son begotten of the Father, had as God aseity, Arminius says that He is in both respects from the Father, and therefore not *a se ipso*, that He has with the Holy Ghost only a communicated divine nature, not $αὐτοθεότης$. The subordination, which is herein contained, was afterwards worked out more decidedly by Simon Episcopius and Philip von Limborch, and in like manner by Vorstius, whilst Clericus, under the name of Liberius a St. Amore, cherished Sabellian (and afterwards Arianizing) views.

But especially has the Arminian *doctrine of atonement* won for itself a certain name. Its chief defenders are, besides Arminius, *Hugo Grotius, Episcopius, Limborch* and *Curcellaüs*.[3] *Arminius* denies the infinitude of the guilt to be atoned. Sin does not offend against God, but only against a command of God, which, as we saw, stands in his view in accidental connection with the nature of God itself. Still he allows the inflexibility of righteousness and the hatred against evil to abide alongside of the mercy of God, and the denial of the infinitude of guilt is supposed to give the ascendancy so much the more surely to the

---

[1] Conr. Vorstius, *de Deo*. Cf. my treatise on the immutability of God. *Jahrb. für deutsche Theol*. 1857, p. 478, ff.

[2] God is, in the view of Vorstius, not *infinitus, immensus;* there is in Him a *diversitas*, also an *accidens, contingens*, to which he reckons joy, anger, sorrow. Not even the ethical is according to him immutable in God. Cf. The works of John Howe, iii. 216, ff., "The Living Temple."

[3] Hugo Grotius, *Defensio fidei catholicœ de satisfactione Christi* against the Socinians. Similarly, Arminius, *de Sacerdot*. Cf. Episcopius, *Instit*. iv. 3, 11, p. 407, 423. Limborch, *Theologia Christ*. lib. iii. 18-23, p. 250-269. Curcellaüs, *Religionis Christ. instit*. iv. 19, 15.

mercy of God and to facilitate the atonement, which was in itself effected by the wisdom of God through the satisfaction rendered by the humanity of Christ. Whilst he leaves it in doubt in what sense an inflexibility (*inflexibilitas*) of righteousness can be spoken of, seeing that sin has not an infinite significance, an explanation is given by Episcopius, who goes back upon the supreme sovereignty of God. As αὐτοκράτωρ, God could have forgiven and punished, as He would, for He is under obligation to no man. His glory consists in His free power. There is no necessity, whether of forgiveness or of punishment, founded in Him. But since there is in God a motion towards mercy and righteousness, and since He has actually given a commandment with punitive sanctions, the enfeebling of which would not consist with His truthfulness, He has in some measure satisfied both considerations by a *temperamentum*, *i.e.* a propitiatory sacrifice (*sacrificium propitiatorium*), which He required neither to give nor to accept, but which He regards as if a price had been paid to Him. The sacrifice of the sufferings of Christ shows that God gives no free pass (*liberum commeatum*) to sin, but pardons us upon condition of improvement.

In opposition to him, however, *Hugo Grotius*, turning round more decidedly to subjectivity, declares that in the whole work of atonement the glory of God is not the matter in hand. The point of view of injured glory would place God over against man as an equal party (*pars offensa*). The injured party however has not the right to punish, but only a higher one who is not a party. As little can the right of punishment be derived from God's supreme sovereignty (*absolutum dominium*), for then it would be a right on account of His own majesty, that is to say on His own account; but a right of punishment exists rather, not on account of him who inflicts it, but on account of society. Essential righteousness as necessary holy goodness he excludes from God, and so there remains left to him an empirical basis of punishment. It has for its end the universally best, the general weal, the maintenance of good order. As supreme governor of the world (*summus Rector*) God cannot leave evil unpunished, nor pardon capriciously. On the other hand, however, the fulfilment of the punishment would bring destruction. How then is help possible? In this way, he says, that there is also a *dispensatio* from the laws or a *relaxatio*, without their becoming thereby invalid. For this end he defines the idea of the law so as to describe the law given to our first parents as a positive (*i.e.* accidental) law, whilst positive laws, and especially the punitive sanctions connected with them, are always relaxable, capable of being modified or even suspended. The law is not something inward in God, nor even the will of God itself, but only a certain expression of His will; consequently, the nature of God is not changed with the law: the latter is for God merely accidental. As the highest sovereignty, He can punish evil or not punish it, for He can relax the law. The general weal decides His action. The difficulty indeed is thus only brought into another form; for the general weal requires on the one hand punitive sanctions, and by implication punishment, for the relaxation always weakens the authority of the law, whilst punishment conserves it; and the general weal requires on the other hand the remission of the punishment, because its fulfilment would bring destruction upon the world. Here, however, Grotius continues, the governing wisdom of God (*prudentia rectoria*) has found a solution through Christ. Christ indeed has not procured the atonement. Punishment was neither in itself nor on God's account necessary. As little has Christ brought it about that God is under obligation to forgive. But since God would not, in the interests of the general weal, remit the punishment without an illustrious example (*non sine insigni exemplo*), Christ is made an example of punishment, which places before our eyes the abominable nature of sin, and accordingly unites with forgiveness the impression of the punishableness of sin, so that the general weal is not purchased through the shattering of the authority of the law. A compensation is thus effected. For the law does not indeed receive the same as it threatened, satisfaction through the punishment of the sinner; but the next thing to the identical (*idem*) is the equivalent (*tantundem*). No doubt the punishment thus falls upon the innocent, whilst the guilty is forgiven; and hence Socinus demands that there must be here a connection between the guilty and the punished. But in fact there is this connection, for Christ is not only our kinsman, but another very different and higher community is preordained between Him and us. For He was designated by God to be the Head of the body of which we were to be the members. The transferability therefore of our punishment to Him and of

His punishment to us rests not merely upon the bodily connection, but also upon the mystical bond between us and the Lord, just as a similar connection exists between a people and its king. This theory,—which in Curcelläus and others restricted more and more the idea of equity, and brought into the place of the eternal law the idea of a changing covenant,—this hovering between pure equity and caprice, was designed to oppose Socinianism, but only forms an intermediate stage which conducts to it, especially since not only has the *liberum arbitrium* the supreme place in God, just as it is with Socinus, but also the human *liberum arbitrium* assumes in Arminianism an important place, and natural corruption is not regarded as strictly sin and guilt, whilst regeneration is transformed into improvement, and the communication of the Holy Ghost into assistance by Him.

The *General Synod of Dort*, which was meant to be an œcumenical Reformed Council, but at which only few Remonstrants were admitted, and that without the right of voting, dealt with the Arminian controversy in 154 sittings, from 13th November 1618 to 9th May 1619, and in the end the decision went completely against the Arminians.[1] Besides England, France, Geneva, and German Switzerland, there were represented at the Synod, Hesse, Nassau, the Palatinate, East Friesland, and Bremen. The *Dort* theologians teach more cautiously than Calvin, and especially than Beza, namely, in infralapsarian manner. Adam was created perfectly pure and holy, but falling from God through the instigation of the devil and his own will, he robbed himself of those splendid gifts. In Adam, however, all have sinned and become exposed to eternal wrath. God would not be unjust if He allowed all to perish, but according to His utterly free good pleasure He has, out of pure grace, elected out of the whole human race a definite number unto salvation in Christ, appointed

---

[1] The Arminians wished only a Provincial Synod of South and North Holland, where they were powerful. But in opposition to them a Netherlandish General Synod was determined upon, under the name, "Synodus nationalis ecclesiarum belgicarum." Not only were the foreign Reformed Churches invited to depute members to it, so that the Arminians might not appeal to their possible agreement with them, but the subscriptions of the foreign deputies were treated as the "chirographa" of their churches, and the public edition of the acts (*acta synodi nationalis*, 1620) says, at the close of the *Prefatio ad Reformatas Christi ecclesias:*
"Rogantur autem Ecclesiæ omnes Reformatæ, ut doctrinam hanc orthodoxam, tam solemniter in hæc Synodo ex verbo Dei explicatam confirmatamque amplecti, conservare, propagare, atque ad omnem posteritatem transmittere veluit."

Him to be the Head of the elect, and ordained for them by the Holy Ghost their calling, justification, and perseverance. Others, again, He has passed over and given up to their wickedness and obstinacy. The effectual cause of their destruction however is not God, but their own guilt. Neither are they passed over because possibly the saving power of the death of Christ had not sufficed for them; it is of infinite value, and in itself is sufficient for the sins of the whole world. Still, however, Christ did not die for all: His redeeming will is confined within the limits of particular election. The condemnation of the Arminians was now sealed by medals, and by their banishment from Holland. They had to seek an asylum in Antwerp and Holstein, and obtained places of refuge in Friedrichstadt and Nordstrand, until Maurice secured to them, in 1636, free worship again in Holland, where their silent influence made itself felt, not only in the theology of Holland, but also in France, to say nothing of its subsequent influence upon English theology, where Arminianism gave rise to the so-called Latitudinarianism, and upon the Lutheran Church.

The logical *sequence* of the Arminian tendency lies in *Socinianism*, which arose indeed already in the sixteenth century, but prematurely for the other confessions, and which first became an operative factor in the history of the Evangelical Church through the mediation of the Arminians. For it was owing to Arminianism that Socinianism, which was much hated in Germany even after the seventeenth century, found entrance in the Reformed Church in ever wider circles, and first of all in Holland and England.[1]

Socinianism sprang originally from the Italian Reformation movements of the sixteenth century, whose peculiarity consists in this, that the clearing-up [*aufklärung*] of the understanding and æsthetic culture had the ascendency over the ethical and religious. The Humanism of Italy, given up to the world of beautiful forms in art and language, essayed through the imitation of the ancients or out of its own resources to give a harmonious

---

[1] In Holland even Conrad Vorstius, and afterwards Curcelläus, approximated to Socinianism. Besides, Holland was the rendezvous for those of Socinian views out of different lands, even as already in Germany Zwicker and Christopher Sand, father and son, thought like Socinus. Their manner of thinking found entrance afterwards in England, through Thomas Chubb, Thom. Emlyn, John Biddell, and Arthur Bury, *The Naked Gospel.* Cf. Patrick Fairbairn in his appendix to the translation of my christological work, 1863, p. 341.

form to life; the æsthetic spirit covered, as with a luxuriant overgrowth, the moral consciousness; the subject-matter of Church dogma furnished an unpleasant admonition of sin and need of atonement; the scholastic form of Church doctrine instigated the reason to contradiction, and in the first instance to contradiction of the doctrines, which had been wrapped up in pure mystery, and so lay like an alien burden upon the mind, which sought to be clearly and freely master of itself. Familiarity with the Aristotelian and Platonic philosophy fostered an idea of God, with which the Trinity and the incarnation of God did not consist, whilst the Church doctrine bore in itself only too many traces of these pre-Christian ideas of God, which did not accord with the general system of dogma, nay, whilst even the great movement of the sixteenth century had done little or nothing for the recasting of the idea of God. Men like *Paleario, Paul Vergerius,* even *Contarini,* were rare in Italy.[1] As the Church doctrine of the Trinity contains an union of the Sabellian and Arian currents, with an exclusion of their Judaistic and heathen elements, the immediate result of opposition to that doctrine was, that a Sabellian doctrine of God and Christology revived again in men like Campanella and Giordano Bruno, and advanced even into Pantheism; whilst men like Bernhard Ochino and Valentin Gentilis favoured Subordinationism. Both currents came to rest in a sort of higher Ebionitism; their crushed condition was exchanged for a firmer form in Socinianism. Persecuted in Italy, they found reception in particular in Sclavonic countries and in Siebenbürgen.

The intellectual founder of Socinianism is *Lelio Sozzini*. His nephew, *Faustus Socinus* († 1604), brought the adherents of his views into an ecclesiastical organization after that *George Blandratta* had, in opposition to *Franz Davidis,* succeeded in carrying out the worship of Christ. Their school at Rakow was very celebrated, but in 1658 they were driven by John Casimir from their principal settlement in Poland, and fled partly to Siebenbürgen, where they have maintained themselves in considerable numbers, and partly to Holland and England. They had a number of important teachers, who were principally reinforced by accessions of Germans who had fallen out with the doctrine

---

[1] Paleario, *die Wohlthat Christi.* Cf. Sixt, *Paul Vergerius,* 1855. Regarding Contarini, cf. Lämmer, *die vortridentinische kath. Theologie,* 1858, p. 63, ff.

of the Church. Amongst them there are especially to be named Valentin Schmalz, Volkel, Ostorodt, Johann Crell († 1631), Andreas Wissowatius († 1678), v. Wolzogen, and Schlichting (†1661).[1]

Socinianism, although it did exercise till about 1700 an important influence upon the large Church communities, yet demands here a few words, since, muttering, as it were, from the distant background, it threateningly points at the dogmatic system of the Evangelicals the question, whether objective doctrines can be taken over thus unchanged out of the old into modern times,—whether the authority of the Church may, in virtue of an old tradition or one to be formed anew, still rule a part of the system,—whether biblical criticism and the investigation of the canonicity of the sacred books must remain free or be decided dogmatically,—and, finally, whether the ethical department is sufficiently considered in the evangelical system? It itself is indeed a marvellous compound of purely supernatural and of rational pieces of work, governed by the practical points of view of a comparatively superficial and legal ethics. A supernatural revelation is, according to it, not necessary on account of the need of salvation, but because we are by nature blind regarding the will of God, upon obedience to which everything depends. More exactly viewed, however, it regards our inability to know the will of God as having its reason in the constitution of the law. No one could say beforehand what God will command as good, for the commands of God have no internal necessity, but God is the absolute *liberum arbitrium*. He can determine what is to be esteemed good by us; accordingly, we can only know what we ought to do, by the way of matter of fact, through a positive revelation which promulgates His law. Thus the evangelical *actus Dei forensis* for the justification of man, according to which God can for Christ's sake pronounce good a sinner who believes, has here placed over against it an *actus Dei forensis*, according to which God, according to His free sovereignty, pronounces good what is not in itself good. This revelation of His will is given, according to the Socinians, in the New Testament; the Old Testament is depreciated in proportion as Socinianism itself still remains essentially upon a legal footing. For through the perfect law the imperfect is deprived of its

[1] *Bibliotheca fratrum Polonorum, Irenopoli*, 1656, ff.

importance. It is not without the feeling that the ethical is the absolute ultimate end of the world; and this is made regulative for that which the revelation can contain, or is at least applied to the interpretation of the New Testament. But Socinianism has a very imperfect and inadequate knowledge of the ethical itself, not merely in its principle, in so far as it places it ultimately under the character of might, but also because it contemplates it only under the form of law and obedience to law, and places it in a very loose connection with religion, which furnishes the knowledge of the law, and because it has no knowledge of goodness in the form of a God-filled power of virtue and of a good state of being. No wonder that Socinianism also knows nothing of an evil state of being, of corruption as a condition, but rather conceives of the free will of man as perfectly equal to the actions which the positive law of God requires. By all this the questions affecting the natural need of salvation, the inward operations of the Spirit, and regeneration, are already decided. Nevertheless, it still seeks an eminent position for Christ. It views Him, indeed, as only a man born of a virgin, by the co-operation of the Spirit; the doctrine of the two natures is as repugnant to it as the doctrine of the Trinity; but partly by nature, partly through being subsequently caught up into heaven before entering on His office of teacher, Christ had the most perfect knowledge of the will of God, and communicated it in teaching; He also through His holy life set up a pattern of the obedience that, amid the hatred of the world, is faithful to God, and finally died as a martyr for the truth of His doctrine. To this there is to be added still further: Man has not in fact, as he might, fulfilled the will of God; and so far as he persists in evil, he goes forward towards eternal destruction. For the godless are swept away and destroyed by divine punishment. In the event of their improvement, God could forgive them without any punishment or atonement being necessary; but without the sure information given us on this point, the improvement itself and confidence in God would be rendered infinitely difficult, if not impossible. God has thus, through the appearance of Christ, remedied this need; He has made proclamation through Him of His grace towards those who repent; and as His whole doctrine was attested by Him as a faithful witness to the truth through His martyr death, God has set the resurrection of Christ to be the seal of His doctrine. Those who continue in the faith and strive to fulfil His law are justified by God on account of the good will, which He looks upon as righteousness, and have bestowed upon them by Him that eternal life, which Christ promised, as a reward or natural consequence, but not as their desert. Christ Himself, however, who was thus approved to be the Holy One through suffering and death, is deemed worthy of being exalted into heaven to the right hand of God, in order to be now the Governor of the world in the place of God, and to be worshipped according to the will of God, who is Himself thereby glorified. Upon earth His work was prophetic, now it is kingly; and with His kinghood is united His heavenly High Priesthood, whilst there is no earthly one. He is thus, as it were, a man become God; for though the nature of God escapes Him, and there abides only one nature in Christ, the human nature, still the divine *attributes*—though not the divine *nature*—come to be communicated to him.

As almost everything is in the Socinian theory of redemption put upon self-improvement, so the sacraments, too, are here purely subjective performances; baptism, a praiseworthy custom, though not instituted for ever; and every one belongs to the Church who makes the *professio fidei*.[1]

[1] Otto Fock, *der Socinianismus nach seiner Stellung in der Gesammtentwicklung des christl. Geistes nach s. historischen Verlauf und nach s. Lehrbegriff.* Kiel, 1847.

APPENDIX.

APPENDIX.

NOTE A, to p. 31.

THE brevity of the sentences adverting to the relation of the Councils to the Papacy seems to call for a few remarks on a subject which has scarcely received the attention it ought in any English works treating of the development of the papal sovereignty. After the Sixth Œcumenical Council, held in Constantinople, A.D. 680, had condemned the Monothelites, two other Councils (2nd of Nice, A.D. 787, and the 4th of Constantinople, A.D. 869) were held, which were recognized as œcumenical, but which were of inferior importance. In all of these, as well as in those which preceded them, there is a certain independence of style and action, which indicates the absence of any rival claimant to ecclesiastical supremacy. They were no doubt unduly dependent on, and subservient to, the power of the Emperor, and were shamefully influenced by the intrigues of the imperial court, but within the Church itself their supremacy was unchallenged either by pope or patriarch. The Bishop of Rome, indeed, had already claimed for his bishopric an œcumenical character, but the claim was very far from being recognized in theory or allowed in practice. Before the papacy could secure the possession of ecclesiastical sovereignty, two things were necessary. First, it had to make itself in *fact* the dominant power and authority in the Church, and then it had to secure for the position it had assumed that sanction and consolidation which could only be imparted through the subservient action of councils, as these were still in theory the highest legislative authority. And this was what actually took place. At the time the last-named Œcumenical Council was held, the forged Isidorian decretals were obtaining currency, and, being universally received as genuine, facilitated the actual assumption of the papal supremacy which they asserted. For two centuries and a half thereafter, no council which even pretended to be œcumenical, was summoned, and during that time power was being gradually gathered into the hands of the Pope. If at some of the numerous provincial and national synods held during this interval, especially in France, there was the strongest repudiation of the authority claimed by Rome, there were others which showed as humble submission to it as even a Hildebrand could have wished. It was after that able and resolute man had become the ruling spirit of the papal court, that the papacy fairly asserted and in action proved itself to be supreme over the Catholic Church. This was seen especially in the reformation of the clerical orders. The Pope did not, however, act altogether independently of synodical concurrence. During the latter half of the eleventh century,—the period of Hildebrand's ascendency—there were general synods held in Rome (especially under Leo IX., Nicholas II., and Hildebrand himself, whose design, as Gregory VII., was to assemble a Lent synod every year), which, although not possessing œcumenical rank, gave effect to papal decisions affecting the whole Church, and thus lent a certain synodical recommendation to decrees, whose real claim to universal recognition was the fact of their being issued by authority of the Pope. When at length, after the lapse of two and a half centuries, an œcumenical council was again assembled, the whole concomitant circumstances showed the greatness of the change which had been effected in the government of the Church. The place of meeting was in Rome,—in the church which was then pre-eminently the parish church of the Pope, and the business of the council was not to give an independent decision upon the important questions occasioning its meeting, but simply to endorse and approve the decisions which had been already arrived at. The four Lateran Councils, so far from being free parliaments of the Church, were nothing more than an enlarged privy council of the Pope; and the very form in which the decisions of the last and greatest of them were expressed indicates the nature of its relations to the papal sovereign,—" sacra universali Synodo approbante sancimus." (See Gieseler's *Church History*, translated in Clark's F. T. Library, vol. iii. p. 163, note 8. Compare Hefele's *Conciliengeschichte*, bk. v. p. 785 ; also Gieseler, Third Period, Fifth Div., ch. i. § 136.)

Thus it was that both by the long interval which elapsed before the first œcumenical council of the Western Church was summoned, and by the dependent character imposed upon those which were at length assembled, the papacy was assisted in arrogating to itself the possession of absolute sovereignty.

The three following councils were equally dependent upon the papacy. Those of Pisa, Constance, and Basle, on the other hand, asserted more or less that freedom of action which had characterized

Appendix. 437

the earlier councils of the Church. But the papacy was now too powerful to be thwarted or opposed in its designs by any council whatsoever, and the completeness of its triumph was seen in the Fifth Lateran Council.—*Tr.*

NOTE B, to p. 64.

These sentences are evidently intended to refer to the Lollards. There were no doubt Waldensian preachers and followers in England as early as the middle of the twelfth century, and there are traces of a Waldensian settlement in Kent towards the end of it, which paid rent to the see of Canterbury. There is also ample evidence of their existence at the same time in Holland. But they can scarcely be said to have acquired a distinct and recognized place in England as a society holding peculiar views and distinguished by peculiar practices until after the end of the fourteenth century, when they became known by the name of Lollards. The account given by Dr. Dorner of the character they desired for the Church, of the discipline they proposed, and of the emphasis laid by them on personal holiness in order to the efficient administration of the ministerial office, very accurately describes the tenets held by the Lollards, in subordination to the cardinal doctrine that the Bible is the only rule and source of faith. But I have been unable to find any authority for the statement in the text, which imputes to them an ecclesiastical organization with bishops and presbyteries. So strong and frequent is the language used by them in reference to the qualification of personal piety necessary for the ministerial office, that one would naturally infer from it the setting up on their part of a distinct church organization. But I have found no evidence of it.—*Tr.*

NOTE C, to p. 66.

It may be thought to be beyond the province of the translator to bring under review the statements he has undertaken to reproduce, but I can scarcely allow Dr. Dorner's account of Wycliffe to pass, without observing that in one important point his language seems to me to convey an inadequate impression of the theology of the great English Reformer. In general, the estimate he presents of Wycliffe is singularly fair and truthful. But it is scarcely correct to say that "he does not yet know the nature of justification, and does not yet understand the free grace of God." It is no doubt the case that none of his writings is formally devoted to the treatment either of the one or of the other, and that the "righteousness of faith"—of which Melanchthon, in a letter to Myconius, declared Wycliffe to be ignorant—is by no means so frequently adverted to as that righteousness of life which was opposed to the many and crying sins of the age in which he lived. But nevertheless his treatises show that the cardinal doctrines of grace were clearly apprehended by him, and his "postils" that they were as distinctly taught. Dr. Dorner himself confesses (p. 65) that Wycliffe rejected the idea of all self-wrought merit. But besides exhibiting the truth negatively, the Reformer also manifested a profound and constant sense of the goodness and grace of God, especially in connection with redemption (cf. *e.g.* Vaughan's *Life and Opinions of Wycliffe*, vol. i. p. 306), and a clear conception of the necessity, nature, and sufficiency of the atonement rendered by Christ (cf. *Tracts and Treatises of Wycliffe*, published by the Wycliffe Society, p. 84). It is viewed by him as the only ground of acceptance for guilty man, and where could a plainer statement of the truth of justification by faith be found than is contained in the following words, "As a right looking on that adder of brass saved the people from the venom of serpents, so a right looking by full belief on Christ saveth His people" (see Vaughan's *Life*, vol. ii. p. 356)? Equally plain is the statement that the assurance of forgiveness is a direct fruit of faith, "It is manifest that the Christian, by his trust in the compassion of Jesus Christ, and in his pain and holy purpose, may know from within himself that his sin is removed, and that he is contrite in spirit" (*Trialogus, Tracts and Treatises*, p. 181). It is farther to be observed that he ascribes not only the atonement of Christ, but also faith and every good work to the free grace of God (*Tracts and Treatises*, p. 87). The statement made by Dr. Dorner, that he is "not without a religious vein," and that "the religious element does not attain to an independent development with him," can only mean that there is no distinct exposition of the great doctrines of grace *per se*, for certainly Wycliffe could never have been the consistent and dauntless Reformer that he was, despite his solitariness, had not his whole life been built upon strong and fully developed religious principle. His writings, too, show him to have been a man of intense and devout piety. Many of his expositions of the abuses of the times are in the form of a prayerful complaint to God, and Vaughan remarks that "rarely does he conclude a composition, however brief, without recording a fervent prayer for the blessing of God on its design, and as rarely does he advert to his sufferings, without expressing his gratitude to the Author of the Gospel for the encouragements afforded by that record of mercy" (Vaughan's *Life and Opinions of Wycliffe*, vol. ii. p. 373).—*Tr.*

NOTE D, to p. 67.

When Hus (for such is the proper spelling of his name) was commissioned by the Archbishop of Prague, as a mark of honour and trust, to deliver the admonition to the clergy of the diocese at their synod in 1407, he demanded of all the clergy that they should exhibit to the people a pattern of Christian perfection in the observance of these Counsels. There were other evidences that he failed to perceive the full bearing of his evangelical ideas; not a word is said by him, for example, against the worship of saints, or against monasticism. It may be well to explain for the sake of some readers, that the *Consilia Evangelica* are, in the ethics of the Roman Catholic Church, distinguished from the *Præcepta*,—the latter being obligatory upon every Christian, whilst the former were injunctions, which did not belong to the code of universal duty, but were necessary in order to perfection. Whoever had once bound himself by them was bound by them always. By complying with them, he reaches a higher stage of holiness than can be strictly demanded of him, and acquires an additional merit which can be transferred to others. At first, they were commonly restricted to chastity, poverty, and obedience, as the opposites of the three chief forms of sin, the lust of the flesh, the lust of the eye, and the pride of life. Afterwards the number of these counsels was supposed to be twelve, there being added the three already mentioned, the abstaining from oaths, non-resistance to evil, giving to all that ask, &c.—things said be counselled by Christ in order to our being "perfect," but not enjoined as necessary to salvation. Usually, however, the number is restricted to these. How far Hus, in urging the *Consilia Evan.*, as such, upon the clergy, fell short of the evangelical view of good works and of perfection, may best be made apparent from the language of our Confession,—which is here completely in accordance with the language of the Conf. Aug.. and the Formula of Concord. Believers are not to grow negligent "as if they were not bound to perform any duty unless upon a special motion of the Spirit" (W. C. ch. xvi. s. 3). "They who in their obedience attain to the greatest height which is possible in this life, are so far from being able to supererogate, and to do more than God requires, as that they fall short of much which in duty they are bound to do" (W. C. ch. xvi. s. 4).

Even the XIVth Article of the Church of England says, "voluntary works, besides, *over and above God's commandments,* which they call works of supererogation, cannot be taught without arrogancy and impiety." It is therefore somewhat remarkable to find that in the *Dictionary of Doctrinal and Historical Theology,* recently published, and edited by the Rev. J. H. Blunt, the "Counsels of Perfection" should be spoken of as if the distinction were really a valid one, and there were a morality essentially optional. The article concludes: "They are called counsels of perfection, because our Blessed Lord commends them to us by word and example, although not enforcing them upon us by universal command, and they are instruments of perfection to such as are really called by God to follow them out."—*Tr.*

NOTE E, to p. 67.

Whilst the Brethren of the Law of Christ were formed out of the Calixtine party, it is to be remembered that they are not to be regarded as preserving the distinctive views and tendencies of the Calixtines. On the contrary, the movement to which they owed their origin grew out of a revived opposition to Rome, and an increasing dissatisfaction with the compromise entered into between the Calixtines and the Council of Basle. It naturally gathered round it the remnants of the Taborite party, and when its adherents became numerous and powerful, they were persecuted avowedly upon the ground that they were in reality the Taborite party revived. And although the accusation was unjust, in so far as it imputed to them the planning of fanatical and violent measures, still the three confessions which they shortly afterwards issued, show that their doctrine was essentially that of the Taborite confession. The founders of the Brotherhood were, as Dr. Dorner says, originally Calixtines, but they gathered round them the scattered remnants of the Taborite party, and without its fanaticism, adopted its doctrine and perpetuated its opposition to Rome, and are therefore justly regarded as its historical successors. They entered also into friendly relations with the Waldensians living in the neighbourhood of Bohemia and Moravia, and obtained ordination for their first pastors from a Waldensian bishop. The Calixtines continued to regard the Brethren with an unfriendly eye, and it was the German Reformation which first drew them together in a common confession —the Confessio Bohemica, 1575.—*Tr.*

NOTE F, to p. 67.

These translations were much more numerous than is generally supposed. Turning first to Germany, we find that in the beginning of the fifteenth century there certainly existed a complete translation of the Bible into German, and that within the last half of the fifteenth century and the early years of the sixteenth, previously to Luther, there were no fewer than at least fourteen different editions of the complete Bible published in High German, and four in Low German. These different editions seem, however, according to Kehrein (*zur Gesch. der deut. Bibeluebers. vor Luther*), to be all founded ultimately upon one translation, though varying somewhat from one another. In France, where Guyar's translation of Comestor's Bible history forms the basis of the earliest translations of the Bible proper, there appeared within the latter half of the fifteenth century two editions of the New Testament (Lyons, 1477), and then a complete Bible (that of De Rely, published in Paris), which went through at least twelve editions. The translations of Le Fèvre and Olivetan belong to the Reformation period. In England, Wycliffe's translation had appeared in the end of the fourteenth century, but had of course been circulated only in MS. copies. To a somewhat later period than that spoken of in the text belongs Tyndale's New Testament, as it was not published till 1526, and that at Wittenberg. In Italy, again, two translations were published in the period referred to, the one known only by its title, the other that of Di Malherbi (1471), who in his introduction speaks of older translations. Vernacular translations of the Bible appeared also, within the same time, in Bohemia, Poland, and Holland. But in order to have a just conception of the extent and influence of this movement, it must still further be remembered that, in addition to these translations of the complete Bible, there were in all the countries that have been named, and also in Spain and Denmark, even more numerous translations into the vernacular of larger or smaller portions of the Scriptures.—*Tr.*

NOTE G, to p. 125.

The offertory prayers (*Opfergebeten*), properly so called, are those belonging to the third division of the ritual of the mass. Originally they had reference to the consecration and acceptance of the offerings presented by the congregation, and to which, at the time the ritual was drawn up, an expiatory power was attributed. But when offerings were no longer brought by the congregation, the whole character of the offertory was changed, and it became the mere presentation and preliminary consecration of the natural elements which were afterwards to be changed into the body and blood of Christ. The prayers —five in number, the first of which was offered in connection with the laying of the yet unconsecrated host upon the paten, and the last, after the hands had been washed in preparation for the transformation of the elements—still adverted to these elements in their *natural* state, and spoke of them *as an expiatory offering for the sins of the priest and congregation, and of living and dead believers.* Prayers like these, which were on the face of them either meaningless or profane, naturally roused the indignation of the Reformers, and formed one of those offensive elements of the mass which incited to its abolition. See Herzog's *Realencyclopädie*, bk. ix. p. 400-402.—*Tr.*

NOTE H, to p. 139.

The view which is presented here, and in p. 141, of the relation between Montanism and the fanatics of the Reformation period is interesting and instructive. The former is not to be looked upon as a separate and isolated heresy, nor does it find a sufficient explanation in the circumstances peculiar to the place or time of its origin. It was in general sympathy with Christian truth, but carried to an extravagant and untenable extreme the principle of the possession of the spirit by believers in this, the final dispensation, and insisted upon direct and immediate revelations from God, upon the moulding of the present conditions of life in a manner befitting the immediate setting up of the kingdom of God upon earth, and upon a rigorous and ascetic discipline. It was a reactionary protest—and the protest found eloquent expression in the writings of Tertullian—against the Church assuming in its existing condition the character of a seemingly permanent institution, and adapting itself to the prospect of a prolonged continuance and work in the world. The Church, on the other hand, while disavowing the belief in the immediate and forcible reorganization of all things by the appearance of Christ, and refusing to adopt the exclusive and rigorous character urged upon it, gave what seemed a fatal blow to Montanism by finding the security for the possession of divine powers by the Church, not in the immediate communication of the Spirit to individual believers and the manifestation in them of His extraordinary influences, but in visible and settled forms of constitution and worship, in sacramental rites and in the apostolical succession. It was necessary that the idea of office should be preserved and the law of order asserted against a system which placed the whole Church at the mercy of sporadic and unreliable spiritual influences. But the development of the Episcopal hierarchy in the Church, and the regulation of the whole Church life in accordance with the hierarchical principle, led to the other extreme and brought about the reassertion of the rights and powers of the individual believer in the Reformation. It then became apparent that the principles of Montanism, so far from being dead, had only been suppressed and benumbed by the power of the hierarchical constitution of the Church, and were in reality only partial and extreme views of the nature of Christianity, such as are fostered by an appeal to the impatience, pride, and party enthusiasm natural to the human heart in every age. As Dr. Dorner truly and suggestively observes, the fanatical movements of the Reformation age were simply the revival of Montanism in a form determined by the circumstances of the times, as soon as, in consequence of the Reformation, the historical conditions allowed of its reappearance. And the same tenets have never disappeared from the field of Protestantism, but still— as, for example, in certain forms of Plymouthism—disturb, though perhaps they serve in some measure to keep awake and stimulate, the life of the Church.—*Tr.*

NOTE I, to p. 405, Note 3.

The accuracy of this statement in reference to R. Wilberforce and Pusey depends, of course, upon the meaning assigned to the word *Justificatio*. We generally take it in a forensic sense, and conceive that in doing so we are adhering to the usage of Scripture and of the earliest of the fathers. Even before Augustine, however, the word *justificatio* was being taken to include the infusion, as well as the imputation, of righteousness; and it was mainly the example of Augustine which made this use of the word common in the Middle Ages and traditional in the Roman Catholic Church. (Justificat impium Deus non solum dimittendo quæ male fecit sed etiam donando caritatem, quæ declinat a malo et facit bonum per Spiritum sanctum. *Aug. Opus Imperf.*) If we take the word in its apostolic and Reformation sense, according to which it describes the objective act of acquittal and acceptance on the part of God, the statement made by Dr. Dorner in this note would be obviously inaccurate. If, however, we take it in the meaning assigned to it by Augustine (and in which Schleiermacher also uses it), then the statement need not be impugned.

What R. Wilberforce and Pusey distinctly teach, is that baptism ingrafts the infant into the body of Christ in such a way that not only is his guilt removed but he is actually as well as forensically made righteous. Pusey prefers to represent it as the implanting of the new life in man by virtue of which he becomes a new creature in Christ Jesus. "Our life is throughout represented as commencing, when we are by baptism made members of Christ and children of God. A commencement of spiritual life after baptism is as little consonant with the general representations of Holy Scripture, as a commencement of physical life long after our natural birth is with the order of His Providence." (Pusey, *Scriptural Views of Baptism*, p. 14; compare also pp. 12-32, 84-89, 162-3.) R. Wilberforce prefers to represent it as the reconstructing of the nature of man, so that it, being regenerate, exercises a suasive influence on that ultimate principle of responsibility in man which must by faith and love accept the gift of a renewed being. "This view of Holy Baptism, as the commencement of man's spiritual history, may show the inadequacy of the notion which is sometimes adopted, that Baptism is the extinction of guilt, but not the recreation of nature." (R. Wilberforce, *Doctrine of Holy Baptism*, p. 43; compare also pp. 22-28, 40-46.)—*Tr.*

www.ingramcontent.com/pod-product-compliance
Lightning Source LLC
Chambersburg PA
CBHW071136300426
44113CB00009B/995